Revisiting Ecuador's Economic and Social Agenda in an Evolving Landscape

Revisiting cuador's conomic and Social Agenda in n Evolving Landscape

ente Fretes-Cibils Marcelo Giugale Eduardo Somensatto

THE WORLD BANK
WASHINGTON, DC

1818 H Street NW
Washington DC 20433
Telephone: 202-473-1000
Internet: www.worldbank.org
E-mail: feedback@worldbank.org

1 2 3 4 5 11 10 09 08

ISBN-13: 978-0-8213-7145-9
eISBN-13: 978-0-8213-7146-6
DOI: 10.1596/978-0-8213-7145-9

Cover art: *Dueños de la Noche* (1987) by Gonzalo Endara Crow.

Library of Congress Cataloging-in-Publication Data

Revisiting Ecuador's economic and social agenda in an evolving landscape / edited by Marcelo M. Giugale, Vicente Fretes-Cibils, Eduardo Somensatto.
p. cm.
Includes bibliographical references.
ISBN 978-0-8213-7145-9—ISBN 978-0-8213-7146-6 (electronic)
1. Ecuador—Economic policy. 2. Ecuador—Economic conditions—1972–3. Ecuador—Social policy. 4. Ecuador—Social conditions. I. Giugale, Marcelo. II. Fretes Cibils, Vicente, 1956– III. Somensatto, Eduardo.
HC202.R477 2008
330.9866—dc22

2007041806

Contents

Tables

Figures

Boxes

Preface

Ecuador is at a crossroads in the early years of the new millennium. Political, economic, and social instability have long affected the country's path of development. Though it is rich in cultural traditions and natural endowments, the stop-and-go cycles of past public policies have prevented the country from realizing its potential for economic prosperity and social equity. Ecuador has the opportunity to define a development agenda that will benefit all of its citizens. In this agenda, stability, growth, competitiveness, social development, decentralization, and transparency would constitute the mileposts. We at the World Bank feel honored to contribute to the public policy debate through publishing the follow-up to *Ecuador—An Economic and Social Agenda in the New Millennium.* We have updated this book to provide an account of Ecuador's current key development challenges, many of the reasons behind those challenges, and some options to overcome them. The analysis here does not claim to provide definitive solutions to all of Ecuador's challenges. Rather, we hope that this second edition can enrich the national discussion among Ecuadorans as they search for their own solutions to these challenges.

The work presented here is organized around three overarching themes: fiscal consolidation and growth, social development, and quality of government. The main messages within each of these themes are summarized and brought together in an opening synthesis. The importance of these three broad themes has become increasingly evident around the world during the past decades and has been accentuated by global integration (financial and commercial) and by the information technology revolution. Understanding those forces is critically important because, in the end, their value will be measured by one simple yardstick—their impact on people's quality of life, especially among the poor.

This second edition is the product of the analytical work of a large number of World Bank staff members. It documents Ecuador's main development trends, policies, and options, and places the country in the context of relevant international comparisons. Extensive dialogue, reflection, and direct operational work with our counterparts in Ecuador and elsewhere are detailed in this volume, which spells out critical lessons and challenges that are relevant for the country and for Latin America as a whole. Finally, the book's second edition proposes policy matrices for each sector and topic, including a proposed sequencing of policy steps.

I am extremely grateful for the cooperation and contributions of our many friends in Ecuador to this very important endeavor, both directly and through several years of working side by side with us. I would like to thank the staff members who have worked to compile this book—editors, authors, and producers. Their work reveals not only their professional talents, but also, and more importantly, their passion for poverty reduction.

Pamela Cox
Vice President
Latin America and the Caribbean Regional Office
Washington, D.C.
May 2007

Acknowledgments

This volume is the result of a team effort and, as such, it has benefited from an array of invaluable contributions. Thanks are therefore due to a large number of people. First, the chapter authors not only provided material of outstanding technical quality, but also made a remarkable effort, working in record time and thus enriching the Ecuador debate at a critical period. We consider ourselves fortunate to share this book with these principal authors—Susan Bogach, Jean Clevy, Elizabeth Currie, Franz R. Drees-Gross, Jonas Frank, Conrado Garcia-Corado, Michael Goldberg, Christopher Humphrey, Julio Ricardo Loayza, Eleodoro Mayorga-Alba, Edgardo Mosqueira, Monique F. Mrazek, Francisco J. Pichon, Rashmi Shankar, and Eloy Eduardo Vidal. All authors are affiliated with the World Bank Group unless otherwise indicated in their respective chapters. Other authors of individual chapters are recognized in the credits of each specific chapter.

While this book reflects the authors' views (and not necessarily the views of the World Bank, its Board of Directors, or its member countries), its production was institutionally housed at the World Bank. We thus benefited greatly from the general guidance of Guillermo Perry (Chief Economist for the Latin America and the Caribbean Region) and from the auspices of the office of Pamela Cox (Vice President for Latin American and the Caribbean Region).

This volume commenced with an internal workshop held on January 18, 2007, in Washington, D.C. The discussion allowed all the authors to present their findings in a friendly forum and to explore various synergies. In addition to the authors, many others participated. Our thanks are extended to: Alejandro Alcala Gerez, Maria Dolores Arribas-Banos, Garry Charlier, Henry Forrno, Fernando Lecaros, Jeffrey Rinne, Marco Scuriatti, Samuel Taffesse, Marco Varea, Eduardo Velez Bustillo, Ian Walker, and David Warren. During this initial exercise, the early stages of the volume benefited from the comments of peer reviewers, who were: Robert Bacon, Franz Drees-Gross, Pablo Gottret, Jose Luis Guasch, James Hanson, Jorge Munoz, and Fernando Rojas. We also recognize the importance of the workshop held on March 19th and 20th, 2007, in Quito, Ecuador, and thank its participants. This workshop not only brought together a majority of the authors under one roof for a day of candid discussions but also, and more importantly, included officials and consultants from government administration. Among the consultants and government officials present at the workshop, we would especially like to thank the following: David Alorris, Victor Arrar, Manuel Badillo, Winston Balanos, Gustavo Bedon, Caria Caiero,

Nicholas Castellianos, Rita Decy, Sylvia Diaz, Roberto Esteves, Grace Fuerrgo, Doris Gordon, Carlos Julio Jarce, Fausto Jordain, Diego Manchero, Jose Martinez, Julio Oleas, Pedro Montalvo, Pabel Munoz, Viviano Munoz, Juan Nieto, Jorge Orbe, Ruben Paez, Nicolay Pastelanos, Rene Ramirez, Guido Rivadeneira, Paulina Romau, Wladimir Rosero, Hugo Ruiz Coral, Malki Saenz, Maria del Pilar Trayat, Eugenia Vallejo, Galo Viteri, Katiuushka Yanez, and Guido Zambrano. Their comments, suggestions, and input, along with those from the many others who attended this workshop, added greatly to this volume.

We are especially thankful to Marcelo Romero and Nelson Gutiérrez for their exceptional work in preparing the Spanish version of this publication as well as piecing together the English version. We are very grateful for the work of Michael Geller, who gave key administrative and logistical support to the process of this work, as well as to Chris Humphrey for having collaborated on the technical editing of the English version of various chapters. The World Bank team in Ecuador should also receive a well-deserved thank you for their outstanding support and help in coordinating the March 19–20 workshop in Quito: Alexandra Del Castillo, Cinthia Guzmán, Daniela Jaramillo, Pilar Larreamendy, Vinicio Valdivieso, Lucy Vargas, and Ana Maria Villaquirán. Without them, achieving the right environment for these important discussions would not have been possible. The World Bank team in Washington was also a strong component during this whole process.

Finally, we would like to thank the World Bank publication team: Santiago Pombo-Bejarano, Stuart Tucker, and Rick Ludwick supervised the entire process and provided key information and assistance at all stages of publication. We extend our sincere thanks to all.

Vicente Fretes-Cibils, Marcelo M. Giugale, and Eduardo Somensatto
Washington, D.C.
May 2008

Editor Biographies

Marcelo Giugale, an Argentine/Italian national, holds a PhD and MSc in economics from London School of Economics, and a BA in economics from Universidad Catolica Argentina. After a spell in academia, he joined the World Bank's Young Professionals Program in 1989 as an economist in the financial research department. From 1990 to 1994, he was a Senior Economist in the Middle East Operations Vice Presidency, supervising Egypt's structural adjustment program and leading the Bank's reconstruction work in postwar Lebanon. From 1994 to 1998, Mr. Giugale was Principal Economist in the Europe and Central Asia Region, responsible for the Bank's lending and analytical economic work in Lithuania and Kazakhstan. In September 1998, he became the Lead Economist for the Colombia-Mexico-Venezuela Department. From December 2002 to June 2007, he was the director of the Bank's Andean Countries Department (Bolivia, Ecuador, Peru, and República Bolivariana de Venezuela). Currently Mr. Giugale is the Bank's Director for Poverty Reduction and Economic Management in the Latin America and the Caribbean Region. He has held teaching positions at London School of Economics and American University in Cairo, and has many publications in the areas of applied econometrics, finance, business economics, and economic development.

Vicente Fretes-Cibils, a native of Argentina, completed his undergraduate work at the Universidad Nacional del Nordeste, in Argentina, and subsequently pursued postgraduate studies at the University of Pennsylvania and North Carolina State University, where he received, respectively, a master's degree in business administration and a PhD in economics. Following his university studies, he joined the World Bank in 1987 through the Bank's Young Professionals Program. Following stints in the Bank's Office of the Vice President for Europe and the Middle East and its Treasury Department, he served from 1988 to 1992 as Economist in the Office of the Vice President for West Africa Operations. Later, from 1992 to 1996, he served as Chief Economist in the Department of Operations for Andean Countries, supervising adjustment programs and heading up economic and analytical missions to Bolivia. From 1996 to 2002, Mr. Fretes-Cibils served as Senior Economist for República Bolivariana de Venezuela, and subsequently for Colombia and Mexico. From 2002 to 2007 he was Lead Economist in the Poverty Reduction and Economic Management sector for the Andean Countries Department (Bolivia, Ecuador, Peru, and República Bolivariana de Venezuela). He is currently a Division Chief of Fiscal and

Municipal Management, Institutional Capacity and Finance at the Inter-American Development Bank. Additionally, he has taught at Argentina's Universidad Nacional del Nordeste and at North Carolina State University, and has published numerous works addressing topics in finance, applied econometrics, public finance, international economics, and economic development.

Eduardo Somensatto, a Brazilian national, did his doctoral work at Georgetown University (1980), where he also earned his MA (1977), and earned a BS in Economics Development at the University of Michigan (1974). He joined the World Bank in January 1988 as an Economist in the Development Economics and Chief Economist's Office. He has since held various positions in the Bank and the International Finance Corporation; he has been responsible for the preparation of several economic studies and country strategies, mostly for Latin America and Eastern European countries. Most recently, he was Country Manager in Guatemala and Country Manager in Ecuador. Before joining the Bank, Mr. Somensatto taught at Georgetown University and was Assistant Director of Economic Policy Studies at the American Enterprise Institute.

Acronyms and Abbreviations

AADT	annual average daily traffic
ADR	alternative dispute resolution
ADV	added distribution value
AE	Eat Well Ecuador (*Alimentate Ecuador*)
AFTA	American Free Trade Agreement
AGD	Deposit Guarantee Agency (*Agencia de Garantia de Depositos*)
ALADI	Latin American Integration Association
ALNAFT	Agency for the Valuation of Hydrocarbon Resources
AME	Association of Municipalities of Ecuador
API	American Petroleum Institute
APRENDO	academic achievement testing
APTDEA	Andean Trade Promotion and Drug Eradication Act
ARPEL	*Asociación Regional Petrolera Empresarial Latinoamericana*
AUS	Universal Health Insurance
BCE	Central Bank of Ecuador (*Banco Central de Ecuador*)
BdE	*Banco del Estado*
BDH	conditional cash transfer (*Bono de Desarrollo Humano*)
BE	*Beca Escolar*
BEDE	Ecuadoran Development Bank
BEV	*Banco Ecuatoriano de Vivienda*
Boe	barrels of oil equivalent
BNF	National Development Bank (*Banco Nacional de Fomento*)
bpd	barrels per day
BS	*Bono Solidario*
CAE	Ecuadoran Customs Corporation (*Corporación Aduanero de Ecuador*)
CAF	Andean Development Corporation
CAN	Andean Community of Nations (*Comunidad Andina de Naciones*)
CATEG-D	*Corporación para la Administración Temporal Eléctrica de Guayaquil* (formerly *Empresas Electricas del Ecuador*—EMELEC)
CCCC	Civil Commission for the Control of Corruption (*Comisión Civica de Control de la Corrupción*)

CEDEGE	Center for Development of the Guayas Basin
CEL	Special Bidding Committee
CELADE	Latin American Demography Center Centro (*Latinoamericano de Demografía*)
CEMs	Educational Matrix Centers (*Centros Educativos Matrices*)
CENACE	National Center for Energy Control (*Corporación Centro Nacional de Control de Energía*)
CEREPS	Special Account for Productive and Social Reactivation (*Cuenta Especial de Reactivación Productiva y Social*)
CESA	*Central Ecuatoriana de Servicios Agrícolas*
CET	Common External Tariff
CETES	short-term Treasury Certificates
CETUR	Ecuadoran Tourism Corporation
CFN	National Finance Corporation
CNJ	National Council on the Judiciary
CNRH	National Council on Hydraulic Resources
CNPC	China National Petroleum Company
CNTTT	National Land Transit and Transport Council
CODAE	Council for Afro-Ecuadorian Development
CODENPE	Council for the Development of the Indigenous Nations and Peoples of Ecuador
COICA	*Coordinadora de Organizaciones Indígenas de la Amazonia*
CONADES	National Wages Council (*Consejo Nacional de Salarios*)
CONAM	National Modernization Council
CONAREM	National Council for Public Sector Remuneration
CONARTEL	National Council of Radio and Television
CONATEL	National Telecommunications Council
CONCOPE	Consortium of Provincial Councils of Ecuador
CONELEC	National Electricity Council (*Consejo Nacional de Electricidad*)
CONSEP	National Council for the Control of Substances
COPEFEN	Coordinator of the Emergency Program to Cope with the El Niño Phenomenon
CORPEI	Exports and Investment Promotion Corporation (*Corporación de Promoción de Exportaciones e Inversiones*)
CPC	Code of Civil Procedure
CPI	Consumer Price Index
CPI	corruption perception index
CREA	Center for the Economic Reconversion of Azuay
CRM	Center for the Reconversion of Manabí
CSO	civil society organization
CTI	Technical Commission on Investments of the IESS (*Comisión Técnica de Inversiones*)
CTH	Mortgage Titling Company
DAC	Civil Aviation Office

DECEVALE S.A.	depository institution
DGVD	Decentralized Roads Management Unit
DIGMER	maritime transport administration
DINEPP	National Directorate of Continuing Popular Education (*Dirección Nacional de Educación Popular Permanente*)
DNH	National Hydrocarbons Directorate
DNP	National Personnel Directorate
DRC	domestic resource cost
DVP	delivery versus payment
EAP	Energy, Environment, and Population Program
EAP	economically active population
ECOPETROL	Colombian Petroleum Company (*Empresa Colombiana de Petróleo*)
ECORAE	Eco-Development Institute of the Ecuadoran Amazon
EDAP	pension savings deposit institutions (*Entidades Depositarias del Ahorro Previsional*)
EEQ	*Empresa Eléctrica de Quito*
EIS	environmental impact study
EITI	Extractive Industries Transparency Initiative
EMAPS	environmental management action plans
EMBI	Emerging Markets Bond Index
EMPROVIT	Empresa Nacional de Comercialización de Productos Vitales (National Agency for Vital Products)
ENAC	Empresa Nacional de Almacenamiento y Comercialización (National Agency for Storage and Commercialization)
ENAP	National Petroleum Enterprise (Empresa Nacional del Petróleo), Chile
ENDEMAIN	Survey on Demographics and Maternal and Infant Health (*Encuesta Demográfica y de Salud Materna e Infantil*)
ENFE	Ecuadoran National Railway Company
ENSO	El Niño–Southern Oscillation
EPHF	Essential Public Health Functions
EPR	effective protection rate
FAC	Savings and Continguency Fund (*Fondo de Ahorro y Contingencia*)
FASBASE	Strengthening and Expanding the Scope of Basic Health Services in Ecuador (*Fortalecimiento y Ampliación de los Servicios Básicos de Salud en el Ecuador*)
FATF	Financial Action Task Force
FDI	foreign direct investment
FEIREP	Fund for Stabilization, Social and Productive Investment, and Reduction of Public Debt (*Fondo de Estabilización, Inversión Social y Productiva, y Reducción del Endeudamiento Público*)

FEISEH	Ecuadorian Fund for Investment in the Energy and Hydrocarbons Sectors (*Fondo Ecuatoriano de Inversión en los Sectores Energéticos e Hidrocarburos*)
FENAJE	National Federation of Judicial Officials
FEP	Petroleum Stabilization Fund (*Fondo de Establización Petrolera*)
FEPP	Fund for the Progress of the People (*Fondo Ecuatoriano Populorum Progressio*)
FERUM	Fund for the Electrification of the Rural and Urban Marginal Areas
FISE	Social Investment Fund (*Fondo de Inversión Social Ecuatoriano*)
FLAR	Latin American Reserve Fund
FODESEC	Sectional Development Fund (*Fondo de Desarrollo Seccional*)
FODETEL	Telecommunications Development Fund (*Fondo de Desarrollo de las Telecomunicaciones*)
FONDIFA	National Children's Fund
FOPEDEUPO	Permanent Fund for University and Polytechnic Development
FOSE	*Fondo de Compensación Social Eléctrica* (in Peru)
FRTL	Fiscal Responsibility Law
FTAA	Free Trade Agreement of the Americas
FTA	free trade agreement
GCR	Global Competitiveness Report
GDP	gross domestic product
GEF	Global Environmental Facility
GGFR	Global Gas Flaring Reduction
GNP	gross national product
GOE	government of Ecuador
GSP	General System of Preferences
GSRT	gross settlement in real time
GUO	Global Urban Observatory of the United Nations
HACCP	Hazard Analysis and Critical Control Point
HDI	Human Development Index
HRM	human resources management
ICE	special consumption tax (*Impuesto sobre Consumos Especiales*)
ICSID	International Center for Settlement of Investment Disputes
ICT	information and communications technology
IADB	Inter-American Development Bank
IEOS	Ecuadoran Institute for Water and Sanitation Works
IESS	Ecuadoran Social Security Institute (*Instituto Ecuatoriano de Seguridad Social*)
ILDIS	*Instituto Latinoamericano de Investigaciones Sociales*
ILO	International Labour Organization
IMCI	Integrated Management of Childhood Illness
IMF	International Monetary Fund

INEC	Survey on Employment, Unemployment, and Underemployment
INECEL	National power company
INEN	Ecuadoran Standardization Institute
INGALA	National Galápagos Institute
INIAP	National Institute for Agricultural Research
INNFA	National Child and Family Institute
INTERAGUA	International Water Services Guayaquil
IOC	international oil companies
IPO	indigenous people's organization
ISP	Internet service provider
ISR	income tax (Impuesto Sobre la Renta)
ISSFA	Social Security Institute of the Armed Forces (*Instituto de Seguridad Social de las Fuerzas Armadas*)
ISSPOL	Social Security Institute of the Police (*Instituto de Seguridad Social de la Policia National*)
ITT	Ishpingo-Tambococha-Tiputini
ITU	International Telecommunications Union
IVA	value-added tax (*Impuesto al Valor Agregado*)
JAPS	water users associations (*Juntas de Agua Potable y Saneamiento*)
JASS	water and sanitation councils
LAC	Latin America and Caribbean Region
LEXI	Law on Foreign Trade and Investment
LIBOR	London interbank offered rate
LMG	Law on Free Maternity Care (*Ley de Maternidad Gratuita*)
LOAFYC	Law on Financial Administration and Control (*Ley Orgánica de Administración Financiera y Control*)
LPG	liquid petroleum gas
LRFP	Law on Reform of Public Finances
LRSE	Reform Law of Electricity Sector Legislation (*Ley Reformatoria de la Ley de Régimen del Sector Eléctrico*)
LSCCA	Civil Service and Administrative Career Law
LSMS	Living Standards Measurement Study
M&E	monitoring and evaluation
MAG	Ministry of Agriculture
MBS	Ministry of Social Welfare
MCCH	*Maquita Cusinchi*
MDMQ	Municipality of the Metropolitan District of Quito
MDGs	Millennium Development Goals
MDOGs	government ministries, departments, and agencies
MEC	Ministry of Education and Culture
MEF	Ministry of Economy and Finance
MEM	Ministry of Energy and Mining

MFI	microfinance institution
MICIP	Ministry of Industry and Competitiveness
MIDUVI	Ministry of Urban Development and Housing (*Ministerio de Desarrollo Urbano y Vivienda*)
MIVI	Ministry of Housing
MODERSA	Modernization and Development of Comprehensive Health Services Networks (*Modernización y Desarrollo de Redes Integrales de Servicios de Salud*)
MOP	Ministry of Public Works
MSP	Ministry of Public Health
NAP	network access point
NFPS	non-financial public sector
NGO	nongovernmental organization
NOCs	national oil companies
NTB	nontariff barrier
OCP	Heavy Crude Oil Pipeline (*Oleoducto del Crudo Pesado*)
ODEPLAN	Planning Office
OECD	Organisation for Economic Co-operation and Development
OLADE	Latin American Energy Organization
ONN	National Standardization Agency
OPEC	Organization of Petroleum Exporting Countries
ORI	Children's Rescue Operation (*Operación Rescate Infantil*)
OSCIDI	Civil Service and Institutional Development Office
PACMI	Supplementary Food Program for Mothers and Infants (*Programa de Alimentación Complementaria Materna-Infantil*)
PAE	School Meals Program (*Programa de Alimentacion Escolar*)
PAHO	Pan-American Health Organization
PAN	Food Program for Boys and Girls (*Programa de Alimentacion de Niños y Niñas*)
PDI	Children's Development Program (*Programa de Desarrollo Infantil*)
PDM	Municipal Development Program
PPS	Social Protection Program (*Programa de Protección Social*)
PRAGUAS	Water and Sanitation Program for Rural Communities and Small Municipalities—financed by the World Bank
PRG	reference generation price
PROAUS	Universal Health Insurance Program (*Programa de Aseguramiento Universal en Salud*)
PROBONA	Native Andean Forests Program
PRODEPINE	Proyecto de Desarrollo de los Pueblos Indígenas y Negroes del Ecuador (Development Project for Indigenous and Black Peoples of Ecuador)

PROFDs	Associative Products of Promotion
PROJUSTICIA	*Unidad de Coordinación para la Reforma de la Administración de Justicia*
PROLOCAL	Poverty Reduction and Local Rural Development Project
PROMECEB	Program for Better Quality Basic Education (*Programa de Mejoramiento de la Calidad de la Educación Básica*)
PROMSA	Agricultural Services Modernization Program
PRONEPE	National Preschool Education Program (*Programa Nacional de Educación Preescolar*)
PROST	Pension Reform Options Simulation Toolkit
PSP	private sector participation
PT	transmission toll
PUCE	Catholic University of Ecuador
RER	real exchange rate
RFR	*Red Financiera Rural*
RGP	referential generation price
RISE	Ecuadoran Simplified Tax System (*Régimen Impositivo Simplificado Ecuatoriano*)
ROA	return on assets
ROAA	return on average assets
ROAE	return on average equity
RUC	centralized taxpayers registry (*Registro Único de Contribuyentes*)
SAPYSB	Sub-Secretariat of Potable Water and Basic Sanitation
SAPSyRS	Sub-Secretariat of Water Supply, Sanitation, and Solid Waste
SBS	Superintendency of Banks and Insurance (*Superintendencia de Banca y Seguros*)
SCP	Subsecretariat of Public Credit (*Secretaría de Crédito Público*)
SelBen	System of Identification and Selection of Beneficiaries (*Sistema de Identificación y Selección de Beneficiarios*)
SENATEL	National Secretariat of Telecommunications
SENDA	Secretariat for National Administrative Development
SENDOSEP	National Secretariat for Organizational Development of the Public Sector
SENRES	National Technical Secretariat for Human Resources Development and Compensation in the Public Sector
SESA	Ecuadoran Animal and Plant Inspection Service
SGO	General Obligatory Insurance (*Seguro General Obligatorio*)
SG	sectional government
SIAN	Integrated System of Food and Nutrition (*Sistema Integral de Alimentacion y Nutricion*)
SIAP	Integrated Personnel Administration System
SICA	Agricultural Information and Census Service

SIGEF	Integrated Financial Management System
SIISE	Integrated System of Social Indicators of Ecuador Social Indicators System of Ecuador (*Sistema Integrado de Indicadores Sociales de Ecuador*)
SIPREM	Public Sector Compensation Budgetary System
SINOPEC	China Petrochemical Company
SIV	Housing Incentives System
SME	small- and medium-sized enterprise
SODEM	MDG Secretariat (*Secretaria de Objectivos del Milenio*)
SOTE	TransEcuadoran Pipeline System (*Sistema de Oleoducto Transecuatoriano*)
SP	service provider
SPC	service-providing company
SPNF	*Sector Público No Financiero* (see NFPS)
SPNG	Galápagos National Park Service (*Servicio del Parque Nacional Galápagos*)
SRI	Internal Revenue Service
SSC	Rural People's Social Security Program (*Seguro Social Campesino*)
SSO	Obligatory Social Security (*Seguro Social Obligatorio*)
STFS	Social Sector Technical Secretariat
SUMA	Single Environmental Management System (*Sistema Unico de Medio Ambiente*)
SUPTEL	Telecommunications Superintendency
TROLE	Economic Transformation Law
TFP	total factor productivity
UCV	Local Road Works Unit
UDENOR	Development Unit of the North
UOST	Trolleybus System Operating Unit
URC	Credit Restructuring Unit (*Unidad de Reestructuración de Créditos*)
USAID	United States Agency for International Development
VAD	value-added distribution
VAT	value-added tax
WLL	wireless local loop
WRM	water resource management
WTI	West Texas Intermediate
WTO	World Trade Organization

Context and Executive Summary

Eduardo Somensatto

I. Introduction

The World Bank has prepared this series of notes as a contribution to the policy debate in Ecuador. The notes were written by experts from both within and outside the World Bank, who offer a broad perspective on the issues confronting Ecuador, while taking into consideration international experiences. The notes presented here are not intended to be exhaustive, but rather analyze and present policy options for a limited number of topics considered to be critical for the country's social and economic development. The policy notes for Ecuador are part of a series of books that the Bank prepares periodically summarizing its accumulated knowledge on the economic and social issues of member countries. The timing of the notes, early 2007, coincides with a new presidential period, which offers the country the opportunity to consolidate many of the gains of the past few years, while building the basis for a more dynamic, equitable, and inclusive growth process.

The current volume updates the policy notes prepared four years ago, presented in the book *Ecuador: An Economic and Social Agenda for the New Millennium.* Much of the analytical work presented in the earlier book remains relevant today, and as a result, certain sections of the current document essentially update that material. The conditions in many sectors have not changed dramatically, and many of the policy recommendations presented in the previous notes are still applicable. Thus, while the current volume can be read as a freestanding work, it has greater analytic power and policy impact when used in tandem with the previous policy notes.

Several of the notes in the current volume are based on recently produced World Bank studies. In the past few years the Bank prepared analytical work for Ecuador in several areas. The list is quite extensive and includes an Ecuador poverty assessment, a public expenditure review (jointly with the Inter-American Development

Bank—IADB), a country financial accountability assessment, a country procurement assessment (jointly with the IADB), a social security analysis, a rural development strategy, a labor market study, a country economic memorandum, and a nutrition study. These studies represent a wealth of analytical work and contain greater detail than some of the notes presented here.

The policy notes that follow cover many areas and issues and are grouped under three broad themes:

- *Preserving stability and accelerating growth.* The topics addressed include (i) maintaining fiscal discipline to ensure the continuity of a stable macroeconomic framework; (ii) accelerating and broadening economic growth through increased competitiveness, expanded opportunities, and greater employment generation; (iii) dealing effectively with the myriad problems affecting the energy sector; and (iv) broadening the benefits of growth through more inclusion, particularly for the rural sector of the economy.
- *Promoting sustainable and equitable social development.* The discussions cover human, natural, and social capital. Particular attention is devoted to the education and health sectors, as well as the social protection system, all sectors that offer the greatest opportunities for reducing the country's deep and ingrained inequalities. The notes also cover other facets of the development challenge, such as ensuring the sustainability of reforms and preserving Ecuador's unique environmental and natural resource base. In a country with such a rich and diverse cultural base, broadening the benefits of development will entail giving greater voice to the country's increasingly empowered ethnic and social groups and making the state more accountable.
- *Improving governance and strengthening institutions.* The topic encompasses a broad range of issues, including institutional reforms aimed at building a high-quality and efficient system of government, the challenges of decentralization, and effective measures to reduce corruption.

II. Overview

The analysis contained in the policy notes indicates that Ecuador is a country with great potential, with a society that has exhibited incredible resilience and the ability to adapt to new challenges. The Ecuadoran society has overcome adversity with great determination in the past few years. Periodic economic crises, external shocks, and even natural disasters tested the country's ability to cope with difficulties. Despite these challenges, the country has maintained a forward-looking perspective and has achieved some important goals. Economic stability in the past few years has given Ecuador the opportunity for a period of sustained economic growth. During this period several development indicators have improved, and several sectors of the economy have demonstrated the dynamism and entrepreneurship that are present in the Ecuadoran culture. In general, surveys show that Ecuadorans feel that their individual conditions are likely to improve in the future.

Many factors have precluded the country from fulfilling its full economic potential. Foremost among them is political instability. A major obstacle to achieving a higher level of development has been the lack of political constancy and policy continuity. Frequent changes of authorities and policy reversals have stifled economic performance by generating uncertainty and harmful economic cycles. Political instability and discord have precluded the country from agreeing on a long-term national agenda and have prevented the pursuit of consistent policies to reduce Ecuador's long-time problems of exclusion, inequity, and lack of opportunity for much of the population. Among the factors driving this instability are deep social, ethnic, and regional divisions, along with weak political institutions. In the past 10 years, the political environment has been particularly volatile in Ecuador. Starting in 1996, none of the elected presidents have been able to complete their constitutionally mandated term. There have been no fewer than six presidents and numerous cabinet ministers during this period. Several factors contributed to this volatility, including questioned ethical conduct, economic crisis, the loss of public confidence, and unstable coalitions. The developments of the past 10 years reveal the challenges the country faces in strengthening its democratic institutions.

Today Ecuador has a unique opportunity to consolidate and improve on the recent economic gains. The country is currently experiencing a period of improved economic and social conditions unmatched since the return of democracy in 1979. Thanks in part to greater macroeconomic stability achieved through dollarization in 2000, the increase in petroleum prices, and greater remittance flows, social and economic indicators have risen considerably in the past five years. The improvement has been particularly noteworthy in levels of consumption; in the growth of imports and nontraditional exports; and in investments, housing, construction, and the recovery of the financial sector. The economy seems to have sufficient momentum to ensure continuity in these trends. The financial situation of the government is also better. In fact, the current administration, of President Rafael Correa, is the first, during the new democratic period, that will inherit a relatively favorable fiscal position. Though the financing requirements of the central government will be significant, ways could be devised to finance many of the newly proposed initiatives and to enhance the role and design of those programs that benefit the needy. Several layers of the state apparatus are in better condition to assume certain responsibilities. In particular, the subnational governments have shown the ability and the competence to handle many of the public sector services and have been extremely successful in responding to their constituencies. This trend, which has given rise to calls for greater regional and local autonomy, offers an opportunity to build a new, more efficient and effective system of political administration and public service delivery.

However, important challenges remain to be tackled if Ecuador is to take advantage of the current favorable economic environment. These challenges range from implementing policies that will sustain and broaden the benefits of current growth, to dealing with inequality and institutional weakness and modernizing the public sector. Other major areas include expanding and improving the quality of public services, ensuring a more inclusive development pattern, and addressing the needs of the rural areas. An overarching objective is to make effective use of the country's rich natural resources, particularly of its diminishing hydrocarbon resources. The current windfall from higher petroleum revenues offers a major opportunity to use those resources more equitably and efficiently. From an intergenerational perspective, equality may require using the current revenues from extracting resources to endow future generations with the higher level of assets and greater opportunities. Today, a large proportion of the petroleum revenues are being enjoyed by the current generation and are financing large universal subsidies, increases in public spending, and a pro-cyclical fiscal policy. Ample opportunity exists to consider alternatives, such as targeting the subsidies, saving some of the additional revenues, pursuing countercyclical fiscal policy, and investing in activities that are certain to have high rates of return for society.

To broaden and sustain the benefits of the recent economic performance, the country could spur growth in sectors that promote employment creation and improve its competitiveness. Ecuador, as all countries that are participating in the inexorable process of global integration, will confront increasingly competitive markets for its products. Special efforts made now would improve the investment and business climate in the country, which is ranked one of the worst in Latin America. To preserve the effects of dollarization under such an environment, it will be crucial to adopt measures to increase productivity, particularly since the country's cost structure is being artificially lowered by significant subsidies that might not be sustained. In addition, the lagging performance of the agricultural sector and the special needs of small rural producers will require specific programs to incorporate the sectors more effectively into the national and international markets.

Expanding the benefits of development and making opportunities more equitable will work only if the country devotes special attention to those who have been excluded in the past. Ecuador is a country with deep social and regional divisions. It has historically excluded large segments of its society from the benefits of development. This is especially true for the case of indigenous peoples and Afro-Ecuadorans. Both exclusion and inequality fuel much of the resentment and discontentment that prevail in some segments of society that are looking for new political directions. While many parts of the country have seen great improvement, many provinces did not get the assistance necessary to lift their population from poverty. Most of those are predominantly rural provinces, with an inefficient agricultural base and a large number of small producers who lack access to credit and services. Besides the support those sectors require, the regions have deficient infrastructure that can only be improved by significant public investment.

To reduce inequality and break the intergenerational poverty trap, it will be important to make more effective use of the country's social programs. Despite the improvements of the past few years, Ecuador still lags behind many Latin American countries in terms of its social indicators. An important segment of the population, essentially the poor, lacks access to basic services. However, the country has an array of social programs that, if properly managed, could be the foundation for helping the poor to become more active participants in the development process. For example, Ecuador has in place the largest cash transfer program in Latin America, in terms of percentage of population covered. Making the program conditional, requiring beneficiaries to demonstrate that their children are attending school and using the health services available, can help reduce school desertion, particularly at the crucial secondary level. Ecuador is also just starting to ensure health access to the poorest people through a universal health insurance program that will change the budgeting for the sector, basing reimbursements on services provided. These programs, along with the effective use of the free maternity care program, can help accelerate the very important trend of reduced infant and child mortality rates, as well as reduced fertility rates, which have declined dramatically in the past two decades. This trend of smaller families is becoming one of the most important factors in improving conditions of many families.

Another critical challenge will be to strengthen the institutional and delivery capacity of the public sector. Currently, many of the government agencies and public enterprises face organizational difficulties that prevent them from providing effective and efficient public services. In particular, several social sector programs can be reformed and be structured with the aim not only of improving services, but also of helping to expand opportunities and becoming more inclusive. The country now has an opportunity to take greater advantage of the management abilities that have been demonstrated by several municipalities and provinces, and begin to consider using a more decentralized process of service delivery.

These challenges will be encountered in an environment of increasing expectations, in a country full of contrasts. In the past few years, individuals and households have seen their welfare improve. Polls show that individuals and households anticipate that their economic conditions will continue to get better, particularly given the prospect of petroleum revenues and remittances remaining high. This positive individual expectation, however, does not seem to be reflected in the attitude of society as a whole. Polls also show a certain level of collective pessimism. There is an interesting contrast of collective uncertainty versus a more positive individual outlook. A dichotomy exists whereby individuals feel they might be better off in the future, but they do not necessarily feel that the country will. One possible explanation is that dollarization has introduced stability, which now allows for longer-term planning and reduces individual uncertainty. The public also now has a sense that the economy is shielded from political instability, the factor that had created most individual uncertainty in the past.

The policy notes presented in this book take into consideration the context presented above, and identify many of the challenges the country will face in the near future. The notes cover many areas and subjects but are grouped into three broad themes: preserving stability and accelerating growth, promoting sustainable and equitable social development, and improving governance and strengthening institutions. The remainder of this chapter summarizes the main findings and recommendations of the policy notes.

III. Preserving Stability and Accelerating Growth

Many individual policy notes cover issues that come under the broad umbrella of stability and growth. This summary focuses on macroeconomic policies, growth and job creation, the business climate, labor markets, the financial sector, trade and commercial policy, the energy sector, agriculture, and rural development. Each chapter follows a similar pattern, with a description of recent and current developments in the sector, along with policy proposals.

Recent Economic Developments

Despite political difficulties, Ecuador's economic performance of the past few years has been impressive. Fueled by increasing oil revenues and recovery from the deep financial crisis of 1998–99, the economy has grown at an average of 5 percent per year since 2000. Consumption has grown even faster, averaging close to 6 percent per year. Inflation, which peaked in the middle of 2000 at 100 percent, declined to 3 percent in 2006. Several other economic indicators reveal widespread improvement in economic conditions. Deposits in the banking sector, along with credit, have more than doubled and now are above the precrisis level. Many sectors of the economy, such as construction, agriculture, and nontraditional exports, also have recovered, with nontraditional exports growing at an impressive 15 percent a year since 2002.

The recovery during the current decade is in sharp contrast to the performance of the 1990s. The economy at the time had experienced protracted fiscal, inflationary, and financial difficulties that were fueled by external shocks, lax policies, and natural disasters. Those conditions culminated in the deepest financial and foreign exchange crisis in the country's recent history, leading to financial costs of 15 percent of gross domestic product (GDP). To address the crisis, the government enacted a series of policies, the most drastic of which was to replace the domestic currency with the dollar in 2000. Other measures included a series of laws that improved the flexibility of markets and allowed for greater participation of the private sector in certain sectors of the economy. More important, the Fiscal Responsibility and Transparency Law that was passed in 2002 called for saving extra resources from increased petroleum revenues and reducing the budget financing vulnerabilities. The law was based on fiscal policy rules that placed limits on the growth of expenditures, while providing for priority programs even in the face of cyclical changes in revenues.

The outcome of the dollarization and the supporting policies has been a period of macroeconomic stability. The country has enjoyed the benefits of a favorable external environment, which has meant low rates of inflation and declining interest rates. Domestic interest rates have fallen to single digits, and a more stable economic environment has given rise to a rapid extension of long-term financing, including mortgages. Real wages have grown by more than 20 percent in the past four years, as has GDP per capita. Employment has grown in line with the growth of the labor force.

Macroeconomic stability and growth have also been driven by increases in both the production and the price of petroleum, Ecuador's largest export product. The September 2003 opening of a privately financed heavy crude oil pipeline allowed private companies to increase exports from around 20,000 barrels a day in 1998 to about 350,000 barrels a day in 2005. Coupled with the output from PetroEcuador, total production in the past three years has averaged around 550,000 barrels per day, an increase of more than 50 percent from the levels at the beginning of the decade. This increase in production was accompanied by a surge in prices, which have almost doubled in the past three years.

Both the fiscal positions and external accounts have improved substantially as a result of the higher oil revenues. The primary balance of the central government reached 5.5 percent of GDP in 2006 (while the overall balance rose to 3.3 percent), compared with about 1 percent in 2001. Ecuador also recovered creditworthiness, with the decline in its debt burden. Public sector debt as a share of GDP fell from 90 percent in 2001 to 33 percent in 2006. In the external sector, the trade balance showed a surplus of over 4.5 percent of GDP in 2006, despite significant increases in imports. The current account balance also recovered and now has a similar surplus, after having reached a deficit of over 2 percent of GDP in 2001. Foreign exchange reserves now exceed US$2.3 billion, compared with the dangerously low levels of 2000.

The confluence of higher oil revenues, dollarization, and the accompanying policies established the basis for a rapid recovery from the financial crisis of the late 1990s. The improvements in the economy have been steady and fairly broad since 2000. Some of the examples are the impressive increases in imports, which have doubled in the past five years. Their strong growth has been present in all categories, particularly imported capital goods, which grew at a remarkable 30 percent annually during this period. The latter reflects the strong performance of investment, especially foreign investment, which has been assisted by greater opportunities in infrastructure and natural resources development, and by better financing mechanisms. The economy's improvements also generated new jobs and helped lower the unemployment rate to approximately 10 percent of the labor force.

The prospects in the near term are favorable. With the price of petroleum expected to remain at current levels for the foreseeable future, the economic outlook is still positive in the near term. Growth is likely to remain above 4 percent for the year. Many of the other macroeconomic indicators are also expected to remain within reasonable ranges. Inflation seems to be under control for the moment, and the external position of the country should be sound enough to preserve the dollarization.

Despite the recovery of the economy, a general perception persists that the policies of the past few years have not benefited all of the groups in society. This is one of the factors that led the new administration to change the course of economic policy in 2005. The thrust of the new policy is to use public spending to reactivate the economy and to channel the additional petroleum revenues to social programs and projects that could benefit the most disadvantaged of the population.

Macroeconomics: Risks and Policy Proposals

Uncertainties challenge the sustainability of the recent trends. Part of the good economic performance of the past few years has been a recovery from depressed economic levels during the 1998–99 crisis. Once that process, now in its final stages, is completed, continued economic growth will depend much more on the expected policy environment. Given the variability in policies and the lack of definition of a longer-term national agenda, the path of future policies is uncertain. The main concerns are the preservation of macroeconomic stability, improvement in the business climate, and a more stable legal and regulatory framework.

The relaxation of fiscal policy in the past couple years could strain macroeconomic stability in the future. Recent measures to raise expenditures and reduce the savings of the public sector have placed fiscal policy in a more vulnerable position. Expenditures have risen by more than 50 percent in the past four years. This has been driven in great part by impressive increases in revenues, owing to additional petroleum income. The expenditure structure, however, is fairly rigid, and any possible decline in the price of petroleum could wipe out the current surpluses being generated by the nonfinancial public sector. Containment of expenditure increases that have averaged close to 10 percent a year will be essential to maintaining macroeconomic stability, since in a dollarized economy, fiscal policy is the primary policy tool for macroeconomic management.

Recent policy measures have liberalized the fiscal management framework as well as liquidity of Ecuador's treasury and public debt management. The amendment of the Fiscal Responsibility and Transparency Law, along with many other measures to ease the use of the oil stabilization funds, lifted the limitations on expenditure growth and modified the allocation of oil revenues in a manner that discouraged public savings. While the funds can now be used for public investments, it is essential that the fund be channeled for productive alternatives, and not current expenditure. As such, the use of the savings could facilitate short-term liquidity management, while making fiscal management more vulnerable to adverse international conditions or other adverse shocks.

The key to ensuring continued stability will be to consolidate Ecuador's fiscal position. In a dollarized economy, fiscal policy is the centerpiece of macroeconomic management. In a petroleum-based economy, fiscal policy is also a key collective instrument to generate savings for future generations. In this context, the course of fiscal policy depends on the decision of how much to save from the current petroleum revenues and how those savings will be allocated. The creation of many savings funds in the past has obscured fiscal decisions and has added to the already saturated system of earmarking. Consolidating the funds and easing the earmarking would aid the management of fiscal policy. It would give greater flexibility and also a clearer picture of the overall surplus of the nonfinancial public sector. Such a surplus is necessary if the country decides to transfer current wealth to future generations, which can also be effected by bequeathing a lower public debt. The country has made great progress in the past few years in lowering the debt burden, when measured as a share of GDP. This does not mean the country has reached a manageable level of debt. The central government still confronts considerable financing needs, given the scheduled amortizations, particularly of domestic debt. To deal with this condition, there are different options, including lengthening the amortization schedules of domestic debt and relying on lower-cost and longer-term-maturity external debt. To carry out such policy, it would be important to have a group of professionals, equipped with the tools and the legal basis, to carry out an active debt management program. The note on debt management in this book highlights the need to develop a strategy to minimize risks and better develop both the primary and secondary markets for public debt.

Achieving the goals of fiscal consolidation will require restraining the growth of expenditures while continuing to improve tax administration. The trend of growing expenditures of the nonfinancial public sector has been accelerating in the past few years. Most of this growth has taken place in current expenditures, without much consideration of their social effectiveness. The continuation of such a trend is not consistent with the objective of using the petroleum windfall for the benefit of future generations. It would be preferable to devote more to public investments, but even in that case, it is essential to ensure that those outlays have high social rates of return and are properly managed.

Much of the increase in the cost of public investment in Ecuador is due to an inefficient system of procurement, deficient administration, and delays in construction. Many of these problems could be overcome by introducing a transparent, more technologically advanced, and more competitive system of procurement throughout the public sector. Similarly, the country has an excellent opportunity, given the advancements in technology, to introduce a system of monitoring the advancement of public works. This system could be coupled with a better process for evaluating the merits of individual components of the public investment program, that is, by consolidating those responsibilities within a single agency or vice ministry.

The past few years' improvements in the management of tax administration are an excellent example of what can be accomplished in the Ecuadoran public sector. Its modernization process has been an unparalleled success, mainly as a result of the continuity in the administration and the determination of its leaders to effect changes. As a result, tax revenues have increased fourfold in seven years, and the efficiency of the tax administration system is one of the best in Latin America. Despite these improvements, much remains to be done, such as reducing tax evasion and avoidance, and incorporating into the formal systems a large segment of the economy that is still operating in the informal markets and not paying taxes. Estimates show that up to 60 percent of the Ecuadoran economy is still laboring outside the formal structures. As discussed in the next section, incorporating informal activities into the economy will require reducing the barriers to formality, such as business registration and tax administration burdens. Another major policy change will involve the effective joint management of customs administration, with the proper cross-checking of information, and the application of systems similar to those introduced in the tax administration area.

Economic Growth and Job Creation—Current Conditions and Policy Proposals

Perhaps Ecuador faces no greater challenge than to improve its growth prospect and promote greater employment generation. The growth of the average real per capita income in the past decade has been extremely low, around 1 percent per year, essentially the same as productivity growth. With such performance it would take more than 70 years to double per capita income. Whereas, if the country could raise per capita income growth to 4 percent per year, incomes would double every 17 years and would rise eight times over the 70-year period. Ecuador has all of the natural and human conditions to achieve higher growth rates, but it needs to improve the environment and framework that could generate such growth. It will be important to implement policies to expand markets and thereby increase productivity and job creation.

To achieve higher growth rates it will be critical to expand the levels of investment (both public and private). Despite the barriers to doing business (discussed below), investments have grown solidly in the past four years. During this period, overall capital formation has been growing twice as fast as GDP. The investment rate today is about 22 percent of GDP. The performance of investment is highlighted by significant increases in the importation of capital and industrial goods, which have increased by more than 60 percent in just four years. Sector data are not easily available, but large investments have taken place in the petroleum sector.

With respect to job creation, the evolution of (urban) labor markets has been closely associated with macroeconomic conditions. After reaching a high of 14.4 percent at the height of the economic crisis in early 2000, the unemployment rate declined to less than 10 percent in 2006. During the same period the population classified as economically active rose by an average of 3 percent per year. Thus, employment creation has mirrored the growth in the economy (the long-term output elasticity of employment is slightly smaller than 1). Most of the employment creation, however, occurred in the informal and temporary job market, which currently accounts for more than half of the economically active population. Most disconcerting are the underemployment figures, which are above 45 percent. Despite the timid employment creation in the formal sector, figures show that most employment creation occurred in those firms that are more productive, use foreign technology more intensively, have a higher exposure to international competition, and have employees with a higher level of education. As in many other countries, productivity increases and employment creation are associated with educational levels and technology use. Ecuador has a number of barriers to job creation, such as high levels of labor protection and entitlement profit sharing, among others. As a result, there has been tremendous growth in the use of temporary workers, who do not enjoy similar guarantees. Removing or reducing these barriers, as well as improving the regulation of the temporary workers markets, will be key to improving job creation.

The lack of significant policy reforms in the past few years could limit future growth and investment. After the initial adoption of some reforms following the financial crisis of 1999, the government has not undertaken significant recent efforts to address the pressing issues that afflict certain sectors of the economy. A number of strategic sectors are in need of fundamental reforms. This is most evident in the energy sector, where both the electricity and hydrocarbon sectors face major challenges. Investors are discouraged by a deficient legal and regulatory structure, arbitrary decisions by the government, the management of public enterprises, the lack of prompt payments, and the large number of nontransparent subsidies being channeled through the sector. In general, political instability and discretionary policies have generated one of the worst business and investment climates in Latin America. Ecuador ranks low in essentially all measures used to qualify countries in terms of their attractiveness to investment. Unless the country addresses many of the factors that influence the business climate, it will be harder to bolster private investment and accelerate economic growth.

Many other areas and sectors require attention if the aim is to accelerate growth. Although the financial sector has improved considerably in the past few years, it still suffers from many shortcomings, such as poor access to credit markets, segmented and incomplete markets, low innovation, high operational costs, poor protection of creditors' rights, weak supervision, among others. Similarly, international trade policy suffers from the lack of a long-term strategy of integration and from the failure to open the markets to greater competition. Also, the agricultural sector is hampered by low levels of technology, underdeveloped rural financial systems, lack of competitiveness in some products, protected markets, and a price support system that distorts the function of the markets. The supporting infrastructure system needs to be modernized. Ports and customs facilities are some of the most inefficient in Latin America. The time delays for processing both imports and exports raise production costs, and the labyrinth of discretionary policies that are applied in the processing of trade can be a source of corruption. The road network is also deficient and increases operational costs. Science and technology policies are lacking, particularly those that spur innovation and increases in productivity. Complementary to this, and as discussed in the next section, are the insufficient improvements in secondary education enrollment and the quality of education in general.

The current environment provides an excellent window of opportunity to carry out the reforms necessary to make growth more sustainable and broader.

International economic conditions are favorable. The momentum in the economy will afford some time for the implementation of the reforms. The new administration has a chance to redefine economic policy and has a mandate to implement key reforms. Below are just a few recommendations and options that could lead to improvement in the growth prospects.

Business Climate and Labor Markets

There is a pressing need to generate an environment propitious to investment, both domestic and foreign. The business climate ranks very low when compared with other countries and tends to discourage greater investment. In the *Doing Business 2007* rankings, Ecuador ranked 123 out of 175 countries in the sample. This makes the country the fourth worst in the region, after Venezuela (164), Haiti (139) and Bolivia (131). Ecuador lags far behind regional leaders such as Chile (29), Peru (65), El Salvador (71), Colombia (79), and Panama (81). Despite the urgent need to improve the business climate, the country has not made reforms in any of 10 principal areas tracked by the Doing Business database.

The cost of doing business and barriers to business formation are still high and burdensome. Registering property was the only area in which Ecuador improved significantly in 2006, moving from 106th to 84th in the international ranking. However, this gain was insignificant when compared with very poor performances in employing workers (161st of 175 in the sample), starting a business (139), closing a business (134), protecting investors (135), and trading across borders (126). Ecuador has a rigidity employment index of 51, compared with a regional average of 32. This index measures labor market regulations and practices related to the costs of hiring and firing workers. For example, in Ecuador the cost of letting an employee go is 135 weeks of wages, when the average for Latin America is approximately 60 weeks.

Perhaps the greatest source of uncertainty and cost of doing business lies with the lack of judicial certainty, contract security, and the enforcement of legal agreements. The prevalence of the rule of law and confidence in the judiciary are among the lowest in Latin America. Ecuador ranks in the lower one-third of the countries when measured by the index of the rule of law. Business activity in Ecuador has to contend with arbitrary nullification of contracts, unilateral and retroactive changes of these contracts, failures to collect on payments, and, more generally, considerable complexity in handling matters related to intellectual property, insolvency and bankruptcy, antitrust actions, consumer protection, and environmental degradation. These have high economic and social costs, and their application often overwhelms the capacity of civil courts.

The traditional resources and capacity of a civil court are clearly inadequate to meet demand. Although the Judiciary Organic Law allows specialization of certain courts or judges for the rapid adjudication of more complex cases, this power has not been fully exercised and could be extended to new areas that have high economic or social impact. The institutional framework for creditor rights and insolvency proceedings is weak, and the prestige of the judiciary is very low. The most frequent complaints of users of the system are as follows: (i) judges lack sufficient knowledge of business issues and commercial law matters; (ii) in practice, judges lack training and continued education; (iii) most judges exert a pro-debtor tendency in commercial cases; (iv) undue political influence on judges often affects their decisions; (v) corruption issues often affect the court officials and some judges; (vi) inefficiencies abound in court organization; and (vii) issues involving lack of transparency and unpredictability in the judicial decision-making process are frequent. The enforcement of creditors' rights is a particular concern, since it is weakened by an outdated and ineffective registration system of property rights and the lengthy procedures to enforce unsecured credits. The municipal cadastres and registries of immovable properties are segmented and not easily accessible, making them difficult to use effectively in enforcement proceedings.

The country could undertake several measures to improve its investment climate ranking, such as preparing an action plan to respond to the key findings of the *Doing Business 2007* report. Among the main measures are to lower the cost of starting and operating a business and to improve labor flexibility and mobility. The regulatory burden in Ecuador is quite high, and a complete review of these required procedures is warranted. The government had prepared a list of the many procedures mandated to start a business, which amounts to 14 steps that take over 90 days and cost 10 times the per capita income in the country (one of the highest costs in the region). These steps can be simplified and the time reduced. Similarly, Ecuadoran businesses spend 15 percent of their time dealing with government regulations, more than in any other country in Latin America. Such requirements increase the possibility of corruption. One approach would be to embark on an administrative simplification program aimed at expediting the granting of licenses and permits. Another would be to reduce the number of visits by regulators, through a process of inspections based on noncompliance risks.

Reforms could involve great efforts to modernize the judicial system's handling of the civil code and to provide greater security for contract and legal agreements. Many legal and administrative reforms can be carried out to modernize the judicial system. In the area of the civil code, they include reviewing the bankruptcy and corporate restructuring laws and the laws governing creditors' rights. The Code of Civil Procedure, which governs bankruptcy processes, is hardly ever used, and the alternative of administrative restructuring under the Preventive Measures Law has failed to achieve its objectives. Hence, an urgent task is to review the laws in order to modernize and facilitate the restructuring procedures. Similarly, new laws and regulations governing secured transactions could make possible the use of a broad range of assets as collateral (e.g., accounts receivables, farm equipment and durable products, and warehouse receipts). Also urgent is the effort to update and upgrade the information systems of title and land registries, lower registration costs, and simplify foreclosures. In general, an essential course is to change the cumbersome legal framework that still favors debtor over creditor rights and to address the lack of speed and predictability of the court system. In this same vein, the public sector itself can take the lead in reducing the degree of arbitrariness and unilateral discretionary management of its contracts. One alternative to reduce discretion and possible corruption (discussed in greater detail in section IV) would be to modernize the public procurement system by introducing an Internet-based transactional system that would promote greater transparency and the participation of more service providers.

Labor market reforms could be the most critical and difficult. The core issue is how to deal with the divisions and differences that exist between permanent and temporary contracts. In a recent study, "The Ecuadorian Labor Markets; Tendencies and Recommendations," the World Bank analyzed the different options of maintaining the status quo, restricting temporary contracts, and making permanent contracts less costly and more flexible. Each combination has its advantages and disadvantages. The basic proposals would be to limit temporary contracts to purely temporary activities, limit the number of consecutive temporary contracts any individual can have with a single firm, and have a different social security contribution for temporary workers. For permanent workers, the options are to reduce the compensation for job losses, consider economic reasons as just cause for dismissal, establish an independent arbitration system to resolve conflicts, make the profit system more flexible and the accounts more transparent, and make the firm pension system more equitable among workers. The choice among these options should be based on criteria aimed at making the overall labor market system more flexible, less costly, more equitable, and geared toward employment generation.

The Financial Sector

The improvement in investment and consumption of the past few years has been assisted in part by the recovery of the financial sector. Since the crisis of 1999–2000 the financial intermediation role of the banks has been restored and the sector has performed relatively well. Deposits have grown rapidly (at an average rate of more than 20 percent per year). The growth of credit has been very similar and has been accompanied by a diversification of the loan portfolio. The sector has had significant increases in nontraditional credit instruments, such as housing and microcredits. Ecuador now has a vibrant home mortgage market, with tenure of more than 10 years, and historically low interest rates are perhaps the most important factor driving the construction sector. The financial sector today is also on a more solid foundation, with sufficient liquidity, reserves, and high rates of return. The quality of credit has improved, with the share of nonperforming loans now down to below 5 percent (from 15 percent in 2001). The system risk ratio is lower, and credit ratings of banks have risen.

Despite the recovery of the financial sector, and its more healthy condition today, important issues are still to be addressed. Financial depth is still rather low, with total assets of the financial sector around 40 percent of GDP, and credit to the private sector only around 18 percent of GDP. The system lacks adequate mechanisms to deal effectively with a liquidity crisis. This is a particular problem in a dollarized economy. Liquidity management remains problematic for Ecuador since the Deposit Guarantee Agency is bankrupt and has no liquidity to honor its obligations. The current proposals to reform the liquidity fund are too expensive or fall short of providing adequate insurance against a systemic liquidity risk. Banking sector vulnerabilities are also exacerbated by the concentration of the investment portfolio and by the country's volatile economic and political environment.

Markets are shallow and narrow, with limited competition and differentiated access to financial services. The sector still caters mostly to large firms and well-established credit clients. While new products, such as long-term mortgages, have grown rapidly, innovation in the capital markets has been slow, stifled in part by the lack of instruments to reduce credit risks. Capital markets can be deepened in many areas, particularly pension and retirement services, insurance, contractual savings, and the stock market. Pension reforms could be a catalyst to much-needed capital market development, particularly given the absence of mutual funds and other pooling mechanisms. Though interest rates have declined overall (mostly owing to lower inflation), the cost of credit remains high compared with other dollarized economies. The large spreads between borrowing and lending rates, along with the complex system of fees used by the banks, have generated concerns about the inadequate protection of consumers and the lack of transparency.

The challenge of the sector is to develop better and more efficient services to small and medium enterprises, and within the whole structure of microcredits. Although Ecuador has a fairly established microfinancing structure (through cooperatives and other institutions), and the formal banks have considerably increased their presence in the sector, most microenterprises still lack access to the formal market. Small and medium enterprises count on financial credit for only 25 percent of their financing needs. This figure is even smaller for microenterprises. Most of the loans are of short duration, and have a high cost. The greatest barrier to a wider market remains the lack of solid credit histories of or information about potential borrowers and the lack of collateral. Many of the solutions recently proposed are to strengthen the role of the public sector banks and the system of public cooperatives. But other options also exist.

One near-term focus might be on promoting private institutions that are already involved in microfinancing to raise credit availability to the small and medium enterprises. Although existing public financial institutions might play a role in direct lending, a more effective means would be to strengthen the existing system of cooperatives and to concentrate on credit information systems and on risk-sharing mechanisms. The cooperatives and other alternative providers offer a base for delivery, but they are limited by liquidity and their ability to pool and share risk. The government could consider allowing for mutually owned institutions and provide incentives for the creation of pooled networks, for example, by reducing capital requirements for those who pool. Partnering with other possible delivery systems, such as the forthcoming network of 1,000 telecommunication centers, could be an alternative, although much training of providers would be needed. Unquestionably, one of the urgent measures is to create better information on small borrowers by establishing effective credit information bureaus that share their credit histories with lenders. The great barrier remains risk, and if public institutions are to be directly involved in the delivery of small credits, their primary role should be to help participants develop a solid credit history.

To strengthen and expand the role of the financial sector, the government can pursue a number of other policies. Most important is to ensure the stability of the system through sound macroeconomic policies and adequate liquidity management mechanisms. The latter may require either a fund that covers at least 20 percent of deposits or the internationalization of the Ecuadoran banking system. The opening of the sector would allow for greater reliance on international liquidity management. However, this approach would require a change in the law. It also would be important to raise capital requirements. The current deposit insurance system must be reformed with the adoption of a more credible arrangement. This could entail greater contributions, complemented by innovative methods of insurance, such as with contingent funds. Naturally, the reforms of the bankruptcy laws and creditors' rights discussed earlier could also strengthen the system. Finally, so as not to undermine the health of the system, care should be taken in adopting recently proposed reforms that place ceilings on interest rates and eliminate all noninterest charges. The reforms should seek transparency and simplification of the processes.

Pension reforms and innovation are essential for the future expansion of the financial system. The complexity of the social security system and the need for reforms constitute a very broad subject that deserves special attention and is beyond the scope of this exercise (it has been dealt extensively in the World Bank's 2005 publication *Ecuador: Policy Options for the Social Security System*). A key element of any reform would be the transparent separation of the system's health and other social protections from its retirement funding role. These are separate systems that should be managed separately. Whereas in both programs there is a cause for expanded coverage and a minimum guarantee, there is also a need to continue to promote the role of pension funds and individual contributions. The social security system in Ecuador is at a stage of accumulating surpluses, given the demographics of its working population. Hence, the system continues to be a key net creditor to the government, which means that future liabilities are dependent on the ability of the government to finance the pay-as-you-go system. In the future, other possible uses of the surpluses could be considered. The Ecuadoran Social Security Institute (IESS) could assist in promoting the mortgage market, not necessarily by direct lending to members, but in mortgage portfolios or backed securities, thus promoting securitization.

Trade Sector and Commercial Policy

Although Ecuador's trade openness is similar to that of other countries in the region and to countries with similar levels of income, the country's external performance is significantly weaker when only non-oil exports are considered. The ratio of non-oil exports to non-oil GDP has declined from 25 percent in 1990–94 to 21 percent in 2000–04 and currently is below the regional average. This decline, combined with strong import growth, has resulted in rising non-oil current account deficits. Coverage of imports by exports fell to 85 percent in the period 2001–03. Moreover, trade volumes were not very responsive to trade liberalization efforts of the early 1990s. Growth of trade volumes as a percentage of GDP was similar in the eight years prior to and after the reforms. In contrast, other countries that have recently opened their economies to trade exhibit rapid increases in trade volumes following these changes.

Limited trade growth is the result of the structure of Ecuador's exports (concentration on oil and traditional agricultural products) and inadequate trade and commercial policies. Ecuador's export concentration ratio is significantly higher than that of its regional competitors, with 95 percent of all non-oil exports being accounted for by only 24 products, and the speed of diversification is slow. Moreover, its exports are much less sophisticated than those of countries with similar levels of income per capita as a result of the relative bias toward extractive and low-value-added exports. Finally, high tariffs on imported intermediate and capital goods and extensive use of nontariff instruments, together with deficient transport infrastructure and ineffective customs services, have increased the cost of accessing modern technologies and, more generally, curtailed the international competitiveness of Ecuadoran firms.

Unfavorable conditions in international markets and the country's inability to diversify its export base have also contributed to hampered trade growth. In recent years demand for Ecuadoran products has been weak, mainly as a result of the decline in the demand for traditional commodities (bananas, fish, crustaceans, cocoa, coffee, and textiles) and because of slower productivity gains relative to other countries. In fact, Ecuador's internationally competitive position in the U.S. market has deteriorated over the past few years. In addition, Ecuador has failed to adapt its export basket to changing conditions in international markets. This contrasts with Eastern European countries, which have pursued an aggressive policy of export diversification targeted to strengthened economic integration with the European Union. Both increased diversification and deepened markets appear to be correlated with economic growth, suggesting that Ecuador is forgoing an opportunity for higher economic growth through greater international trade integration, particularly with the United States.

The international experience shows that more open economies tend to be more productive. Firms that export and actively participate in the international markets are more efficient, with higher rates of productivity. They also tend to innovate more often, by making effective use of technology transfer. Ecuadoran firms have demonstrated a keen ability to compete internationally. Hence, measures and agreements that open the markets, with the appropriate support and compensation to those adversely affected, should be pursued. Besides agreements on market access with other countries, Ecuador can unilaterally adopt several measures to open its markets, such as reducing tariffs on capital goods, lowering the dispersion of tariffs on intermediate and capital imports, and limiting the "effective protection" in low-value-added activities. It can sharply reduce unnecessary import authorizations and bans, which would permit lower prices and enhanced competition in the market for agricultural inputs.

In addition, the system of mandatory technical norms should be reviewed. Other measures could include refocusing institutions' traditional export promotion and competitiveness promotion to place a higher priority on their activities toward new exports. This could be done by (i) promoting business associations, R&D in agriculture and food, incubator programs, fiscal incentives for diversification (revising traditional free trade zone incentives and eliminating other tax exemptions not considered in the diversification strategy), and export consortia of small and medium enterprises; (ii) by improving capital risk financing; and (iii) by revamping the quality and standards institutional system.

Agreements of market access should be complemented with a set of policies aimed at modernizing services and improving standards. One of the benefits of market access agreements has been the inclusion of complementary measures that are equally as important as trade promotion. These measures include adopting international standards, modernizing the system of product quality control, reforming customs services, and improving transport and port facilities. The adoption of international standards can be a very important vehicle for technology diffusion and application of good practices, and the standards embed the right incentives for increasing competitiveness of local firms in international markets. Quality control ensures speedier market access and acceptance. Reforms of the customs system can reduce costs and corruption. The same is true of the improvements in the transport infrastructure, which should begin with the port facilities. With both customs and ports, the government could review the regulatory and administrative measures that lengthen clearance times, such as extreme physical inspections, the involvement of many institutions, and the lack of competition among service providers. The most pressing issue is to eliminate discretion and the curse of corruption. Although the initial thrust in customs should be administrative reforms (as previously done in Internal Revenue Service [*Servicio de Rentas Internas*—SRI]), modern systems and techniques of random and risk-adjusted inspections, as well as cargo handling and port management, can assist in the modernization process.

The Energy Sector—Petroleum and Electricity

The importance of the petroleum sector for the future of the Ecuadoran economy cannot be overstated. The sector produces approximately 24 percent of GDP and accounts for 30 percent of the nonfinancial public sector revenues and 60 percent of total exports. Through the sector, the government heavily subsidizes the consumption of energy, in the amount of almost 5 percent of GDP. The sector has attracted most of the foreign investment in Ecuador. Private petroleum companies pay one-third of income taxes. With proven reserves estimated to last 23 years at current levels of production, the sector will continue to have a predominant presence in the economy and would still be one of the most important sources of revenues for the country. The variability of government oil revenues, however, will continue to be the main source of the risks to macroeconomic management.

Despite its importance, the sector is going through a very difficult situation that does not portend well for the future. The state petroleum company, Petro-Ecuador, is facing a crisis of significant proportion. Its production, which covers the best sites, is declining, and its investment capacity is limited. Its facilities have deteriorated, and the company is inefficient. Hence, the sector underperforms compared with international standards. Low productivity in the state-owned oil sector is particularly worrisome at present, when oil prices in international markets are hitting record highs, meaning that the opportunity cost of producing below potential is particularly high. While private sector investment has been the main source of increased production in the past few years, it has leveled off since the opening of the new pipeline. Ecuador has not signed a new production-sharing contract in the past eight years, and recent decisions by the government could discourage additional investment. Decisions to unilaterally change contracts retroactively, as well as the controversial decision to nullify the contract with a large multinational oil company, have generated doubts about the security of contracts.

The investment needs of the sector are substantial, particularly if the country is to reduce its dependence on imports of refined products. A new refinery could cost upwards of US$4 billion, and to maintain production of crude oil, the whole sector may need an average of US$1 billion a year. These funds are not readily available in Ecuador's public sector, and other partners will be needed. Finally, the oil companies face challenges in managing both the environmental impact of production and the community relations in the sparsely populated and fragile ecological zone of the Amazon.

Because of high levels of subsidies and the complex system of earmarking the distribution of petroleum revenues, most of the benefits are accruing to the current generation and upper income levels. It has been well established that the energy subsidies in Ecuador are provided mostly to the top two quintiles of the population (the top 40 percent in the income level). Despite many efforts to reduce and redirect the subsidies, all have failed, and with today's high international prices and frozen domestic prices, the country is spending more in subsidies than at any time in the past 20 years. The financial burden of the subsidy is hidden in the finances of PetroEcuador and is not explicit in the public budget. The country also loses an estimated 2 percent of GDP through contraband petroleum products shipped to neighboring countries. The earmarking of petroleum revenues is so complex that it is almost impossible to analyze the beneficiaries. Just the four petroleum funds that were created in the past few years have intertwined financing allocations, whereby funds are difficult to trace. In general, the recent decisions by the government have been to reduce the savings from revenues and increase the benefits to the current generation. Though much of the revenues are allocated to investment in other sectors, the returns from some of those investments are uncertain. Under current policies, future generations are not likely to benefit much from the use of a depleted resource.

The petroleum sector is in urgent need of reforms and clear policy direction. The principal objectives of the reforms would be to increase investment, production, and efficiency while making better use of the resources and improving the environmental management of the sector. The core of the reforms would be to separate the regulatory and production functions by reforming the institutional, regulatory, and contractual functions of the state and allowing PetroEcuador to become an independent enterprise subject to clear rules, preferably similar to rules imposed on other companies.

Under the proposed system, the definition of policies and norms would be the responsibility of the central government, and application of the policies and the regulatory function would be assumed by a specialized agency or ministry. This agency could be modeled after regulatory agencies in other countries, which have highly professional and independent regulatory systems. Its main responsibilities would be to administer reserves by assessing the level and economic value of existing oil reserves, promoting the exploration for new reserves, publishing transparent information, designing and implementing adequate policies regarding the management and exploitation of reserves, and entering into contracts with PetroEcuador and other companies. It would also be responsible for the enforcement of existing contractual arrangements and for the collection of royalties or other payments.

PetroEcuador would be an independent public enterprise. It would operate under an autonomous board of directors and have transparent and independent finances. It would have to follow clear rules and regulations, as all other enterprises in the sector do, and could enter into alliances with other companies. Its finances would be transparent and not include the subsidies of refined products. It would eventually compete in the market (of both supply and distribution) of refined products. In the meantime, the state company would still be responsible for improving existing facilities and handling distribution.

Making the current subsidies transparent in the budget and reviewing them along with budget earmarking could generate support for reducing them. The attempt to reduce energy subsidies in Ecuador has always been frustrated by public opposition, which has rarely considered other alternatives. Under the proposed reforms, the explicit inclusion of the subsidies in the budget would require approval by the Congress and the executive branch and would reveal the true magnitude of the cost, thus generating possible support for reducing the subsidies and making better use of the funds. Needless to say, the subsidies should be reduced and better targeted. The same applies to the earmarking process, which creates a very rigid allocation. One of the main objectives of the financial reform of the sector would be to make more of the resources available for economic and social projects, as well as for future generations.

An important element of any reform in the sector is to improve environmental management of the operations and the relations with the affected communities. This requires a more active role of the Ministry of Environment and new legislation and regulation, along with explicit norms in the contracts. One part of the operation that would be addressed is the associated gas flaring, which can be used more efficiently with the proper application of technology. Reforms also could resolve the existing environmental liabilities through fees and particular arrangements with the communities.

In fact, it would be advisable for the environmental authorities to have a greater participation in the definition of the policies governing petroleum companies' operations.

The electricity sector is also in a deep and growing crisis. The reforms in the 1990s helped to attract some private investment in generation, but they did not lead to the expected increases in competition, expanded capacity, and efficiency. The reforms were incomplete and did not fundamentally alter the public structure of the distribution system, which is fraught with inefficiency and technical and financial losses. The private sector's interest in generation has been limited by the problems of the sector, by political instability, and by a lack of contract security and prompt payments. The best performance has been in transmission, where modernization of the new structure has been consistent, and a new wholesale market has been introduced.

Investment in generation has been insufficient, and the sector is vulnerable to hydrological conditions. Installed capacity has grown by a bit more than 10 percent in the past five years, while demand has increased by almost 20 percent. Part of the increase in demand came from the greater number of connections, with about 90 percent of households in the country now having access to electricity. Per capita use, however, is still low, approximately half the Latin American average. Most of the recent investment in generation has been in high-cost thermal generation that relies on subsidized diesel. The country must now import about 12 percent of the electricity used. Hydroelectric generation still accounts for 45 percent of supply, but it has been declining in importance. As a result, the cost of generation has increased. The projected needs of the sector are significant, and plans are under way to increase capacity by about 1 megawatt. Unfortunately, financing is secured for fewer than half of the projects. Given the gestation period of the investments, the country could face interruptions in the short term, before two hydropower plants come onboard in two years. Thus, it is critical that reforms deal with the financing needs of the sector.

The sector's main problem is its dysfunctional distributional system. The 22 regional distribution companies incur considerable losses and are highly inefficient. Average losses for the system, between theft and technical shortcomings, are about 24 percent of total distribution, while actual collections hover around 90 percent of delivered electricity.

As a result, the sector's losses continue to mount. The accumulated deficit and arrears for the past five years (mainly to PetroEcuador, generators, and suppliers) are over US$1.3 billion and rising by US$200 million a year. Though tariffs have been adjusted, they are not sufficient to cover the cost of operation of the sector. The average tariff of 8.7 cents per kWh is about the midpoint for Latin American countries but below the real cost of the sector, which is about 10.8 cents per kWh. A recent legal reform included dispositions for the government to recognize the accumulated deficits and include in the public budget adequate resources to cover the annual deficits. It remains to be seen, however, how this will be implemented.

Although recently enacted legal changes should help correct many pressing problems, fundamental reforms still must be carried out before the sector is on a sound footing. The change of the Electricity Law in 2006, besides addressing the issue of the accumulated deficits, also introduced guarantees for payments, penalties for theft, new tariff calculations, and incentives for efficient management of the distribution companies. These must now be implemented and complemented with additional measures. The new law did not include many measures to attract needed private capital or management to the sector. Means to do that should be considered. Twining arrangements or concessions could improve the efficiency of the sector. To achieve economies of scale, the government could also merge some of the distribution companies and have joint contracting for services and equipment. Forcefully applied penalties could be charged on nonpaying customers or those not properly connected to the system. Given the losses, tariff adjustments and rebalancing might be needed. To increase electricity generation, the government could support the construction of additional hydroelectric capacity. One mechanism, besides public funds, would be to partner with potential investors or provide more certain guarantees of payments to potential and current suppliers. Finally, a continued review of the regulatory and administrative structure of the system is needed, with the aim of creating management incentives and providing greater independence to regulators.

The Agricultural Sector and Rural Development

Although quite urbanized, Ecuador still has a large rural population, and a significant portion of the workforce is in the rural sector, living off both agricultural and nonagricultural activities. The most basic characteristic of the rural sector is that rural incomes are very low and poverty rates are high. This condition has numerous reasons, among them extremely low productivity, low levels of investment in the countryside, limited access to human and financial capital, and poorly designed protection mechanisms. Policies encourage products without comparative advantage and do not support those with comparative advantage. These obstacles need to be addressed for the country to face the opportunities and challenges posed by the global marketplace.

Agriculture remains a key part of Ecuador's economy, labor force, and exports. Well over half of the rural labor force of 1.7 million persons is dependent on agriculture or food processing. The agricultural sector is highly diverse, including traditional domestic consumption–oriented sectors such as maize, beans, and potatoes; traditional export sectors such as bananas and cacao; and more recently, strongly growing nontraditional export sectors, including flowers and shrimp. Yet the competitiveness of much of the rural and agricultural sectors is being challenged from many directions: low productivity growth; lack of access of the rural poor to productive factors (land, capital, and technology); poor infrastructure; the legacy of weak institutions; and an unstable policy environment. Ecuador's rural and agricultural sectors will thrive or suffer as a result of the country's success in dealing with these challenges.

However, the agricultural sector has not performed well recently. Agriculture has been lagging in the past few years, and the conditions in the rural areas have been slower to improve compared with more dynamic urban settings. Agriculture, which accounts for 20 percent of GDP, has grown at less than half the rate of other sectors.

The productivity of the agricultural sector is low compared with other countries, and for basic crops such as rice, corn, and potatoes, it is below its neighbors Peru and Colombia. Some of these basic products could have difficulty as part of a more open trade system, which is the main reason those sectors seem to have protectionist tendencies. Though the sector has had many successes, such as the development of new crops and diversification, it is still mostly dependent on a few export products. The sector is still characterized by unequal land distribution and a very high Gini coefficient (0.8). Small agricultural producers are particularly disadvantaged because they lack ready access to credit and services, thus limiting their opportunity to integrate more fully into organized markets. In fact, only 10 percent of the formal agricultural sector relies on formal credit and technical services. Despite these shortcomings, the country is blessed with fertile soils, plentiful water for irrigation, distinct climatic regions, and an able workforce. These combined factors create excellent potential for a dynamic agricultural sector

Domestic resource cost (DRC) indicators show some degree of actual or potential comparative advantage. Overall, for 2003 the DRC indicators of comparative advantage show some degree of actual or potential comparative advantage in its traditional perennial crops (coffee, bananas, and cacao) and in African palm, as well as in labor-intensive seasonal crops such as broccoli, beans, cotton, and dairy production. On the other hand, Ecuador does not appear to have a comparative advantage in traditional seasonal crops such as rice, yellow maize, soybeans, and wheat, most of which use high volumes of imported inputs. Those crops don't enjoy the economies of scale that characterize production in more competitive nations such as Argentina and Brazil.

Despite its relatively small size, Ecuador has a wide diversity of ecological and ethnic regions, each with its own particular needs. Indigenous groups share a strong belief in a territorial or geographically based development approach. They believe that development must be approached from an integrated, territorial perspective, acknowledging the social, cultural, economic, and geographical heterogeneity of rural Ecuador, and through a highly participatory and decentralized governance framework. The indigenous preference for a territorial focus is not surprising given their attachment to land and nature and their patterns of economic and social organization. Geography has been an integral part of their daily life and their cultural beliefs.

Rural nonfarm employment is important in Ecuador, as in other Latin American countries. In 1995, some 40 percent of rural incomes were derived from rural nonfarm employment, with 37 percent of males and 50 percent of females having primary or secondary employment outside agriculture. According to the 2001 population census, some 65,000 people are self-employed in the small industry and handicrafts sector in rural *cantones*. At the time of the 2000 agricultural census, there were 1.9 million occupied workers living on farms, of which nearly 30 percent worked off-farm (41 percent in agriculture and 59 outside agriculture).

According to the 2000 agricultural census, the availability of financial and technical services for farmers is very low, which is unquestionably one of the main reasons for the country's low agricultural productivity. Only about 10 percent of farms and agricultural land are reported to be served by either formal or informal sources of financing. In terms of technical assistance, all sources together provide assistance to only 6.8 percent of farmers, covering 17.8 percent of all farmland. The decline in the subsidized public provision of these services, which has occurred over the past decade or more, has not been compensated by the development of private markets for these services. The vacuum has been filled in part by nongovernmental organizations (NGOs), whose resources, however, are extremely limited. Ecuador urgently needs to improve the organizational capacity of small producers and the marketing structures (such as clusters) that are present in the country.

Ecuador's national system for agricultural research and technology development is one of the most limiting factors in the growth of agricultural productivity. Public and private investment in science and technology are very low. Weak institutional capacity is accompanied by the lack of an effective long-term vision for national research investments and an orientation toward medium- and large-scale producers. At the root of these problems is the low and unstable national financial investment in agricultural research. Total investment in agricultural research is estimated to be below 0.5 percent of agricultural GDP, a low level by any standard and less than half the level (1 percent) that exists across Latin America generally.

This book recommends strategies in three related areas considered vital to promoting sustainable and inclusive development in Ecuador. These areas are (i) adopting a policy framework based on a territorial approach for sustainable and inclusive local development; (ii) improving access of the poor, especially its weakest segments—indigenous and Afro-Ecuadorans—to productive investments and services needed to generate employment and income; and (iii) confronting the challenges of environmental health, oil-related pollution, and conservation and protection of critical ecosystems. Of particular importance to nontraditional exports will be the implementation of domestic regulatory measures and industry best practices to conform with international plant and animal health and food safety standards. Conformance with these measures will be an increasingly important criterion to successfully meet potential foreign market demand.

IV. Promoting Sustainable and Equitable Social Development

The most effective way to sustain the development process is to continuously improve the quality of the human capital of the society. By addressing the deficiencies of service delivery in the social sectors and by expanding coverage, the country can ensure a more equitable outcome.

Human Capital

The areas covered here that are included under the realm of human capital are education, health, and the plethora of social safety and welfare programs. As in the previous section, the analysis covers the recent developments in each sector and the current conditions, and presents the summary of policy proposals.

Recent Developments

With the recovery and improved conditions, the country has been able to reestablish a pattern of poverty reduction. During the crisis years poverty rose from 34 percent in 1995 to 56 percent in 1999, but it has since declined. Preliminary data from a new survey measuring living standards shows that the poverty rate is once again below 40 percent. Extreme poverty, defined as those making less than US$1 a day, is now estimated to be below 10 percent of the population. These figures mask the considerable differences that exist between the urban and rural areas, where extreme poverty can exceed 30 percent in some of the poorest provinces.

Inequality and lack of opportunities continue to be a major characteristic of the social and economic structure. With a Gini coefficient of 0.44, Ecuador has one of the higher levels of inequality in the distribution of income in Latin America. Today, the top quintile average income is 23 times higher than the lowest quintile. Also, the top quintile receives 27 percent of the social expenditures, versus only the 12 percent for the lowest quintile. Ecuador spends more on subsidies for cooking gas for the rich than it does on cash transfers for the poor.

Nevertheless, the country has made progress in several of the social indicators in the past few years. Life expectancy has risen, from 64 years in 1990 to almost 70 years in 2005. Infant mortality has decreased from 30.3 per 1,000 people to 23 per 1,000 during the same period. Education has also experienced an important improvement. Literacy rates have risen from 88 percent in 1990 to 93 percent in 2005, while school enrollment rates at the primary level has grown from 65 percent to 93 percent in the past 25 years. Even more impressive were the gains in secondary and tertiary education, 50 percent and 17 percent attendance, respectively.

Successive governments have devoted greater attention and increasing resources to the social sectors. Recent administrations have created several new agencies, such as the Technical Secretariat of the Social Front (*Secretaría Técnica del Frente Social*—STFS), which is made up of the ministers from the social sectors and is supported by a secretariat that coordinates policy in the social sector. They have also introduced or expanded many new programs, such as the conditional cash transfer under the Human Development Bond (*Bono de Desarrollo Humano*—BDH), which reaches 40 percent of the population, and the free maternity services and universal health insurance programs, which are aimed at the same targeted population. The amount of funding to the social sectors has increased steadily in the past few years, from 3.4 percent of GDP in 2000 to 5.4 percent in 2005. In terms of expenditure per person, spending rose from US$70 in 2001 to approximately US$130 in 2005.

Greater expenditures and new programs have raised coverage levels, but they have made little headway toward improving quality. Higher enrollment in education has not been accompanied by better education. Measurements such as the retention rate (in fifth grade), years to completion (of primary school), and the efficiency coefficient (at sixth grade) are essentially the same today as they were 10 years ago. In terms of learning outcomes, the quality of education is the lowest among 19 Latin American countries. One contribution to these poor results is the extremely high level of teacher absenteeism, estimated to be near 14 percent (at any one time). The rigidity in human resource management in the sector has led to a sharp increase in the average age of the Ecuadoran teacher, which today stands at 48 years old. Four out of 10 teachers are 50 years or older.

A similar picture emerges in the health sector. The coverage of services by the Ministry of Health and the Social Security system has grown in the past few years. Part of this progress has been driven by the introduction of new programs, such as the Free Maternity Law in 1999, which now provides 33 basic services of primary health care to all expectant mothers and children under the age of five. The innovative mechanism of this program, which is now being applied by the new Universal Health Insurance Program, is to reimburse providers for the cost of services. Under the program, 30 percent of pregnant women received services in 2003. However, service is not uniform, and rural indigenous populations are not as well served. Over the past decade, the composition and the number of health staff in the public system has changed little, and as a consequence of the decision in 2004 to halve the working hours of doctors (from eight to four hours a day), there has been a reduction in medical consultations from 861 to 787 per thousand people.

Over the past few years, Ecuador has begun to build an effective social assistance program. The country now has a plethora of programs, including a series of feeding and nutrition interventions, and most importantly the large conditional cash transfer program, the BDH. The BDH reaches 40 percent of the population and is the largest program of its type in Latin America when measured in terms of population coverage. The program costs 0.7 percent of GDP and accounts for 80 percent of total welfare expenditures. The program is relatively well targeted, and it is particularly beneficial to the poorest 20 percent of the population. Impact evaluations have found that the program reduces child labor and increases the years of schooling of the children of beneficiaries. Families tend to spend 70 percent of the funds on food. The government is introducing a much-needed coresponsibility requirement on the BDH, which will ensure that beneficiaries enroll and keep their children in school, as well as take them for periodic exams in health clinics. In the past few years Ecuador has shown a tremendous ability to construct and manage complex welfare programs, which bodes well for the country's ability to continue reducing inequality and to target its interventions to those most in need.

Basic public services such as water, sanitation, electricity, and telecommunications have also improved. With the sustained increases in budgetary allocations, more than 90 percent of urban populations now have access to potable water (compared with approximately 45 percent in rural areas). Sewerage has similar coverage, albeit slightly lower. In terms of electricity connections, today more than 90 percent of the households have access to the grid, compared with 77 percent just 15 years ago. In the area of telecommunications, Ecuador has one of the highest penetrations of cellular phones in Latin America, with more than 55 percent of the population possessing a cell phone. Internet use, while still very low, is growing rapidly, with more than 8 percent of the population having access. Although the focus, correctly, is on what is missing and remains to be done, nevertheless a proper analysis of the situation must begin by recognizing the many achievements of the past few years.

Current Conditions

Despite the improvements of the past few years, the current levels of human development in Ecuador remain near the middle of the group of countries measured. The country is ranked 83 (out of 146 countries) in the United Nations' overall Human Development Index, which is a comparative measure of life expectancy, literacy, education, and standards of living. This relative measure has not changed much in the past few years, revealing that the country's progress in these areas is consistent with those indicators in many other countries. Ecuador's ranking is also below what would have been expected from its levels of income, revealing that other countries at a similar level of economic development are performing better in the human development area. Part of the reason for this underperformance is the sharp differences that exist within the country. Considerable inequalities of treatment and of access by different groups tend to lower the averages for Ecuador.

Ecuador spends less on social sectors than most of the other Latin American countries. The performance of the country in the human development index could have been better if Ecuador were to devote similar amounts of resources to the social sector. The average expenditure by Latin American countries in the health and education sectors is about 7.4 percent of GDP, compared with 4.5 percent for Ecuador. Ecuador is next to last in Latin America in terms of expenditures per capita in the social areas, spending approximately one-third what other countries spend. The recent efforts to establish as policy priority a commitment to systematically increase the expenditures (through the approval of a popular referendum), plus the recent creation of new programs aimed at increasing coverage, should raise Ecuador's relative position in these areas.

Ecuador's social sector indicators lag behind many of its Latin neighbors'. Areas in which the country has made impressive gains still do not compare well. For example, net enrollment in secondary schools is close to 70 percent for Latin America, whereas Ecuador is at about 50 percent. This is perhaps one of the most critical measures related to the country's ability to compete in the world markets, be open to innovation, and generate productivity improvements. The gaps that exist in secondary education enrollment are also significant and tend to perpetuate the inequality of opportunities that is prevalent in the country. Indigenous and Afro-Ecuadorans have a much lower level of enrollment, 22 and 31 percent, respectively, than the rest of the population. The same is true in health and social protection. Infant mortality is higher than in other neighboring countries, mainly because of the high incidence in the rural and indigenous areas. Child mortality is three times the rate among indigenous populations, compared with nonindigenous, with an almost similar ratio between rural and urban areas. Some indicators, such as stunting and chronic malnutrition, are similar to those reported by some Sub-Saharan countries (a stunting rate of 23 percent approaches those of Botswana, Ghana, and South Africa). Again, these rates reflect more than anything the tremendous disparities that exist between the rural and urban population, as well as the poor and nonpoor.

The educational sector is burdened by an obsolete structure and suffers from many deficiencies. The four critical areas are the organization of basic education, grade repetition, learning outcomes, and the school management model. With 75 percent of the students attending public schools, the national public system is essentially controlled by provincial directorates that are in charge of teachers' assignments, a process that faces various challenges, from union coercion to political patronage. These directorates also control one-third of the expenditures in the sector, with another third going directly to more than 2,400 secondary schools in the system. The Ministry of Education has little power over the human resources management or budget administration, handling only about 5 percent of the total sector budget. Currently, there is no system of teacher evaluation, and little in terms of accountability for results. As a consequence, test scores are relatively low, as is the overall quality of education. Recent measures to rejuvenate the teaching profession and introduce a system of evaluation should help in improving quality.

The health sector provides limited coverage and is fairly fragmented. The Ministry of Public Health provides health services to only about 30 percent of the population, while the Social Security Institute covers 18 percent (but not the dependents of members), and other institutions, including the armed forces, cover another 10 percent. As a result, more than 30 percent of the population has no access to basic services, and 70 percent are uninsured. The failure to have a coherent set of policies in the sector has led to the dispersion of services that disproportionately benefit some sectors of the population.

On social protection, Ecuador now has the basis to begin developing an effective welfare system. Despite the shortcomings of many existing programs, several elements are in place to create a more rational and better-targeted system of social protection. Budding institutional capacity, now armed with an advanced system of information, is a solid start. Continued professional staffing of the Technical Secretariat of the Social Front and the Program of Social Protection should strengthen the ability of these recently created agencies to provide technical guidance for the management of some of the programs. The government also has at its disposal a powerful and very useful information instrument, the System of Identification and Selection of Beneficiaries (SelBen), which contains a wealth of information on the households that make up the last two quintiles of the population. This information has been used effectively to target the conditional cash transfer program, and can now form the basis for focusing many of the other social protection programs.

The availability of the information on the poorest households now allows authorities to better target subsidies. Ecuador is currently expending more than US$2 billion in general energy subsidies that benefit primarily the upper income classes. These subsidies are extended mostly through mandated prices for derived petroleum products and electricity. It is widely recognized that these subsidies not only introduce significant inefficiencies, distort consumption, generate contraband, and affect the environment, but also are a source of great inequality. Perhaps the most important action a new government could take would be to gradually reduce these subsidies and use the SelBen to improve their targeting, thus benefiting the lowest 40 percent of the population, that is, those below the poverty line.

Policy Proposals

The policy proposals below are a summary of the more detailed proposals on education, health, and social protection programs presented in the section on sustainable and equitable development.

EDUCATION

The government should ensure that the proposals of the Plan Decenal, which was recently supported by a national referendum, are implemented. The plan calls for expanding early childhood education, achieving universal coverage in primary education, reaching a 75 percent enrollment in secondary education, eradicating illiteracy, upgrading school facilities, and improving quality through a system of teacher evaluation and training. This effort is to be accompanied by an increase in annual allocations to the education budget, excluding universities, until it reaches 6 percent of GDP by 2012. The goals are lofty but reachable, and there is no greater priority for long-term development than education.

The successful implementation of the proposals requires a series of supporting measures. To begin, the Ministry of Education needs to improve its institutional and resources management capacity. New information systems will allow the ministry to manage both financial and human resources. The most pressing need is to have an updated personnel registry with all of the capacity to monitor staff employment history, accomplishments, development, evaluation, supervision, and retirement. To complement the proposals, the ministry could introduce a new general formula in which it has more say on hiring and posting teachers, according to the needs of the sector. In general, quality of education can only begin with greater accountability for results on the part of administrators and staff. On the institutional front, the Ministry of Education's needs are many, varying from better coordination between central and provincial levels to the ability to deliver coordinated actions on early childhood education services, which is now offered by no less than five government agencies. Naturally, the most important role of the ministry is to set teaching standards, curriculum guidelines, and evaluation parameters, among others. All of these activities need to be reinforced and the leadership of the ministry accepted by others. On the financial front, the formula for allocating budget funds to schools should be based on the number of students and the needs of the facilities, and not on historical trends and teachers' allocations. A better financial management should also ensure prompt payments of salaries and benefits.

HEALTH

In the health sector, there is the possibility of achieving important progress in terms of coverage and financing. The adoption of recent programs, such as the Free Maternity Law and the Universal Health Insurance program (AUS) offer an opportunity to increase coverage and change the form of financing. In its initial stages the AUS targets the poorest 40 percent of the population, with a simple package of primary care. The goal is to eventually expand the program to the entire population. The program is in its early stages of implementation and is effectively working in only parts of the largest cities of Guayaquil, Quito, and Cuenca. The first experiences show that many providers, other than those in the public sector, are interested in participating in the program. With the government supporting the demand for health services, instead of the supply, the program could attract the many new participants in the provision of services.

A fundamental change brought about by the new programs is the separation of service delivery and health financing. Under the original design, a key characteristic of the programs is that providers (whether public or private) would be financed according to services provided, instead of the existing standard budgetary system of allocating funds according to historical levels or size of the facility. This innovation is the most significant reform that could occur in the health sector. The new administration will have the chance to build on these initial stages of the program and thus will provide the direction of the reforms in the sector. The challenge will be to negotiate contracts with both private and public providers to reach the 1.4 million providers scheduled for the first phase. In addition, an urgent need is to build the capacity to manage the program by expanding the unit in charge of its implementation.

In line with modern tendencies, the new programs require better monitoring and evaluation systems and a clear focus on results and performance. The way contracts with providers are to be designed offer an opportunity to introduce performance-related incentives to providers and thus increase the efficiency of the system. The results-based approach to compensation should be a guide to providers to focus on coverage and quality of services. To ensure compliance with the contracts, the programs need to have very complex information systems to monitor, among other things, the beneficiaries and providers, the quantity and quality of services provided, and the reimbursement process. The monitoring and eventual evaluation of the participants in the program require a well-staffed organization and capable independent personnel with the capacity to manage this new system.

Many other broad sector reforms are needed. An important part of the overall strategy should be the expansion of the coverage by social security system. Family members, particularly the children of beneficiaries, should be included. The focus solely on the principal member severely limits the effectiveness of having a separate program under the IESS. Expansion of coverage will entail higher expenditures and may require additional facilities. Better tracking of the health program's costs will require that the health fund be clearly separated from the pension fund. The Ministry of Health also will have to ensure that hospitals and health centers have the capacity to provide the additional services that might be required for the expanded coverage considered under the Universal Health Insurance program. Other efficiency measures would include more transparent and bulk procurement of products along with better financial allocation to hospitals and clinics. The other component of the strategy is the promotion of generic medicines. Medication is a major item in household budgets. Though the law mandates that doctors and pharmacists prescribe or offer generic medication, they do not have the incentives to do so. Liberalizing the market and offering the proper incentives for distribution of generics will aid in reducing the cost of medicines.

SOCIAL PROTECTION SYSTEM

Creating an effective social welfare system will require that the government rationalize and improve the coordination of the many programs now in place. The administrative structure for creating a more effective and rational system of social protection and improving coordination already exists. The Secretariat of the Social Cabinet and the Social Protection Programs has the capacity to promote such coordination and rationalization. At the most basic level, they have the means to improve the targeting of the programs. The SelBen is an effective tool, but it needs to be updated, in terms of the information on beneficiaries, the methodology used to qualify them, and certification of eligibility. At the broader level, the BDH would be the centerpiece of a new strategy to break the perpetuation of intergenerational poverty. This would entail linking the program to educational and health attainments, to a program of savings, to the old-age basic security coverage, and to other programs such as the protection of the disabled. Complementary to this effort should be consolidating the nutrition programs under a single umbrella.

The conditional cash transfer program, BDH, as now structured, can be used more broadly to break the poverty cycle. The program has the capacity to channel greater resources to those in extreme poverty, and any future expansion of payments should be concentrated on the first quintile. Recent evaluation studies have shown that the program has the greatest impact and yields the greatest benefits when focused on the first quintile. The coresponsibility program, which requires beneficiaries to ensure school enrollment and attendance by their children, along with periodic visits to health centers, can also be very effective in improving the program's impact. For the other beneficiaries, such as those in the second quintile, the best use of the funds would be to promote savings in order to eventually graduate them from the program (no other country covers such a large segment of the population with cash transfers). These requirements should be accompanied by programs to help beneficiaries participate in productive activities, such as gainful employment and small business. Differentiating the beneficiary groups, such as those with disabilities and senior citizens, is important for demonstrating that the program is not an acquired entitlement but a means to protect vulnerable groups and help them graduate from those conditions. Other government institutions and programs, such as the IESS, could be required to work in conjunction with the program to expand the services provided to those groups. Another example is the support and follow-up that the more vulnerable groups would need to ensure their compliance with the requirements of the program, such as school attendance and better health treatment.

The other key element in breaking the intergenerational poverty cycle is to improve nutritional standards. Ecuador can achieve considerable efficiency and effectiveness in this area by consolidating its three major programs—Food Program for Boys and Girls (PAN2000), the School Meals Program (PAE), and Eat Well, Ecuador under the newly created Integrated System of Food and Nutrition (SIAN). Besides having unified administrative structures, the programs should also work more effectively to bring better services to targeted populations by avoiding duplications or failure to provide services to the needy. The programs should have a single target instrument (using poverty maps and the SelBen) and minimum goals for service provision.

All social sectors programs will benefit from greater transparency and accountability. The government has worked to provide information on social expenditures, but its timeliness and quality could be improved. Spending data, by program, and in particular coverage and outcomes, could be included in more frequent periodic Web reports. The information could also be more consistent and broader in its coverage and include all programs. Another new development that should be reinforced is the use of impact evaluations of programs. The Technical Secretariat of the Social Front has been given the responsibility to carry out this function; it should now be given the resources and a broader mandate. All of the programs should have expected, measured outcomes and should be able to report their achievements. The evaluations should also rely on a more participatory approach, in which beneficiaries participate in the process. Already, evaluations for the Bono (BDH) and rural primary education have been done by beneficiaries, using scorecards to rank the quality of services provided. Overall, further reforms in the sector will require greater participation and consultation, as beneficiaries gain greater voice and influence in the process of redesigning the programs. Grassroots consultation and an effective communication strategy will help generate awareness and consensus about the need for constant refinement of the programs, such as the process of graduation or periodic certifications.

V. Improving Governance and Strengthening Institutions

The policy notes cover several areas where the authorities could make significant inroads into improving governance and strengthening the institutions in the country. The focus is mostly on the public sector, where reforms could be undertaken in the areas of budgeting, financial management, procurement, civil service administration, service delivery, performance outcomes, administration, and justice. Among other broad themes, the volume provides a recent history, current conditions, and proposed policy coverage in each area.

Current Conditions

Ecuador's development is hindered by institutional weakness. It is widely recognized that institutions in Ecuador have considerable deficiencies. Most often this perception is associated with the ineffectiveness of the state institutions. But, in a broader sense, weak institutions also reflect the failure to obey and enforce rules or the law, to achieve a certain level of moral and ethical conduct necessary for the operation of a market economy, and in general to have an established set of norms and incentives that govern behavior. The institutional context here refers only to those associated with governance, or the ability of the state to exercise its authority to provide public goods and services.

Ecuador has one of the lowest rankings internationally in many areas of governance. More than 75 percent of countries have a higher ranking than Ecuador in the areas of government effectiveness, political instability, and corruption. In the latter two categories there has been a deterioration of the country's relative position in the past six years. With respect to the rule of law, Ecuador is among the lowest 30 percent of the 213 countries analyzed by the World Bank, and its ranking has remained at these low levels since the surveys began in the mid-1990s. The two areas where Ecuador has improved its rankings are for regulatory quality and for voice and accountability. The regulatory regime, particularly in the financial sector, is much better following the crisis of 1990, and Ecuador has a long tradition of wide participation by civil society in public affairs, and more recently a growing tendency for governments to be more transparent and accountable.

Studies have shown a strong correlation between governance and economic growth and development. Those countries that have high and rising rankings in all of the areas described above also experience, on average, higher levels of economic growth. Ecuador's economy is actually performing better than would be expected based on its rankings, mostly because of petroleum. But to sustain its economic development, Ecuador must address the issues of government effectiveness, the rule of law, and corruption.

Ecuador has shown that it can improve government effectiveness. Some of the experiences with institutional and organizational reforms in Ecuador have been positive. The most evident is the improvement of the Internal Revenue Service (SRI), which has gone through a process of modernization and is today a much more professional organization that is yielding positive results. The efficiency of tax collection has improved considerably in the past few years. The lessons from the SRI are that reforms require a firm political commitment, strong leadership, and unyielding persistence. Patience is also required, since the results become evident only over time.

Another example of the ability to improve government effectiveness has been the performance of some local governments. It is generally accepted that the local governments have been more responsive and innovative in providing services to the population. This has been the case mostly where the administrative capacity has been strongest, that is, in the largest cities and in the more populous provinces. These governments have counted with more stable governments and more continuous plans and policies. Since their responsibilities are still rather limited, the areas of best performance have been in local transport and in water supply and sanitation. Local governments are also expanding their role, increasingly providing services that heretofore have been the responsibility of the central government, such as in health and education. There are also many initiatives, being supported by development partners, to help the local governments improve their financial and budgetary management and embrace a more participatory process of budget formulation.

Progress has been made in the modernization of the Public Finance Management System. After 1999, public institutions began using the Integrated Financial Management System (SIGEF), which comprises both the budget and accounting systems. It is currently being used in 168 institutions, managing 78 percent of the central government's budget. A total of 2,300 institutions feed their information to the central level each month to integrate it and enable the elaboration of comprehensive reports. Given these developments, at present 99 percent of the central government's aggregated budget information is available.

The development of SIGEF induced an important positive change in the management of public finances. Information was standardized. The management capacity of the institutions was strengthened, leading to better internal controls. Still, problems related to the processing and timely provision of information spawned strong critiques against the system from within the very financial administration of the state. The system does have weaknesses and is now outdated technologically. It is not Web-based and relies on the information provided by the operating units, which do not report full information on time. Information is very fragmented, given the large number of operating units. To deal with these problems, the Ecuadoran government reached an agreement with the Guatemalan government to transfer its more modern system, a process that is under way.

Public administration remains deficient in several areas. Despite recent reform efforts, many facets of the operation of the public sector can be significantly improved. Those range from the management of the budget to the provision of services. The list is extensive. They include, besides the budget, the public sector procurement system, the civil service system, the program of public investment, and specific agencies such as customs administration and the operations of the many ministries. The deficiencies are found in the planning stages, in the implementation of the programs, and in the supervision and control.

The budget system is archaic. The process of budget preparation and approval relies on historical patterns, not on newly established priorities. Significant earmarking makes the budget structure very rigid. There is little room for reallocation of budgets when the laws link expenditure items to specific sources of financing. Congress often fails to allocate for required payments, for example, for debt service, to make room for other programs. These decisions are reversed by the Ministry of Finance, frequently in a discretionary manner. The lack of proper financial programming leads to allocations during the year on the basis of political and other pressures, and the information on expenditures is not up-to-date. The current system does not track commitments or the true floating debt. There is no system for evaluating the budget implementation, and the systems of control are designed to oversee particular transactions instead of ensuring the application of the norms and regulations. Given the predominance of the state in the economy and the use of the budget as a key instrument to promote national objectives, modernizing the budget process and public sector financial management system are critical needs.

The systems of public sector procurement and civil service administration are not uniformly applied and vary considerably across institutions. The public procurement policies allow for the use of distinct forms of purchase, including non-competitive single-source contracts. Many transactions are not transparent and are prone to possible manipulation. The public procurement system is perhaps the single most important source of corruption within the public sector. Although Ecuador uses a Web-based system of procurement, Contratanet, it is used on a limited basis, and until recently its use was not legally required. In the civil service, recent legal reforms have set the basis to standardize salaries for similar job categories and to apply standard recruitment procedures, both processes that are being implemented. Human resource management still requires the creation of an information system that includes the history of public employees, a process of performance evaluation, and norms for promotion and demotion.

Many agencies throughout the public sector provide poor-quality services. The problem afflicts many functions of the state, from customs administration to the property registry, agricultural extension, health services, even the system of justice, not to mention some public sector enterprises. Several factors account for the service quality: antiquated systems of information and management, lack of resources, distorted incentives, entrenched interests, and others. The result is the widespread sense that the public sector lacks transparency and accountability (in one survey, more than 90 percent of civil society groups share this view). The general feeling of the population is that under the current system corruption is rampant, and they are pessimistic that progress can be made in combating corruption. Ecuador is ranked 128 (out of 163 countries) in the Transparency International corruption index.

Though many measures are necessary to improve service delivery and combat corruption, what are most lacking in Ecuador are transparency and accountability. While efforts have been made, particularly with the passage of the Law of Transparency and Access to Information in 2002, much needs to be done to comply with the mandates of the law. Many agencies are embarking on processes to make their operations more transparent, particularly through the use of Web pages, but surveys have shown that most public institutions fail to respond to inquiries by civil society (only 14 percent were answered), and none of the Web pages displayed the information mandated by the law. Generally, the majority of the sites do not contain information on budget management, procurement, collective contracts, salaries, and so forth. The information systems and the agencies' ability or willingness to provide public information are still nascent. There is no culture of transparency, and incentives to disseminate information are absent.

The lack of accountability stems in part from the failure to measure results. Very few public institutions in Ecuador align their operations to preestablished targets and goals. In most instances, systems needed to track the results of operations or projects are not available, and baseline information on existing conditions is absent. The focus on the Millennium Development Goals (MDGs), which establish fairly explicit targets, is raising the consciousness regarding the need to begin measuring results and tracking performance. Though some of the MDGs are broad, governments at different levels (including, recently, the local governments) are beginning to articulate their activities in terms of their contribution to reaching the MDGs. The possibility of generating baseline information for many programs will be enhanced by the information being obtained through the comprehensive Living Standards Measurement Survey that is being carried out by the government. This sample of over 10,000 households should provide a wealth of information that will allow some comparisons over time in many areas of welfare and service delivery.

The perception of institutional failing in Ecuador is fueled by the general sense that rules are applied and enforced unevenly, and that the justice system is ineffective and inefficient. Despite the progress made in the past few years with the management of the judicial branch of government, the population still does not see tangible results. Access and application of justice is seen as politically influenced, discretionary, and vulnerable to corruption. Many recent scandals within the national policy or the court system have undermined the credibility and the authority of these institutions. The current Supreme Court is gaining public trust and is cognizant of the need for reform. The areas that seem most lacking are the management capacity, inadequate case administration, low professional standards and personnel qualifications, lack of resources, and ineffective oversight systems. The number and complexity of the cases being handled by the courts is overwhelming the ability of the current system to dispose of the cases in a reasonable period of time. There are still significant barriers to exclusion stemming from the high cost and time required to handle and review cases. The new procedural code establishes the basis for some reforms, including the adoption of an oral argument–based system, which should improve efficiency and transparency. There is also ample room for professional improvement and development through systems of evaluations and merit-based hiring. Finally, the oversight of the justice system is anomalous, with some agencies subject to congressional control. The new administration will find the moment propitious to carry out reforms in the judicial system, with the leadership of the Supreme Court.

Policy Proposals

The democratic future of Ecuador depends on the ability of the authorities to strengthen the country's institutional structure and system of governance. Without fundamental institutional reforms, there is a real danger that citizens will become further disillusioned with current systems of governance. It is imperative that the government demonstrate that institutions can be modernized and can become more efficient, more responsive, more transparent, more accountable, and free of corruption. The key is to embark on a participatory process of fundamental reforms of the public administration. Such reforms should include the introduction of a modern system of budgetary management, a more transparent process of public procurement, and a more effective civil service administration. Ecuador can make public entities more efficient. The country can create a more independent, efficient, and just judicial sector. The process of rebuilding the institutional capacity of the state should have as a goal regaining the trust of the citizens. To achieve such goal the process has to be inclusive, by ensuring public participation.

The conditions are present for improving the budget management system. The arrangements are in place to introduce a modern financial management system, which will serve as the basis for a more transparent and efficient handling of public funds and for reforming the budget process. The interchange agreement with the Guatemalan government to transfer the newest financial management system in Latin America to Ecuador is well under way, with the new system already in its testing phase. The process broadly seeks to (i) attain full coverage of the public sector (handling the financial management of more than 2,300 institutions); (ii) provide an instrument that offers integrated management solutions to diverse sectors (for example, defense, police); (iii) perform all budgetary transactions in a Web-based environment; (iv) introduce the concepts of commitments, accruals, and cash management and accounting; (v) give the central government treasury the opportunity to perform cash programming, perform wire transfer operations, use different payment processes, and operate on a single account system; and develop an integrated framework between the financial system and other administrative and management systems of the government. Some of the new procedures can be implemented in 2007, but the full system should be in place with the start of the 2008 budget year. The key to achieving these goals will be committed leadership by the government to proceed with implementing the current arrangement. The new system offers an excellent opportunity to comply with the promise to make the operations of the public sector more transparent. The system would offer real-time information and could be accessed from any point (depending on security access). The introduction of the new system will also require an update of the rules and norms of budget management, which will offer the opportunity to change the procedures.

One of the most effective tools to combat corruption would be to implement a more transparent and competitive public procurement system. As with the financial management system, the process is also under way to introduce a new system in Ecuador. The government has the opportunity to build on the latest systems introduced with great success by other Latin American countries. The electronic Web-based systems now provide the opportunity to create a truly open procurement process, which can increase transparency, improve competitiveness, reduce transaction costs, shorten delivery cycles, and, more importantly, decrease corruption. Although legal reform is required, much can be accomplished with the introduction of new technology along with the administrative and procedural changes. The technology is available and can be introduced rapidly through an upgrading of Contratanet. The other measures require first an institutional arrangement whereby the Ministry of Economy and Finance (MEF), the Corruption Commission, the SRI, and the General Management Office come to an agreement on the basic roles and responsibilities of each entity. It is essential that the new system ensures close coordination among the agencies and links the system to other public systems. In other countries, for example, suppliers cannot participate unless they are in a registry, which contains all information on their compliance with other contracts and tax liabilities. Payments are not made unless the procurement has been done through the new system. Naturally, many other norms and regulations also must be applied, along with conflict resolution procedures, and it would be important to create an independent oversight entity.

To complete the modernization of the administration of the public sector, it would be essential to accelerate civil service reforms. The Ecuadoran government has made great progress in this area, but much remains to be done. The goal would be to have a professional, efficient, well-managed, and well-paid cadre of civil servants. One of the first actions should be to review the staffing of many agencies and ministries, since there are many with shortages of capable personnel and others with excess employees. An incentive system, such as recently adopted by the Ministry of Education, can be part of a broader severance package to eliminate overemployment or to change skill mixes. The government needs an updated human resource database, with all information on service and salary history, performance and evaluations, and retirement and other benefits. Such information, while partially available, is critical for many purposes: to cross information with the budget on salaries, to implement a true process of hiring and promoting on the basis of merit, and to apply sanctions.

Reforming the judicial system is at the core of building a credible and effective governance and institutional structure. Although the judiciary has embarked in a modernization process, many other measures could be taken that would visibly demonstrate Ecuador's ability to construct solid and respected institutions. The application and respect for the rule of law is essential for the governance of the country. The reforms that could be undertaken range from administrative measures to fundamental changes in access.

Administrative reforms would require improving judicial sector management and supporting the sector's human capital development. There is a need to update the court management system to align it with the proposed new procedural handling system (away from written to an oral argument–based system). Moving to an oral argument system requires new internal policies and procedures and a reorganization, redefinition, and redistribution of functions and responsibilities, essentially an overall process reengineering. A major input into the integrated management system will be to collect, analyze, and disseminate statistical information generated by judicial districts and specific court offices on caseloads, individual and court performance, impact and outcome indicators, and users' profiles. Complementary measures to strengthen the judiciary's managerial function and enhance its efficiency in case processing include (i) monitoring and evaluating judges' performance as proactive managers of caseloads and courtrooms, (ii) experimenting with different courtroom staffing patterns, and (iii) analyzing medium- and long-term user demands (for example, possible revisions of jurisdictional rules, or incentives for the use of alternative dispute resolution [ADR] mechanisms).

Other measures to reform the judiciary include developing and implementing standard information and communication systems at the central level so that information from decentralized units can better inform sector authorities' decision-making. Information should also be more broadly disseminated. Human capital reforms should include recruiting and retaining quality judicial human resources and providing them with appropriate professional development. The sector also needs to introduce modern concepts of human resources planning and management (including the use of incentives) and develop managerial capabilities within the judiciary. This could be similar to the public sector's overall effort to develop a coherent selection methodology, review job profiles, adopt consistent selection criteria, and create appropriate examination mechanisms. Naturally, such efforts should be accompanied by enhanced training of judges, now that the judicial training unit is set up.

Although administrative reforms are necessary, it will be the fundamental changes in the access and delivery of justice that will build public trust in the institution. The success of the reform process will be measured by the respect attained by the judiciary and the general compliance to the law. As such, within the framework of an inclusive governance approach that would protect the interests of marginal groups, sector authorities should seek to address obstacles preventing such groups' access to justice (for example, high costs of attorneys or long delays in the functioning of family and tenancy jurisdictions). This could be accomplished by (i) strengthening legal aid; introducing more accessible mechanisms, such as small claims courts and justices of the peace in selected geographical areas that have major transportation or communication barriers; (ii) expanding mediation centers ascribed to superior courts as an expeditious ADR mechanism in civil and commercial matters; and (iii) strengthening other ADR mechanisms (conciliation and arbitration) in partnership with the private sector and civil society organizations. These activities should take into account Ecuador's rich cultural diversity and any progress made in the area of indigenous justice systems. Specific actions to be considered for the benefit of indigenous peoples would include studies of gender issues and strategies to handle intrafamily violence cases, and strategies for the effective recognition of traditional dispute resolution mechanisms of indigenous communities. Such an approach requires a more effective outreach program that makes public the information about the system's functioning. The sector should start complying with the current transparency law by providing information on judicial decisions, compensation packages, performance indicators of judges, administrative and court staff, attendance records, court dockets, and so forth.

The expansion of judicial sector services should include increasing the capacity to handle highly complex cases for relevant economic development. This is essential to create a predictable decision-making process that protects the interests of economic agents and the integrity of contractual agreements. Given the lack of capacity in this area, it would be essential to increase the capacity of selected personnel from fiscal, labor, and civil courts to handle complex cases involving the enforcement of market-oriented laws, such as intellectual property rights, antitrust, insolvency and bankruptcy, consumer protection, and environmental degradation.

The proposed reforms would increase the credibility of the justice system and restore faith in the country's ability to improve its institutions. To build its credibility, the justice system needs to begin with internal reforms that ensure accountability and integrity in the handling of justice. The judicial authorities should ensure that any incident of corruption, gross nepotism, and mishandling of justice is promptly sanctioned. Hence, it is necessary to ensure the creation of effective investigative capacity and, more importantly, the adoption of clear disciplinary measures. To build the integrity of the system, it would be important to work together with other groups and partners, outside the system, who could assist with civil oversight of the system. Finally, the judiciary can set the example to society by promoting the highest level of ethical standards in its operations, through the adoption of an ethical value system second to none.

In conclusion, improving governance requires that Ecuador build credibility, integrity, and trust in public institutions. Many of the recommendations above may seem to be focused on administrative and procedural matters. However, they are designed to create the conditions for a fundamental change in the institutional structure of the country. Institutions must be seen not as organizations or agencies but as a set of relational arrangements that guide public sector behavior and activities. These arrangements can be formed by formal constraints (such as rules, laws, or constitutions) or framed by informal constraints (such as behavioral norms, codes of conduct, or conventions).

The proposals presented here must accompany or strengthen these formal and informal arrangements. The measures of transparency, responsiveness, accountability, and integrity are just some of the instruments needed to build the public institutions that can be honored and trusted, and of which citizens can proud. Ecuador is going through a phase of deep reflection about the failures of its institutional structure and governance. Some people question whether these deficiencies are cultural and deeply ingrained in the society, and will require considerable time to change. Others note, however, that the failures reflect the design and functioning of the institutions themselves. Hence, changing the operational rules of the public administration apparatus could begin to correct many of the shortcomings. In reality, both positions have valid arguments. The changes in institutions imply new rules, norms, and incentives to guide behavior, which, once ingrained in the conduct of society, become part of its culture. Ecuador has all of the means to build a country with strong and respected institutions that will improve governance and bring about a more inclusive economic and social development.

Summary of Some Policies for Improving Economic and Social Development in Ecuador

Preserving stability	*Promoting sustainable and equitable social development*	*Improving governance and institutions*
• Preserve fiscal position by generating surpluses in the nonfinancial public sector. • Restrain growth in public expenditures. • Reduce and focus energy subsidies. • Consolidate petroleum funds and reduce earmarking. • Improve debt management and lengthen debt amortization structure. • Expand tax base. • Reveal medium-term macroeconomic program. • Introduce system of expenditure evaluation. • Set up affordable liquidity fund for banking sector. **Accelerating Economic Growth** • Prepare an action plan to improve business climate. • Lower costs of starting and operating a business. • Introduce legislation to increase labor flexibility and mobility. • Reform bankruptcy and corporate restructuring laws governing creditors' rights.	**Education** • Ensure the implementation of education "Plan Decenal." • Increase education expenditures to 6% of GDP by 2010. • Promote universal primary enrollment and enrollment of 75% in secondary schools. • Improve institutional and resource management of the Ministry of Education. **Health** • Expand health access services to the poor. • Broaden the Universal Health Insurance program beyond major cities. • Improve the Ministry of Health's ability to manage the sector. • Separate service delivery and health financing (focus on payments for services provided). • Introduce monitoring and evaluation systemsof services provided. • Expand IESS health coverage to family members. • Separate health from pension system in the IESS.	• Embark on modernization process of public institutions. • Make public entities more effective in provision of services. • Introduce results-based budgeting. • Modernize budget management with the introduction of a new system. • Implement a new, more transparent and competitive public procurement system. • Make all budgets transparent and available in Web-based systems. • Accelerate civil service reforms. • Review staffing of all agencies and ministries, and update human resource databases. • Modernize the judicial system. • Eliminate political influence on control agencies. • Introduce a new court management system. • Implement new procedural handling system (using oral arguments). • Expand mediation centers and create a legal aid program.

(*Table continues on the following page.*)

Summary of Some Policies for Improving Economic and Social Development in Ecuador (*continued*)

Preserving stability	*Promoting sustainable and squitable social development*	*Improving governance and institutions*
• Expand financial services to small and medium enterprises. • Strengthen role of credit cooperatives and improve systems of credit information and risk sharing. • Introduce measures to open markets and compensate those adversely affected by integration. • Reduce dispersion of tariffs. • Modernize systems of quality control and adopt international product standards. Make PetroEcuador an independent public enterprise. • Adopt a new energy regulatory scheme, treating all companies alike. • Reduce losses of electricity companies. • Attract more investment into electricity sector. • Expand the agricultural service network to small producers. • Strengthen clusters and producers' association.	**Social Protection** • Rationalize and improve coordination of different programs. • Make the Human Development Bond (*Bono de Desarrollo Humano*—BDH) the centerpiece of the package of programs. • Focus BDH on the first quintile, disabled, and elderly. • Introduce coresponsibility by recipients in education and health. • Consolidate nutrition programs under the Integrated System of Food and Nutrition (SIAN). • Expand evaluation by beneficiaries to all welfare programs.	• Introduce specialized courts to deal with complex business cases.

1

Fiscal Sustainability and Debt Management in Ecuador

Vicente Fretes-Cibils, Rashmi Shankar, and Elizabeth Currie

Executive Summary

The key fiscal policy challenges confronting Ecuador are the narrow tax base, fast-growing expenditures, and weaknesses in budgetary management. Revenues are dominated by income from oil, and expenditure increases are largely due to irreversible growth in salaries and subsidies. Greater flexibility in fiscal assignments from the petroleum funds has reversed some of the progress in revenue management, and reduced the central government's ability to put in place countercyclical measures and to manage contingencies. Debt management is faced with three significant hurdles: excessive contingent liabilities; the high proportion of floating rate debt, which is subject to interest rate risk given the high country risk premium; and refinancing risk due to the need to roll over debt. Debt administration is also deficient, indicating the need for a coherent medium-term strategy and a functional debt management committee. Additionally, the domestic debt market is poorly developed, and urgent reforms to financial infrastructure are required. This note recommends setting the following priorities: tighter budgetary management; complementary institutional, market, and regulatory reforms; elimination of policy-induced disincentives to the expansion of the non-oil sector; and strictly enforced legal separation of the petroleum funds from budgetary expenditure. Failure to address these issues will leave Ecuador vulnerable to shocks, given the necessity for fiscal robustness in the dollarized context, and will reverse the improvement in the debt ratio. Prompt action to resolve problems will help create sufficient fiscal space for investment in the social and productive sectors and enable effective income stabilization, reducing the probability of a crisis during the downturn of the business cycle.

Section IV: Public Debt Trends is a summarized version of "Ecuador: Public Debt Management and Domestic Debt Market Development Report," prepared by Elizabeth Currie, Antonio Velandia, Anderson Silva, Catiana García, and Andrés Huby.

I. Background and Current Context

Macroeconomic Indicators

Despite political difficulties, Ecuador's economic performance has been impressive in recent years. Fueled by increasing oil revenues and a recovery from a deep financial crisis, the economy has grown at an average of 4 percent per year since 2000. Consumption has grown even faster, averaging close to 6 percent per year. Inflation, which peaked in the middle of 2000 at 100 percent, declined to single digits by 2005. Deposits in and loans from the banking sector have more than doubled as a percentage of GDP and are currently above the precrisis level. Many sectors of the economy, such as construction, agriculture, and nontraditional exports, have also recovered, with the latter growing at an impressive 15 percent a year since 2002.

The recovery during the current decade is in sharp contrast to the performance of the 1990s, when the economy experienced protracted fiscal, inflationary, and financial difficulties, caused by external shocks, lax policies, and natural disasters. These culminated in the deepest financial and foreign exchange crisis in the country's recent history, with sharp economic declines and inflation nearing 100 percent.

To address the crisis, a series of policies were enacted, the most significant of which was to replace the domestic currency with the U.S. dollar in 2000. Other measures included a series of laws that improved the flexibility of markets and allowed greater participation of the private sector in certain sectors of the economy. A Fiscal Responsibility and Transparency Law passed in 2002 mandated fiscal assignments from surplus petroleum revenues, including allocations for debt reduction. The law also established rules to limit expenditure growth while providing for priority investments and contingency management even during cyclical revenue downturns.

The 2002 law was an essential component of the dollarization strategy, given the lack of an independent monetary policy. The fiscal authority is the effective lender of last resort, and fiscal policy is the only countercyclical instrument available. In 2005, the Fiscal Responsibility and Transparency Law II was introduced, which weakens the separation of the petroleum funds from the management of current budgetary expenditures and is therefore disquieting.

The outcome of dollarization and energetic postcrisis reforms has been a period of relative macroeconomic stability. Growth in GDP, measured in 2000 U.S. dollars, averaged 4.9 percent over the 2002–06 period, compared with 3.3 percent for all Latin America and Caribbean (LAC) countries. Ecuador's growth in 2006 was slightly lower than the LAC average and considerably below Panama, a more mature dollarized economy, but was comparable with Chile, which is also a primary commodity exporter (table 1.1). Inflation and interest rates have fallen to single-digit levels, and change in the consumer price index (CPI) was 3.3 percent in 2006. Real wages have grown by more than 20 percent in the past four years, though there is some concern that labor productivity has not kept pace. The period also shows sustained

Table 1.1. Ecuador Macroindicators, International Comparisons

	2002	*2003*	*2004*	*2005*	*2006*
Annual real growth (%)					
Ecuador	**4.3**	**3.6**	**7.9**	**4.7**	**4.2**
Chile	2.2	3.9	6.2	6.4	4.3
Panama	2.2	4.2	7.6	6.4	7.5
Mexico	0.8	1.4	4.1	3.0	4.7
LAC (weighted average)	0.0	1.6	5.8	4.2	4.9
Change in CPI (%)					
Ecuador	**9.4**	**7.9**	**2.7**	**2.1**	**3.3**
Chile	2.8	1.1	2.4	3.7	2.5
Panama	1.8	1.7	1.1	3.8	2.1
Mexico	5.7	4.0	5.2	3.3	3.9
LAC (weighted average)	12.2	7.4	6.9	5.7	4.8

Sources: Banco Central de Ecuador (BCE) and World Development Indicators (WDI).
Note: LAC average is weighted by 2005 GDP. The 2006 change in the CPI was estimated in November, except for Ecuador, which was observed.

job creation, with 2006 annual average unemployment in the three major cities at 5.8 percent, compared with 6.9 percent in 2005.

Banking Indicators

Financial sector solvency and continued expansion are essential to any strategy of overall fiscal sustainability. In the effective absence of monetary policy in a dollarized context, the banking sector is the first line of defense against shocks and potentially a key source of support to fiscal policy. Any vulnerabilities that increase the probability of a costly banking crisis also threaten fiscal viability. The banking sector's profile has strengthened since the 1999–2000 crisis (table 1.2). Total assets have recovered to a level slightly higher than 2000 as a proportion of GDP, after plunging in 2001. Investments, total intermediation (loans plus deposits), and liquidity have also improved, while the proportion of nonperforming loans has decreased significantly since the financial crash. Profitability has improved from a return on assets of −2.8 percent in 2000 to a positive return of 2.3 percent. The stability provided by de jure dollarization—Ecuadoran banking assets and liabilities were already highly dollarized de facto – may have been a determinant of the improved robustness of the financial sector.

However, key challenges remain (see chapter 3 of this book). Liquidity management is a significant concern for three reasons: absence of an interbank market, limited role of the central bank under dollarization, and lack of resources with the Deposit Guarantee Agency to back insured deposits. Since short-term deposits are

Table 1.2. Banking System Indicators
(percent)

	2000	*2001*	*2002*	*2003*	*2004*	*2005*	*2006*
Total assets/GDP	28.2	23.4	23.3	23.3	24.9	27.0	29.1
Available Funds plus investment/total assets	34.0	36.7	35.1	39.0	38.1	37.0	35.3
Bank business/GDP	29.3	26.9	28.2	28.3	31.5	34.9	38.0
Return on assets	–2.8	–0.5	0.1	1.5	1.6	1.8	2.0
Cash plus reserves/ total assets	4.0	3.0	5.0	3.0	4.0	4.0	4.3
LAC average	12.0	14.0	13.0	15.0	13.0	11.0	. . .
Private domestic credit/GDP	41.0	30.0	20.8	18.9	20.7	23.2	23.9
LAC average	47.0	46.0	51.0	50.0	49.0	52.0	. . .
Bank nonperforming loans/total loans	31.0	28.0	9.4	8.8	6.9	5.3	3.4
LAC average	7.0	9.0	9.0	8.0	5.0	. . .	. . .

Sources: Superintendencia de Bancos y Seguros del Ecuador, WDI, and authors' calculations.

predominant, banks must maintain high levels of liquid assets, largely in foreign banks. This reduces available resources for lending and domestic investment and is a constraint on financial deepening and widening.

The level of domestic credit is low—24 percent of GDP and declining—compared with a LAC average of 52 percent of GDP and the East Asia average of 110 percent of GDP. Another indicator of poor financial depth is that loans and deposits add up to only 38 percent of GDP, and banking assets are 29 percent of GDP. These numbers represent an improvement over the situation immediately following the crisis, but they are tiny compared with Panama, where domestic banks alone generated intermediation and total assets of 136 percent and 105 percent of GDP, respectively, in 2006.

The vulnerability of the banking system leads to higher risk of a deposit run in response to a shock or even to increased uncertainty. Small banks are especially vulnerable because, unlike the largest banks, they do not have access to external lines of credit. Contagion effects fueled by depositor nervousness are also likely, since there is no mechanism for liquidity recycling across banks. A vulnerable banking sector is more likely to magnify the effects of shocks, rather than cushion the economy (Rigobon 2006). In this context, any uncovered liabilities resulting from individual bank insolvencies risk becoming a contingent liability of the fiscal authority.

The fiscal authorities must therefore maintain an adequate liquidity cushion against all contingencies, including a financial crisis. The size of this cushion could approach US$3 billion if a crisis occurred comparable to the one in 1998–99.[1] Even if the banking system exhausted all available funds and was able to liquidate private investments at no cost (including net foreign assets), there would be a significant shortfall. To restore full confidence in the banking system while freeing banks to allocate assets in line with improved returns, the authorities should maintain contingent liquid funds of no less than 8 percent of GDP.[2]

Institutional recommendations (see chapter 3) include reforms of the bankruptcy law, alignment of taxation policy with international best practices, enforcement of loan collection, and elimination of court delays in implementing contracts, all of which are essential to improving systemic robustness and credibility. The reforms would permit closer relations with foreign correspondent banks, which would facilitate liquidity management while allowing domestic banks greater flexibility in arranging their portfolios. These results in turn would release credit to the domestic private sector, allowing wider access to credit and especially benefiting small firms, which are unable to access international financial markets.

External Indicators

Overall, external indicators have improved significantly between 2003, when Ecuador had a trade deficit of 0.1 percent, and 2006, when the trade surplus was at 4.2 percent of GDP and the current account balance was at 3.7 percent of GDP (table 1.3). However, a decomposition of the trends reveals continued reliance on oil exports. In 2006, the non-oil trade balance stood at –8.6 percent of GDP, and the non-oil current account balance stood at –9.1 percent of GDP. Oil prices, which doubled between 2002 and 2005, increased by an additional 25 percent, to an average price of US$52.30 per barrel in 2006. At 12.8 percent of GDP, the balance on trade in petroleum and petroleum products was nearly twice that in 2003, even though cumulative growth in real GDP over the same period was almost 18 percent.

Table 1.3. Key External Indicators
(% of GDP, except as noted)

	2003	*2004*	*2005*	*2006*
Crude petroleum exports unit value (US$/barrel)	25.8	29.9	41.1	52.3
Change in merchandise terms of trade	5.2	3.4	26.9	11.0
Trade balance	0.3	0.9	2.0	4.2
Non-oil	–6.3	–9.1	–9.4	–8.6
Current account	–1.5	–1.7	0.8	3.7
Non-oil	–8.0	–11.6	–10.5	–9.1
Petroleum balance	**6.5**	**9.9**	**11.4**	**12.8**
Direct inward investment (foreign direct investment)	5.4	3.6	4.5	5.1
Portfolio investment	0.0	0.0	1.6	–1.8
Remittances from emigrants	5.7	5.6	6.7	7.1
International reserves coverage (months)	1.5	1.5	2.0	2.0

Sources: BCE, WDI, and authors' calculations.

The reversal of capital flows in 1998 had forced the current account into surplus in 1999 and 2000. Capital inflows resumed in 2001, improving steadily until slowing down in 2006, largely because of a US$1.3 billion fall in portfolio investment. Foreign direct investment increased to 5.1 percent of GDP in 2006, but it was concentrated in the energy sector. Remittances from emigrants, a significant source of external financing in recent years, continued to increase, reaching 7.1 percent of GDP, the largest source of revenue after net petroleum exports. The international reserve position has stabilized relative to imports, largely because of a sharp increase in inflows starting in 2004, and was at US$2.05 billion as of January 8, 2007. However, in 2006, worsening of the overall balance of payments position led to reserve decumulation of US$123 million, as opposed to reserve accumulation of US$709 million in 2005.

The breakdown of trends in external indicators reveals Ecuador's biggest hurdle: an inability to sufficiently diversify production and trade away from reliance on the oil sector.[3] Exports of goods remain concentrated in crude oil; gross oil and derivatives exports were 18.5 percent of GDP, compared with non-oil exports of 13.5 percent of GDP in 2006. Compared with LAC and lower- and middle-income countries, Ecuador's non-oil goods exports have been decreasing as a percentage of non-oil GDP (figures 1.1a and b), with the trend reversing only in 2005. A concentration on raw material exports reduces growth potential in several ways: commodity price volatility, limited job creation in a capital-intensive industry, few opportunities for technical progress and productivity gains,[4] the potential appreciation effects of natural resource exports on the real exchange rate, and rent-seeking behavior that is often associated with natural resource–based sectors. Long-term macroeconomic stability is unlikely without economic diversification, which is also a prerequisite to successful expansion of the tax base and sustainable public revenues. At the same time, it should be recognized that significant steps have been made in the right direction: non-oil GDP and exports have shown brisk growth in recent years in response to a benign external environment, suggesting potentially high capacity to diversify.

Overall, the current macroeconomic context is characterized by mixed trends. Stabilization of inflation and improved economic growth are clear positives. However, significant challenges remain: lack of sufficient economic and trade diversification, leading to vulnerability to oil shocks; relative inability to attract foreign direct investment in sectors of the economy other than mining and limited external financing through other channels compared with other emerging markets; and continued financial sector weaknesses.

II. Fiscal Trends and Challenges

Ecuador's fiscal performance has strengthened in recent years, in large measure because of improved GDP growth, more efficient tax collection, and increased income from oil (for a discussion of specific fiscal issues, see chapters 2 and 12, on tax

Figure 1.1a. Non-oil Exports, 1995–2005
(% of non-oil GDP; 1995 = 100)

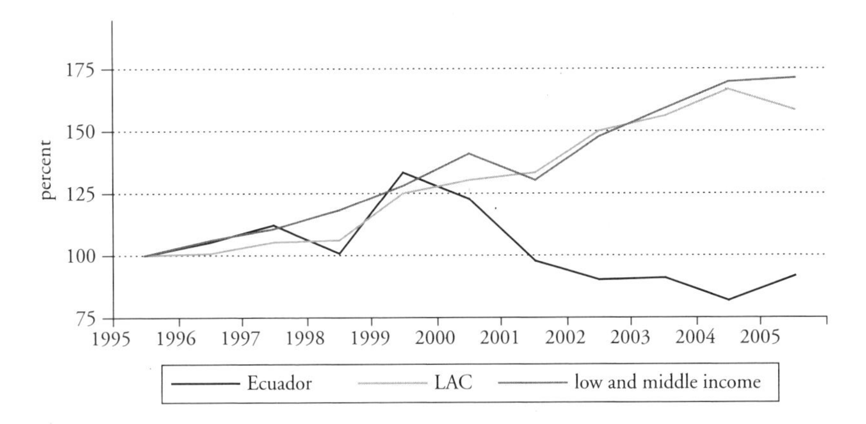

Figure 1.1b. Noncommodity Exports
(% of noncommodity GDP; 1995 = 100)

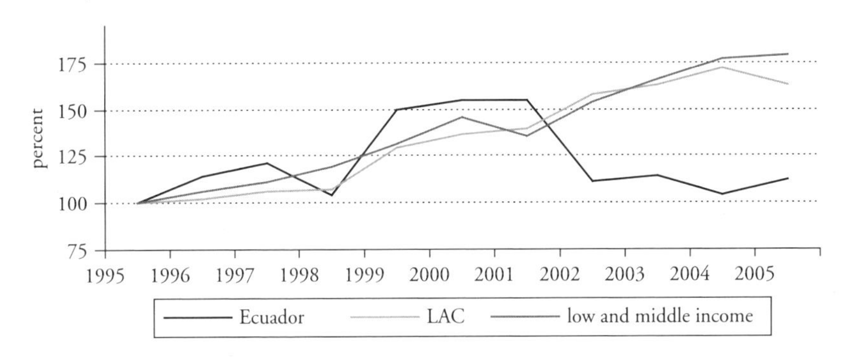

Source: Authors' calculations using data from WDI.

policy and decentralization). Between 1995 and 2000, the nonfinancial public sector (NFPS) overall balance improved from a deficit of 3.3 percent to a surplus of 1.5 percent of GDP; between 2000 and 2006, the overall surplus more than doubled, increasing to 3.3 percent of GDP. The primary surplus was 5.5 percent of GDP in 2006 (table 1.4), the highest since 2001.

NFPS revenue increased slightly, from 25.6 to 27.6 percent of GDP between 2002 and 2006, or from US$6.4 billion to US$11.2 billion. Oil revenues have increased from 22 percent to 29 percent of NFPS revenues since 2002, or from US$1.4 billion to US$3.2 billion, suggesting that dependence on income from oil remains a cause for concern in spite of improvements in non-oil tax revenue.

Table 1.4. Main Fiscal Indicators
% of GDP (except as noted otherwise)

	2000	*2001*	*2002*	*2003*	*2004*	*2005*	*2006*
			Central government				
Overall balance	0.1	–1.1	–0.7	–0.4	–1.0	–0.5	–0.2
Primary balance	6.5	3.4	2.6	2.5	8.6	1.9	2.1
Non-oil balance	–8.6	–7.1	–6.2	–5.8	–5.8	–4.8	–4.4
Non-oil primary balance	–2.3	–2.7	–2.9	–2.9	3.9	–2.5	–2.1
Salaries	4.4	5.1	6.7	6.5	6.3	6.3	6.3
Salaries (% of non-oil revenues)	38.2	42.4	52.1	58.1	56.6	51.3	49.9
			Nonfinancial public sector				
Overall balance	1.5	0.04	0.8	1.6	2.1	0.7	3.3
Primary balance	8.1	4.7	4.2	4.5	4.5	2.9	5.5
Non-oil balance	–7.7	–6.3	–4.8	–4.2	–4.4	–5.3	–4.6
Non-oil primary balance	–1.1	–1.6	–1.4	–1.4	–2.0	–3.1	–2.4
Revenue	**25.9**	**23.3**	**25.6**	**24.1**	**25.1**	**25.1**	**27.6**
Petroleum	9.2	6.4	5.6	5.8	6.5	6.1	7.9
Value-added taxes	5.6	6.9	6.7	6.1	5.8	5.9	6.0
Income taxes	0.5	0.7	0.9	0.9	0.8	0.8	0.9
Expenditure	**24.4**	**23.3**	**24.7**	**23.0**	**23.0**	**24.3**	**24.3**
Salaries	4.8	6.4	8.1	8.0	7.9	8.0	7.8
Interest	6.6	4.7	3.4	2.9	2.4	2.2	2.2
External	5.4	3.6	2.7	2.2	1.9	1.8	1.8
Memorandum items:							
NFPS salaries (% of NFPS non-oil revenues)	28.6	37.7	40.4	43.6	42.6	42.0	39.4
Petroleum (% of NFPS revenue)	35.4	27.3	21.9	24.1	25.9	24.2	28.7

Source: BCE and authors' calculations.

The data provide clear evidence of continued fiscal dependence on the petroleum sector, with oil revenues rising from 5.8 percent to nearly 8 percent of GDP between 2003 and 2006.[5] The non-oil primary deficit of both the central government and the NFPS, though persistent, decreased between 2005 and 2006, both in nominal terms and as a percentage of GDP. The high exposure of budgetary revenues to oil price risk remains a concern, however. A 12 percent decrease in the price of oil in 2007, to US$45 per barrel, combined with a 5 percent fall in production could reduce Ecuador's primary surplus by nearly 1 percent of GDP.

Poor product and trade diversification is responsible for increased fiscal vulnerability to oil price volatility and has restricted the tax base. This chapter contains some recommendations on greater diversification; a more detailed analysis of the issue can be found in chapter 5, on competitiveness.

Figure 1.2. NFPS Oil Revenues and Primary Expenditure
(% of GDP)

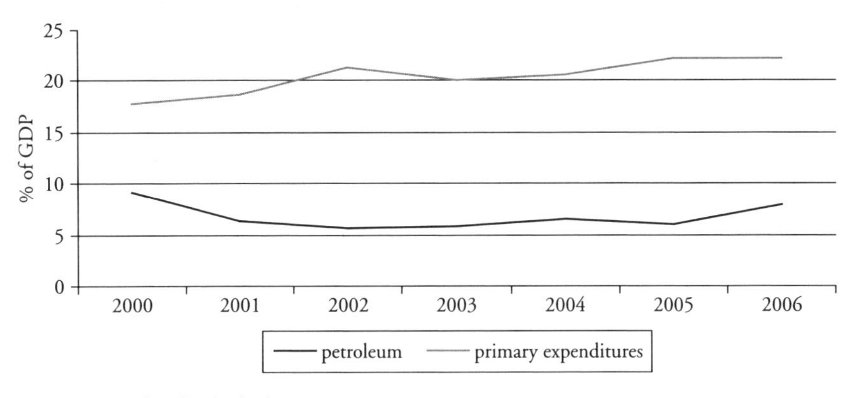

Source: BCE and authors' calculations.

The share of primary expenditures in GDP remained more or less constant between 2002 and 2006, rising slightly from 21.4 percent to 22.1 percent. Volatility of primary expenditures has grown in recent years, however. Noninterest expenditures grew from 19.0 to 21.4 percent of GDP between 1995 and 1999, averaged 19.5 percent of GDP over 2000–03, and averaged 21.6 percent of GDP over 2004–06. In nominal terms, total expenditures increased from US$6.1 billion to US$9.9 billion, while primary expenditures rose more dramatically, from US$5.2 billion to US$9 billion over the same period.[6]

The main source of primary expenditure growth during this period was the increase in public sector salaries, which more than quadrupled in nominal terms between 2000 and 2006, from US$762 million to US$3.2 billion. This represents an increase in the salary bill from 4.8 percent to 7.8 percent of GDP. Salaries rose from an average of 6.8 percent of GDP between 2000 and 2003 to an average of 7.9 percent of GDP between 2004 and 2006. As a consequence, the share of non-oil revenues consumed by public salaries has increased over time (table 1.5). This has created additional and likely irreversible expenditure obligations that will persist even after windfall oil revenues disappear.[7] In the current political context, it is highly improbable that salary growth will slow down, at least in the medium term.

Subsidies and transfers, as budgeted by the central government, have increased from 55 percent to nearly 78 percent of total central government revenues since 2003 (not including public financing through debt issuance). As a percentage of GDP, the budgeted shares have increased from 9 percent to 11.8 percent. Because 44 percent of this disbursement is earmarked or required by law, the result has been reduced budgetary flexibility. The growth in central government subsidies and transfers therefore represents a permanent burden on government revenues (figure 1.3).

Table 1.5. Evolution of Public Wages and Salaries

	Salaries (% of GDP)	*Salaries (% of non-oil revenues)*	*Salaries (% of primary expenditure)*
2000–04	7.0	38.6	35.4
2005	7.9	41.9	36.0
2006	7.8	39.4	35.1

Source: BCE and authors' calculations.

Figure 1.3. Ecuador's Share of Transfers and Subsidies in GDP

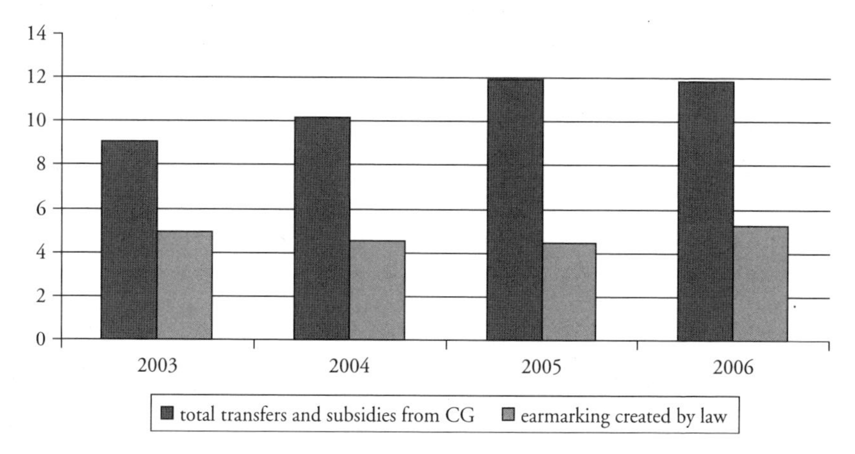

Source: Authors' calculations based on Ministry of Economy and Finance (MEF) Budget Proposal 2006.

Of particular concern are the regressive price subsidies on energy consumption and university education. In 2003, subsidies on liquid petroleum gas (LPG) and diesel stood at 1.7 percent of GDP, increasing to 3 percent of GDP according to the 2006 budget. If the correct crude price is taken into account, this figure is likely to be closer to 5 percent of GDP (for more details on these subsidies, see chapter 4, on the oil and gas sector). Even using understated numbers from the Pro-forma 2006, and based on benefit incidence analysis done in recent years on the impact of subsidies, nearly US$256 million in university subsidies and transfers is captured by the wealthiest 40 percent of the population, along with an additional US$240 million in LPG subsidies.[8] This US$500 million should be compared with a total budgeted outlay of US$1.4 billion on health and community development, education, and culture. Other costly fuel subsidies to gasoline and diesel are also disproportionately captured by the wealthy. By contrast, the Human Development Bond (*Bono de Desarrollo Humano*—BDH), a well-targeted cash assistance program for the poor, had a budget of merely US$200 million in 2006.[9]

Previous recommendations have included a suggestion that the SelBen (System for Identification of Social Program Beneficiaries), a welfare index that ranks households according to their demographic and structural characteristics, also be used to target gas subsidies. This would be politically more feasible than eliminating the gas subsidy, because only a small proportion reaching the poor might represent a significant percentage of their consumption expenditures. In 2004 the Ecuador Poverty Assessment calculated, based on 1999 household survey data, that not only would improved targeting lead to a tripling of the share of gas subsidies that reached the poor, it could also generate savings of up to 75 percent of subsidy expenditure.

Overall, therefore, the budgetary situation has improved, largely because of rising oil revenues through 2005 and the first three quarters of 2006, and because of improved economic growth. The fiscal surplus remains exposed to oil price risk. Key sources of fiscal pressure are rapid growth in primary expenditures and the narrow revenue base. Sound fiscal policy would be designed around a strategy for providing fiscal space to increased social and productive sector spending and for maintaining a sufficient cushion for stabilizing incomes and managing contingencies. Weaknesses in the banking sector are an additional source of vulnerability, given that the fiscal authority is also the lender of last resort. Fiscal profligacy and financial sector vulnerabilities are the greatest threats to the dollarization regime and therefore must be resolved as early as possible.

III. Fiscal Policy and Public Debt Sustainability

Ecuador's public debt situation has improved significantly overall, declining to less than 34 percent of GDP from more than 100 percent in 1999. However, the country will have to continue to generate fiscal surpluses in order to reduce the debt servicing burden. The Fiscal Responsibility and Transparency Law that passed in 2002 helped contain expenditure increases, and oil revenue above a certain level was diverted to a fund, with a portion directed to repurchases of public debt. These provisions played a major role in reversing Ecuador's difficult fiscal landscape, stabilizing the economy after the crisis, and helping the country regain access to international capital markets after the debt default. At the same time, the country built up contingent reserve assets.

In 2005 lawmakers passed a new Fiscal Responsibility and Transparency Law setting up a new oil fund called the Special Account for Productive and Social Reactivation (*Cuenta Especial de Reactivación Productiva y Social*—CEREPS).[10] The new law loosened fiscal restrictions in several ways, including by easing caps on primary expenditure growth related to capital spending, returning social security reserve funds to individual beneficiaries, and increasing financing of public spending.[11] The Savings and Contingency Fund (*Fondo de Ahorro y Contingencia*—FAC) became based on oil revenue levels as opposed to oil prices and remained capped at 2.5 percent of GDP, which seems inadequate. For example, under severe crisis conditions such as those that prevailed in 1999, the direct and indirect fiscal cost could be more than 7 percent of GDP.

Of even greater concern is a recent proposal to allow use of funds in the Fund for Investment in the Energy and Hydrocarbons Sectors (FEISEH) (created out of income received from the nationalized Occidental Petroleum oil fields) to purchase short-term government securities (CETES). This would in effect damage the wall between current budgetary expenditure management and surplus oil revenues. It should be noted that the success of contingency funds and income stabilization funds depends critically on the credibility of the separation between budgetary financing and funds' resources. In this context, the recent declaration by the new government that agriculture, roads, health, and education require emergency spending has led to the signing of decrees allowing additional commitments out of the FAC. If unchecked, this tendency could damage the central government's fiscal situation.

These recent changes, coupled with the narrow tax base and increasing expenditure rigidities discussed previously, make it all the more important for the government to keep a tight rein on primary expenditure to ensure continued reduction of the public debt burden and generate surpluses for the savings of future generations. In this context, table 1.6 (a and b) presents four-year projections of public debt as a ratio of GDP under alternative scenarios.[12] The assumptions on oil revenues are broadly consistent with those in chapter 4, on oil and gas, but the scenarios are constructed under different assumptions, because the objective here is to examine the sensitivity of the public debt ratio to the primary surplus and to GDP growth rather than to analyze the impact of potential reforms on oil production.

It should be noted that the primary surplus averaged 4.4 percent of GDP between 2003 and 2006, and was 5.4 percent of GDP in 2006. As noted in the previous section, oil revenues were primarily responsible for improvements in the fiscal position in 2005 and the first three quarters of 2006 and stood at 7.8 percent by the end of that year.

The debt ratio is sensitive to changes in the assumptions on the primary surplus, which in turn are determined by assumptions on oil revenues, subsidy projections, and increases in public wages and salaries. The simulations in table 1.6 do not assume any decline in the average price of Ecuadoran crude in 2007, but allow for a 5 percent fall in the price of oil in 2008 under the extreme shock scenario.

In the short and medium run, improved expenditure management will clearly be critical to maintaining Ecuador's surpluses, whereas in the medium to long run, policies to increase non-oil revenue will be the key to sustainability. In addition to policies focused directly on expenditure containment and revenue enhancement, reform in fiscal institutions should continue at all levels of tax collection, to ensure that the performance of subnational governments is in line with national priorities. The authorities also should renew their commitment to greater transparency and accountability in fiscal decisions. One important step has been the timely dissemination of fiscal data. However, it should be possible to provide a programmatic classification of expenditures as well as the standard functional classification that is currently available. Considerable

Table 1.6a. Assumptions Underlying Debt Simulations, 2007–10

Scenario	*Oil-related assumptions*	*Other assumptions*
Optimistic	Reforms in oil sector cause oil revenues/GDP to increase by 28 percent between 2007 and 2010 and require additional public investment of US$1.5 billion; oil revenues average 10.06 percent of GDP.	Real growth rate averages 4.6 percent between 2007 and 2010; NFPS revenues average 30.6 percent of GDP, and primary expenditures average 25.1 percent of GDP, implying an average primary surplus of 5.4 percent of GDP.
Baseline	Partial reforms in oil sector cause oil revenues/GDP to stagnate, and no additional public investment is required; oil revenues average 8.01 percent of GDP.	Real growth rate averages 3.5 percent between 2007 and 2010; NFPS revenues average 28.5, and primary expenditures average 23.4 percent of GDP, implying an average primary surplus of 5.1 percent of GDP.
Pessimistic	No reforms in oil sector cause oil revenues/GDP to decrease by 45 percent between 2007 and 2010; oil revenues average 5.5 percent of GDP.	Real growth rate averages 2.4 percent between 2007 and 2010; NFPS revenues average 26.2 percent and primary expenditures average 24.1 percent of GDP, implying an average primary surplus of 2.1 percent of GDP.
Extreme shock	No reforms in oil sector cause oil revenues/GDP to decrease by 53 percent between 2007 and 2010; oil revenues average 5.1 percent of GDP;	Real growth rate averages 1.4 percent between 2007 and 2010; the shock to the economy leads to a jump in public spending of US$1.5 billion in 2008; NFPS revenues average 24.4 percent and primary expenditures average 24.6 percent of GDP, implying an average primary surplus of –0.3 percent of GDP.

Table 1.6b. Sensitivity of Debt Projections to Fiscal Assumptions[a]
% of GDP

	2006	*2007*	*2008*	*2009*	*2010*
I. Primary surplus: *Optimistic*	5.4	4.37	2.6	6.9	7.9
Public debt	33.5	27.6	23.7	17.5	11.6
II. Primary surplus: *Baseline*	5.4	4.5	4.9	5.3	5.7
Public debt	33.5	27.5	23.2	19.8	17.0
III. Primary surplus: *Pessimistic*	5.4	3.3	2.6	1.7	0.9
Public debt	33.5	29.7	28.7	29.2	31.3
IV. Primary surplus: *Extreme shock*	5.4	2.9	–1.3	–0.7	–2.1
Public debt	33.5	30.4	35.3	38.1	40.4

Source: Authors' calculations.

a. Contingent liabilities, which could total as high as 11 percent of GDP (discussed in more detail in the next section), are not accounted for in these calculations.

progress has already been made in administrative reform and fiscal reporting, and it is vital that the process be carried still further. (See chapters 2, on tax policy, and 10, on public sector transparency and efficiency.)

IV. Public Debt Trends

Ecuador's public debt ratio has declined sharply in recent years: in December 2006, public debt amounted to 33 percent of GDP, a significant decrease from 100 percent of GDP in 1999. The continuous decrease in debt-to-GDP levels (figure 1.4) is explained by (i) a sustained economic recovery, partly due to high oil prices; (ii) debt reduction achieved in 2000 after a successful restructuring in which Ecuador exchanged US$6.4 billion of Brady bonds for US$3.9 billion of new global bonds; and (iii) restricted access to new financing. (See the annex for a detailed analysis of debt management issues and recommendations.)

If central government debt and financial assets are netted (table 1.7), the reduction in the debt/GDP ratio is even more impressive.[13] In turn however, this calculation underestimates central government debt because budget arrears and nonrecognized liabilities of the central government to the rest of the public sector are excluded.[14] In

Figure 1.4. Total Debt Levels as a Percentage of GDP

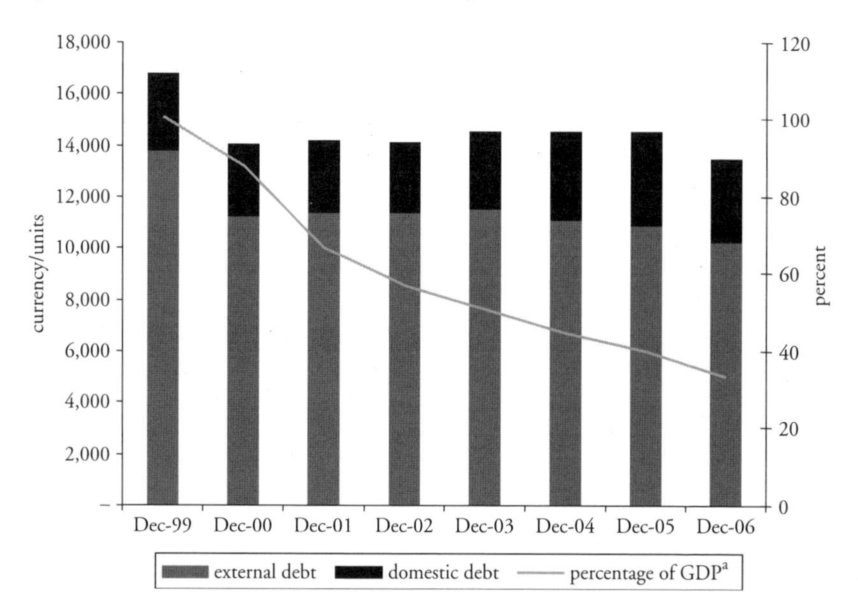

Source: MEF and World Bank staff calculations.

a. Estimate for 2006 is based on data available December 2006.

Table 1.7. Net Central Government Debt

Year	*Gross debt*	*Deposits*	*Net debt*	*Percentage of GDP*
2003	14,507	655	13,852	48
2004	14,549	754	13,795	42
2005	14,416	1,377	13,039	36
2006	14,031	2,078	11,953	31

Source: BCE.

Table 1.8. Credit Sovereign Debt Rating

	2004	*2005*	*2006*	*Jan-07*
Moody's	Caa1	Caa1	Caa1	Caa2
Standard and Poor's	CCC+	B	CCC+	CCC
Fitch	CCC+	B–	B–	CCC+

Source: Bloomberg.

sum, although public sector finances have strengthened as a result of the oil price increase, with growing deposits in the central government accounts and the FAC, these gains are partly offset by arrears and growing contingent liabilities of the central government.

Ecuador's credit sovereign debt rating is very low (table 1.8). Although the credit rating agencies value the economic stabilization and resumption of growth under dollarization, they penalize Ecuador for its political instability, poor track record in meeting its debt obligations, the volatile and uncertain political environment, limited fiscal flexibility with vulnerability to a downturn in oil prices, policy constraints due to dollarization and for an economic growth vulnerable to external shocks, as a small, commodity-dependent economy.[15]

Spreads for Latin American emerging markets have narrowed considerably since 2002 (figure 1.5). Ecuador's spread decreased from 1,013 basis points in October 2002, down to 654 basis points in early April 2005. However, as of January 23, 2007, following repeated statements by the incoming administration that Ecuador was seriously considering an Argentine-style debt restructuring, the spread widened to 1,051 basis points. This implied that secondary financial markets considered Ecuadoran debt to be riskier than either Lebanon's or Iraq's. Following timely coupon payments on the global bonds in February, the spread narrowed again.

Debt Structure and Risk Analysis

The structure of Ecuador's debt in terms of funding sources has been relatively stable over the past few years: external debt—mainly from multilateral and bilateral sources—represents 75 percent of total debt, and the remaining 25 percent corresponds to

Figure 1.5. EMBI Plus Ecuador and Latin America

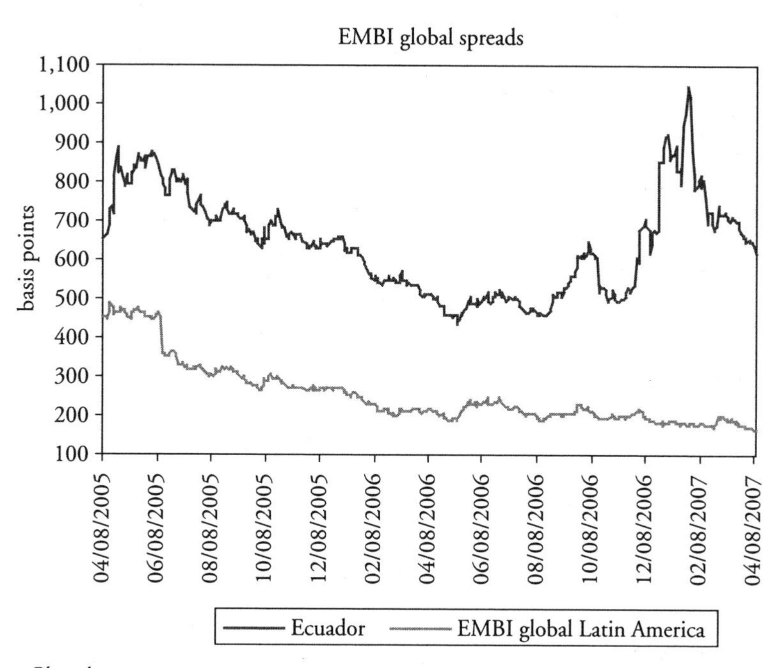

Source: Bloomberg.
Note: EMBI = Emerging Markets Bond Index.

domestic debt placed largely with public institutions (table 1.9).[16] Private market funding sources are limited. Following the 1999 debt default, Ecuador's access to lending was severely restricted. The international capital markets reopened to the country only in 2005, while the domestic market remains virtually closed in terms of private sector demand. The debt has been refinanced almost exclusively with new borrowing from multilateral investors and the social security system.

Multilateral lending represents 40.5 percent of the country's external debt, which amounts to US$10.2 billion. The Inter-American Development Bank (IADB) and Andean Development Corporation (CAF), which are the largest creditors, have combined outstanding loans with Ecuador for US$3 billion. Bilateral lending accounts for another 18 percent of external debt, and the remaining 41 percent comprise mainly debts restructured in previous crises: Brady bonds in the 1980s and Paris Club agreements reached after 1994. Among outstanding bonds, US$650 million of global bonds 2015 issued in December 2005 represents Ecuador's return to the international capital markets, though it amounts to only 6.5 percent of total external debt.[17]

Domestic debt in December 2006 amounted to US$3.3 billion, or 25 percent of total public debt. Of that, US$2.8 billion is medium or long term (of maturity longer than 1 year). Amortization of domestic debt is due in the amount of US$1.1 billion

Table 1.9. Total Debt, by Source of Funds

	2000	*% Total debt*	*2001*	*2002*	*2003*	*2004*	*2005*	*2006*	*% Total debt*
Multilateral orgs.	**4,122**	**29.3**	**4,272**	**4,213**	**4,514**	**4,297**	**3,888**	**4,142**	**30.7**
IBRD	863	6.1	916	853	910	853	817	762	5.6
IADB	1,932	13.7	1,958	1,985	2,084	1,994	1,819	1,838	13.6
CAF	878	6.2	1,038	1,029	1,110	1,139	1,155	1,202	8.9
IMF	147	1.0	190	307	387	289	79	23	0.2
FLAR	291	2.1	154	17	—	—	—	300	2.2
Bilateral orgs.	**2,713**	**19.3**	**2,629**	**2,777**	**2,641**	**2,426**	**2,000**	**1,830**	**13.6**
Original agreements	1,394	9.9	1,351	1,472	1,382	1,244	987	897	6.6
Paris Club	1,319	9.4	1,278	1,306	1,259	1,182	1,013	933	6.9
Eurobonds	**3,950**	**28.1**	**4,079**	**4,078**	**4,077**	**4,076**	**4,723**	**4,163**	**30.9**
Brady bonds	133	0.9	129	128	127	126	123	120	0.9
Global 2012	1,248	8.9	1,250	1,250	1,250	1,250	1,250	510	3.8
Global 2015	—	0.0	—	—	—	—	650	650	4.8
Global 2030	2,569	18.3	2,700	2,700	2,700	2,700	2,700	2,700	20.0
Domestic bonds	**2,738**	**19.5**	**2,704**	**2,506**	**2,529**	**2,983**	**2,832**	**2,825**	**20.9**
Long-term bonds	903	6.4	704	636	853	1,449	1,375	1,390	10.3
AGD bonds	1,410	10.0	1,326	1,242	1,242	1,242	1,242	1,242	9.2
CFN bonds	425	3.0	392	374	318	247	196	175	1.3
Filanbanco bonds	—	0.0	282	254	116	45	19	19	0.1
Treasury certificates	**19**	**0.1**	—	**123**	**302**	**415**	**681**	**293**	**2.2**
Others	**511**	**3.6**	**484**	**452**	**444**	**350**	**413**	**241**	**1.8**
Total	**14,053**	**100.0**	**14,168**	**14,148**	**14,507**	**14,547**	**14,536**	**13,493**	**100.0**

Source: MEF.

over 2007, including payments of US$130.4 million in March and of US$292.7 million in April.

Most domestic debt is held by public entities, notably the Central Bank of Ecuador (BCE) and the social security agency (*Instituto Ecuatoriano de Seguro Social*—IESS).[18] Private domestic investors own only an estimated US$300 million of government paper, or less than 10 percent of total domestic debt. Large private banks' risk management strategy, for example, includes minimizing Ecuadoran paper in order to hedge their portfolio against country risk. As a result, they have significant investments in U.S. Treasury bills and Fannie Mae paper. Among the public debt holders, the BCE holds close to US$1.4 billion (approximately half of domestic debt) in bonds issued for the recapitalization of banks and for repayment of deposits in banks that closed during the 2000 financial crisis.[19] The outstanding balance of domestic bonds has remained fairly stable, and changes in borrowing requirements have been funded by short-term Treasury Certificates (CETES). The volatility of CETES stock over the past few years reflects the difficulty in forecasting funding requirements, which in turn relates to a budgetary policy affected by earmarked revenues and little control of budget execution.[20]

At least two types of risks are relevant for Ecuador's public debt: (i) the potential volatility of debt-servicing flows due to the refinancing and market risk of the debt portfolio, and (ii) the presence of significant contingent liabilities, some of which may materialize, thereby potentially increasing debt levels.

The financial risk generated by the debt portfolio is essentially the exposure to interest rate risk of both external and domestic debt and the refinancing risk posed mainly by the CETES.

Interest Rate Risk

More than US$6 billion, or 45 percent of total debt, is either held at variable rates—mainly the London interbank offered rate, or LIBOR[21]—or will come due within one year (figure 1.6 and 1.7). Accordingly, an increase of 1 percent in this reference rate will add US$60 million to the interest bill, which means that the increase of four percentage points in LIBOR over the past four years must have had a significant impact on the budget. Thus, the current debt redemption profile and the relatively high proportion of variable-rate debt leave the government significantly exposed to interest rate shocks. This exposure is not easily apparent in terms of the debt portfolio's average duration of 2.1 years, which is relatively long due to debt held by the BCE and long-term fixed-rate external debt. (See, for instance, Deposit Guarantee Agency bonds [*Agencia de Garantia de Depositos*—AGD] issued to deal with the financial crisis of 1999–2000.) Rising country risk premiums are serious cause for concern.

Refinancing Risk

This exposure arises mostly from the need to roll over US$850 million of CETES. Although the main investor of these securities, the IESS, can be considered a captive investor, the sheer size of the paper to be rolled over, the uncertainty of the interest

Figure 1.6. Composition of Total Public Debt, by Interest Rate

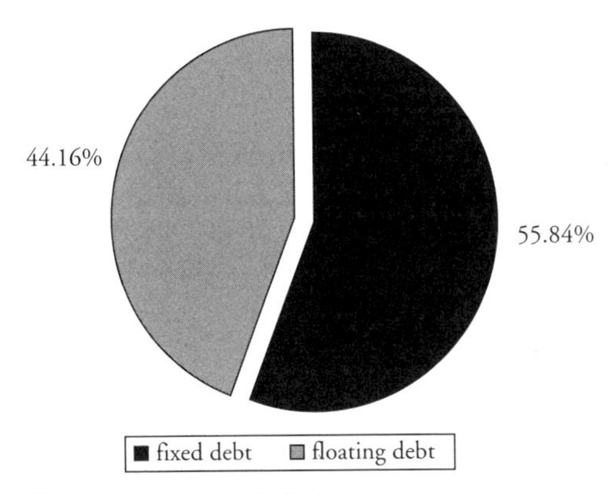

Source: World Bank staff calculations, August 2006 data.

Figure 1.7. Amortization Profile
(% of GDP)

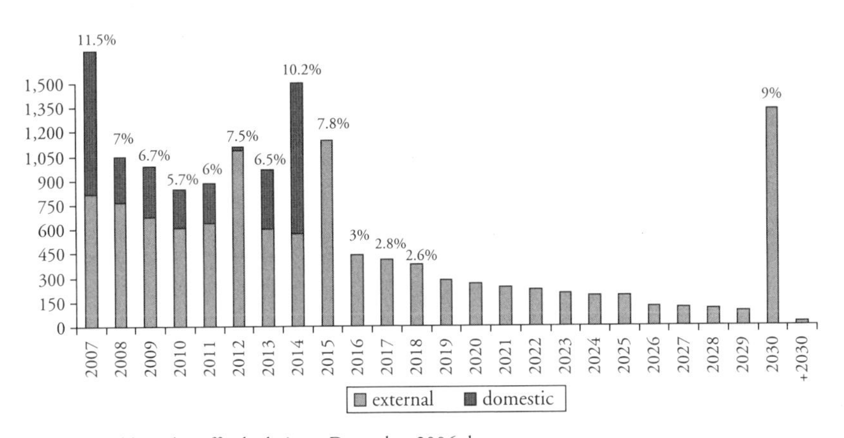

Source: World Bank staff calculations, December 2006 data.

rate negotiations, and the decrease of the IESS's assets generate significant risk to the budget.[22]

Exchange Rate Risk

As almost 90 percent of total debt is U.S. dollar denominated, and Ecuador has a dollarized economy, debt currency risk seems low (table 1.10). A more specific quantification of the government's currency exposure will require having a benchmark for the currency composition of the government debt. Such a benchmark could be developed by taking into account the impact of alternative currency baskets on the volatility of debt service payments relative to government revenues and their corresponding costs.[23]

Table 1.10. Public Debt by Currency
(percent)

U.S. dollar	89.4
Currency basket[a]	4.3
Euro	2.8
Yen	2.2
Others	1.3

Source: MEF and World Bank Staff Calculations, December 2006 data.
a. Borrowed from the IADB.

Finally, public finances also were exposed to contingent liabilities risk, which could trigger financial obligations of up to US$4.5 billion from three sources: (i) potential actuarial deficit and arrears;[24] (ii) the current level of government guarantees, US$902 million, of which US$284 million are already a financial obligation for the government; and (iii) the arbitration claim of Occidental Petroleum, which was filed with the International Center for Settlement of Investment Disputes for the oil fields seized by the government earlier in 2006 (if accepted, the claim would cost more than US$1 billion).

In sum, interest rate risk represents the main exposure of the government debt portfolio, followed by domestic debt refinancing risk. Given the binding macroeconomic and market constraints, debt managers in Ecuador have limited room to address these risks. Though ad hoc strategies adopted in the past appear reasonable, further progress could be made if a more proactive approach were adopted, especially to push back current domestic market constraints. Unfortunately, recent attempts by the authorities in this direction have been hampered by continuous changes in the government and the lack of institutionalized processes for debt management.

A detailed analysis of Ecuador's debt management, with policy recommendations, is presented in the annex.

V. Policy Options to Strengthen Fiscal Sustainability

Maintaining fiscal space for high-priority growth-enhancing expenditures is an important objective of sustainable fiscal policy. Additionally, fiscal robustness is a key component of dollarization, given the limited role for independent monetary policy in stabilizing income over the business cycle. Previous sections therefore analyzed macroeconomic, fiscal, and debt trends and challenges and examined the sensitivity of the public debt ratio to various assumptions about primary surplus generation. This section outlines a multipronged strategy aimed at achieving the goals of fiscal and debt sustainability with stable and accelerated growth.

The short- and medium-run focus of policy should be containment of current expenditure, revenue management, transparency, and accountability, and the statement of clear fiscal targets. In the long run, fiscal sustainability depends on the expansion of the non-oil sector and of the tax base, and on revenue diversification in line with the goal of maintaining fiscal prudence while accelerating growth and enhancing competitiveness.

Immediate measures should include setting caps on current capital expenditures and allowing only capital spending that has a high social rate of return. The fiscal authorities should specify mandated transparent use of CEREPS for social spending that minimizes discretionary increases in spending. This approach will also contribute to the medium-run goal of increasing accountability and transparency at all levels.

Wage growth should be targeted so that the public wage bill is no more than 7 percent of GDP, compared with 8.9 percent as of 2006. In addition, unifying the public personnel laws into a single central regime will restrict rapid increases in the number of public sector employees.

The other major source of high public expenditures is subsidies. Poorly targeted, regressive subsidies should be reduced or eliminated to release funds for creating an effective social safety net while easing budgetary pressure. Pro-poor retargeting of gas subsidies through the use of the SelBen would create fiscal space while ensuring the desired benefits.

In the medium term, expenditure management will require the implementation of a credible regulatory and institutional framework that assigns expenditure management to subnational governments in line with their administrative capacity. The framework also conditions resource transfers on timely reporting.

The weakness of the banking sector and the lack of independent monetary policy (due to dollarization) place a burden on fiscal policy to stabilize the economy from external shocks, meet domestic growth objectives, and manage debt. As of now, excessive dependence on oil revenues implies that the NFPS budget is highly exposed to oil price shocks. Revenue management aimed at building up a liquidity cushion is therefore necessary to guard against crises and catastrophes while managing debt effectively to retain continued access to international financial markets. This liquidity cushion should be built up, through the FAC, toward 8 percent of GDP, instead of being capped at 2.5 percent, as it is now. The effective utilization of windfall oil revenues must be a priority.

Policies need to be implemented to expand the tax base and reduce oil revenue dependence, which are likely to have an impact only in the medium and long term. These policies would include targeted subsidies and tax benefits to non-oil investment in new product lines, and they would be in place for limited periods and with performance-based benchmarks in order to avoid a return to import substitution. Policies should be implemented that encourage both foreign direct investment (FDI) and domestic investment in the non-oil sector. Measures to promote the non-oil economy are analyzed in more detail in chapter 5, on productivity and competitiveness.

The following matrix summarizes the policy recommendations discussed above. Long-term institutional and market structure reforms for public debt management are found in the annex.

Policy Matrix

Issue	*Problems*	*Policy options*
Managing public expenditures with credible, transparent policies	After a period of sound, sustainable fiscal policy that was critical to help the economy recover from the 1999 crisis, Ecuador appears to be moving toward loosening controls on spending. This, in turn, could have serious long-term implications, as the rising spending bill will be difficult to lower when oil revenues decline.	• Establish clear, well-defined fiscal targets to provide credibility to government policy. • Impose a cap on all capital expenditures, with no exception for infrastructure spending, and establish clear rules and objective criteria for project selection, both for regular budgetary resources and for CEREPS resources. • Set clear, simple rules for the use of the FAC. • Design and implement a strong regulatory and institutional framework that clearly assigns expenditure responsibilities to subnational governments in line with their administrative capacity, and condition resource transfers on timely and reliable reporting. • Improve budgetary transparency and accountability at all levels.
High growth in public wages and salaries	Wages and salaries are forming a large and growing portion of the budget. The pressure to increase real wages is likely to continue in the coming years.	• Unify the various public personnel laws under a single, transparent regime in order to halt wage bill growth. • To limit nominal wage growth, and as part of the fiscal rules, establish a cap on wage growth in relation to GDP (around 7 percent of GDP would seem adequate, down from the current 9 percent).
High budgetary earmarking for transfers and subsidies	As of 2006, a high proportion of regressive, untargeted subsidies remains, particularly in higher education (0.9 percent of GDP) and on gasoline, diesel, and natural gas (over 3 percent of GDP), which benefit primarily the richest 20 percent of the population. The high cost of these subsidies increases as the international oil price increases.	• Eliminate, or at least target, fuel and other subsidies to allow for the financing of priority programs without straining the budget. A proposal to set domestic oil prices based on the opportunity cost of raw materials and/or to create a special consumption tax on fuels that would be paid for and collected at the refineries could also constitute a step in the right direction. The SelBen household survey data, which supplies information for targeting the conditional cash transfer program for the poor (BDH), could be used to improve targeting of oil and gas subsidies.

Fiscal management to protect the economy from shocks and reduce public debt	The current design of the oil funds (CEREPS and FAC) is insufficient to insulate the economy from potential future shocks, and it does not continue the former practice of using oil revenues to reduce the stock of public debt. Instead, much of the extraordinary oil revenues are now being channeled to capital and current spending.	Use windfall profits from high oil prices wisely both to reduce the risk of crisis by lowering debt and to provide a cushion in the event of any type of economic shock, including banking crises, natural catastrophes, and terms-of-trade deterioration: • Assign a fixed proportion of CEREPS revenues to debt repurchases, comparable to the provision under the old Fund for Stabilization, Social and Productive Investment, and Reduction of Public Debt (FEIREP). • Build up the FAC oil fund to at least 7 percent of GDP (up from 2.5 percent currently), the estimated loss to NFPS revenues in case of a severe crisis, in order to provide a credible liquidity cushion against economic and natural catastrophes.
Narrow tax base, undiversified economy, and oil revenue dependence	Ecuador's fiscal panorama is excessively dependent on oil revenues, while the non-oil tax base is extremely limited. Numerous obstacles limit the ability of the economy to diversify, including upcoming expiration of preferential access to the U.S. market under the Andean Trade Promotion and Drug Eradication Act (ATPDEA), uncertainties for foreign investors, and weak or poorly designed public programs to support diversification.	Promote economic diversification through: • Transparent and consistent policy commitments to maintain credibility with international investors and encourage FDI in tradable non-oil sectors. • Pursuit of continued preferential access to the U.S. markets and trade opportunities in other markets. • Limited subsidies to domestic investment in new non-oil industries that are targeted at the sector and are not firm specific, with clear performance benchmarks and sunset clauses. Tax benefits for product line upgrades, development of new product lines, and investment in new sectors with clear performance-based benchmarks and, for a limited time, with periodic review to ensure that all benchmark conditions are satisfied.

Annex. Public Debt Management

Over the past four years Ecuador has achieved some progress in the management of its public debt. The country has regained access to the international capital markets and has lowered the cost of external debt by prepaying a portion of expensive bonds using cheaper multilateral loans and a new bond issuance. At the same time, the authorities are maximizing the use of multilateral funding and trying to ensure that the funding has a smooth refinancing profile. In addition, they are attempting to extend the maturity of short-term domestic debt placed with the public sector. However, authorities are well aware of the need to strengthen debt management in several key areas. For example, the de facto debt strategy mentioned above is not based on a systematic risk analysis of the debt portfolio. Authorities plan to introduce a more structured process for designing and implementing a debt management strategy. At the same time, they are conscious of the need to further strengthen institutional capacity, governance, and institutional arrangements in public debt management and have taken some important steps in this direction based on analyses and reforms proposed by the IADB and the Andean Development Corporation.

The domestic debt market is still incipient, with very limited access to voluntary investors, and a carefully sequenced plan for domestic debt-market development is still lacking. The main priorities are the development of a money market and an issuance policy that builds upon current standardization plans of the Ministry of Economy and Finance (MEF), with a special focus on credibility measures to increase demand for public debt from private sector investors. These actions should be designed in harmony with the other reforms related to a secondary market and infrastructure to be developed in a second phase.

Several actions could be included in a carefully sequenced reform plan to help public debt management and markets in Ecuador advance in the direction of international sound practice. These could complement and enhance the effectiveness of reforms already being recommended and implemented by other multilateral lenders.

Public Debt Management Issues and Recommendations

As a start, the legal framework should be revised to address three main issues. The first would include typical debt management objectives related to cost reduction within preestablished risk limits and to the development of the domestic debt market. Currently, objectives are couched primarily in terms of fiscal policy and investment projects. The second would require that the MEF create a medium-term debt management strategy for approval by the minister and that it periodically inform Congress and other third parties on strategy design and implementation. Third, the legal framework would establish an institutional process for the design, authorization, implementation, and review of the debt strategy and create and institutionalize a debt management committee.

The BCE would be advised to discontinue short-term paper issuance in the primary market so as to consolidate all debt issuance in the MEF, and to conduct its liquidity management intervention using repurchase agreements, or repos, with government securities as collateral. If the BCE continues debt issuance, it should have a formalized agreement with the MEF on strategy. In spite of dollarization, the BCE still issues its own short-term paper in the primary market to help recycle interbank liquidity. Although this issuance is small, it competes with CETES issued by the MEF in the same short end of the yield curve in a very small domestic market.

The MEF should design a business plan that consolidates strategic activities within the Subsecretariat of Public Credit (*Secretaría de Crédito Público*—SCP)—of both the middle and front office—and institutionalizes a formal coordination mechanism in the MEF between the SCP and Treasury regarding CETES issuance. Although by law SCP consolidates public debt management functions, its analytical skills are scarce.

Both the MEF and the BCE should provide more comprehensive public debt information and produce quarterly and annual reports, including a complete debt profile.

In the area of risk quantification and debt strategy development, SCP should summarize the current strategy in a document to initiate the debate in a formal, institutionalized manner, ideally within a public debt management committee. Although SCP has no formal public debt strategy, it has a de facto funding strategy that has met the borrowing levels targeted in the Fiscal Responsibility and Transparency Law. SCP should periodically undertake cost-risk analyses and subsequently propose and implement a comprehensive medium-term debt management strategy. The analysis and discussion should be based on the cost and risk analyses of the debt portfolio and on an evaluation of macroeconomic and financial market constraints. A first step in this direction is for SCP to periodically produce debt statistics and risk indicators, accompanied by analyses of how to address different risks, including those of contingent liabilities.

Coordination between debt management and fiscal policy could be strengthened. Currently, they are coordinated mainly through the Fiscal Responsibility Law, but coordination and information flows could be improved in two areas: (i) risk analysis of the debt portfolio, because SCP currently cannot perform a sensitivity analysis for borrowing requirements and for the projected debt-to-GDP ratio; and (ii) comprehensive information on the fiscal context, because information on government assets and liabilities is incomplete.

A liquidity cushion could be created at the beginning of the budget cycle, and a cash forecasting model could be implemented. Also, better coordination between debt and cash management could be promoted by creating a cash management committee. A review of cash management covering the entire public sector could be undertaken. The proposed measures should help delink debt issuance from cash outflows without holding excessive cash balances.

As for institutional capacity, SCP should be restructured along functional lines, with a front, middle, and back office structure, and a comprehensive training program should be designed and implemented to strengthen staff technical capacity. SCP's current distribution of responsibilities makes it difficult to promote specialization and the development of analytical and execution functions.

Domestic Debt Market Issues and Recommendations

To develop the money market, the authorities should encourage current plans intended to increase the connectivity of local and international liquidity through a single correspondent bank for the BCE and Ecuadoran banks. Poor connectivity with international markets, in spite of Ecuador's being a dollarized economy, is a major problem for the country. Money markets are very small and fragmented. Underdeveloped domestic liquidity markets and the fact that BCE cannot be a lender of last resort make banks hold most of their precautionary liquidity in correspondent banks abroad. Other recommended measures include using a reporting scheme for off-exchange money market transactions and building an adequate settlement infrastructure (bilateral and real time).

In the primary market, the issuance process should be addressed with a high-level three-to five-year issuance plan of standardized securities that emphasizes a communication and placement strategy to increase credibility of public debt policy. The current strategy of primary market issuance is irregular, is not standardized, lacks a strategy to build market benchmarks, and is subject to a serious lack of credibility among the general public and private investors.

To further enhance credibility, the MEF should implement an investor relations program and study the viability of retail placements focused on eliminating the negative political connotations of investing in public debt. This program should be complemented by debt management instruments that support the sustainability of the placement process, such as a liquidity fund, or a regular debt-for-debt swap program with the objective of smoothing the concentration of maturities and of increasing the liquidity of outstanding issues.

Additionally, the auction mechanism at the exchanges should be simplified and a more market-oriented placement scheme should be built. The pricing process in the primary market is distorted by having the Ecuadoran Social Security Institute (IESS) often be the only buyer of public debt, and by the "50 percent rule" obliging the public sector to split the volume of its issues and investments equally between the two existing exchanges. Also, there is no de facto interconnection of the two exchanges' trading systems, so auction prices for the same securities can be different, and the auction rules are complex and foster collusion.

To develop the secondary market, the public sector should design a plan—in dialogue with market participants—to improve the institutional organization of the secondary market to allow the development of an off-exchange wholesale market with direct participation of banks. The average size of transactions in the exchanges is very low, confirming that they are not used for wholesale transactions. Operational and regulatory changes can only be effective if they are planned in dialogue with all market participants, including the exchange.

Regarding the investor base, in the short term the participation of the IESS—the main investor in public debt—in the government securities auctions should be made more transparent. Banks and mutual funds are a relevant potential investor base, provided a more market-oriented approach is implemented. Primary market quotas for the IESS can also be considered. In the long term, the rules that oblige the IESS to split its investments equally between both exchanges should be analyzed.

As for market infrastructure, the BCE should take a leading role in establishing institutional and functional infrastructure guidelines to build a central depository. This should be done independently of the entity that is responsible for the central depository, either the BCE itself or a private entity. Market infrastructure (trading and central depository) is currently fully dependent on the exchange, with a design that is not adequate for a wholesale public debt market.

Finally, a pragmatic agenda of regulatory changes should be developed that balances feasibility with priority in relation to development of the public debt market. The first phase should emphasize regulation of custodial arrangements, unification of regulatory frameworks for the exchanges, and prudential regulation for brokers. The Securities Market Law, enacted in 1998, has wide coverage of all issues but needs to change custodial arrangements, opening the monopoly of exchange, unifying the regulatory framework for both exchanges, clarifying the definition of public offers, and using a more gradual approach to sanctions.

Notes

1. The estimate assumes that a crisis would entail a run on deposits of similar magnitude as during the last crisis, with adjustments to account for the current preponderance of short-term liabilities. See chapter 3, "The Banking System," for a detailed calculation under various scenarios.
2. See chapter 3 on the banking system. Because banks are forced to maintain relatively high liquid assets, potential average yield on investments is lower.
3. For a detailed discussion and comprehensive literature survey on related issues, see World Bank (2006).
4. Frankel and Romer (1999) find that openness improves income through its effect on total factor productivity; several studies find a positive impact of increased trade on income growth (Alesina, Spolaore, and Wacziarg 2005; Dollar and Kraay 2004; Loayza, Fajnzylber, and Calderón 2005). Raw material exports are found to have a negative impact on growth (Sachs and Warner 1995), whereas trade diversification increases growth through its positive impact on productivity or learning by exporting (Feenstra and Lee 2004; Hausman, Pritchett, and Rodrik 2004; Hernández and Pierola 2006; Kaufman, Kraay, and Zoido-Lobaton 1999; Klinger and Lederman 2004; and Van Biesenbroek 2003).
5. A roughly 6 percent decrease in gross income from petroleum is envisaged in the Pro-forma 2007 relative to the codified figure for 2006. At the same time, non-oil revenue is projected to increase by 5.2 percent.
6. The GDP figures used in this calculation increased from US$15.9 billion to US$24.9 billion between 2000 and 2002 and to US$40.8 billion by 2006.

7. The Pro-forma 2007 assumes an 8.3 percent increase in central government salaries relative to codified 2006 expenditure in the same category.

8. Benefit incidence numbers come from the "Ecuador Poverty Assessment" (World Bank 2004b) and the "Ecuador Development Policy Review: Growth Inclusion and Governance—the Road Ahead" (World Bank 2004a),. According to Bank calculations based on actual fuel prices rather than on the budget estimates, the LPG subsidy going to the wealthiest 40 percent is US$344 million, while the total amount spent on fuel subsidies (LPG, gasoline, and diesel) totaled an estimated US$1.9 billion in 2006.

9. The Pro-forma 2007 budgets an increase from US$175 million to US$360 million in central government transfers to the BDH. Total central government transfers are budgeted to increase 4.7 percent over codified 2006 expenditures.

10. Assumed to provide US$601 million in the Pro-forma 2007 compared with codified receipts of US$235 million in 2006.

11. With the new Hydrocarbon Law of April 2006, 50 percent of oil revenue accrued above US$22 a barrel (or "windfall oil revenue") goes to the public accounts, to be spent on social, technology, and ecological programs.

12. The assumptions in table 1.6 do not account for the estimated US$4.5 billion in contingent liabilities (see next section) or the US$2.5 billion estimated to be required in additional electricity sector investments (see chapter 6, on the electricity sector). These expenditures would require resource mobilization of over 17 percent of 2006 GDP.

13. Central government deposits held in the BCE, in financial institutions, and in the FAC.

14. Arrears with the social security agency and utility companies are unsettled and therefore not completely registered in the official debt statistics. The IESS indicates that the government's debt is around US$2.5 billion and the government recognizes only US$549 million.

15. See for example, Standard & Poor's July 2005 research note on Ecuador, and Moody's Global Credit Research Rating Action, January 2006.

16. The International Monetary Fund (IMF) paper "The Level and Composition of Public Sector Debt in Emerging Market Crises" (IMF 2006b), which analyzed the case of 12 emerging-market countries before and after a financial crisis, observed an increase in the share of multilateral creditors and a greater exposure of the domestic banking system to sovereign debt. In the case of Ecuador, the banking system is wary of investing with the government, so domestic debt is mostly placed with public sector institutions.

17. In May 2006, Ecuador bought back US$740 million of global bonds 2012, using US$400 million from the Latin American Reserve Fund (FLAR) and US$340 million raised from the global bonds 2015 issuance. This transaction will reduce interest payments by US$20 million per year.

18. The IESS may only hold half its stock in government paper. As of March 6, 2007, the market value of their holdings of public sector paper amounted to US$1.275 billion (no change from end-February), about 39.7 percent of their portfolio. They could increase their holdings by US$330 million and still comply with the 50 percent legal ceiling on public sector paper. As of March 8, the central government was trying to roll over US$315 million extended maturity debt (10-year).

19. Deposit Guarantee Agency (*Agencia de Garantías de Depósitos*—AGD), Filanbanco, and National Finance Corporation bonds.

20. For instance, in 2006 NFPS revenues of US$2 billion could not be used in the budget process and were earmarked to prepay domestic debt.
21. Floating paper includes CAF, IBRD, Children's Development Program (PDI), Brady bonds, and domestic bonds.
22. The IESS started to pay back the *Fondo de Reserva*, a mandatory saving fund, to its affiliates. For more on this issue, see chapter 8, on pensions.
23. At present, the impact of a 10 percent devaluation of the Japanese yen and the euro would be an increase of US$73.5 million in total outstanding debt, or approximately 0.2 percent of GDP.
24. From 1985 to 2000, financial restrictions resulted in the government discontinuing its legally determined contributions to the IESS. The government considers these arrears to amount to US$549 million, while the IESS calculates them at US$2.5 billion. Other arrears with the IESS and utility companies are estimated to be on the order of US$1 billion.

Bibliography

Agencia de Garantía de Depósitos. http://www.agd.gov.ec.

Alesina, Alberto, Enrico Spolaore, and Romain Wacziarg. 2005. "Trade, Growth and the Size of Countries." In *Handbook of Economic Growth*, 1st edition, ed. Philippe Aghion and Steven Durlauf, 1499–1542. Elsevier.

Asociación de Bancos Privados del Ecuador. http://www.asobancos.org.ec.

BCE (Banco Central del Ecuador [Central Bank of Ecuador]). http://www.bce.fin.ec.

———. 2005. Pareja Canelos Mauricio, Gerente General (e). SE-2490-2005.

Dollar, David, and Aart Kraay. 2004. "Trade, Growth, and Poverty." *Economic Journal* 114 (493): F22–49.

ECLAC (Economic Commission for Latin America and the Caribbean). 2004. *Base de datos macroeconómicos del estudio económico de América Latina y el Caribe.* Santiago, Chile: ECLAC.

Feenstra, Robert, and H. L. Lee. 2004. "On the Measurement of Product Variety in Trade." *American Economic Review, Papers and Proceedings* 94 (2): 145–49.

Frankel, Jacob, and D. Romer. 1999. "Does Trade Cause Growth?" *American Economic Review* 89 (3): 379–99.

Hausman, R., L. Pritchett, and D. Rodrik. 2004. "Growth Accelerations." Photocopy, Harvard University, Cambridge, MA.

Hernández, Fernando, and Martha Denisse Pierola. 2006. "Trade, Diversification and Growth in Ecuador." Photocopy.

IMF (International Monetary Fund). 2006a. "Ecuador: Staff Report for the 2005 Article IV Consultation." IMF.

———. 2006b. "The Level and Composition of Public Sector Debt in Emerging Market Crises." Working Paper, IMF, Washington, DC.

Kaufman, D., A. Kraay, and P. Zoido-Lobaton. 1999. "Governance Matters." Policy Research Working Paper 2196, World Bank, Washington, DC.

Klinger, B., and D. Lederman. 2004. "Discovery and Development: An Empirical Exploration of New Products." Policy Research Working Paper 3450, World Bank, Washington, DC.

Ley de Beneficios Tributarios para Nuevas Inversiones Productivas, Generación de Empleo y Prestación de Servicios. November 18, 2005.

Ley Orgánica de Responsabilidad, Estabilización y Transparencia Fiscal . June 4, 2002. Reglamento. February 10, 2003.

Ley Orgánica Reformatoria a la Ley Orgánica de Responsabilidad, Estabilización y Transparencia Fiscal. July 27, 2005. Reglamento, October 12, 2005.

Loayza, N., P. Fajnzylber, and C. Calderón. 2005. *Economic Growth in Latin America and the Caribbean. Stylized Facts, Explanations, and Forecasts.* Washington, DC: World Bank.

Notaría Primera, Cantón Quito. 2005. *Liquidación del Contrato de Fideicomiso Mercantil Fondo de Estabilización, Inversión Social y Productiva y Reducción del Endeudamiento Público, Fideicomiso FEIREP.* September 28, 2005.

Rigobon, Roberto. 2006. "Ecuador's Stabilization Policy." Mimeo, Sloan School of Management, MIT, Cambridge, MA.

Sachs, J., and A. Warner. 1995. "Economic Reform and the Process of Global Integration." *Brookings Papers on Economic Activity.*

Servicio de Rentas Internas. http://www.sri.gov.ec.

Superintendencia de Bancos y Seguros del Ecuador. http://www.superban.gov.ec.

Van Biesenbroeck, J. 2003. "Exporting Raises Productivity in Sub-Saharan African Manufacturing Plants." NBER Working Paper 10020, Cambridge, MA: National Bureau of Economic Research.

World Bank. 2000. "Ecuador: Crisis, Poverty and Social Services." Report 19920-EC, World Bank, Washington, DC.

World Bank. 2003a. *Doing Business in 2004: Understanding Regulation.* Cambridge: Oxford University Press for the World Bank.

World Bank. 2003b. "Ecuador. An Economic and Social Agenda in the New Millennium." Report 19920-EC, World Bank, Washington, DC.

World Bank. 2004a. "Ecuador Development Policy Review: Growth Inclusion and Governance—The Road Ahead." Report 27443-EC, World Bank, Washington, DC.

World Bank. 2004b. "Ecuador Poverty Assessment." Report 27061-EC, World Bank, Washington, DC.

World Bank. 2005. *Ecuador, Creating Fiscal Space for Poverty Reduction: A Fiscal Management and Public Expenditure Review.* Washington, DC: World Bank.

World Bank. 2005. *Ecuador Investment Climate Assessment.* Washington, DC: World Bank.

World Bank. 2006. "Ecuador Country Economic Memorandum: Promoting Stable and Robust Economic Growth." Report 36412-EC. World Bank, Washington, DC.

World Bank and International Monetary Fund. 2005. Financial Sector Assessment Program. Ecuador: Technical Notes: Banking System.

2

Tax Policy and Administration

Osvaldo Schenone

Executive Summary

The three principal tax policy problems in Ecuador are the lack of simplicity, the country's small tax base, and inefficient use of resources. The reasons behind these problems are, first, the proliferation of taxes, a trend that lacks transparency and hides inequity and inefficiency in the allocation of resources. A second reason is the tax exemptions, which introduce distortions and do not comply with any of the tax policy objectives, especially with respect to redistribution, in the case of the value-added tax (VAT), and with respect to promoting socially equitable undertakings, in the case of income tax exemptions or import duties. The third and final reason is the tax revenue preallocations, which do not allow for the efficient use of tax resources and discourage the collection efforts of those jurisdictions that prefer to count on transfers from the central government. A tax simplification—by abolishing minor taxes, broadening the base by eliminating exemptions, and reorienting taxes by eliminating preallocations—would result in lower administrative costs for collecting taxes, an increase in tax revenues, and more efficient allocations. Regarding tax administration, the two most serious problems are the inadequate institutional design of the Internal Revenue Service (SRI), which makes the SRI vulnerable to constant pressures from private interests, and the poor antievasion efforts by customs officials. Although reforms by the Ecuadoran Customs Corporation (CAE) board in 2006 made steps toward improving the CAE's tax collection performance by addressing modernization and tax compliance, it still has not had the same dynamism as the SRI. Good practice would suggest reinforcing the independence of the SRI and merging with customs under a single authority.

This chapter was prepared by Osvaldo Schenone, tax specialist and World Bank consultant.

I. Background

The advent of the new millennium not only brought a new monetary system—that is, dollarization—to Ecuador, but also put an end to the deficit in the nonfinancial public sector, which characterized the final decades of the past century. One of the important factors contributing to the primary surplus of the past few years was an increase in tax revenues, primarily the VAT.

The nonfinancial public sector comprises the central government, the municipal governments, the Ecuadoran Social Security Institute (*Instituto Ecuatoriano de Seguridad Social—IESS*), and a multitude of other public enterprises. The income from taxes and nontax revenues (primarily from oil) of the nonfinancial public sector amounted to over 25 percent of GDP in 2004 and 2005, and will reach almost 28 percent in 2006, as indicated in table 2.1. The table also shows the portion of the income received by the central government from oil and from taxes. The income from taxes are separated into those collected outside the Internal Revenue Service (*Servicio de Rentas Internas*—SRI) and those collected by the IESS—that is, income tax (ISR), VAT, and special consumption tax (*impuesto a los consumos especiales*—ICE), and others.

As indicated in table 2.1, the increased income by the central government and, in general, by the entire nonfinancial public sector in 2001 was primarily due to the increase in VAT revenues, since the increases in ISR, ICE, and others were significantly less, in terms of percentage of GDP. VAT revenues accounted for about 63 percent of

Table 2.1. Total Income by the Nonfinancial Public Sector and the Central Government, 1995–2006
(percentage of GDP)

		Central Government							
				Taxes					
					Within the SRI				
Year	*Nonfinancial public sector*	*Total*	*Oil*	*Outside the SRI*	*Total*	*ISR*	*VAT*	*ICE*	*Other*
1995	22.7	15.5	5.9	3.6	6.0	2.0	3.1	0.5	0.3
1996	21.8	15.2	7.0	2.6	5.6	1.9	2.9	0.5	0.3
1997	19.9	14.6	5.1	3.5	6.0	1.8	3.2	0.6	0.4
1998	17.2	13.9	3.8	3.9	6.2	1.8	3.5	0.5	0.3
1999	20.8	16.1	6.0	1.8	8.3	0.7	3.7	0.5	3.4
2000	25.9	20.4	7.8	2.2	10.4	1.7	5.8	0.5	2.3
2001	23.3	18.1	5.9	1.2	11.0	2.8	6.9	0.9	0.3
2002	25.6	18.4	5.3	2.2	10.9	2.7	6.8	1.0	0.3
2003	24.1	16.7	5.4	1.1	10.2	2.7	6.1	1.0	0.4
2004	25.1	15.9	4.0	1.9	10.0	2.8	5.9	1.0	0.4
2005	25.1	16.6	4.3	1.5	10.8	3.4	6.0	1.0	0.4
2006[a]	27.9	16.6	3.7	1.8	11.1	3.7	6.1	1.0	0.3

Sources: BCE and SRI.
a. Estimate based on data up to November 2006.

all SRI collections. However, although VAT revenues have remained the central government's largest source of income since 2001, accounting for 55 percent of total SRI revenue, ISR revenues as a percentage of GDP doubled between 2001 and 2006, increasing from 25.5 percent of total SRI revenue to 33.3 percent.

At present, the tax income of the central government not administered by the SRI consists primarily of customs tariffs, collected by the CAE.[1] The SRI director is a member of the CAE board, and though this was interpreted as indicating the intention to merge the two institutions several years ago, this has not yet occurred.

The fact that the improvement in the VAT collection efforts was not accompanied by a parallel improvement in ISR in 2000 may be attributed to several factors, one of which is the zigzagging policy that first abolished and then readopted the ISR in 1999. Another factor is that, as indicated in a later section, the ISR had suffered the effects of repeated and varying exemption proposals more severely than other taxes had. However, the ISR has increased from 1.7 percent of GDP in 2000 to 3.7 percent of GDP in 2006, increasing from 25.5 percent of total ISR revenue to 33.3 percent—equivalent to an increase from 1.7 to 3.7 percent of GDP.

The tax administration also showed a change in orientation during the final years of the 1990s. The SRI was created in December 1997 as a replacement for the discredited Internal Revenue Office. Likewise, in 1998, the CAE was created as a replacement for the previous National Customs Office. At the time of its creation, the SRI did not have a central taxpayers registry—only several registries at the different regional offices throughout the country. This used to make it possible for a delinquent or tardy taxpayer to simply register at another regional office and avoid punishment for previous delinquencies.

A number of improvements have been made since then. A centralized taxpayers registry (*Registro Único de Contribuyentes*) has been created, with 1.1 million registrants (80 percent of them individuals and 20 percent legal entities). The number of personnel was reduced, and training was increased. More than 95 percent of the print shops authorized to print sales and withholding receipts have been verified since 2002 (with an electronic authorization system for printing invoices, which shortens the process—including taxpayer verification—to just a few minutes). The large taxpayers (approximately 4,168 companies in 2006, up from 3,055 in 2001) are subject to special procedures, since a special unit is now considered necessary to attend to their needs.

The SRI started making use of third-party information to increase taxpayer compliance during 2001 and 2002, when it detected that approximately 100,000 persons had not registered in the taxpayers registry. Companies and public entities are subject to VAT, making cross-checking of information possible, because when these entities request a reimbursement of VAT credits, they automatically reveal their identities to their suppliers. Because the government purchases large volumes, the resultant information to be cross-checked is also very large. Table 2.2 shows the results of improvements in information-gathering measures, along with satisfactory tax administration levels.

Table 2.2. Selected Tax Administration Indicators, 2001–03
(percent)

	2001	*2002*	*2003*
Debt collected versus outstanding debt	23	41	n.a.
Forced collections versus collections under management	1.70	2.80	5.70
Taxpayers who declare nothing versus taxpayers who declare a gain	47.20	41.40	43.50
Taxpayers who declare versus taxpayers who should declare	43.40	33.50	53.70
Notifications to actual nonfilers versus (special) nonfilers	94	89	n.a.
Notified taxpayers with cross-checked differences versus planned notifications	47	91	n.a.

Source: SRI.
n.a. = not available.

The SRI is a proponent of the strategy of limiting to a minimum any visits to companies, in order to avoid needless discussions among its auditors and the accountants of the companies, which (it is feared) could lead to opportunities for corruption. Visits have been replaced with information cross-checking and subsequent notifications of irregularities to the taxpayers.

Unfortunately, the Ecuadoran Simplified Tax System (*Régimen Impositivo Simplificado Ecuatoriano*—RISE), an initiative for small producers and informal vendors, was vetoed in 2002. Under RISE, taxpayers would pay a monthly sum based on their estimated income and would be responsible for issuing and receiving invoices, but they would not be obligated to maintain an accounting system. The veto accompanied the veto of an increase in VAT, from 12 to 15 percent, which was declared unconstitutional by the Constitutional Court in 2002. RISE was expected to generate an additional US$20 million, or 0.1 percent of GDP, in that year.

II. Three Primary Problems of Ecuador's Tax Policy

Although the Ecuadoran tax system has various problems, three stand out because they are important and urgently require a solution. They are the proliferation of taxes, tax exemptions, and preallocation of tax revenues. Among the problems not chosen for detailed treatment in this note—despite their importance—are the limited progressiveness of personal income tax and the repercussions of reduced customs tariffs.[2]

The underlying difficulty of Ecuador's economic policy is its subordination to political urgencies. A description by the Ministry of Economy and Finance provides a good example (Badillo and Salazar 2002):

> Once the goal of economic stability was reached, the national political front became complicated again. By not having a political party or a majority in

> Congress, the government was obliged to incur expenses and recruit economic authorities that provided it with greater discretionary space. This produced a reduction in the primary fiscal surplus which would have been better used as a contingency fund, but which unfortunately was used to guarantee the short-term political governance in the absence of a long-term national pact. (5)

Regarding tax policy specifically, this subordination has led to the creation of multiple taxes to satisfy the demands of different interest groups, while at the same time conceding exemptions to those groups for the same purpose. What remains of tax revenues after exemptions is preallocated to different beneficiaries, again to expand the accommodation of interest groups. This balancing act leaves the government with fewer resources for public goods and infrastructure to benefit the entire population.

The Problem of Tax Proliferation

Though nearly all of the country's tax revenues stem from 10 different taxes, and half of them (VAT, ISR, ICE, customs tariffs, and the vehicle tax) generate about 75 percent of the central government tax revenues, the SRI has identified more than 80 taxes that fall into the classifications shown in table 2.3. This situation implies unnecessarily high

Table 2.3. The Structure of the Tax System

		Beneficiaries			
Type of tax	***Number of taxes***	***Central gov.***	***Munici-palities***	***Provinces***	***Others***
Income and capital earnings tax	6	4	1	1	
Payroll tax	1			1	
Property and net worth tax	26	1	11	2	12
Real estate transfer tax	24		8	2	14
Financial asset tax	6	1			5
Sales tax on goods and services	19	10	2		7
VAT	1	1			
ICE	10	9			1
Telecommunications	1				1
Electricity	4				4
Public entertainment	1				1
Betting	2		2		
Foreign trade tax	1	1			
Various taxes	4	2	1	1	
Totals	87	19	23	7	38

Source: SRI.
Note: The Others column is composed of an enormous variety of institutions. For example, the Guayaquil Beneficence Council, the State University of Guayaquil, the Guayas Transit Commission, the Ecuadorian Social Security Institute, the Osvaldo Loor Foundations, the Potable Water Company, the National Promotion and Development of Sports, the Superintendency of Companies, the Superintendency of Banks, the Ecuadorian Tourism Corporation, the National Children's Fund, and so on.

administrative costs for both the taxpayers and the administration. It discourages payment on the part of the taxpayers and supervision on the part of the tax authority.

The proliferation of taxes then makes it necessary for tax authorities to fine-tune the tax policy, including carefully selecting who pays the tax, who is exempt, and who gets the benefits. Having a large number of taxes leads to having exemptions and more exemptions. This type of tax policy lacks transparency and hides inequity and inefficiency in the allocation of resources.

The Recurring Problem of Exemptions

Despite the difficulty of eliminating exemptions, during 1999–2001 Ecuador successfully reduced the number of exemptions granted. The government eliminated ISR exemptions for the financial sector (on the income from securities and shares issued by the government), for cooperatives and provident societies (except for the ones established by farmers or officially recognized indigenous people), and for promoters of development (directed primarily at tourism and industrial endeavors). Also, the list of items subject to VAT was replaced with a tax list of VAT-exempt services (fundamentally, housing rentals and financial services), which left all other services subject to VAT.

Nevertheless, within a little more than a year, the government renewed efforts to reinstate the exemptions. The most important of these exemptions were as follows:

- To exempt interest on mortgage loans from paying income tax.
- To reinstate exemptions in the tourism sector. Actually, article 31 of the Tourism Law of December 12, 2002, already established that tourism services would have zero tariffs, and sales would be taken as service export sales.
- To defer VAT payments on the import of goods until the sale or use of such goods generate a tax debit against which the VAT can be credited. According to article 72, published on November 17, 2004, VAT on export activities will be reimbursed.
- To exempt from income taxes investments in key strategic sectors and regions. Congress passed the Tax Incentives Law in November 2005, under which investments in Pichincha and Guayas provinces are exempt from income taxes for 10 years (for other provinces the period is 12 years). The exemption is directed to investments in hydroelectric generation projects, oil refineries, airports, and others.
- To grant a subsidy of up to 5 percent on the free-on-board value of the exports of the Export and Investment Promotion Corporation (*Corporación de Promoción de Exportaciones e Inversiones*—CORPEI).

In 2004, provisional calculations of the internal VAT exemptions (that is, excluding the VAT on imports) were made on the basis of a sample of 3,055 large taxpayers during 2001, which represented 84 percent of the SRI tax revenues. That estimate, presented in table 2.4, indicated a tax cost of approximately US$237 million for the year (1.1 percent of GDP) as a result of the exemptions. Approximately half of that cost came from the commerce and industry sectors. A more recent calculation in 2006 gives a lower-bound estimate of the cost of the VAT exemptions, which are on the order of US$735 million the equivalent of 1.7 percent of GDP.

An alternative estimate, which uses National Accounts data for 2000 and 2005 (see annex), gives a tax cost of 2.2 percent and 3.4 percent of GDP, respectively, as the combined result of the exemptions and tax evasion. This result is not inconsistent with tax costs shown in table 2.4.

According to a estimate by Ministry of Economy and Finance (MEF) for 2000 and 2001, the exemptions on customs tariffs and on VAT on imports[3] are concentrated in five tax codes, which account for 93 percent of these types of exemptions (table 2.5). The tax cost of those exemptions represents approximately US$123 million and US$148 million (for 2000 and 2001, respectively), or 0.7 percent of the GDP of these years, without including the exemptions for commercial agreements, such as the Andean Community Nations (*Comunidad Andina de Naciones*—CAN), or the Latin American Integration Association (ALADI).

Table 2.4. Estimated Tax Cost of the Internal VAT Exemptions in 2001
(US$ millions)

Sector	*Total income*	*Export of goods and services*	*Taxable income before exemptions*	*Income actually taxed*	*Exempted estimated income*	*Tax credit on purchases*[a]	*Fiscal cost*[b]
Agriculture	1,339	363	976	86.6	889.4	533.6	42.7
Commerce	7,162	507	6,655	5,148.6	1,506.4	903.8	72.3
Construction	523	1	522	467.8	54.2	32.5	2.6
Energy and gas	572	0	572	89.9	482.1	289.3	23.1
Energy and mining	571	431	140	65.3	74.7	44.8	3.6
Finance and insurance	1,499	63	1,436	1,190.0	246.0	147.6	11.8
Industry	5,468	899	4,569	3,469.9	1,099.1	659.5	52.8
Others	25	1	24	13.0	11.0	6.7	0.5
Commercial services	3,089	909	2,180	1,982.4	197.6	118.6	9.5
Transportation and communication	1,405	30	1,375	998.7	376.3	225.8	18.1
Total	21,654	3,204	18,450	13,512.4	4,936.6	2,962.2	237.0

Source: Ministry of Economy and Finance.

a. The tax credit for purchases was estimated as 60 percent of the estimated exempt income.

b. The fiscal cost was calculated as 12 percent of the difference between the estimated exempt income and the tax credit for purchases.

Table 2.5. Tax Cost of Exemptions on Customs Tariffs and on the VAT on Imports, 2000 and 2001

Code number and name of the exemption	*CIF value of imports (US$ millions)*		*Tax cost rate*			
	2000	*2001*	*Tariff (%)*	*VAT (%)*	*2000*	*2001*
407—Exempt from VAT	712.8	848.4		12	85.5	101.8
395—Pharmaceutical products	29.0	27.0	5	12	5.0	4.6
464—Public sector	115.2	161.9	10	12	25.3	35.6
343—Public sector donations	1.8	11.6	10	12	0.4	2.6
413—Exempt from VAT (public sector)	59.1	30.5		12	7.1	3.7
Total	917.9	1,079.4			123.3	148.3

Source: Ministry of Economy and Finance.
Note: The tariff is the average of the tariff positions involved.

Nevertheless, including the VAT exempted from imports would overestimate the tax cost of the exemptions. Leaving only the exempted tariffs in the previous calculation, the final costs of the exemptions on the imports under tax codes 395, 464, and 343 are estimated at 5 and 10 percent, respectively, for 2000 and 2001. This makes for a total tax cost of between US$13 million and US$18 million, or approximately 0.1 percent of the GDP, for 2000 and 2001, respectively.

The exemptions based on trade agreements, on the other hand, represented a tax cost, in 2001, of approximately 90 percent of the tariff revenues of that year—or 1.4 percent of GDP—broken down as follows: Exemptions by the CAN are US$247 million. Exemptions for trade with Chile are US$18 million; with Mexico, US$11.2 million; with Argentina, US$6.2 million; and with Brazil, US$12.8 million.

The promoters of exemptions generally draw on two arguments. First, the exemptions promote a certain select activity whose competitiveness must, presumably, be safeguarded and increased through tax or tariff policies; and second, they promote equity by proposing exemptions on VAT for a variety of products. The first argument is generally used when exemptions to the ISR or to the customs tariffs are proposed.

Neither of the two arguments is particularly valid. Promoting business through tax or tariff exemptions requires the identification of those ventures whose promotion would be beneficial to the society as a whole and not only to the investors involved. The errors of identification that might result would be too costly for taxpayers who were not selected. Furthermore, there is no mechanism to ensure that only involuntary and honest mistakes would be committed, which thereby opens up opportunities for corruption and is another disadvantage of the exemption policy.

Exemptions on customs tariffs have, in general, strongly prejudicial effects on economic efficiency, as they can generate widespread protection and, therefore, create business opportunities that may be profitable, but are disastrous to the national economy (Giugale, Lopez-Calix, and Fretes-Cibils 2003).

The equity argument in favor of exemptions also has limited validity. VAT exemptions on popular consumer goods constitute a highly inefficient way of introducing progressiveness into the tax system. Although it is generally true that the exempted consumption represents a greater percentage of the total consumption by poorer families, it is the richer homes that benefit more from the exemptions. In the case of Ecuador, it was calculated in 1999 that out of every 100 sucres the tax office did not collect because of the exemptions on education, books, health, transportation, water, and electricity (in other words, except basic food items, house rental, and financial services), 43 sucres benefited the richest 25 percent of the population and only 14 sucres benefited the poorest 25 percent (Kopits et al. 1999). Techniques have to be found to get the 14 sucres to the poorest sector without automatically awarding the richest sector 43 sucres.

Moreover, VAT exemptions complicate the tax administration for the taxpayers and the SRI alike. Taxpayers who sell exempted products as well as taxed products have to attribute the credits for VAT paid on their purchases on some of their sales, thereby complicating their business's accounting system. Furthermore, the exemption creates a temptation to claim all of the VAT credits, as if all of the purchases were dedicated to the supply of taxed products. This greatly complicates the taxation task of the SRI and the CAE.

The Problem of Preallocations

Income preallocations, whether they are from tax revenues or oil, are found scattered throughout 50 pieces of legislation—laws, decrees, or ministerial agreements. In July 2005, Congress passed a new Fiscal Responsibility, Stabilization, and Transparency Law. Under the new law, a government account under the Ministry of Finance (CEREPS—Special Account for Productive and Social Reactivation) replaced the Fund for Stabilization, Social and Productive Investment, and Reduction of Public Debt (FEIREP). Under CEREPS up to 80 percent of the trust fund will be earmarked and allocated through the budget, exacerbating the problem of earmarking and preallocations in Ecuador (for detailed comparison of FEIREP and CEREPS, see World Bank 2006).

In 2001, preallocated tax revenues were US$303 million, or 1.4 percent of GDP, of which $112 million corresponded to VAT and $133 million corresponded to ISR. In 2004, Almeida, Gallardo, and Tomaselli (2006) reported preallocated tax revenues of 2.3 percent of GDP, and in the case of oil revenues, they estimated them to be 1.5 percent of GDP, for total preallocations of 3.8 percent of GDP. In the Pro-forma 2006, the government estimated total preallocations of about 5 percent of GDP.

For 2006, the percentage of preallocated VAT revenues was 12 percent (1.5 percent to the SRI, 10 percent to the Permanent Fund for University and Polytechnic Development, and 0.5 percent to the state universities), about equal to the average preallocation for all taxes (14.3 percent of total tax revenues in 2001).

In the case of the ISR, in 2006, the percentage of preallocation was at least equal to 28.5 percent of the tax revenues designated for various purposes. Furthermore, taxpayers have the right to request, in writing to the tax authority, that up to 25 percent of their taxes paid be transferred to their municipality. If all taxpayers made use of this right, 53.5 percent of the ISR's tax revenues would be preallocated. Data for 2002 indicate that the average preallocation of all taxes increased to about 19 percent of the total tax revenues, possibly because taxpayers used this right. In 2006, the central government's share of tax revenues was 71.5 percent, with 10 percent allocated to the Unversidades y Escuelas Politecnicas Estatales, 1 percent to Universidades Particulares, 10 percent to the Sectional Development Fund (FODESEC), 6 percent to the Comision de Transito del Guayas, 6 percent to the Corporacion Reguladora de Manejo Hidrico de Manabi, 6 percent to the Fondo de Salvamento del Patrimonio Cultural de los Municipios del Pais, and 1.5 percent to the SRI.

As shown in table 2.6, of the six categories of goods and services subject to the special consumption tax (ICE), only one (telecommunications) does not provide any income to the central government. The other five provide income that fluctuates between 83.5 percent and 88.5 percent of their respective tax revenues. Tax revenue

Table 2.6. Preallocation Percentages of the ICE Tax Revenues, 2006

Preallocation recipient	*Cigarettes*	*Beer*	*Soft drinks*	*Alcohol*	*Telecomm.*	*Luxuries*
Hospital equipment	10[a]	10	10	10[a]	—	10
Free maternity care	3[a]	3	3	3[a]	—	3
Osvaldo Loor Foundation	—	—	—	2[a]	—	—
Internal Revenue Service	1.5[a]	1.5	1.5	1.5[a]	1.5	1.5
Potable water company	—	—	—	—	66.67	—
National sports	—	—	—	—	33.33	—
IESS retirement pension increases	100% of increase[b]	—	—	100% of increase[b]	—	—
Central govt. share from ICE revenues	85.5[a]	85.5	85.5	83.5[a]	—	88.5

Source: Ministry of Economy and Finance.

a. Percentages are approximate.

b. According to Law 39, the retirement pension increase of the IESS will be financed with an increase in the ICE for cigarettes (up to 98 percent tax rate) and alcoholic products (up to 32 percent). The additional increase in these taxes will be allocated directly to the retirement pension according to the law published in the Registro Oficial on July 28, 2004. The law establishes that the pension increase will also be financed with interest from bonds Deposit Guarantee Agency (AGD), US$25 million from the Fondo de Solidaridad). The law also stipulated financing the increase with resources from FEIREP, if necessary, but that has been replaced by CEREPS, so financing may have to come from CEREPS in the future.

from telecommunication services has increased; it provides about 41 percent of the total ICE revenues, equal to about US$190 million in 2007 according to the Pro-forma 2007, up from about US$169 million in 2006.

Only about 6 percent of the customs tariffs for 2006 were preallocated, distributed between the Water Resources Council of Jipijapa, Pajan, and Puerto Lopez; Autoridad Portuaria de Manta; and FODESEC. The other 94 percent went to the central government. According to the Pro-forma 2007, the shares will be about 7 percent and 93 percent, respectively.

Preallocation procedure prohibits the tax resources from being oriented to where their productivity would be greatest. It promotes inefficient, and possibly also inequitable, use of the tax resources. The problem is particularly dire in the case of the funds allocated to regional governments, since the automatic transfers discourage these governments from collecting their own taxes. As a result, they promote irresponsible fiscal behavior, since the governments do not have to face the political costs of collecting taxes.

In March 2001, the government sent Congress a bill under the name of Fiscal Discipline and Prudence. Article 22 of this bill abolished preallocations. Likewise, the bill stated that "the General State Budget for the year 2002 would compensate, in the same amount, the Public Sector entities or organisms for the allocation actually received by them during the previous year." The proposed mechanism for eliminating the preallocations attempted to soften the transition, preventing the public sector entities or organizations from suddenly experiencing a shortage of financing.[4] Nevertheless, this component of the bill was not approved, leaving the preallocation regime unchanged.

III. Modernization of the Tax Administration— Two Priority Reforms

The institutional designs of the SRI and the CAE are the most pressing issues of the tax administration. The reforms of the SRI and CAE at the end of the 1990s resulted in a notable improvement in the tax evasion controls of the SRI; however, the CAE did not show evidence of significant improvement. To modernize its information system and collect taxes more efficiently, the SRI adopted an Internet-based tax filing system that, by 2006, was already being used by more than 40,000 taxpayers. The information system, which was upgraded and modernized by the SRI in the late 1990s, included online tracking information from the moment the merchandise was shipped from the point of origin. Thus, the taxes could be paid and the merchandise liberated from customs at the moment of arrival in the port, preventing storage problems and their corresponding delays. Other methods also will result in improved controls of tax evasion, such as the use of checking accounts for each taxpayer, and for each type of tax, so that individuals' payments and reimbursements can be electronically reported to the SRI without delay.

Background—The Independence of the SRI

The SRI board consists of six members (with a voice and vote), and the executive director, with a voice but no vote. The members of the board include the minister of finance (with two votes in case of a tie); the superintendent of companies; the superintendent of banks; the undersecretary of the budget; the minister of industrialization, commerce, integration, fishing and competitiveness; and one representative of the private sector. Additional reforms to reinforce the SRI board—allowing members to resist pressures from the public sector itself and, naturally, from the private sector—would ensure its independence. Although the board would not be breaking the law by responding to interest group pressures, it would be satisfying objectives that are outside the scope of the board's function, collecting taxes. For example, making a profit from promoting the competitiveness of a given sector, or improving the distribution of tax revenues to make them more equitable, are outside the objective of tax collection and may impede the board's effectiveness.

Efforts of the CAE to Control Evasion of Taxes and Tariffs

The CAE's efforts to control tax evasion did not have the same dynamism as the SRI's, even though it shared the SRI's computerized information tracking system and Internet-based tax filing system. However, in 2006 the CAE took measures to address corruption and better control tax evasion. Resolution No. 7-2006-R3 of the board of the CAE created two anticorruption units to coordinate complaints, follow investigations, and monitor acts of corruption. The CAE also has created an executive commission with technical support from a Chilean expert in customs modernization.

Unlike the SRI, which by 2001 had replaced practically all of its personnel, the CAE was prevented by labor regulations from dismissing employees unless the department in which the employees worked was being abolished. The tax reform legislation of March 2001 merged the two institutions, but Congress rejected the initiative following strong pressure from the import sector interest groups. In November 2001, a law passed making the SRI executive director president of the CAE board.

A procedure for uncovering cases of VAT evasion or contraband was introduced by Law 41 of 1999, which provided that the merchandise in warehouses or storage areas may be inspected by CAE personnel to verify whether the property is backed by documents proving ownership (a commercial invoice if it is national, or a shipping bill in the case of international shipments). Transporters who move the merchandise from one place to another also were required to show these documents, and without the documents the merchandise could be seized. However, the procedure has rarely been used. An independent evaluation should be done concerning the advantages of merging the CAE with the SRI, without endangering the efforts of the latter.

For individuals and companies to be considered eligible to issue sales receipts and be constituted as resident taxpayers, they are required to register with a centralized taxpayers registry prior to any import or export transaction. Proper enforcement will lead to improvements in tax compliance and efficiency in tax collection. According to the Central Bank of Ecuador, if the structure of imports and tariffs in 2007 is the same as in 2006, tariff collection could increase 14.8 percent in 2007 from 2006 because of an increase in imports greater than the increase in GDP and because of more efficient collection by the CAE.[5] Should the trend toward modernization and improvement in tax compliance and efficiency by CAE continue, this could be a substitute for the disappearance of the customs office and its merging with the SRI.

IV. Recommendations

The adoption of the following recommendations would produce a less complicated, broad-based tax system that is consistent with an efficiently functioning economy.

Simplification of Tax Structures

Eliminate minor taxes. We recommend that the government discontinue the collection of minor taxes and disbursement of their funds. Although the financial effects of eliminating them would be insignificant, their elimination would allow the tax authority and taxpayers to reduce administrative costs and to concentrate on the truly important taxes. The tax revenue effect is uncertain, but efforts aimed at improving compliance with the important taxes may provide more tax revenues than efforts spent administering and collecting the minor taxes.

Eliminate exemptions. We recommend that VAT exemptions be applied only to unprocessed basic food items and to residential rentals that are in addition to a primary home. Consequently, we recommend eliminating exemptions on the following: agricultural input items (such as seeds, balanced feed, tractors, fungicides, herbicides, plows, harrows, and so on); financial services; different types of paper, books, and magazines; medicines and their raw materials; transportation services, electricity, water, and sewage; public entertainment events; professional services; tolls; fumigation services; the cooling and storage of foods; and all other services used in the preparation of foods or other goods. This list is not exhaustive, but it illustrates the exemptions to be eliminated. The tax revenue increase of this elimination was estimated at 0.9 percent of GDP in 2001, with a conservative lower bound of 1.4 percent of GDP in 2006.

We also recommend eliminating the ISR exemptions and the customs tariff exemptions for their prejudicial effects. Although the primary purpose of eliminating tariff exemptions is not to increase tax revenues but to reduce protection, we estimate revenue from elimination of customs duty exemptions to be about 0.1 percent of GDP. We did not calculate the revenue effect of eliminating the ISR exemptions.

Eliminate preallocations. We recommend eliminating the majority, if not all, of the preallocations, except for the payroll tax, which is allocated to the Ecuadoran Social Security Institute. The measure could take place gradually, in the manner described in Article 22 of the Discipline and Fiscal Prudence Act of March 2001. This measure would have the effect of permitting (although not guaranteeing) a more productive use of tax resources. The amount involved in 2001 was US$112 million of VAT and US$133 of ISR, plus other preallocated taxes, for a total of US$303 million, the equivalent of 1.4 percent of GDP (this increased to 3.8 percent of GDP in 2004 and to about 5 percent of GDP in 2006). Eliminating preallocations would lead not only to better use of tax resources but also to increased productivity in the public sector and the economy.

Tax Administration Recommendations

Propose and approve the RISE legislation. The Ecuadoran Simplified Tax System (*Régimen Impositivo Simplificado Ecuatoriano*—RISE) legislation would allow greater control over the suppliers of small taxpayers in the system, because they have to have invoices from their suppliers. As the number of taxpayers in the tax system grows, it will be more difficult for the suppliers to avoid registration with the SRI, since the demand for invoices will be greater for sales made to taxpayers in the RISE. It was estimated in the first edition of this publication that at the outset of its implementation, RISE would have generated tax revenues of US$20 million, or 0.1 percent of GDP in 2001. Assuming that the number of small taxpayers has remained unchanged, a rough estimate gives extra tax revenue of about US$65 million in 2006, or 0.15 percent of GDP.

Correct delays in internal processes. Delays on account of information cross-checking (among different taxes paid by the same taxpayer and among different taxpayers) must be reduced, as must the delays in sending notifications to taxpayers regarding incorrect tax returns.

Reinforce the independence of the SRI board. The purpose of this recommendation is to prevent the SRI resolutions from being used as instruments for introducing discriminatory and distorted tax treatments. The SRI must not get involved in satisfying any objective other than the strict collection of the taxes created by law. In particular, the competitiveness of any sector, or the promotion of industry, agriculture, or a given region, should never be an element of judgment in the deliberations of the SRI board of directors.

Consider the merger of the SRI with the CAE. Because VAT contributors make up the majority of taxpayers who pay customs duties, and because they are satisfactorily controlled by the SRI, this institution could take advantage of economies of scale to also supervise the collection of customs duties from the same group of taxpayers. Certainly, this result could also be achieved through a close collaboration between the

SRI and CAE. The question is whether this collaboration could be more easily obtained under a single authority that governs both institutions.[6]

Amend the Customs Act. Reforming the customs office labor system would permit a restructuring similar to the one that has worked so well at the SRI.

Promote strict compliance with Law 41 of 1999 and the latest resolutions by CAE. This mechanism for controlling VAT evasion contraband requires official backing at the highest level so that it can be applied without exceptions or discretion. Official support would include compliance with the latest resolutions by the CAE board to address corruption and tax compliance.

Summary Table of the Estimated Tax Revenue Effects of the Recommendations in 2006

(percentage of GDP)

Recommendation	*Tax revenue increase*
Reduction of VAT exemptions	1.4
Reduction of customs duty exemptions	0.09
Elimination of preallocations	0.5
Ecuadoran Simplified Tax System	0.15
Total	2.14

Source: Author's estimations.

Summary Table of the Priority of the Recommendations

Essential and immediate recommendations	*Medium-term recommendations (during 2008–09)*
Eliminate exemptions	Eliminate minor taxes
Eliminate preallocations	Consider the SRI-CAE merger
Corrrect the delays in cross-checking information in the SRI	Promote the strict compliance with Law 41 of 1999 and 2006 resolutions by the board of CAE
Reinforce the independence of the SRI board of directors	Approve the RISE
Amend the labor system of the Customs Act	

Recommendation Matrix

Problems (including annual tax cost—if applicable)	*Policy Measures*		*Progress indicators*	*Objectives and goals*
	Short term (2007)	*Medium term (2007–10)*		
Exaggerated number of minor taxes, low tax revenues, and preallocations	Eliminate the minor taxes and their corresponding collections	Gradually eliminate the minor taxes	Approval of repealed laws	Reduce administrative costs for the tax authority and for the taxpayers
Exemptions of ISR, VAT (except unprocessed basic foods, financial services, and home rental, and customs tariffs)	Eliminate the exemptions that create less conflict politically	Completely eliminate exemptions (except unprocessed foods, financial services, and home rentals)	Approval of repealed laws	Reduce distortions in the economy; increase the tax revenues by 1.5 percent of GDP
Preallocation of taxes (except preallocations to the IESS)	Eliminate the preallocations that create less conflict politically	Completely eliminate preallocation (except the IESS)	Approval of repealed laws	Increase productivity of fiscal resources used by 0.5 percent of GDP
Small producers and merchants that are not taxpayers	Adopt the RISE		Approval of the law	Reduce the informality and generate estimated tax revenues of 0.15 percent of GDP
Vulnerability of the SRI to private interest pressures	Strengthen the SRI institutionally		Development of a set of qualitative and quantitative institutional indicators for internal revenue entities, for comparison across countries	Prevent erosion of the tax base through administrative means

CAE low efficiency and efforts in customs revenue collection	Evaluate the improvement of customs revenue collection given the 2006 initiatives by CAE to improve its customs collection; if the results are not satisfactory, evaluate merger between the CAE and the SRI		Number of persons or companies registered with the taxpayers registry to import and export; customs collections; adoption of modern customs procedures; increase in monitoring of corruption complaints and follow-up of investigations with proper enforcement of the laws	Improve contraband control
Delays in information cross-checks and in notifications sent to taxpayers	Start resolving the delays	Complete elimination of the delays and prevent new delays	Continued adoption and use of modern procedures	Improve tax collection
Labor system of the Customs Act	Approve a legal reform that allows the restructuring of personnel	Restructure customs personnel, similar to the way it was done at the SRI	None	Improve efficiency

Annex

Estimates of the tax cost of the VAT exemptions are presented here for 2000 and 2005.

Using the information from the National Accounts—Final Consumption of Households, a maximum potential VAT income can be estimated, which will be different from the tax income observed for two reasons: exemptions and evasion.

Table A.1. Value of VAT Exemptions, 2000
(US$ millions)

Final consumption of households	*Value*	*Potential tax revenues*
Bananas, coffee, and cacao	53.88	6.47
Grains	54.00	6.48
Flowers	18.45	2.21
Other crops	408.24	48.99
Breeding animals	229.14	27.50
Forestry and lumber	14.26	1.71
Fish and shellfish	183.40	21.99
Mineral products	2.63	0.32
Meat and meat products	728.71	87.45
Processed fish and shellfish	104.31	12.56
Oil and fats	204.83	24.58
Milk products	236.01	28.32
Grain milling and bakery products	549.04	65.89
Refined sugar	127.93	15.35
Candies and chocolates	67.99	8.16
Other foods	185.18	2.22
Drinks	384.12	46.09
Tobacco and cigarettes	52.21	6.27
Textiles and clothing	844.93	101.39
Wood products	26.24	3.15
Paper and related products	184.88	22.19
Petroleum products	197.02	23.64
Chemical products	620.41	74.45
Rubber and plastic products	109.06	13.09
Nonmetal minerals	39.45	4.73
Products made of metal	209.83	25.18
Machinery and equipment	319.75	38.37
Transportation equipment	201.40	24.17
Other manufactured items	401.86	48.22
Electricity and water	142.20	17.06
Hotels and restaurants	438.23	52.59
Shipping and storage	1,216.34	145.96
Mail and telecommunications	329.15	39.50

(*Table continues on the following page.*)

Table A.1. Value of VAT Exemptions, 2000
(US$ millions) (*continued*)

Final consumption of households	*Value*	*Potential tax revenues*
Financial and insurance services	130.98	15.71
Home rentals	683.88	82.07
Other activities	51.24	6.15
Public administration	10.36	1.24
Education	274.80	32.98
Social and health services	182.05	21.85
Other social, personal, and domestic services	138.88	16.66
Total	10,357.52	1,242.90

Source: Calculations based on Central Bank of Ecuador data on final consumption of households of the national accounts.
Note: Using the 2000 data, it is calculated that the tax income results together with exemptions and evasion end up being equal to the difference between US$1,242.90 million and the effective tax income for this year, US$893.4 million; that is, US$349.5 million, or approximately 2.2 percent of GDP. The amounts estimated in the text of this report, which attributes a tax cost of 1.1 percent of GDP to the exemptions, is not inconsistent with the results of this annex.

Table A.2. Value of VAT Exemptions, 2005

Final consumption of households	*Value (US$ millions)*	*Potential tax revenues (US$ millions)*
Bananas, coffee, and cacao	73.7	8.8
Grains	116.7	14.0
Flowers	27.1	3.3
Other crops	671.0	80.5
Breeding animals	384.6	46.2
Forestry and lumber	20.7	2.5
Fish and shellfish	348.8	41.9
Mineral products	4.4	0.5
Meat and meat products	1,086.3	130.4
Processed fish and shellfish	176.8	21.2
Oil and fats	323.2	38.8
Milk products	432.8	51.9
Grain milling and bakery products	871.7	104.6
Refined sugar	176.8	21.2
Candies and chocolates	138.5	16.6
Other foods	230.2	27.6
Drinks	778.0	93.4
Tobacco and cigarettes	116.5	14.0
Textiles and clothing	1,049.6	125.9
Leather and leather products	274.0	32.9
Wood products	36.4	4.4
Paper and related products	349.6	41.9

(*Table continues on the following page.*)

Table A.2. Value of VAT Exemptions, 2005 *(continued)*

Final consumption of households	*Value (US$ millions)*	*Potential tax revenues (US$ millions)*
Petroleum products	633.8	76.1
Chemical products	1,113.1	133.6
Rubber and plastic products	138.9	16.7
Nonmetal minerals	54.8	6.6
Products made of metal	354.7	42.6
Machinery and equipment	776.6	93.2
Transportation equipment	514.0	61.7
Other manufactured items	814.4	97.7
Electricity and water	532.8	63.9
Hotels and restaurants	996.1	119.5
Shipping and storage	2,583.0	310.0
Mail and telecommunications	1,489.3	178.7
Financial and insurance services	584.2	70.1
Home rentals	3,263.7	391.6
Other activities	119.3	14.3
Public administration	67.9	8.1
Education	1,546.3	185.6
Social and health services	621.4	74.6
Other social, personal, and domestic services	340.1	40.8
Total	24,231.7	2,907.8

Source: Calculations based on Central Bank of Ecuador data on final consumption of households of the national accounts.

Note: The above table uses 2005 data. As in the previous table in this annex, we calculate the cost of tax exemptions with tax evasion to be the difference between US$2,907.8 million and the effective tax income for 2005, US$1,683.4 million; that is, US$ 1,224.4 million, or approximately 3.4 percent of GDP.

Notes

1. Other sources of tax income, which are of less significance in terms of size, are two taxes on transportation and oil by SOTE, administered by the central bank, and the taxes on lubricants and aviation fuel for international service and the airport tax, administered by the Civil Aviation Office.

2. The reasons that the customs tariffs must be reduced and made more uniform are discussed in *Commercial and Competitiveness Policy, An Economic and Social Agenda in the New Millennium* (Giugale, Lopez-Calix, and Fretes-Cibils 2003).

3. The exemption of VAT on imports has a limited tax revenue effect, since the majority of the import operations are not performed by end users but by wholesalers. The result is that when they pay VAT they would claim the corresponding tax credit when they sell the products to retailers. In this way, the net VAT collection on import operations tends to disappear and show up as VAT on domestic operations (that is, in the retail sales to the end consumer).

4. This proposal is not consistent with the recommendation included in this study: not exceeding the proportion of preallocated revenues by the Constitution to the sectional governments effectively reached in 1999 (9 percent of the current income, instead of 15 percent preallocated), and not exceeding the preallocation for educational expenses above the effectively reached percentage in 1999 (12.5 percent of the current income, instead of 30 percent preallocated). Finally, the abolition of all other revenues preallocated by law was recommended, except the revenues of the Ecuadoran Social Security Institute (Kopits et al. 1999).

5. Report to the Honorable National Congress, Pro-forma Report of the Central Government, 2007, and Limit of Public Debt, Central Bank of Ecuador, February 2007 (Pro-forma 2007).

6. In 1999 the International Monetary Fund recommended the evaluation of this merger. See Kopits et al. (1999), p. 9.

Bibliography

Almeida, Maria Dolores, Veronica Gallardo, and Andres Tomaselli. 2006. *Governabilidad Fiscal en Ecuador.* New York: United Nations, Instituto Latinoamericano y del Caribe de Planificacion Economica y Social (ILPES).

Badillo, D., and R. Salazar. 2002. "Economic and Public Investment Balance from January 2000 to January 2003." Ministry of Economy and Finance, Quito.

Gallardo, J. 2001. "Tax Reform: Guaranty for the New Generations." Ministry of Economy and Finance, Quito.

Giugale, Marcelo, Jose Roberto Lopez-Calix, and Vicente Fretes Cibils, eds. 2003. *Ecuador: An Economic and Social Agenda in the New Millennium.* Washington, DC: World Bank.

Kopits, G., E. Haindl, E. Ley, and J. Toro. 1999. *Ecuador: Modernization of the Tax System.* International Monetary Fund, Washington, DC, Department of Public Finances.

World Bank. 2006. "Promoting Stable Economic Growth in Ecuador." Country Economic Memorandum. World Bank, Washington, DC.

3

The Banking System: Current Context and Remaining Challenges

Rashmi Shankar and Jean Clevy

Executive Summary

Ecuador's banking sector faces three key challenges: (i) liquidity management, in particular, the need to monitor solvency risks while stimulating financial widening and deepening; (ii) establishment of an effective and timely crisis resolution framework; and (iii) regulatory and institutional changes focused on improving risk management and thereby the robustness of the system. In the context of dollarization and the resultant limited role for the Central Bank, banks in Ecuador are seriously constrained by the absence of an interbank market that can recycle liquidity. Over three-quarters of total liabilities are short term, causing individual banks to favor liquid assets, thereby lowering both yield and intermediation. Smaller banks, with limited access to external financing, are especially vulnerable. Institutional weaknesses persist in spite of the momentum provided to reforms by the previous crisis. This chapter suggests broad-ranging initiatives to resolve several issues: the lack of a crisis resolution framework, the effective absence of resources to back deposit guarantees, inadequate staffing at and poor coordination across the supervisory agencies, insufficient definition of the scope and mandate of the key regulators, and the need for complementary legal reform, especially in enforcement of creditor rights and bankruptcy law. Addressing problems now will provide the country with a financial sector that can cushion the economy from adverse events, fuel investment and growth, and channel financing to needed sectors in a cost-effective manner. Failure to act will leave the sector and the economy vulnerable to external shocks and the risk of a costly crisis.

I. Profile of Ecuador's Financial System

A healthy financial sector facilitates growth, absorbs shocks, and plays a key role both in maintaining price stability and in enabling an efficiently functioning payments system. A financial sector with systemic weaknesses, on the other hand, may magnify the effects of external shocks and also be unable to fully facilitate potential investment (Rigobon 2006).[1] In Ecuador, given the history of macroeconomic volatility and the particular severity of the 1998–99 financial crisis, building a robust banking system is a priority for policy makers.

The 1999 banking crisis in Ecuador was followed by a large drop in economic output and slow recovery to "normal" growth rates over three years. The direct fiscal cost of restructuring the banks was estimated at over US$2 billion in 2002, based on generous assumptions on asset values, and the process of liquidating insolvent banks continues. The crisis resulted in a dramatic contraction in the size of the banking sector. The number of private banks declined 30 percent between 1998 and 2002 (table 3.1), although this has since stabilized. The contraction in sectoral size reduced total assets (as a proportion of GDP) by half (figure 3.1). The value of the maturing portfolio dropped to 11 percent of GDP, with only two-thirds channeled to the commercial and industrial sector. Deposits fell by more than 7 percent of GDP between 1998 and 1999.

By 2006, the situation had improved considerably, with gross bank assets more than doubling in nominal terms between 2000 and 2006, though, at less than 30 percent of GDP, still short of precrisis levels. Total loans improved from 11 percent to 16 percent

Table 3.1. Number of Entities in the Financial System

	Dec. 1998	*Mar. 2002*	*Dec. 2006*
Financial intermediaries	**114**	**81**	**90**
Private banks			
Operating (including Filanbanco until 2002)	38	21	22
Operating with public capital		2	2
Offshore	15	6	4
External banks	4	4	5
Public banks			
Operating	1	1	2
Second level	1	2	2
Finance companies	23	11	12
Cooperatives	25	27	36
Mutual funds	7	7	5
Other entities in the financial system	**72**	**62**	**54**
Exchange houses	13	8	1
Bonded warehouses	8	7	4
Public institutions	5	4	4
Credit cards	1	1	1
Securitization houses	1	1	1
Insurance companies	42	39	41
Reinsurance companies	2	2	2
Total	**212**	**193**	**104**

Source: Superintendency of Banks and Insurance (SBS).

Figure 3.1. Bank Assets, Loans, and Deposits
(% of GDP)

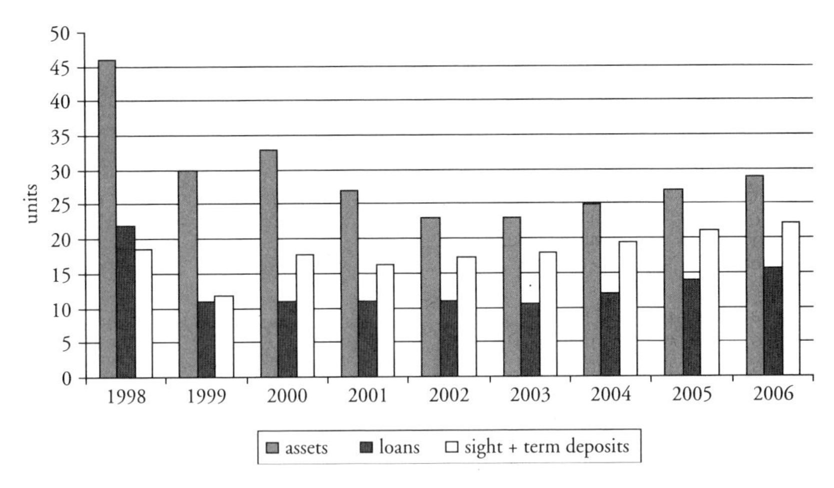

Source: SBS.

between 2002 and 2006. Over the same period, total deposits increased from 17.3 percent to 22.3 percent of GDP, which implies that gross intermediation is currently about 38 percent of GDP.

Private domestic credit has grown only sluggishly, however (figure 3.2). While financial depth has improved, it remains below the norms for comparator countries. In Latin America and the Caribbean as a whole, for example, the share of private domestic credit in GDP is more than twice that in Ecuador. As of end-November 2006, domestic bank assets are over 100 percent of GDP in Panama (which dollarized over a century ago) and are matched by foreign bank asset holdings, so that total banking assets are at more than 200 percent of GDP. Gross intermediation of domestic Panamanian banks is 138 percent of GDP (again almost matched by foreign banks' lending plus deposits). At the end of December 2006, total banking assets and total intermediation were 75 percent and 50 percent of GDP, respectively, in El Salvador, which dollarized in 2001. Improving financial depth will be an essential component of any strategy designed to guarantee wider access to finance in Ecuador.

In addition to the slow but steady improvement in the volume of intermediation, there has been increased diversification of the loan portfolio. The share of housing and microcredit loans in the loan portfolio increased from 9.9 percent to over 18 percent between 2002 and 2006, indicating improved access to credit and higher demand for noncommercial loans (table 3.2).

The absence of a true last-resort lender under the dollarization regime has resulted in the maintenance of a liquidity cushion that reached US$2.9 billion in December 2006. Bank net foreign assets, excluding Central Bank of Ecuador (*Banco*

Figure 3.2. Financial Depth
(% of GDP)

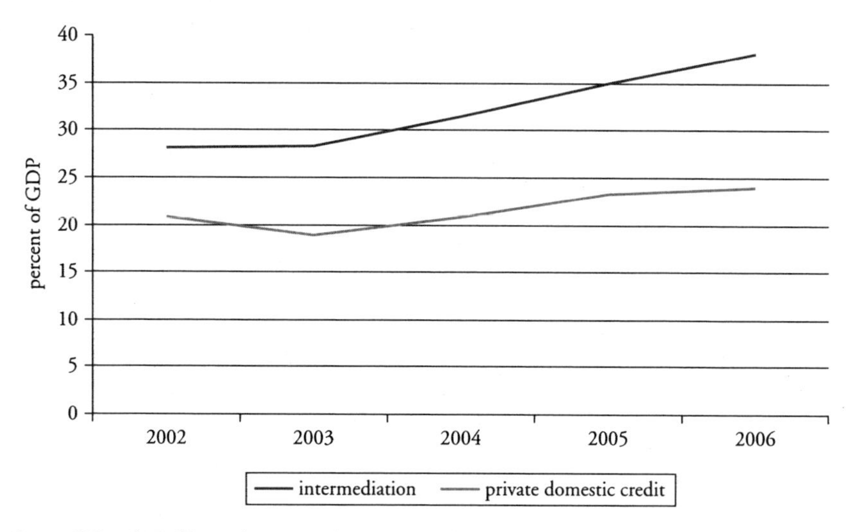

Source: SBS and World Development Indicators (World Bank).

Central de Ecuador–BCE) reserves, were US$2.5 billion at end-2006. As of end-2006, the ratio of available funds (mostly held abroad) to short-term deposits was 27 percent for the private banking system, even though required reserves are currently only at 4 percent.

The maintenance of a high level of foreign assets and of a relatively liquid asset portfolio is necessary, given that dollarization has limited the role of the BCE and there is no interbank market. At the same time, diversion of investible resources into liquid funds restricts portfolio growth and reduces yields. Investments plus available funds—typically a measure of broad liquidity—have remained at 35 percent of total assets since 2002.

Between 2002 and 2006, the share of productive assets (loans and investments) rose from 63 percent to 71 percent of total. Nearly half of all investments are in public sector securities, which exposes the sector to sovereign risk. However, the largest private banks hold a high proportion of U.S. government securities, as part of a risk management strategy that seeks to hedge against country risk by minimizing holdings of Ecuadoran paper. U.S. bonds were held by only six banks in December 2006 but were over 21 percent of total investments, since these banks accounted for 65 percent of the total system's investments (and 59 percent of total deposits).

It should be noted that BCE securities gain banks access to liquidity recycling through the reverse repurchase agreement (*reverse repo*). However, in the event of a systemic shock, domestic paper may not be easy to liquidate.

Table 3.2. Private Banking System: Consolidated Balance Sheet

	Oct. 2002		*Dec. 2006*	
TOTAL ASSETS	**5,726,339**	**100%**	**11,890,163**	**100%**
Available funds	1,115,639	19	2,138,489	18
Net investments	890,550	16	2,053,721	17
With the private sector	336,632	6	815,488	7
With the public sector	436,913	8	972,794	8
Of limited availability	131,025	2	321,594	3
Net loan portfolio	2,683,543	47	6,379,867	54
Gross loans	3,016,617	53	6,789,545	57
Commercial	1,879,947	33	3,542,168	30
Consumer loans	863,406	15	1,978,918	17
Housing	237,632	4	781,421	7
Microenterprise	35,632	1	487,037	4
(Provisions for unrecoverable loans)	–333,074	–6	–409,678	–3
Fixed assets	324,905	6	387,868	3
Other assets	708,582	12	625,230	5
Of which: Allocated goods	88,164	2	69,895	1
TOTAL LIABILITIES	**5,143,995**	**90%**	**10,654,424**	**90%**
Debts to the public	4,265,304	74	9,146,595	77
Sight deposits	2,929,933	51	6,251,881	53
Term and other deposits	1,335,371	23	2,871,853	24
Other liabilities with cost	462,831	8	1,017,110	9
Of which: Foreign lines	222,584	4	417,563	4
Convertible obligations and contributions for capitalization	194,655	3	112,612	1
Other liabilities	217,205	4	371,840	3
CAPITAL	**539,550**	**9%**	**1,235,739**	**10%**
Notes				
Total nonperforming loans	287,213	5	224,286	2
Commercial	204,809	4	98,783	1
Consumer loans	62,293	1	88,467	1
Housing	18,281	0	10,801	0
Microenterprise	1,829	0	26,235	0

Source: SBS.
Note: Includes Banco del Pacífico, with public capital. Total assets equals total liabilities plus capital (US$).

Table 3.3 suggests that the increase in the gross financial margin has been considerably larger than the increase in the net interest margin. This is mostly because of the increase in income from fees and commissions. Operational costs as a proportion of total assets were at 6.2 percent at end-2006, compared with 6.4 percent at end-2005, and only 2.6 percent in October 2002, but earnings ratios have increased as well.

The quality of the net portfolio has improved significantly. The nonperforming proportion of the portfolio (matured plus portfolio not earning interest) to gross portfolio dropped from 17.5 percent in December 2001 to 9.5 percent in October 2002, and to 3.3 percent in December 2006 (table 3.4). By type of loan, the

Table 3.3. Private Banks: Income Statement
(US$ thousands)

	2001	*Oct. 2002*	*Dec. 2006*
Interest earned	383,857	173,954	791,088
Interest paid	158,588	49,588	249,580
Net interest margin	225,268	124,366	541,508
Income and commissions for services	160,167	67,879	532,490
Expenses and commissions paid	69,808	14,606	25,782
Gross financial margin	315,627	177,639	1,048,216
Operating expenses	348,336	150,361	732,624
Other net operating income	61,309	25,469	146,084
Net operating margin before provisions	28,600	52,746	461,675
Provisions	123,250	27,851	198,180
Net operating margin	–94,650	24,895	263,496
Net extraordinary income	69,050	28,270	59,451
Pretax profits	–25,600	53,165	322,946
Taxes and employee profit-sharing	—	10,371	97,065
Earnings or loss for the business year	–25,599	42,794	225,881
Notes			
Operating expenses/gross financial margin	1.1	0.85	0.70
Provisions/gross financial margin	0.39	0.16	0.19

Source: SBS and authors' calculations.
Note: Includes Banco del Pacífico, with public capital.

Table 3.4. Private Bank Financial Indicators
(percent)

	Oct. 2002	*Dec. 2006*
Broad financial health indicators		
Capital/assets	9.4	10.4
Nonperforming loans/total loans	9.5	3.3
Net loans/deposits	62.9	69.8
Profitability		
Net interest margin/gross income	38.8	33.4
Operating costs/gross income	48.3	45.2
Operating costs/average assets	3.8	3.3
Return on average assets	1.5	2.2
Return on average equity	15.3	25.0

Source: SBS (preliminary data) and authors' calculations.
Note: Includes Banco del Pacífico, with public capital.

nonperforming portfolio is no longer concentrated in commercial loans—consumer loans have nearly doubled their share. Profits were about US$43 million in 2002, compared to a loss of US$25.6 million in December 2001, and stood at US$225.8 million in 2006 (table 3.3). Return on average assets improved from 1.5 percent to 2.2 percent between 2002 and 2006.

The decomposition of return on assets suggests that the improved profitability between 2002 and 2006 was due to both an increase in revenues and a proportional decrease in expenses. On the revenue side, higher charges under fees and commissions (as a percentage of average assets, 4.9 in 2006 compared to 2.9 in 2002) have allowed income to increase without an increase in exposure to credit risk. On the expenditure side, there have been substantial improvements in cost management, reflected in lower provisioning and administration expenses.

The strengthening of bank capital resulted in solvency indexes of 10.4 percent for the system by December 2006, above the 9 percent regulatory minimum. Although the Superintendency of Banks and Insurance (*Superintendencia de Bancos y Seguros*—SBS) has made great progress, largely because of concerted efforts made since the 1998–99 crisis, the system is not yet close to compliance with Basel core principles. Regulatory and institutional reform must continue in order to achieve effective compliance with international best practices in terms of capital adequacy and risk management, an issue examined in greater detail in section III.

In terms of funding, private banks have improved access to foreign lines of credit, though the extent of financing remains less than half of the precrisis level (figure 3.3). Access to external lines of credit depends on relations with foreign correspondent banks and may facilitate liquidity smoothing in the short term. External finance cannot substitute for a domestic interbank market, however, since access is limited to a small number of institutions.

Deposits from the general public remain concentrated in sight deposits (70 percent of the total), revealing the preference for short-term assets owing to political and macroeconomic uncertainty. The share of short-term deposits in total deposits

Figure 3.3. External Lines of Credit

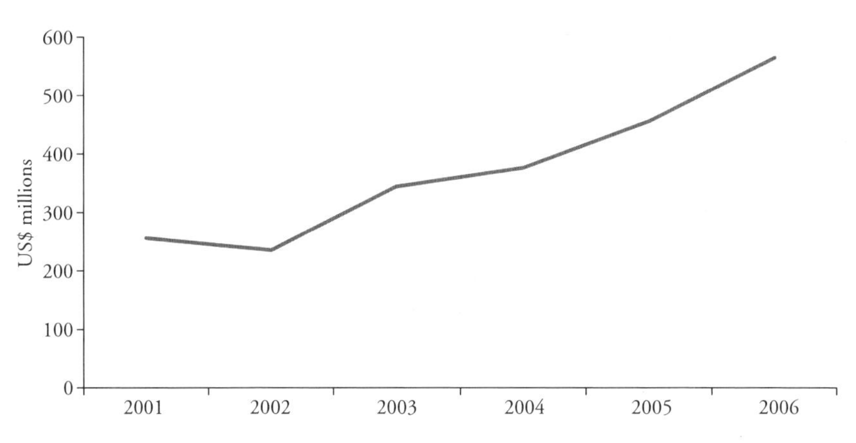

Source: SBS and BCE.

Note: External credit is the sum of lines 2603, 2605, and 2607 in the balance sheet. All years are year-end.

increased from 79 percent to 87 percent between 2002 and 2006, while the coverage of short-term deposits by available funds fell from 35 percent to 27 percent.

Overall, although there has been improvement in asset penetration and intermediation since the crisis, financial depth is relatively low. The loan portfolio reveals greater diversity across loan type and improved quality of loans, as indicated by share of nonperforming loans. The structure of the balance sheet displays a preponderance of short-term, volatile liabilities and a corresponding high portfolio allocation to liquid assets, since the absence of a lender of last resort and of an interbank market necessitates individual liquidity management. Larger banks have shifted investments to U.S. Treasury bills and Fannie Mae paper in recent years, while smaller banks continue to hold domestic securities, partly as a means to access credit lines to smooth liquidity. Larger banks also have the advantage of accessing external lines of credit, which may function, in the short-term, as a partial liquidity-smoothing mechanism.

II. Structure of the Financial Sector

By October 2002, the 24 existing private banks had 82 percent of the total financial assets in the country (table 3.5), concentrated in turn in the four largest banks (which held 63 percent of the total assets in private banks). These banks include Banco del Pacífico (the largest in 1998), which is state-owned (by the BCE) as a result of its restructuring but has been under the administration of a team of international bankers that has improved its operations.[2] The system includes two midsize foreign banks (Citibank and Lloyds) that remained in Ecuador. Another two foreign banks left the system by selling their assets to other banks or through mergers (ABN-AMRO and ING), owing to high perceived country risk postcrisis and because they had not achieved sufficient scale to justify operating as retail banks. The remaining institutions have a small share in the system, particularly the state-owned banks—National Financing Corporation (CFN), Banco Nacional de Fomento (BNF), Banco del Estado, and Banco Ecuatoriano de la Vivienda—whose operations are directed toward specialized areas. The increase in the number of financial institutions is because of the rapid expansion in the number of cooperatives, from 27 to 37 between 2002 and 2006.

As of 2006, the shares of private banks in total banking assets had fallen slightly to 79 percent. Between 2002 and 2006, the four largest banks' shares fell from 64 percent to 52 percent of total banking assets, indicating that the system is still highly concentrated. Additionally, the majority of institutions are members of a small number of financial groups. These groups include private banks (typically the main component), foreign branches, finance companies, securities houses, fund administrators, real estate companies, insurance companies, bonded warehouses, and computer service companies.

An important feature of Ecuadoran banking before the 1999 crisis was a substantial offshore sector. Offshore banking declined in importance with the exit of almost

Table 3.5. Number and Size of Institutions in the Financial System

	Number		*Total assets*				*Net credit portfolio*				*Net investments*				*Deposits with the public*			
			2002		*2006*		*2002*		*2006*		*2002*		*2006*		*2002*		*2006*	
	2002	*2006*	*US$ 000s*	*%*	*US$ 000s*	*%*	*US$ 000s*	*%*	*US$ 000s*	*%*	*US$ 000s*	*%*	*US$ 000s*	*%*	*US$ 000s*	*%*	*US$ 000s*	*%*
Total (in the country)	**69**	**81**	**6,951,074**	**100**	**14,699,115**	**100**	**3,559,719**	**100**	**8,223,401**	**100**	**996,496**	**100**	**2,251,484**	**100**	**4,919,225**	**100**	**10,598,307**	**100**
Private banks	22	24	5,726,339	82	**11,890,163**	**79**	2,683,543	75	6,187,591	75	890,550	89	1,966,671	87	4,242,060	86	8,934,347	84
Pichincha			1,529,505	22	2,938,135	19	707,217	20	1,590,881	19	195,905	20	435,939	19	1,189,434	24	2,206,463	21
Guayaquil			841,932	12	1,742,804	11	353,185	10	658,476	8	136,744	14	348,360	15	567,203	12	1,147,174	11
Pacifico[a]			621,985	9	1,330,498	9	154,366	4	542,149	7	190,377	19	325,398	14	325,709	7	1,035,849	10
Produbanco			601,615	9	1,154,752	8	314,666	9	547,388	7	89,569	9	330,243	15	463,060	9	864,610	8
Public banks[b]	2	3	493,020	7	766,943	5	310,365	9	519,316	6	54,842	6	61,972	3	192,464	4	284,578	3
Finance companies	11	12	327,201	5	783,740	5	231,689	7	582,968	7	16,459	2	31,614	1	199,872	4	312,785	3
Savings and loan institutions[b]	27	37	246,481	4	1,001,402	7	176,089	5	719,551	9	19,715	2	114,559	5	169,091	3	687,970	6
Mutual associations	7	5	158,033	2	463,278	3	158,033	4	213,975	3	14,930	1	76,668	3	115,739	2	378,626	4
Total (abroad)	**9**	**9**	**1,284,057**	**100**	**2,136,548**	**100**	**571,169**	**100**	**1,084,702**	**100**	**393,683**	**100**	**626,011**	**100**	**946,248**	**100**	**1,601,724**	**100**
Offshore	5	4	476,937	37	278,090	13	222,260	39	97,945	9	146,467	37	120,171	19	367,113	39	209,439	13
Operating abroad	4	5	807,120	63	1,858,458	87	348,910	61	986,758	91	247,215	63	505,840	81	579,135	61	1,392,285	87
Total	**78**	**90**	**8,235,131**		**16,835,663**		**4,130,888**		**9,308,103**		**1,390,179**		**2,877,494**		**5,865,474**		**12,200,031**	

Source: SBS.

Note: 2006 data refer to December except for offshore and external banks, for which latest available information is October.

a. Includes Banco del Pacífico, with public capital.

b. Does not include second-tier institutions.

half the private banks with which it was associated, through reorganization, merger, or liquidation. By the end of 2002, the four offshore banks still open belonged to the largest banks in the system, although their growth was limited by a new restriction stipulating that the asset level of March 2000 would be the upper limit allowable to each individual offshore bank. The share of offshore banks in total private banking assets (within the country and abroad) fell from 6.8 percent to 1.9 percent between December 2002 and December 2006.

Four new foreign banks have entered the system (table 3.5), operating mostly abroad—while the offshore banks focused on operations with domestic banks—and are subject to the regulatory authorities of their base countries (Colombia and Peru). All four belong to the Pichincha financial group, whose bank held nearly 25 percent of total assets in the private banking system, as of 2006. Pichincha bank has acquired two small banks through one of its foreign banks. Owing to Pichincha's rapid growth (by acquiring banks that experienced troubles during the restructuring process) and to foreign banks' decision to leave the system over the years following the crisis, the Pichincha group became the system's largest, with 35 percent of the total assets of the financial groups by 2002, declining slightly to 31 percent by November 2006. The owners of this group also own the system's largest finance company (Diners Card), with 64 percent of all finance company assets in 2002 and 66 percent in 2006.

The Herfindahl-Hirschman Index (HHI) across loans, deposits, and total assets provides a more accurate picture of the trend in market concentration, which is increasing for all indicators (figure 3.4). The sharp increase in the index following the crisis was the result of the contraction in the number of banks and increased consolidation within the sector. The jagged nature of the indexes plotted in the figures is because of the use of annual rather than high-frequency data; however, it appears that the index is less volatile over investments than over loans. Although deposit concentration has declined since peaking in 2002, it is still considerably higher than before the 1999 crisis.

In spite of dollarization and improved access to world capital since 2002, integration of the financial sector with global markets has not improved significantly. There are two main potential advantages of higher foreign bank participation in the sector: more liquidity, which would generate improved ability to withstand shocks and greater supply to finance, and greater competition, which may reduce borrowing costs to domestic investors and increase smaller borrowers' access to credit (BIS 2004). Other possibilities include better risk management and the perception that the benefits of doing business in the country are higher because of visible improvements in financial infrastructure. Currently, only a small number of dominant banks have access to external lines of credit through their relationships with foreign correspondent banks.

The growth of foreign bank participation is hindered by the weakness of the business environment, which raises the risk exposure of investment in financial services: FDI in non-oil sectors in general has lagged behind that in oil and mining. Essentially, the obstacle to foreign bank entry is the perceived risk of doing business

Figure 3.4. Concentration Ratios (HH Index) for Ecuadoran Banking System

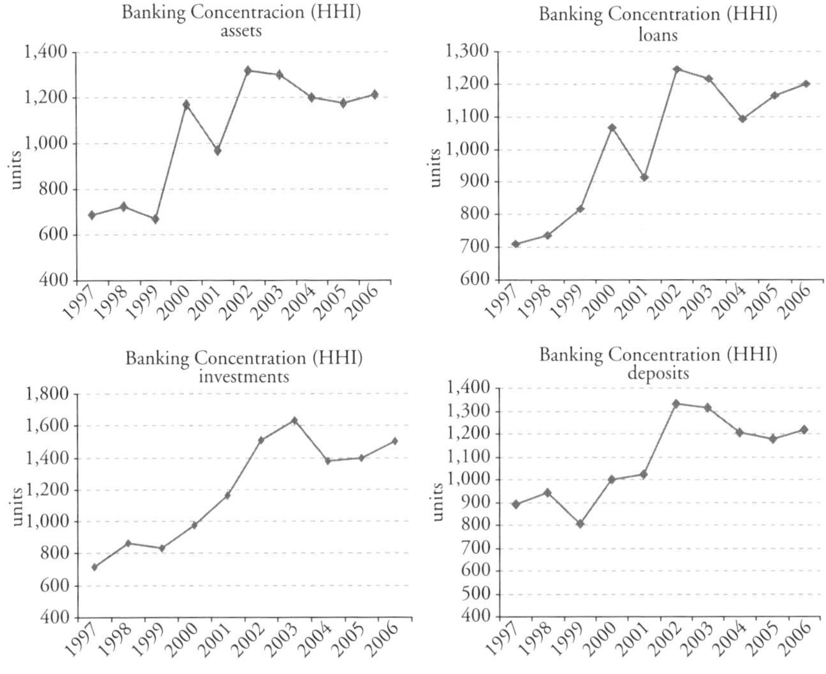

Source: SBS and authors' calculations.

in Ecuador and the small size of the market. The largest banks enjoy access to external lines of credit through their relations with the foreign correspondent banks.

Comparisons with the two other dollarized economies in the region show that Ecuador is comparable with El Salvador, but Panama is considerably ahead of both Ecuador and El Salvador across all measures (table 3.6). In Ecuador, as discussed above, the trend has been lower foreign bank participation over time. In 1998, Ecuador had four foreign banks with assets at nearly 2.5 percent of GDP. In 2001, the remaining two banks that are still in operation today (Citibank and Lloyds) had assets at 1.6 percent of GDP. This figure declined to 0.9 percent of GDP by December 2006.

Overall, since the crisis the sector has advanced in terms of financial indicators and intermediation, though the growth in financial depth has been slow. The sector is highly concentrated, with a small number of banks dominating in terms of access to external financing and share in deposits and assets. The risk profile has also improved, as measured by quality of loan portfolio and capital adequacy indicators. However, important concerns remain and are explored in detail in the following sections.

Table 3.6. Integration with Global Financial Markets (November 2006)

	Panama[a]	*El Salvador*[b]	*Ecuador*
Total assets (% of GDP)	214.8	73.5	29.1
Assets owned by foreign banks	109.4	1.1	0.9
Profits (% of total assets)	4.1	1.7	2.2
Of foreign banks	5.0	0.7	5.5
Total loans (% of GDP)	83.8	49.9	15.6
By foreign banks	30.4	0.3	0.3
Total deposits (% of GDP)	78.3	47.6	22.4
In foreign banks	26.9	0.6	0.7

Source: Banking Superintendencies in Ecuador, El Salvador, and Panama.

a. Total loans and deposits refers to loans to residents and domestic deposits for Panama.

b. Data are for December 2006 for El Salvador.

III. Liquidity Management and Solvency

Stress in the payments and settlements system can compromise systemic stability in the Ecuadoran context for three reasons: postdollarization, the Central Bank is no longer able to function as lender of last resort, there is no interbank market, and the Deposit Guarantee Agency (*Agencia de Garantia de Depositos*—AGD) does not have the resources to back deposit guarantees. Individual banks are responsible for managing liquidity, which they do by maintaining available funds well in excess of required reserves (which are fixed at 4 percent of reservable deposits). Monitoring liquidity in order to identify potential stress points is therefore a key component of risk management in the Ecuadoran context.

This section has two components: (i) an examination of actual liquidity trends; and (ii) a comparison across different potential mechanisms of liquidity management.

Liquidity Indicators

Overall liquidity, as defined by available funds relative to short-term deposits (less than three months maturity), has been declining since December 2005, but remains at a relatively high level (table 3.7). Available funds net of reserves were 18 percent of total deposits at the end of 2006, while required reserves are only 4 percent. This is because of the banking system's experience during the crisis, the absence of a lender of last resort, the lack of resources with the AGD, and the preponderance of short-term deposits, which were 74 percent of total liabilities and 86 percent of total deposits at the end of 2006. Efficient management of liquidity would be assisted by stronger links with foreign correspondent banks, which have the resources to assist when frictions arise. As of now, a small number of banks have access to external credit, leaving the smaller banks with more limited options.

Table 3.7. Analysis of Liquidity

	Dec. 2005	*Dec. 2006*
Available funds (cash + liquid deposits as % of GDP)	5.9	5.2
of which deposits abroad (as % of GDP)	3.8	3.0
Available funds (% of short-term deposits)	31.3	27.0
Available funds (% of total deposits)	27.9	23.4
Available funds (% of total assets)	21.8	18.0
Short-term deposits (% of total deposits)	88.9	86.9[a]

Source: SBS and authors' calculations.
a. The deposit run was concentrated in sight deposits.

Coverage of large deposits has also shown a declining trend. Between end-2005 and end-2006, coverage of the 100 largest deposits declined from 113.4 percent to 91.6 percent. Distinguishing by function as opposed to size yields significant variation as well. Coverage of the 100 largest depositors was 86.8 percent, 61.9 percent, 29.1 percent, and 42.9 percent, respectively, for banks specializing in commercial, consumer, housing, and microenterprise loans. These figures suggest some vulnerability in coverage, especially for small banks and for banks specializing in housing loans.

Overall, therefore, liquidity is high but declining, and there are significant variations by size and type of institution. While the current context highlights the vulnerabilities of small banks and of consumer, housing, and microenterprise banks, the purpose has been to motivate longer-term policy reform, with a view to preventing problems before they occur.

Liquidity Management: Drain on Yield and Intermediation

To build credibility, the banking system needs a transparent mechanism for liquidity management. Individualized liquidity management by each bank has two potential negative effects on the economy. The first is that it reduces the funds available for investment, which has negative consequences for yield. The second is that it reduces the proportion of retained earnings that can be invested or lent domestically. This hinders growth in domestic credit and limits access to finance, thereby constraining both financial deepening and widening.

One proposal is for a centralized liquidity fund under the management of the Central Bank. The issue that needs to be addressed, therefore, is how a centralized system would work and how the BCE could effectively support it. The idea of centralized liquidity management is not new—it emerged from the postcrisis discussion of reforms and is revisited every time there is reason to be concerned about inadequate liquidity management. The scheme, still entirely hypothetical, is based on access to reserves managed by the Latin American Reserve Fund (FLAR) via a contingent line of credit, which could be as high as US$500 million based on Ecuador's current participation in the reserve fund (table 3.8).

The current reserve requirement of 4 percent could be diverted to the liquidity fund without further private contributions. However, this implies contingent fiscal costs and higher risk of moral hazard than if the liquidity fund were both privately financed and managed. The increase in the liquidity fund could be matched by an equal decline in available funds maintained by private banks, leading to a potential freeing of funds of US$500 million. The scheme could release credit into domestic financial markets, or the funds could be invested, for example, in high yield bonds, permitting a better bank yield. Based on an 8 percent spread between yields, bank income could increase by up to US$40 million (0.34 percent of total private banking assets).

While this example highlights the negative consequences on yield and intermediation of individualized liquidity management, a public liquidity provision scheme faces two fundamental difficulties that must not be underestimated, because they require changes in the legal framework. The first requirement for the viability of a centrally managed liquidity fund is to instill, in the commercial banks, full confidence in the BCE's capacity to manage this fund with the required level of confidentiality. Furthermore, to date, the legal restriction that prevents the BCE from managing trusts has made it necessary to delegate management of the liquidity fund to the CFN, a state-owned bank experiencing problems in its balances. In addition, the BCE's share in ownership of the third largest bank in the system (Banco del Pacífico) creates potentially significant conflicts of interest that could hinder the full effectiveness of the liquidity fund. A second requirement is the need for close monitoring of the liquidity fund's investment policies, which could be delegated to a reputable—preferably international—financial institution that would act as trustee and administrator of these funds.

The proposal for centralized liquidity management and the current dependence on individual resources are symptoms of a larger institutional gap: the absence of an interbank market that can recycle liquidity.

Table 3.8. Liquidity in the Banking System (December 2006)

	Dec. 2006		*Hypothetical centralized scheme for liquidity management*	
	US$ million	*% of deposits*	*US$ million*	*% of deposits*
Private resources	**1,773**	**19.4**	**1,273**	**14.0**
Voluntary reserves	72	0.8	72	0.8
Available funds net of reserves	1,701	18.6	1,201	13.2
Public resources	**530**	**5.8**	**1,030**	**11.3**
Obligatory reserves	365	4.0	365	4.0
Liquidity fund	165	1.8	165	1.8
Contingent credit	0	0.0	500	5.5
Total liquidity	**2,303**	**25.2**	**2,303**	**25.2**

Source: SBS, BCE, and authors' calculations.

Liquidity Management: Missing Market and Vulnerabilities of Small Banks

The effectiveness of liquidity management, in particular, the depth and resilience of the payments system, will determine whether the banking sector is robust with regard to shocks and to upsurges in systemic volatility, and, most important, whether idiosyncratic stress is likely to escalate into systemwide distress (Box 3.1). The interbank money market is typically the cornerstone for smoothing liquidity flows within the sector and recycling liquidity from surplus to deficit banks. Such a money market is practically absent in Ecuador, where large banks rely on lines of credit from foreign correspondent banks to assist with temporary problems in flows and have limited incentives to assist small domestic banks, which typically do not enjoy ready access to external financing.

One main institutional arrangement to tide over liquidity problems is the reverse repurchase arrangement with the BCE, access to which is determined by government securities holdings. The other is through drawing on the liquidity fund and is limited by participation. Each bank contributes only 1 percent of deposits. The overall size of the fund is barely US$165 million, clearly insufficient to support the system. The need for a substantially larger fund cannot be overstated.

The AGD has almost no effective means to back insured deposits, which, in the eyes of the depositors, reduces the credibility of both deposit guarantees and the regulators. The bulk of bank contributions to the AGD cover administrative expenses. Guaranteed deposits were at nearly 8 percent of GDP by end-2006 and are largely viewed as a contingent fiscal liability.

Figure 3.5. Evolution of Deposits

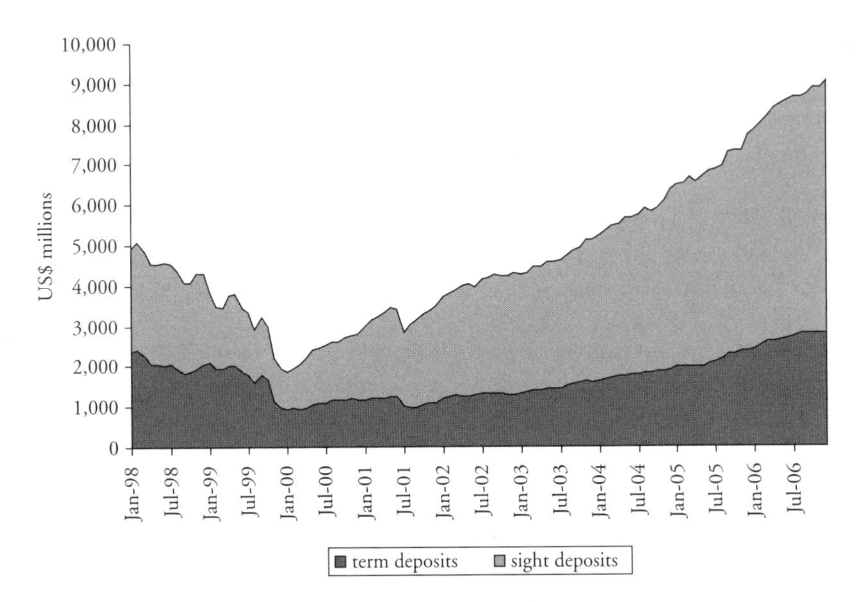

Source: SBS and authors' calculations.

Box 3.1. Liquidity Management and Payment System

The smooth functioning of the payments system is a critical component of a robust financial system. It is the mandate of supervisory authorities to promote and safeguard an efficient and safe payments and settlements system, especially under situations of liquidity shortfalls, and especially in the Ecuadoran context.

Banks fulfill two functions in this context: they intermediate payments between various economic agents, and they manage the means of payment on behalf of customers for future transactions. The vulnerability of the payments system is determined largely by the depth of the interbank money market, which in turn determines the risk that liquidity stress on an individual bank might be transmitted to the rest of the sector. Under scenarios of deposit withdrawal, which may trigger liquidity shortfalls within the banking system, weaknesses in the payments system can be destabilizing. The banking system has increased the liquidity of its asset portfolio in response to the shortening of the term structure of its liabilities, with available funds at nearly 18 percent of total assets at end-2006, although over half of this liquidity is held abroad.

Under stress scenarios, the assumption about the sources of liquidity has implications for the effectiveness of the payments system's response to deposit runs. Current accounts held by banks at the BCE consist of the compulsory reserve requirement (4 percent of reservable deposits) and voluntary reserves. During the course of daily operations, these accounts are debited and credited as orders flow through the settlement system. In practice, surplus reserves are used by banks to ensure a smooth settlement of their payment flows. This approach is consistent with the assumption that each bank will always provide enough liquidity to honor its debts and keep the payment system working properly. However, that is not always the case. For example, a bank, even with high liquidity coverage, could let its reserves at the BCE draw down until it defaults on its payments to depositors. In Ecuador, where balances are monitored based on the average over one week of the month, banks may fall below their legal requirement without attracting immediate attention. Then, despite the apparent solvency of the bank, its temporary default could trigger a contagion effect and create financial distress even before the aggregate level of liquidity reaches a warning threshold level. Alternatively, individual bankers may choose not to divert their net assets abroad to distressed banks with limited resources. Large banks may prefer not to lend to small banks when they might instead have an opportunity to purchase the best loan assets of a distressed bank. If several banks are

(Box continues on the following page.)

Box 3.1. (continued)

affected at the same time, the payment system may be damaged, with disruptive effects on the rest of the economy. Typically, under stress situations, interbank money markets stop recycling liquidity, further hurting vulnerable banks. In Ecuador, interbank lending is limited even during normal circumstances: the daily peak of interbank lending has never exceeded US$9 million in recent years (or 0.15 percent of sight deposits).

IV. Risk Profile of the Banking System

This section analyzes the risk profile of the banking system's loan portfolio and indexes of capital adequacy. A significant component of risk management in banking is regulation driven. The standard risk indicators do provide a measure of the evolution of the system's robustness, largely by monitoring the management's ability to conform to basic requirements, and by evaluating the structure of the balance sheet. However, without strong governance and well-coordinated institutions, meeting capital adequacy requirements is not sufficient to ensure that the sector can rise to meet future challenges.

Risk Indicators

Overall, since the crisis, there has been a tremendous improvement across all risk indicators (see table 3.9). There have also been improvements in transparency and data reporting. Regulatory authorities must now evaluate the modalities of risk analysis and strengthen in place mechanisms for resolving stress to ensure that the gains become resistant to shocks.

An analysis of the portfolio in table 3.9 suggests a dramatic improvement both in the quality of loans and in the coverage of unproductive loans. However, the ratio of unproductive assets to total assets is still high, at just over 13 percent, as is the ratio of unproductive loans to total capital, at 18 percent. Additionally, the expansion in microcredit has been accompanied by an increase in the proportion of nonperforming microloans. As pointed out earlier, liquidity indicators have worsened over time, though Ecuadoran banks are still relatively liquid. The burden of individual liquidity management is risky in itself, however, since there is no interbank lending to speak of.

The capital necessary to maintain confidence in the banking system in Ecuador is considered to be higher than the standard 8 percent recommended by Basel I, unless the system is highly liquid and well integrated, as is the case in Panama. (The 1988 Basel Accord recommended 8 percent of risk-weighted assets as the minimum capital

Table 3.9. Risk Indicators for the Banking System

	2002	*2003*	*2004*	*2005*	*2006*
Asset quality (%)					
Net nonperforming assets/total assets	80.9	82.5	14.6	13.4	13.0
Portfolio at risk (C, D, and E)	***11.0***	***9.4***	***6.0***	***4.7***	***3.5***
Commercial loans overdue (%)	9.5	8.2	7.5	5.5	2.8
Consumer loans overdue (%)	6.6	8.5	6.0	4.4	4.5
Housing loans overdue (%)	6.4	4.7	2.7	1.6	1.4
Microenterprise loans overdue (%)	7.0	4.5	4.9	7.4	5.4
All loans	8.4	7.9	6.4	4.9	3.3
Provisioning for problem loans (%)					
Commercial	155.1	107.8	76.6	83.8	270.7
Consumer loans	57.4	53.6	57.5	70.6	104.1
Housing loans	60.8	43.8	67.5	96.1	187.2
Microcredit	80.8	62.0	76.9	60.5	114.3
All problem loans	131.4	127.3	119.0	143.7	182.7
Capital adequacy (%)					
Gross unproductive loans/total capital	46.1	38.9	33.9	28.1	18.1
FK = (capital + results − extraordinary income)/total assets	8.3	9.1	9.0	9.0	9.8
FI = 1 + (unproductive assets/total assets)	119.3	117.5	114.6	113.4	113.0
Net Index of Capitalization: FK/FI	6.9	7.7	7.8	7.9	8.7
Capital to assets weighted by risk	11.8	12.2	12.0	11.6	12.0
Liquidity (%)					
Available funds*/short-term deposits	34.7	30.9	31.7	31.3	26.9
Available funds/25 largest deposits		152.8	143.0	163.3	128.8
Available funds/100 largest deposits		106.6	101.2	113.4	91.6

Source: SBS.

Note: Dates are end-December.

*Available funds are highly liquid assets maintained as demand deposits, cash, and reserves.

requirement for banks with an international presence.) Ecuadoran banks have accordingly maintained a surplus of capital (figure 3.6). The smallest and most vulnerable banks, which have smaller clients and limited or no access to global markets, maintain the largest surplus in capital ratios. As of end-2006, the net capital-asset ratios—calculated as (capital + profits – extraordinary income)/total assets—were above the regulatory minimum of 9 percent for all banks, by asset class and function, except for housing.

In perceived systemic risk, a measure of success or failure that is more responsive to changing market conditions than regulatory capital is the rate of change in the domestic interest rate. Domestic interest rates have been decreasing since 2003, largely because of the success of dollarization in reducing inflation. Market-based interest rates typically incorporate a risk premium and also reflect monetary market conditions. A risk perception index can be constructed based on the spread between

Figure 3.6. Banking System's Capital Adequacy, 2006

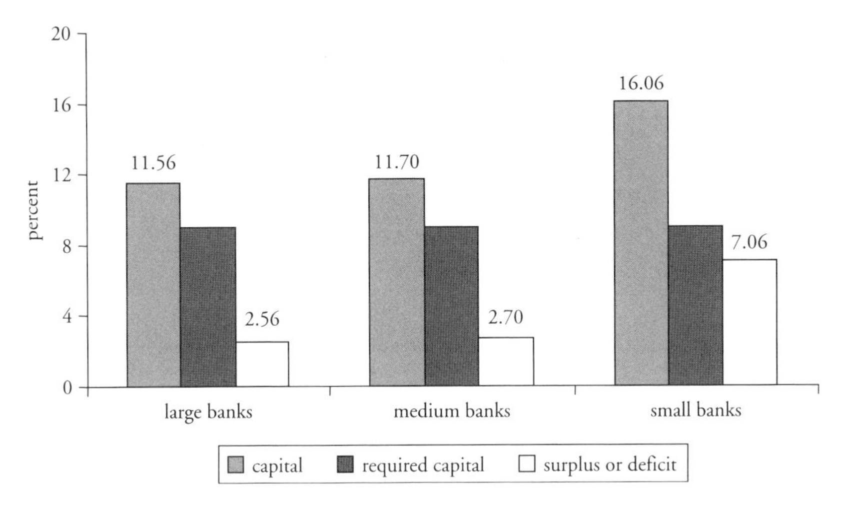

Source: SBS and authors' calculations.

domestic deposit rates and the U.S. Treasury bill rate (figure 3.7). That the index shows an overall trend of decline is a positive indicator. This decrease in perceived risk is due in part to the fall in macroeconomic volatility between 2001 and 2006. However, the decline in vulnerability should be interpreted with caution, given the high proportion of sight deposits in the system.

Institutional Issues

One of the most important tasks of bank supervisors is to ensure that banks maintain an adequate capital cushion against losses, especially during times of financial instability or stress. However, establishing capital adequacy ratios is insufficient, in itself, as a guarantee against systemic risk. Banks and the regulatory authorities have to take complementary steps to protect the financial sector from the adverse effects of any potential shock. Effective risk management is rooted in effective regulation and supervision. Monitoring and supervisory mechanisms are designed to improve solvency and market discipline. In the process, through timely and detailed reporting on key indicators, the system builds up the credibility critical to the functioning of the financial sector.

Building the desired level of trust between regulated institutions and regulators is an important component of enhancing the system's credibility. The role, mandate, and relationship of the main financial regulatory agencies (BCE, SBS, and AGD) should be clearly defined during normal and crisis periods. A transparent demarcation

Figure 3.7. Risk Perception Index

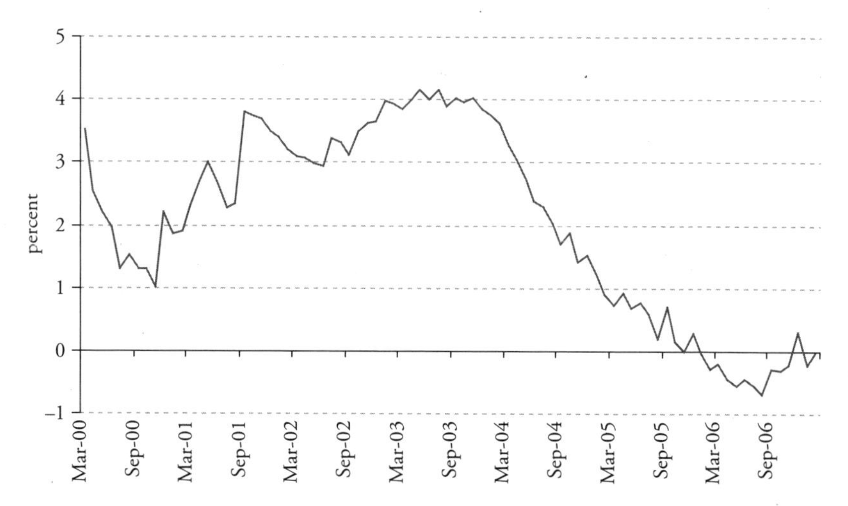

Source: Authors' calculations based on data from SBS and BCE.
Note: Represents 90-day deposits vs. three-month U.S. T-bill (%). Risk Perception Index = $(1/(1+r^{TB}))-(1/(1+r^{ECU}))$ where r is the 90-day interest rate, TB is U.S. Treasury bills, and ECU is the Ecuadoran deposit rate.

of responsibility is necessary to ensure that each agency is held accountable for its actions and policies.

Under the dollarized regime, the BCE is responsible largely for supervising the payments and settlements system. It uses more or less static indicators as ex post indicators of problems in liquidity flows, such as inadequate funds to settle obligations in an individual bank's current account, requests for funds to pay clients, continued transfers to or from abroad, bankwise risk analysis and tracking of deposit volatility, and settlement indicators relative to normal trends. Since private banks dominate the system but do not participate in the payments mechanism to the same extent as small banks, there is typically not enough centralized liquidity to extend lines of credit to deficit banks during times of need. The Central Bank also lacks the authority to sanction individual banks if they fall below legal reserve requirements, currently at 4 percent of deposits. The Central Bank must inform the SBS, which may levy a fine in case of persistent failure to meet reserve requirements over an extended period. It is the SBS that is responsible for monitoring and regulating individual banks.

The SBS has made significant progress toward strengthening on-site and off-site supervision, including building the capacity of its employees. However, it is still not a fully independent regulatory agency with sufficiently trained professional regulators who are well versed on the latest developments of increasingly complex financial services offered worldwide. Nor does the SBs have a clear and coherent legal framework for bank resolution. This is a serious gap, given the failure of the AGD to complete liquidation of banks in a timely manner following the previous crisis. Currently, risk modeling is updated once a month, and monitoring based on high-frequency data is only possible with a one-week lag. There can be a lag of several weeks by the time a bank experiencing payments and settlements problems is faced with suspension of lending operations.

Regarding the AGD, the institution's lack of resources is preventing it from acting as a proper guarantee of deposits, which in turn encourages banks to tie up significant resources to protect against deposit withdrawals instead of increasing lending. The delay in resolving banks that were taken over during the crisis was only partly because of the need to raise resources to settle with depositors and largely because of the lack of a legal and institutional framework to deal with delinquent borrowers (or of the political will to do so). Currently, the AGD has effectively no resources, and its reputation has suffered because of the many years it has taken to liquidate bankrupt banks and settle its obligations. Banks perceive the AGD as using contributions not to back deposits but to settle administrative expenses.

Institutional capacity, inadequate market development for liquidity recycling, and the absence of a credible and transparent crisis resolution framework are persistent problems that still need to be addressed. The performance of the banking sector in terms of meeting regulatory requirements such as capital adequacy ratios and in terms of reducing the weight of the nonperforming portfolio has improved considerably since the 1998–99 crisis.

V. Policy Recommendations

This note has identified positive trends in the income and balance sheet profile of the banking sector, but has also outlined key weaknesses that must be resolved before the system can fully consolidate the gains of recent years. Some of the issues that arise in the Ecuadoran context are the by-product of dollarization. Others have more to do with inadequacies in regulatory and legal institutions.

Liquidity Management: Demand and Supply

Typically, policy recommendations address supply-side management and ignore problems arising from volatile liquidity demand (World Bank 2003). Since banks are more likely to be liquidity-constrained when they are at the bottom of their income cycle, Ecuador could consider a more dynamic pro-cyclical loan-loss provisioning policy. This would increase the volume of reserves against portfolio losses during periods of high portfolio growth (and high bank yield) and reduce it during periods of weak or negative growth (and low bank yield), as experimented with successfully in Spain. As a policy mechanism, the idea is similar to that of an income stabilization fund.

The only viable long-term strategy to reduce overall volatility of liquidity demand is to improve the credibility of the regulatory authorities and thereby of the system. This can be done by making crisis containment and resolution transparent and by backing emergency-response plans with adequate resources. In addition, reforms designed to improve the sustainability and credibility of deposit guarantees may encourage a lengthening of the term structure of deposits, and a proportionate reduction in the weight of volatile liabilities.

The management of liquidity supply would hinge around two key components—clarification of the regulators' role in monitoring and supervising the payments and settlements system, and a centralized liquidity fund on a much larger scale than the current centralized liquidity fund—that make up for the lack of interbank lending by creating a pool of dollar reserves for deficit banks to draw on as needed.

The consensus among the authorities seems to be that (i) the BCE could keep its central position in the management of the payments system and of the system's liquidity needs, and (ii) the AGD could be reduced to a pay box for deposit guarantees that delegates the settlement and solution of responsibilities to the SBS, while the SBS would maintain responsibility for individual—but not systemic—interventions in the financial sector.

Under the new scheme, the BCE would be responsible for managing the overall liquidity of the economy, including supervising the payments system and managing system liquidity. To reduce the need for individual banks managing liquidity, proposals have been made for implementing a centralized liquidity fund under the management of the BCE. The reserve requirement of 4 percent would be contributed to the liquidity fund without further private contributions, which implies that this is a contingent fiscal cost and that the risk of moral hazard is greater than it would be if banks were financing and managing the liquidity fund. Such a scheme could release credit into domestic financial markets, or could be invested, for example, in high yield bonds, permitting a better bank yield.

An alternative mechanism that has the advantage of reducing the risk of moral hazard, but may not be feasible for the smaller and more vulnerable banks, is a privately funded and managed trust fund. Participation would be through securitization of the loan portfolio. The SBS is consulting with the Federal Reserve Bank of Atlanta on how the fund may be created and leveraged, but the scheme is still at an incipient stage.

Institutional reform aimed at strengthening the payments system will also facilitate liquidity management by reducing perceived risk and allowing the system to manage large transactions swiftly. The security of financial transactions and assets could be increased significantly. The role of the BCE in the management and supervision of the payment system is not yet fully defined, since Ecuador has not yet implemented regulations specifying the Central Bank's supervisory responsibilities over the payment system.

Two significant constraints limit the ability of the BCE to play an effective role as the manager of system liquidity and payments. The first is the conflict of interest associated with BCE ownership of the Banco del Pacífico, the fourth largest bank in the country. The second feature is the legal restriction that prevents the BCE from administering a trust and that has made it necessary to delegate the management of the liquidity fund to the CFN. The BCE could remove the first obstacle by divesting its share in Banco del Pacífico. To overcome the second, the BCE is sponsoring a modification of the legal impediment to manage trusts.

The capacity of the SBS to monitor liquidity and act swiftly in response to individual stress can be strengthened. Reducing lags in data reporting, pooling information and data, and improving coordination with the BCE will allow regulators to work in tandem to enforce requirements and encourage the confidence of both the banks and the public.

With guaranteed deposits at 7.5 percent of GDP and almost no resources to effectively back deposit insurance, reform of the AGD is of paramount importance. Currently, banks' contributions are largely used for administrative support. The AGD could channel deposit premiums into a transparently managed fund that will support the credibility of its deposit insurance schemes. An additional possibility is market-based reinsurance for deposits, though that is not likely to be feasible without a concerted effort by authorities to make the necessary concomitant regulatory and institutional changes.

Risk Management

The key issues pertaining to risk management have to do with strengthening oversight along technical lines and through building staff capacity, developing a credible action plan in case of contingencies (including mandatory coordination and information pooling by all regulators), and introducing the supporting legislative reforms. Key priorities are as follows:

- Clearly define the role, mandate, and relationship of the main financial regulatory agencies (BCE, SBS, and AGD) during normal and crisis periods.
- Strengthen the training of SBS regulators so they can adequately assess both individual and systemic risk and ensure adequate staff for high-frequency updating.
- Continue the ongoing process of strengthening SBS's internal processes of supervision. For example, the use of new manuals for on-site and off-site supervision has had a positive effect on the institution's reputation, which is crucial to increasing confidence in the system.
- Ensure that regulators have legal protection against lawsuits having to do with the performance of their duties.
- Design a clear legal framework for bank resolution in the event of problems, with effective provision and enforcement of property rights, bankruptcy provisions, contractual agreements, credit information, and creditors' rights. This framework would provide the additional benefits of encouraging domestic intermediation and widening access to finance, while facilitating foreign direct investment in banking.

The AGD's role in crisis management could be made more effective if it is relieved of the responsibility for managing banks in the process of liquidation or restructuring. The legislature's decision to not put any more banks under the AGD's management was a positive development, but as 2006, it was still responsible for 10 banks that were currently being liquidated.

The AGD would focus on strengthening the deposit insurance fund (with the premiums that are being charged to active banks), instead of having to use these premiums to pay the debts and administrative expenses of banks under reorganization. The resolution of banks outside of the AGD was already put into practice in response to Filanbanco's second and final fall, which ended with its liquidation in July 2002. One possible policy recommendation would have the AGD hand over the management of the portfolio and the sale of allocated goods and buildings to an international professional administrator with experience, benefits of scale economies, and state-of-the art knowledge of tools and best practice. It would also help to have distance between the agency responsible for asset liquidation and the system's debtors (particularly the largest).

To summarize, the recommendations are presented in the following policy matrix, with additional operational details and suggestions on prioritization.

Policy Matrix

Areas of focus and goals	Policy measures and progress indicators	
	Short term (by June 2008)	*Medium term (2007–11)*
Liquidity fund		
Transparently managed, centralized liquidity fund with pooled resources; two alternatives.	Transfer of management to the BCE could increase public confidence in the liquidity fund.	
Managed by Central Bank.	Reduced risk of moral hazard, but small banks may not be able to leverage their way in.	
Legal authorization permitting the BCE to manage trusts. The present law does not permit this, which is why the CFN was assigned the role of trustee for management of the liquidity fund.		
Managed by CAF privately, and funded privately. Trust fund would invite participation by all banks with access determined by bank's ability to securitize loan portfolio.		
Definition of a new organizational structure for management of the liquidity fund.	Create a financial system oversight committee comprising the BCE, SBS, and Ministry of Economy and Finance.	Create an agency to manage and/or supervise the middle office responsibilities (technology and portfolio risk management) of the liquidity fund.
Coordination of responsibilities between the lender of last resort (the manager of the liquidity fund) and the bank supervisor.		
Efficient exchange of information between the BCE, SBS, AGD, and oversight committee (to be created).	Prepare for the creation of a pooled data bank that the different agencies can access. Mandate procedures for information exchange between the agencies.	
Elimination of the Central Bank's conflict of interest as owner of Banco del Pacífico.	Sustain progress in the bank's restructuring plan.	Revise the plan for the bank's privatization in the medium term.

(*Table continues on the following page.*)

Areas of focus and goals	Policy measures and progress indicators	
	Short term (by June 2008)	*Medium term (2007–11)*
AGD		
Finalization of AGD activities related to the crisis. Payment of outstanding liabilities, sale of portfolio and other assets.	Contract with external international consultants to sell assets to prevent their rapid erosion, taking advantage of best practice experience, state-of-the-art tools, and distance from debtors.	
No further responsibilities toward asset liquidation in banks under restructuring.		
Restructuring of the AGD and redefinition of its role.	Mandate transparent use of bank deposit premia.	
Allow AGD to focus on partial deposit insurance. Revise its structure; consider converting it into a pay box for deposit guarantees.	Effective use should be made of online information to sustain public confidence.	
Superintendency of Banks and Insurance		
Legal protection for the superintendent and other functionaries in performing their duties.	Modify the Banking Act, to include explicit protection.	
Improvement of the SBS's reporting.	Include a section in its annual report with statistics that reflect the oversight activity of the SBS.	
Compliance with international standards against money laundering (coordinating efforts with the related authorities). Guaranteeing that the SBS can carry out legal actions in this sphere within a fully integrated legal system.	Introduce a law to bring the country into compliance with Financial Action Task Force (FATF) principles of money laundering.	Introduce regulation to be implemented by banks and insurance companies.
Strengthening of mechanisms for credit risk analysis, for both on-site and off-site inspections (to improve risk monitoring and containment at the level of the individual bank).	Employ training programs for existing staff and coordination of training between the BCE and the SBS.	

Protection for debtors		
Implementation of Bankruptcy Act *(Ley General de Concurso Preventivo)* in line with the best international practices. This has been subject to political influence, weakening achievement of the objective of improved debtor rights.	Perform an analysis of corporate insolvency (Reports on the observance of standards and codes: Insolvency).	
Payments system		
Formulation of a strategic vision of the payments system beyond operational aspects, focused on improving payment services. Extend the scope of the reform to include legal issues, the oversight function, securities, government payments, and so on.	Formulate a strategic vision for the settlement of payments and securities that is comprehensive and goes beyond operational aspects.	
Legal protection of the payments systems against individual bankruptcy, purpose of liquidation, and legal basis for collateral, legal recognition of the estimation of net balances, and so on.	Perform in-depth review of the legal framework of the payments system and supporting institutions, and design a plan of action for implementing the necessary reforms.	Incorporate into the legal framework all aspects identified for increasing the soundness of the payments and settlements system.
Establishment of the oversight function by the Central Bank. Address the lack of legal capacity and practical oversight of the payments system by the Central Bank. A reform cannot be considered complete unless this function has been activated, which permits effective control of the risks and checks and balances to ensure that flows are efficient and secure at all times.		Have the Central Bank establish the function of oversight of the payments system and coordinate with other regulators (on the subject of securities, for example).

(*Table continues on the following page.*)

Areas of focus and goals	Policy measures and progress indicators	
	Short term (by June 2008)	*Medium term (2007–11)*
Overall coordination		
Coordination by the Central Bank with other related parties. Improve the existing organizational arrangements through the Central Bank's Inter-Institutional Committee.	Establish a mid-level committee that provides a better liaison between the high-level committee and the present technical committees.	
Clear specification of crisis resolution framework.	Mandate roles and responsibilities for all regulatory agencies in the event of systemic stress.	
	Design a concrete prevention plan that is transparent and publicly accessible and that draws on all of the above measures.	

Note: CAF = Corporation Andina de Fomento. (Andean Development Corporation).

Notes

1. Shocks may be magnified if the banking sector is unable to intermediate and therefore "finance volatility." Any increase in volatility may lead to higher costs and interest rates to a greater extent than if the banking sector is robust, leading to sharper declines than warranted in financial activity.

2. The restructuring of this bank's operations is still in progress, but it has already logged significant achievements. It continues to work with two consultants from the international team that managed the bank until October.

Bibliography

BIS (Bank of International Settlements). 2004. "Foreign Direct Investment in the Financial Sector of Emerging Market Economies." CGFS Publication 22, Bank of International Settlements, Basel.

Rigobon, Roberto. 2006. "Ecuador's Stabilization Policy." Photocopy, Sloan School of Management, MIT, Cambridge, MA.

World Bank. 2003. *The Banking Sector in Ecuador: An Economic and Social Agenda in the New Millennium.* Washington, DC: World Bank.

4

The Oil and Gas Sector

Eleodoro Mayorga-Alba, Alfredo Monge,
Oscar Arrieta, Jorge Albán, and Horacio Yépez

Executive Summary

Reforming Ecuador's oil and gas sector would increase its contribution to the national economy to its full potential. In particular, modifying the institutional framework would create conditions that are conducive to public and private investment. Recommended reforms include decisive interventions to improve the management of the sector, to address environmental and social impacts, and to adjust fuel prices, limiting subsidies to the poor. An urgent overhaul of PetroEcuador could turn it into a productive, efficient company. These measures will require both political will and a degree of social consensus, and they could well be implemented if the distribution of rents is made transparent and the population is rightly informed. Indeed, the proposed measures in this note have, in one way or another, been suggested by a number of Ecuadorans. Without reform, the sector's contribution to the economy could diminish, jeopardizing the country's social stability. In contrast, a sound reform of the sector, which draws on the experiences of neighboring countries, would generate sustained, significant funds in the short and long term.

I. Current Situation

The oil and gas sector is very important to the Ecuadoran economy. Exports of crude oil and petroleum derivatives accounted for 58 percent of the country's total exports in 2005. The notable increase in the price of crude oil on the international market explains how revenues increased by 39 percent, despite an increase of less than

---

This chapter was written with contributions from numerous Ecuadoran experts.

2 percent in the volume exported. Efforts to reform the tax system have not succeeded in freeing the budget from dependence on volatile funds generated by the oil sector. In 2005, 30 percent of general budget revenues derived from the oil and gas sector, and the industry generated one-third of all taxes collected.

Despite its importance, the sector is in a critical situation. In particular, the government-owned company PetroEcuador is undergoing a major crisis. PetroEcuador is operating with restricted budgets, has poorly maintained installations and numerous wells on which production has been halted, and causes significant environmental damage. Probably the most profitable investment option is the reactivation of oil and gas production in the areas under the control of Petroproducción, an affiliate of PetroEcuador.

Upstream Sector Issues

Ecuador has sufficient reserves to almost double production in the coming years. The National Direction for Hydrocarbons estimated remaining oil and gas reserves at 4.5 billion barrels as of December 31, 2005. Of that, 3.8 billion barrels correspond to fields operated by PetroEcuador, while the rest are in fields exploited by private companies (table 4.1). In the short term, increased production depends on PetroEcuador's upstream (production) investments. Production in 2005 was 194 million barrels, representing an increase of 0.9 percent from 2004. Petroproducción holds 84 percent of reserves and produces 54 percent of the country total, taking into consideration that it has now added the production of Occidental Petroleum (Oxy) in Block 15, which contributes 18 percent. Private companies hold only 16 percent of the remaining reserves and extract 46 percent of Ecuador's total daily production.

The construction of the Heavy Crude Oil Pipeline (*Oleoducto del Crudo Pesado*—OCP), added to the existing Trans-Ecuadoran Oil Pipeline System, has increased crude oil transportation capacity to almost 850,000 barrels per day (bpd). However, average production is currently about 500,000 bpd. If the current pace of extraction continues, proven reserves guarantee production for the next 25 years.

Table 4.1. Ecuador Hydrocarbon Reserves
(barrels)

	In production	*Not in production*	*Unified fields*	*Total*
Petroproducción	1,906,772,418	1,545,787,000		
Block 15	332,125,000			
Total Petroproducción	2,238,897,418	1,545,787,000		3,784,684,418
Private companies	363,091,000	192,197,000	178,011,582	733,299,582
Total	**2,601,988,418**	**1,737,984,000**	**178,011,582**	**4,517,984,000**

Source: Ministry of Energy and Mines.

Considering the potential of unexplored areas in several basins, if investments are renewed, Ecuador's oil wealth will last for many years.

Not only is PetroEcuador making few investments, but the private sector also is making few investments because of a lack of legal stability. The effort to attract capital and technology for certain upstream projects has not been successful. The following events during the past year have weakened the investment climate.

- Oxy, the leading private producer, decided to sell 40 percent of its rights to a Canadian company. Previously, Oxy had won a court judgment for a US$75 million refund in value-added tax (VAT) that was improperly retained by the previous administration. Arguing that Oxy had not followed the correct procedure in this sale, the government declared its contract terminated and obligated the company to return the wells and production installations of Block 15, without any compensation. An international arbitration procedure is now under way to resolve the issue.
- Encana (Canada), another major producer, sold its assets to Andes Petroleum Ecuador, a consortium of China National Petroleum Company (CNPC; 55 percent) and China Petrochemical Company (SINOPEC; 45 percent), which is unlikely to mobilize significant investments, given present conditions.
- In response to high prices, the government introduced an additional reform in the tax regime applicable to oil and gas. Though many countries have made tax adjustments based on extraordinary profits, Ecuador established a new tax on gross revenues, calculated on the basis of the excess revenues derived from higher prices than the ones initially in effect when contracts were signed.
- In response to pressure from local indigenous communities, the government has negotiated specific contributions with private companies for social and infrastructure investments in oil and gas production.

Viewed as a whole, the resulting tax regime is complicated and, together with the legal instability, discourages private investment in production and transportation. The complex tax regime also is the result of other modifications and additions over recent years (see box 4.1). By comparison, neighboring countries such as Colombia and Peru have tried to improve their institutional framework and contract model, adapting them to situations of volatile prices and of production costs and characteristics that vary from one field to another. In resource-rich countries such as Ecuador, contract stability is as important, or even more important, than explicitly favorable fiscal terms as a factor in successfully attracting risk capital. No new contracts have been signed in more than a decade, other than minor agreements over marginal fields.

Downstream Sector Issues

The downstream sector also operates under greatly inefficient conditions. On the one hand, refineries and logistical installations run by PetroEcuador operate with serious

Box 4.1. Fiscal Terms Applicable to Oil and Gas Production

- Participation in production, exported by PetroEcuador.
- Half of the differential income attained through price increases, comparing the price in effect when the contract was signed with the price now in effect, adjusted for inflation.
- Profit sharing with employees, at 15 percent of earnings.
- Income tax (25 percent).
- VAT, on which withholdings have been disputed.
- The Amazon tax, equivalent to US$0.50/barrel, to be distributed between the authorities of the production area (90 percent) and the Eco-Development Institute of the Ecuadoran Amazon (*Instituto Ecodesarrollo de la Región Amazónica*—ECORAE; 10 percent).
- Contribution to the Roads Fund.

limitations, because of their configuration and insufficient maintenance. Domestic production of fuels does not meet environmental specifications. This means that better quality products must be imported, or else air quality standards in the cities cannot be met. As a result, imports of refined products are growing, which seriously affects the balance of payments.

PetroEcuador's crude-oil processing refineries generate a high volume of heavy residual fuel as a result of their configuration. This inability to produce more highly refined products—such as gasoline, diesel, and liquid petroleum gas (LPG)—necessitates imports. This situation also exacerbates the balance of trade and diminishes the sector's contribution to the national economy. Even though the country has a nominal refining capacity of 64 million barrels, in 2004 the actual refining volume was only 51 million barrels, and in 2005 that figure dropped to 47 million barrels. (In early 2007 the fluid catalytic cracking unit of the Esmeralda Refinery was stopped for major repairs, which will result in increased deficits of LPG, gasoline, and diesel.) National consumption of derivative products is rising at an average annual rate of 5 percent, with growing imports. Imports of subsidized products (LPG, gasoline, and diesel) have practically doubled since 2001 (table 4.2).

High, indiscriminate subsidies have become a determining factor in the downstream situation, accounting for 25 percent of the national budget (table 4.3). Fearful of being rejected by the citizenry, recent administrations have subsidized fuel consumption, providing an incentive for wasteful use and unprecedented levels of contraband moving toward Colombia and Peru. The subsidies distort energy consumption and PetroEcuador's accounts, and are disproportionately captured by the rich. In 2004, an estimated 33 percent of the LPG subsidy was captured by the wealthiest 20 percent of the population, while the poorest 20 percent received only 8 percent of subsidies

Table 4.2. Production, Imports, and Exports of Refined Products
(millions of barrels)

		LPG	*Gasoline*	*Diesel*	*Fuel oil*	*Others*	*Total*
2001	Production	2.2	10	13.4	23.8	2.9	52.3
	Import	5.5	2.9	4.2	—	0.2	12.8
	Export	—	—	—	12.4	1.6	14
2002	Production	2.2	9.9	13.2	23.5	3	51.8
	Import	6.2	4.1	4.2	—	0.1	14.6
	Export	—	—	—	10.9	2.4	13.3
2003	Production	2.2	9.5	12.9	22.5	3.2	50.3
	Import	6.5	4.8	5.8	—	0.2	17.3
	Export	—	—	—	9.1	2.8	11.9
2004	Production	2.4	7.4	13.4	22.9	4.9	51
	Import	7.2	4.7	5.5	—	—	17.4
	Export	—	—	—	10.9	2.7	13.6
2005	Production	2.3	7	13.1	21.3	3.5	47.2
	Import	8	6	8.1	—	0.1	22.2
	Export	—	—	—	10.7	2.3	13
2006/e	Production	2.2	6.4	11.4	20.8	5	45.8
	Import	8.4	6.4	8.2	—	0	23
	Export	—	—	—	10	2.2	12.2

Source: Ministry of Energy and Mines (http://www.menergia.gov.ec).

Table 4.3. Estimate of 2006 Subsidy Levels (without VAT)
(U.S. currency)

	Current price to end users (cents/gal)	*Import or export parity pricing to the end user (cents/gal)*	*Subsidy (cents/gal)*	*Total subsidies (US$)*
Super gasoline	150.0	165.3	–15.3	–19,730,340
Extra gasoline	116.9	165.0	–48.1	–227,813,586
Diesel	80.4	178.9	–98.5	–885,161,033
LPG	6.7	140.3	–133.5	–594,362,945
Fuel oil	62.0	101.6	–39.6	–176,467,457
Total subsidies	—	—	—	**–1,903,535,361**

Source: Author estimates based on parity prices as of October 2006.
Note: Simulated for West Texas Intermediate Crude (WTI) at US$55/bbl.

(World Bank 2004, 124). With the higher international prices, this pervasive impact on the revenue distribution would have increased, with the richer consuming more subsidized energy, and thereby receiving larger benefits. The subsidies also limit spending that would otherwise service the poorer segments of the population. Successive administrations have all had good intentions of benefiting the population and

Table 4.4. Average Gasoline and Diesel Prices Paid by Domestic Consumers
(US$/gallon, including VAT)

	Gasoline				*Diesel*			
	2000	*2002*	*2004*	*2006*	*2000*	*2002*	*2004*	*2006*
Ecuador	1.17	1.50	1.50	1.77	0.68	1.02	1.02	1.48
Colombia	1.85	1.67	2.73	3.70	1.32	0.91	1.36	2.16
Peru	3.03	2.80	4.24	4.62	2.04	1.82	2.88	3.26
Venezuela, R. B. de	0.45	0.19	0.15	0.11	0.23	0.19	0.08	0.07
United States	1.78	1.51	2.04	2.39	1.82	1.48	2.16	2.61

Source: GTZ.
Note: International fuel prices. Countries' gasoline octane numbers differ.

national industry, yet they have failed to take into consideration that fuels are non-renewable products whose price is set on a global market, and they ignore the highly regressive nature of fuel subsidies. Finally, as shown by the rapid changes of governments in general and of sector ministers in particular, the policy, which distorts energy demand, creates enormous losses for the treasury, and exacerbates corruption clearly has failed to preserve political stability.

Subsidies in 2006 were estimated to be US$2 billion; the total subsidy of the second half of 2006 was US$1.3 billion. (For the 2007 national budget, the estimated cost of fuel subsidies exceeds US$2.3 billion.) By comparison, the 2006 budget allocated slightly over US$1 billion to education and US$400 million to health care. The subsidies result in domestic fuel prices significantly lower than elsewhere in the region, apart from República Bolivariana de Venezuela (table 4.4). The price of a 15-kilo cylinder of LPG in Ecuador is US$1.60, while smaller cylinders (10 to 12 kilos) in Colombia and Peru cost more than US$10. The price to the public of a gallon of gasoline in Ecuador in 2002 was about the same as in Colombia and almost half the price of gasoline in Peru; currently the price of gasoline in Ecuador is well below the Colombian price and almost one-third of the Peruvian price. The same trend is observed in the price of diesel. The current diesel price in Ecuador is less than half that in Colombia and less than one-third the price in Peru. These low prices also lead to an estimated public loss due to fuel smuggling to Peru and Colombia of almost US$700 million. This contraband also distorts demand and contributes to corruption.

Management and Distribution of Oil Rents

The Ecuadoran system for the management of rents lacks transparency. A study by the Energy Sector Management Assistance Program (2005), prepared with data from 1997 to 2003, compared how Bolivia, Colombia, Ecuador, and Peru collected and distributed oil and gas earnings. The study showed that Ecuador had the least transparent system, involving an endless number of beneficiaries based on preallocations, many of which were neither monitored nor audited by the budgeting system. Over the past three years, an effort has been made to reduce the number of preallocations and, to a certain extent, to rationalize budget expenditures.

Despite production declines and high subsidies, Ecuador's economy has been able to once again generate financial surpluses and experience a cycle of expansion as a result of increased crude oil prices. One sign of this phenomenon is that Ecuador is reportedly requesting to rejoin the Organization of Petroleum Exporting Countries (OPEC). This cycle of expansion will continue as long as crude oil prices remain high, provided that the sector's operating conditions do not deteriorate further.

Efforts to isolate the oil surplus and prevent inflation, which have provided the basis for the stabilization and savings funds, have been hampered by the propensity of previous administrations to satisfy short-term spending priorities. Frequent political changes have limited the ability to create rules with sufficient consensus for a more reasonable system of managing oil revenues.

In an attempt to address dependency on oil and fluctuations in the price, the government has created a variety of funds. The first fund, created in 1998, was the Petroleum Stabilization Fund (*Fondo de Estabilización Petrolera*—FEP). It was intended to stabilize fiscal resources derived from petroleum revenues, and it is liquidated at the end of each year. The fund fills up when oil prices are higher than expected for a given year and it is used to compensate budgetary accounts in case of higher-than-expected costs, which are often due to the price of imported refined petroleum products. If any resources are left at the end of the year, half are directed to another fund (CEREPS, see below), and the remainder are divided among specified development projects. In recent years, the FEP has been almost entirely used up by the budget.

The Fund for Stabilization, Social and Productive Investment, and Reduction of Public Debt (*Fondo de Estabilización, Inversión Social y Productiva, y Reducción del Endeudamiento Público*—FEIREP) was created in 2002 and was aimed at capturing the surplus brought in by the OCP pipeline operations and extraordinary petroleum revenues. Administered by the Central Bank, 70 percent of its resources were earmarked to pay external debt and the public debt to the Social Security Institute; 20 percent went to the Savings and Contingency Fund (*Fondo de Ahorro y Contingencia*—FAC) to be used in the event of an economic downturn; and 10 percent was earmarked for education and health spending.

In 2005, Congress converted FEIREP into a new fund, called the Special Account for Productive and Social Reactivation (*Cuenta Especial de Reactivación Productiva y Social*—CEREPS), which is under the direct control of the Ministry of Economy and Finance (MEF). With its stronger emphasis on pro-cyclical spending, the uses of this fund are not established in a clear, specific way, allowing much greater discretion, and it does not establish any minimum amount to be spent on debt buy-back. As with FEIREP, 20 percent of CEREPS is to be diverted to the FAC, although the rules for withdrawing from the FAC were loosened. Additional portions are allotted to scientific research, road infrastructure, and repair of environmental damage caused by hydrocarbon operations.

To guide the use of the resources generated by the former Oxy fields (Block 15) and prevent a new increase in current spending, a law was enacted in 2006 to create a new fund, the Ecuadoran Fund for Investment in the Energy and Hydrocarbons Sectors (*Fondo Ecuatoriano de Inversión en los Sectores Energéticos e Hidrocarburos*—FEISEH). FEISEH is expected to capture approximately US$1.2 billion in earnings annually, to be channeled for the following purposes:

- To compensate the treasury for revenue losses due to termination of the contract on Block 15. An annual amount of US$145 million will be earmarked as tax obligations in favor of the budget.
- To cover the operating costs incurred by PetroEcuador for operations of the block and/or unified neighboring fields.
- To develop the National Microfinances System program, a one-time allocation of US$50 million will be made.
- For strategic hydrocarbon infrastructure and generation projects (capacity of at least 25 megawatts) in the hydroelectric and alternative energy sector.
- To the FAC.
- To cover the costs of constituting, registering, and executing trust operations to promote productive investments, as well as for oversight and auditing of the trust funds' financial statements.

Social and Environmental Issues

The sector faces a significant negative environmental legacy, especially in the northeast of the country, as well as the impacts of current operations. It is also held responsible for a negative social legacy reflected in the degraded living conditions of communities in the zones of production. These factors create continual conflicts. Environmental and social impacts of oil and gas activities are especially complex in the case of Ecuador, because they are taking place in a fragile tropical rainforest with extensive biodiversity, which contain the most important protected areas of the country. These production zones often overlap with the protected areas, which are mainly inhabited by indigenous peoples. Colonization processes have expanded the agricultural frontier and led to confrontation with indigenous peoples, and government services and enforcement are often weak.

Oil operations have left behind environmental and social impacts that form a part of the collective memory of the country, exacerbating distrust over new operations and generating social conflicts that are difficult to resolve. PetroEcuador, which absorbed the Texaco fields and has carried out its operations with very few controls, is currently the largest producer in the northeast region. Unfortunately, a good part of its operations apply technological and environmental management standards from the past, perpetuating environmental deterioration. The operations of Petroproducción continue flaring associated gas and dumping formation water into rivers. Currently, almost 50 percent of the associated natural gas is flared (more than 60 million cubic feet per day), even though LPG could be extracted to reduce imports or, together with natural gas, could be used to generate electricity in production areas (box 4.2). The operation of submerged pumps, which increase crude oil extraction, generates a major demand for electricity in the zones of production, a greater proportion of which could be provided through gas-fired thermal generation.

Though private companies have significantly improved their technical production standards and (unlike PetroEcuador) reinject formation water, the activity of the entire industry continues to have indirect impacts on the territory and the local populations. These impacts, added to accumulated distrust and the fact that concessions have been granted in protected areas, helps explain the numerous social conflicts. The absence of the state and the lack of a preventive policy have caused social conflicts to evolve, in certain cases, into real security treats. Close to the Colombian border the lack of security is becoming a major challenge to industry operations.

Environmental authorities have serious political, budgetary, technical, and operating limitations. The creation of governmental agencies to address environmental problems is relatively recent, and those agencies have yet to attain sufficient institutional and social influence to play a decisive role in formulating policy and resolving social conflicts. Although Ecuadoran society is increasingly concerned about more reliable environmental operations, the authorities do not have the rules, laws, and funds needed to fulfill their mission. In addition, some companies are playing the role that should be assumed by the government (helping supply education, health care, roads, and so forth). This situation has completely distorted the relationships among the various companies, the peoples inhabiting the region of the hydrocarbon reserves, and the central and subnational governments.

The absence of clearly defined environmental legislation complicates the obtaining of environmental licenses for oil and gas exploration and exploitation. The collective rights section of the Constitution establishes the right of people "to be consulted on plans and programs for exploration and exploitation of nonrenewable resources on their lands that might affect them environmentally or culturally; the right to participate in the benefits of these projects to the extent possible, and receive indemnification for the socioenvironmental damages that these projects occasion upon them." In practice, this constitutional right boils down to haggling over compensation amounts, without any parameter to objectively establish those amounts. Everything is left to the capacity and negotiating strength of the affected communities with the companies. At last report, three companies have their production operations halted. No clear regulation addresses a permanent solution to the conflicts, only isolated actions that skirt the underlying issue: the lack of government attention in these zones.

A clear legal framework on environmental protection that permits the sustainable development of the sector is indispensable, and would best be conceived by consensus of all the stakeholders—indigenous peoples and nationalities, local governments, and the companies. Such a framework could be based on successful experiences in other countries with similar environmental and cultural characteristics. In the region, the

Box 4.2. Reducing Flaring of Associated Gas in Ecuador

In 2002, the World Bank established a public-private initiative called the Global Gas Flaring Reduction (GGFR) partnership to support national efforts to reuse associated gas that is currently flared. The effort promotes effective regulatory frameworks and tackles constraints on gas utilization, particularly in developing countries.

Ecuador has been a member of GGFR since 2003, and in January 2007 it endorsed the Global Voluntary Standard, which provides guidance to both companies and governments on how to achieve flaring and venting reductions. Parties supporting the standard agree to work with GGFR partners to seek solutions to barriers that prevent greater utilization of flared and vented natural gas. In 2003, GGFR commissioned a study on small-scale opportunities for use of flare gas in Ecuador (World Bank 2003). The study highlighted key constraints and assessed the technical and economic feasibility of using flared gas in various applications, ranging from rural electrification and LPG to commercial and industrial uses.

As next steps, to adopt the voluntary standard, the new administration could jointly involve the Ministry of Energy and Mining (MEM), Ministry of the Environment, and PetroEcuador, and use the knowledge and experience of the GGFR initiative to implement the standard, including actions such as the following:

- Establish goals for eliminating flaring and venting from new projects
- Prepare a country implementation plan
- Prepare associated gas recovery plans for existing projects and producers
- Publish figures about flaring and venting volumes through a Web-based data tool developed for GGFR partners (already rolled out in several partner countries)

Significant environmental and economic benefits can be gained by eliminating the vented or flared associated gas in the Oriente fields and by increasing the production of both LPG for domestic markets and dry gas to substitute for imported diesel in electricity generation. Any effort to recover crude oil production in these fields will require additional amounts of electricity, which can be conveniently generated from currently flared natural gas.

Source: World Bank 2004b.

Box 4.3. The Energy, Environment, and Population Program

The Energy, Environment and Population (EAP) program was created to address issues related to the impacts of the hydrocarbon industry and its potential contributions to sustainable development of the Amazon Basin. A process of tripartite dialogues was set up by the *Coordinadora de Organizaciones Indígenas de la Amazonia* (COICA), the *Asociación Regional Petrolera Empresarial Latinoamericana* (ARPEL), and the Latin American Energy Organization (OLADE), representing, respectively, indigenous peoples, industry, and government. The goal of the EAP was to improve the communication and cooperation between the parties at the regional, national, and local levels. Inspired by the International Labour Organisation (ILO) Convention No. 169, six regional tripartite conferences took place from 1999 to 2003. Since then, national workshops of representatives from the three sectors have made contributions toward better consultations, socioenvironmental regulations, and the general improvement of the industry's contribution to the life of indigenous peoples.

In some countries the national dialogues have made important contributions to the understanding and solution of social conflicts. This is the case of Colombia, República Bolivariana de Venezuela, and Peru. Government stability, political leadership, and a serious commitment to enforcing contractual arrangements and obligations that resulted from the dialogues have been important factors in maintaining a social climate in the oil regions necessary for both the industry to operate and the community to launch sustainable projects. After a period of intense social conflict and changes in governments, the parties are again working together to establish the regional EAP program.

Source: http://www.olade.org.ec/.

experience of tripartite dialogues—conducted in a balanced manner and led by government officials committed to solving this problem—has resulted in improvements in the formation of indigenous leaders, a better understanding of problems, and the development of sound consultation and civic participation practices (box 4.3; ESMAP 2002a, 2002b).

II. Principal Aspects of Sector Reform

The proposed sector reform encompasses changes in the institutional framework and in the role of the sector institutions. With regard to PetroEcuador in particular, reforms would change the way subsidies are allocated and rents are distributed and change the policies in place for the mitigation of social and environmental impacts. This section addresses these changes in detail.

Separation of Roles between the Government and PetroEcuador, and Reform of the Sector's Institutional Framework

Ecuador's oil and gas sector has an organizational structure that fails to clearly separate the functions of the state. Sector institutions include the Ministry of Energy and Mines (MEM), which defines policy for the sector, and the National Hydrocarbons Directorate (*Dirección Nacional de Hidrocarburos*—DNH), which applies that policy. Also playing a role is the government-owned company PetroEcuador, which functions as a contractor, regulator, exclusive wholesaler, subsidies administrator, and operator of the most important crude oil reserves. Finally, branch agencies of the Ministry of the Environment and the Ministry of Economy and Finance (MEF) address specific issues.

This poor organizational structure has been overcome in almost all countries of the region. Ecuador, in designing its reforms for the sector, can benefit from the experiences—both good and bad—of the institutions and oil companies in other countries of the region, whose sectors operate with greater efficiency and transparency, attracting the investments they need. The cases of Brazil, Colombia, and Peru, and of the leading companies, can be useful for defining needed institutional changes to the sector. Those changes involve clearer delineation of functions and the creation of a new agency to administer resources and oversee contracts (table 4.5).

Government entities at the top of the institutional framework of the sector would have a regulatory and oversight role, essentially consisting of the following:

- Ensure the supply of hydrocarbons to the local market; develop plans for the exploration and conservation of hydrocarbon reserves (MEM).
- Propose and enforce regulations concerning distribution and marketing (DNH).

Table 4.5. Institutional Structure Proposed for the Oil and Gas Sector

Define policies and regulations for the sector	Ministry of Energy and Mines
Oversee the policy's implementation	National Hydrocarbons Directorate
Administer hydrocarbons resources and promote, sign, and supervise contracts	New agency
Engage in production and commercial operations, directly or through joint ventures	National company
Define environmental policy and ensure its implementation	Ministry of the Environment
Manage prices and subsidies, distribution of revenues, and economic regulations	Ministry of Economy and Finance

Source: Authors.

- Approve downstream activities and regulations for hydrocarbon transportation and storage; carry out expropriation procedures and declarations of national need (DNH).
- Evaluate hydrocarbons potential; publish the Book of Reserves (DNH).
- Set hydrocarbon prices—as long as a price-controls system remains in effect—and, in general, define policy for the sector (MEM-DNH and MEF).

The functions of the proposed new agency can be defined based on examples from neighboring countries such as Brazil, Colombia, or Peru. A new technical body, unaffected by changes in administrations and with financial autonomy, would be in charge of the following:

- Maintain a database and information system.
- Sign contracts with PetroEcuador and with private contractors.
- Promote new blocks once they have the environmental license, and contract only through tender processes.
- Encourage exploration in offshore areas.
- Qualify exploration and production contractors, and supervise the performance of the contracts.
- Facilitate transparency in the collection of revenues, allowing the collecting entities (MEF) to efficiently fulfill their task.

Experiences in other countries (see annex for details) suggest that the agency should be led by a board of directors with no more than five members, most of whom would be qualified representatives of the sector. One member of the MEM would lead this body, but the participation of the MEF is also important. The following are recommended:

- The term for which the members of the board are designated should be one year longer than the presidential term. Any new governmental administration would be allowed to replace only two members during its term in office.
- The agency would be administered by a general manager.
- The number of professionals would not surpass 50, and their functions would be strictly defined.

The agency would help resolve environmental and social problems. The new contracts signed would be in areas that have an environmental license, and would be the result of a tender process, without privileges for private Ecuadoran companies or government-owned companies of other countries. As noted below, training efforts for the sector's entities should be extended to the environmental entities as well.

Looking toward the future, contracts must respond to volatile prices and stricter environmental standards. Given the current complicated tax regime, a new contract model may be required that predominantly taxes excessive earnings and is adapted to the cases of large and small fields and to low and high production costs. The new agency could request that the Congress adopt fiscal terms for new contracts that simplify the existing regime and respond to price volatility, leaving open the option for current contractors to migrate to the new model. The new contract should contemplate the creation of a fund to remedy environmental damages when fields are abandoned.

Reorganization of PetroEcuador: Focus on Investments to Increase Production and Improve Refineries

PetroEcuador could migrate into fulfilling a strictly business mission. Its accounting would no longer serve for managing subsidies; the numerous receivables from other government entities in deficit would be eliminated, and as any private operator, it would be obligated to fully comply with technical and environmental standards. Given the complexity of the proposed changes outlined below, it would be necessary to prepare a business reform plan, with the help of consultants, based on audits of reserves, operations, finances, and environmental considerations. The plan would include indicators and partial goals. Among other aspects, the plan would take into account the new economic reality in which the operations would be taking place, the selection of priority projects, relations of PetroEcuador with the MEM and other governmental entities, organizational and administrative aspects, and a projection of the cash flow over the next five years and for the long term. Efforts to reorganize PetroEcuador would benefit from the experiences of other major national and international oil companies (box 4.4).

Upstream

Investments to improve future, or upstream, conditions include the following:

- PetroEcuador, in contracts with the new agency, would keep the areas it is capable of operating, in particular the mature fields of the northeast, and would allow the rest of the areas to revert to the state. PetroEcuador would compete with other companies to bid in tender processes for new areas.
- The development of the reserves of the Ishpingo-Tambococha-Tiputini (ITT) field would be subject to an open, competitive bidding process. The process would have a high priority to ensure longer-term revenues. The role of PetroEcuador in this process needs to be clarified.
- PetroEcuador should have a certified audit of reserves, making it possible to valuate the company and allowing it access to credit.
- In its contracts, PetroEcuador would have to obtain the necessary funds to remedy environmental liabilities, improve installations, and, in general, efficiently operate the company.

A sound reform could turn around the decline in production, increasing the current level of 530,000 bpd to nearly 750,000 bpd in the next five years (figure 4.1).

Box 4.4. Efficient State Oil Companies

Throughout the past two decades, economic liberalization, market reforms, and corporatization have characterized the oil and gas industry worldwide. National oil companies (NOCs) have emerged as hybrid firms, controlling a majority of the remaining proven resources. In terms of world production, however, only six of the top firms are NOCs, whereas international oil companies (IOCs) represent among the largest producers worldwide and appear to be achieving a dramatically higher return on capital than NOCs of similar size and operations.

NOCs are in the process of reevaluating and changing business strategies, with substantial consequences for international oil and gas markets and for their respective local economies. It is a time of great change inside the leadership of these companies, and goals and priorities will be different from those of the international major companies, with potentially serious consequences for market stability and oil geopolitics. Established IOCs as well as newcomers (from China, India, Republic of Korea, and others) are interested in strengthening ties with emerging NOCs to diversify their operations, access resources, and enhance supply security. Depending on the rules in place, strategic alliances have been difficult to form.

In Latin America, the renewal and new importance of NOCs in certain countries have been accompanied by a strong nationalistic appeal. However, sustainable longer-term results will be driven by the NOCs' economic results and, more important, their contribution to the national economy. The search for efficiency has become the new NOC paradigm. Governments and communities will not accept heavier financial deficits or a loss of national rents, nor will they support poor environmental performance.

An examination of the conditions under which efficiency could be achieved points to (i) sound technical management, (ii) an institutional framework restricting political interference, (iii) accountability and transparency, and (iv) respect for technical, environmental, and economic regulations equal to those applied by private companies. The successful modernization of certain companies in the region (Petrobras, Ecopetrol) has been accompanied by higher autonomy and private participation. The issuing of a package of shares on local and international stock markets is bringing a healthy investor scrutiny of the operations of these companies.

Figure 4.1. Production

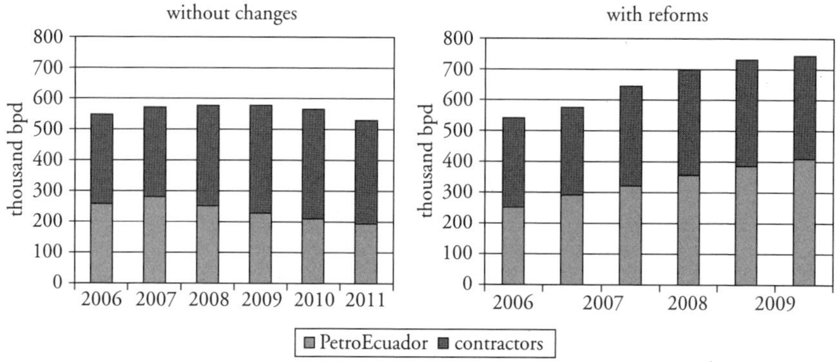

Source: Author's estimate.

Most of the increase will have to come from PetroEcuador, which now controls up to 80 percent of proven reserves. The production by private contractors would be essentially maintained, based on new investments that would prevent a decline in the current fields. PetroEcuador, in the case it receives the required funding and operates with the appropriate procurement regulations, could invest in highly profitable work-overs of older wells and on delayed projects to rapidly improve its production.

Downstream

The reforms needed in the downstream sector also require a certain period of time. Given the difficulty of establishing competitive conditions in the short term, Petro-Ecuador will likely continue being the exclusive entity in charge of the country's supply of petroleum products. It is therefore important that the government facilitate financing to PetroEcuador to modernize refining activities and facilities for transportation, storage, and dispatching of products. Whereas upstream financing will accompany the contracts PetroEcuador will sign over for areas with proven reserves, for the downstream more direct financing instruments are needed.

At the same time, to the extent that PetroEcuador gains corporate independence, the government must introduce standards for improving fuel quality by performing environmental audits and establishing programs for environmental remediation and adaptation.

The growing importation of LPG, gasoline, and diesel, and the need to improve fuel quality, make new downstream investments essential. To accomplish this, this note suggests the following:

- Eliminate restrictions on refining that affect private companies.
- Study the modernization of the refinery of Esmeraldas, financed by Petro-Ecuador, principally to supply the domestic market.

- Consider replacing the old units at the refinery of La Libertad with a new refinery, preferably financed by a private company, with approval for exports.

To cover demand and to reverse decapitalization, investments can be sought to modernize and expand the pipeline system and product storage terminals. These installations—which constitute natural monopolies—should be open to third persons in nondiscriminatory conditions that are based on regulated fees and operations. In the first stage, PetroEcuador will have to assume the initial investments to modernize infrastructures, but later the fees of the operators would provide funding to recover the current investments and future ones, depending on the market growth. As reforms progress, the margins of the end distributors, together with wholesale rates and prices, could be deregulated.

Elimination of Fuel Subsidies and Focalization of New Subsidies in Favor of the Poor

An essential condition for the success of the proposed reforms is that subsidies would no longer be administered by PetroEcuador, but rather be managed through a separate account of the MEF. That would make it possible to study and implement policies for the elimination of blanket subsidies or for their conversion into direct, targeted subsidies. Clearly, the treatment of subsidies calls for decisions with a heavy political content. The current subsidies provide incentives that support contraband and wasteful use of fuels. Furthermore, as noted in previous chapters, their greatest beneficiaries are the middle and upper classes. Since the subsidies drastically deplete the national budget, they are detrimental to the poorer classes, who depend upon publicly funded social services (education, health, and so forth).

Proper targeting of subsidies would have a major impact on increasing fiscal resources for antipoverty programs, reducing contraband, and eliminating opportunities for corruption.

- *LPG subsidies*—These subsidies would be targeted by raising the price of LPG until it covers both the real cost of a cylinder of gas and the cost of increasing the Human Development Bond (Bono de Desarrollo Humano—BDH) cash subsidy program to cover the new LPG price and its impact on inflation, as other fuel subsidies are also to be eliminated. The list of beneficiaries of the BDH should be revised to incorporate rural populations and its increase tied to an extension of education and health services. Transparent accounting and information are key actions to making the measure a success.
- *Gasoline and diesel subsidies*—These subsidies would be eliminated. An exception would be made for certain consumers who would have a temporary right to obtain a direct reimbursements based on their level of activity (such as electricity generators and cargo and passenger transportation companies).

LPG distribution activities should be formalized through enrollment of the companies involved, the registration of volumes, and the respective accounting. But that would not be sufficient to eliminate wasteful consumption and contraband. Given the current level of incentives, experience shows that control measures will not significantly reduce wasteful consumption. The government would start an aggressive information campaign even before the price changes are introduced, similar to the one undertaken in Indonesia prior to removing its fuel subsidies. A vital step in generating popular support would be giving the public information on the highly regressive nature of existing subsidies, the exact mechanism by which the new price will be estimated, and the social uses for the new fiscal resources. This could include posting on a Web site the calculation of the new BDH, the new price of the LPG, and the estimated amount and use made of the remaining funds once subsidies are phased out.

One possible step toward removing subsidies would be to make them transparent and include them in the budget approval. If they become part of the budget accounts, the executive and the Congress would have to approve the amounts allocated to subsidies rather than to social infrastructure and investments.

Over time, it should be the market that sets prices, not the government, which does not control the key variables of price. One of the reform objectives is to create these recommended conditions as soon as possible, so that fuel prices will no longer be controlled. As part of the economic regulations, retailers would become accustomed to regularly reporting their prices; the government would be limited to supervising the market and to enforcing rules to prevent monopolistic abuses.

Targeting subsidies would decelerate the growth in demand. The elimination of subsidies would appear in the statistics as a temporary fall in consumption, followed by growth at a slower pace. Projections for this note assume an initial decrease of 10 percent, followed by growth at an average rate of 3 percent, rather than the current 5 percent (figure 4.2). The rise in prices would force consumers to improve efficiency and energy conservation. Such programs are impractical in Ecuador today, as there is no incentive to conserve fuels at current subsidized prices.

Increased Oil and Gas Revenues through Reform and Improved Revenue Use

Failing to change the sector's institutional framework and costly subsidies will result in a decline of the sector's contribution to the economy. The balance of payments would be the first to suffer following a fall in production and growing imports of refined products. An evaluation of the balance of payments in the sector and of the sector's contribution to the economy explored three scenarios (see figures 4.3 and 4.4): no change (Case A), targeting of subsidies, but no reform to sector institutions or PetroEcuador (Case B), and reforms plus changing of the subsidies framework (Case C). Three assumptions were used to compare the scenarios: that prices remain at approximately US$50/bbl over the next five years, that margins and prices on fuels are consistent with this, and that the tax situation for the oil and gas sector does

Figure 4.2. Consumption of Petroleum Products

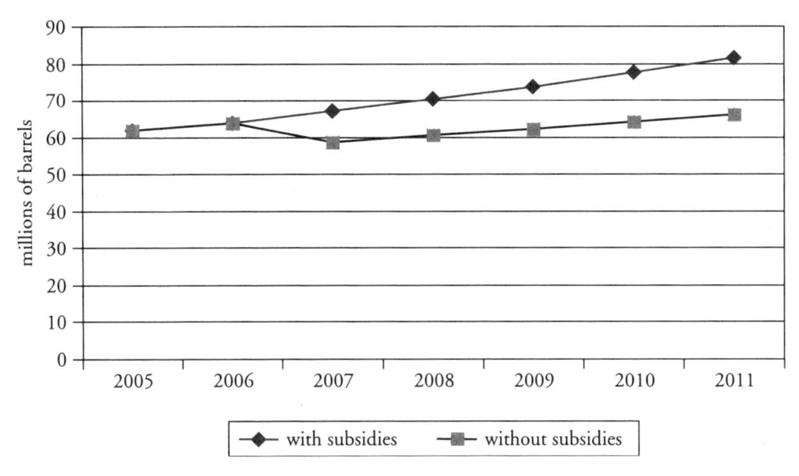

Source: Authors' estimates.

Figure 4.3. Balance of Trade, Oil and Gas Sector

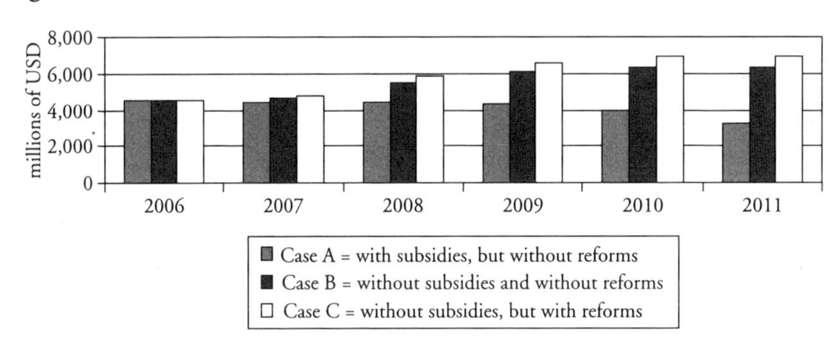

Source: Model for the sector developed by authors.

Figure 4.4. Sector's Contribution to Public Revenues

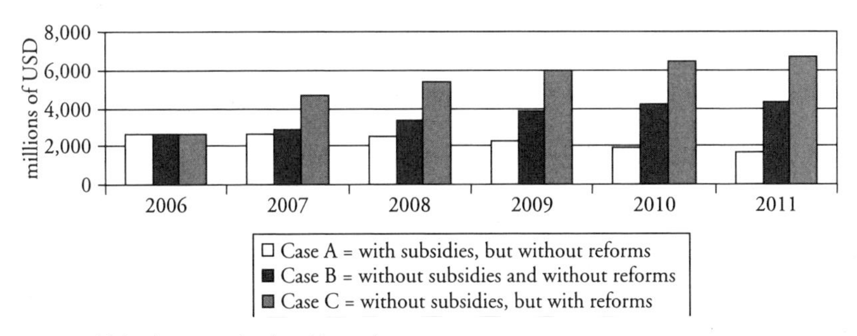

Source: Model for the sector developed by authors.

not change. In the results, reforms to the sector and the targeting subsidies (Case C) offer the possibility of almost tripling the sector's contribution to public revenues over the next five years. Increased exports of crude oil as well as decreased imports and contraband would stop the sector's balance of trade from diminishing, and would allow the trade surplus to nearly double.

The above model assumes that oil prices stay at the relatively high and stable level of US$50/bbl in the coming years. The reforms would be much more difficult if prices fell even modestly from these levels (box 4.5).

In the context of the proposed reforms, with PetroEcuador's role redefined, distribution of the increased revenues generated by the sector must be made more transparent, both by the government and by private companies. The use of extraordinary revenues derived from hydrocarbons is a critical issue in most oil producing countries. In the past, as with many other resource-producing countries, Ecuador has used various funds as a way to ensure that windfall profits are not wasted and to limit the pro-cyclical impact of these profits on the economy. As with many other countries

Box 4.5. Sensitivity Analysis: The Impact of Lower Oil Prices

An alternative set of projections of the sector trade balance and its contribution to the economy has been prepared using an average price for the reference crude oil WTI (West Texas Intermediate) of US$37.50/bbl instead of US$50.00/bbl. Under the scenario of no reform to the sector or subsidies (Case A), the trade balance would drop significantly.

Trade balance	*2006*	*2008*		*2011*	
Reference price for the WTI crude (US$/bbl)	*+60.00*	*50.00*	*37.50*	*50.00*	*37.50*
Case C (reforms), US$ million		5,908	3,858	6,976	4,561
Case A (no reforms), US$ million	4,586	4,459	2,696	3,282	1,808

At the same time, the fiscal contribution of the sector under a lower price projection would fall marginally if reforms were undertaken (Case C) but would drop precipitously if no reforms occurred (Case A), to only US$1.05 billion a year. Such a contribution, less than half of the current one, would induce a drastic cut of government expenses, with political and social implications.

Million US$	*2006*	*2008*		*2011*	
Reference price for the WTI crude (US$/bbl)	*+60.00*	*50.00*	*37.50*	*50.00*	*37.50*
Case C (reforms), US$ million		5,429	4,274	6,650	5,145
Case A (no reforms), US$ million	2,596	2,528	1,660	1,617	1,053

that also face a volatile political context and a weak governance environment, the rules governing use of oil funds have been frequently changed for political reasons, and the destination of these resources has not been transparent. In such a context, the first and best use for extraordinary oil revenues would be to pay down public debt. This policy has a number of important virtues:

- Resources are not misspent through inefficiencies, for political reasons, or because of corruption.
- The economy is sterilized from the inflationary impact of pro-cyclical oil revenue inflows.
- The public debt burden is reduced, lowering country risk, improving overall macroeconomic stability, reducing debt service payments, and clearing space for future borrowing during more difficult economic times.

Should the decision be made that a fund of some type is the best way for Ecuador to manage windfall hydrocarbon profits, a number of changes should be made to the current management of funds. First, and most importantly, the CEREPS should have specific, clear, and objective criteria for allocating resources. The current rules allow too much discretion, which opens the door for political influence and allocations made for political reasons, rather than for the best interests of the entire populace. Second, it would be best to limit the very high number of recipients of fund resources, many of whom would be better served with more reliable, steady allocations out of the annual budget to allow for long-term planning. And third, the income and allocations by the CEREPS, the Petroleum Stabilization Fund (FEP), and FEISEH should be absolutely transparent, with figures published regularly on the Web and available to all. International experience has shown (for example, in Canada, Chile, and Norway) that natural resource funds work best with simple, clear, and open rules for their management (ESMAP 2006).

Regarding the Eco-Development Institute of the Ecuadoran Amazon (*Instituto Ecodesarrollo de la Región Amazónica*—ECORAE), management should also be made more transparent, as well as the benefits currently being allocated to the subnational governments. The idea is not to reduce amounts, but to ensure their rational use:

- The distribution of earnings should be based on revenues generated by operations in the region, priority investment needs, and verification of the administrative capacity of the executing agencies.
- The appropriation and application of benefits should be made within the budget and be based on criteria of efficiency and social development.
- The rights of communities directly affected by the operations to participate in the earnings must be borne in mind.

In the effort to create transparency in the management of oil and gas earnings, the private sector and civil society should become involved. The World Bank has

Box 4.6. Criteria of the Extractive Industries Transparency Initiative

- An independent review of payments made to governments by oil, gas, and mining companies and revenues received by governments from those companies. This review would be made by an institution that enjoys an unblemished reputation and unquestioned independence. Depending on the specific conditions of each country, this institution could be an auditing firm, although that would not be necessary in all cases.
- Reader-friendly publication of payments made by companies and of revenues received by governments from those companies, as well as the accounts of regional governments and the civil society institutions involved.
- Extension of transparency concepts to all companies, including any government-owned oil or gas company.
- Active involvement by civil society in the design, monitoring, and public discussion of the implementation process.
- Commitment to work within the plan and the agreed upon implementation time frames.

Source: http://www.eitransparency.org.

been assisting some 25 countries in the design and implementation of the Extractive Industries Transparency Initiative (EITI; box 4.6). With a focus on publicly disclosing earnings generated by the sector, the EITI is facilitating complex communication processes among stakeholders in several countries. Ecuador can benefit from this experience.

Social and Environmental Issues

The oil and gas industry has a poor relationship with civil society, and in particular with indigenous communities, who denounce environmental damage and the lack of respect for their rights. The social and environmental situation is quite serious, as described in the previous section. The government can begin to recover credibility in the eyes of the population regarding oil and gas production by offering the following:

- Clearly define functions of governmental entities, coordination procedures, and budgets of government entities responsible for environmental management.
- Create definitive solutions to the problem of environmental liabilities.

- Work in consensus with the parties involved in reviewing environmental regulations.
- Agree on a law addressing issues of consultation, compensation, and benefit-sharing with peoples living in the areas surrounding the industry's operations.
- Introduce standards for the abandonment of installations.
- Require technological improvements and eliminate emissions of gas (following the Global Gas Flaring Reduction project guidelines), and improper disposal of formation water.
- Develop environmental management action plans (EMAPs) that are realistic for the current operations.
- Resolve the case of operations already in existence in protected areas, such as Block 18 and Tarapoa, through compensations, and define a particular framework for the exploitation of the Ishpingo Tambococha Tiputini (ITT) field.
- Establish the consensus needed to enact a new law and regulations for full compliance with ILO Convention 169.
- Create mechanisms to inform and ensure the participation of representatives of communities and civil society.

Until new policies and necessary capacities are developed, the government should not award any contracts—whether to PetroEcuador or to private companies—outside the traditional areas of operation. In relation to territorial rezoning, the assignment and use of areas must be defined, separating between those of current contractors and those of PetroEcuador; protected areas that will remain untouchable in the coming years; and areas available for exploration, subject to an environmental license and prior consultation, if they overlap indigenous community lands.

III. Final Recommendations

Many of the proposed reforms discussed in this note have been studied in the past and have been successfully implemented in other countries. The proposed policy changes are not new and do not involve resources that would cause financing problems. Nonetheless, reforms of this scope will unquestionably need strong political support. The administration would be advised to appoint a high-level commission that will finalize the reforms' conception and direct their implementation. In order to efficiently fulfill that task, a calendar and reform plan would be needed, setting forth the reforms' stages, intermediate and final goals, and the necessary funds.

All changes come up against a certain social inertia, distrust of the government, and stakeholders who need an explanation to acknowledge the benefits of change. Without information being given to all interested parties, without transparency and a search for consensus, reforms cannot advance. The team in charge of the project must make a decided effort to thoroughly explain the reforms to the population.

Among other tools, the legal changes must be incorporated into a single codified legal text, accompanied by the essential regulations for their application. A suggested order in which the reforms could take place follows:

Initial measures

- Replace existing subsidies with direct subsidies administered by the MEF.
- Announce the new institutional framework, explaining the new vision of PetroEcuador and the goal of attracting more upstream and downstream investors.
- Call on the parties involved to reach a consensus on the new treatment of environmental and social impacts.
- Form a team with professionals of acknowledged competence and honesty who are thoroughly familiar with the proposed measures and are able to explain them.

First year

- Change the law on the sector and the law on environmental management; prepare model contract(s) and review fiscal terms.
- Create a new agency to administer resources and contracts.
- Implement measures to ensure transparency in the collection and distribution of earnings.
- Contract studies on refining, EMAPs, and the reengineering of PetroEcuador.

Second year

- Sign new contracts between the new agency and private companies, and between the agency and PetroEcuador.
- Introduce new environmental regulations.
- Contract the modernization of the Esmeraldas Refinery.
- Implement the reengineering of PetroEcuador.
- Prepare new bidding competition rounds, including for the ITT field.

Third year

- Advance in the remediation of environmental liabilities.
- Evaluate the new institutional framework, and adjust as needed.
- Hold new bidding competition rounds.
- Deregulate the downstream and marketing sectors.

Matrix of Policy Options

	Problem	Options and recommendations
Issue		
Institutional, regulatory, and contractual framework	Insufficient separation of responsibilities between the entities of the sector and the government-owned company.	Establish a team to take charge of the reform, and provide it with a plan and with adequate resources. Review laws and regulations. Create a new contracting agency.
	Shortage of public and private investment. Lack of an institutional and contractual framework and of legal stability to attract investments.	Review the model contract for exploration and production, bearing in mind the volatility of prices, productivity, and conditions that are determinant for operations. Offer private contractors incentives for migration to the new model or renegotiate contracts.
	Problems in applying social and environmental standards.	Work with interested parties to achieve a consensus that makes it possible to review environmental regulations as a substantial part of the reform. Budget sufficient resources for the competent entities. Prepare EMAPs for all operations, with independent experts.
Proposed measure		
Organization of PetroEcuador	Current crisis, poor reputation, poorly maintained installations, and accumulated accounts receivable.	Reengineer PetroEcuador based on a plan with precise goals. Develop a public information campaign on the reform's proposed changes and objectives, and on the future of PetroEcuador, to improve the company's image.
	Lack of investment capacity.	Define key activities and evaluate the company's capacity and investment priorities. Sign upstream contracts. Define the type of financial support for downstream projects.

(*Table continues on the following page.*)

	Problem	Options and recommendations
	Environmental past liabilities of mature fields.	Limit areas assigned to PetroEcuador to those for which PetroEcuador has the technical capacity and where the contracts would give it economic capacity. Attach to this the remediation of past liabilities. Define the bidding competition for the ITT field. Introduce clauses into the contracts regarding the proper manner for abandoning fields.
	Refineries with insufficient capacity that produce low-quality products, forcing imports to increase.	Authorize PetroEcuador to design and execute the modernization project for the Esmeraldas Refinery. Prepare the bidding competition for the construction of a new refinery to replace the La Libertad refinery.
Transparency in the management of the sector's accounts	Preallocations that do not come under budget controls. Lack of accountability and information on the use of revenues and the functioning of the FEP and the FEISEH.	Adhere to the EITI, creating a platform of dialogue among the parties and reporting on revenues and transfers to the population. Make the necessary regulatory changes.
	Transfers to subnational governments and ECORAE without a sustainable vision or a system to control expenditures.	Create mechanisms for preparation of projects, transparent management of accounts, and systematic accountability of results.
Social and environmental problems	Lack of a competent authority with sufficient funds. The state only appears when conflicts arise, raising security issues for certain operations.	Review laws and regulations with a view to clearly defining functions of governmental entities, coordinating procedures, and ensuring sufficient budgets of government entities responsible for environmental management.

	PetroEcuador does not have funds, its infrastructure is functioning with a high environmental risk in zones with a compromised environmental past. Associated gas is being flared and formation water is being dumped into rivers.	Sign the Global Initiative on Natural Gas Flaring Reduction. Prepare a plan of action to prohibit dumping of formation water within a certain period. Provide the funding to PetroEcuador to meet the standards. Develop participatory environmental monitoring schemes.
	Operations in protected areas and deficient territorial zoning.	Redefine the areas of oil and gas operations. Have the new contracting agency head up strategic regional environmental studies and consultations prior to opening new areas to tender processes.
	Poor relationship with indigenous communities and a high level of mutual distrust.	Create conditions for constructive dialogue with the interested parties. Better manage revenues, with allocations to indigenous communities based on effective local development plans.
Convert the indiscriminate subsidies into direct subsidies that only benefit the poor.	One-quarter of the budget earmarked to cover the cost of the subsidy. Contraband of LPG, diesel, and gasoline reported to amount to US$700 million. Problems associated with corruption.	Increase the social bond to cover the additional cost of a cylinder of LPG, plus additional funds that make it possible to bear potential price increases on liquid fuels. Open downstream activities (refineries and wholesale transportation and marketing installations) to private companies in order to create competitive conditions and withdraw the government from the task of setting prices.

Annex. International Experiences with Contracting Agencies and Tax Regimes

	Agency for the Valuation of Hydrocarbon Resources (ALNAFT), of Algeria	*National Petroleum Agency, of Brazil*	*National Hydrocarbons Agency, of Colombia*	*Perupetro, of Peru*
Law creating the agency	Law No. 05-07, of April 28, 2005	Law 9478, of August 6, 1997	Law 1760, of June 28, 2003	Law 26221, of August 20, 1993, and Law 26225, of August 24, 1993
Legal structure	Publicly administered legal entity	Publicly administered legal entity	Publicly administered legal entity	Privately administered legal entity
Corporate governance	A board of directors consisting of a president and five directors, designated by presidential decree based on the proposal of the Ministry of Hydrocarbons. Decisions are adopted by a simple majority.	Self-sufficient entity, administered by a managing director and four directors-at-large, nominated by the president and approved by the Senate. The period for which they are designated is four years.	Administrative unit under the MEM with administrative and financial autonomy, administered by a board of directors composed of a managing director and five members: the minister of energy and mines, who presides over the board, the minister of the treasury, the director of the department of planning, and two representatives of the president.	Private corporation, governed by a shareholders board with three members, appointed by the MEM. Perupetro is administered by a board of directors with five members: three representing the MEM (one of whom is its president) and two representing the MEF.
Funding	Has its own capital and financial autonomy. Its funds consist of 0.5 percent of the taxes established in each contract, as well as revenues produced by its own activities.	Income regulated by the budget, including transfers from the budget, special credits, and bonds for the signing of the contracts; revenues derived from pacts, agreements, and contracts; donations,	Has its own capital comprising technical information revenues, contractually established fees, property assigned to it by the state, and the contributions allocated to it under the budget.	Budget approved by the MEM, for which 1.5 percent is earned from contractually set royalties and from interest on amounts received.

		bequests, and subsidies; and the product of fees, fines, and penalties, pursuant to law.		
Common objectives and particular objectives *Common objectives:* – Promote investments in exploration and production. – Qualify interested investors. – Engage in contracting procedures (direct, tender, or bidding competition). – Negotiate and enter into exploration and production contracts. – Approve modifications of exploration and production contracts. – Supervise the performance of the contracts. – Collect, develop, administer, and disseminate technical information received from investors. – Create a data bank and place it in operation.	Authorize prospecting. Collect taxes and turn them over to the Treasury. Cooperate with national industry and promote research and development. Collaborate on the policy for the sector. Grant SONATRACH preference rights in case of transfer of interests or of the contract. Authorize joint operations. Authorize anticipated production. Limit production volumes. Periodically establish the reference price of natural gas. Oversee the supply of hydrocarbons for the local market. Develop 10-year plans for all the reserves in keeping with the needs of the local market. Establish the volume of gas available for exportation.	Promote regulation. Implement policy for the sector. Regulate and approve geology and geophysical services. Approve downstream activities, including hydrocarbon imports and exports. Establish criteria for calculating transportation fees. Oversee exploration and production activities. Carry out expropriation procedures and public usage declarations. Stimulate research and development. Annually consolidate information on reserves. Specify hydrocarbons quality standards. Regulate biodiesel activity. Administer rights over hydrocarbons.	Evaluate hydrocarbon potential. Collect royalties and monetary compensation; hold them and remit them to the corresponding entities. Set production volumes and hydrocarbon prices for local refineries and petrochemical plants. Approve technical and economic studies. Help define the hydrocarbons policy. Perform other activities established by law.	Hold royalties, in kind, in the event that the contractor fails to pay them in a timely fashion.

(Table continues on the following page.)

	Agency for the Valuation of Hydrocarbon Resources (ALNAFT), of Algeria	*National Petroleum Agency, of Brazil*	*National Hydrocarbons Agency, of Colombia*	*Perupetro, of Peru*
Contracting processes and models	The contracting takes place following a tender process.	The contracts are entered into following a bidding competition.	Both contracting through a tender process or bidding competition and direct contracting.	Both contracting through a tender process or bidding competition and direct contracting.
Tax regime	**Royalty**, based on systems defined in the law for the sector. The agency turns the royalties over to the treasury. Annual payment of **surface rights**, in accordance with the table that appears in that same law. **Transfers** of an investor's participation in a contract, in whole or in part, taxed at 1 percent of the transaction price. Tax on **authorizations for natural gas flaring**, and for the use of potable water. **Income tax**, called supplementary tax, as established in each contract.	**Bond**, for submission of proposals in the bidding competition, paid at the signing of the contract. **Royalties** of 10 percent, to be paid monthly on the volume of production as of the start of production of each field. This royalty may be reduced to 5 percent, based on the characteristics of the area. **Special participation**, to be established by presidential decree, for large fields. **Payment for occupation** or withholding of areas.	**Royalties** of up to 25 percent of production, based on average daily production. **Participation by ECOPETROL**, in joint production contracts, according to factor R (ratio of accrued revenues to accrued expenditures). **Income tax** **Tax on transportation** for use of the pipelines. **Social support** contribution, whose amount is established at the time of the environmental impact study (EIS).	**Royalties**, whose percentage is determined as a function of the ratio of accrued revenues to accrued expenditures (factor R), or based on accrued production. **Income tax**, according to the general tax regime. **Training** contribution. Agreements for **social support** to local communities.

Bibliography

ESMAP (Energy Sector Management Assistance Program). 2002a. "Ecuador—Programa de Entrenamiento a representantes de Nacionalidades Amazónicas en temas hidrocarburíferos." Technical Paper 25. ESMAP, World Bank, Washington, DC.

———. 2002b. "Population, Energy and Environmental Program: An Initiative for Understanding and Sustainable Development in the Amazon Region." Technical Paper 20 (27, Spanish). ESMAP, World Bank, Washington, DC.

———. 2005. "Estudio comparativo de la distribución de la renta petrolera en Bolivia, Colombia, Ecuador y Perú." ESMAP, World Bank, Washington, DC.

———. 2006. "Experiences with Oil Funds: Institutional and Financial Aspects." Report 321/06.

World Bank. 2004a. "Ecuador Poverty Assessment." Report 27061-EC. World Bank, Washington, DC.

World Bank. 2004b. "Flared Gas Utilization Strategy: Opportunities for Small-Scale Uses of Gas." Report 5. World Bank, Washington, DC. http://www.worldbank.org/ggfr (under Publications).

5

Economic Growth through Improved Competitiveness and an Enhanced Investment Climate

Mike Goldberg, Juan Carlos Mendoza, José Guilherme Reis, and Eric Palladini

Executive Summary

Economic growth is critical to creating jobs, relieving poverty, and improving Ecuador's living standards. During the past 25 years, Ecuador's economic growth has been stagnant, while almost every other country in Latin America has experienced gradual growth. Although the economy grew at an average annual rate of 5.2 percent between 2000 and 2005, much of this growth was based on high oil prices and increased remittances from workers abroad. Further economic diversification is essential to generate stronger growth in the long term and reduce vulnerabilities to shocks. Promoting diversification requires policy changes to improve the business climate, facilitate the expansion of credit, and take advantage of opportunities offered by international trade.

This policy note reviews the current situation from the perspective of the business and investment climate, the small and medium enterprise (SME) sector, the informal sector, rural sector competitiveness, and the financial sector. On the basis of this analysis, the note provides recommendations to address these issues. A top priority should be to lower the costs of doing business in Ecuador to promote the growth of formal sector employment, particularly in SMEs, including reforming the drawback system and considering changes in the tax regime. To promote exports, programs should be developed to promote quality, certification, and technological changes—such as efficient competitive matching grants mechanisms. Labor market and regulatory improvements are extremely important to the competitiveness of firms, including a government-supported market-oriented mechanism to enable greater labor mobility as sectors change as a result of international trade.

To strengthen the financial sector, key recommendations include supporting the development of capital markets, contractual savings, and the insurance, pension, and retirement systems. Moreover, public intervention in microfinance and rural microfinance should focus on subsidizing information and innovation and addressing risk. Finally, the

Superintendency of Banks and Insurance (Superintendencia de Bancos y Seguros—SBS) should develop capital rules for investments in mortgage-backed investments, and the Ecuadorian Social Security Institute (Instituto Ecuatoriano de Seguridad Social—IESS) should support the mortgage market through long-term funding, but not lend funds directly to its members or at below-market interest rates.

I. Introduction

Ecuador's recent economic growth performance has been disappointing. During the past 25 years, economic growth has been stagnant, while almost every other country in Latin America has experienced gradual growth. Although the economy grew at an average annual rate of 5.2 percent between 2000 and 2005, much of this growth was based on high oil prices and increased remittances from workers abroad. Employment growth has been minimal, with underemployment rising from 43 percent at end-2004 to 50 percent by mid-2006, and with unemployment expected to grow from an estimated 10 percent in 2006 to 12 percent by 2008. Considering the country's heavy dependence on capital-intensive commodity exports, this is no surprise. Economic diversification is essential to generate the jobs that Ecuador needs to reduce poverty and create opportunities, as well as to reduce the vulnerability to shocks.

Low productivity growth is a key underlying cause of this poor economic performance. As the World Bank's *Ecuador Development Policy Review* (2004b) states, "Economic stagnation has been caused by low productivity of investment in physical and human (especially secondary and tertiary) capital. Among LAC countries Ecuador has had some of the lowest growth in total factor productivity." This productivity roadblock is caused by a number of factors that can be improved through policy changes, including start-up and operation of a business, facilitation of exports, contract security, credit expansion, and the overall governance environment.

The next section reviews Ecuador's performance in key areas of competitiveness, revealing several areas where the country lags behind competitors. The second section provides a detailed assessment of the financial sector, including banks, finance companies, microfinance institutions and the products that have not yet been developed in the country. The financial sector's recent past and potential to contribute to improved competitiveness merit special attention. The final section is devoted to recommendations and presents a matrix of policies and activities that would improve the country's competitiveness in the short and medium term.

II. Competitiveness Challenges

Business and Investment Climate

Ecuador's business and investment climate is weak and has shown few signs of improvement in recent years. In the Doing Business 2007 rankings, Ecuador

Table 5.1. Changes in Competitiveness Rank, 2005–06

Ease of...	*2006 rank*	*2005 rank*	*Change in rank*
Doing business	123	120	–3
Starting a business	139	139	0
Dealing with licenses	60	61	+1
Employing workers	161	162	+1
Registering property	84	106	+22
Getting credit	65	59	–6
Protecting investors	135	133	–2
Paying taxes	53	52	–1
Trading across borders	126	124	–2
Enforcing contracts	96	91	–5
Closing a business	134	127	–7

Source: Doing Business 2006, and WB and IFC (2007).

ranked 123 out of 175 countries in the sample, down from 120 in the previous year (table 5.1). This makes the country the fourth worst in the region, after Venezuela (164), Haiti (139), and Bolivia (131). Ecuador lags far behind regional leaders such as Chile (29), Peru (65), El Salvador (71), Colombia (79), and Panama (81). Despite the urgent need to improve the business climate, the country has not made reforms in any of 10 principal areas tracked by the Doing Business database.[1] Registering property was the only area in which Ecuador improved significantly in 2006, moving from 106 to 84 in the international ranking. However, this ranking compares with very poor performances in employing workers (161 of 175 in the sample), starting a business (139), closing a business (134), protecting investors (135), and trading across borders (126).

Ecuador also performed poorly in other international competitiveness rankings. Del Ecuador ranked 107 in the Business Competitiveness Index, in a sample of 116 countries. The only countries in the region with lower ratings are Paraguay (114), Bolivia (113), and Guyana (110). Regional competitors are ranked significantly higher, including Peru (81), Uruguay (70), and Mexico (60). Of 100 countries ranked by Fitch Ratings as of September 2006 for sovereign default risk, Ecuador was classified as a B– with a negative outlook, sharing this negative combination of rankings with only Bolivia. Similarly, Standard & Poor's rates Ecuador as a high-risk country, assigning it a CCC+ rating (among the lowest). These low ratings strongly affect investor decisions.

Firms confirm these poor assessments, based on results of the Investment Climate Assessment for Ecuador (World Bank 2005), which included interviews with 451 manufacturing firms in the provinces of Manabi, Guayas, Pichincha, and Tungurahua. When asked to rank the biggest barriers to growth, the firms identified the top four binding constraints as policy uncertainty, cost of financing, macroeconomic instability, and corruption (table 5.2).

Table 5.2. Constraints to Doing Business in Ecuador

Constraint	*Companies citing constraint (%)*
Policy uncertainty	61
Cost of financing	56
Macroeconomic instability	54
Corruption	49
Anticompetitive and informal practices	47
Access to financing	43
Tax rates	38

Source: World Bank (2005).
Note: Constraints listed were identified by more than 30 percent of firms.

Table 5.3. Cost and Difficulty of Starting a Business
(% of gross national income GNI)

Indicator	*Ecuador*	*Colombia*	*Peru*	*Bolivia*	*Chile*	*Region*	*OECD*
Procedures (number)	14	13	10	15	9	10.2	6.2
Time (days)	65	44	72	50	27	73.3	16.6
Cost (% of income per capita)	31.8	19.8	32.5	140	9.8	48.1	5.3
Minimum capital requirement	7.7	0	0	3.8	0	18.1	36.1

Source: World Bank and IFC (2007).

Starting a Business

Starting a business in Ecuador requires more procedures than the regional average, but it takes less time, has lower costs, and requires less minimum capital than the regional average (table 5.3). The low cost of entry may explain, in part, why the size of the informal sector in Ecuador is reported to be below the regional average and only half the size of the informal sector in Bolivia, where the costs of establishing a business are exorbitant. However, the informal sector is growing, both in size and economic importance.

Ecuador's informal sector was responsible for about 37 percent of the country's gross national product (GNP) in 2002, placing it seventh of 17 Latin American countries (Schneider 2002). The trend shows moderate growth in informal-sector participation in the GNP, from 34.4 percent in 2000, a jump of 2.3 percentage points in only two years. In addition, the gap between informal and formal sector income was high. Data from 2000 show the informal sector per capita GNP was only US$416, compared with an overall GNP estimate of US$1,210 (Atlas method).

The steady growth of the informal sector has high social and economic costs. Numerous studies have shown that a large informal sector can limit the productivity gains in an economy. In other countries in the region, the informal sector causes distortions and lowers overall productivity. More than 30 percent of GDP and 70 percent of the labor force are typically involved in informal activities. The high economic and social costs include (i) a lack of labor protection (social security, severance pay, minimum wage, and appropriate working conditions); (ii) a lack of vocational training; (iii) product informality (affecting the quality of water quality, food inspections, and medicines); and (iv) a lack of access to credit, due to property registration imperfections and costs (Palmade 2005; Schneider and Klinglmair 2004). It will be important for Ecuador to take policy measures to facilitate the creation and growth of formal businesses.

In terms of licenses, Ecuador ranks very well in the world, at 61. This is comparable to Bolivia (57) and Colombia (60), and outperforms Peru (121). In fact, Ecuador's performance is close to the OECD average (table 5.4).

Operating a Business

Regulations and costs of employing workers are a major constraint to competitiveness in Ecuador (table 5.5). Labor regulations make it difficult to hire workers and almost impossible to fire them. According to the Doing Business 2007 benchmarks, Ecuador is ranked 161 out of a sample of 162 countries for costs of employing workers, which reflects the level of benefits and the costs of firing workers. Ecuador has a rigidity-of-employment index[2] of 51, compared to a regional average of only 31.7. Firing costs are among the highest in the world and given the rigidity index and difficulties encountered in hiring workers, firms are far less competitive than those in neighboring countries. For example, a firm that fires a worker must pay the equivalent of 135 weeks of wages, compared to an average of only 59 weeks of wages in the region.

Table 5.4. Business Licensing

Indicator	*Ecuador*	*Region*	*OECD*
Procedures (number)	19.0	15.4	14.0
Time (days)	149.0	198.7	149.5
Cost (% of income per capita)	83.7	246.2	72.0

Source: World Bank (2007).

Table 5.5. Employment and Competitiveness

Indicator	*Ecuador*	*Colombia*	*Peru*	*Bolivia*	*Chile*	*Region*	*OECD*
Difficulty of Hiring Index	44	22	44	61	33	34.0	27.0
Rigidity of Hours Index	60	40	60	60	20	34.8	45.2
Difficulty of Firing Index	50	20	80	100	20	26.5	27.4
Rigidity of Employment Index	51	27	61	74	24	31.7	33.3
Hiring cost (% of salary)	12.2	27.6	9.8	13.7	3.4	12.5	21.4
Firing costs (weeks of wages)	135.4	58.6	52.0	99.5	52.0	59.0	31.3

Source: World Bank (2007).

These operational costs and regulatory requirements contribute directly to the poor competitiveness of many Ecuadorian firms.

Taxes are not excessively high, but tax procedures consume too much time. Although the number of payments for a medium-size firm is about half those required in OECD countries, the time required is three times as high (table 5.6). Nonetheless, compared with Peru and Colombia, Ecuador performs well in terms of number of payments and the total tax rate.

Importing inputs and goods in Ecuador is more time consuming than the regional average (table 5.7). Even the most efficient firms can lose a competitive edge as a result of import and export services, and the costs involved in bringing in imported inputs and exporting final goods. Export processing is relatively efficient in Ecuador, but the costs are equal to those of landlocked Bolivia and twice those incurred by exporters in Chile.

Inadequate investments in electricity and telephone service hurt competitiveness. The Investment Climate Assessment of Ecuador (World Bank 2005) compared the country with 10 others in the region. Low investment in the electricity sector (only 0.16 percent of GDP between 1996 and 2000) has resulted in an average of 41 days to obtain connection. Transmission and distribution losses added up to poor service provision and had a strong negative effect on the productivity of firms (see chapter 6).

Table 5.6. Tax Burden

Indicator	*Ecuador*	*Peru*	*Colombia*	*Region*	*OECD*
Payments (number)	8	53	68	41.3	15.3
Time (hours)	600	424	456	430.5	202.9
Total tax rate (% of profit)	34.9	40.8	82.8	49.1	47.8

Source: World Bank (2007).

Table 5.7. Requirements and Costs for Importing and Exporting

Indicator	*Ecuador*	*Colombia*	*Peru*	*Bolivia*	*Chile*	*Region*	*OECD*
Documents for export (number)	12	6	7	12	7	7.3	4.8
Time for export (days)	20	34	24	26	20	22.2	10.5
Cost to export (US$ per container)	1,090	1,734	800	1,110	510	1,068	811
Documents for import (number)	11	11	13	12	9	9.5	5.9
Time for import (days)	41	35	31	36	24	27.9	12.2
Cost to import (US$ per container)	1,090	1,773	820	1,230	510	1,226	883

Source: World Bank (2007).

Private investment in the sector is low, leaving the financial burden for improvement largely in the hands of the government. For telephone service, delays totalled 130 days for new connections, and frequent cuts in service cost firms an estimated 7.6 percent of sales (see chapter 13 on infrastructure).

Investor Protection

Ecuador is ranked very low in the area of investment protection—135th in the world, well below most of South America. This lack of protection is revealed through several different indexes on transparency of transactions, liability for self-dealing, and shareholders' ability to sue officers and directors for misconduct, and overall investor protection (table 5.8). The indexes vary between 0 and 10, with higher values indicating greater disclosure, greater liability of directors, greater powers of shareholders to challenge the transaction, and better investor protection.

Contract enforcement is difficult by international standards but compares favorably in the region (table 5.9). Owing to generally poor performance in Latin America, Ecuador does not fare badly in this area of the business climate. Though the number of procedures is high (41), the costs are relatively low. The estimated time for a standard commercial case is almost 500 days, but it is 150 days less than the regional average. However, there is a lot of room for improvement in these areas, possibly leading to a competitive advantage in the investment climate in the future.

Business Closure and Insolvency

Closing a business is costly, and recovery rates are relatively low (table 5.10). The time and cost of declaring bankruptcy and resolving the asset and registration issues are a major problem in Ecuador. The average time required is eight years, compared to

Table 5.8. Dimensions of Investor Protection

Indicator	*Ecuador*	*Colombia*	*Peru*	*Bolivia*	*Chile*	*Region*	*OECD*
Disclosure Index	1	7	8	1	8	4.3	6.3
Director Liability Index	5	2	5	5	6	5.1	5.0
Shareholder Suits Index	6	9	7	7	5	5.8	6.6
Investor Protection Index	4.0	6.0	6.7	4.3	6.3	5.1	6.0

Source: World Bank (2007).

Table 5.9. Contract Enforcement

Indicator	*Ecuador*	*Colombia*	*Peru*	*Bolivia*	*Chile*	*Region*	*OECD*
Procedures (number)	41	37	35	47	33	39.3	22.2
Time (days)	498	1346	300	591	480	641.9	351.2
Cost (% of debt)	15.3	20.0	34.7	10.5	16.3	23.4	11.2

Source: World Bank (2007).

Table 5.10. Closing a Business

Indicator	*Ecuador*	*Colombia*	*Peru*	*Bolivia*	*Chile*	*Region*	*OECD*
Time (years)	8.0	3.0	3.1	1.8	5.6	2.6	1.4
Cost (% of estate)	18.0	1.0	7.0	14.5	14.5	13.6	7.1
Recovery rate (cents/dollar)	12.7	57.7	31.8	37.6	20.0	25.7	74.0

Source: World Bank (2007).

only three in Colombia and Peru. The costs are 40 percent above the regional average and more than twice the cost in Peru. For firms that manage to complete the bankruptcy procedures, salvage value (recovery on assets) is among the lowest in the region.

The insolvency system neither facilitates the reorganization of viable insolvent enterprises nor allows the efficient liquidation of nonviable ones. Insolvency legislation is fragmented, incomplete, and contradictory. The Commercial Code, which establishes the suspension of payments for merchants, is rarely used because it is an obsolete proceeding. The Code of Civil Procedure governing bankruptcy is a highly inefficient liquidation process and is also rarely used. The same is true of the Law of Reorganization Proceedings (*Ley de Concurso Preventivo*), enacted in 1997, that provides for an administrative reorganization proceeding applicable to commercial companies under the supervision of the Superintendency of Companies. Until the end of 1999, 40 reorganizations were conducted in Guayaquil and only 17 were filed in Quito; the majority of them failed in their intended reorganization objective. Since 1999, this reorganization proceeding has not been used in any significant case. As a result, public opinion is largely unfavorable of both the law and its implementation by the superintendency.

Ecuador lacks a favorable environment for informal corporate restructuring agreements to rehabilitate insolvent or financially distressed enterprises. Though several financial institutions have favorable views of and some experience in collective informal corporate negotiations, there is no adequate legal framework to support them or incentives to such informal negotiations. On the contrary, some rather rigid banking regulations tend to discourage the use of such informal arrangements. For example, reductions in debt service granted to the reorganizing debtor and even an agreement establishing a very low interest rate may be interpreted, according to banking regulation, as presumptions of special arrangements, which would entail unfavorable consequences to that enterprise in its normal relationship with the banks.

The enforcement of creditor rights is significantly weakened by an old-fashioned and ineffective registration system for property rights and securities. In addition, lengthy, unpredictable, and complicated enforcement proceedings face unsecured and mortgaged creditors. Registration methods are outdated, and there is no countrywide unified and computerized consultation mechanism. The Municipal Real Estate Survey (*Catastros Municipales*) is separate from the Registries for Immovable Assets (*Registros de la Propiedad*) and, with a few exceptions, is not well-connected to this registry. The average length of the enforcement proceedings before final judgment can be between one and three years. Debtors frequently delay the process using numerous appeals. Enforcement procedures are also lengthy and complicated, and the challenge of the appraisal of collateral value, by the creditor or by the debtor, results in a potentially long conflict.

As a result of these very serious shortcomings, the institutional framework for creditor rights and insolvency proceedings is weak and the prestige of the judiciary is very low. Users of the system complain that (i) judges lack sufficient knowledge of business issues and commercial law matters; (ii) there is no training and continuing education for judges; (iii) most judges have a pro-debtor tendency in commercial cases; (iv) undue political influence on judges often affects their decisions; (v) corruption issues often affect court officials and some judges; (vi) numerous inefficiencies abound in court organization; and (vii) issues of transparency and unpredictability in judicial decision-making processes are frequent.

Governance

Other governance issues reveal further weaknesses in Ecuador's regulatory system. These include voice and accountability, government effectiveness, and regulatory quality. Chapter 10 provides a thorough discussion of the governance indicators compiled by the World Bank. They reveal that the main weaknesses include the rule of law, control of corruption, political stability, and government effectiveness. The two areas where there have been improvements since the mid-1990s are in (i) the regulatory quality and (ii) in voice and accountability, a measure of civil society's involvement in governance issues.

Small and Medium Enterprises

From the perspectives of both efficiency and equity, small and medium enterprises (SMEs) must play an important role in the economic growth of the country. However, a review of the national budget in 2005 found that the ministries charged with supporting SMEs (particularly the Ministry of Industry and Competitiveness—*Ministerio de Industria y Competitividad*, formerly MICIP) did not have adequate programs to take a leading role in stimulating competitive practices by SMEs. Only a few isolated programs to promote artisans and small tourism projects are on the MICIP budget, rather than significant sectoral or regional efforts. Government efforts also have little coordination or complementarity to other ongoing efforts, with no institutional mechanism to coordinate efforts in rural areas, for instance, between the Ministry of Agriculture, MICIP, and the ministries responsible for infrastructure development. Key topics such as quality enhancement, the promotion of international standards, and laboratories were largely ignored, revealing a passive government approach to promoting SME competitiveness. In other countries in the region, such as Bolivia, Chile, Guatemala, and Nicaragua, the government has taken the lead in promoting associative private sector clusters and value chains. The results have included SME participation in exports, as well as increased employment.

In recent years, SMEs have been slow to integrate and innovate. A 2002 survey of SMEs identified many barriers to improved productivity (MICIP/INSOTEC 2002). Four central problems were identified: (i) lack of association and subcontracting between firms, including weak value chains; (ii) lack of information about export opportunities and requirements; (iii) lack of training for business managers and workers (61 percent had not invested in skills upgrading of any kind); and (iv) low levels of in-firm infrastructure. The vast majority of firms do not reinvest in improved machinery—only 3.8 percent of machinery was computerized, and 72 percent consisted of manual tools or basic semiautomatic machinery. Other findings included a lack of quality control systems, the dominance of informal decision making by managers, and a lack of appreciation for market research. These factors were responsible for a drop in SME productivity (by 0.5 percent) in the period from 1995 to 2004.

The Investment Climate Assessment (World Bank 2005) found similar results. The survey found that SMEs were more affected by the low levels of credit than other firms. For example, access to financial services was better for microbusinesses than for SMEs, thanks in part to a growing microfinance sector. And the regulatory burden—including the frequency and cost of inspections and licensing processes, and management time dedicated to such requirements—was greater for SMEs, especially those with fewer than 20 employees. SMEs also reported having to spend a larger share of sales in bribes to secure government contracts and comply with licensing and other requirements (11.3 percent of sales for firms with 51 to 100 employees).

Despite the market, infrastructure, and regulatory issues, SME exports amounted to US$125.4 million (with little value added) in 2003. Agricultural goods led the export list (US$88 million), followed by agro-industry (US$18.7 million) and wood products (US$9.1 million). Surprisingly, other sectors with large export potential, such as leather goods and ceramics, exported relatively little in 2003 (FENAPI 2005). Raw materials continue to dominate exports, with very low value-added content, demonstrating a weakness in SME productivity and investment.

Important changes in international markets could dramatically affect SMEs. The end of the Multi-Fiber Agreement, the continued Andean Trade Partnership and Drug Eradication Agreement (APTDEA) and the possibility of negotiating further trade preference agreements all increase the importance of SMEs investing in improvements and integrating with other firms. At the same time, government administrative systems could be adjusted to give SMEs an incentive to export. For instance, simple changes in the duty drawback system and adjustments to the value-added tax might be helpful, although a review of the fiscal impact would be an important first step to assess these incentives. Since many SMEs are more likely to export indirectly, linkages to larger producers and to brokers could play an important role in improving their competitiveness.

Clusters are most successful when they become inclusive, involving raw material suppliers, producers, buyers, suppliers of specialized services, financial institutions, specialized universities, research centers, and policy makers. Cluster organization and coordination can increase a sector's overall efficiency, integration, and exports. Often, small investments are required to resolve these bottlenecks using market intelligence services and technical assistance for specific sectors. For example, the Nicaraguan government, with World Bank support, has successfully supported 10 clusters, resulting in concrete benefits for firms, including a significant number of SMEs (box 5.1).

Another example of sectoral improvements is the Associative Projects of Promotion (*Proyectos Asociativos de Fomento*—PROFOs) in Chile. The model includes a matching grant to cover the cost of a full-time professional manager to coordinate marketing strategies, branding, quality control, and certifications that enable the participating firms to increase exports and employment. Some industries have developed PROFOs without government support (pharmaceuticals, wine), while others have leveraged short-term government support to form inclusive sectoral associations. An evaluation by the University of Chile found that firms in PROFOs increased sales by 12.9 percent on average from 1996 to 1999, whereas a control group increased sales by only 2.1 percent during the same period.

One important example of such approaches in Ecuador is the Export and Investment Promotion Corporation of Ecuador (CORPEI). The corporation has carried

Box 5.1. Successful Clusters in Nicaragua: Gains in Income, Exports, and Jobs

Clusters are groups of firms within a sector that are participating in a project. In the case of the Nicaragua Competitiveness project, the results in terms of legal and regulatory framework, jobs creation, and certification have been important, as noted by the specific examples provided below.

- Increased exports (ranging from 23 percent for coffee to 85 percent for tourism, 68 percent for meat, and 85 percent for cheese)
- Increased employment (from 38 percent for tourism to 67 percent for light manufacturing)
- Four original clusters strengthened (policies, strategies, and projects)
- Cluster strategies included in National Development Plan (2003)
- Laws drafted for tourism, light manufacturing, and dairy sectors
- Indicators established in light manufacturing to promote the formalization of commercial contracts
- Five white cheese firms beginning ISO and Hazard Analysis and Critical Control Point (HACCP) certification (first in sector)
- Four new clusters (shrimp, wood, beef, and cocoa) organized and received training, technical assistance and institutional support

Source: World Bank 2007.

out sectoral studies to identify export opportunities for national producers. Notable successes include textiles, artisan products, broccoli, shrimp, mangos, cocoa, and bananas. The methodology includes studies, promotional campaigns, and promotion of standards and certification to ensure access to U.S. and other markets. The results have been impressive increases in exports and certifications. CORPEI also provides a database with sectoral and general information on legal frameworks and requirements, norms, and national sanitary and environmental requirements.

The Rural Sector

Rural sector competitiveness remains elusive. During the 1980s, Ecuador's parastatal organizations for basic commodities maintained an interventionist regime in domestic food and agricultural markets. In the 1990s, fixed prices and producer support prices were eliminated, and agriculture tariffs (both import and export) declined substantially. Ecuador joined the Andean Community in 1994, which included the adoption a common external tariff at four levels (5, 10, 15, and 20 percent), a reduction of tariff dispersion and nontariff barriers, and harmonization of its agricultural price policies with those of other member countries through the establishment of the Andean System of Price Bands.

Despite these reforms and recent dynamism in the sector, low productivity reduces the sector's competitiveness and prevents Ecuador from taking full advantage of its rich and diverse agricultural resources. The low level of productivity reinforces persistent rural poverty, which in 2005 included almost 70 percent of the rural population. Low productivity especially affects cereal grains, pulses, tubers, and other traditional staples. Ecuador's productivity in traditional export crops is below most of its competitors. The reasons include underdeveloped support services, a high degree of protection, a very unequal land tenure system, weak organization of producers, and little integration of value chains. Political and economic instability in the country have also limited agricultural investment and modernization.

An impressive example of a rural cluster in cocoa in coastal Ecuador could be a model to improve competitiveness in other sectors. In 2002, Ecuador had 60,000 cocoa farmers who farmed 300,000 hectares of cocoa, and 54 percent of these farms were smallholdings of less than 10 hectares. Ecuadorian cocoa is marketed without government interference. Local prices are driven by international prices and by local supply and demand. Most producers are located far away from exporters' operations and are unable to sell directly to these brokers. Transport costs and intermediaries' margins limit the prices they can get from brokers, leaving producers with a very small share of the export price. In more remote areas, growers with limited quantities of produce to sell have even less bargaining power.

Maquita Cusinchi (MCCH) has had significant success, specifically in the development of a cocoa and chocolate value chain in coastal areas of Ecuador. This nongovernmental organization (NGO) was founded in 1985, initially focusing on improving cocoa yields of small producers. It has been exporting cocoa grown by small producers from Esmeraldas and Manabí provinces since 1992 through its export company, *Agroexportadora Maquita.* MCCH's cocoa operations have been subsidized to a small extent. The intention of MCCH was to establish a marketing system in parallel with the export of cocoa with the explicit aims of working with farmer organizations, securing a fair price and weight, and receiving a premium for any good-quality cocoa produced. Donor grants initially provided the organization with capital to invest, both in its marketing operations and in improving cocoa bean quality at the farm level.

The part of Maquita's profits that is not reinvested in the company goes through MCCH to farmers, funding farmer training and other socially motivated activities. MCCH operates a vertically integrated marketing system that it claims rewards the loyalty of affiliated smallholder cooperatives. The criteria for becoming affiliated are that the association should operate in remote areas, it should be well organized, and its members should possess smallholdings of less than approximately seven hectares. MCCH also purchases from regular sellers on nonpreferential terms to realize economies of export scale. They offer training related to cocoa growing, including improving production, postharvest activities, and marketing. Farmers involved in this fair trade effort have benefited in the following ways:

- Higher price paid for cocoa or influence on local prices
- Elimination of middlemen
- Fairer and more accurate weighing system
- Provision of market information
- Cash payments
- Access to transport
- Incentives for the production of better quality cocoa by smallholders

III. The Financial Sector

Background

The financial sector shows slow signs of recovery. Ecuador liberalized its financial sector in the early 1990s, but bank supervision capacity lagged, particularly when portfolios grew quickly. Related-parties lending, high portfolio concentrations, and increased dollar commitments of bank clients combined to create a financial sector crisis from 1997 to 1999. As a result of bank failures, the number of active banks dropped from 38 in late 1998 to 22 by the end of 2002. During the same period, bank assets dropped by 50 percent as a share of GDP. (For a broader assessment of financial services, see chapter 3.)

More recent positive macroeconomic developments have helped the financial system recover from the 1998–99 crisis and adapt to the new currency regime, but the crisis overhang (including outstanding unresolved claims) still needs to be resolved. Concrete steps, such as improved financial regulations and supervision, need to be taken to rebuild confidence in the sector. This will require continued monitoring of solvency ratios of banks and mutual financial institutions (such as savings and loan cooperatives), and finance companies. Dollarization has removed exchange rate volatility and has modified but not eliminated exposure to exchange and interest rate risk.

Issues Limiting Credit Expansion

Difficult access to credit by the corporate sector is related to the very poor protection of creditor rights, which acts as a powerful disincentive to lending in general and to lending to small firms in particular. Although the legal framework for traditional secured transactions (mortgage and pledges) and for more modern security legal methods like guarantee trusts (*fideicomiso de garantía*) is largely sound, problems are found at two stages. Registration mechanisms are outdated, and procedural enforcement mechanisms are plagued by flaws, making the recovery of defaulted loans difficult, lengthy, and costly.

Moreover, current liquidity management in Ecuador suffers from the lack of appropriate tools to address systemic bank liquidity needs. Dollarization deprives the banking system of a lender of last resort. Consequently, banks face a trade-off between holding liquidity to avoid systemic liquidity risk (that is, the risk of bank runs) and offering more credit. The higher the credit volume, the higher the systemic liquidity risk, and vice versa. In response to liquidity regulations and banks' own policies, banks addressed the trade-off by limiting credit expansion—bank loans represent only 40 percent of bank assets and 11 percent of GDP. The authorities plan to set up a liquidity fund for use in the case of systemic deposit withdrawals.

Poor access to the credit market and greater exposure to external shocks are deepening the divide between large and small firms. Large firms, through their participation in holding groups, have created an alternative intragroup circuit of finance that avoids the uncertainty and the cost of external credit, while optimizing cash management. These groups may include cash-rich sectors (department stores or commercial banks) and cash-poor sectors (construction). Moreover, large groups enjoy productive diversification benefits, the international visibility required to access foreign credit, and the clout to obtain better conditions from domestic suppliers of credit. Together, these features provide large firms a substantial monopoly in the access to foreign capital. In contrast, the decline of supplier credit—together with bank credit—after the crisis has been particularly harmful to small firms, as they often do not have access to bank credit and rely mostly on retained earnings and trade credit to finance working capital and new investments.

Wider access to the credit market also requires improvements in credit information and specific regulations for microlending activities. Better information and a wider scope of coverage through an integrated system of credit registries and credit bureaus would improve lenders' knowledge of borrowers and increase competition in the small loan market. It would also increase the incentive for small borrowers to repay and maintain a good credit rating. A parallel effort should aim at reducing regulatory costs for small formal lenders and at providing incentives to share fixed costs through the participation in common central networks. For example, the current ceiling on lending rates imposed by the usury law needs to be made less stringent.

Beyond standard credit products, there is little innovation in financial services. Leasing, warehouse receipts financing, weather-based agricultural insurance, and factoring all offer important advantages to producers, especially SMEs, but all are underdeveloped in Ecuador. The lack of a legal and regulatory framework for partial credit guarantees is especially problematic, since this approach to extending credit to new clients has been successful in other countries in the region. Under an enabling framework, partial credit guarantees can overcome collateral constraints, offset risks of lending to SMEs, address information constraints, compensate for initial low profit margins, and induce experimentation by commercially oriented financial institutions (Gudger 1998).

One critical factor to improve micro- and rural credit is a stronger legal and regulatory framework. Particular problem areas include inadequate land registry and titling programs, especially in the rural coastal region and urban *barrios*; limited ability to broaden the range of assets used as loan collateral beyond land; inadequate and limited legal registries; high registration costs; and complex, lengthy foreclosure procedures.

Sharply reduced inflation and interest rates, rising real salaries, and the restructuring of the banking industry have created substantial potential for the growth of residential mortgage finance in Ecuador, from its currently low level of 1.7 percent of GDP. While real salaries have risen by 33 percent since 2000, close to half of the population has inadequate housing, and 32 percent of the population live in units considered critically overcrowded. The vast majority of units are single family homes, with 67 percent of units owned by their occupants. An estimated 30 percent of urban units are substandard and lack legal title. Studies have estimated that Ecuador has an overall housing deficit of 1.6 million units, or an annual production deficit of 50,000 units.

Obstacles to further development of the housing market include (i) the usury ceiling, which particularly inhibits microfinance; (ii) taxes on title transfer that reach up to 35 percent of the property value; and (iii) ineffective foreclosure procedures. Permitted ceilings on interest rates on any kind of credit are 1.5 times the Central Bank's posted lending rate. This arbitrary ceiling inhibits the development of risk-based pricing of credit and reduces the amount of credit available for microlending for housing or for enterprises. Taxes on title transfer of up to 35 percent of property value obstruct the sales of existing housing and other properties from resolved institutions. These problems also lead to a dramatic underassessment of official property values. Finally, inefficient foreclosure procedures (discussed in the previous section) have induced lenders and regulators to develop alternative arrangements such as a maximum loan-to-value ratio established at 70 percent; clauses requiring arbitration to avoid courts in the case of default; placement of property titles in trusts that are dissolved once the loan is repaid; and use of leases that transfer title to the buyer only at the end of the lease term.

Financial Institutions

Despite the presence of innovative commercial banks with microfinance pilots and products, and despite some relatively strong microfinance institutions serving rural markets, SMEs are largely an untapped market for formal financial institutions. When firms do manage to get credit, the loan maturity is reported to average 17 months, far below levels for Guatemala (41 months), Honduras (38 months), and Brazil (42 months). Such short loan terms make it difficult for SMEs to invest in technologies and processes that would transform them into competitive firms. A further complication is the collateral requirement, which averages 177 percent of loan value (compared to 115 percent reported by Guatemalan firms and 122 percent by firms in Peru).

Public banks have not followed sound practices, with the National Financial Corporation (*Corporación Financiera Nacional*—CFN) and National Development Bank (*Banco Nacional de Fomento*—BNF) providing limited outreach at high cost, instead of sizable outreach at low cost. Even though BNF has one of the largest branch networks of any bank, the coverage of cooperatives is five times higher. Meanwhile, the provision of microcredit from private banks has increased to nearly US$100 million. BNF has prioritized disbursing resources over recovering them, with major consequences for the credit histories of rural clients. Activities to spread risks or promote intermediation have been neglected. Credit subsidies through BNF and CFN have been ineffective and inequitable (failing to reach the poor), and have created incentives for corruption. The losses of public resources of the two banks could have financed thousands of rural health centers, primary schools, or major rural infrastructure projects. The dysfunctional role of Ecuador's public banks in rural and microfinance needs to be reconsidered.

Through its discount window, the Ecuadoran Housing Bank (*Banco Ecuatoriano de la Vivienda*) currently provides long-term financing for 3.5 percent of the industry portfolio. In a positive move, the bank bought US$400,000 of the recent Mortgage Titling Company (CTH) mortgage securitization. As a second-tier institution, it should play a more active role in long-term financing for private sector lenders. However, it should not subsidize interest rates nor reenter the primary market.[3] Weaknesses in its portfolio remain in its direct loans, which it no longer makes.

Cooperatives offer a good option for reaching rural clients and poorer urban households. Yet most are informal, face liquidity constraints, are limited in their ability to pool and share risks, and cannot offer their clients a broad range of financial services. One solution may be legal and regulatory reforms and incentives that encourage the formation of licensed, mutually owned banks along Brazilian lines. The result would be the formation of effective central (apex) institutions that can facilitate delegated supervision, establish quality standards, upgrade technology, and improve liquidity management. The US$200,000 capital requirement could be reduced for cooperatives that form part of a cooperative network headed by an apex organization approved by the Superintendency of Banks and Insurance (*Superintendencia de Bancos y Seguros*—SBS). A more immediate concern is to increase training for both supervisors and market players and reduce the onus of detailed reporting on small loans that imply little systemic risk.

The IESS has announced its intention to support the development of mortgage finance by investing in mortgage portfolios (*cédulas*), and mortgage-backed securities when they become available. This is an appropriate role for IESS and would provide important support to the market's development, although it should be prevented from lending directly for mortgages at an interest rate equal to its estimated actuarial rate of return, which is currently 6 percent below market rates for mortgages. Setting the mortgage note rate equal to the IESS's required actuarial rate of return fails to reflect the risks and returns of the mortgage lending business. Lending at below-market interest rates conflicts with the IESS's stated goal of ensuring adequate benefits for its members, inhibits the development of a sustainable supply of private sector financing, and will lead, as in many other countries, to substantial losses for fund beneficiaries.

IV. Policy Recommendations

The following policy recommendations include public sector legal and regulatory adjustments, as well as short-term public sector incentives to the private sector to improve productivity, competitiveness, and integration. Given the problems reviewed above, this combination of policies and activities promises to help Ecuador's private sector prepare for the fundamental challenges ahead in a cost-effective manner. A key message to policy makers is that a proactive approach is far more likely than a passive stance to lead to significant changes in the currently disappointing competitiveness level of the country. A joint public-private approach in both competitiveness and financial sector improvements could generate enormous gains for the country.

Competitiveness

To improve the investment climate in Ecuador, several aspects of registering and operating a business could be streamlined. Though the number of procedures is not significantly different from the regional average, the costs of business registration are excessive. The government should develop an action plan as a response to the *Doing Business 2007* report, which identifies specific areas in need of improvement. Building a consensus between the various ministries involved in business establishment and operation could have very high payoffs. This report also recommends that duty drawbacks be promoted for SMEs, through chambers of commerce and business associations (as has been done successfully in Chile). Finally, the government should study the fiscal impact of changes in the value-added tax system, to see if a favorable rate for SMEs would make sense from a countrywide economic perspective.

To increase exports, firms need to meet the increasingly challenging international standards for goods and production processes. A campaign led by the government to stimulate SME certifications (such as ISOs, HACCPs) would help firms to export. Laboratories and other service providers should be supported in the development of their services. Subcontracting arrangements are another avenue for SMEs that hope to export, and it would be important to foster these associative arrangements by reviewing regulations that might present barriers to such business links.

In term of labor market reforms, Ecuador's strict labor regulations have become a barrier to greater competitiveness, especially in terms of firing workers. Though this note does not advocate a wholesale change in labor regulations, it would be very beneficial for the government and the private sector to jointly review the labor regulations in other countries in the region, to find middle ground between protecting workers and allowing market mechanisms to rationalize labor use. In addition, developing a more functional regional labor agency could help workers identify new opportunities, gain access to specific skills training (including on-the-job training with firms), and relocate to fast-growing regions of the country.

Ecuador has in the past used matching grants to improve access to market information, with significant success. A good reform would build on this experience, using a transparent, competitive matching grants mechanism to promote firms' investment in quality control and technology improvements, laboratories, certifications, and other business development services. At the same time, investments in laboratories to ensure that they meet international standards would have a large payoff in terms of firms' competitiveness.

Finally, closer collaboration between the public and private sectors would provide large dividends in terms of the business and investment climate and firms' performance. A striking example of building such a consensus and a forum for ongoing dialogue comes from Guatemala. From 2000 to 2003, the government and the private sector rarely met and had an adversarial relationship. The new government formed a large public-private steering committee (*Comite Ampliado de Competitividad*) and launched a monthly meeting to hear private sector concerns and present projects and accomplishments. This group of 60 representatives, including four ministers and representatives from leading business chambers, associations, unions, and indigenous groups, has been instrumental in forging joint plans that have resulted in major gains in the country's competitiveness.

Finance Sector

Strengthening capital markets, contractual savings, insurance, and pension and retirement services will improve Ecuador's financial system. The extreme segmentation of the domestic stock markets between Quito and Guayaquil, together with the burdensome rules for issuers and investors in the domestic markets, are pushing Ecuadoran issuers and investors to foreign markets. Lack of stocks and bonds makes mutual funds useless. The weak regulatory framework and fiscal obstacles limit the development of contractual saving by life insurance companies and general risk coverage by all insurance products with the exception of life insurance. The abortive 2001 pension reform should be reconsidered to eliminate the current limits to the supply of pension services on the part of private financial entities.

Direct public interventions to promote greater access to finance should take the form of subsidizing information and innovation and of addressing risk. Better information on small borrowers, through a credit information bureau, would allow lenders to know about their borrowers at lower cost and increase competition in the small loan market. It would also improve the incentive for small borrowers to repay to maintain a good credit record. Together with the improvements in the legal framework with regard to titling and execution of collateral to improve creditor rights, these improvements in information would help increase the flow of microcredit and reduce nonperforming loans.

To improve rural and microlending, recommended reforms include (i) designing programs to title and register land, especially in the rural coastal region and in urban barrios where this is a bigger problem; (ii) reforming laws and regulations governing secured transactions to ensure that a broad range of assets can be used as collateral (for example, accounts receivables, farm equipment and durable products, and warehouse receipts); (iii) reforming legal registries and expansion of the scope for private operation; (iv) reducing the valuation standards for collateral on loans under US$5,000; (v) lowering registration costs (typically up to 5 percent of loan amounts); and (vi) simplifying foreclosures, which are cumbersome in a legal framework that still favors debtor over creditor rights, and where the court system is slow and unpredictable.

The SBS should be encouraged to regulate market risk, and it should develop capital rules for investments in mortgage-backed securities to take into account recourse and subordination. Once the SBS has developed a binding rule governing market risk that incorporates liquidity shortfalls, it should provide an important motivation for mortgage lenders to hedge market and liquidity risks. As the mortgage securitization market develops, it will be essential to develop risk-based capital rules for financial institutions that reflect the concentration of credit risk that is built into the subordinated bonds issued by the CTH.

The IESS should provide long-term funding to the mortgage market, but it should not be permitted to offer mortgages directly to its members, or to offer below-market interest rates. The IESS should not lend directly for mortgages at an interest rate equal to its estimated actuarial rate of return (currently 6 percent below market rates for mortgages), which would fail to reflect the risks and returns of mortgage lending.

Policy Recommendations Matrix

Technical area	*Objective*	*Specific activities*
Investment climate	Lower the costs of starting and operating businesses; improve the attractiveness of foreign investment in Ecuador.	• Develop an action plan to rapidly respond to key Doing Business 2007 findings. • Promote a duty drawback system to SMEs through chambers or associations (such as is done in Chile). • Study the fiscal implications of adjusting VAT for SMEs.
Identification of supply-side constraints for exports	Improve SME product quality and raise the share of businesses meeting quality and process requirements (ISOs, HACCPs).	• Launch promotional campaigns on importance of ISOs, HACCPs, and national standards. • Improve the availability and quality of private sector business development services. • Review regional experiences in government-led export promotion (pro-Chile, pro-Nicaragua). • Strengthen the CORPEI system of export market identification. • Review the legal framework for subcontracting. • Provide incentives for sectors to improve value chain efficiency.
Labor market regulation	Reduce high cost of existing labor regulations; facilitate movement of labor to sectors with growth potential.	• Have government and private sector jointly review labor regulations in other countries in the region to find middle ground between worker protection and allowance for market mechanisms to rationalize labor use • Through improved market intermediation, increase labor market information to employers and workers, especially in vulnerable sectors and provinces. • Encourage private sector retraining in sectors with growth potential. • Increase the government's role in monitoring performance of intermediation agencies to ensure compliance with regulations.

Supply and demand for quality and technology	Facilitate technology adoption, changes in production processes, use of quality control systems and certifications.	• Provide short-term matching grants to SMEs for quality and technology enhancement, certification, and integration. • Upgrade laboratories to meet international certification standards. • Review the case of Maquita Cusinchi as an example of improving rural competitiveness resulting in export growth. • Coordinate with CORPEI, chambers, and associations to improve the provision of technology services.
Financial sector	Promote increased access to financial services by SMEs.	• Investigate the need for a partial risk guarantee mechanism and the related legal and regulatory framework. • Reform collateral and bankruptcy proceedings to offer greater incentives for SME lending by banks. • Provide information on best practices in agricultural and weather insurance, and in leasing to commercial banks and nonbank financial institutions. • Provide short-term incentives (training, technical assistance, output-based subsidies) to banks interested in SME lending. • Consider a short-term second-tier government program to improve access to financial services by SMEs (especially for technology transformation, relocation, worker training). • Evaluate the microfinance lending and guarantee schemes of the National Financial Corporation (*Corporación Financiera Nacional*) and the Andean Development Corporation (*Corporación Andino de Fomento*).

Notes

1. The areas for reform are (i) starting a business, (ii) licenses, (iii) labor, (iv) property registration, (v) access to credit, (vi) protecting investors, (vii) paying taxes, (viii) trading across borders, (ix) contract enforcement, and (x) closing a business.

2. This index measures labor market regulations and practices related to the costs of hiring and firing workers in formal sector firms, with a higher number representing a more rigid labor market.

3. The recommendations for the Ecuadoran Housing Bank contained in this section are still valid in the case the bank is merged with other state-owned banks to form a single development bank. In that case, these recommendations will apply to the housing-related lending activities of the new institution.

Bibliography

Economist Intelligence Unit. 2006. *Ecuador Country Profile.* London. http://www.eiu.com.

Enriquez, Francisco. 2004. *Caracterización del Impacto del TLC en el Empleo Manufacturero a Nivel Provincial en el Ecuador.* Quito: Indigenous Nationalities (CONAIE). http://www.conaie.org/revista/es/2006_01/reportaje01c.html.

FENAPI (Federación Nacional de la Pequeña Industria). 2005. 2003 survey results. FENAPI.

Fitch International. 2006. Benchmarking and Country Risk Profiles. http://www.fitchratings.com.

Gudger, Michael. 1998. "Credit Guarantees: An Assessment of the State of Knowledge and New Avenues of Research." Agricultural Services Bulletin 129, FAO, Rome.

Jatobá, Jorge. 2006. *Labor Mobility for Low-Skilled Urban Workers: Enhancing Job Search and Training Programs.* Quito: World Bank.

Loayza, Norman, Pablo Fajnzylber, and César Calderón. 2005. *Economic Growth in Latin America and the Caribbean.* Washington, DC: World Bank.

MICIP (Ministerio de Industria, Comercio, Integración y Pesca) and INSOTEC (Instituto de Investigaciones Sociolocos y Tecnologicos). 2002. *Diagnósitico de la Pequeña y Mediana Industria.* Quito: INSOTEC.

Palmade, Vincent. 2005. *Why Worry about Rising Informality? The Biggest and Least Well Understood Impediment to Economic Development.* Washington, DC: Foreign Investment Advisory Service, World Bank.

Rodas, Andrea. 2005. *Relación Sintética de Proyectos Dirigidos al Fortalecimiento de la Competitividad de PYMEs.* Background study. Quito: World Bank.

Schneider, F. 2002. "Size and Measurement of the Informal Economy in 110 Countries around the World." Paper presented at the Workshop of Australian Tax Centre Conference, Canberra, July 17, 2002.

Schneider, F., and R. Klinglmair. 2004. "Shadow Economies Around the World: What Do We Know?" CESIFO Working Paper 403. Johanes Kepler University of Linz, Austria.
Standard & Poor's 2006. International Benchmarking and Country Risk Profiles. http://www.standardandpoors.com.
World Bank. 2004a. "Chile: Una Estrategia para Promover la Pequeña y Mediana Empresa Innovadora." Report 29114-CL. World Bank, Washington, DC.
———. 2004b. "Ecuador Development Policy Review: Growth, Inclusion and Governance—The Road Ahead." Report 27443. World Bank, Washington, DC.
———. 2004c. "Ecuador Investment Climate Assessment." World Bank, Washington, DC.
———. 2005. "Ecuador Investment Climate Assessment." World Bank, Washington, DC.
———. 2006. "Agricultural Competitiveness and Sustainable Rural Development Project." Project Appraisal Document. World Bank, Washington, DC.
———. 2007. Implementation Completion Report, Nicaragua Competitiveness Learning and Innovation Loan, January 17, 2007, World Bank.
World Bank Institute. 2004. "Worldwide Governance Indicators." Washington, DC: World Bank.
World Bank and IMF (International Monetary Fund). Ecuador Financial Sector Assessment Program. Washington, DC: World Bank.
World Bank and IFC (International Finance Corporation). 2007. *Doing Business 2007: How to Reform.* Washington, DC: World Bank.
World Economic Forum. 2006. *Global Competitiveness Report 2006–2007.* Geneva: World Economic Forum.
Zettelmeyer, Jeromin. 2006. "Growth and Reforms in Latin America: A Survey of Facts and Arguments." Working Paper 210. International Monetary Fund, Washington, DC.

6

Electricity Sector

Susan V. Bogach and Eduardo H. Zolezzi

Executive Summary

Ten years after the Electricity Law of 1996 was approved, the electricity sector continues to be run by public companies, with minimal private presence. The sector is in a deep and growing financial crisis, created by high levels of nonbilling and nonpayment in certain distribution companies and a tariff below economically efficient costs. The combined loss of income from these factors amounts to 40 percent of the sector revenues; about half of that is because of unbilled services and low collection rates and half is from a tariff that is below costs. This unsustainable deficit in revenues has undermined the ability and willingness of sector companies to invest in generation and distribution to meet future demand and to keep the sector functioning.

If action is not taken in the near future, the sector's deteriorating infrastructure and unreliable generation are expected to cause power outages, seriously affecting Ecuador's competitiveness. Therefore, sufficient investments in maintenance and in new generation to supply requirements during the dry season are high priorities in the short and medium term, together with investments in energy efficiency and renewable energy in the long term. Achieving these results would require improvement of sector governance, including regulations for price and tariff setting.

Pressure has been growing to solve the immediate problems in the sector by using public resources (largely from petroleum revenues) to compensate the sector for past tariff deficits, as well as to finance the annual tariff deficit in the sector and finance new investment. Though compensation for the past tariff deficit appears unavoidable, it is estimated that at least half of these expenditures could be financed from the sector itself if the tariff deficit was eliminated and policies to encourage public and private investment were put in place in the sector.

The following options are recommended for reforming the sector:

- *Make the distribution system function efficiently to collect the revenues from customers that are essential for the sector.*
- *Compensate the sector for past accumulated deficits and increase tariffs to eliminate future annual financial tariff deficits.*
- *Ensure that investment in generation is adequate to keep the lights on, especially during the dry season.*
- *Improve sector regulation for price and tariff setting.*
- *Improve sector governance to facilitate overall efficiency in the sector.*
- *Develop cost-effective new and renewable energy sources.*
- *Improve efficiency of electricity consumption.*

I. Overview of the Current Situation

As in several other Latin American countries, Ecuador followed the path of reforming its electricity sector in the mid- and late 1990s. The national power company, the Ecuadoran Electrification Institute (*Instituto Ecuatoriano de Electrificación*—INECEL), was shut down in 1999, and several public hydroelectric and thermal generation companies were created, together with a transmission and interconnection company. Public distribution companies, which follow roughly provincial boundaries, were kept unchanged. The 1996 Electricity Law also introduced a competitive wholesale electricity market, with agents that included generators, distributors, a transmission company, a market and system operator, and large consumers (see figure 6.1).

Figure 6.1. Institutional Setup of the Electricity Sector

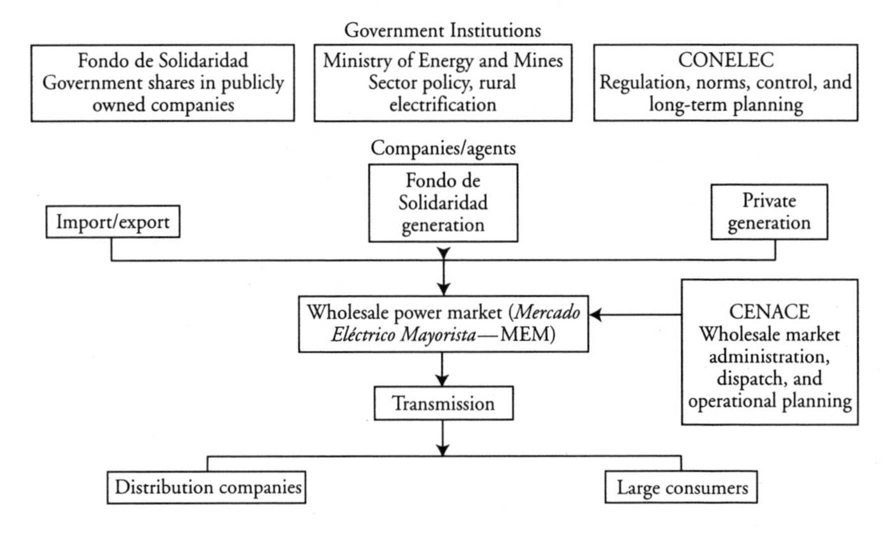

Sector governance was radically reformed, with a sharp reduction in the state's role in providing electricity services and a major increase in its regulatory role. Policy making was entrusted to the Ministry of Energy and Mines (MEM). Sector planning and regulatory functions were entrusted to the National Electricity Council (*Consejo Nacional de Electricidad*—CONELEC), a body whose members were, for the most part and until recently, directly or indirectly appointed by the country's president.

As part of the 1996 reforms, INECEL was unbundled vertically and horizontally, resulting in the creation of seven new companies: Transelectric, in charge of the transmission system; three hydroelectric companies, Hidropaute, Hidroagoyan, and Hidropucara (which was absorbed by Hidroagoyan in 2001); and three thermoelectric companies: Termoesmeraldas, Termopichincha, and Electroguayas. Transmission and distribution companies were considered regulated monopolies. Generation was to be developed in an open, competitive market. Regional and local distribution companies continued to operate unchanged as publicly owned, operated, and managed enterprises based on roughly provincial boundaries. Most publicly owned companies in the sector were put under the ownership and management of the Solidarity Fund (*Fondo de Solidaridad*), which now holds their majority shares.[1] Private sector participation up to 51 percent of ownership was allowed. The National Center for Energy Control (*Corporación Centro Nacional de Control de Energía*—CENACE) was created for dispatching and managing wholesale market functions.

One of the reform's fundamental objectives, in addition to introducing incentives to improve the performance of the players, was to create conditions to attract new capital, especially for the generation of electricity, and to improve efficiency and management of companies through private participation. This was intended to have the beneficial effect of relieving the government from its investment and subsidy burdens, making it possible to channel government funds into social services. It was hoped that market mechanisms and rational rate rules would attract funds, thereby contributing to the sustainability of the electricity sector.

Although the recipe for reform was followed closely, the expected results—competition, private sector participation and investment, and greater efficiency—have not materialized. Ten years after the Electricity Law was approved, the electricity sector continues to be run by public companies, with minimal private presence. The electricity sector is in a deep and growing crisis caused by (i) high levels of nonbilling and nonpayment in certain distribution companies, resulting in serious revenue loss to the sector; and (ii) a tariff kept below economic costs for years, which has created a sectorwide financial deficit.

A study carried out in 2003 on the investment climate in Ecuador showed that the reliability of electricity service is perceived by companies as an important problem for their operations and an important limitation to economic growth (World Bank 2005). About 30 percent of the companies surveyed indicated that electricity service poses a major or severe obstacle to their operation and growth, the worst ranked among the infrastructure services. More than 70 percent of companies had experienced at least one power cut during the previous year. Production losses from power outages were estimated at 2.6 percent of annual sales values.

Many reasons have been invoked to explain the failure to reach the intended objectives of reform. Privatization of state-owned companies has never been able to gather enough momentum to overcome opposition by unions, some civil society organizations, and indigenous groups. The private sector had little interest in investing in Ecuador, partly because of political instability, but in particular because the electricity sector is plagued with myriad problems. The small size of the Ecuadoran power system, together with few dominant producers, limits the possibilities of genuine competition. Finally, the executive branch's interference in the tariff, plus the pricing system embodied in the law from which distribution companies aren't assured of recouping their costs, do not provide the climate necessary to attract investment.

The absence of private sector interests, together with the absence of strong centralized control (similar to the type existing before reform), has led to a progressive reduction in governance standards and poor performance of some distribution companies. An indication of the seriousness of the problem is the level of unbilled energy and the level of uncollected bills. Together, they show that only 65 percent of the kilowatt hours purchased by companies is paid for by their customers. Healthy companies should receive payment for at least 85 percent of the energy they purchase, the remainder being accounted for by physical losses and a small percentage of nonpaying customers. This means that 20 percent of overall sector revenues are being lost through a combination of nonbilling of customers, theft, and low payment rates.

Contributing to the sector's deepening financial crisis is the continuous interference by past governments to limit tariffs to levels below economic costs, plus intervention in other aspects of the sector. The situation is not satisfactory, supply security is at risk. The sector will continue to deteriorate if important changes are not introduced soon; however, some good examples of other electricity sectors in the Andean region could be used as lessons for developing policies to correct the situation in Ecuador.[2]

One step that was taken by the previous government to put the sector in order was Congress's approval of the Electricity Sector Reform Law (*Ley Reformatoria de la Ley de Régimen del Sector Eléctrico*) in September 2006. The new law, which corrects some of the most critical sector issues, includes dispositions regarding (i) government recognition of its responsibility for the sector debt caused by the tariff deficit, for the period from April 1999 till December 2005; (ii) the obligation of the government to incorporate in the annual national budget any future annual financial deficits to the sector that would result from setting tariffs below economic costs; (iii) guaranteed payment to generators for energy supply under term contracts with distribution companies in which the government has more than 50 percent ownership; (iv) change in the composition and appointment of the CONELEC board; (v) revision of the method of calculating retail tariffs; (vi) establishment of mechanisms to ensure efficient management of distribution companies; and (vii) penalties for unauthorized manipulation of metering equipment and illegal connections (electricity theft). However, the 2006 reform law perpetuated the concept of maintaining the tariff below economically efficient levels and failed to introduce changes needed to mobilize commercial investment.

Electricity Supply

Installed generation capacity has increased only 11 percent in the past five years, while power demand has increased 18 percent in the same period. Furthermore, effective capacity for power production is considerably lower than installed capacity, especially in hydropower plants whose output depends on hydrological conditions, which vary seasonally and annually. A case in point is Paute, the largest plant, with a nominal capacity of 1,075 megawatt (MW). In 2005 Paute's output during the dry season averaged 357 MW, whereas in October 2006 its reported effective capacity was less than 100 MW.

The local reserve margin (the difference between the effective capacity installed in the country and demand) has been decreasing since 2002 to a level below 10 percent in 2005; a level that is insufficient for security of supply. To meet demand, there is an increasing dependence on international interconnections. These interconnections give the system a reasonable reserve margin of roughly 25 percent, when available, but since they are based on contingent and not firm contracts, they cannot guarantee a stable security of supply.

There has also been a constant reduction of the share of hydropower in the electricity supply, and consequently an increase in thermal generation. While hydroelectricity production has been about 7,000 gigawatt hours per year (GWh/yr) in the last five years, total gross generation (including imports) has gone from about 11,000 GWh in 2001 to 15,000 GWh in 2005, an increase of more than 36 percent. The incremental production is from thermal plants and imports, both of which have increased rapidly. The situation in 2005, in this respect, was particularly severe. Hydroelectricity generation in 2005 represented only 45.5 percent of total supply, considerably less than in 2001, for which the proportion was close to 64 percent.

The consequence of this reduction in hydroelectric generation (in particular, in the last two years, when oil prices have increased sharply) has been a significant increase in the fuel bill, which has contributed to the deterioration of the already negative finances of the sector. For example, the cost of petroleum used in power generation increased 30 percent from 2004 to 2005, from US$202 to US$263 million.[3] Energy imports represented US$150 million in 2005. The main fuels used for thermal generation in 2005 were fuel oil (about 52 percent of thermal generation used this type of fuel), diesel (38 percent) and other (10 percent—made up of natural gas, residual, and crude oil, of which about one-third was natural gas). This has also been the proportion, with minor variations, in recent years.

A main loop of 230 kilovolt (kV) double-circuit lines constitutes the trunk transmission system, which connects the main supply sources and the major demand points in the national interconnected system. At this highest voltage level, there is some redundant transmission capability. The remainder of the transmission system is made up of radial lines of 138 kV and 69 kV. Interties of 230 kV link the system with neighboring Colombia and Peru. Although some local reinforcements are necessary, in general, the existing transmission system is considered adequate, and no serious problems are foreseen.

Growth in Demand

Electricity demand has grown steadily from 2001 to 2005 at about 4.4 percent a year, on average. Electricity consumption in 2005 was 9,450 GWh, 6 percent more than in 2004. The distribution of this consumption by type is as follows: 39.1 percent residential; 20.8 percent commercial; 18.9 percent industrial; 7.6 percent public lighting; 9.2 percent other; and 4.4 percent large users. Annual per capita consumption in 2003 was about 627 kilowatt-hour (kWh), about half the average for Latin America and representative of the low industrialization of the country (see Table 6.1).

Considering a moderate annual growth of 5 percent in the next five years, about 500 MW of capacity and 12,610 GWh of new energy would be needed to serve the expected final demand (at generation level, the requirements would be higher, considering the existing gross inefficiency in the system, estimated at about 715 MW and 18,000 GWh).

Distribution System

The distribution companies are fundamental to a well-functioning electricity sector because they collect the revenue needed to operate the system and justify new investments in the sector. Ecuador has 20 distribution companies that are dissimilar in size of service area, number of clients, and level of consumption. The largest are Empresa Eléctrica de Quito (about 641,000 clients in a service area of 15,000 km^2) and CATEG-D, serving Guayaquil (423,000 clients in a service area of only 1,400 km^2). Because of the large number of companies, even the largest Ecuadoran distribution companies are too small to achieve the economies of scale possible in systems that serve several million users.

Table 6.2 shows the overall energy balance of distribution companies during the five-year period 2001–05. By any standards, the overall level of distribution losses reported is extraordinarily high. In 2005, losses represented close to 24 percent[4] of energy available for distribution, of which 14 percent were black losses, that is, nonbilled energy use. By comparison, Latin America and Caribbean (LAC's) regional average is about 15 percent losses, and well-performing companies have losses of around 10 percent (in both cases, these losses do not include nonpayment). These issues are discussed in detail in the following sections.

Electricity Tariffs

One of the main objectives of sector reform was the establishment of an independent regulator in charge of determining efficient tariffs based on economically efficient cost of service. However, CONELEC has calculated tariffs reflecting the economic cost of service at levels consistently higher than the rates actually approved and applied. In 1998 the gap was approximately US$0.037/kWh, which increased to some US$0.06/kWh due to the economic crisis of 1998–99. The sector operated under the assumption that the government would provide for the difference between

Comparative Energy Statistics in Latin America

Country	Final energy consumed[a] Boe (000)	Per capita GDP[b] 1995 US$	Per capita final consumption Boe/ inhabitant	Energy intensity[c] Boe/1995 US$ (000)	Consumption: Electricity Final GWh	Consumption: Electricity Per capita kWh/ Inhabitant	Consumption: Oil products Total Boe (000)	Consumption: Oil products Per capita Boe/ inhabitant
Argentina	314,726	6,423	8.2	1.3	80,026	2,084	174,210	4.5
Barbados	1,897	6,826	7.0	1.0	782	2,895	2,495	9.2
Bolivia	19,599	954	2.2	2.3	3,665	412	15,280	1.7
Brazil	1,146,394	4,285	6.5	1.5	329,771	1,860	595,385	3.4
Colombia	168,338	2,312	3.8	1.6	36,518	819	90,881	2.0
Costa Rica	18,381	3,833	4.3	1.1	6,708	1,580	12,764	3.0
Chile	148,738	6,102	9.4	1.5	41,895	2,656	91,453	5.8
Dominican Republic	38,587	2,072	4.4	2.1	11,893	1,349	41,070	4.7
Ecuador	**48,047**	**1,780**	**3.6**	**2.0**	**8,366**	**627**	**49,048**	**3.7**
El Salvador	23,114	1,760	3.5	2.0	4,839	729	14,259	2.1
Guatemala	50,523	1,551	4.1	2.6	5,808	472	22,298	1.8
Honduras	23,637	717	3.4	4.7	3,817	545	13,725	2.0
Mexico	701,409	4,689	6.8	1.4	160,384	1,553	636,419	6.2
Nicaragua	16,308	785	3.0	3.8	1,653	301	9,204	1.7
Panama	16,678	3,159	5.4	1.7	4,359	1,399	12,893	4.1
Paraguay	26,853	1,474	4.5	3.1	4,315	729	9,006	1.5
Peru	77,056	2,436	2.8	1.2	20,206	744	51,622	1.9
Suriname	4,188	1,390	9.9	7.1	1,339	3,166	4,151	9.8
Uruguay	16,035	4,892	4.7	1.0	5,970	1,752	9,719	2.9
Venezuela, R. B. de	256,399	2,485	10.0	4.0	62,477	2,445	181,508	7.1
Total	**3,280,308**				**820,706**		**2,367,420**	
Regional Avg.		**3,782**	**6.1**	**1.6**		**1,529**		**4.4**

Sources: Organización Latinoamericana de Energía (OLADE), 2004; estimate based on energy balances.

a. Final consumption + transformation center consumption + own consumption.

b. Final energy consumption per unit of gross domestic product.

c. Information from 2003 (base year 1995).

Boe = barrels of oil equivalent.

Table 6.2. Energy Balance of Distribution Companies, 2001–05

Year	*Energy available (GWh)*	*Energy billed (GWh)*	*Energy losses (GWh)*	*Losses (%)*	*Maximum demand (MW)*	*Change (%)*	*Load factor (%)*
2005	12,347	9,456	2,947	23.9	2,344	2.2	60.1
2004	11,706	8,901	2,805	24.0	2,294	5.2	58.3
2003	11,134	8,522	2,613	23.5	2,174	4.0	58.5
2002	10,575	8,140	2,435	23.0	2,087	5.1	57.8
2001	10,293	7,966	2,327	22.6	1,980	2.0	59.3

Source: CONELEC 2005.

the cost-based tariff calculation and the tariff applied (tariff deficit), as a subsidy to consumers. In May 2000 the rate increased from US$0.025/kWh to US$0.042/kWh, and a 4 percent per month adjustment plan was implemented, with a view to reaching cost levels by the end of 2003. In April 2002 the rate was frozen. In October of 2002, CONELEC approved a rate for the period of November 2002 to October 2003, with monthly increases of 5 percent as of January 2003 until it reached a level of US$0.1038/kWh. Nonetheless, in January 2003 the plan was discontinued, and the increase was reduced to 1.6 percent per month. Box 6.1 shows the structure of the tariff and the situation for 2006.

Box 6.1. Explanation of Tariff Deficit

The regulated tariff consists of the reference generation price (PRG) plus the average costs of transmission, known as the transmission toll, plus the charge for distribution value-added (VAD). CONELEC calculates and sets tariffs annually, based on the PRG, as calculated by CENACE using a simulation of the future operation of the system, and the transmission toll and VAD, which are calculated by CONELEC. The same PRG and transmission charges are applied nationwide, while the VAD is different for each distribution company,[a] depending on service costs. The VAD is based not on the real costs of a company but on the costs of an efficient model company. Therefore, the actual losses of each distribution company (or any other inefficiency) are not factored into the VAD. The regulations allow for a maximum of 12 percent distribution losses. (As the 2005 numbers show, the average overall distribution losses amounted to 24 percent, resulting mainly from theft and illegal connections.)

The annual period for tariff regulation is November to October of the following year. The last regulation was in October 2005, when CONELEC approved the tariffs in the table below. The average nationwide retail tariff is US$0.108/kWh. However, CONELEC (under instruction from the past government) has kept the tariff frozen at the values used during the previous period (and since the freeze ordered in April 2003). This reduction of 24 percent in the tariff would need to be offset by direct subsidies from the government to cover the actual cost of the service. However, the government has not been providing the subsidy to cover the indicated tariff deficit.

Tariff Structure, November 2005–October 2006

	Real tariff		*Subsidized tariff*		*Subsidy*	
Component	*%*	*Value US$/100*	*%*	*Value US$/100*	*%*	*Value US$/100*
• Generation	52.8	5.70	48	4.16	37.00	1.54
• Transmission	6.1	0.66	8	0.71	0.00	0.00
• Distribution	41.1	4.44	44	3.84	16.00	0.60
• Current tariff	100	10.80	100	8.71	24.13	2.14

The Electricity Law also established a 10 percent subsidy to residential users with monthly energy consumption below the average in each distributor's concession area (the national monthly consumption average is about 130 kWh). The subsidy is financed through an equal increase in tariffs to users with consumptions above the average (technically, a cross-subsidy).

a. The new reform law of the sector, approved by Congress in August 2006, has modified the VAD calculation, establishing a kind of "average uniform VAD" for all the distribution companies.

One of the arguments for keeping tariffs below costs is the perception that tariffs in Ecuador are higher than in other countries in the region. However, table 6.3 shows that the perception that the electricity price in Ecuador is high compared with other countries of the region does not correspond to reality. The table shows that electricity prices in countries in the region vary considerably. Only a few countries—Argentina, Honduras, Paraguay, and República Bolivariana de Venezuela—have consistently lower prices than Ecuador, and those have tariffs that are subsidized overall or have been affected by devaluation of the local currency (as is the case in Argentina). In others, industrial tariffs are particularly subsidized, as in Brazil and Uruguay.

Regarding electricity prices in the wholesale market, table 6.4 shows the average price of the spot (or occasional) market and that of fixed-term contracts during the five-year period 2001–05. Distribution companies bought 78 percent of their supply requirements from the spot market, assuming a high risk owing to the volatility and high prices on this market. Very few bilateral contracts exist between generators and distributors, mainly because there is no price pass-through mechanism (the generation price in the wholesale market for distributors is a calculated value, which does

Table 6.3. OLADE Electricity Prices in LAC (US¢/kWh), 2004

Country	*Residential*	*Commercial*	*Industrial*
Argentina	3.75	6.11	3.77
Bolivia	7.20	10.45	4.97
Brazil	9.94	8.77	5.04
Chile	8.79	8.43	5.72
Colombia	9.40	11.28	9.05
Costa Rica	6.40	8.50	5.89
Dominican Republic	17.70	21.83	14.15
Ecuador	**9.84**	**8.27**	**7.42**
El Salvador	12.90	11.89	12.00
Guatemala	16.17	12.27	11.53
Honduras	4.47	2.92	3.49
Mexico	8.66	17.87	8.44
Nicaragua	14.08	16.86	12.93
Panama	12.10	11.80	9.90
Paraguay	5.56	5.93	3.73
Peru	12.71	9.77	8.77
Uruguay	12.45	10.35	5.98
Venezuela, R. B.	4.50	4.02	3.17

Source: OLADE 2005.

Table 6.4. Average Price of Electricity for Distributors in Spot Market and Fixed-Term Contracts (US¢/kWh)

Year	*Average*	*Spot Market*	*Contracts*
2005	8.00	12.04	3.69
2004	7.35	12.33	3.29
2003	6.89	11.12	4.34
2002	5.87	8.12	3.76
2001	5.3	6.5	2.95

Source: CONELEC 2005.

not consider the contractual relations between generators and distributors). This factor contributes to the financial difficulties of the distribution companies.

Access to Electricity

One success story in the electricity sector is the increase in electricity coverage over the past 15 years, especially between 2000 and 2005, during which the increase in the electrification rate has been almost 8 percent. The percentage of households with electricity increased from 77.7 percent in 1990, to 78.8 percent in 1995, 82.0 percent in 2000, and 89.7 in 2005. This important increase in electrification represented about 65,000 new household connections per year. The progress is financed by the Fund for the Electrification of the Rural and Urban Marginal Areas (FERUM),[5] which charges a tariff surcharge of 10 percent on industrial and commercial electricity consumption. FERUM is administered efficiently by CONELEC, using clear and transparent criteria for project selection. If FERUM continues to operate at similar levels over the next five years, the electrification rate in Ecuador could surpass 95 percent by 2011. Ecuador's present electrification rate compares favorably with Peru's but is less than Colombia's.

Renewable Energy and Energy Efficiency

Renewable Energy

Renewable energy has considerable potential in Ecuador, especially for hydropower and geothermal power, but little systematic investigation of that potential has been done. Table 6.5 shows the estimated potential capacity and installed capacity of renewable-energy projects that have been built or are under study.

The 1996 Electricity Law established that the state will stimulate the development and use of nonconventional energies and energy efficiency through the public sector, development banks, universities, and private institutions, and that FERUM resources would be used for rural electrification projects using nonconventional power resources such as solar energy, wind, geothermal, and biomass. Since 2002 FERUM has financed 104 projects using renewable resources, providing modern energy services to about 8,300 dwellings.

As of January 2007, CONELEC has approved promotional prices for electricity produced using nonconventional sources and a compensation mechanism to promote renewable energies in areas not connected to the grid. The system operator, CENACE, will dispatch with priority the energy generated up to 2 percent of the total installed capacity in the generation system. If the total capacity of these plants exceeds that limit, the extra energy will be dispatched according to its economic merit, based on its variable production cost.

Table 6.5. Estimated Renewable Energy Potential for Electricity Generation

Renewable energy source	*Estimated potential (MW)*	*Projects built and under study (MW)*
Wind	High	40
Small hydroelectric	10,000	100
Biomass	400	55
Solar[a]	High	12
Geothermal	70,000	534
Total	80,400	741

a. Assumes solar home systems are installed in 15 percent of remote rural homes without access.

Energy Efficiency

Energy efficiency programs encourage market penetration of energy-efficient equipment and processes, as well as of companies that provide and install them, and new financing instruments. Energy efficiency makes it possible to postpone investments in power supply facilities, increase economic productivity, and reduce the environmental impacts of conventional energy and traditional fuels at the local and global levels. Together with renewable energy sources, energy efficiency provides a path toward increased independence from hydrocarbons. Growing awareness of climate change risks is a forceful driver for promoting sustainable energy.

The low load factor of Ecuador's electricity system (61 percent) increases the capital cost of supplying electricity to final users. Demand management techniques can help improve the load factor but have not been used in Ecuador—except in a project a few years ago that involved replacing incandescent lamps with compact fluorescent lamps, implemented by the distribution company Centro Sur. In addition, sodium lamps have been used in parts of the public lighting system. In energy audits performed by the Ministry of Energy and Mines in the industrial, commercial (hotel), and public sectors, investments in energy efficiency with a repayment period of about one year reduced electricity use by 5 percent. If the sample was representative, moderate penetration of energy efficiency measures in 30 percent of the industrial sector could potentially save up to 130 GWh a year by 2012. But several barriers (discussed below) have precluded energy users and the country from benefiting from these opportunities, including the lack of a national energy efficiency strategy that is fully integrated with the overall energy strategy.

II. Key Challenges

The problems of the electricity sector have been well documented in a number of sources (see the bibliography), most recently in the electricity chapter of the World Bank's "Ecuador: Creating Fiscal Space for Poverty Reduction" (2004). The following section examines some of the challenges, how they have progressed in the past two years, and their present status. It also examines the potential impact of the recently enacted legislation of the sector, mainly the Electricity Sector Reform Law and the Organic Law for the Creation of the Ecuadoran Fund for Investment in the Energy and Hydrocarbons Sectors (*Fondo Ecuatoriano de Inversión en los Sectores Energéticos e Hidrocarburos*—FEISEH).

What Makes the Electricity Distribution System Dysfunctional?

If asked to identify the most critical issue of the Ecuadoran electricity sector, most professionals, government authorities, and the private sector will point to the disastrous situation of some distribution companies, which has negative consequences for the entire sector. All segments of the electricity supply business are important, and their being sound both operationally and financially is indispensable for a well-functioning system. Nevertheless, distribution is the critical link of the chain. The distribution companies supply electricity to final users, plus do billing and collections. These companies are the public face of the sector. The revenues they collect from consumers are needed to finance all other segments of the sector.

For these reasons, the practice has been to start the sector reform process by introducing efficiency improvements in distribution companies. Different options exist, for example (i) a "contract plan" between the government and the public-owned company's internal management, with clear and detailed efficiency targets, premiums, and penalties; (ii) external management contracts; (iii) management partnership agreements with well-run companies; (iv) direct private participation through concessions; and (v) private ownership of partial or total assets. Quite a few successful experiences demonstrate some of these options in Latin America and worldwide.

Table 6.6 shows characteristic efficiency indexes of all the distribution companies in Ecuador for 2005. When the companies are examined individually, marked

Table 6.6. Efficiency Indexes of Distribution Companies, 2005

Distributor	*Number of employees*	*Clients per employee*	*MWh sold by employee*	*Losses (%)*	*Collections (%)*
Ambato	311	536	991	14.3	97.6
Azogues	122	212	279	5.0[a]	94.9
Bolívar	164	257	257	18.3	89.3
CATEG-D	1,516	279	1,624	27.4	93.7
Centro Sur	477	512	992	9.5	100.0[b]
Cotopaxi	280	304	507	13.4	100.0[b]
El Oro	487	310	708	30.4	85.8
Esmeraldas	311	262	770	30.4	73.4
Galápagos	56	107	375	7.8[a]	99.0
Guayas-Los Ríos	563	303	877	38.1	88.1
Los Ríos	560	129	297	31.2	77.0
Manabí	468	434	1,169	40.1	64.7
Milagro	288	358	738	41.9	100.0[b]
Norte	328	486	915	14.6	97.9
Quito	1,484	441	1,635	13.1	99.2
Riobamba	321	376	448	19.6	97.9
Sta. Elena	313	257	672	31.0	82.7
Sto. Domingo	245	421	943	19.0	93.4
Sucumbíos	228	145	341	38.1	79.4
Sur	385	332	437	13.9	100.0[b]
Total/Average	**8,896**	**340**	**1,017**	**23.9**	**93**
LAC average		**559**	**2,343**	**15.3**	**97**

Source: CONELEC 2005.

a. This figure is not representative given the very small size of the companies.

b. The companies with a 100 percent collection rate indicate previous year's recuperation of collection arrears. For example, Cotopaxi's real collection figure for 2005 was 120 percent.

differences in efficiency can be seen, especially between the largest two companies. Empresa Eléctrica de Quito has reasonable operational and financial indexes (losses were 13 percent and bill collection was 99 percent), while CATEG-D of Guayaquil is in very bad shape, both operationally and financially (losses were 27 percent and bill collection was 94 percent).

According to a recent research study, the indexes in table 6.7 for Ecuador compare badly with those of other distribution companies in the Latin America region (World Bank 2006). For example, the average number of clients per employee in the region is 559, and in Ecuador the average is 340. The best-ranked Ecuadoran company with respect to this index is Ambato, with 536, still lower than the average in the region. The average energy sold per employee annually in Ecuador is less than half of the regional average of 2,343 MWh. Not even the two largest companies (Quito and CATEG-D) have efficiency indexes that could be considered satisfactory. Although the 2006 study did not obtain data regarding bill collections, a collection percentage lower than 97 percent is considered, in general, to be financially unsatisfactory. The average of this index in Ecuador is 92.8 percent, and eight companies have bill collections of less than 90 percent, indicating a relatively high level of nonpayment.

At 24 percent average total losses, Ecuador has one of the highest levels of nationwide distribution loss in Latin America. If this percentage were to be reduced to the regional average of 15 percent, the distribution companies' revenues would be increased by about US$100 million annually. Improving bill collection from 93 percent to 97.5 percent would contribute another US$40 million to annual distribution revenues. To illustrate the impact of the problem, table 6.7 compares a standard efficient company, the Ecuadoran average, and what would be considered a very efficient company.

Reforms to implement the necessary efficiency improvements in distribution companies would include modernizing the distribution companies' information systems; improving billing systems; reducing losses, theft, and illegal connections; improving collections; and reducing operation and maintenance costs. Privatization is one way to achieve these changes. However, several times over the past four years, governments have backed away from plans to privatize electricity distributors because

Table 6.7. What Happens to 100 kWh Purchased by a Distribution Company (kWh)

	Standard company	*Ecuador average*	*Very efficient company*
Purchased energy	100	100	100
Heat losses	10	10	8
Remaining energy for sale	90	90	92
Stolen or unmetered	3	14	1
Billed	87	76	91
Paid	86	68	91

Source: Authors' estimates.

of strong opposition by labor unions and regional and municipal governments. Three separate efforts to outsource the administration of electricity distributors, while maintaining state control of the assets, failed in 2003, 2004, and 2005. The result of new efforts in 2006 to arrange concessions with some companies did not materialize.

One of the major problems is that, in parallel with management improvements, investments are required, and the negative cash flow keeps that from happening. The outlook is therefore one of continued deterioration for many distribution companies, unless measures are taken. The reform law of September 2006 contemplated some measures directed at improving distribution companies, such as establishing mechanisms to ensure efficient management and penalizing electricity theft, unauthorized manipulation of metering equipment, and illegal connections. But this legislation also has brought some potential problems to the distribution companies; for example, it established a new mechanism to calculate the VAD as a national average applied to all companies, not specifically related to the particular cost components of each company, which penalizes the most efficient companies.

Tariff Shortfalls and Growing Accumulated Deficits

As noted under "Electricity Tariffs," the financial problems of the distribution companies come not only from the poor performance of some companies, but also from a permanent tariff deficit, meaning the establishment of electricity tariffs below the economic cost of service. The accumulated financial impact of the tariff deficit from April 1999 to December 2006 has been about US$1,260 million. This deficit caused nonpayment and arrears of distribution companies to the other agents of the wholesale electricity market, that is, the generators and the transmission company, making the whole system dysfunctional.

The problems in tariff setting and the resulting financial deficit stem from discretionary application of the rules, combined with constant interference by past governments in tariff setting decisions that are the regulator's responsibility. This situation generates distrust in the regulatory system and jeopardizes the independence of the regulator. What is more important, it creates undesirable precedents, discouraging the entry of private investors or operators.

As shown in table 6.8, the accumulated deficit as of December 2005 was US$1,059 million, and the expected tariff deficit for 2006 is about US$200 million. Successive governments have promised to cover the deficits. However, past deficits were only partially compensated by debt-offset procedures, or not compensated at all, resulting in a large and accumulating deficit. For example, in 2002 and 2003 the executive office enacted decrees by which the government, through the Ministry of Economy and Finance, recognized and ratified the obligation to pay the difference in income that was generated by the tariff deficit. However, no funds were finally allocated.

In 2004, an executive decree authorized the Ministry of Economy and Finance to recognize, through the escrow accounts system, an amount up to US$15 million for the period September–December 2004, to compensate the difference between the

Table 6.8. Distribution of Tariff Deficit and Arrears to the MEM
(December 31, 2005, US$ except where noted)

Company	*Tariff deficit*	*Arrears to the MEM*	*Difference*	*Losses (%)*
Ambato	40,896,367	8,308,950	32,587,417	14.33
Azogues	7,146,593	1,639,469	5,507,124	5.57
Bolívar	9,902,192	5,195,502	4,706,690	18.34
CATEG-D	288,549,670	659,655,768	–371,106,098	27.36
Centro Sur	75,891,849	1,166,080	74,725,769	9.48
Cotopaxi	20,525,166	1,385,985	19,139,181	13.44
El Oro	37,850,908	67,718,683	–29,867,775	30.35
Emelgur	21,788,436	139,547,396	–117,758,960	38.13
Esmeraldas	21,810,789	43,113,301	–21,302,512	30.42
Los Ríos	19,067,000	40,435,170	–21,368,170	31.15
Manabí	41,071,421	161,429,426	–120,358,005	40.12
Milagro	15,163,669	43,916,818	–28,753,149	41.85
Norte	37,928,263	14,546,123	23,382,140	14.58
Quito	316,114,525	105,952,205	210,162,320	13.14
Riobamba	33,875,612	470,002	33,405,610	19.60
Sta. Elena	20,504,781	35,177,902	–14,673,121	31.00
Sto. Domingo	15,708,985	21,491,365	–5,782,380	18.97
Sur	35,119,325	11,390,293	23,729,032	13.86
Total	**1,058,915,552**	**1,362,540,439**	**–303,624,887**	—

Source: CONELEC 2005.

reference generation cost that is paid through the tariff and the actual generation cost (see box 6.2). This decree also authorized allocation of all necessary resources to cover the difference between the generation cost applied in the tariff and the actual generation cost in the proposed national budget of 2005. Despite this decree, only US$80 million was allocated in the 2005 budget, with specific instruction on how to allocate funds (for example, Hidropaute, Hidroagoyan, and CATEG-D were favored in allocation over private generators, remaining public generators, the distributors, and PetroEcuador).[6] During 2004 and 2005 the government allocated US$95 million to cover the tariff deficit, but this amount is less than 10 percent of the total accrued deficit.

In the Reform Law of September 2006, the government committed to compensate the sector for the tariff deficit from April 1999 to December 2005, up to a limit of US$950 million (taking into account the US$95 million allocated previously). The prescribed funds would be used to (i) pay PetroEcuador the amount owed by thermal plants for their fuel bill (about US$170 million); (ii) balance cross-debt accounts of public hydroelectric generators and the Ministry of Economy and Finance (related to external hydropower generators' debts assumed by the government, and to the tariff deficit); (iii) establish a loss reduction program and management improvements of distribution companies; and (iv) allocate the remainder to distributors

Box 6.2. Payment Priorities from Distribution Companies and Accumulating Debts

As a result of a series of executive orders, the distribution companies deposit into individual escrow accounts their entire revenue from electricity sales to their customers. The EA administrators make payments to generators supplying electric power to the Ministry of Energy and Mines, as dispatched by CENACE.

Since December 2004, the first priority for payment is reserved for each distributor's VAD payment, then payment to Transelectric for transmission services, and third, payment for electricity imports and private generation (priority 3A and B, respectively). Payments are to be made in the defined order of priority, applying the payment priority to the bill for the month preceding the one in which the amounts are collected. Payment on bills pending from previous months is moved to the lowest payment priority. This change, introduced in the priority table under the amendment of October 2003, has caused the older bills to go unpaid. Their settlement moved to the lowest priority, to be settled out of any remaining balance after all other categories have been satisfied. As electric power collections are significantly lower than the value of the electricity purchased by the distribution companies, outstanding bills from previous months turn into bad debts.

This has resulted in an accumulation of debt to PetroEcuador for fuels as well as for purchase of electricity from publicly owned hydrogeneration companies, which are last in the order of payment.

with positive balance between their corresponding tariff deficit and what they owe to the wholesale market.

As can be seen in table 6.8, the deficits at the level of individual companies again show considerable differences. CATEG-D, Emelgur, and Manabi show large negative balances, while other companies such as Quito and Centro Sur actually show positive balances because of their relative efficiency.

The table also shows the accumulated arrears to the wholesale market (MEM) of US$1,362 million as of December 2005, which is greater than the accumulated tariff deficit. This means that even if the government provides the necessary funds to cover the accumulated tariff deficit, a negative difference (a deficit) would still remain in the accounts of some distribution companies. Not surprisingly, the distribution companies with the largest remaining deficits are the ones with the largest distribution losses.

Another important tariff issue is related to the way in which CENACE calculates the generation cost (the reference generation price, or PRG) and its direct translation into tariffs by CONELEC. Both policies affect distribution company finances that are already in bad shape owing to inefficiency and management problems and to the tariff deficit. CENACE calculates the RGP as the expected average marginal operating cost of the system for a four-year period of estimated supply and demand conditions, plus a capacity charge related to a peaking unit. This calculated value of the RGP does not coincide with the actual price at which distribution companies buy energy, which is based on contractual prices with generators and purchases in the spot market. For example, in 2005, purchases had a mean cost of US$0.08/kWh, compared with an RGP of US$0.057/kWh, resulting in a loss of US$28.4 million.[7]

A final point regarding tariffs is the average consumption cross-subsidy described in box 6.2. Although this type of subsidy is common practice in many countries (by setting a minimum or social tariff), usually the subsidy is limited to lifeline consumption and targeted to poor households. One such example, which is close to Ecuador's, is the Peruvian FOSE (Fondo de Compensación Social Eléctrica) subsidy (see box 6.3). Lifeline consumption in many countries is established at around 50 kWh/month, compared with about 130 kWh/month for eligibility for the subsidy in the case of Ecuador.

The cross-subsidy, as described in the Electricity Law and applied by CONELEC, has some regressive characteristics that favor users with higher consumption rates over

Box 6.3. Peru's Fondo de Compensación Social Eléctrica

In the restructuring of the Peruvian electricity sector, the electricity tariff scheme was designed for full cost recovery. Until the middle of 2001, there were no explicit subsidies to the electricity rates. In 2001, legislation was passed, establishing a "social tariff" for electricity consumption (the so-called FOSE) which applied beginning in November 2001, with a temporary duration of three years.

In July 2004, the Congress extended indefinitely the application of the subsidy, increasing the levels of tariff reductions. The current subsidy consists of 25 percent and 62.5 percent tariff reductions for monthly consumption up to 30 kWh for urban users supplied by the interconnected system and for rural users supplied by isolated systems, respectively. For consumption between 31 kWh and 100 kWh, the reduction is gradual, from a maximum of 31.25 percent to a minimum of 7.5 percent, for rural users supplied by isolated systems, and for urban users supplied by the interconnected system, respectively. Consumption above 100 kWh per month would pay a proportional cross-subsidy to finance the FOSE discount.

Statistics indicate that just over 60 percent of households (about 2.4 million electricity service users) are beneficiaries of FOSE. The FOSE cross-subsidy amounts to about US$25 million annually, which represents a slightly over 3 percent increase in the retail full-cost residential electricity tariff for the users providing the subsidy.

those who consume less. In practice, electricity clients of Empresa Eléctrica de Quito and CATEG-D (serving Guayaquil) are favored by the subsidy scheme. Figure 6.2 shows the situation of the cross-subsidy for two distribution companies, CATEG-D (with users with the largest average monthly consumption—194 kWh/month) and Bolivar (with users with much lower average monthly consumption—60 kWh/month).

As the figure shows, CATEG-D's clients receive a larger proportional subsidy (as a percentage of the kWh tariff) than Bolivar's for each range of monthly consumption. Furthermore, CATEG-D clients with consumption in the range 60–145 kWh/month receive a subsidy of between 40 percent and 15 percent of their kWh tariff, whereas Bolivar clients in this range of consumption have to pay for the subsidy, with an increase in the kWh tariff of about 10 percent. In the case of CATEG-D, only its clients with monthly consumptions above 200 kWh pay the subsidy. All this indicates the lack of equity in the subsidy mechanism and the need to revise it to be more clearly targeted to benefit low-income households and to be equitable across distribution companies. There are many examples of efficient and effective cross-subsidies in the electricity sector, such as the FOSE scheme in Peru described in box 6.3.

Inadequate Investment in Generation—How to Keep the Lights On

The Electricity Law of 1996 charged CONELEC with sector planning, in addition to regulatory functions. Under this mandate, CONELEC publishes each year a National Electrification Plan (*Plan Nacional de Electrificación*), which covers a period of 10 years. In this document, CONELEC analyzes alternatives of transmission and

Figure 6.2. Cross-Subsidy Scheme for Bolivar and CATEG-D

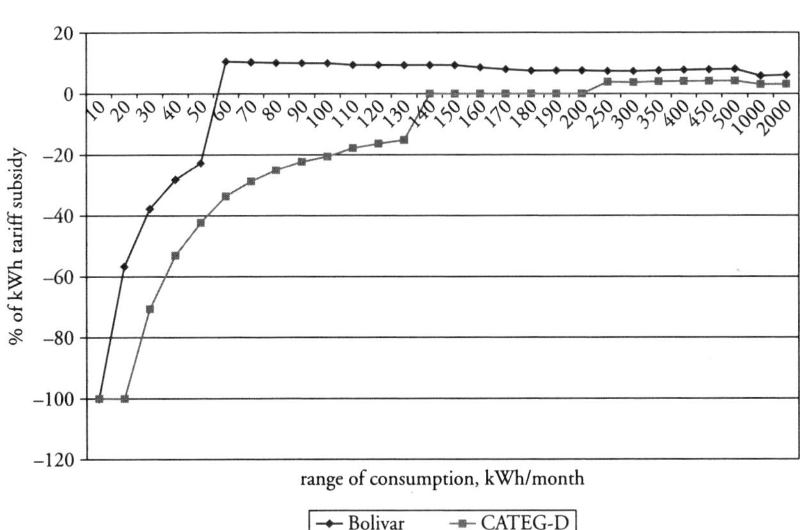

Source: Authors' elaboration.

generation expansion to deal with expected electricity demand requirements. The expansion of the generation system for 2007–11, as analyzed by CONELEC in its latest plan, is based mainly on construction of six new plants: Termoguayas (150 MW), San Francisco (212 MW), Bajo Alto (95 MW; Machala), Mazar (190 MW), Machala 3rd stage (87 MW), and Termoriente (270 MW), plus other private developments consisting of small hydropower, one wind power, and one thermal plant (total of 144 MW). The overall expected expansion of local generation would be 1,050 MW, if all proposed projects are implemented. Projects under way are the publicly owned San Francisco, which is financed through Brazil; Mazar, whose implementation has begun but stalled through lack of financing; and Termoguayas, which should start operation in December 2006 (totaling 550 MW). None of the other privately owned projects (totaling about 500 MW) have obtained financing for implementation. Furthermore, about 820 MW of the existing thermal generating units are now reaching the limit of their useful life and are very expensive to operate, requiring replacement, or rehabilitation and repowering. If not replaced, the spot market price will continue to reflect the high cost of these plants.

The most important development of the expansion program is Mazar, not because it would contribute 190 MW to generation capacity, but because the reservoir associated with it will secure the available capacity of Paute during the dry season. Thus, Mazar represents in practice an additional 193 MW of capacity during this critical period and 1,182 GWh of energy production annually for the system.

If the expansion program as foreseen by CONELEC is fully implemented, the situation during the dry season is critical in 2006 and 2007, when production capacity and energy availability are just enough to cover the demand plus a 10 percent reserve (see figures 6.3 and 6.4). In 2008 and 2009 the balance of demand and production capacity improves noticeably, in particular in 2009 with Mazar's double impact—its own production and the increase in capacity and energy availability in Paute. The reserve situation in 2009 and thereafter improves considerably, reaching 53 percent in capacity and 38 percent in energy.

With improved conditions anticipated in the sector from 2009 onward, it would be possible and advisable to program the retirement of the old, inefficient diesel-powered thermal plants after 2009. This action would reduce the excess reserve to a more reasonable level. Of the 510 MW total capacity of the thermal plants that could be retired, 130 MW belong to distribution companies. Also, the import requirements would be reduced, to apply only in emergency situations.

The generation system also requires an adaptation to have a more efficient plant mix and to reinforce the energy availability of hydrogeneration during the dry season. CONELEC's expansion program complies with these requirements, although it will require a great investment of over US$1 billion in the next five years, of which about US$350 million is expected to come from the private sector.

Of the 1,050 MW planned by CONELEC, 500 MW have not yet been financed; therefore, the critical supply situation could extend beyond 2006–07. The financing of Mazar is especially critical, given its importance to increasing production capacity.

Figure 6.3. Maximum Demand Balance, 2006–11 during Critical Month in Dry Season
(under dry-year hydrology, medium demand, and normal capacity availability)

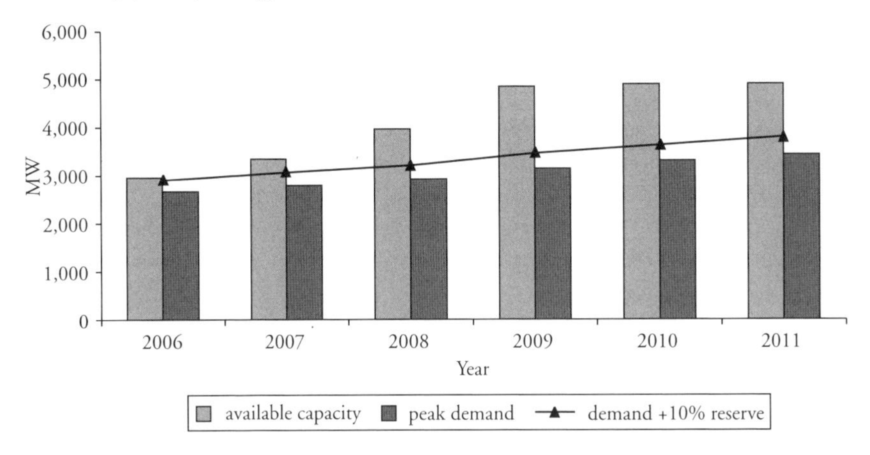

Source: Authors' elaboration of CONELEC data.

Figure 6.4. Energy Balance, 2006–11 during Critical Month in Dry Season
(under dry-year hydrology, medium demand, and normal energy availability)

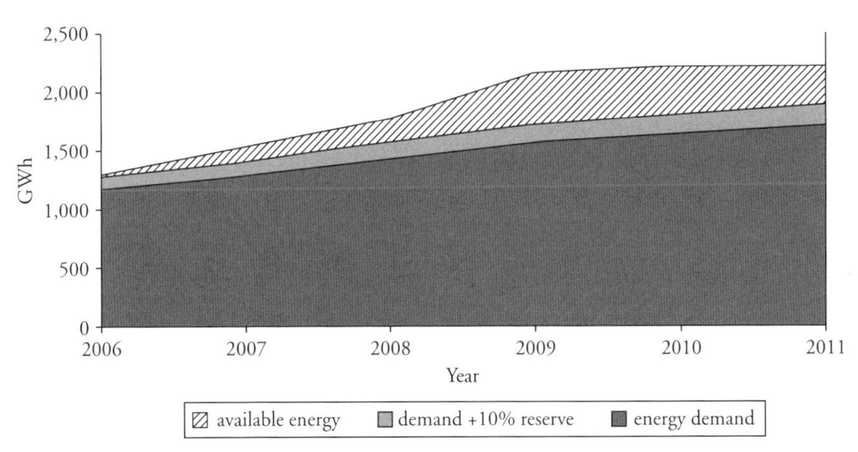

Source: Authors' elaboration of CONELEC data.

Much depends on sufficient availability of funds from petroleum revenues through newly established mechanisms, especially FEISEH. If sufficient financing is not made available for Mazar very quickly, dry season shortages will be exacerbated, and rationing and brownouts will be necessary.

Governance Issues That Contribute to Inaction on Resolving Long-Standing Problems

The design of the institutional framework in the 1996 electricity law followed most of the basic principles concerning the structure of the sector and separation of functions; however, certain aspects of the institutional setup, the allocation of functions, and the very limited participation of the private sector contributed to the government's retaining a significant role in all activities of the electricity industry. In the past, one of the most visible government interventions in the sector has been the setting of electricity tariffs, showing in practice CONELEC's lack of real independence.

Also, as originally envisioned, the Solidarity Fund was established to act as a fund manager of the proceeds resulting from the privatization of the publicly owned companies, to be a social projects financier, and to ensure equitable distribution of the fund's profits among Ecuadorans. In practice, as a result of the failure of privatization, the Solidarity Fund has become the owner and de facto administrator of public companies, functions not foreseen in its constitution. The administration of the electricity companies by the fund has not improved the operations and management of those companies but may instead have added an additional layer of bureaucracy to the sector.

Another aspect of the electricity sector framework that has contributed to the difficulty of correcting problems in the sector is the lack of a central governmental institution with a final responsibility in setting national sector policies and proposing legislation. In the 1996 reform, the Ministry of Energy and Mines was stripped of almost all electricity sector policy and planning functions except rural electrification. Even sector planning, which is a ministerial function in other LAC countries, was transferred to CONELEC. As a consequence, with time, the ministry's role in the electricity sector was weakened, and it proposed few new policy initiatives. High-level decision making in the sector was dispersed, leaving the solution of most pressing problems in the hands of the executive branch.

Barriers to Development of Renewable Energy and Energy Efficiency

While development of renewable energy and energy efficiency has considerable potential in Ecuador, such development has been hampered by a number of factors.

Renewable Energy

Ecuador has the potential to develop new and renewable sources of energy, especially small and medium hydropower, wind power, and biomass fuels for grid-connected systems, plus mini-hydroelectric grids and solar home systems for providing electricity to isolated communities. The inventory of viable small hydroelectric projects, originally prepared by the national power company INECEL, includes 200 projects with combined capacity of 10,000 megawatts. Of these, 80 projects would generate more than 10 megawatts each, and 120 would generate less. About 40 mini-hydroelectric plants have been built, with total capacity of about 100 megawatts, but some are out of service. The Ministry of Energy and Mines has conducted technical and financial prefeasibility studies of 15 small hydropower plants included in the above inventory to facilitate future participation by private investors.[8]

Geothermal resources are abundant but underdeveloped in Ecuador. Total potential geothermal energy is estimated at about 1,450 metric tons of oil equivalent, while economically viable energy is estimated at about 55 metric tons of oil equivalent, or about 70 gigawatts. Viability studies for three projects are under way—Cachirimbo, Chalupas, and Chiles-Cerro Negro—with combined capacity of 534 megawatts.

Although renewable energy has considerable potential in Ecuador, several barriers have been identified:

- Capital costs are significantly higher for renewable energy sources than for conventional sources, and long-term financing is not easily available. This situation is complicated in Ecuador by the dysfunctional situation of the distribution companies, which means that payment for generation is not assured.
- Some renewable energy options—such as solar and wind—have variable production, depending on the availability of the resource, and therefore require backup. However, the use of small renewable energy plants that are geographically dispersed throughout the system increases the system's aggregate reliability.
- Because renewable energy is usually site specific, lack of access to or lack of reliable records and data—such as on wind intensity and permanency data, or geological data on sites proposed for hydroelectric projects—are a barrier to a site's development.
- Lack of information and unclear regulations can increase costs of project identification, design, and implementation, affecting small projects in particular. Unclear procedures for negotiating, approving, and contracting projects may further increase costs.

Energy Efficiency

Demand-side management programs can reduce consumption at peak demand times, and thereby improve load factors and result in postponement of investments in supply facilities. Properly executed demand-side management could substantially increase residential consumers' use of efficient compact fluorescent lamps, reducing peak demand by about 125 megawatts. Another demand management program, aimed at using efficient lamps in street lighting and replacing about 300,000 inefficient incandescent and mercury vapor lamps, could reduce peak demand by about 25 megawatts. A medium-term program supporting energy service companies, and facilitating efficiency investments by them and by the commercial, industrial, and public sectors, could reduce peak demand by another 30 to 100 megawatts by 2012, depending on the program's intensity and penetration. Acceleration of the current standardization, measurement, and labeling program, which aims to increase the efficiency of electrical appliances and equipment and the thermal insulation of buildings, as well as promote the adoption of solar water heaters—could also help reduce peak demand and the carbon content of the country's energy sector. If implemented soon, mandatory standardization and labeling of refrigerators alone could reduce peak demand by 40 megawatts by 2012. Combined, these interventions could reduce peak demand by 220–290 megawatts.

Several additional barriers must be addressed in order to realize the energy efficiency potential described above:

- The main economic and financial barriers are the lack of commercial financing for energy efficiency projects, the high cost of developing in-house technical capacity to identify and implement energy efficiency projects, and subsidies on electricity tariffs and inadequate use of time-of-day tariffs that fail to give correct price signals to consumers.
- The main technological barriers are the lack of efficient technologies and equipment in the market, the lack of information and knowledge on efficient technologies, and the lack of confidence in the effectiveness of efficient technologies to improve processes and lower costs.
- The main sociocultural barriers are the lack of an energy efficiency culture; ignorance of energy efficiency options, particularly among small and medium enterprises; perceived risks of and lack of confidence in energy efficiency projects; lack of training and experience in implementing energy efficiency projects; lack of demonstration projects; a conservative mentality toward adopting energy efficiency projects; and fear among informal enterprises of fiscal consequences if they share information or open their processes to energy audits.

The Reform Law of the Electricity Sector

The National Congress recently approved a law to amend the existing electricity law, in force since 1996. The stated objective of the new reform law of 2006 is to correct some existing structural problems of the sector. The new legislation stipulates the following:

- The Ministry of Energy and Mines will be the governmental entity in charge of formulating and coordinating the electricity sector's national policy as well as preparing the energy master plan for the country.
- Criminal penalties will be set for those who use electricity for fraudulent purposes (theft).
- The government may directly develop new generation projects, with its own resources, and in association with specialized companies.

- Only one of five members of CONELEC's board of directors will be appointed by the president. The other four members will be selected through a competitive process carried out by an independent committee.
- The Ministry of Economy and Finance has the obligation to guarantee contractual payment to generation companies, for electricity supply under term contracts with distribution companies, in which the government has more than 50 percent share participation. This guarantee only applies if the selling price is lower than the reference price in force at the contract date.
- The law modifies the method of calculating the energy price for regulated final consumers. The applicable distribution value added (VAD) will be determined as the average VAD of all distribution companies of the country. Companies with a VAD higher than the average will reduce their VAD to the average. Companies with VAD lower than the average will maintain their VAD.
- The members of the boards of directors and managers of energy sector companies in which the government has a majority share will be appointed through competitive public processes.
- The government recognizes the tariff deficit. The Ministry of Economy and Finance (MEF) will establish a mechanism to pay the tariff deficit produced from April 1999 and December 2005, up to a limit of US$950 million.
- CONELEC is given five years to execute an energy sector stabilization program for the incorporation of new and efficient generation and to improve the management of distribution companies. During this period distribution companies must buy at least 70 percent of their annual energy needs through long-term contracts.

Although the new sector legislation has positive aspects that are directed at correcting some of the sector's most visible problems, it leaves many important issues, such as the tariff deficit in the future and the fiscal impact of that deficit, unsolved. Also, recognizing the past tariff deficit as a government debt is not enough, if the government does not or cannot allocate the necessary resources to pay tariff subsidies (for example, payment of the tariff deficit by the government has been limited to the estimated amount through December 2005, without establishing a mechanism to compensate the 2006 and later deficits). Since the annual deficit in 2006 was US$200 million and growing, over the next five years the cumulative deficit could easily total US$1.5 billion, requiring additional resources of this magnitude from the treasury. The government does not have a good track record on the issue of tariff deficits. In any case, making the tariff deficit official may not be the solution to the sector's financial problems. Furthermore, with the law's intention of establishing a nationwide VAD, it has proposed a new cross-subsidy.

The new law has no promotional or incentive measures to enable the sector to mobilize commercial financing or attract needed private capital or management to the sector. Even the law's guarantee-payment mechanism for supply contracts with distribution companies is restricted to contract prices not greater than the regulated reference generation price (RGP). In practice, therefore, a generation price cap for contracts has been introduced in the legislation. As a consequence, payment to generators for electricity supply to the spot market is not guaranteed, leaving these companies unprotected from the commercial risk of nonpayment by distributors to the wholesale market. This lack of guaranteed payment for generation is clearly a disincentive to commercial investment in new generation.

Another recent law that could have a profound impact on the electricity sector, mainly in the expansion of generation supply, is FEISEH, which created the Ecuadoran Energy and Hydrocarbons Investment Fund. This law, approved by Congress in September 2006, provides a legal framework for the administration and use of revenues coming from production by the oil fields previously operated by Occidental Petroleum Company (Oxy) and recently taken over by PetroEcuador. The legislation allows for the creation of a trust fund whose resources will be partly invested in the country's electricity and hydrocarbons sectors. It aims to protect public cash resources flushed from this new oil revenue from growing pressure to increase state spending.

FEISEH proposes to channel all the revenues from the fields to the trust fund that would be administered by the central bank and run by a commission of five representatives from several public entities, and presided over by the vice president of the country. From those revenues, some 27 percent would be earmarked to compensate the Special Account for Productive and Social Reactivation (*Cuenta Especial de Reactivación Productiva y Social*—CEREPS) for lost revenue after cancellation of the Occidental contract. The necessary operating and investment expenses for production and management of the fields will also be charged to the fund. PetroEcuador estimates US$250 million of operating expenses annually (Occidental's latest estimate, including necessary additional drillings, was US$400 million). Expected annual revenue after operating expenses is between US$1.3 and US$1.5 billion. A one-time assignment of US$50 million for the national system of microfinance from the fund is also stipulated.

The most important part of the law, concerning the energy sector, is the provision to use part of the FEISEH resources to finance strategic hydroelectric, renewable energy, and hydrocarbons projects of enterprises in which the state has more than 50 percent ownership (including CATEG-D). The private sector could participate in these projects together with state-owned companies, in a minority partnership agreement. Potential projects will be approved by a special technical committee.

The fund would finance hydroelectric projects of not less than 25 megawatts of installed capacity, up to an incremental total of 2,300 megawatts. Considering the expected revenues of the fields, the production and operating expenses, and the other assignments of fund resources, it is estimated that about US$3 billion could be invested in this type of hydroelectric project over six years (some US$500 million per year), thus ensuring financing for the important hydroelectric project of Mazar, and the availability of funds from FEISEH would represent a very important boost to expanding generation. It is not yet clear whether the 2006 reform law and the law creating FEISEH will be implemented.

III. Policy Options

Making the Distribution System Functional

Low billing and collection in a number of distribution companies, especially CATEG-D and small companies, are resulting in significant losses of revenue to the distribution companies. The large number of distribution companies and the small size of many of them prevent economies of scale for efficient operation, resulting in a distribution system that is dysfunctional. Because the distribution companies generate revenue needed for all stages of investment in electricity generation, transmission, and distribution, it is essential to restore their function as the system's cash register. Some key issues and options are outlined in each table on policy options.

Eliminating Accumulated and Annual Tariff Deficits

Because tariffs do not cover costs, distribution companies are not able to pay all their bills and are accumulating growing debts to PetroEcuador for fuel and to publicly owned hydroelectric companies for electricity purchases. This in turn impedes new investment. Paute, for example, is unable to finance essential investment in Mazar because of a lack of capital, yet it is unable to mobilize debt financing because of the uncertainty of final payment for future electricity sales. The result is growing pressure on the public sector to (i) make retribution to the sector for the past accumulated deficit of US$1.3 billion and (ii) continue to finance an annual deficit currently estimated at US$240 million and growing (compared with an annual budget expenditure on health, which is US$400 million). It should be noted that in most Latin America and the Caribbean countries, including neighboring countries such as Colombia and Peru, the electricity sector is self-financing, requiring no support from the national budget. Table 6.9 outlines several options to address these issues.

Ensuring That Investment in Generation Is Adequate to Keep the Lights On

Ecuador is experiencing increasing shortages in the dry season that are making it difficult to maintain electricity supply. A study carried out on the investment climate in Ecuador in 2003 showed that the reliability of electricity service is perceived by companies as an important problem for their operations and an important limitation to economic growth (World Bank 2005). Also, some thermal plants are reaching the end of their economic life and are expensive to operate, requiring replacement or rehabilitation. While plans exist for system expansion, financing has not yet been secured for most of the investments, including the most important investment required in Mazar. Unless financing is secured rapidly, rationing and power cuts will worsen in the dry season, negatively affecting the country's competitiveness. Table 6.10 outlines several options to address these issues.

Table 6.9. Options to Eliminate Accumulated and Annual Tariff Deficits

Issue	*Options*	*Responsibility*
Low billing and collection in some distribution companies	Introduce competitive and professional selection of board members and management of public distribution companies.	Solidarity Fund
	Create a culture of payment, while enabling cutoff of electricity to nonpaying customers.	Solidarity Fund, distribution companies
Poor performance of some distribution companies	Create a custom solution for CATEG-D: sell off or concession as already planned.	CONELEC
	Outsource management of distribution companies through concession, management contract with private firm, or performance-based contracts with top management and staff.	Solidarity Fund
Size of companies; lack of economies of scale	Merge large and small companies serving similar size market territories or put small companies under control and supervision of larger efficient companies.	Solidarity Fund
Annual tariff deficit because of past interference that limited tariff to level below CONELEC's calculation	Select majority of CONELEC board members by independent committee.	MEM
	Increase tariffs to reach the necessary level for financial sustainability or include annual subsidy in national budget.	CONELEC, MEF
Accumulation of US$1.3 billion in wholesale market debt from past	Assign the MEF to make payment to sector for accumulated debt.	MEF
No fiduciary responsibility of distribution company managers for sectoral debt	Enable cutoffs of distribution companies that do not pay generation companies for electricity purchases (follow Colombian example) or require posting of guarantee by buyers.	MEM, Solidarity Fund

Improving Sector Regulation for Price and Tariff Setting

Existing regulations for electricity price and tariff setting could be improved. No specific rules address competitive supply contracting by distribution companies, to ensure economic efficiency and adequate pass-through of generation costs to consumers and cost recovery by distribution companies. Regarding electricity tariffs to final consumers, the existence of cross-subsidies may distort the economic signal necessary for efficient energy use and for tariffs that reflect costs. The present scheme

Table 6.10. Options to Ensure Adequate Investment in Generation

Issue	*Options*	*Responsibility*
The need to meet demand during the dry season	Activate FEISEH regarding use of petroleum revenues for financing hydropower projects on a debt-financing basis.	MEM, MEF
	Develop long-term storage for hydroelectric facilities; ensure adequate financing for Mazar.	MEF, MEM
	Mobilize financing for hydropower using public-private partnerships and regulations; ensure reasonable return on efficient investment.	MEM
Old thermal plants that are nearing the end of their economic life and expensive to operate	Replace, rehabilitate, or repower old publicly owned thermal plants.	MEM, Solidarity Fund
	Mobilize private financing for new, efficient thermal plants using public-private partnerships.	MEM, generation companies
	Guarantee payment by public distribution companies of energy bill and regulations ensure reasonable return on efficient investment.	MEM, MEF

of cross-subsidy favors users of distribution companies with larger consumption. Also, the subsidy is provided to users with consumption above a reasonable lifeline level focusing on the poor and therefore is contrary to an efficient governmental social policy. It is not surprising that those paying the subsidy resent the scheme. One other issue on price regulation is the present arrangements to import electricity from neighboring countries. Although the imports have had positive effects in avoiding potential power cuts, their effect on electricity pricing has been limited, mainly because of a lack of regulation of long-term contracting, which subjects the purchases to relatively high opportunity prices in an occasional market (see Table 6.11).

Improving Governance to Facilitate Efficiency in the Sector

Policy making in the sector has not always been consistent and effective. The fact that CONELEC is charged with both policy making and regulation for the sector may create a conflict of interest. A second part of the problem could be that the Solidarity Fund, which was intended to be both owner and manager of the publicly owned distribution companies, has an important de facto role in commercial management of the sector that it is not well equipped to play (see Table 6.12).

Table 6.11. Options to Improve Sector Regulation for Price and Tariff Setting

Contracting of electricity supply by distribution companies	Establish new regulation for efficient and competitive contracting of electricity supply by distribution companies.	MEM, CONELEC
Tariffs not reflecting actual costs of distribution company energy purchases	Change regulations to allow pass-through of actual reasonable (e.g., competitively bid) energy purchases.	MEM, CONELEC
Inefficient subsidies	1. Rationalize cross-subsidy to avoid regression characteristics of present scheme. 2. Limit subsidy to lifeline consumption.	MEM, CONELEC
High price of electricity imports	Establish long-term contracts for imports rather than occasional supply at expensive opportunity price.	MEM, distribution companies

Table 6.12. Options to Improve Governance to Facilitate Efficiency in the Sector

CONELEC charged with both policy making and regulation for the sector	1. Implement policy-making function in MEM including policy setting for tariffs.	MEM
	2. Strengthen capacity of MEM for policy making and planning.	MEM
Tariff decisions made on discretionary basis by political authorities in the past	1. Assign CONELEC to set tariffs independently, following transparent and efficient cost-based price regulations.	MEM, CONELEC
	2. Ensure price protection for the poor (lifeline subsidy).	MEM, MEF
Solidarity Fund's role in commercial management	Implement independent management of companies the, with Solidarity Fund would be owner and administrator of the fund.	MEM, Solidarity Fund

Developing Cost-Effective New and Renewable Energy Sources to Facilitate Sustainability in the Sector

Many ongoing and previous initiatives supported by public and private local and international stakeholders have prepared the field to capitalize on current opportunities. Also, the government has declared its commitment to making sustainable

Table 6.13. Options to Develop Cost-Effective New and Renewable Energy Sources

Legal and regulatory barriers to renewable energy development	Define a legal, institutional, and regulatory framework for sustainable energy.	MEM
	Strengthen the Subsecretariat of Renewable Energy and Energy Efficiency.	MEM
	Transform current maximum participation of renewable energies as defined by CONELEC—2 percent—into a mandatory target, and consider increasing this participation in the future.	MEM, CONELEC
Long-term financing not available to finance high capital costs of renewable energies when regulatory risks are perceived as high	Set up a financial facility to provide project financing or limited guarantees to banks lending on commercial terms. Increase use of FERUM.	MEM, MEF
	Allow the MEM, CONELEC, and others to act as aggregators to reduce transaction costs of trading certified emission reductions.	MEM, CONELEC
Lack of access to or lack of reliable resource records and data	1. Make available to potential investors the inventory of renewable resource records and data.	MEM, CONELEC
	2. Collect, prepare, and publish data such as wind and solar maps and inventory of hydroelectric resources and biomass in Ecuador.	MEM, CONELEC

energy a key component of its energy strategy and created a Subsecretariat of Renewable Energy and Energy Efficiency under the MEM. However, creating the momentum necessary to overcome the barriers to developing renewable energy will require a strategic and programmatic effort by the MEM, with a number of elements (Table 6.13).

Maximizing Energy Efficiency

Together with renewable energy sources, energy efficiency provides a way to increase independence from hydrocarbons and reduce emissions that increase risks of climate change. To promote renewable energy and energy efficiency, electricity tariffs must the reflect full economic costs of energy supply if they are to provide adequate signals to investors and consumers. Time-of-day tariffs should

Table 6.14. Options to Maximize Energy Efficiency

Economic and financial barriers	Create a facility to finance studies of energy efficiency measures and provide grants and loans to finance their implementation (audits, studies, and investments), as well as partial guarantees to facilitate commercial lending for energy efficiency projects.	A special window in the new National Micro Finance System, supported by FEISEH, that provides loans and guarantees for study and implementation of energy efficiency projects.
	Expand time-of-day tariffs to medium-size and large consumers able to modulate their load to reduce demand at peak times.	MEM, CONELEC
Technological and information barriers	Implement a standards and labeling program to promote efficient appliances, equipment, and construction materials.	MEM
	Support energy service companies, increase energy audits, and disseminate best practices.	MEM
	Promote and implement demand-side management programs by utilities.	MEM, CONELEC
Limited awareness of and commitment to energy efficiency	Disseminate best practices and success stories among commercial, public, and industrial users. Support research, implement educational programs in schools and universities, organize training and public information campaigns.	MEM, CONELEC
	Increase scale of efficient lighting campaigns directed at residential and commercial customers.	Distribution companies

be expanded to all consumers able to modulate their use to reflect changing energy costs during the day and promote peak reduction and energy efficiency. Demand-side management programs allow utilities to reduce demand at peak times, improve their load factors, and postpone investments in supply facilities. Scaling up existing programs to promote the use of 6 million compact fluorescent lamps to replace incandescent lamps could reduce peak demand by 120–240 MW, saving 285–570 MWh and eliminating 380,000 tons of carbon dioxide emissions every year. Necessary measures to overcome the barriers are outlined in table 6.14.

Problems and Recommendations Matrix

Issue	*Options*	*Responsibility*
Options to eliminate accumulated and annual tariff deficits		
Low billing and collection in some distribution companies	Introduce competitive and professional selection of board members and management of public distribution companies.	Solidarity Fund
	Create a culture of payment, while enabling cutoff of electricity to nonpaying customers.	Solidarity Fund, distribution companies
Poor performance of some distribution companies	Create a custom solution for CATEG-D: sell off or concession as already planned.	CONELEC
	Outsource management of distribution companies through concession, management contract with private firm, or performance-based contracts with top management and staff.	Solidarity Fund
Size of companies; lack of economies of scale	Merge large and small companies serving similar size market territories or put small companies under control and supervision of larger efficient companies.	Solidarity Fund
Annual tariff deficit because of past interference that limited tariff to level below CONELEC's calculation	Select majority of CONELEC board members by independent committee.	MEM
	Increase tariffs to reach the necessary level for financial sustainability or include annual subsidy in national budget.	CONELEC, MEF
Accumulation of US$1.3 billion in wholesale market debt from past	Assign the MEF to make payment to sector for accumulated debt.	MEF
No fiduciary responsibility of distribution company managers for sectoral debt	Enable cutoffs of distribution companies that do not pay generation companies for electricity purchases (follow Colombian example) or require posting of guarantee by buyers.	MEM, Solidarity Fund
Options to ensure adequate investment in generation		
The need to meet demand during the dry season	Activate FEISEH regarding use of petroleum revenues for financing hydropower projects on a debt-financing basis.	MEM, MEF

(*Table continues on the following page.*)

Issue	*Options*	*Responsibility*
	Develop long-term storage for hydroelectric facilities; ensure adequate financing for Mazar.	MEF, MEM
	Mobilize financing for hydropower using public-private partnerships and regulations; ensure reasonable return on efficient investment.	MEM
Old thermal plants that are nearing the end of their economic life and expensive to operate	Replace, rehabilitate, or repower old publicly owned thermal plants.	MEM, Solidarity Fund
	Mobilize private financing for new, efficient thermal plants using public-private partnerships.	MEM, generation companies
	Guarantee payment by public distribution companies of energy bill and regulations ensure reasonable return on efficient investment.	MEM, MEF
Options to improve sector regulation for price and tariff setting		
Contracting of electricity supply by distribution companies	Establish new regulation for efficient and competitive contracting of electricity supply by distribution companies.	MEM, CONELEC
Tariffs not reflecting actual costs of distribution company energy purchases	Change regulations to allow pass-through of actual reasonable (e.g., competitively bid) energy purchases.	MEM, CONELEC
Inefficient subsidies	1. Rationalize cross-subsidy to avoid regression characteristics of present scheme. 2. Limit subsidy to lifeline consumption.	MEM, CONELEC
High price of electricity imports	Establish long-term contracts for imports rather than occasional supply at expensive opportunity price.	MEM, distribution companies
Options to improve governance to facilitate efficiency in the sector		
CONELEC charged with both policy making and regulation for the sector	1. Implement policy-making function in MEM, including policy setting for tariffs.	MEM
	2. Strengthen capacity of MEM for policy making and planning.	MEM
Tariff decisions made on discretionary basis by political authorities in the past	1. Assign CONELEC to set tariffs independently, following transparent and efficient cost-based price regulations.	MEM, CONELEC
	2. Ensure price protection for the poor (lifeline subsidy).	MEM, MEF

Solidarity Fund's role in commercial management	Implement independent management of companies, with Solidarity Fund would be the owner and administrator of the fund.	MEM, Solidarity Fund
Options to develop cost-effective new and renewable energy sources		
Legal and regulatory barriers to renewable energy development	Define a legal, institutional, and regulatory framework for sustainable energy.	MEM
	Strengthen the Subsecretariat of Renewable Energy and Energy Efficiency.	MEM
	Transform current maximum participation of renewable energies as defined by CONELEC—2 percent—into a mandatory target, and consider increasing this participation in the future.	MEM, CONELEC
Long-term financing not available to finance high capital costs of renewable energies when regulatory risks are perceived as high	Set up a financial facility to provide project financing or limited guarantees to banks lending on commercial terms. Increase use of FERUM.	MEM, MEF
	Allow the MEM, CONELEC, and others to act as aggregators to reduce transaction costs of trading certified emission reductions.	MEM, CONELEC
Lack of access to or lack of reliable resource records and data	1. Make available to potential investors the inventory of renewable resource records and data.	MEM, CONELEC
	2. Collect, prepare, and publish data such as wind and solar maps and inventory of hydroelectric resources and biomass in Ecuador.	MEM, CONELEC
Options to maximize energy efficiency		
Economic and financial barriers	Create a facility to finance studies of energy efficiency measures and provide grants and loans to finance their implementation (audits, studies, and investments), as well as partial guarantees to facilitate commercial lending for energy efficiency projects.	A special window in the new National Micro Finance System, supported by FEISEH, that provides loans and guarantees for study and implementation of energy efficiency projects

(*Table continues on the following page.*)

Issue	*Options*	*Responsibility*
	Expand time-of-day tariffs to medium-size and large consumers able to modulate their load to reduce demand at peak times.	MEM, CONELEC
Technological and information barriers	Implement a standards and labeling program to promote efficient appliances, equipment, and construction materials.	MEM
	Support energy service companies, increase energy audits, and disseminate best practices.	MEM
	Promote and implement demand-side management programs by utilities.	MEM, CONELEC
Limited awareness of and commitment to energy efficiency	Disseminate best practices and success stories among commercial, public, and industrial users. Support research, implement educational programs in schools and universities, organize training and public information campaigns.	MEM, CONELEC
	Increase scale of efficient lighting campaigns directed at residential and commercial customers.	Distribution companies

Notes

1. Corporación para la Administración Temporal Eléctrica de Guayaquil (CATEG-D) is an exception; it is under CONELEC and overseen by the municipality.

2. The International Monetary Fund, the Andean Development Corporation (*Corporación Andina de Fomento*—CAF), World Bank, and other multilateral institutions have supported development of strategies to resolve the present crisis (e.g., CAF assisted in the preparation of the reform law of the electricity sector (*Ley Reformatoria de la Ley de Régimen del Sector Eléctrico*), sector conditions were introduced in the IMF standby negotiations and Bank's programmatic loan. Additionally, the Bank's PROMEC project includes investment support for improving the dispatch center, monitoring and supervision of the wholesale market, and technical assistance to the sector on regulatory issues.

3. This amount considers the fuel price adjustment (reduction) decreed by the government (DE 338 of July 2005). The fuel bill would otherwise have been around US$330 million, if fuel market prices had been considered instead.

4. If transmission losses and self-consumption are added, the overall systemwide losses are close to 30 percent.

5. Although FERUM has been a well-funded resource for electrification (about US$150 million in the past five years for network expansion, reinforcements, and renovation, and another US$30 million for generation), this subsidy, actually a tax, is resented by the productive sector. In other countries, electricity service expansion in rural and remote areas is financed by direct allocation of funds in the national budget, or through investment obligations of distribution companies, not by requiring a cross-subsidy.

6. Later, the government partially corrected the discriminatory allocation, providing assignment of funds to private generators as a second priority. In addition, the 2004 decree and government provision altered the priority payment order established in the escrow accounts agreements described in box 6.3.

7. If instead an RPG of US$ Cents 4.16/kWh is assumed, which is the value considered in the official tariff finally approved, the loss would has been US$47 million.

8. These studies were financed under the Ecuador Modernization of the Energy and Telecommunication Sectors Project, supported by the World Bank and Global Environment Facility.

Bibliography

CENACE. 2001–2005. "Plan de Operación del Mercado Eléctrico Mayorista de Ecuador." CENACE, Quito.

CENACE. 2001–2005. "Reservas de Energía en el Mercado Eléctrico Mayorista de Ecuador." CENACE, Quito.

CONELEC. 2005. "Resumen de la Estadística del Sector Eléctrico Ecuatoriano." CONELEC, Quito.

Lecaros, Fernando. 2004. "Expectativas, Realidad y Futuro del Sector Eléctrico Ecuatoriano: Strategia de Desarrollo." Photocopy, PROMEC Project, Quito.

"Ley Orgánica de Creación del Fondo Ecuatoriano de Inversión en los Sectores Energético e Hidrocarburífero—FEISEH." Registro Oficial del Ecuador No. 386, Quito, October 2006.

"Ley Reformatoria de la Ley de Régimen del Sector Eléctrico." Registro Oficial del Ecuador No. 364, Quito.

"Memorias de las VII Jornadas de Funcionamiento del Mercado Eléctrico Mayorista de Ecuador: Transacciones Internacionales de Electricidad." Cuenca, May 2006.

OLADE. 2004. "SIEE—Energy Statistics 2003." OLADE, Quito.

World Bank. 2001. "Power and Communication Sectors Modernization and Rural Services Project." Project Appraisal Document Report 22519-EC, World Bank, Washington, DC.

World Bank. 2004. "Ecuador: Creating Fiscal Space for Poverty Reduction." Report 28911-EC, World Bank, Washington, DC.

World Bank. 2005. *"Ecuador, Investment Climate Assessment."* Report No. 31900-EC, World Bank, Washington, DC.

World Bank. 2006. "The Impact of Privatization on the Performance of the Infrastructure Sector: The case of Electricity Distribution in Latin American Countries." Policy Research Working Paper 3936, World Bank, Washington, DC.

7

Boosting Sustainable and Equitable Social Development

Monique F. Mrazek

Executive Summary

This chapter reviews the developments in the social sectors—education, health, and social protection—during the past four years, and makes recommendations to address ongoing challenges. The main goals of social sector reform have been to increase efficiency in sector programs, while expanding coverage to basic education and health care so as to begin tackling the large inequalities that have historically excluded large segments of the Ecuadoran society. Despite some improvements, Ecuador's social sector indicators still lag behind those of many Latin American countries. Reforms should continue to focus on reducing the deep inequalities that have contributed to an intergenerational poverty trap, particularly among those in rural areas, and the indigenous and Afro-Ecuadoran populations. Ecuador has a number of social programs in place, including the largest conditional cash transfer program in Latin America, which can be used for making further progress if adequately supported and managed. The quality and performance of social sector programs could also be improved by increasing transparency and accountability.

In the education sector, inequalities in primary and secondary education remain between poor and nonpoor, between urban and rural areas, and between ethnicities. Critical organizational deficiencies in the system have resulted in major problems in human resource management and teacher distribution. Consequently, the performance and quality of the education system are poor. Progress toward some of the most urgent challenges facing the sector will require improvements in financial and management responsibilities, human resource management, equitable resource allocation, and standards of teaching for early childhood education.

The health sector has seen improvements in maternal and child mortality rates, along with significant system developments to improve coverage. Solidifying these advancements will require additional steps. Both the Law on Free Maternity Care

(Ley de Maternidad Gratuita—LMG) and the Universal Health Insurance Program (Programa de Aseguramiento Universal en Salud—PROAUS) are anticipated not only to improve coverage, but also to generate important changes in the way resources are allocated in the system. However, the effective implementation of these and other programs will depend on building management capacity, updating monitoring and information systems, strengthening culturally sensitive approaches to increase LMG coverage rates, expanding health coverage provided through the Ecuadoran Social Security Institute, and improving access to and the rational use of medicines, including least-cost generics.

Ecuador has many social assistance programs, including a series of feeding and nutrition programs, and a conditional cash transfer program, the Human Development Bond (Bono de Desarrollo Humano—BDH). However, nutrition outcomes remain poor, and without a coherent national nutrition strategy, Ecuador will be unlikely to achieve its declared goal of halving stunting to 12 percent by 2015. Only a quarter of Ecuadorans are covered by the current social insurance arrangements for old-age protections, yet the state subsidies of these pensions are increasing. Social protection programs could be strengthened by reviewing the methodology and framework to improve targeting, strengthening institutional structures and capacities of the BDH and improving health and education coresponsibilities, implementing a coherent, well-monitored national nutrition strategy, and expanding old-age security through existing structures and through a new scheme for informal workers.

Developing a culture of transparency and accountability in the social sectors depends on the availability of timely information on social expenditures. This effort could include strengthening the institutional and technical capacity of the Social Sector Technical Secretariat (STFS), which is essential to the sustainability of the reform agenda, plus completing impact evaluations for other social programs, continuing to consult with relevant stakeholders to ensure the sustainability of reforms, and continuing participatory evaluations.

I. Sector Overviews, Trends, and Diagnostics

The social sectors confront the twin challenges of high poverty and inequality plus low access to basic education and health services among the poor and indigenous groups. In 2003, the government designed a reform agenda for the social sectors structured around three pillars: (i) improved targeting of poor households using a proxy-means test; (ii) implementation of the BDH conditional cash transfer program; and (iii) increased coverage of basic health and education services. The strategy has promoted more efficient use of existing resources in the social sectors. The following subsections address the three social sectors, major trends, and diagnostics.

Overview of Social Sector Strategy, Spending, and Priority Programs

Social sector spending increased steadily between 2002 and 2005. Total spending in the social sectors rose in real terms from US$830 million in 2002 to US$1.1

billion in 2005. In constant per capita terms, budgeted spending rose from US$92 per person in 2002 to US$130 in 2005 (figure 7.1). As a percentage of GDP, social spending increased from 4.8 percent in 2002 to 5.4 percent in 2005 (figure 7.2). This is mainly attributable to spending linked to the BDH; the education and health budgets held stable as a share of GDP. The fact that overall social spending rose relative to GDP is noteworthy, as real GDP increased quickly in this period because of the oil price boom. As a percentage of nonoil GDP, the increase in social spending was even greater, rising from 5.4 percent in 2002 to 6.5 percent in 2005.

In nominal terms, expenditures on staff employed in the social sectors increased by 42 percent between 2002 and 2005, compared with 63 percent for other nonstaff spending, such as goods and services, current transfers, investments and capital transfers (table 7.1). In real per capita terms, staff spending rose from US$45 a year to US$53 over the same period (17 percent), while nonstaff spending rose from US$20 to US$27 (34 percent). As a result, the share of nonstaff spending rose, mainly owing to the increased spending on the BDH, which is classed as a current transfer and forms part of nonstaff expenditure. Investment spending was flat in real terms.

Seven priority programs were defined by the government in 2003 to target poverty reduction and achieve the Millennium Development Goals (MDGs) for health, education, and nutrition (table 7.2). Real spending for these programs fell from US$342 million in 2003 to US$302 million in 2005 (in constant 2000 U.S. dollars). However, this was offset by improved budget execution of priority programs, up from 72 percent in 2003 to 93 percent in 2004.

Education Trends and Developments

Ecuador has made strides in education, with literacy rates rising from 88 percent in 1990 to 93 percent in 2005. There has also been progress toward the MDG of achieving

Figure 7.1. Ecuador Real per Capita Social Expenditure

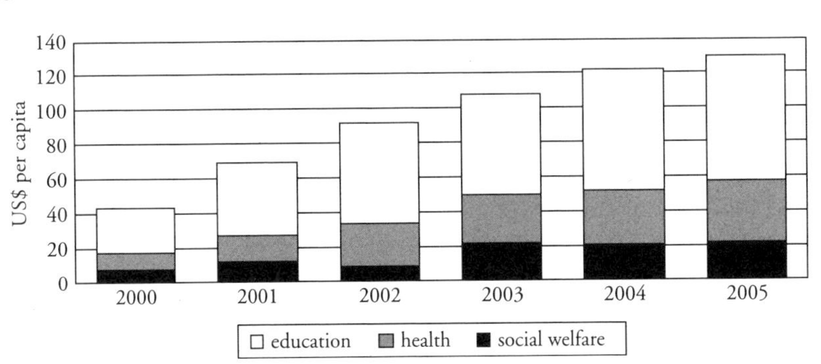

Source: STFS, MEF.

Figure 7.2. Ecuador Social Sector Spending

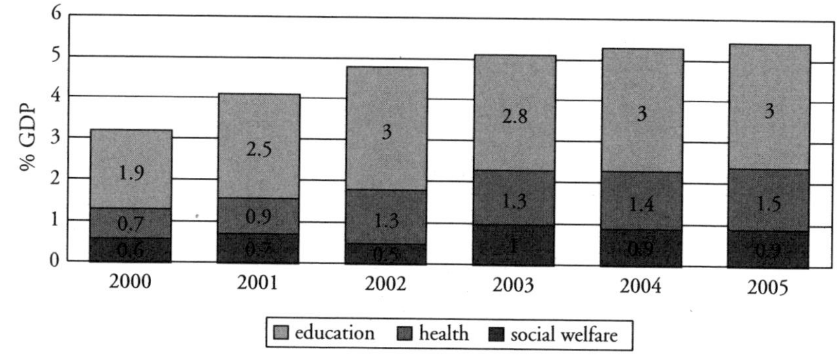

Source: STFS, MEF.

Table 7.1. Increase in Social Spending by Expenditure Group, 2002–05 (%)

	Nominal	*Real*	*Real per capita*
Total spending	48	28	22
Staff	42	22	17
Nonstaff	63	40	34
Goods and services	71	48	41
Current transfers	283	230	216
Investment	16	0	–4
Capital transfers	–14	–26	–29

Source: STFS, MEF.

Table 7.2. Real Change of Priority Program Budgets (constant 2000 US$)

	2003	*2004*	*2005*
Human Development Bond	189.5	180.6	173.2
Nutrition <2 years (PANN2000 food program)	1.3	1.3	8.8
Nutrition 2–5 years (Eat Well, Ecuador)	11.4	14.3	14.0
School meals program	28.6	27.4	13.2
Immunization program	9.3	4.5	5.3
Free maternity care	17.5	17.8	17.3
Education investment	84.7	80.1	70.2
Total	**342.4**	**326.1**	**302.0**

Source: STFS, MEF.

net universal primary education by 2015, reaching an enrollment rate of 93 percent in 2004 (table 7.3). Nevertheless, this places Ecuador behind wealthier countries such as Argentina, Uruguay, and Chile, all with net primary enrollment of 98 percent, and also behind its neighbors Peru (95 percent) and Bolivia (96 percent). Ecuador continues to

Table 7.3. Net Enrollment Rates
(percent)

Year	*Net primary enrollment*	*Net secondary enrollment*	*Net tertiary enrollment*
1982	68.6	29.5	7.4
1990	88.9	43.1	10.9
2001	90.1	44.6	11.9
2004	93.1	49.2	17.9

Source: STFS and National Survey on Employment, Unemployment and Underemployment (*Encuesta Nacional de Empleo, Desempleo, y Sub-Empleo Urbano*—ENEMDU 2004).

lag behind in secondary enrollment, with a net enrollment of 49 percent, compared to the Latin American average of 70 percent. Furthermore, Ecuador's education expenditures, at 2.8 percent of GDP, place it below several other Latin American countries such as Bolivia (6.8 percent), Brazil (4.3 percent), and Peru (3.3 percent).

Inequalities in access to education at all levels remain between poor and nonpoor, between urban and rural areas, and between indigenous and Afro-Ecuadorans and the rest of the population. The gap in net enrollment rates between the wealthiest and the poorest quintiles is 10 percent in primary education and 60 percent in secondary. By ethnic group, primary school enrollment is 92 percent among whites, 85 percent among the indigenous populations, and 83 percent among Afro-Ecuadorans, and for secondary education these figures are 54 percent, 22 percent, and 31 percent, respectively (SIISE 2000). About 50 percent of rural students (20 percent of urban) do not make the transition from primary to lower secondary education. The education requirements (*conditionalities*) of the BDH should have a positive effect on school attendance. At the tertiary level, 70 percent of the public subsidy goes to the richest quintile. Reallocation of this subsidy is urgently needed if opportunity of access is to be expanded to those most in need.

Critical deficiencies have also been revealed in the quality of education, as reflected in poor learning outcomes. The quality of education in Ecuador is the lowest among 19 Latin American countries. The results in 2000 of Ecuador's national assessment system, APRENDO, for grades 2, 6, and 9, were 8.2, 9.3, and 11.1, respectively, for Spanish, and 8, 5, and 5.5, respectively, for mathematics, out of a possible 20 points (MEC 2001). Other measures of quality, such as retention rates and years to completion, remain relatively unchanged (table 7.4). Rural women have disproportionately poor outcomes, with illiteracy rates of 50 percent. Educational outreach opportunities for this group are needed urgently. Poor performance outcomes are partly a problem of poor organization, where most schools fail to offer the first grade of basic education and the upper section of basic education (8th to 10th grades). In early childhood education, services are currently offered by a number of ministries in addition to the Ministry of Education and Culture (MEC). Having other ministries involved, including the Ministry of Social

Table 7.4. Internal Efficiency Indicators

Indicator	*1995*	*2001*
Fifth-grade retention rate (%)	84	81
Years to complete sixth grade	6.8	6.9

Source: World Bank (2005b).

Welfare, Ministry of Labor and Human Resources, Ministry of Public Health, and Ministry of Urban Development and Housing, undermines necessary quality improvements such as uniform curricular parameters and teaching standards for early childhood education.

The MEC is responsible for setting the overall direction of the sector, yet it has little control over assignment of teachers or other aspects of human resource management, which is currently the biggest bottleneck to improving equity, quality, and performance of the sector. While the MEC establishes policy, its provincial directorates are in charge of implementing policy, including teacher assignments. MEC also has limited budgetary authority, as teachers are paid by the Ministry of Economy and Finance (MEF) based on information from the provincial directorates. However, communication and the flow of information from the provinces to the center are weak. Although a division of responsibilities between the center and the provinces has been designed, no explicit decentralization strategy has been specifically articulated, despite programs such as *Centros Educativos Matrices* and *Redes Amigas* (Education Centers and Friends Network). One consequence of the current structure is significant delays in salary payments to teachers. These delays are one of the main causes of strikes by teachers, a situation that was particularly difficult in 2003, and underlying causes have not been resolved. The MEF and MEC need to work more closely to resolve accumulated delays and to devise a system to reduce future delays.

The MEC's limited role is also reflected in the education budget (table 7.5). The central level of the MEC has direct control over only 5.4 percent of total education expenditures. One-third of education expenditures are outside the MEC's mandate. Almost one-third of the education budget goes directly to provincial directorates and roughly another third goes directly to each secondary school. With the MEC's lack of control over a budget, or controls over the information flows between provincial directorates and the MEF, it is difficult to have high expectations about the performance of MEC or the education sector in general.

The distribution of public teachers currently does not adequately address needs and significantly limits improvements in the sector's performance overall. The poor distribution of teachers is more critical in some parts of the country than in others (figure 7.3). Resource allocation in the education sector has traditionally responded to historical trends and budgetary inertia rather than to real needs. Unions have also played a central role in limiting changes to the current regime. To date, no effective

Table 7.5. Total Education Sector Budget

Ministry of Education and Culture (67.2%)				*Autonomous and decentralized entities (32.8%)*	
Central administration	*Provincial directorates (schools)*	*Secondary schools*	*Other*	*Higher education*	*Cultural institutions and others*
5.4%	30.2%	28.9%	2.7%	21%	11.8%

Source: MEC and MEF.

Figure 7.3. School-Age Population without Teacher Coverage

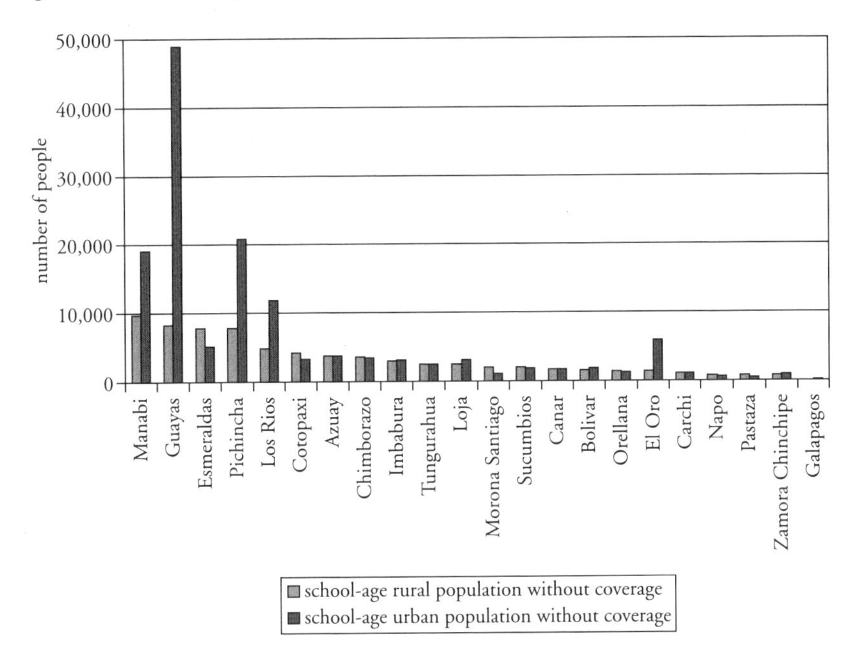

Source: MEC.

formula has been developed that would improve distribution and equity in response to demand. Instead, teacher assignment is usually determined by the provincial directorates following various forms of pressure, from union coercion to political patronage. Administrative custom has transformed teaching posts into portable entitlements for teachers, further exacerbating bad distribution and inaccurate information on teacher allocation. Net teacher transfer flows are invariably from rural and marginally urban areas to central urban schools. This has resulted in central urban areas with very low student–to-teacher ratios, while entire rural areas are devoid of teachers. The MEF rightly does not authorize new teaching positions to replace transferred ones, arguing that the national treasury cannot pay for poor personnel management by the education sector.

An additional consequence of the rigidity of human resource management is that the teaching force has become old and therefore expensive. The average age of a teacher is 48.3 years, and four out of every 10 teachers are 50 years or older. To address this problem, the MEC successfully launched the first round of invitations to teachers for voluntary retirement under certain criteria, including age and years of service, in September 2006. To date, approximately 1,200 teachers have signed up for the program, under which they will receive an incentive of US$12,000. The MEC plans to use the funds released from these retirements to hire new teachers in rural areas. Furthermore, the education sector, like the health sector, has not been included under the Organic Law of the Civil Service and Administrative Career (*Ley Organica de Servicio Civil y Carrera Administrativa, 2003/04*), and doing so would also aid in expanding common salary scales for full reform of civil service human resource management.

Improvements in the quality and performance of the sector are also hindered by the lack of a system to evaluate teachers or ensure accountability of results. Evaluation and accountability require information, but currently the information system at the central level is not fully integrated with the provincial level, leading to lags in information processing and information loss. Even at the level of human resources, the data on education personnel exist in several different databases and are often inconsistent, unreliable, or incompatible.[1] Data on quality and performance are absent from the system to any meaningful and effective extent. Weak capacity to manage existing information at the central and provincial levels compounds these problems.

Health Care Trends and Developments

Ecuador has made important progress toward achieving health-related MDGs. Both infant and child mortality are about half of what they were in 1990 and are below the Latin America average (table 7.6). Maternal mortality also showed a downward trend, falling from 117 deaths per 100,000 births in 1990 to 76.4 per 100,000 in 2004.[2] Despite these aggregate improvements, inequalities in health outcomes remain consistent with economic inequalities associated with Ecuador's demographic, cultural, and social heterogeneity.

Ecuador's health care market suffers from a number of distortions, in particular, high fragmentation, which has led to a system that is inefficient, inequitable, of poor quality, and largely inaccessible. Until 2006, only 23 percent of Ecuadorians were covered by some type of public or private health insurance (Consorcio Care–Johns Hopkins University 2004).[3] Of these, the Ecuadoran Social Security Institute (IESS) covered the largest share of the population (18 percent), followed by the Social Security Institutes of the armed forces and police (covering 3 percent together), and

Table 7.6. Trends in Selected Health-Related MDG Indicators

	1990	*1995*	*2000*	*2004*	*Latin America average 2004*
Immunization, DPT (% of children ages 12–23 months)	68	74	89	90	91
Immunization, measles (% of children ages 12–23 months)	60	73	84	99	92
Mortality rate, infant (per 1,000 live births)	43	34	27	23	27
Mortality rate, under 5 years (per 1,000)	57	43	32	26	31
Incidence of tuberculosis (per 100,000 people)	202.4	174.9	146.7	138.4	—
Tuberculosis cases detected under DOTS (%)	—	—	—	42	62

Source: World Development Indicators database (2004).

private insurance (2 percent). More people in urban areas had health insurance coverage (58 percent). Furthermore, 91 percent of children younger than five years of age did not have health insurance. Of the health insurance provided by the IESS, 38 percent was in Rural People's Social Security Program (*Seguro Social Campesino*—SSC); enrollment has been closed for a decade. The poor and children have the lowest rate of access to health insurance.

To begin to address the lack of health insurance and improve health outcomes related to achieving Ecuador's MDG targets for maternal and child health, the government established the Law on Free Maternity Care (LMG) in 1999 to provide free access to primary health care for all expectant mothers and children under five. The LMG is run by the Ministry of Public Health (MSP), which finances the provision of 33 basic services for the maternal-child population. The LMG's executed budget in 2005 was US$20 million, about 4 percent of the total budget of the MSP. Through this mechanism, the MSP reimburses providers (mainly MSP health centers and hospitals) for the cost of services with funds from the Solidarity Fund and a portion of sales tax revenues. In theory, all women and children under five have coverage, but in practice, only those that have physical access to MSP facilities are covered. Through the LMG, 30 percent of pregnant women were reached in 2003; however, coverage of indigenous and rural women was 19 percent, and for the poorest quintiles it was 20 percent.

To address these cultural barriers, a monitoring and evaluation (M&E) system and strategy have been designed and piloted, and are presently being rolled out nationwide. It is already fully operational in the departments of Bolivar, Chimborazo, Cotopaxi, and Tungurahua, where some of the largest concentrations of poor indigenous households are found. Strategies to reduce cultural barriers to access LMG services have been developed, including provisions that reimburse services provided by traditional midwives (through the LMG) who refer their patients for prenatal consultations, institutional births, and postnatal consultations. In 2005, over 1,600 such services were paid for, mainly in the provinces of Sucumbios, Pichincha, and Cañar.

In 2005, contracts were signed with two nongovernmental organizations (NGOs) to deliver LMG services for the Ministry of Public Health. This is an important development, as it potentially signifies a new stage in the strategy to expand the coverage of the LMG, as well as to separate purchasing and provision of health care services. It will be important to closely follow the experience with these two NGOs if this is to be replicated, as it is the only example of service provision of the LMG outside the MSP. Although the ministry signed an agreement with the SSC to provide LMG services to non-SSC affiliates, that agreement was never implemented.

In 2005, the government launched the Universal Health Insurance (*Aseguramiento Universal en Salud*—AUS) to increase coverage through existing social health insurance schemes. The AUS also complemented those schemes with other forms of coverage and additional sources of financing so that, together, they would constitute an overall framework for universal health care coverage. Through this program, the government envisioned an expansion of coverage that would extend Obligatory Social Security (*Seguro Social Obligatorio*—SSO) to affiliates' families and independent workers (increasing its coverage from 9 percent to 38 percent of the population) and an expansion of private insurance (from 3 percent to 6 percent of the population). In addition, the strategy included the development of insurance coverage for the most vulnerable segments of the population, which led to the development of the Universal Health Insurance Program (*Programa de Aseguramiento Universal en Salud*—PROAUS).

PROAUS was established in 2006 to further strengthen the financing of basic health services for the poor. The program was to be limited to households in quintiles 1 and 2, paying for services not covered by the LMG. It included financing a set of basic guaranteed services defined in the National Health System Law, at an initial rate of US$45 per capita. Initially the service was to be principally delivered by the MSP, the SSC, and the municipalities of Quito, Guayaquil, and Cuenca, with additional services as the program expanded. Those would potentially be delivered by NGOs, other social insurance institutions, and other private institutions. An impact evaluation of the program would be done alongside the BDH-conditional cash transfer program. It was expected that PROAUS would become the basis for fundamental changes in the health care system by increasing transparency and efficiency in the way that resources are allocated and health care services are purchased and delivered.

PROAUS was an important first step toward developing universal health coverage, serving to address key problems of efficiency and inequality in the system. The challenges faced in the implementation of PROAUS are twofold. First, to cover the targeted 1.4 million beneficiaries by the end of the first phase of the program, the implementing agency would need to negotiate and sign contracts for services with the MSP, SSC, municipalities, and private agencies. It would be important to develop performance-related contracts with providers to improve the efficiency of the system.

The contracting phase for PROAUS should build on experience with the LMG program in separating the purchasing and service-provision functions. As part of the LMG program, the MSP has contracted with two NGOs. Also, within the context of PROAUS, the municipality of Guayaquil has contracted a private Colombian firm to manage its insurance responsibilities. Although the scope of services contracted to this private firm is limited for the time being, it is an interesting management experiment worth monitoring with the view of potential replication elsewhere.

The second challenge in the implementation of PROAUS is that its success would depend on effective information systems that can accurately collect performance data from providers. This capability is essential, as reimbursement is linked to the achievement of agreed-upon performance targets. Similarly, the LMG needs data to monitor provider performance. Both the LMG and PROAUS also need reliable data to ensure that benefits are reaching the poorest families and are not impeded by cultural barriers. Given the structural similarity between the LMG and PROAUS (both programs reimburse MSP facilities against the delivery of specified health services), an information system could be shared between the two programs, increasing coordination. In addition, the effort to expand health care coverage for the poor could benefit from the experiences of other countries in the region, notably Colombia (box 7.1).

Expanded coverage by the IESS is an important part of the overall strategy of increasing access to health insurance generally and the wider goal of universal health insurance. However, reforms of the IESS's health coverage have not advanced satisfactorily. The IESS has yet to separate the health fund from the pension fund, which would clear the way for increased emphasis on expanding health services. Nor has the IESS law been amended to permit the provision of health services to its affiliates' families, which would require that the IESS expand hospital capacity in Quito and Guayaquil.

In 2000, the Generic Medicines Law was introduced to increase access to low-cost pharmaceuticals by encouraging the development of a generic drugs market, yet the penetration of generics remains low (25–30 percent of the market by value). There are several explanations for this: rates of prescriptions that include a generic are as low as 5 percent; there are concerns over the quality and reliability of generic equivalency; and pharmacists do not have the financial incentive to dispense a low-cost generic. Further reforms in this area are required to ensure that the objectives of the law are achieved.

Social Protection Trends and Developments

Ecuador has a number of social assistance programs, including a series of nutrition programs and a large conditional cash transfer program, the Human Development

Box 7.1. Expanding Health Coverage to the Poor: Lessons from Colombia

Colombia expanded health coverage to the poor in much the same way as Ecuador plans to do, with an overall positive experience, but some pitfalls should be avoided. Prior to 1993, the Colombian health care system was segmented according to social groups in three categories—Ministry of Health, Social Security Institute, private sector—with much of the population being without coverage (76 percent), as is currently the case in Ecuador.

By 2000, following radical reforms, Colombia was ranked first of 191 countries by the World Health Organization in terms of fairness in financing, with health insurance coverage expanding to 54 percent of the population. The reforms involved creating a new system characterized by universal health insurance coverage, with cost-sharing on the financing side and pluralistic public-private provision. Quintiles 1 and 2 are covered under a subsidized scheme and receive basic benefits.

Despite the successes in Colombia's reforms, some key problems have arisen:

- A complicated transfer system led to payment delays from the implementing agency and providers.
- One-third of the eligible population was not covered because they lacked information on the affiliation process.
- Manipulation of the enrollment system has occurred through connections. It has been difficult to verify enrollment information. If the economic situations of enrollees improve, they are unlikely to acknowledge this and lose the subsidy.

Source: Escobar and Panopoulou (2003).

Bond (*Bono de Desarrollo Humano*—BDH). The country assigns a considerable amount of resources to these programs, although resource distribution is heavily skewed toward the BDH (table 7.7). In the area of social insurance, just over a quarter of Ecuadorans contribute, but among the poor it is less than half of this average. At the same time, the state is spending increasing amounts to subsidize the pensions of middle- and higher-income retirees. These social protection programs are a key mechanism by which unequal allocations of resources to the poor can be tackled.

Feeding and Nutrition Programs

Ecuador, like Peru and Guatemala, has failed to convert its middle-income status into improved nutritional outcomes for its population and registers persistently

Table 7.7. Social Assistance Spending, 2003–06

				% of total		
Year	*Total (US$)*	*Total (%)*	*School feeding (PAE)*	*PANN2000*	*Aliméntate Ecuador*	*BDH*
2003	189.81	100	8.0	3.0	3.7	85.3
2004	221.76	100	12.6	5.8	3.4	78.2
2005	217.10	100	12.5	4.2	3.7	79.7
2006[a]	239.77	100	9.6	10.4		80.0

Source: MEF.
Note: PAE: *Programa de Alimentación Escolar.* PANN2000: *Programa de Alimentación y Nutrición.* BDH: *Bono de Desarrollo Humano.*
a. Budgeted. In the proposed budget for 2006, the funds for PANN2000 and *Aliméntate Ecuador* have been fused.

Table 7.8. Nutrition Outcomes of Children under Five in Selected Countries

	Argentina 1995/96	*Brazil 1996*	*Bolivia 2003*	*Chile 2004*	*Colombia 2000*	*Ecuador 2004*	*El Salvador 2002*	*Peru 2000*
Stunting (deficient height for age)	12.8	10.5	26.5	1.4	13.5	23.2	18.9	25.4
Wasting (deficient weight for height)	3.3	2.3	1.3	0.3	0.8	1.7	1.4	0.9

Source: ENDEMAIN (2004) (cited in World Bank (2007)).

high rates of childhood nutritional deficiency (table 7.8). In 2004, nearly one-quarter (23 percent) of Ecuador's children under the age of five, and nearly half of indigenous children (47 percent) faced chronic malnutrition (stunting). To meet its MDG target to halve malnutrition by 2015, Ecuador needs to triple reduction of stunting to over 5 percent a year.

The prevalence of stunting varies greatly between socioeconomic groups and by geographical location, and it is particularly severe in rural, highland indigenous communities. The stunting rate is higher in rural populations than urban (31 percent versus 17 percent) and higher in the mountain region (32 percent) than on the coast (16 percent) or in Amazonia (23 percent). Stunting is far higher for indigenous children (47 percent) than for those of any other racial group. It is also higher for poor families (28 percent) than for the nonpoor (17 percent). In 2007 the World Bank completed a study to evaluate the causes of malnutrition in Ecuador (box 7.2). The central argument of the study was that the causes of nutritional failure are the product of policy failure. Despite many programs to address nutritional problems, too much emphasis has been placed on programs that are often poorly targeted by age range or nutrition-risk status. For example, 67 percent of households do not benefit from any of the six principal programs, while 21 percent benefit from one

Box 7.2. Major Causes of Malnutrition in Ecuador

An in-depth econometric analysis was undertaken of the causes and correlates of malnutrition, using the Survey on Demographics and Maternal and Infant Health (ENDEMAIN) (2004—in World Bank [2007]) household survey data set. The main findings are as follows:

- The critical window of opportunity for interventions to prevent stunting in Ecuador is during pregnancy and in the first year of a child's life.
- Every Ecuadoran girl rescued from stunting now reduces the likelihood of a future child being born stunted.
- The mother's expectation regarding her child's height is highly relevant to stunting outcomes. Counseling at community level to improve nutritional knowledge should be a main plank of nutrition strategy.
- Children in urban areas have much better growth prospects than rural children. Nutrition strategy should concentrate on rural communities.
- Altitude has a strong negative association with nutritional status. Nutrition strategy should give high priority to the isolated communities of the Sierra.
- Household resources are an important determinant but offer a "long route" to improved nutrition outcomes. Other, more direct strategies to improve nutrition are needed to complement income growth.
- Stunting is positively correlated with the number of household members and the number of preschool children in the household. Adequate birth spacing and reduced family size are relevant strategies.
- The availability of toilets has a positive impact on nutritional status. Investments in rural sanitation are likely to yield positive returns in nutritional status.

Source: World Bank 2007.

program and 13 percent benefit from more than one (ENEMDU 2005). Further, a coherent national nutrition strategy has not been developed nor has attention been given to measuring outcomes. The last national nutrition survey was completed in 1986. Implementing a strategy with clear goals would strengthen the accountability framework for holding relevant agencies responsible for service production and quality.

At an institutional level, the Food Security Law passed in 2006 has led to confusion about the future role of the MSP-led Integrated System of Food and Nutrition (*Sistema Integral de Alimentacion y Nutricion*—SIAN). SIAN was established in 2003, and formalized by an executive decree in 2005, grouping the School Meals Program

(*Programa de Alimentacion Escolar*—PAE), Eat Well, Ecuador (*Alimentate Ecuador*—AE), and the Food Program for Boys and Girls (*Programa de Alimentacion de Niños y Niñas*—PANN2000). SIAN aims to rationalize feeding programs, to promote more rigorous targeting and impact evaluations, and to articulate feeding interventions with the primary health network and with nutrition outcomes. Although the new law recognizes the existence of SIAN, it has created confusion over SIAN's future role; the law specifies that the budget of PAE should not be consolidated with those of PANN2000 or AE as originally planned. As the government redefines the role of SIAN, one option is to make SIAN the focal point for a goal-based national nutrition strategy. This, combined with revamping the SISVAN (Food and Nutrition Monitoring System) growth monitoring system, would increase transparency and accountability in generating improvements in nutritional outcomes, as has been the experience elsewhere (box 7.3).

Targeting of Social Sector Programs

The system of beneficiary selection (*Sistema de Selección de Beneficiarios*—SelBen) is administered by the Social Sector Technical Secretariat (STFS) within the Ministry of Social Welfare (MBS) and has been a vital tool in the retargeting of social programs

Box 7.3. Chile's Use of Monitoring Systems—A Nutrition Success Story

Chile experienced rapid and significant improvements in health and nutrition between 1965 and 1980. Growth retardation (under 75 percent of standard) dropped from 24 percent in 1965 to 2 percent in 1980. Today, only 1.7 percent of children are stunted in Chile. The integration of nutrition interventions and primary health care appears to have contributed most to these impressive outcomes. The provision of potable water and sewage control in urban areas also led to reductions in infant mortality. Food supplementation (in the form of milk) benefited the poorest quintiles. Furthermore, the country has perhaps one of "the most sophisticated nutrition surveillance systems in the world. Data on approximately 400,000 children and 200,000 mothers are regularly collected, collated, analyzed, and used for decision-making by the Ministry of Health. There is a regular flow of information from every unit of the health system to the central computer service and back to each source, with appropriate comments when justified." Other factors in the success of this effort included: sustained political commitment; explicit attention to social equity; and outreach to isolated households and communities (for example, mobile health units).

Source: Horwitz (1987), cited in World Bank (2007).

in Ecuador. SelBen is a proxy-means test that uses information on demographic composition, assets, and other variables to classify households according to welfare levels. All households in the first and second quintiles of SelBen constitute the potential target population of various social programs. The bulk of beneficiary certification took place during 2001–02, when the first round of the SelBen survey was administered (SelBen I). Since then, a few thousand more interviews have been conducted, bringing the total number of households in the SelBen I database to 2 million. Making SelBen the only source of data by which beneficiary households are identified would minimize political manipulation.

The methodology of SelBen was evaluated by an independent consulting firm, Habitus, which noted several areas where SelBen could be improved: (i) SelBen variables should be reviewed to exclude those with little discriminatory power; (ii) additional variables could be included to capture more accurately welfare levels of households headed by the elderly; and (iii) the risk that respondents may tailor their responses should be evaluated and adapted to future rounds of surveys. Furthermore, SelBen I has uneven coverage across urban and rural areas, and procedures for verifying and updating information are imperfect. These recommendations should be incorporated into recertification efforts under SelBen II.

SelBen also needs updating for reasons of durability. Although enough evidence shows that SelBen I accurately identified the poorest households in the country when it was first used to target the BDH in 2003, positive economic growth and other developments, including changes in household composition, have rendered some of the information obsolete. Existing evaluations indicate that information should be updated approximately every five years.

Income Support Programs

The BDH was created in 2003 by merging two previously existing programs, the Solidarity Bond (*Bono Solidario*) and the student scholarships (*Beca Escolar*). In practical terms, this involved three important changes: (i) increasing the amount of benefits paid to certain households, which was done immediately; (ii) retargeting the benefits to the population's 40 percent poorest households as identified by SelBen; and (iii) conditioning receipt of benefits to fulfillment of certain schooling and health visit standards among households with children ages birth to 16. The BDH is administered by the Social Protection Program (*Programa de Protección Social*—PPS), an independent unit within the MBS.

The PPS's campaign to retarget beneficiaries through SelBen was implemented as the second step of transforming the BDH. This reduced resource leakage, as more than 500,000 households (or 50 percent of the Solidarity Bond beneficiaries in 2003) were disqualified while another 500,000 households were newly registered and started receiving benefits. Consequently, the share of BDH expenditures accruing to the poorest households increased, and the increases in beneficiary households was more pronounced in poor parishes than nonpoor parishes.

A recent development was the creation of an old-age and disability pension (*Pensión Asistencial para Personas de Tercera Edad o con Discapacidad*) for BDH beneficiaries with an elderly or handicapped head of household. These households were part of the Solidarity Bond and were temporarily part of the BDH through the grandfathering process. The objective in separating these beneficiaries was to ensure that the BDH could properly focus on families with children from birth to 16 years of age.

One area of the BDH implementation that is still lagging is the monitoring of education and health coresponsibilities. BDH payments to households are conditional on fulfillment of certain health and education coresponsibilities, such as health checkups and school attendance. This implementation delay can be attributed to several factors: (i) insufficient technical capacity, exacerbated by constant changes in the PPS team for political rather than technical motives; (ii) a lack of political support for the reform within the MBS; (iii) technical limitations of current information systems; and (iv) a lack of coordination and understanding of the program within the MEC and MSP.

Other challenges have been in the coordination between SelBen and the PPS, which suffers from the poor quality of their communication networks, and from a lack of unique identifiers within the SelBen database that would allow for fluid and timely information exchanges and updates between both institutions. Also, a lack of clear information among beneficiaries and others about eligibility rules and other operational aspects of the program remains a constraint to the success of the BDH.

Several initiatives to evaluate the potential impact of the BDH were carried out over the past few years. Schady and Araujo (2005) reported that receipt of the BDH transfer was associated with a 17 percent decrease in child labor among the recipient households. In the area of school enrollment, a joint World Bank-STFS evaluation of the BDH, conducted during 2003–05, showed that the BDH had a large, positive impact on school enrollment (about 10 percent; Schady and Araujo 2005). Finally, although an adequate system to monitor BDH coresponsibilities is not yet in place, interviews with households carried out for the evaluation found that the impact of the BDH was largest in households that understood transfers to be conditional on school enrollment.

Social Protection for Old Age

Ecuador's social insurance system suffers from a number of major shortcomings, which affect access, equity, and quality of services (for more details on Ecuador's social security system, see chapter 8). The social insurance system is composed of four contributory schemes—the Obligatory Social Security (SSO), Rural People's Social Security Program (*Seguro Social Campesino*—SSC), and armed forces and police social security schemes—to which workers in the formal labor market contribute and receive old age and health protection. Those who do not contribute to one of the four institutions are excluded (table 7.9). Labor markets in Ecuador are

Table 7.9. Overview of Social Security Network

Insurance	*Managed by*	*Coverage*	*Number of affiliates*
Obligatory Social Security (SSO)	IESS	Health insurance and pension for formal sector wage earners only	1.3 million affiliates
Rural People's Social Security Program (SSC)	IESS	Covers rural workers with pension for head of household and basic health care for household members	870,000 affiliates
Armed Forces Social Security	Instituto de Seguridad Social de las Fuerzas Armadas	Covers contributor's pension and basic health care for household members	50,000 active and 45,000 retired members, jointly
Police Social Security	Instituto de Seguridad Social de la Policía Nacional	Covers contributor's pension and basic health care for household members	

Source: World Bank (2005b).

highly informal and, consequently, most workers and their families have no access to social insurance. Only 27 percent of the labor force contributes to one of the four social insurance programs, but among the poorest workers, it is less than half this average. Only 16 percent of those 65 years or older received a retirement benefit in 2004, a very low rate compared with high performers in the region (Argentina, Brazil, Chile, and Uruguay), where coverage exceeds 60 percent, and even compared with middle performers (Costa Rica, Panama, Peru, and Venezuela) where 25–40 percent of the elderly receive pension benefits.

In 2005, the World Bank completed a review of social security in Ecuador (World Bank 2005b). The diagnosis and recommendations are centered on three areas: coverage, financing, and institutional organization. The allocation of resources in the system needs to be examined with particular care, since the expansion of coverage inevitably depends on the availability of funds. Actions also must address the contradiction of insufficient spending on health and protection of the poorest while pensions of higher income groups are subsidized.

Fewer than one in four Ecuadorans participate in the system, yet the society as a whole makes a significant effort to subsidize the system. Almost two-thirds (65 percent) of contributors are in the top two income quintiles; however, as a group these affiliates receive an annual subsidy equivalent to about 2 percent of GDP. Furthermore, the 40 percent contribution by the government exerts permanent fiscal pressures and has a regressive distributive impact. In fact, this subsidy makes the system one of the most regressive mechanisms in the economy. Most social security agencies in Latin America have some sort of subsidy, such as transfers from the budget or revenues from specific taxes that are assigned to finance these expenditures.

The Ecuadoran pension system appears to be fiscally sustainable as long as the main parameters remain within the assumed ranges. The most serious medium-term risks are related to the aging population and maturation of the system. The 2001 Social Security Law included a provision incorporating a mechanism for continuous adjustments of the retirement age every five years, starting in 2006. This article would permit adjustments to one of the most critical variables in the system and prevent the aging of the population from disrupting IESS finances. However, it will undoubtedly prove very difficult politically to implement. If the law is applied literally, retirement ages should be increased by nearly six years for males and 10 years for females and then be corrected by approximately 0.4 years every five years.

Design and financial problems are compounded by a dysfunctional institutional setting, where the main actors in the social insurance system (the MEF, MSP, three social security institutes, Central Bank, and Bank and Insurance Supervision) rarely collaborate and coordinate policies or initiatives. This lack of communication results in continuous conflict among government agencies that should be working together to solve the system's problems. The situation is further complicated by the degree of political autonomy of the IESS, which appears to have extended far beyond what is usual in other countries. As a result, IESS authorities are in a position to make decisions, without appropriate political oversight, that far exceed management of the system.

A necessary step is to design a fiscally sustainable strategy for expanding social protection to the elderly, through the IESS or other mechanisms. To date, the IESS has been reluctant to participate in any exercise the institution perceives as undermining its autonomy. Little has been achieved on this matter despite the creation of an interinstitutional working group. Given the difficulties in working with the IESS, solutions must involve developing alternative ways to strengthen policies on old-age income support.

Trends and Developments in the Transparency and Accountability of the Social Sectors

Over the past few years, important advances have been made in improving transparency and accountability of the social sectors. The government has worked to improve the quantity and quality of the information available to policy makers and others on social sector spending, the performance of social programs, and social outcomes. The STFS has been made responsible for monitoring social spending and has put in place the social sector statistics system (SIISE—*Integrated System of Social Indicators*). These have been important advances, but they can work only if the system is continually updated and made publicly available to improve monitoring and transparency.

This trend to increase transparency has also translated into support for impact evaluations in the social sectors. The STFS has been given formal responsibility for evaluating social programs. An impact evaluation for the BDH program was concluded in 2005, and it showed that the program increases school enrollment and reduces the incidence of child labor. An impact evaluation of PAE is currently in the field, and a joint impact evaluation of the BDH and PROAUS is already in the early stages of implementation. Similar approaches should be taken for other social programs.

As is to be expected, reforms of social sector services in Ecuador face resistance from some interest groups who stand to lose as a result of necessary changes and who are well organized and outspoken. In contrast, many of the potential beneficiaries of reform lack information and have no access to forums where they can voice their support, undermining the political viability of reforms. Therefore, an essential strategy is to build consensus in support for reforms by holding stakeholder and civil society consultations that will increase public awareness of problems and opportunities in the social sectors, correct misapprehensions, and identify valid concerns. To date, a consultation has been undertaken with stakeholder groups on the conceptualization of the reform program. In 2004–05 the government conducted a consultation with the civil society group *Contrato Social por la Educación* to identify measures to improve rural primary education. These consultations have proved an effective tool to ensure grassroots support.

Finally, the government has begun a series of participatory evaluations that involve complementing the use of quantitative surveys and studies with qualitative beneficiary appraisals. Evaluations have been carried out by the NGO Esquel for the BDH, the LMG, and rural primary education programs, using a scorecard methodology. The results are expected to be discussed between the government and civil society representatives and should be incorporated into the respective programs.

II. Policy Recommendations

Despite some improvements, Ecuador's social sector indicators still lag behind those of many Latin American countries. Reforms should continue to focus on reducing the deep inequalities that have contributed to an intergenerational poverty trap, particularly among those in rural areas, and the indigenous and Afro-Ecuadoran populations. The following section makes some recommendations to further advance developments in the social sectors.

Education Sector

The 10-year plan (*Plan Decenal*) recently supported by a national referendum calls on the government to achieve some of the most important goals for the education sector: expanding early childhood education, achieving universal coverage in primary education, reaching a 75 percent enrollment in secondary education, eradicating illiteracy, upgrading school facilities, and improving quality through a system of teacher evaluation and training. To achieve these important goals, a series of changes are necessary.

One of the most urgent challenges facing the education sector is human resources, which currently accounts for 90 percent of the education budget. Without tackling human resources, it will not be possible to expand coverage to poor rural areas, because even if additional resources were to flow to the education sector, they would be assigned to an urban area by default under the current approach. Furthermore, changing the way resources are allocated in the sector could help by pushing the 10 percent currently allocated to infrastructure, books, and capacity building to really improve quality. One method could include evaluation of performance against sector goals. Such changes would also align the management model more appropriately with a decentralized education model. Given this context, measures essential for achieving the *Plan Decenal* include (i) improved institutional capacity and resource management, (ii) human resources management information systems, (iii) improved resource assignment, (iv) timely salary payments, and (v) strengthened early childhood education.

- ***Strengthen the MEC's role in the financing and management of resources in the education sector.*** The current structure—under which the MEF pays directly for teachers, and the MEC has little control over human resource management—undermines the MEC's institutional capacity to control and monitor sector resources. The reform would include strengthening the MEC's oversight role and technical capacity. There is also a need to improve coordination and define responsibilities between central and provincial levels of the MEC, particularly in the area of human resource management. A balance in this area would acknowledge the provincial-level reality where most teacher-related activities occur, while ensuring normative, evaluative, and oversight roles of the central level.
- ***Implement a human resource management information system.*** Currently, there is no way to adequately monitor human resources, making transparency and accountability difficult. The system should contain real-time data on staff assignments to schools and posts and data on staff attendance. The system would need to be implemented and validated at the national and provincial levels. The information system would include a human resource component with the following functions: personnel registry, staff development, staff supervision, staff performance evaluation, and retirement.
- ***Develop a formula for hiring and posting teachers.*** The formula would be designed to allocate resources on a per student basis that takes account of coverage deficits and other equity considerations, including the ethnicity and gender composition of the school-age population. The formula would be used

to create new teaching posts at understaffed schools. The allocation of new teachers to schools to which they were assigned should be binding.

- ***Improve coordination between the MEF and MEC to ensure timely payment of salaries in the education sector.*** The implementation of the information system described above would make possible the planning and monitoring of salary payments. The design should include systems for cost and budget, attendance control, and coverage. These data could be combined with the National Statistics and Census System (SINEC III) to provide a picture of the system's performance.
- ***Strengthen the MEC's capacity to evaluate and coordinate the delivery of quality early childhood education.*** This could be achieved through printing and disseminating curricular parameters, designing pedagogical standards and competencies, and training educators. These standards need to be monitored and evaluated to ensure compliance, learning, and policy adjustment.

Health Care Sector

The establishment of PROAUS was an important development toward improving health outcomes by expanding coverage to the poorest Ecuadorans. PROAUS was not only a strategic basis for moving toward universal health coverage, but was also a vital part of improving efficiency in the sector and reducing its fragmentation. Furthermore, this program was anticipated to generate several other important positive spillover effects, or externalities. It was expected to change resource allocation in the system away from budget allocations based on historical costs to allocations based on production of services and performance, generating more effective and active participation of the health care system in a decentralized context. However, for PROAUS to be effectively implemented, and for health care coverage and system performance to improve more generally, the following challenges would need to be addressed: (i) strengthening capacity to manage PROAUS; (ii) implementing a monitoring and evaluation system to improve performance and accountability for both the LMG and PROAUS; (iii) addressing IESS health service reform as part of a broader strategy to expand health care coverage; and (iv) improving access to medicines by promoting generic medicines.

- ***Focus on building capacity to manage PROAUS and ensure adequate staffing levels of the implementation unit.*** Unless immediate attention is given to ensuring that sufficient resources are available within the implementation unit, the effectiveness of the program's rollout could be jeopardized. In addition to ensuring adequate numbers of staff, it is essential that they be given the capacity to appropriately address the challenges they face.
- ***Update the ENDEMAIN survey to provide additional indicators to monitor improvements in health access in the beneficiary populations of the LMG and PROAUS.*** To ensure the effectiveness of both the LMG and

PROAUS, the ENDEMAIN should be updated so that it can be used for the ongoing monitoring of health outcomes and access goals in target populations with specific measurable indicators that are relevant to the two programs.

- ***Develop a new interinstitutional monitoring and information system for the LMG and PROAUS.*** This should be an integrated M&E system capable of collecting data on coverage rates, identifying cultural or other barriers to access, and monitoring reimbursement payments. The information system should be uniform so that it can be used by both the LMG and PROAUS, with modifications to accommodate the differentiated needs of the two schemes. The M&E system should be piloted and rolled out nationwide, with priority given to Bolivar, Chimborazo, Cotopaxi, and Tungurahua, which have large numbers of poor indigenous households.
- ***Implement culturally sensitive approaches to increase LMG coverage rates.*** A strategy to reduce cultural barriers to access LMG services should be developed, including provisions allowing the LMG to pay for services provided by traditional midwives who refer their patients for prenatal consultations, institutional births, and postnatal consultations. The LMG could develop a training module to help traditional midwives deal with hemorrhaging and other postnatal complications. A working group on indigenous health could be established to identify other services that could be geared to the needs of indigenous communities.
- ***Expand coverage of the social security system as part of the overall strategy to expand health care coverage.*** Coverage should include family members, particularly children, who are the most vulnerable and are most often excluded from any coverage under the current system. Such expansion would entail additional expenditures and facilities, and careful planning and cost management would be essential to long-term sustainability.
- ***Design policies to correct the disincentive facing pharmacists to dispense low-cost, generic-equivalent drugs.*** Putting the right incentives in place for pharmacists would likely lead to a significant increase in the use of generics and increase competition, lowering drug prices. Incentives would be part of a wider set of policies designed to promote generic prescribing and rational drug use. Further efficiencies could be achieved by undertaking a facility survey of health posts and hospitals to improve forecasting and the procurement process.

Social Protection Systems

The opportunity to rationalize and improve coordination of the social protection system exists within the Secretariat of the Social Cabinet and the Social Protection Program. To accomplish these objectives, regular updating and recertification of SelBen is essential to reorient subsidies to where they can be used most effectively to rehabilitate and create social opportunities. The transformation of the BDH from an unconditional cash-transfer program to a program dependent on education and health requirements, or conditionalities, will be a key strategic accomplishment not only for the program itself but, more important, for the potential benefits it will bring in terms of access to and use of education and health care services as a means to break the perpetual cycle of intergenerational poverty. These accomplishments will be strategically important for graduating families from the programs by improving their socioeconomic status. Improved nutritional standards are also an important element in improving this status. The important challenges for the sector require targeting the following objectives: (i) strengthening program-targeting instruments; (ii) making the BDH more effective through institutional strengthening and capacity building; (iii) revising nutrition strategies and promoting transparency and accountability in feeding and nutrition programs; and (iv) expanding access to old-age income support.

- ***Improve targeting by revising the methodology to be implemented under SelBen II and by strengthening its legal and institutional framework.*** This would include the methodological recommendations of Habitus to improve SelBen II recertification, as mentioned earlier. Methodological improvements would also benefit from a review to better understand how other programs and agencies are using and feeding into the SelBen database. Strengthening the legal and institutional framework of SelBen would help guarantee periodic recertification and develop clear rules for updates at national and local levels. The government may want to interview some additional households using a revised methodology prior to implementing SelBen II. It would be advisable to minimize ad hoc inclusion of additional beneficiaries before implementing the SelBen II recertification process.
- ***Evaluate different methodological approaches to increase the size of BDH payments.*** An analysis of options and scenarios, along with a logistical plan, should be done before BDH payments are increased. Prioritizing payment increases to quintile 1 (the poorest) would generate the greatest impact. These changes to the BDH would need to be incorporated into the impact evaluation that is under way. Simultaneously, policies should be designed to graduate beneficiaries in quintile 2 from the BDH.
- ***Continue to strengthen the core institutional structures and capacities for the BDH.*** For the BDH to be successful, the government should ensure that necessary institutional and legal conditions are in place to guarantee a successful consolidation of the BDH reform program. In particular, reform should focus on the institutional capacity of the PPS and its ability to coordinate with the MEC, MSP, and STFS, including SelBen. This strategy also should include the development of a communications strategy to improve beneficiaries' and others' understanding of rights and responsibilities under the program to improve transparency and accountability.
- ***Review plans and implement a comprehensive system to monitor BDH education and health co-responsibilities.*** This should be part of a comprehensive

M&E system, with the capacity for process monitoring and quality control. This system would benefit from increased coordination with the MEC and MSP.

- ***Implement a goal-based, coherent national nutrition strategy with SIAN as the focal point.*** A new national nutrition strategy is essential to reducing stunting by 12 percent by 2015. This strategy should be led by the MSP and SIAN. To be fully effective, it should not be limited to feeding programs, but integrate all relevant interventions, including community-level growth monitoring and counseling, primary health, and micronutrient supplementation. The strategy should have differentiated interventions by risk group, and the highest priority should be in the rural mountain region. Culturally sensitive health- and nutrition-related counseling to pregnant women and mothers of young children should be a central tool of the strategy. The micronutrient strategy should be overhauled, including updating of statutory norms and enforcement for fortification of mass-consumption foods with iron and iodine. A strategy also is needed to improve delivery (reliability and quantities) of therapeutic micronutrient supplements (iron, folic acid, calcium, and zinc) through the health system. Finally, the role of the BDH in the nutrition strategy needs to be reconsidered, particularly in light of the commitment to increase the amount of the fund transfers; a mother's participation in growth counselling sessions might be an appropriate conditionality to consider.
- ***Strengthen the monitoring of nutrition outcomes to increase transparency and accountability.*** The SISVAN growth-monitoring system should be revamped to generate real-time data on the growth trajectory of children. This measurement should be done at the same time as nutritional counseling is given to mothers. In doing so, children not growing properly could be identified and appropriate follow-up given through the health system. These data on growth outcomes should form a key part of the nutrition strategy's results and accountability framework. Improvements should be prioritized as part of a stronger M&E system at program level that would include rigorous impact evaluations to strengthen transparency and accountability.
- ***Expand old-age security in the country.*** The World Bank (2005b) supported a comprehensive review of the current social insurance coverage in the country and identified several options for expanding coverage, including expanding coverage through existing social security schemes as well as through a new social insurance scheme for informal workers. The study also recommended a series of additional structural and institutional reforms to improve performance in this area.

Transparency and Accountability in the Social Sectors

Continuing to develop a culture of transparent, evidence-based decision making in the social sectors requires the production and publication of timely information on social expenditures and their outcomes, the systematic evaluation of priority programs, and the strengthening of the STFS's institutional and technical capacity. Sustainability of the reform agenda would be supported through stakeholder consultations, and improved accountability would be achieved through participatory evaluations.

- ***Further strengthen STFS social sector data systems to ensure appropriate monitoring and transparency.*** Social sector spending data, organized by program and funding source, should be published on a Web page on a quarterly basis, in collaboration with the MEF, the sector ministries, and the managing units of social programs. The STFS should also continue designing a new generation of the SIISE Web-based social statistics system. At the same time, the STFS should improve the definitional consistency of social spending data generated by the different subsystems. Finally, to update statistics on social outcomes, the government should plan a Living Standards Measurement Study (LSMS) and a new health and nutrition survey (ENDEMAIN) in 2007. The results could be fed into the SIISE.
- ***Continue the use of impact evaluations to monitor program outcomes in the social sectors.*** Ensure completion of the PAE and the joint BDH-PROAUS impact evaluations that are under way. Ensure that impact evaluations are also carried out for other social programs.
- ***Continue to consult with relevant stakeholders to ensure the sustainability of the reform programs in human development.*** Such consultations have been an important part of ensuring wider ownership and responsiveness of social sector programs.
- ***Maintain the practice of participatory evaluations.*** This should include a new round of participatory evaluations for the BDH, LMG, and rural primary education programs and also for the SIAN programs. The results and recommendations from the evaluation that is already under way should be incorporated into their respective programs and projects.

Policy Matrix

Area	*Issues/problems*	*Policy recommendations*
Education	• The education sector has a confused management structure with little central control. • Human resource policies and resource allocation are not always based on need, negatively affecting rural areas in particular. • Illiteracy and access to basic education is high in some regions and among some sectors. • The overall quality of education is low, with weak performance evaluations of teachers and inadequate teacher training. • Early childhood education programs are limited.	• Strengthen the MEC's role in the financing and management of resources in the education sector to gain better control over human and financial resources. • Implement an information system for human resources management, with real-time data on staff assignments to schools and posts and data on staff attendance, as well as components on (i) personnel registry, (ii) staff development, (iii) staff supervision, (iv) staff performance evaluation, and (v) retirement. • Develop a clear, rational formula for hiring and posting teachers, based on education sector need. Newly created teaching posts should be prioritized using this formula to address understaffed schools. • Improve coordination between the MEF and MEC to ensure timely payment of salaries in the education sector. • Strengthen the MEC's capacity to evaluate and coordinate the delivery of quality early childhood education.
Health	• Inadequate staffing and staff training could negatively affect the rollout of PROAUS. • Monitoring and evaluation systems are currently insufficient to track performance and accountability for both the LMG and PROAUS. • The IESS health system has limited coverage and does not include the families of members. • Some aspects of the health system do not adequately account for cultural sensitivities among indigenous people, limiting their use of these services.	• Urgently focus on building capacity to manage PROAUS and ensure adequate, well-trained staff for the implementation unit. • Update the ENDEMAIN survey to provide additional indicators to monitor improvements in health access in the beneficiary populations of the LMG and PROAUS with specific measurable indicators that are relevant to the two programs. • Develop a new interinstitutional monitoring and information system for the LMG and PROAUS. This

(*Table continues on the following page.*)

Area	*Issues/problems*	*Policy recommendations*
	• Incentives currently work against the use of low-cost generic medicines that could significantly reduce the cost of medical care.	should be an integrated M&E system capable of (i) collecting data on coverage rates, (ii) identifying cultural or other barriers to access, and (iii) monitoring reimbursement payments. The M&E system should be piloted and rolled out nationwide with priority to Bolivar, Chimborazo, Cotopaxi, and Tungurahua, where there are a large number of poor indigenous households. • Implement culturally sensitive approaches to increase LMG coverage rates. A working group on indigenous health could be established to identify services that could be geared to the needs of indigenous communities. • Expand health coverage provided by the social security system to include family members, in particularly children who are the most vulnerable and most often excluded from any coverage under the current system. • Design policies to correct the disincentive facing pharmacists to dispense low-cost generic equivalent drugs.
Social protection	• The SelBen targeting system, though good, could be improved to ensure that social programs reach those who need them most. • The BDH is being increased sharply without adequate assessment of the way to do so to have the greatest impact on the poorest people. • The BDH component on education and health coresponsibilities is weak. • The proliferation of different nutrition programs has made it more difficult to address Ecuador's goals in this area.	• Improve targeting by revising the methodology to be implemented under SelBen II and by strengthening its legal and institutional framework, including the methodological recommendations of Habitus. • Continue beneficiary recertification efforts under SelBen II using a revised methodology to ensure improved targeting. • Analyze methods for increasing the size of BDH payments. Prior to the implementation of this commitment, analyze options and scenarios and create a logistical plan to facilitate rollout. Prioritizing payment increases to quintile 1 (the poorest) would generate the largest impact. • Continue to strengthen the core institutional structures and capacities for the BDH.

		• Review plans and implement a comprehensive system to monitor BDH education and health coresponsibilities. This should be part of a comprehensive M&E system, with the capacity for process monitoring and quality control. • Implement a goal-based, coherent national nutrition strategy with SIAN as the focal point. A new national nutrition strategy is essential to halving stunting to 12 percent by 2015. This strategy should be led by the MSP and SIAN. To be fully effective, it should not be limited to feeding programs but should integrate all relevant interventions. • Strengthen the monitoring of nutrition outcomes to increase transparency and accountability.
Cross-cutting social sectors	• Although recent years have seen improvements, Ecuador needs to work harder to develop a culture of transparent, evidence-based decision making in the social sectors. This could be achieved by producing and publishing timely information on social expenditures and their outcomes and systematically evaluating priority programs.	• Further strengthen STFS social sector data systems to ensure appropriate monitoring and transparency. Social sector spending data by program and funding source should be published on a Web page on a quarterly basis, in collaboration with the MEF, the sector ministries, and the managing units of social programs. The STFS should also continue designing a new generation of the SIISE Web-based social statistics system. A new LSMS and ENDEMAIN surveys should be undertaken in 2007. • Ensure completion of the PAE and the joint BDH-PROAUS impact evaluations that are under way and ensure that impact evaluations are also carried out for other social programs. • Continue to consult with relevant stakeholders to ensure the sustainability of the reform programs in human development. • Maintain the practice of participatory evaluations.

Notes

1. The MEF and MEC for payroll, Human Resources for the personnel system, DINEIB and DINAMEP for training, and the provincial directorates for teacher placements.

2. However, the reliability of infant and maternal mortality data based on vital statistics records has been disputed, and estimates based on demographic surveys indicate rates that are significantly higher. For example, in 2004, the infant mortality rate was estimated at 40 per 1,000 by the United Nations Population Division of the Department of Economic and Social Affairs, almost twice the official figure, and PAHO estimated a maternal mortality ratio of 81 per 100,000 births in the same year.

3. Data from ENDEMAIN (2005) estimate that only 19 percent of the population surveyed had health insurance coverage.

Bibliography

Consorcio Care–Bloomberg School of Public Health, Johns Hopkins University. 2004. Consultoria Proyecto de Modernización de los Servicios de Salud (MODERSA). Quito.

Escobar, M-L, and P. Panopoulou. 2003. "Health." In *Colombia: The Economic Foundation of Peace*, eds. M. M. Guigale, O. Lafourcade, and C. Luff. Washington, DC: World Bank.

Horwitz, Abraham. 1987. "Comparative Public Health: Costa Rica, Cuba and Chile." *Food and Nutrition Bulletin* 9(3), September. The United Nations University Press.

MEC (Ministry of Education and Culture). 2001. *APRENDO: 2000—Resultados Nacionales/Resultados por Destrezas.* Quito: APRENDO (mayo).

INEC (National Institute of Statistics and Censuses). 2005. "Encuesta National de Empleo, ENEMDU." Quito, Ecuador.

Ordoñez J., P. Stupp, G. Angeles, A. Valle, D. Williams, R. Monteigh, and M. Goodwin. 2005. "Encuesta Nacional de Demografía y Salud Materna Infantil—2004 (ENDEMAIN). Informe Final." CEPAR, Centers for Disease Control, MEASURE Evaluation. Quito, Ecuador.

Rofman, Rafael, and Leonardo, Lucchetti. 2006. "Pension Systems in Latin America: Concepts and Measurements of Coverage." Social Protection Discussion Paper 0616. World Bank, Washington, DC.

Schady, N., and M. C. Araujo. 2005. "Cash Transfer, Conditions, School Enrollment and Child Work: Evidence from a Randomized Experiment in Ecuador." World Bank, Washington, DC.

SIISE (Integrated System of Social Indicators of Ecuador [*Sistema Integrado de Indicadores Sociales del Ecuador*]). 2000. Quito: SIISE.

World Bank. 2005a. *Creating Fiscal Space for Poverty Reduction in Ecuador: A Fiscal Management and Public Expenditure Review.* Washington, DC: World Bank.

World Bank. 2005b. *Ecuador: Expanding Social Insurance to Protect All.* Washington, DC: World Bank.

World Bank. 2007. *Nutrition Failure in Ecuador: Causes, Consequences and Solutions.* Washington, DC: World Bank.

8

The Pension System

Rafael Rofman

Executive Summary

The Ecuadoran pension system has three types of problems—in its design, management, and institutional makeup—that need to be resolved in the short and medium term. The first problem involves the program's effective coverage. The proportion of the economically active population and the elderly who are protected by the Obligatory Insurance of the Ecuadoran Social Security Institute (IESS) is one of the lowest in the region. In part, this low coverage is the result of a very high rate of labor informality in Ecuador, which is estimated to be over 60 percent of the economically active population. Noncontributive programs, such as the Rural People's Social Security Program (Seguro Social Campesino) or the Human Development Bond (Bono de Desarrollo Humano—BDH) cash subsidy, extend the coverage, although benefits are relatively low.

A second problem is the financial management of the IESS. On the one hand, the state has failed to pay certain contributions to the IESS for more than a decade. Yet according to the institute's accounting, this debt is listed as an asset. The amount of the debt differs significantly, depending on whether it is calculated by the IESS or by the Ministry of Economy and Finance (MEF). The discrepancy in question has a major impact on the actual size of reserves. Also, the state is mandated by law to contribute 40 percent of the benefits of retired persons each year, even though the IESS's pension program clearly has a surplus, and despite the fact that the subsidy could be better spent on more progressive programs. As such, unnecessary pressure is being placed on government revenues.

This chapter was written by Rafael Rofman, senior economist and specialist in pension systems at the World Bank, and was updated by Chris Humphrey, consultant LC6/PREM, based on information from the IESS and the government of Ecuador.

A third problem is in the system's institutional framework, which gives the IESS excessive autonomy in policy design (as opposed to administration) without sufficient oversight. In addition, the government does not have a centralized entity to analyze and design policies for the social security system. This policy note proposes measures for broadening the scope of coverage of the insured in a manner that is fiscally and socially responsible, while improving the financial management of the IESS and strengthening the system's institutional stability.

I. System Diagnostic

The following section reviews aspects of the current pension system, including institutional organization and structure, financial situation, level of benefits, coverage, and the failed reforms of 2001.

The Institutional Organization of Ecuador's Pension System

Ecuador's system for protecting the income of the elderly comprises three contributive-type programs, a fourth program that is nominally contributive but has a major subsidy component, and a fifth program that is noncontributive. The principal contributive program is Obligatory Social Security (*Seguro Social Obligatorio*—SSO), which covers workers from the formal sector of the economy. The other two are the pension systems of the armed forces and of the police. The voluntary Rural People's Social Security Program (*Seguro Social Campesino*—SSC), which covers peasants who work independently or are members of communes, cooperatives, or other community organizations, is nominally contributive, but the contributions made by the beneficiaries cover a minimal part of the expenses. Finally, a fifth program, which was not created as part of the pension system but in practice plays an important role in the economic safety net for the elderly, is the old-age component of the BDH cash subsidy program.

The SSO was initiated during the first two decades of the 20th century, when certain government workers obtained the right to receive pensions upon retirement. This program expanded to sectors of public servants and private employees in the following decade, and other coverage was added, including sick pay, maternity benefits, disability insurance, death benefits, workman's compensation, and severance pay. The SSO has been administered by the IESS since the early 1970s. The IESS also administers the SSC, which was created about 1980 with the intention of extending social security coverage to families belonging to communal farms or other rural organizations. The SSC is financed through contributions from workers and employers enrolled in the SSO, as well as through contributions from the government and minimal contributions from the participants themselves. Benefits under the SSC are much lower than benefits under the SSO. Members of the armed forces and the police enjoy a protection similar to that of the SSO, through programs administered by independent entities, the Social Security Institute of the Armed Forces (ISSFA) and the Social Security Institute of the Police (ISSPOL). The BDH subsidy program, which grants a noncontributive monetary subsidy to low-income elderly persons, is administered through the Ministry of Social Welfare.

The IESS is autonomous and is relatively impervious to pressures by either the executive or legislative branches. This autonomous status is greater than what is usual in other countries, since IESS authorities make decisions far beyond the management of the system, such as defining the value of pension benefits themselves, with little oversight. This detracts from the quality of system management. Some decisions appear to be made without proper analysis, and procedures are not always transparent or efficient. One example of this is the lack of up-to-date information on IESS performance on the institute's Web site, in contrast to the pension systems for the military and police.

In 2001, the Congress passed a significant reform of the country's social security system, introducing the concept of universal coverage through different modalities. However, several critical provisions of the law—in particular, those related to the creation of personal pension accounts—were declared unconstitutional by the courts. Since the court decision, attempts have been under way to pass new reform legislation, which as yet have not been successful. In the meantime, the IESS has implemented a number of the provisions of the 2001 law, despite the fact that its regulations have not been issued. However, the major proposed change in the system, creating individual accounts administered by the IESS with investments by private companies, was never enacted.

Structure of the Pension System

The SSO protects its affiliates against the risks of disability, old age, and death, as well as risks related to health, maternity, workman's compensation, and job loss. Participation in the program is obligatory for all public and private sector employees. Its financing is derived from personal contributions from workers and employers. In addition, the state contributes the equivalent of 40 percent of the pensions paid by the IESS, which in 2006 amounted to 0.94 percent of GDP. (This does not include the 0.3 percent of GDP paid out of the budget to the armed forces and police pensions.) This public contribution originated in the 1950s and was intended to cover an expected future actuarial deficit, which has not yet materialized. Total contributions from workers and employers are made at the rate of 28.5 percent of the base wage, out of which 8.5 percent is earmarked to cover disability, old age, and death benefits. Of that 28.5 percent, private sector employees contribute 9.35 percent, while the rest is covered by the employer; public sector employees pay 11.35 percent. Employers also pay 8.3 percent to a reserve fund that is returned to workers every three years (see below for more on this). Voluntary affiliates, who pay the entire contribution themselves, pay 20.15 percent of base wages.

Workers of both sexes can retire with full benefits at age 60, provided that they had 30 years of contributions credited. The two limits (age and years of contributions) are flexible. For each year that a worker puts off retirement, one fewer year of contributions is required, to the point that a person can retire at age 70 with only 10 years of continuous contributions. As well, a person with 40 years of contributions can retire regardless of the age limit. The monthly old-age retirement benefit was proportional to 75 percent of the average of the five best years of the worker's contributions, and is further determined per years of contributions. Workers who reenter the labor force after retirement are eligible for a reentry bonus.

Disability and death benefits have their own structure. The amounts of these benefits are not established as an automatic percentage of prior wages, but they also increase as a function of the age of the disabled person or decedent. In the case of disability, workers with a minimum of 60 monthly contributions have a right to a pension once they are declared disabled by the IESS. Death benefits are made to a widow or female cohabitant, and to a widower or male cohabitant if he is disabled and a dependent of the decedent, as well as to children who are under 18 years of age or disabled. Death benefits for widows, widowers, or cohabitants are 40 percent of the pension that the decedent would have been receiving or would have been entitled to collect, and 20 percent of that amount for each child. The rules and regulations also provide benefits to other family members under exceptional circumstances.

Contribution rates and benefits are both determined on the basis of taxable wages. Until recently, this reflected only a part of the workers' actual income, as, in recent decades, workers' wages were often adjusted not through direct increases to their pay, but through the creation of new forms of remuneration. New remunerations (such as bonuses, vouchers, and the like) were created by employers over time and formed a part of the worker's total income but were not considered taxable wages. This practice was especially pronounced in the public sector, where there were 28 items for which compensation was received, but contributions were only made on base wages. The complementary remunerations, which represented 36.5 percent of total remunerations in 1990, grew to the point that they reached 92.5 percent in 1999 (IESS 2001). This problem severely reduced the resources available to the IESS for financing benefits, and it also affected the future benefits of those making contributions during those years.

In 2000, a new law began the unification of salaries in the private sector, including many of these myriad components, into base wages. By 2005, wages accounted for more than 95 percent of total remuneration of private sector workers. As a result, private sector contributions to the IESS have increased significantly in recent years, improving the institution's financial balances. The 2003 Civil Service Law similarly unified wages for the public sector, which has also led to a significant increase in IESS income from public sector affiliates.

Up to 2005, pursuant to the Labor Code, the IESS was administering a reserve fund generated through a monthly contribution from employers, equivalent to one-twelth of monthly wages. The purpose of the fund was to provide resources to salaried workers during times of unemployment. The failed 2001 pension reform had intended these resources to be managed by the workers themselves in individual accounts. Because this reform did not move forward, in July 2005 the Congress passed a law calling for the devolution of accumulated funds to affiliates every three years, over a scheduled period, to smooth the financial impact. As of December 2006, US$712.2 million had been devolved to 1.1 million affiliates, and roughly US$30 million remained to be devolved to about 100,000 more affiliates. This measure has not had any direct impact on pension system sustainability, since the resources are not part of the system, now or in the future. The large amount paid out in such a short period of time had a fairly significant macroeconomic impact, particularly in terms of household consumption, and contributed, along with high oil income, to economic growth. In the future, contributions to this fund will continue to accumulate in special accounts in the Central Bank and will be paid out every three years.

The SSC, in contrast to the SSO, requires minimal (essentially symbolic) contributions for benefit entitlement. Heads of households contribute 1 percent of the basic minimum wage to finance worker benefits, which works out to 4 cents on a dollar each month. Workers and employers enrolled in the SSO were required to contribute 0.35 percent of wages. In addition, 0.30 percent of that same wage base is provided as a contribution from the state, and the state also makes another direct contribution. Enrollment in the SSC entitles the beneficiary to health services for his or her family unit. The head of household is also entitled to disability or old-age benefits, in an amount equivalent to 75 percent of the basic minimum wage. The right to an old-age pension is acquired at age 65, provided that the beneficiary has made at least 10 years of contributions. Under the 2001 law, although never implemented, this requirement is gradually phased out starting at 71 years of age, and at age 75 or more, only five years of contributions are required.

Finally, the BDH cash subsidy program offers a benefit in the form of assistance granted through the Ministry of Social Welfare. The subsidy was originally created in 1998 as the Bono Solidario, to replace subsidies on consumption of energy, which were eliminated that same year (although the energy subsidies were reestablished shortly afterwards). In 2003, the government created the BDH, a conditional cash-transfer program targeted to the poorest 40 percent of the population. Although mainly directed toward mothers and children from this population segment, it also granted benefits to households with elderly people (defined as 60 years and above). However, only one grant per household was permitted, even if an elderly person, mother and child all lived together. In September 2006, the BDH component for the elderly was changed; it is now targeted to the elderly individuals themselves, leaving the rest of the household eligible for the regular BDH, if they qualify. In early 2007, the elderly benefit was increased from US$11.50 per month to US$30, along with the regular BDH.

Financial Situation

The overall IESS system has had a surplus in recent years. The surplus was smallest in 1999, when it amounted to only 0.1 percent of the GDP, and largest in 2002, when it amounted to 2.0 percent. Since then, surpluses have declined, to about 0.4 percent of GDP in 2004 (figure 8.1).

An analysis of trends in insurance for the old age, disability, and death subcomponents is more complex, because the IESS did not keep a separate accounting of the various funds, as indicated above. Nonetheless, estimated financial values indicate that there has also been a surplus since 1993, with balances ranging from 0.1 percent of the GDP in 1999 to 0.7 percent of the GDP in 2001. However, because of increases in benefits, which were partially but not totally offset by increasing contributions from wage unification, the IESS pension system funds declined in 2004, with a deficit of 0.6 percent of GDP (figure 8.2).

Figure 8.2 shows the estimated results for the SSO pension system, without considering transfers from the state. If the total results of policies aimed at generating income for the elderly were included, the estimated deficit would be larger, as disbursements are also made from the military and police retirement systems, pensions granted through the SSC (about US$900,000 in 2006), and the BDH benefits for the elderly (US$2.2 million in 2006, although that is expected to increase sharply in 2007 to US$6 million or more).

The improvement in capturing revenues as of 2000 is due to two effects. On the one hand, since March 2000, a wage standardization process was commenced, which tends to simplify the structure of remunerations and to classify the majority of wages as taxable income for purposes of social security contributions. Furthermore, in 2001 the state started paying the contributions it owes as an employer and as a third party, causing collected revenues to rapidly increase. In 2006, the state contributed 0.94 percent of GDP (US$384 million) to the SSO, and a further 0.3 percent (US$123 million) to the police and military pension funds.

Figure 8.1. Overall Financial Performance of the IESS Pension System, 1993–2004

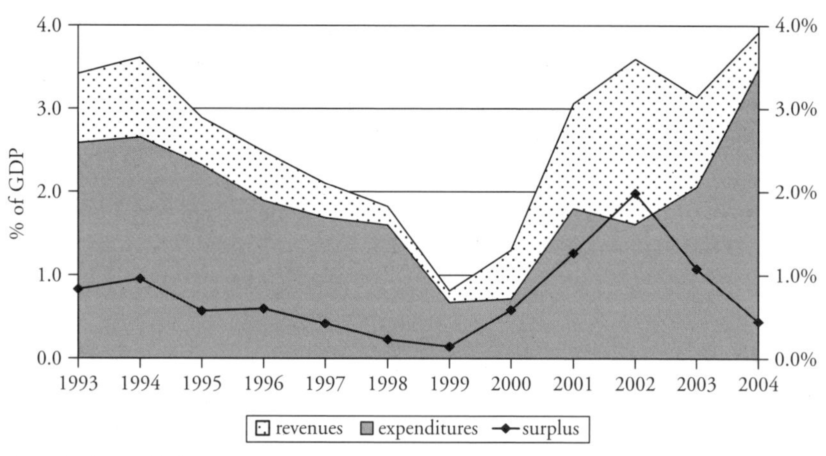

Source: Rofman (2005).

Figure 8.2. Financial Performance of the IESS Pension System, 1993–2004

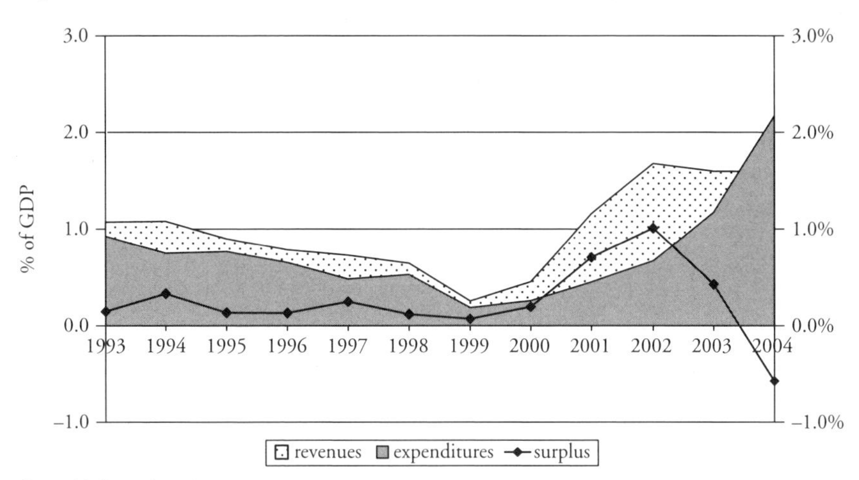

Source: Rofman (2005).

The positive results obtained by the IESS have led to an accumulation of reserves. In 2005, the General Insurance reserve (which includes disability, old age, and death), according to the IESS's own accounting, was US$930.5 million, up from US$586 million the previous year. This does not include the debt from the state for past unpaid contributions, which the IESS estimates is US$2.6 billion, but the government contends is only US$549 million. The final amount of this debt will be decided through negotiation between the MEF and IESS, although this has yet to take place.

The ability of the IESS to invest reserves is strictly controlled by law in various ways, leading to relatively low rates of return on investment. For example, the special workman's compensation fund that accumulates and devolves to workers every three years, amounting to several hundred million dollars, did not receive any return at all until the end of 2006, as it was deposited in non-interest-bearing accounts in the Central Bank. This has recently changed, and the accounts will accrue some interest. During the day, resources are available to the IESS for current needs, and at night the funds are invested in interest-bearing overnight repurchase instruments. Pension fund reserves are heavily oriented toward public debt because no low-risk corporate debt is available in the domestic market. Investment outside of Ecuador is allowed only up to a maximum of 15 percent of reserves, and this only in exceptional circumstances and with the unanimous approval of the Technical Investment Committee and IESS Directive Council.

The IESS has announced its intention to invest in mortgage portfolios and mortgage-backed securities, when they become available. This is an appropriate role for the IESS and would provide important support to the market's development. However, it should be prevented from lending directly for mortgages at an interest rate equal to its estimated actuarial rate of return, which is currently 6 percent below market rates for mortgages, because the rate fails to reflect the risks and returns of the mortgage lending business. Lending at below-market interest rates conflicts with the IESS's stated goal of ensuring adequate benefits for its members and inhibits the development of a sustainable supply of private sector financing. As in many other countries, such lending could lead to substantial losses for fund beneficiaries.

One important and problematic aspect of Ecuador's pension system is the large amount paid into the system by the government each year (40 percent of system benefits). In recent years, this cost has been rising significantly, totaling 0.94 percent of GDP in 2006 (figure 8.3), or 1.25 percent of GDP if the contribution to military and police pensions are added. This practice was instituted in the 1950s to cover expected actuarial deficits in the future, and the contributions are not necessary to fund day-to-day operations. Considering that the pensions cover a very small portion of society (about one-fifth of the economically active population), and a nonpoor portion at that, it is worth considering the appropriateness of having society as a whole cover an expected future actuarial deficit out of current revenues. Despite the regressive nature of this transfer (as pensions predominately go to the nonpoor), the reality is that the IESS finances much of this transfer by using its own investment resources to buy public debt. Consequently, although these fiscal resources could be used more progressively in other areas, changing this contribution may also require the government to find other sources of financing for its public debt.

The Level of Benefits

One of the reasons why the IESS has been able to maintain a certain degree of financial stability despite the problems discussed in the previous section is that benefit amounts were also severely affected by macroeconomic dynamics. In the mid-1990s the average old-age pension benefit was approximately US$100 per month (after accounting for the special payments); however, it fell rapidly between 1998 and 2000, to less than US$30 per month. As of 2001 the IESS started to pursue a policy of restoring

Figure 8.3. Government Contribution to IESS Pensions

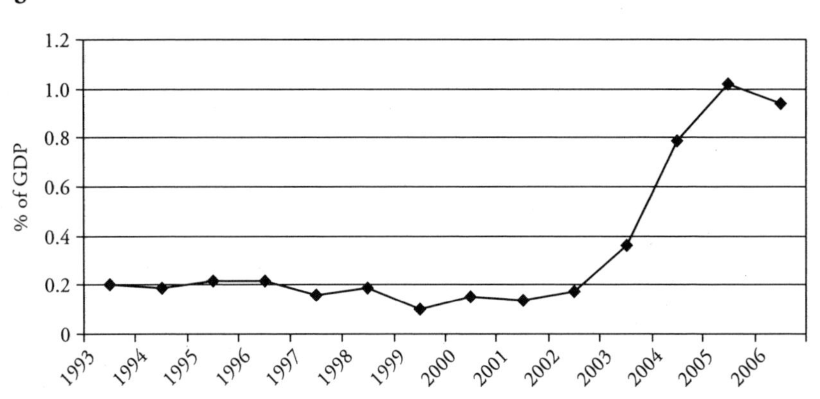

Source: MEF.

benefit levels (table 8.1). In 2006, the average benefit was US$281 per month. Disability benefits in 2006 averaged US$238, and death benefits were US$125. The amount of the benefit is defined by the IESS; the government is not able to intervene. Although the average benefit payment has increased in recent years, it is still significantly less than that promised under 2001 reform law.

Retirees eligible for the rural people's pension (SSC) receive a benefit payment equivalent to 75 percent of the basic minimum wage, but the amount has not been adjusted since the dollarization. The average pensions under this program in the mid-1990s were slightly greater than US$20 per month. But then the amounts fell, in a manner similar to what occurred with benefits under the SSO, reaching levels of US$3 per month in 2001. The pension amount has yet to be corrected.

Finally, beneficiaries of the BDH cash subsidy program received US$11.50 per month in 2004, up from US$7 in 2000. The payment increased significantly, to US$30 per month, in February 2007.

Coverage

The core objective of a pension system is to provide income for persons who, by reasons of age (or disability or death), are unable to generate the income they need for their subsistence and the subsistence of their family group. Therefore, a system's coverage is a central issue. A pension system that fails to protect a significant proportion of the population has failed to meet its principal objective.

The coverage of Ecuador's pension system is one of the lowest in South America. The coverage indicators customarily utilized (such as the proportion of the economically active population that pays into the contributive system, or the proportion of persons age 60 or more with benefits) indicate values that are lower than those of other countries in the region. Indeed, only Bolivia, Peru, and Colombia (as well as Paraguay, not included) have a lower percentage of contributors (figure 8.4).

The problem of low coverage in Ecuador worsened in recent years, given that macroeconomic difficulties affected the degree to which workers had formal employment.

Table 8.1. Average Monthly Pension Benefits, 2000–06
(U.S. dollars)

	SSO old-age pension	*SSC old-age pension*	*BDH*
2000	25	6	4.5
2001	44	3	7
2002	120	3	7
2003	184	3	7
2004	234	3	11.5
2005	266	3	11.5
2006	281	3	11.5

Source: IESS.

Figure 8.4. Percentage of the Labor Force Participating in Contributive Pension Programs in South America

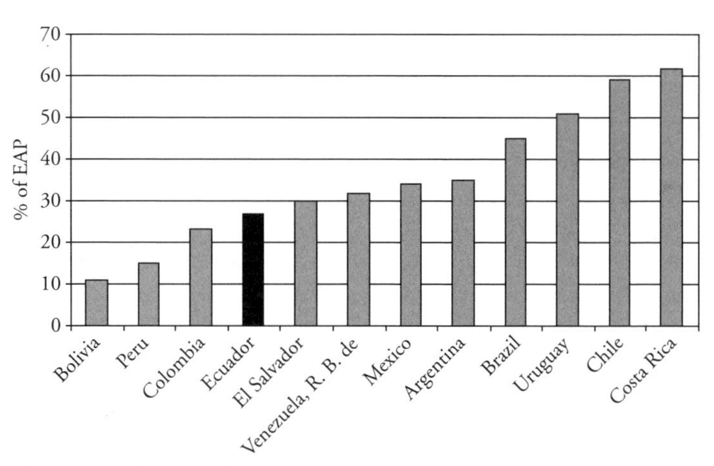

Source: Rofman and Lucchetti (2006).
Note: Country data are from about 2000, as available.

This provoked stagnation in the number of contributors to the SSO in the mid-1990s, at a time when the economically active population was growing steadily. As a consequence, the proportion of the economically active population covered by the SSO declined between 1995 and 2005 from 34 percent to 19 percent—1.2 million Ecuadorans out of an economically active population of 6.3 million. This decline reflects the incapacity of the formal labor market to expand at the same rate of growth as the population (figure 8.5). Currently, an estimated 60 percent or more of the workforce in Ecuador is in the informal sector and by definition does not have any pension coverage (World Bank 2007, 29).

Trends in the SSC during this same period were similar. The program grew rapidly during the first decade of its existence. As of 1995, however, the number of heads of households registered in the program stabilized, and the program's impact diminished in terms of the percentage of the economically active population who benefited. In 2005, the SSC had about 190,000 direct affiliates and 23,000 retirees, along with 820,000 family members of affiliates with medical coverage. The potential membership is about three times larger than the actual membership, with the potential to benefit about 700,000 direct affiliates and 2.4 million family members. The IESS has stated in its plans for the SSC that it intends to increase coverage to 40 percent of eligible families by 2008. However, financial constraints have kept membership growth at almost nil for the past decade. The military and police pensions cover roughly 50,000 active affiliates and 45,000 retirees. The BDH for the elderly currently assists about 200,000 people, although the new targeting program (which allows elderly to claim the benefit even if their family is also claiming the regular BDH) aims to bring that number up to 320,000 in coming years.

Figure 8.5. Pension Coverage of Economically Active Population, 1965–2005

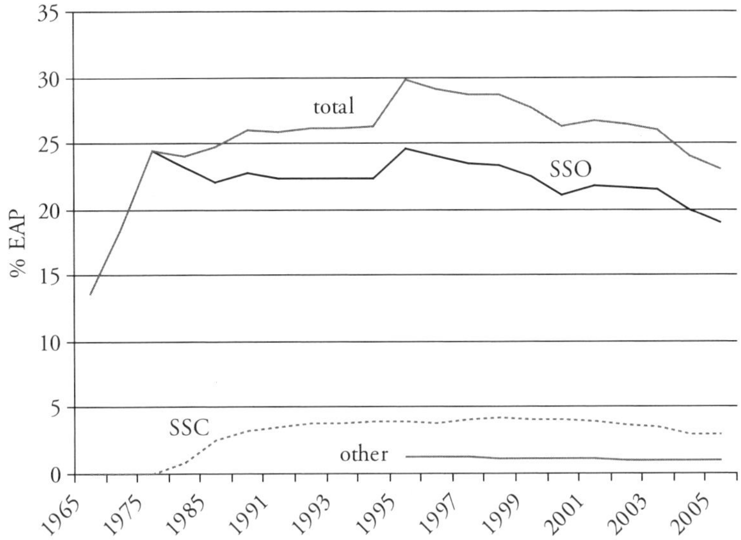

Source: Rofman and Lucchetti (2006), for 1965–2003; ILO and IESS for 2004–05.
Note: Does not include BDH.

The low coverage of the SSO program among active workers is also reflected among elder workers. Indeed, the coverage of this program among persons over 65 years of age was 16 percent in 2004, very low compared with countries such as Argentina, Brazil, Chile, and Uruguay, where coverage is more than 60 percent, or even compared with Peru, Costa Rica, Panama, and Venezuela, with 25–40 percent coverage. If one considers the BDH cash subsidy program, coverage is about 30 percent. Other programs have little effect, either because they are relatively new (in the case of the SSC) or because they are small or cover a younger population, or because of the characteristics of the programs themselves (for example, the retirement systems of the police and the armed forces). An analysis of pension coverage shows the limited coverage of the pension system, broken down by age and gender (figure 8.6). The lower coverage of women is striking.

The Failed 2001 Reform

After a prolonged parliamentary debate, the National Congress passed a new Social Security Act in November 2001. The new Social Security Act was intended to fully supersede the old law, created 60 years earlier, and modify the system's basic structure through changes in parameters, changes in the system's structure, and changes in the system's institutional organization. When some aspects of the new law were overturned by the courts, the government did not proceed with issuing regulations,

Figure 8.6. Coverage of Pension Systems, by Age Group and Gender

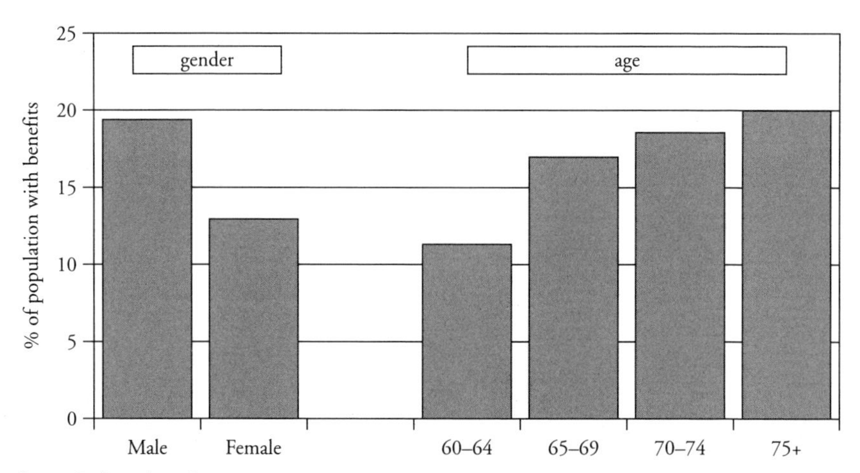

Source: Rofman (2005).
Note: Does not include BDH.

although the IESS did apply some aspects of the law related to contribution rates, procedures, and IESS management. The basic outlines of the reform are as follows.

Structural Reforms

A multitier approach was taken, with a structure similar to that of the reform carried out in Uruguay. As such, all workers would first participate in an obligatory solidarity regime, for which they would make contributions based on their income up to the sum of US$165 per month. At the same time, the totality of employer contributions and personal contributions corresponding to wages in excess of US$500 would be earmarked to finance this regime.

The second tier, or an obligatory savings regime, would consist of capitalizing personal contributions on wages between US$165 and US$500, in individual accounts. These contributions would be administered by pension savings deposit institutions (*Entidades Depositarias del Ahorro Previsional*—EDAP), for which a bidding competition would be conducted by the IESS Technical Commission on Investments (*Comisión Técnica de Inversiones*—CTI).

A new noncontributive assistance benefit would be created for individuals over the age of 70 who have no other funds, and it would be financed by the public budget. The features of this benefit would have been similar to those of the BDH, but the two programs were to be kept separate.

Institutional Reforms

The new law required a separate reserve for each fund administered by the IESS, and prohibited using funds from one program to finance another. A system of dual controls over companies would administer pension funds. The CTI would be assigned the ultimate responsibility for managing the funds. At the same time, supervisory authority would be delegated to the Superintendency of Banks. The new law also granted the CTI an imprecise degree of autonomy, stating that members would be designated by the government, the insured, and employers in an equal fashion.

The most high-profile aspect of the reform, and the one that led to the new law being overturned as well as much public debate, was the creation of private accounts. But rather than simply creating a new, parallel private pension system as has been done elsewhere in the region, the law maintained the overall administration of the IESS over pension accounts, and allowed the private sector in only as the means to invest pension resources. Several proposals were put forward since the court decision to modify the law, while keeping its basic elements, but no legislative action has been taken.

II. Proposed Policy Solutions

The section below offers policy options for addressing problems in the areas of institutional framework, breadth and depth of coverage, and financial management of the IESS.

Institutional Framework

A first general problem is the institutional weakness of the sector, which is due in part to the lack of a hierarchical entity within the government that is politically responsible for designing strategies, coordinating their implementation, and evaluating their execution. Such an entity must have the budgetary and technical resources it needs and should maintain an active policy of coordinating the various programs aimed at economically protecting the elderly. Also, the IESS has excessive autonomy and limited oversight, leading to opaque and inefficient decision making that is not coordinated with national economic policy. It is important to maintain IESS autonomy, to protect it from political influence. However, this autonomy should be limited to administrative issues, while policy-making decisions should be made by the government. These limits would require legal reforms to clearly define the roles in the sector. Apart from these legal reforms, the government should create an office (possibly at the undersecretary level) that would centralize all dialogue with the IESS and other sector institutions, define medium-term goals, coordinate policies, and disseminate information.

Breadth and Depth of Coverage

Even including the BDH program for the elderly, the current system to protect the elderly provides a low level of coverage among the age groups that actively participate in the economy, in part because of the very high level of informality in Ecuador's economy. Only an estimated 19 percent of the economically active population are affiliates of the SSO program, and coverage of the SSC is also low as a share of its target population. Furthermore, the BDH has not permitted new enrollments for several years. As a result, the number of beneficiaries of that program has slowly but surely diminished since its creation, although the government has stated plans to increase coverage in 2007. In total, the SSO pays benefits to about 250,000 elderly Ecuadorans, out of a population of 720,000 people over age 65 in the country.

Even more important is the problem of depth of coverage. The fact that people are formally enrolled as beneficiaries is positive, but if the benefits received are minimal, the practical effect is also minimal. The current monthly benefit payment of the BDH program for the elderly is US$30 (recently raised from US$11.50), whereas under the SSC, the retirement benefit is only US$3 per month. The benefits of the SSO are greater than those for BDH programs. Though the benefits have been increasing since 2001, some beneficiaries receive less than US$30 per month. Thus, a considerable portion of elderly people with pension coverage of some type are receiving a very minimal amount of money, not even reaching the national income poverty line, while another 100,000 or so receive no benefit at all.

The government should make efforts to extend nominal and effective coverage to the majority of the population. For that purpose, five actions in particular could be recommended:

1. Develop a rigorous methodology for analyzing pension policies. This first action is relevant in terms of applying the other recommended actions. It consists of preparing a methodological framework and delineating a critical path through which to implement measures aimed at broadening the coverage proposed below. To do so, it is necessary to evaluate the fiscal cost (as well as the savings) generated by the reform and by the proposed measures in the short term, to plan for their gradual implementation.[1]

2. Broaden the coverage of the SSO. As a result of the 2001 law, all workers are required to participate in the SSO, including the self-employed and employers. However, the number of self-employed individuals affiliated with the SSO is low, around 40,000 in 2005. Further actions are needed to facilitate enrollment by this sector. Furthermore, to ensure effectiveness, capitation mechanisms and procedures for controlling evasion among new affiliates need to be designed and implemented. This measure has no fiscal cost in the short term and will immediately increase revenue collections. Measures to increase transparency and reliability of SSO administration (for example by publishing information, reducing political influence on the board, and making decisions regarding coverage and benefits public), potential contributors to the system would see greater incentives to participate.

3. Implement a program to cover the informal sector. The 2001 law proposed a noncontributive benefit to cover the informal sector, but it was never implemented, nor has the IESS or any other government agency studied the fiscal implications of such a program. Calculations done for a separate study on Ecuador's pension system (Rofman 2005) suggest that a noncontributive program for the elderly who do not receive social security or BDH funds would cost US$100–300 million per year, depending on benefit level. These resources could come from a reorientation of the central government subsidy now paid to the IESS.

4. Broaden the coverage of the SSC. The SSC currently covers close to 20 percent of its target population, estimated at 1 million families. The IESS should develop a mechanism to broaden coverage, bringing in new family groups, individuals, and communities. To do so, an expansion plan must be designed that includes a geographical targeting mechanism to identify the zones with the greatest need. Although this action does entail a fiscal cost, that cost would be limited, considering the low cost of the system at present.

5. Correct benefit payments for retirees under the SSC and BDH. The benefit payments received by these two groups are very low. It is a positive that retirees are offered at least a minimum coverage; indeed, to preserve a reasonable incentive, benefits under these programs ought to be lower than SSO benefits. Nonetheless, the current amount seems to be insufficient. The problem is particularly serious for the SSC, where the retirement benefit is only US$3 per month. The amount of the benefit under both programs should be established using a rigorous criterion, such as a percentage of the poverty line, considering the capacity of the state to finance the assistance.

Although the reforms suggested above would not be fiscally neutral, they would be feasible if the government and Congress were to reform the pension system such that the government no longer contributes a 40 percent share (see the next section).

Financial Management of the IESS

The Ecuadoran Social Security Institute administers reserves for the various insurance programs it offers its affiliates. The management of these reserves is critical for the smooth functioning of the system, as these reserves guarantee the payment of future benefits. Certain problems with these reserves should be carefully considered, as they could have adverse effects.

1. The contribution from the state. Laws regarding the social security system indicate that the state has an obligation to contribute 40 percent of the IESS's pension-payment expenditures, so as to stabilize the actuarial balance. However, this contribution—which amounted to roughly US$500 million in 2006—is not needed at present, given the current healthy financial situation of the IESS and the military and police pension funds. IESS reserves have increased significantly as a result. This contribution is a major fiscal burden in a context in which the state is facing financial difficulties. Furthermore, the transfer is strongly regressive. It consists of a subsidy from the general revenues to the affiliates of the IESS, who make up only 19 percent of the labor force and are clearly middle income, since they are public servants or employees in the formal urban sector. As well, the mechanism of "presubsidizing" the pension system is inefficient. If the state wishes to grant a subsidy to workers in the formal sector of the economy through a pension system, that subsidy should be transferred when needed, and not accumulated in the reserves of the IESS, which generally get a low level of financial return. It would be much more progressive to reorient this subsidy to more vulnerable sectors of society, and if in the future the IESS starts to show a deficit, a government subsidy could be considered. Such a reorientation would not require legal reforms, and the resources could be used progressively to expand coverage and benefit levels of the old-age security system.

2. The debt owed by the state to the IESS. Between 1984 and 2000, the state stopped paying its two obligations with respect to the SSO: the contributions corresponding to its role as an employer and the contribution for 40 percent of the pensions, as required by law. The accrued debt is significant. The IESS estimates the amount at US$2.55 billion (as of December 2006), while the MEF estimates the debt at less than US$549 million. The discrepancy results from applying different criteria to adjust the amount to current money values. The IESS and the MEF should jointly clarify and resolve this issue as quickly as possible—a process that began in 2006 but was not completed before the elections and political transition.

3. Mortgage lending. The IESS should provide long-term funding to the mortgage market, but it should not offer mortgages directly to its members, nor offer below-market interest rates. The IESS should not lend directly at an interest rate equal to its estimated actuarial rate of return (currently 6 percent below market rates for mortgages), which would fail to reflect the risks and returns of mortgage lending.

III. Conclusion

Major reforms to Ecuador's social security system would not be easy, especially in the wake of the failed 2001 reforms and the involvement of the courts. This is particularly true regarding the creation of any type of individual account for pensions. However, there is a growing awareness in the government, Congress, and the IESS that further reforms are needed. Significant progress was made in designing a new proposed law in 2006, but no action was taken before the elections and government transition. The proposal addressed several of the issues discussed above, and also attempted to reformulate the 2001 law's stipulations on creating partial private accounts, while maintaining overall IESS responsibility for the system, in a way that would address the concerns of the courts. This work could form the basis of a new proposal for reform, if the government, the IESS, and the legislature make the effort to achieve some type of consensus and are able to clearly explain both the need for reform and their proposals to the public. Now, during a time of relative economic strength, would be an excellent time to place the country's social security system for the elderly on a more sound footing for the future, rather than waiting for more difficult times to address existing problems.

Policy Matrix

Area	*Problem*	*Policy proposal*
Institutional framework	• The IESS has excessive autonomy, such that it makes not only administrative decisions but also policy decisions, with little oversight by the government. • The government has no central entity to address issues related to the social security system.	• Undertake a legal reform to maintain IESS autonomy and separation from political influence, but limit this autonomy to administrative issues, while giving policy-making authority to the government. • Create a government office (possibly at the undersecretary level) to centralize all dialogue with the IESS and other sector institutions, define medium-term goals, coordinate policies, and disseminate information.
Breadth and depth of coverage	• The pension system covers a very low share of the economically active population. • A large portion of those who are covered receive only a minimal benefit.	• Develop a rigorous methodology and a critical path through which to implement measures aimed at broadening the coverage. Evaluate the fiscal cost (as well as savings) generated by reform and by the proposed measures in the short term, to plan for their gradual implementation. • Broaden the coverage of the SSO by facilitating enrollment for the self-employed, improving control of evasion, and increasing the transparency and reliability of SSO administration (for example by publishing information, reducing political influence on the board, and making public any decisions regarding coverage and benefits) to encourage potential contributors to the system to participate. • Implement a program to cover the informal sector, for example through a noncontributive benefit (costing US$100–300 million per year, depending on benefit level) paid for by reorienting the central government subsidy now paid to the IESS. • Design an expansion plan to broaden SSC coverage, defining a geographical targeting mechanism that identifies the zones with the greatest need so as to target the expansion effort. Although this action does entail a fiscal cost, that cost would be limited, considering the low cost of the system at present.

(*Table continues on the following page.*)

Area	*Problem*	*Policy proposal*
		• Increase benefit payments for retirees under the SSC and BDH, particularly the SSC. The amount of the benefit under both programs should be established using a rigorous criterion, such as a percentage of the poverty line, considering the financial capacity of the state and IESS.
Financial management of IESS	• The 40 percent contribution of the state is not needed for the IESS's financial health, as it was designed for an actuarial deficit that has not materialized. This contribution constitutes a highly regressive transfer to a small, nonpoor segment of society. • The state has a backlog of debt to the IESS after several years of not paying the 40 percent of pensions required by law. The IESS says this amount is US$2.55 billion, while the MEF says it is US$549 million. • The IESS is considering making mortgage loans at below-market interest rates.	• Reorient the state subsidy to more vulnerable sectors of society; if in the future the IESS starts to show a deficit, a government subsidy could be considered. Such a reorientation would not require legal reforms, and the resources could be used to expand coverage and benefit levels of the old-age security system in a progressive way. • Encourage the IESS and the MEF to jointly resolve the debt issue as quickly as possible to clarify this major accounting issue for the IESS. • Have the IESS provide long-term funding to the mortgage market, but not offer mortgages directly to its members, or below-market interest rates.

Note

1. A World Bank simulation tool called the Pension Reform Options Simulation Toolkit (PROST) can evaluate the effects of various policies, based on the system's relevant variables.

Bibliography

Comisión de Seguro Social, Congreso Nacional de Ecuador. 2006. "Informe Primer Debate Reformas Ley de Seguro Social." Oficio 0405-CEPCGPUSS-P-2006. Quito: Congreso Nacional.

Frente Social. 2006. *Pensión Asistencial para Adultos Mayores y Descapacitados.* (Draft). Quito: Unidad de Información y Análisis de la Secretaría Técnica del Frente Social.

International Monetary Fund. 2006. *Ecuador: 2005 Article IV Consultations—Staff Report.* Washington, DC: IMF.

Organización Internacional del Trabajo. 2006. *Análisis y Recommendaciones Técnicas de OIT al Proyecto de Ley de Reforma de la Seguridad Social de Ecuador.* Quito: OIT.

Rofman, Rafael. 2005. "Ecuador: Expanding Social Insurance to Protect All." Report 32771-EC, World Bank, Washington, DC.

Rofman, Rafael, and Leonardo Lucchetti. 2006. *Pensions in Latin America: Concepts and Measurements of Coverage.* Washington, DC: World Bank.

World Bank. 2007. *Informality: Exit and Exclusion. Study by the Office of the Chief Economist, Latin America and Caribbean Region.* Washington, DC: World Bank.

9

Sustainable and Inclusive Rural Development

Francisco Pichon

Executive Summary

Ecuador is generously endowed with natural resources: oil, large forests, abundant water, plentiful fisheries, rich biodiversity, and many varied agroecological environments suitable for different temperate and tropical crops and economic activities. Ecuador is also rich in cultural traditions, and has a physical size and a population adequate to the development of most industries and the generation of an internal market sufficient to act as a strong engine of growth. Yet, these potentially favorable opportunities and rich and diverse natural and cultural resources have not been effectively translated into sustainable economic development for the benefit of most of Ecuador's citizens.

Although urbanizing rapidly, Ecuador still has a large rural population, and a significant portion of the workforce is still in the rural sector, living off both agricultural and nonagricultural activities. However, as a result of extremely low productivity, rural incomes are very low and poverty rates are high. Environmental issues are also an important aspect of development in Ecuador, including the health costs of environmental contamination of water and air, the particular environmental problems posed by the oil industry in the Amazon region, the impacts of climate change in the sustainability of economic development of the country, and the urgent need to protect Ecuador's rich biodiversity while finding ways to sustainably derive income from it.

Ecuador's current institutional setup for rural development is characterized by a marked imbalance between the vitality of rural development initiatives by local

This chapter was written with input from McDonald Benjamin, Pilar Larreamendy, J. C. Belausteguigoitia, and Gabriela Arcos. The chapter draws heavily from Ecuador's Rural Development Strategy, prepared by a team of World Bank staff and external consultants in 2005 and led by Jose Maria Caballero.

governments, civil society organizations, and externally financed projects on the one hand, and weak coordination and capacity at the national government level on the other. A main deficiency of the current system is the lack of a strategic policy framework for sustainable and inclusive local development that could orient the actions of national ministries and agencies and integrate them with the private sector and local authorities.

The movement to define such a policy framework is appropriate for two reasons. First, local development experiences have matured sufficiently to allow a big step forward. It is the lack of an adequate policy framework and institutional architecture that holds back local development. The second reason is the change in the conditions of competitiveness taking place in the country. With dollarization it is no longer possible to cushion competitive disadvantages with monetary and exchange rate policies. Ecuador's improving debt position and a horizon of favorable oil prices also would allow higher availability of public investment resources for rural areas in the medium term.

The strategy proposed in this policy note makes recommendations on the following five related areas that are vital to promoting sustainable and inclusive development in Ecuador: (i) adopt a policy framework based on a territorial approach for sustainable and inclusive local development; (ii) improve access of the poor, especially its weakest segment, the rural poor, to productive investments and services needed to generate employment and income; (iii) improve competitiveness in the agricultural sector; (iv) promote "development with cultural identity" in indigenous areas and in geographic areas with concentrations of Afro-Ecuadoran populations;[1] and (v) confront the challenges of environmental health, oil-related pollution, and conservation and use of critical ecosystems.

I. The Context for Sustainable and Inclusive Development in Ecuador

Ecuador contains a variety of rural territories, with their own geographical features and population, ethnicity, agriculture, economic structure, and governance issues. This diversity suggests that no unique policy recipe for rural development can be applied to the entire country. Addressing this heterogeneity through a territorial approach to local development is a core recommendation of this note.

Population, the Labor Force, and Rural Poverty Trends

As happened in other Latin American countries, Ecuador experienced rapid urbanization in the past two decades. The rural population decreased from 71 percent in 1950 to 51 percent in 1982 to 39 percent in 2001. In absolute numbers, however, the rural population continues to grow, although very slowly—0.1 percent in the past decade, compared with an overall growth rate of 1.3 percent. Ecuador is fairly rural outside the major urban areas of Guayaquil, Quito, and Cuenca. Some provinces have more than 70 percent of their residents in rural areas.

According to the 2001 population census, some 1.7 million people were in the rural labor force, of which about 1 million, about 58 percent, had agriculture as primary employment. Of this rural labor force, 42 percent were self-employed and 29 percent were salaried workers. A noteworthy trend in the last decade is the increase in economic participation due to the changing age structure and an increased presence of women in the labor force. Self-employment and wage employment are unequally distributed in the territory. Family enterprises dominate in most parts of the central and southern *Sierra*, in the Estribaciones, and in the *Oriente*. By contrast, in a narrow fringe of the southern and central *Costa*, in the transition area of the northern Sierra, and in the areas surrounding Quito, employers and wage laborers dominate.

Poverty increased from 40 percent to 45 percent between 1990 and 2001, mostly as a result of the economic crisis. Rural poverty is higher—50 percent in the Costa and 62 percent in the Sierra—and is associated with lower education, larger household size, and agricultural employment. In the Sierra, being indigenous is also associated with poverty.

Rural nonfarm employment is important in Ecuador and is associated with lower poverty. In 1995, some 40 percent of rural incomes were derived from rural nonfarm employment, and 37 percent of males and 50 percent of females had primary or secondary employment outside agriculture. According to the 2001 population census, some 65,000 people are self-employed in the small industry and handicrafts sector in rural *cantones*. In 2000, there were 1.9 million occupied workers living on farms, of which nearly 30 percent worked off-farm, 41 percent in agriculture, and 59 percent outside agriculture.

Migration is an important feature of the country. In 2001, more than 30 percent of Ecuadorans were born in a place different from their place of residence. Urban-to-urban migration is more significant statistically than rural-to-urban migration, but nonetheless 19 percent of the population born in rural areas lived in urban ones in 2001. International migration is a recent phenomenon, and it has grown exponentially since the 1999 economic crisis. In 2001, residents in all 202 cantones reported relatives living abroad, a total of some 378,000. By the end of 2003 this figure had about doubled. Recent international migration has largely taken hold in areas where there was already some tradition of migration, and migrants tend to come from areas where self-employment, small industry, handicrafts, and small farming are dominant.

Agrarian Structure and Production Characteristics

Land is highly concentrated in Ecuador, a country with a strong tradition of *haciendas* (large estates or ranches). Through a combination of relatively timid land reform measures applied over various periods since the late 1960s, the operation of land markets, inheritance, and land distribution has improved over the years, although inequality is still high, with an overall Gini coefficient of 0.80. However, land concentration varies considerably in different parts of the country.

Ecuador can be divided into nine rural territories whose characteristics and Gini coefficients are presented in table 9.1 (see annex table A.1 for more detail). Three areas show land concentrations significantly above the others: the entrepreneurial Costa (an area of commercial farming on the coast), the northern Sierra (traditional hacienda regions around and north of Quito), and the seigniorial areas of the central and southern Sierra (also a traditional hacienda region, around provincial capitals in the southern mountain region; Chiriboga 1988; Gondard and Mazurek 2001).

The Oriente region has the lowest Gini coefficient, which is consistent with its condition as a recently settled frontier area without a tradition of haciendas. Transition areas are mostly dominated by self-employed farmers, and to some extent they share with the Oriente some degree of isolation deriving from a settlement process more recent than that of the core parts of the Sierra and Costa regions. As indicated by their names, the coastal peasant areas and the south and central Sierra peasant areas have in common the strong presence of self-employed small farmers in the local economies, although with varying degrees of economic dynamism.

Because of the high level of diversity of agroecological conditions, land use, and farm types in Ecuador (Huttel, Zebrowski, and Gondard 1999), conditions differ in the three main regions. In the Costa, traditional export crops (bananas, sugar, and oil palm) and basic grains grown in mechanized wage-labor farms dominate, although most parts also have peasant segments, which prevail in some cantones. In the Sierra, livestock haciendas coexist with peasant agriculture of indigenous origin and are oriented to the domestic market. The Sierra region also has a growing presence of new intensive export lines in flowers and vegetables (broccoli in particular). In the Oriente, extensive livestock operations coexist with traditional colonization and indigenous agriculture, wood extraction, and other forms of forest exploitation.

Table 9.1. Selected Characteristics of Ecuadoran Subregions

	Population in 2001			*Pop. growth rate 1990–01 (%)*		*Poverty incidence (%)*		
Subregions	*Total (000s)*	*Rural (000s)*	*Rural (%)*	*Total*	*Rural*	*FGT (0)*	*UBN*	*Land Gini coeff.*
Oriente	193.0	129.9	67.3	4.0	3.7		91.3	0.494
Peasant Costa	1,636.3	1,009.6	61.7	1.3	–0.2	54.9	91.7	0.719
Entrepreneurial Costa	2,829.4	569.7	20.1	2.6	1.0	46.6	88.6	0.779
Northern Costa	348.4	193.0	55.4	2.1	2.9	55.0	89.5	0.608
Transition areas	566.5	328.6	58.0	1.8	0.4	66.5	90.0	0.633
Galápagos Islands	9.8	2.5	25.5	6.0	0.8	19.3	76.0	0.733
Peasant Sierra	737.5	543.0	73.6	0.7	0.2	69.5	90.6	0.732
Entrepreneurial Sierra	2,183.7	765.6	35.1	2.5	2.9	67.0	69.6	0.826
Seigneurial Sierra	964.1	489.3	50.8	1.6	0.8	70.2	84.5	0.819
All Ecuador	**9,468.7**	**4,031.1**	**42.6**	**2.1**	**1.1**	**56.1**	**85.6**	**0.901**

Source: Author's calculation from cantón-level data from population and agricultural censuses, SIISE, Infoplan *Tablas Dinámicas*, and work files of World Bank (2004).

Contrasting Rural Territories

Territorial dynamics in rural areas can be characterized using a combination of economic and institutional criteria. From an economic perspective one can examine whether the areas show high or low economic performance, whether the economic dynamics come from agriculture and agroindustry or the rural nonfarm sector, and whether those dynamics are based on small family-type enterprises or on medium and large businesses.[2] From an institutional perspective one can look at the presence of market organizations that provide ancillary services to productive activities and make production more competitive, and at the presence of organizations favoring the economic coordination of private and public actors active in the territory.

Six core types of rural territories can be defined in the country, the basic features of which are summarized in table 9.2 and explained below. This territorial classification is not the only possible one and it is not exhaustive. The purpose is to illustrate how territories may differ and thus present different policy challenges, and to characterize some core territories that are both typical and important to understanding the varying dynamics of Ecuador's rural areas.

Type 1. Dynamic territories based on medium and large agricultural enterprises with strong market-based support institutions and corporate organizations. Typical territories in this category are the African palm production areas in the Costa, the beef production areas in Santo Domingo de los Caballeros, the flower and dairy production areas close to Quito, the cocoa production areas in Los Ríos, the sugar production areas in Guayas, and the Galápagos tourist area. Policy issues important for these territories are mostly those related to agricultural competitiveness, in particular transport systems and costs, commercial policies, and availability of advanced technological services. Environmental and social issues are important

Table 9.2. Characteristics of Core Rural Territories

	Type 1	Type 2	Type 3	Type 4	Type 5	Type 6
Agriculture/ RNF	Agriculture	Agriculture	Both	Agriculture	Agriculture	Agriculture
Economic dynamism	+++	++	++	+	+	+
Pop. density/ isolation	+	+	+	++	++	+++
Large/small producers	Large	Medium	Small	Small	Large/small	Small/medium
Migration	Retention	Retention	Retention	Out-migration	Out-migration	In-migration
Market-based institution	+++	++	++	+	+	+
Economic coordinated institution	+++	+	+++	++	+	+

Note: (+) indicates minimum and (+++) indicates maximum development of the characteristic.

because of the high contamination with agrochemicals, the environmental fragility of the Galápagos Islands, and issues of child labor on plantations.

Type 2. Dynamic territories based on medium agricultural enterprises, but also some large and some small ones, with relatively good market-based support institutions, but inadequate economic coordination systems. Typical of this type of territories are the grain and banana production areas in the central and southern Costa. Important policy issues are those related to competitiveness mentioned for Type 1, high interest rates and other onerous loan conditions, the availability of good seeds and other inputs at competitive prices (in the case of grains), technical assistance, storage facilities, and competitive imports.

Type 3. Dynamic territories based on small producers both in agriculture and in nonfarm activities with differentiated markets and reasonably good economic coordination mechanisms. Included here are the artisanal areas of Otavalo, the tourist areas of Galaceo and Chordeleg, and the peasant horticulture areas of Chimborazo and Tungurahua. The main policy issues in these territories are the availability of investment and other loans to allow the expansion of activities, the provision of technical assistance and skills training, the enhancement of producers' organizations for commercial purposes, the expansion of links with domestic and export markets, and the development of contract systems with processing and exporting firms.

Type 4. Stagnant peasant economy territories with high out-migration rates where systems of economic coordination are being developed mostly with the assistance of nongovernmental organizations (NGOs) and rural development cooperation programs. Examples are the cantones of Guamote and Alausí in Chimborazo, the cantones of the Cotopaxi province such as Saquisilí, the cantones of Carchi province, and the cantones in the upper part of the Jubones valley in the province of Azuay. The main policy issue in these territories is the identification and development of activities capable of promoting economic dynamism in the local economy, which in turn depends on the availability of credit, technical assistance, and good market connections.

Type 5. Stagnant territories with a combination of peasant production and traditional haciendas with weak economic and territorial organizations. Social systems in these territories are often hierarchical and based on clientelistic ties between *hacendados* (the owners) and peasant farmers, and *cacique* behavior of local authorities. Some of these territories experience much emigration and therefore have a significant inflow of cash from remittances; many cantones in the provinces of Azuay, Cañar, Loja, and Zamora Chinchipe are examples. In addition to the policy issues relevant to Type 4 territories, specific issues include the need to build democratic territorial and economic institutions, access to land for very small holders, and encouragement of traditional haciendas to intensify land use. In territories where remittances are significant there is the additional issue of how to apply part of these funds to local investments.

Type 6. Frontier-type territories with small populations, poor infrastructure, thin markets, and weak institutions. Many of the cantones in the Oriente fall under this description. The main policy issues in these territories is developing communications and access infrastructure, providing basic health and education services, and building a system of territorial and economic institutions.

In some rural territories (for example, Otavalo and Galápagos), economic dynamism is related to nonfarm activities such as handicrafts and tourism, which are important sources of income for the local population. Dynamic territories based on nonfarm activities usually have in common the productive use of assets that are specific to the territory. These assets could be cultural, such as handicrafts related to indigenous and other local cultures, natural resources, including attractive landscapes, archeological and architectural sites, and even unique construction works like the Chimborazo railway. These territories also generally have good access and are promoted by some specific group, such as the tourist industry, supporting NGOs, or the environmental or scientific communities (see annex table A.2 for more details).

II. The Agricultural Sector

Agriculture remains a key part of Ecuador's economy, labor force, and exports. Well over half of the rural labor force of 1.7 million people is dependent on agriculture or food processing. The agricultural sector is highly diverse, including traditional domestic consumption–oriented sectors such as maize, beans, and potatoes; traditional export sectors such as bananas and cacao; and more recently, strongly growing nontraditional export sectors, including flowers and shrimp. Yet the competitiveness of much of the rural agricultural sector is being challenged from many sources: low productivity growth, lack of access of the rural poor to productive factors (land, capital, and technology), free trade initiatives, dollarization and the strength of the dollar to which the economy is now tied, and a legacy of weak institutions and an unstable policy environment.

Sector Evolution

Over the past decade, the agriculture sector's performance has exceeded that of the country as a whole: agriculture grew at 4.3 percent annually on average between 1993 and 2003, while the overall economy grew at only 2.2 percent. However, as in the economy in general, "agriculture" performance has been erratic, with strong growth in some years offset by low growth rates, or even contraction, in other years. Ecuador's GDP totaled about US$17.8 billion in 2003, with agriculture accounting for an estimated US$1.9 billion, representing around 10.4 percent of total economic activity. Ecuador remains highly dependent on agricultural exports, and the agricultural trade balance is consistently positive.

Important changes in agricultural land use have taken place in the last decade. In general, land devoted to importable crops (in particular cotton, maize, and rice) declined, while land devoted to nontradables increased substantially, and land devoted to traditional export crops (bananas, cacao, and coffee) remained about the same, with the exception of coffee, which decreased markedly. A set of developments in the national food marketing and distribution system have had a positive effect on the sourcing of domestic foodstuffs for the growing national market. At the same time, new export-oriented crops, among them African palm, flowers, broccoli, pineapple, palm hearts, and passion flower, increased enormously. The combined export value of these products (US$392 million in 2003) exceeds the combined value of the five traditional food crops: rice, yellow maize, soybeans, beans, and wheat (US$286 million at international prices).

Productivity in agriculture is very low. In the major seasonal crops, yields are far below international levels. For example, maize yields of 2.3 tons per hectare rank Ecuador among the lowest in the hemisphere. In wheat, beans, and soybeans, yields have actually declined since the early 1990s. Yields of rice (3.8 tons per hectare) are also very low, although they have risen significantly over the past decade. Yields of almost all crops in Ecuador are lower than in neighboring Colombia and Peru, and in some cases are markedly lower, such as for important crops like coffee, cacao, sugar cane, and African palm. This disappointing performance is a result of several factors, including lack of investment in agricultural research, the relatively poor functioning of input markets, institutional weaknesses in technology transfer, low levels of schooling of much of the agricultural workforce, and the lack of support for technological development.

A 2000 Central Bank study of total factor productivity estimated the contributions of total factor productivity (TFP), labor, and capital inputs to the growth of value added in agriculture between 1994 and 1999 (table 9.3). The study showed a noticeable decline in TFP growth in most of the selected subsectors, with the exceptions of animal agriculture and forestry.[3] In traditional export sectors (bananas, coffee, and cacao), annual productivity declined, offsetting increases in capital inputs (9.1 percent annually) and a modest increase in labor inputs (1.1 percent). In the case of the flower industry, one of Ecuador's most dynamic industries, both capital and labor inputs are also estimated to have grown strongly (32.5 percent and 7.0 percent, respectively), but these gains were offset by declines in TFP.

These trends illustrate that the growth of production over 1993–1999 was mostly attributable to increases in capital inputs and only modest growth, at most, in labor inputs. This suggests that growth in agricultural production is less labor-intensive than in the past, meaning that this sector should not be looked to as an increasing source of national employment. The agricultural labor force is also becoming more skilled; between 1990 and 2001, it is estimated that the ratio of skilled to unskilled labor in agriculture increased from 0.08 to 0.14 (Vos and León 2003). That increase, combined with a very modest overall increase in sectoral employment (1.8 percent), implies that employment opportunities for unskilled labor in agriculture will likely be limited in the future.

Table 9.3. Total Productivity Contribution of Labor and Capital to the Value-Added Growth, 1994–99 (contribution to the average annual growth of the period)

		Average annual contribution		
	Products	*TFP*	*Capital*	*Labor*
1	Banana, coffee, and cocoa crops	–4.2	9.1	1.1
2	Grain crops	–3.5	0.8	–0.1
3	Flower crops	–8.5	32.5	7.0
4	Other crops	–6.6	9.6	–0.1
5	Livestock	2.0	0.1	0.0
6	Grazing and wood extraction	1.3	3.6	0.0
7	Shrimp production	–4.2	8.6	–0.1
8	Fishing	–1.1	5.1	0.2
9	Elaboration, processing, and conservation of meat and meat products	–1.4	29.9	–1.2
10	Processing and conservation of shrimp	–3.3	0.9	1.1
11	Processing and conservation of fish and fish products	–7.8	3.4	3.6
12	Vegetable and animal oil and grease	1.9	5.7	0.2
13	Milk products	–1.7	2.0	0.3
14	Production and processing of bread and other mill products	–0.5	2.2	1.2
15	Production and processing of sugar	2.9	–0.1	–0.7
16	Production and processing of cocoa, chocolate, and related products	–1.0	–2.1	–0.5
17	Production of other foods	0.9	1.9	0.5
18	Beverages	2.2	2.7	0.5
19	Tobacco products	6.3	–1.7	0.0

Source: Banco Central del Ecuador.
Note: The indicators are constructed according to the national accounts (in sucres), base year 1993.

The patterns characterizing sources of productivity growth in agroindustry differ somewhat from those in agricultural production. On one hand, in five of 11 agroindustries, the contribution of TFP to the growth in production was estimated to be positive. On the other hand, the capital-intensity bias in the growth of agroindustry growth was less than in the case of agricultural production, although in two particularly dynamic cases (meat and meat products, and the oils subsector), growth depended almost entirely on increased capital inputs.

In sum, in the years preceding the major economic crisis of the late 1990s, the majority of agricultural and agroindustry subsectors demonstrated declining productivity and overall efficiency, with the growth in production wholly attributable to the growth in productive inputs, notably capital. The antiemployment bias of this growth should also be noted. To the extent that these trends continue into the present decade, they will limit the ability of the agricultural and agroindustry sectors to generate employment and to address poverty and income distribution problems.

Trends in Food Marketing and Distribution

Food marketing and distribution are also fundamental to understanding Ecuador's agricultural sector. In Ecuador, as in many developing countries, the marketing sector is characterized by an overly complex chain of intermediaries, high marketing margins, low and inconsistent quality, weak sanitary and food safety standards, and recurrent oligopoly and monopsony problems. Farmers, particularly smallholders, often have weak collective strength in negotiating with wholesalers and food buyers. This is a particular problem with growers of fruits and vegetables, cereals, tubers, and export products such as coffee and cacao. The phasing out of parastatal organizations (ENAC and EMPROVIT) in the 1980s has been succeeded by oligopoly in numerous sectors, disadvantaging producers and elevating marketing margins (and consumer food prices). Producers typically have poor knowledge of existing prices and market developments, and they have limited management expertise in marketing, postharvest food handling, and market requirements. Sanitary and food safety standards and regulations are only weakly enforced.

Even with these and other constraints, increased sourcing of national production from domestic agroindustry and food distribution firms has occurred in recent years. Changes in diets and a growing diversity of food demands have generated an increasing demand for processed and packaged foods among urban residents. This has required a more integrated and complex marketing and distribution system to deliver food to urban areas. Marketing methods have become more diverse and sophisticated. Supermarket-based retailing, however, has not grown as rapidly or extensively as in some other Latin American nations. Road access by farmers has increased significantly in a comparison of data from the 1995 and 2001 agricultural censuses. Still, over half of rural roads are poor quality, and only 13 percent of the national road system is paved, elevating transportation costs and transit times.

Agricultural Services

The availability of financial and technical services for farmers is very low, which is one of the main reasons for the country's low agricultural productivity. Only about 10 percent of farms and agricultural land are reported on the 2000 census as being served by either formal or informal sources of financing. Larger farms tend to have access to more credit and credit from formal sources, such as private banks and the National Development Bank (BNF). Formal-sector credit sources such as the BNF, private banks, and financial cooperatives cover only 3 percent of farms, accounting for 7 percent of agricultural land. Smaller farms typically have poorer access to credit, and when they do have it, they use more informal sources; moneylenders, merchants, and family sources are the most common sources. Informal-sector lenders and financial intermediaries are only reported to cover 31.5 percent of farms and 13.2 percent of agricultural land.

All sources of technical assistance together provide coverage to only 7 percent of farmers or about 18 percent of all farmland. The primary sources of technical assistance (table 9.4) are private sources; together, private merchants, individuals, nongovernmental organizations, and other private sources are the primary source of technical assistance to 72 percent of farmers who receive such services. Institutional sources such as the Ministry of Agriculture (through the National Institute for Agricultural Research, INIAP), the BNF, agricultural cooperatives, and universities are a relatively infrequent source of this assistance.

Neither public and quasi-public sources of financial and technical assistance nor private markets for these services are adequate for meeting the demand, whether from small producers or from larger commercial producers. The decline in the subsidized public provision of these services has not been compensated by the creation of institutional conditions favorable to the development of private markets for these services. The vacuum has been filled in part by NGOs whose resources are extremely limited and are not a sustainable long-term solution for making technical and financial services available to the commercial agriculture sector.

The banking crisis of the late 1990s created an environment favorable for the development of rural cooperatives and microfinance services. Rural savings and loans associations, for example, which are present in both the Sierra and the Costa, have more than tripled their share capital, deposits, and loan portfolios since 1996. Other developments, such as the Solidarity Bank, the Rural Financial Network, and other local and regional cooperatives, will need to develop financial products and services that adapt to the limitations of the formal financial system serving particularly small producers in rural communities.

Ecuador's national system for agricultural research and technology development is another serious factor limiting agricultural productivity growth. Total public investment in agricultural research is estimated to be below 0.5 percent of agricultural GDP, a low level by any standard and less than half the level (1.0 percent) that exists across Latin America generally. The Agricultural Services Modernization Program (PROMSA) represents new resources and an institutional innovation

Table 9.4. Sources of Farmers' Technical Assistance

	Farms		*Hectares*	
Sources	*(thousands)*	*%*	*(thousands)*	*%*
National Development Bank (BNF)	1.0	1.8	44.9	2.0
Agricultural cooperatives	1.5	2.5	38.7	1.8
Commercial traders	5.4	9.4	213.0	9.7
Universities	1.0	1.8	30.2	1.4
Others	13.6	13.8	670.7	30.6
NGOs or foundations	13.6	13.7	307.0	14.0
Min. of Agriculture-INIAP	8.8	15.3	350.0	15.9
Other public institutions	3.8	6.6	90.3	4.1
Other private institutions	8.6	15.0	449.6	20.5
Total	**57.2**	**100.0**	**2,194.5**	**100.0**

Source: Agricultural Census 2000, http://www.sica.gov.ec.

through a competitively funded program of applied research, a program of technology transfer, and investments in plant and animal health. As with other recurrent government activities carried out under foreign-financed projects, the problem is sustainability once foreign funding is discontinued.

The markets for farm inputs such as seeds, fertilizers, and pesticides also have several problems. In part because of inadequate research capacity, the seed industry has a limited supply of high-quality, certified seeds. In fertilizers and agricultural chemicals, the absence of scale economies in production and the geographic dispersion of agricultural production across the country create significant diseconomies that have promoted oligopolistic wholesale markets, high margins for merchants, and high prices for farmers. Solutions to these constraints will be addressed only through greater spatial concentration of agroindustry over time and improved organization and coordination of producers to enhance their collective power.

Competitive Conditions and Advantages

Developments in macroeconomic policies are changing the competitiveness of agriculture. Dollarization, in particular, is important because of the impact of the real exchange rate on international competitiveness. Dollarization made evident the substantial economic distortions that had developed in 1998 and 1999. The overall macroeconomic climate has become more stable; following an initial period of high wage increases and high inflation to deal with pressures already in the system, both prices and wages have stabilized, and the greater stability in key macroeconomic variables, notably inflation and the exchange rate, can be expected to continue. At the same time, devaluation can no longer be used as an "easy" way to increase exports, improve competitiveness, and restore equilibrium in the external balances. Genuine competitiveness must now be based on the productivity of the economy and of agriculture. This necessity presents a substantial challenge.

Domestic resource cost (DRC) indicators of comparative advantage show some degree of actual or potential comparative advantage in traditional perennial crops (coffee, bananas, and cacao) and in African palm, as well as in labor-intensive seasonal crops such as broccoli, beans, cotton, and dairy production.[4] On the other hand, Ecuador appears to have no comparative advantage in traditional seasonal crops such as rice, yellow maize, soybeans, and wheat, most of which use high volumes of imported inputs, and which do not enjoy the scale economies that characterize production in more competitive nations such as Argentina, Brazil, and the United States.

Traditional exports, such as coffee, bananas, and cacao, reveal some degree of comparative advantage, with DRC measures between 0.4 and 0.8. In the case of cacao, the more intensive semitechnified system appears to be more competitive than the traditional system of production. Even though this system uses more intensive labor and tradable inputs (fertilizers and pesticides), higher labor productivity more than compensates for greater use of purchased inputs.

In the case of nontraditional exports, DRC calculations also demonstrate some degree of comparative advantage, particularly with palm oil and broccoli. In the case of cotton, estimated DRCs show comparative advantage, which is inconsistent with the fact that production has nearly disappeared from the country. This discrepancy may reflect institutional problems in the productive structure that prevent taking advantage of latent comparative advantage.

In the case of imports, with the exception of sugar cane, beans, and milk in Cayambe, all of the indicators demonstrate a lack of comparative advantage. The degree of comparative disadvantage for rice is high and has worsened considerably since dollarization. In the case of soybeans and maize, Ecuador does not possess comparative advantage. In potatoes, the indicators show that Ecuador does possess comparative advantage, even though agricultural productivity levels are low in almost all zones.

A comparison with neighboring countries Peru and Colombia shows that Ecuador and Colombia possess similar patterns of comparative advantage, indicating competition in products and markets. Peru, on the other hand, exhibits some differences. A comparison of labor costs for selected crops between Ecuador and Colombia showed that in seven of the 10 crops examined (dry land and irrigated rice, yellow maize, soybean, coffee, cocoa, potatoes, cotton, African palm, and sugar cane), the daily labor requirements per hectare are greater in Ecuador than in Colombia. Other measures of comparative advantage for Ecuador's agricultural sector gave similar results.

Trade Policies

Intervention in agricultural foreign trade is carried out through the Andean system of price bands, which is used both for price stabilization and protection. The structure of agricultural protection reflects a bias in favor of the products in which the country has comparative disadvantage. Whatever the reasons in support of this policy, it induces significant inefficiencies in the allocation of resources. Overall, products receiving high levels of price support include sugar, rice, yellow maize, and wheat. African palm and dairy receive moderate support. Soybeans have been relatively unaffected by trade policies, while potatoes and cacao face negative levels of protection.

Trade protection policies for uncompetitive products distort prices and incentives along the agribusiness value chains, many of which have links that are quite sensitive to the prices of agricultural raw material. For example, Ecuador has a comparative advantage in the production of milk, and probably in poultry and pork, but the high prices of agricultural raw materials resulting from protectionist policies threaten their competitiveness, forcing them to be protected too. Furthermore, household spending is quite sensitive to prices of animal products. Spending on these products in low-income households (over half the population) can account for more than a quarter of all spending, making the price of animal products an important determinant of real income and the nutritional well-being of a good part of the population.

The broad effects of trade liberalization on agriculture can be foreseen with some certainty. Impacts would differ significantly by sector and by subregion. Cereal and oilseed crops can be expected to continue to decline in the face of pressure created by cheaper and more globally competitive imports. Traditional exports, notably bananas, can be expected to continue to be a mainstay of the agricultural economy, assuming that future trade negotiations continue to lower tariffs and market access barriers in importing countries. Animal agricultural production should be positively affected by the reduction in prices for primary inputs (feed grains) and by possible market opportunities in the United Status for beef and dairy products, contingent on the eradication of hoof-and-mouth disease.

Of particular importance to nontraditional exports will be the implementation of domestic regulatory measures and industry best practices to conform with international plant and animal health and food safety standards.

Positive export growth in Ecuador will continue to have a positive effect on employment, but particularly on the skilled employment. The salary gap between skilled and unskilled or semiskilled labor will likely continue to grow, worsening the distribution of income. It is necessary to examine in greater detail the effects on employment generated by the export sector. At the same time, it is valuable to remember that scale economies are rarely realized in agricultural export industries, which are labor intensive. To have an impact on small and medium farms and the unskilled labor force, improved access to inputs, productive services, and markets are a precondition.

III. The Institutional Setup for Rural Development

Ecuador's current institutional setup for rural development can be characterized by the following:

- The dominant national political view of rural development is divorced from matters of employment, income growth, and the competitiveness of rural areas, while local governments have become gradually more interested and involved in promoting, coordinating, and regulating productive activities in their rural areas.
- Coordination among relevant ministries is weak. The Ministry of Agriculture and its dependent institutions have distanced themselves from wide rural development concerns, instead concentrating their emphasis on supporting commercial agriculture with little coordination with other institutions working in rural areas.
- Rural development projects and donor assistance have promoted rural development programs, while NGOs and other civil society organizations have an increasing role in rural development as providers of production support services and institutional strengthening.
- Market agents, both private and cooperative, have contributed to the establishment of new economic links and the provision of services in rural areas.

- Ethnicity has been a major engine of institutional development, and the indigenous areas are the ones to experience more consolidation and growth of rural organizations.

Civil Society Organizations and Development

During the past few years Ecuador has experienced an extraordinary flourishing of civil society organizations (CSOs), many of which are involved in the productive aspects of rural development (for more on the overall development of civil society organizations in Ecuador, see chapter 10 on governance). NGO-type service organizations and membership associations of various types have been created: financial entities such as savings and loan associations, territorial organizations embracing local communities or groups of communities, and producer associations to carry out specific activities such as marketing, processing, and water use. Other actors—universities, the Catholic and various Protestant churches, and the private sector—have also expanded their role in rural development.

A major factor in this blooming was the withdrawal of government from many service areas in the 1990s and before, a void partly filled by service firms and civil society service organizations. This surge happened in many areas such as agrarian reform, agricultural extension, and small irrigation development. Also, service organizations have proved to be rather flexible and adaptable to the needs of clients, creating networks, establishing alliances, developing new areas of expertise, and improving the marketing of their services. The availability of funding from bilateral cooperation agencies, financing NGOs from donor countries, and financing from the churches provided the financial backing required for the system to expand. The decision by large development projects to outsource the implementation of many activities to service organizations also helped to create a market for these institutions. In addition, international development entities' increasing recognition of the importance of civil society organizations as development actors boosted the CSOs' legitimacy. Finally, the financial crisis of 1998–99 resulted in the closing of many banks and the reduced operation of others, and opened the ground for the development of microfinance NGOs and savings and loan associations.[5]

The relationship between service organizations, particularly development NGOs, and membership organizations is complex. On one hand, both types of institutions depend very much on each other. NGOs usually derive their legitimacy and income from their support to the creation and functioning of membership organizations. These, in turn, often owe their capacity to carry out economic projects for their members, and even owe their own existence, to the support received from NGOs. This support includes not just technical advice but also an outreach function, for instance, in the search for markets, sources of finance, technical expertise, and innovations. Furthermore, a strong synergy often exists between NGO staff and their CSO clients, who embrace a shared vision and construct a shared project for local development. On the other hand, there is competition between service and membership organizations, mostly because the latter would rather be more independent and self-sufficient. This is particularly the case with some second- and third-level territorial organizations, which feel that NGOs preempt their direct access to the sources of development assistance; they would like to create their own technical teams, financed with donor funds, rather than rely on NGO services.

The simultaneous and synergic development of service NGOs and membership organizations makes it difficult to assess who had a more determinant developmental role. What seems evident is that it was the confluence of both types of organizations that created the conditions for success in many rural development undertakings. It is also evident that territorial membership organizations become important actors in rural development when they administer particular resources or services and are able to break into particular market niches. Several observers have stressed that successful cases are highly correlated with particular market niches, high-value products, and strong local organizations. The challenge is to replicate or scale up these experiences to achieve a significant impact beyond a few localized areas.

Subnational Governments and Rural Development

Perhaps the most significant political development of the past few years has been the stability and improved performance of some local governments. Unlike at the national level, political leadership at the local levels has been much more stable and responsive to local constituencies, and consequently those areas have experienced greater policy continuity. Local governments are also expanding their role, and increasingly are providing services that heretofore have been the responsibility of the central government, such as in health and education. A driving force that has allowed this greater responsiveness has been the additional resources received by local governments following the law that assured them 15 percent of public revenues.

Notwithstanding the limitations of the legal framework for decentralization, some interesting experiments are being carried out by municipal governments in inclusive and participatory processes of local development, resulting in productive investments in their rural hinterlands and in alliances with NGOs, second-tier organizations, and local territorial associations. The use of more participatory processes of budget formulation and planning is growing in different places. These processes are a step toward an inclusive type of local development, but they have the limitation of usually consisting of collections of unrelated investments demanded by the population or of similarly unrelated investments promised by the local authorities, rather than being coherent programs of complementary investments with a strategic orientation.

Because of their closeness to the rural population, the *juntas parroquiales* could play a major role in rural development, becoming critical institutions for more democratic and inclusive development of rural areas as well as for more rural-urban municipal integration. The 1998 constitution provides a favorable framework for this. In fact, the juntas have started preparing local development plans, and

CONAJUPAR, their national association, is orienting them in that direction. However, the juntas are having difficulty getting access to funding and establishing alliances with municipal governments, which often continue to turn their backs on them. They are also very recent institutions and have yet to consolidate themselves and clearly define their development role.

IV. Ethnicity in Rural Development

The political and social development of Ecuador's indigenous groups has been shaped by the complex relationship of cultural networks influenced by Ecuador's diverse topography and ecological niches. Since pre-Colonial times, the indigenous peoples from the Sierra traded with indigenous groups from the Amazon and the Costa. The vertical variation of ecological niches encouraged a system of exchange and cooperation that led to complex forms of social and economic organization and intricate alliances that persist until now. These small groups formed interlinked political societies that fought off several invaders, including the powerful Incas and later the Spaniards. In the process, they demonstrated remarkable capacity to adapt to changing political circumstances while continuing to assert their cultural identity (Salomon 1986).

Indigenous Groups

Indigenous people in Ecuador are concentrated primarily in the Sierra, with smaller groups in the Pacific Costa and Amazon regions. Currently, the indigenous population of the Sierra region is 63 percent, followed by the Amazon region, with 31 percent, and the Costa with 26 percent. The 2001 census estimated that the indigenous peoples make up 7 percent out of the total population of Ecuador, with 60 percent settled in rural areas and the remaining 40 percent in urban centers. Guayaquil and Quito have the largest percentage of urban indigenous population (36 percent and 26 percent, respectively), but these estimates often vary depending on the source and the definition of indigenous.

Ecuador's constitution recognizes 12 "nationalities" and 14 Kichwa peoples (*pueblos*)[6] who are represented through a network of national, regional, and local organizations. These organizations have been capable of mobilizing economic and cultural resources, gradually strengthening their organizational capacities and social capital (Carroll 2002; Bebbington 2002). Despite the increased political prominence gained by the indigenous movement in the past decade, indigenous poverty has not diminished. The indicators of poverty and human development register an important gap when comparing indigenous peoples to nonindigenous populations. Although poverty rates present significant differences when disaggregated by region, living in a predominantly indigenous area is still associated with being poor (Skoufias and Patrinos 2006). Poverty is more generalized in the Amazon region and the central Sierra, where the majority of indigenous people live. These regions register precarious living conditions and restricted access to education, health, and the formal job market (STFS 2006).

Indigenous groups share a strong belief in territorial or geographically based development. A fundamental view shared by indigenous leaders is that the purpose of development is to improve the quality of life of their people, create equity, and protect their collective identity. They believe that development must acknowledge the social, cultural, economic, and geographical heterogeneity of rural Ecuador and use a highly participatory and decentralized framework. This approach has been called "development with identity."[7]

Along with territorial focus, indigenous populations are searching for development practices that incorporate and recognize their values and traditions, their close ties to the land and to natural resources, and their redistribution practices designed to maintain social cohesion. With the encouragement and support of NGOs and external donors, several nonindigenous mayors have begun to adopt many of those governance practices, including participatory planning and budgeting, in a number of municipalities and two provincial governments. The PRODEPINE project, an indigenous movement aimed explicitly at indigenous and Afro-Ecuadoran communities, became a key vehicle for the dissemination of these governance practices; they are also being replicated in nonindigenous communities through the Poverty Reduction and Local Rural Development Project (PROLOCAL) in targeted nonindigenous areas.[8]

The livelihoods and economic activities of indigenous groups are embedded within a complex geographical context and an equally complex network of relationships and social and cultural practices designed to ensure food security and maintain social cohesion. This relative equilibrium is being affected by migration, the degradation of the environment, and the impact of dollarization. However, indigenous communities have shown admirable resilience and adaptability to frequent political, social, economic, or natural changes. This has been possible through the strong social capital that is characteristic of indigenous communities, and through their subsistence and semisubsistence production.

Despite the increasing value attached to education by indigenous parents and the introduction of bilingual education, indigenous people continue to lag behind in school completion and educational achievement. Also, the return on investments in education is lower for indigenous people than for *mestizo* or white Ecuadorans (Larrea and Torres 2004). An indigenous male with the same level of secondary education as a nonindigenous male has a 60 percent chance of being poor compared with 35 percent for the nonindigenous peer. This translates into an intergenerational reproduction of poverty. The incidence of illiteracy is particularly large among rural and indigenous women (23 percent and 53 percent, respectively, versus 15 percent and 31 percent for men). Likewise, access to basic health services is comparatively restricted for indigenous peoples, especially for those living in rural areas. Nearly 36 percent of indigenous women did not have prenatal assistance, compared with 12 percent of their nonindigenous peers.

Afro-Ecuadorans

Despite their historical presence in the country, Afro-Ecuadorans have been invisible from national statistics, making difficult the identification of their living conditions, the characteristics of their community organizations, or their specific needs. Concentrated in the provinces of Esmeraldas, Imbabura, Carchi, and Guayas, Afro-Ecuadorans represent 5 percent of the total population. They are among the poorest of country, followed by indigenous peoples. Over half of the Afro-Ecuadoran population is considered very poor and 26 percent live in extreme poverty. The average years of education is 4.9 in rural areas, limiting their access to good quality jobs. Afro-Ecuadoran women, particularly those in the rural areas, are poorer and earn less. High infant mortality rates, malnutrition, and limited local infrastructure characterize the majority of their communities; basic infrastructure in some areas is almost nonexistent. Migration from rural to urban areas is a direct response to limited job opportunities, the deterioration of livelihoods, and the low level of basic infrastructure in their communities. Nonetheless, over 40 percent of Afro-Ecuadorans live in rural areas and depend primarily on the economic and social opportunities that exist or that can be developed in the territories.

Rural Afro-Ecuadorans live surrounded by rich and complex ecosystems that combine forest, agricultural areas, and coastal marine resources. Those living in the Costa region often make their livelihood from a combination of small-scale agricultural production, seasonal labor in extensive agriculture, particularly in the palm oil agroindustry, and extraction of forest or marine resources including fish and conchs. The expansion of agroindustry in the Costa, particularly the recent growth of the palm oil industry, has led many small-scale producers to become agricultural workers employed by the palm oil industry. Those in the mountainous area of Imbabura are mostly small-scale agricultural producers.

Progress in gaining recognition for the Afro-Ecuadoran population, their living conditions, their direct and indirect contribution to the national economy, and their culture has contributed to the emergence of a number of Afro-Ecuadoran organizations. Local community organizations and NGOs have been formed, many in rural areas that are actively involved in local and territorial development, environmental management, and basic community services. Projects such as PRODEPINE helped in the formation and consolidation of many of these organizations and created avenues for a dialogue between the communities and local and national decision makers. Several municipalities in the Costa pioneered participatory budget planning and budget monitoring based on both demand from communities and a commitment from the municipalities to improve the living conditions and create development opportunities for the communities. The creation of an official government entity that represents the interest of the Afro-Ecuadoran communities is an opportunity to expand their inclusion in rural policies and programs aimed at consolidating their livelihoods and reducing their level of poverty. However, these newly formed organizations need to be strengthened at the local, territorial, and national levels.

V. Environmental and Natural Resources Policy Challenges

Ecuador has exceptional natural resource and environmental advantages and challenges. The country is strategically located and has considerable oil reserves in the interior and the coastal region. Despite being one of the smallest countries in South America, Ecuador combines a tropical coastal region, a fertile highland valley in the Andes, a relatively unspoiled and resource-rich Amazon interior, and the unique Galápagos Islands. Ecuador is one of the most biologically diverse countries in the world, with an estimated 9.2 species per square kilometer and numerous endemic species. This natural wealth has allowed Ecuador to compete in the production and export of cocoa, bananas, coffee, shrimp, tuna, ornamental horticulture, and palm oil, among other products. At the same time, pollution-related health problems are considerable. Waterborne bacterial diseases and ambient and indoor air pollution pose the highest costs, totaling an estimated 2 percent of GDP. Protecting Ecuador's rich but fragile natural resources and environmental quality is critical to the country's long-term economic growth and social progress.

Ecuador has developed several institutions and organizations to manage natural resources and protect the environment, starting with the 1976 Law to Prevent and Control Pollution. Several regulations to prevent and control air and water pollution, based on the 1976 law, were enacted in the ensuing years. The 1994 National Environmental Action Plan established environmental priorities for the first time and started development of a framework for environmental management at the national and local levels. From this process, Ministry of the Environment was created in 1996. The 1998 constitution affirms the right of Ecuadorans to live in a healthy environment, ecologically balanced and pollution free. The 1999 Law of Environmental Management set up the guidelines for environmental policy, and in 2000 the country's Environmental Strategy for Sustainable Development was issued. The strategy stressed protecting fragile ecosystems and consolidated protected areas. Despite these institutional efforts, Ecuador still faces significant environmental challenges.

Environmental Health

Poor Water Quality

Lack of potable water and sanitation services and poor hygiene are associated with various illnesses, including schistosomiasis, intestinal worms, and diarrhea. Although diarrhea is not as serious as some other waterborne diseases, it is far more common and affects more people, constituting the largest share of health loss caused by waterborne diseases. More than 15.5 million episodes of diarrhea are recorded every year (600,000 among children under age five), with 1,100 deaths a year among children under five (13 percent of deaths of children of that age group). At any given time, one-third of children had diarrhea in the previous two weeks. The estimated annual health cost of waterborne disease caused by poor water supply, sanitation, and hygiene amounts to almost 1 percent of GDP.

As a result of infrastructure interventions, 93 percent of Ecuadorans have access to an improved water source and 57 percent have access to improved sanitation (compared with the regional averages of 89 percent and 75 percent). Although these interventions have helped cut the incidence of waterborne diseases and benefited the poor, they provide only a partial response to waterborne diseases. Improvements in water supply and sanitation provide a 30 percent expected decline in diarrheal disease (Fewtrell and Colford 2004). A mean decline in diarrheal illness of about 45 percent would result from hand-washing interventions, highlighting the need to implement hygiene education programs.

Indoor Air Pollution

Two out of 10 households in rural areas burn traditional fuels for cooking and heating, using inefficient stoves in poorly ventilated areas. The health effects include pneumonia, chronic bronchitis, emphysema, other chronic obstructive pulmonary diseases, and lung cancer (Desai, Mehta, and Smith 2004). About one million people in rural areas are exposed to high indoor air pollution, resulting in 200 deaths and close to 1.6 million acute respiratory illnesses each year. The health costs of indoor air pollution are estimated at 0.2 percent of GDP.

Urban Air Pollution

Urban air pollution is one of the leading causes of respiratory illnesses in Ecuador. Air quality is serious in high-altitude cities such as Cuenca and Quito (Quito is among the most polluted cities in Latin America). Outdoor air pollution in the two cities causes about 700 premature deaths a year (Strukova 2006), mainly among adults in these two cities. It also causes about 2,500 chronic bronchitis cases in adults and about 200,000 lower respiratory illnesses in children annually. The health costs of air pollution in these two cities are estimated at 0.5 percent of GDP.

Environmental Impacts of Oil-Related Operations

The environmental and social impacts associated with oil operations in Ecuador are especially complex because of their impact on fragile ecosystems in protected areas. The most frequent problems include clashes with existing populations; inadequate operation of facilities, resulting in leaks and other losses; and land-use changes caused by an accelerated increase in the demand for goods and services. In addition, the environmental authorities linked to oil operations face political, financial, technical, and operational limitations in their working relation with oil companies, particularly with the state-owned PetroEcuador. (These issues are also discussed in detail in the chapter on the oil sector.)

The oil activity in the 1970s and 1980s caused severe environmental and social impacts that increased public awareness of the problems posed by oil-related operations in the country. Aging and deteriorated infrastructure, including production stations, pipes, wells, refinery plants, ducts, and terminals, has caused considerable environmental damage, including (i) constant leaks (more than two hundred have occurred in the past two years); (ii) discharges of untreated water into rivers and swamps (30 percent of processed water by PetroEcuador); (iii) hundreds of untreated petroleum waste–collecting pools; and (iv) burning of gas by-products (approximately 50 percent of the gas produced is flared). In addition, the high level of sulfur, aromatics, and benzene in produced fuels is one of the main causes of air pollution–related health problems in major cities.

Conflicts between indigenous communities and companies over oil operations are frequent. Despite the fact that the constitution grants indigenous people the right to be consulted about potentially harmful exploration and exploitation of natural resources in their lands, there is a weak regulatory framework to enforce these rights. Given the uncertainty caused by that weak regulatory framework, negotiations over permits, compensation, and other relevant issues are frequently unnecessarily lengthy, expensive, and unfair.

Impacts of Climate Change

Ecuador still has large tracts of pristine and secondary forests that act as important reservoirs of carbon, which otherwise would be released into the atmosphere with global warming effects. The country is an important carbon sink (an ecosystem with a net absorption of CO_2 from the atmosphere). The potential for afforestation and reforestation of former forest cover, although not yet sized, is also thought to be significant and could play an important role in efforts to capture carbon.

Ecuador is very vulnerable to climate change impacts. Recent analysis by Miller (2007) indicates that the coastal areas of Ecuador are susceptible to significant flooding as a consequence of sea level rise that could affect extensive agricultural areas and infrastructure. Ecuador's energy and agriculture sectors are also very vulnerable to the El Niño–Southern Oscillation (ENSO) signal, for which mounting evidence shows a link to global warming. More frequent and stronger ENSOs will affect energy costs in Ecuador. Finally, Bradley, Viuille, and Vergara (2006) have indicated faster warming of the Andes as global warming proceeds, with adverse impacts on water supply for mountain cities as well as threats to the integrity of Andean ecosystems. Amphibians and reptiles in the Ecuador Andes are disappearing at a very high rate.

Conservation and Use of Ecosystems

Biological diversity constitutes one of the most important sources of wealth in Ecuador. The country's biological diversity is closely tied to significant cultural diversity, and places Ecuador among the 12 most biologically diverse countries in the world (Ministry of the Environment 2001a). Because of these characteristics, groups have made significant efforts, nationally and internationally, to conserve the country's biodiversity. One of the most important instruments for this purpose is the creation of the National Patrimony of Protected Areas, which covers roughly 18 percent of the national territory and encompasses the most critical and endangered ecosystems (Ministry of the Environment 2001b). Nevertheless, there is a clear trend toward the deterioration of these resources, primarily caused by the alteration and destruction of habitats. In addition, knowledge is lacking about the many ways in which biodiversity can be productively used (Suárez and Josse 2001).

The conservation and sustainable use of biodiversity in rural landscapes demand sustainably productive systems, which need adequate technologies. Sustainable agriculture is a critical issue that will be addressed on a future development agenda. Ecolabeling for agricultural products and ecotourism operators are tools with enormous potential to improve national competitiveness. Ecuador has an opportunity to position itself globally as a custodian of natural resources and a producer of goods and services associated with its environmental capital.

Forest Resources

Forest ecosystems in Ecuador cover more than 11 million hectares (42 percent of the national territory). Forests play a vital role by providing environmental services and values (including biodiversity), supporting the livelihoods of indigenous and other rural communities, and being a potential source for economic development in many rural areas. These important functions, however, have not been adequately recognized and addressed by government policies and programs, which in part has led to their loss, degradation, and underutilization. The current annual rate of deforestation of Ecuador (1.4 percent) is more than three times the regional average.

Some of the main causes of forest degradation and the poor economic performance of the forestry sector have been associated with pressures for conversion of forests to other land uses (for example, agriculture, pasture, oil extraction); land tenure conflicts and poor definition of property rights; limited capacity of local communities and other land owners to manage their forests sustainably; illegal logging; and an inadequate legal and institutional framework.

The Galápagos Islands

The Galápagos Islands possess some of the most unique life forms on the planet. From a total of 5,725 registered species, 1,839 (32 percent) are endemic. This exceptional biodiversity and the dramatic scenery attract more than 120,000 visitors every year. The islands have also attracted thousands of immigrants lured by the prospects of lucrative activities linked to the wildlife. The Galápagos ecosystem has been considered endangered for many years, and a number of programs and actions have been implemented to promote conservation. Despite these efforts, today the Galápagos Islands are under greater pressure than ever before as a result of (i) substantial increases in tourism (cruise ships and frequent shuttle flights have increased the number of visitors); (ii) increased migration (population doubled from 1998 to 2005, reaching close to 30,000 inhabitants); and (iii) the introduction of invasive species.

Overexploitation of fisheries is also changing the Galápagos ecosystem. As many as 40 marine species may soon be classified as threatened, and whole biological communities, rich in endemic species, have been replaced by impoverished sea urchin barrens. The sea cucumber boom of the 1990s generated overcapacity of the fishing fleets. Sharks are vital for the ecosystem and tourism, but they are fished illegally; some species will soon be wiped out commercially and functionally.

Despite the Special Galápagos Law, the Galápagos population continues to grow explosively, driven by labor demands of a growing economy, ever more residency permits (some fraudulently obtained), weak migration controls, and the widening gap in living standards between the Galápagos and mainland Ecuador. Increased population means more transport of people and cargo, hence faster introduction and spread of alien species and more extractive use of resources.

Several of the environmental problems are linked to poor governance and weak institutional capacity. The Galápagos National Park Service (*Servicio del Parque Nacional Galápagos*—SPNG) has been unable to monitor and enforce conservation programs, owing in part to the high turnover of its technical personnel. Local authorities are often pressed to concentrate on the immediate demands of their constituents at the expense of longer-term conservation interests. Until the National Galápagos Institute (INGALA) assumes its role and takes full responsibility for the evaluation and approval of development projects such as roads, airport terminals, urban zone expansion, and zoning, development pressure will continue to overcome conservation concerns.

VI. Conclusions and Recommendations

The strategy proposed in this note makes recommendations on the following five related areas that are considered vital to promoting sustainable and inclusive development in Ecuador:

- Adopting a policy framework based on a territorial approach for sustainable and inclusive local development.
- Improving access of the poor, especially its weakest segments, the rural poor, to productive investments and services needed to generate employment and income.
- Improving competitiveness in the agricultural sector.
- Promoting development with identity in indigenous areas and in areas with a predominance of Afro-Ecuadoran populations.
- Confronting the challenges of environmental health, oil-related pollution, climate change, and conservation and use of critical ecosystems.

Adopt a Territorial Approach for Sustainable and Inclusive Local Development

Ecuador is at a strategic juncture to make major decisions regarding its rural development strategy and the most effective institutional framework to carry it out. The past three decades have witnessed an unparalleled flourishing of different types of rural institutions. However, all this experience is not reflected in a consistent policy framework for sustainable and inclusive local development in the country. Acting at this moment to define such a policy framework is appropriate for two reasons. First, local development experiences have matured sufficiently to allow a big step forward. Second, significant changes in the conditions of competitiveness are taking place in the country. With dollarization, it is no longer possible to cushion competitive disadvantages with monetary and exchange rate policies. Ecuador's improving debt position and a horizon of favorable oil prices also allow envisaging greater availability of public investment resources for rural areas in the medium term.

Given the diversity of rural territories in Ecuador, it is critical that the new policy framework respond to a modern concept of rural development based on a territorial approach. The central purpose of the approach is to facilitate endogenous growth processes, centered on the capacity of local agents to promote territorial development on the basis of existing resources. Elements favorable to this approach are the presence of valuable territorial assets (natural resources, landscapes, culture and traditions, accumulated local knowledge and know-how in certain areas, and others), strong institutional development and social capital, and the potential to generate growth processes around territorial economic linkages.

Territorial planning is also an instrument of economic coordination and should be carried out in a way that involves all relevant local actors in the decision-making process to identify the strategic axes for investment. It is also a way of organizing the local demand for development assistance. Cost-sharing in the investments by beneficiaries, ex ante budgetary restrictions, and effective decision capacity of the planning body are essential elements to arrive at trade-offs between alternative investment options. This type of planning is hence the opposite of the simple collecting and listing of local spontaneous investment requests that are so common in many community-driven development programs.

The experience of the World Bank–funded PROLOCAL suggests that this approach can be successful in promoting comprehensive rural development in a way that involves multiple stakeholders—public, private, and civil society—intervening in local development. Participation of communities and their territorial or second-tier organizations is critical to identify and take advantage of value-added chains, access to markets, and complementary off-farm activities. Particular attention must be paid to enhancing competitive conditions among small producers, who are the majority in rural areas. Targeted investments in human capital formation and empowerment of local actors are also fundamental for proper execution of local investments in the short to medium term, and for the sustainability of local development in the longer term.

The main tenets of territorial development can be summarized as follows:

- A combination of productive transformation and sector coordination at the local territorial level.

- A widening of the concept of rural space to include small rural towns and the links with intermediate cities.
- A multisectoral approach to economic development covering different economic sectors and including farm and nonfarm activities.
- Recognition of the differences among rural territories and the need to tailor productive investments and other interventions to their diverse characteristics and needs.
- A concept of the territory that presupposes some territorial identity and the possibility of building a collective project of local actors and their organizations for development.
- Capacity of local governments to engage in participatory planning, budgeting, and implementation of priority rural investments in their respective constituent areas.
- Conscious involvement of different local actors (public, private, and civil society) and their organizations in the economic coordination process, and alliances between these actors to enhance social accountability and support decentralization.
- Emphasis on territorial competitiveness and on maximum economic use of territorial assets.
- Strengthening of financial services in rural areas through the expansion and consolidation of microfinance institutions to extend coverage, lending, credit products, and involvement in local development.
- A medium- and long-term development horizon.

Promote Access to Investments and Services for Local Development

The first priority for a local territorial approach is to facilitate access of the rural population, especially the rural poor, to investments and services needed to generate employment and income in an increasingly competitive context. To accomplish this, actions in four core areas are recommended: (i) promoting access to assets by the rural poor, including human capital (education and health), natural capital (land and irrigation), and social capital; (ii) promoting development of rural financial services; (iii) promoting competitiveness among small farmers; and (iv) promoting improved environmental management in agricultural areas. This is apart from services such as water, roads, electricity, telecommunications, and other important matters for the well-being of rural populations (see specific chapters in this book for more background.

Access to human capital. Measures are required on both the demand and supply sides of educational services. On the demand side, the recent redesign of the *Bono Solidario* as a Human Development Bond (*Bono de Desarrollo Humano*—BDH) is a positive step to change the funding to a transfer conditional on, among other things, school attendance. Another demand-side intervention would be the provision of grants to children of rural poor households, particularly those who are far from secondary school facilities, to obtain secondary education. On the supply side, other recommendations include continuing to advance the decentralization process of education through the system of education matrix centers (*Centros Educativos Matrices*—CEM) and the expansion of the *Redes Amigas*; the introduction of distance education systems; more training of bilingual teachers; testing of new methodological approaches for single-teacher, multigrade rural schools; and the increase of leadership, technical, and vocational training and capacities in rural areas.

In the area of health, educational campaigns would be useful to encourage the rural population to use more existing facilities, particularly women with respect to child care and reproductive health. As with education, the redesign of the Human Development Bond to include health and nutrition conditionality for mothers and school-age children is a positive change.

Access to natural capital. Five possible lines of intervention could be taken in the area of land. One is the continuation and expansion of market-based access to land programs of the type carried out by Ecuador's Fund for Progress for the People (*Fondo Ecuatoriano Populorum Progressio*—FEPP). Another suggestion is to use land taxation to make land markets more dynamic. Two recommendations are (i) to improve the existing municipal land tax through direct assistance to the municipalities to update their registries and cadastral values and improve collection, and (ii) to study the possibility of introducing a national land taxation system. Another line of action would be to carry out a study to understand the failures of the land rental market, which should include suggestions to stimulate the working of the market. Finally, the intervention should pay particular attention to the problems of young farmers in terms of access to land and the intergenerational circulation of land.

Many challenges must be met to expand and make better use of irrigated lands. The first one is to revise the system of allocating water rights in order to make it more equitable and technically sound. This could be done by adjusting legislation on permits; carrying out studies of water balances, of the distribution of permits, and of the existence of illegal irrigation structures; and linking the withdrawal or reduction of permits to the inadequate use of water, the existence of permits in excess of water availability, and missed tariff payments. A possibility to be explored is the introduction of a system for buying back permits, to be used in the most difficult situations, such as basins with particularly inequitable and conflict-ridden water allocations or with a very negative water balance. Another recommendation is to relate the functioning of the irrigation systems to the management of the basins where they are inserted. This is particularly important in the Sierra, where basin management is more critical. A final recommendation is to link irrigation development with a support system to enhance competitiveness of the irrigated lands, and to move from a concept of irrigation development focused on engineering to one centered on social and production issues.

Access to social capital. In the case of territorial organizations, this note proposes extending to all rural development programs the institutional strengthening components that already exist in many of them, such as PROLOCAL. However, support should be oriented to enhance the functions for which territorial organizations are well suited (representation and dialogue with public institutions, management of local public goods, local governance, the keeping of traditions and local identity, and bridging to other similar organizations), not those for which they are not well suited, such as managing economic enterprises related to productive projects. NGOs have shown that they can be capable of earning their place in the donor finance and service provision markets, so there is no reason why government should subsidize them. The government and donors could, however, strengthen NGOs in many ways, for instance by increasing the outsourcing of developmental functions, and consulting relevant matters with the NGO community.

Rural finance systems. With respect to the microfinance institutions (MFIs), the proposal made by the Central Bank of Ecuador, to create a second-level fund to provide financial resources to MFIs through lending and rediscount facilities, is positive. Also, the unequal regulation of the rural microfinance sector by the Superintendency of Banks should be revised, and a regulatory system more adequate to these institutions should be established. The Red Financiera Rural (RFR), which is already providing support to improve the self-regulation of MFIs, could play an important role in the regulatory system, with the superintendency delegating to it some of the supervisory functions.

A final recommendation is the expansion of the range of financial services offered by MFIs in rural areas to include different saving instruments, some types of insurance, more types of personal loans, money transfers, and others. The RFR could also play an important role in the testing and dissemination of new instruments. Financial support from donors or the government would be required for the RFR to be able to do this. In the case of the National Development Bank, this note recommends that the bank (i) change its constitutional charter to ensure technical autonomy and to insulate it from undue political pressures; (ii)concentrate operations on farming sectors outside the radar screen of commercial banks; (iii) work with industrial associations (*gremios*), chains, and other rural organizations to provide financial backing for integrated programs; and (iv) modernize procedures, reduce transaction costs, and introduce new instruments (such as credit cards).

Competitiveness among small farmers. In addition to the recommendations to improve agricultural competitiveness discussed in the following section, several recommendations are included here that are specific to small farmers. The first is to accommodate the demands of and involve small farmers in agricultural research and technology transfer systems. Another recommendation is for chain organizations and agricultural supporting systems to promote the incorporation of small farmers in value chains and promote contract agriculture systems like the very successful horticultural producers of Gatazo-Zambrano. A final recommendation is to abandon a view of agricultural support systems based on the concept of the viable farm in favor of a more integrated concept, where it is recognized that (i) agriculture is for many rural families only one of the areas of operation and sources of income; (ii) most farms are too small or lacking in soil resources to comfortably support a family; and (iii) farmers should be helped to improve their part-time farming, which (as shown by the European and U.S. experience) can be a competitive activity.

Improved environmental management. Proposals for environmental management in agricultural areas concentrate on five areas:

- *Watersheds.* Expand and replicate the successful experience of El Ángel watershed.
- *Highland páramos.* Make investments to improve the environmental management of páramos through the strengthening of local capacities, the preparation and implementation of management plans, the promotion of ecotourism, the introduction of a set of incentives to improve the management of the páramos, and the support to protected areas with páramos.
- *Soil and water contamination with agrochemicals.* Amend the legal framework related to the importation and use of toxic agrochemicals; collect information on the use and disposal of toxic agrochemicals in agriculture-intensive areas and on related health conditions in those areas; carry out information and education campaigns on the health hazards and safe use and disposal of contaminant agrochemicals; and carry out pilot programs to adopt integrated pest management systems, changes in agricultural practices, and use of biological control methods.
- *Mangroves.* Support the preparation and implementation of integrated mangrove management plans; create a system to monitor the level of recovery of damaged areas; and strengthen the current regime on artisanal exploitation of mangroves to keep it within sustainable levels.
- *Natural disasters.* Undertake prevention campaigns, particularly in relation to anticipated El Niño events, and introduce a natural disasters fund along the lines of the Mexican FONDEN (Fund for Natural Disasters) to assist rural dwellers in the event of large shocks linked to natural disasters.

Improve Agricultural Competitiveness

Agricultural competitiveness will have to be achieved from fundamental improvements in productivity and efficiency, rather than from favorable price policies or currency devaluation, as has been the case in the past. Protected sectors are, for the most part, the same sectors in which the country does not possess comparative advantage, including rice, maize, soybeans, wheat, and animal products. This suggests that future economic competitiveness will be contingent on a reorientation away from supporting traditional cereal crops, and other basic sectors where Ecuador does not have a comparative advantage, and toward those sectors in which the country is better able to compete, given the realities of a globalizing marketplace.

This conclusion also suggests three specific implications. First, agricultural and trade policy will increasingly have to conform to policy directions and national commitments made in response to World Trade Organization (WTO) and regional hemispheric trade initiatives. These are likely to diverge increasingly from the current protectionist price policies based largely on the Andean system of price bands. Second, as the country becomes less dependent on traditional agricultural protectionism and promotes industries and sectors that are globally competitive, it will have to continue to diversify its export sector and modernize domestic production and marketing. Finally, given the country's very low existing productivity levels in most agricultural subsectors, to accomplish these goals Ecuador will have to invest widely in productivity-enhancing technology, and in infrastructure under a territorial development approach. Many of these changes will be most effective if focused at the regional level where agroindustry clusters operate and where strengthened private and public services can be most efficient and mutually reinforcing.

Smooth the Transition and Promote Competitiveness

The exposure of crops that lack competitive advantage to international competition, even if gradual and progressive, will inevitably result in a decline in the area planted. Production would be significantly affected in regions such as the southern and central Costa, where these crops are common and occupy a significant area and share of the workforce. The following recommendations would be more consistent with WTO policies than the status quo as a way to smooth this transition.

Border protection. Use the Andean system of price bands as a price stabilization mechanism only. Reduce its memory (to 30 or 36 months) and shorten band amplitude. Move eventually to a system based on floor prices for importable products, calculated according to the true production cost of international price setters, and on farmer-funded stabilization funds for exportables.

Direct payments. In the event of further trade liberalization, introduce a direct payment program on the Mexican PROCAMPO (Program for Direct Assistance in Agriculture)–cash transfer model to benefit the producers of crops more likely to suffer from liberalization. The program would compensate producers for income losses and also encourage a transition to higher competitiveness. Payments could be on a per hectare basis, delinked from production levels and applied over a transition period of perhaps 10 to 15 years. Eligibility would be defined by historical acreage of the selected crops. Payments might be capitalized (that is, brought to present) conditional on investing the capitalized sum on a farming project that would involve converting traditional cropland to alternative uses or reconverting to improved technology. Progressiveness could be promoted by capping program payments and paying more per hectare to smaller producers. Provisions could be established to make the subsidy acceptable as collateral for loans.

Incentives for agricultural innovation. Also, in the event of further trade liberalization, introduce a temporary (say, five years) incentive program to promote on-farm and agroindustrial modernization. Such a program could focus on new agricultural or agroindustrial enterprises, conversion of land to new crops, or investment in well-defined technological improvements. Eligible investments could be fixed assets, equipment, technical assistance, and training. The program could operate on a matching grant basis and be administered as a competitive bidding fund, or could be channeled to small producers via the banking system as a discount on the principal of loans issued to finance investments associated with innovation. Preference in the bidding process could be lending to small farmers, integrated program investments designed to stimulate particular chains or subchains, investments proposed by farmer and value-chain organizations, investments in comparative advantage sectors with clear linkages to marketing and processing, investments to facilitate productive alliances between small farmers and processing and marketing firms, and conversion to comparative advantage activities.

In addition to financing innovative on-farm investments, resources could be applied to three types of programs: (i) to develop entrepreneurial capacity in agroindustries; (ii) to create or consolidate agroindustries by financing preinvestment studies and administrative costs for the establishment of enterprise; and (iii) to finance fixed assets to increase the competitiveness of enterprises in the product chain with spillover effects in the chain. Resources for programs 1 and 2 may not be recoverable in the case of small farmers, whereas most of the resources going to program 3 should be recoverable. Allocation should be through competitive funding mechanisms. Eligible projects would be those linked to production chains with competitive potential in export markets or in expanding domestic markets, with clear linkages to marketing and processing. Priority could be given to small producers and associated producers.

Whatever the potential costs and configuration of such program alternatives, the point is that they provide policy mechanisms that are realistic in meeting many of the goals of farmers and policy makers: (i) they help farmers who are unable to be globally competitive in a market-oriented environment to make the transition to new enterprises; (ii) they give farmers a transition period to develop favorable competitive conditions by providing public goods and subsidies, conditional on desired policy goals; (iii) they encourage farmers to move into products in which the country has a comparative advantage; and (iv) they have the potential, if designed properly and with progressivity in mind, to protect the weakest sectors during a transition period and help affected producers adjust to new opportunities.

Diversification and higher productivity. Maintaining competitiveness in agriculture will require a renewed focus on diversifying and increasing productivity in those areas in which the country does possess comparative advantage. This aim implies providing more public goods and services, especially to smallholders; increasing the capacity of the private sector to foster diversification and efficiency; and fostering institutional innovations that will help generate regional arrangements to promote productivity and growth.

It remains to be seen whether the recent growth of the nontradable sector will continue or wane. In any case, the growth of nontraditional exports can be expected to be one of the primary vehicles to maintaining agricultural competitiveness in the future.

Targeted infrastructure investments. Promoting competitiveness will also require a subregional focus. Much of Ecuador's agriculture, including both traditional and nontraditional products, has a narrow regional focus, given the country's geographical heterogeneity. Many nontraditional crops need modern integrated infrastructure—roads, air freight service, communications, marketing infrastructure—to be competitive. These two considerations—a subregional focus and a modern integrated infrastructure—mean that a regional focus is needed to support efficiency and growth of product clusters. The territorial approach to rural development is the most appropriate answer to this geographic variety.

Improvements in chain organization. One of the institutional innovations that represents a step in the right direction is the use of consultative councils (*consejos consultivos*), which since 1999 have provided a venue for dialogue, consensus-building, and shaping of pricing and marketing agreements in selected agroindustry clusters. It is important to continue supporting the consolidation of value chains and their consultative councils, mainstreaming the work carried out by the Ministry of Agriculture and its Agricultural Information and Census Service (SICA). It is also critical to encourage industrial associations by drafting favorable legislation to mandate farmers' contributions to their associations and possibly by offering a transitory matching grant.

Technology development and transfer. Increasingly, research, technical, and marketing assistance needs will be defined by "clusters" of producers (large and small), marketers, and processors figuring out how to achieve higher efficiency and productivity throughout their chains of production, marketing, and distribution activities. The research and technology transfer system must be sufficiently flexible and responsible to adapt to these changing needs. The recommendation is to continue and mainstream the support provided by PROMSA (the Agricultural Services Modernization Program) to agricultural research and technology transfer, combining the strengthening of INIAP with the continuation of a research grants fund, and progressively expanding the number of beneficiaries of the technology transfer component.

Sanitary and phytosanitary issues. It is also critical to continue and mainstream the support provided by PROMSA to the strengthening of the Ecuadoran Animal and Plant Inspection Service (SESA). A program must be established to ensure that Ecuadoran producers, processors, and exporters conform to the wide range of Hazard Analysis and Critical Control Point (HACCP) and Codex standards. Monitoring, regulatory controls, and technical assistance in animal and plant health and food safety must continue to be modernized and updated. SESA must work more effectively with private firms and producer and trade organizations to promote best practices in safety aspects of crop and animal production, processing, handling, and packing. SESA should also increase its expertise and ability to work with exporters on certification programs. Cofinancing with the private sector should be encouraged.

Promote Development with Identity in Indigenous and Afro-Ecuadoran Areas

Despite the increased political prominence gained by the ethnic movements in the past decade, poverty among indigenous people and Afro-Ecuadorans has not diminished over time. Living in predominant indigenous and Afro-Ecuadoran areas is still associated with being poor. These regions register precarious living conditions and restricted access to education, health, and the formal job market. This note offers the following recommendations:

- Support training and capacity building to the national secretariat (Council for the Development of the Indigenous Nations and Peoples of Ecuador [CODENPE] and CODAE) in charge of the indigenous and Afro-Ecuadoran public policy design, monitoring, and evaluation.
- Improve access of indigenous and Afro-Ecuadorans to basic services, including health education.
- Improve programs focused on child nutrition.
- Improve quality of intercultural primary education and work to increase the number of indigenous students attending secondary schools.
- Improve access of indigenous and Afro-Ecuadoran populations to social protection programs, especially the Human Development Bond.
- Recognize that the geographic and natural space is a central part of indigenous life, and that the choices and practices of indigenous peoples and Afro-Ecuadorans are directly linked to their connection with their environment and their social relations.
- Promote increased democratic practices while establishing the conditions for a more equitable development impact, given the potential granted by the governance framework advocated by the *alcaldes alternativos*.

Confront Environmental Health, Oil-Related Pollution, and Protection of Critical Ecosystems

This section recommends policy measures in several areas: health problems related to the environment, social and environmental impacts of hydrocarbon production, and conservation and use of forest ecosystems.

Environmental Health

Reduce outdoor air pollution. The urgent need is to update regulations, issue standards, and develop economic instruments that cut the concentration of fine particulate matter in the air in major cities. Some of the most promising options include lowering the sulfur content of fuels, controlling emissions from stationary and nonpoint sources, converting gasoline and diesel cars to natural gas, retrofitting particle-control technology for diesel vehicles, using incentives to encourage people to scrap older cars, and carrying out inspection and maintenance programs.

Reduce indoor air pollution. Cutting these impacts will need cross-sectoral interventions, which could include, for example, cleaner fuels, technical mitigation options such as improved cooking stoves, and policies that promote improved housing design. Experience has shown that the benefits from these interventions are realized quickly.

Address poor water quality. Improvements in water supply and sanitation provide a 30 percent expected decline in diarrheal disease (Fewtrell and Colford 2004). A mean decline in diarrheal illness of about 45 percent would result from hand-washing interventions, highlighting the need to implement educational programs.

Social and Environmental Impacts of Hydrocarbon Production

Targeting the following policy, institutional, and legal reforms would address the social and environmental impacts of hydrocarbon production.

Focus on institutional strengthening. Pressure is mounting to take away the Ministry of Energy and Mines' (MEM) environmental management authority over oil operations and grant it to the environment ministry. However, the discussion about what ministry should have that authority may hide the more relevant question of what resources and coordination mechanisms are needed for either scheme to work properly.

Improve the environmental performance of PetroEcuador. Actions include (i) granting the Environmental Management Unit of the MEM the authority to design and implement plans and programs, (ii) modernizing infrastructure and clean waste collection pools, (iii) implementing programs to use the gas that is currently burned off with no economic benefit and to improve water-processing management, (iv) investing in refineries to increase the environmental quality of their products, and (v) improving waste management.

Improve agreements with local communities (especially with indigenous peoples). Actions include (i) creating the legal and regulatory framework to comply with Convention 169 of the International Labour Organization (ILO), and (ii) developing a strategic plan for oil operations in the Ecuadoran Amazon.

Conservation and Use of Forest Ecosystems

To conserve and protect forest biodiversity while taking advantage of Ecuador's other economic, social, and environmental values, the country could institute policy, institutional, and legal reforms. The following reforms are recommended:

Improve governance, accountability, and transparency of public forestry institutions. Actions include (i) strengthening monitoring and evaluation systems by expanding their scope and raising the participation of civil society, (ii) creating a national consultative forestry council that includes stakeholders, (iii) generating and disclosing public information about the sector, and (iv) developing a decentralization strategy to involve local governments and local stakeholders in decision-making processes.

Support local communities and other producer organizations to improve their capacity to manage forests sustainably and generate forest-related incomes. Actions include developing technical assistance and training programs to improve the capacity of producers to manage forests for timber and nontimber products, agroforestry, and other services such as ecotourism.

Design output-oriented regulations, norms, and incentives to ensure sustainable use and conservation of forests and other ecosystems. Actions include (i) promoting standards and indicators of sustainable forest management, (ii) recognizing and supporting third-party certification schemes, and (iii) promoting market-oriented strategies for payment of environmental services.

Invest in land regularization, territorial zoning, and recognition of customary rights of indigenous peoples. Territorial zoning has been a successful land planning instrument in Ecuador that needs to be strengthened. International experience shows that clearly defining property rights and recognizing customary laws and traditional forms of government of indigenous communities are critical to ensure involvement of landowners in sustainable management and forest conservation.

Improve overall management of the Galápagos Islands. Ecuadorans, and Galápagos residents in particular, can receive a sustainable flow of benefits from a well-conserved natural environment in the Galápagos and from the high demand for unique and highly prized tourism opportunities. For this to occur, the government could step up its efforts and improve its effectiveness in (i) establishing and enforcing strict limits on the number of tourists and their activities, (ii) managing migration, (iii) supporting capacity building for local residents, (iv) ensuring the institutional capacity of its agencies operating in Galápagos, and (v) strengthening its inspection and quarantine systems.

Address impacts of climate change. Stewardship of Ecuador's natural capital is essential to the long-term sustainability of the country's economic development, yet that wealth has traditionally not been counted as part of the capital assets of the country. The global community also has a large stake in the conservation and sustainable use of these assets, because their proper management has global and regional consequences of concern under the biodiversity, climate change, and international water conventions.

Policy Matrix

Area	*Issue*	*Policy options*
Territorial development	Ecuador has not fully incorporated a holistic vision of sustainable and inclusive local development that takes into account the particular economic, social, and environmental characteristics and needs of different territories within the country.	Adopt a policy framework based on a territorial approach for sustainable and inclusive local development, including the following tenets: • Recognize the differences among rural territories and the need to tailor productive investments and other interventions to their diverse characteristics and needs. • Incorporate sector coordination at the local territorial level. • Ensure meaningful involvement of local actors and their organizations in the economic coordination process, so they can enhance social accountability and decentralization. • Build capacity of local governments to engage in participatory planning, budgeting, and implementation of priority investments. • Emphasize territorial competitiveness and sustainable use of territorial assets. • Strengthen financial services in rural areas to increase involvement in local development. • Use a medium- and long-term development horizon.
Access of the rural poor to productive assets	The first priority for a local territorial approach is to facilitate access of the rural population, especially the rural poor, to investments and services needed to generate employment and income in an increasingly competitive context.	• Focus on human capital through education and health programs such as the Human Development Bond, increased distance and bilingual learning, and promotion of existing rural health clinics. • Focus on asset investments that enhance people's economic mobility and encourage adjustment to changing circumstances instead of investments that particular livelihoods. Education and other human capital assets yield returns in multiple occupations and livelihoods that facilitate long-run economic mobility. • Focus on natural capital through land programs, improved land taxation, and better water rights' policies for irrigation. • Focus on social capital through extension of institutional strengthening components to all rural development programs to support representation and dialogue with public institutions, management of local public goods, bridging to other local organizations, and increased outsourcing of developmental functions to qualified NGOs.

		• Focus on rural finance through support to the Central Bank proposal to expand the funding of microfinance institutions; revision of unequal regulatory situation of microfinance institutions; and ensure technical autonomy of BNF, together with modernization of procedures and instruments, and concentration on sectors not on the radar screen of commercial banks.
Rural competitiveness	Future agricultural competitiveness in Ecuador will have to be achieved through improvements in productivity and efficiency, rather than through favorable price policies or currency devaluation, as has been the case in the past. Ecuador's agriculture has been shifting from one focused on traditional exports and grains to one whose future growth will depend on selected traditional exports, increasingly diversified nontraditional exports, and increased productivity in nontradables. The growth of nontraditional exports will be one of the primary vehicles to maintaining agricultural competitiveness in the future.	*Border protection* • Align incentive system with comparative advantage. • Reorient support policies away from border price supports and toward more WTO-friendly systems. • Reduce price band amplitude and shorten memory in the short and medium term. In the medium to long term move to more WTO-friendly stabilization measures. *Compensation schemes and modernization incentives* • Extend possible compensatory income support schemes to main losers from liberalization during transition period (five to 10 years depending on liberalization schedule and agreements). • Extend a possible transitional incentive system for agricultural innovation to operate on a matching grant basis administered as a competitive bidding fund. Show preference to small farmers, to operations based on economic coordination within chains, and to activities that are a conversion to or expansion of comparative advantage activities. *Agricultural research and technology* • Define research, technical, and marketing assistance needs by clusters of producers (large and small), marketers, and processors. • Increase public investment in research and development. • Improve and mainstream PROMSA-type support to research, extension, and sanitary and phytosanitary activities. *Targeted infrastructure investments* • Focus on infrastructure investments (roads, air freight service, communications, marketing infrastructure) to support efficiency and growth of competitive agroindustry clusters.

(*Table continues on the following page.*)

Area	*Issue*	*Policy options*
		Economic coordination and collective action issues • Link SICA-type (Agricultural Information and Census Service) support to value chain organizations and information systems. • Encourage the use of parafiscal systems to strengthen farmers' organizations, avoiding free-riding situations and ensuring financial autonomy and sustainability. • Extend possible transitory matching grant scheme over three to five years to encourage farmers' financial contribution to their organizations.
Development with identity in indigenous and Afro-Ecuadoran areas	Despite the increased political prominence gained by the indigenous movement in the past decade, indigenous poverty has not diminished over time. The indicators of poverty and human development register an important gap when comparing indigenous peoples to nonindigenous populations.	• Support training and capacity building of the national secretariat (CODENPE, CODAE) in charge of the indigenous and Afro-Ecuadoran public policy design, monitoring, and evaluation. • Improve access of indigenous peoples to basic services, including health and education. • Improve programs focused on child nutrition. • Improve quality of intercultural primary education and increase the number of indigenous students attending secondary schools. • Improve access of indigenous and Afro-Ecuadoran populations to social protection programs, especially the Human Development Bond. • Recognize that the geographic and natural space is a central part of indigenous life, and that the choices and practices of indigenous peoples and Afro-Ecuadorans are directly linked to their connection with their environment and their social relations. • Promote the governance framework advocated by the *alcaldes alternativos*, which has potential for increasing democratic practices while establishing the conditions for a more equitable development impact.
Environmental and natural resources' policy challenges	Ecuador has exceptional natural resource and environmental advantages and challenges. Ecuador is also one of the most biologically diverse countries in the world. At the same time,	*Outdoor air pollution.* Update regulations, issue standards, and develop economic instruments that cut the concentration of fine particulate matter in the air in major cities. *Indoor air pollution.* Introduce cleaner fuels, technical mitigation options such as improved cooking stoves, and policies that promote improved housing design.

pollution-related health problems are considerable. The environmental and social impacts associated with oil operations in Ecuador are especially complex due to their impact on fragile ecosystems in protected areas. Protecting Ecuador's rich but fragile natural resources and environmental quality and confronting the impact of climate change are critical to the country's long-term economic growth and social progress.	*Environmental oversight of the oil and mining sectors.* Allocate adequate resources and coordination mechanisms for the MEM and the Ministry of Environment to allow them to perform their respective functions effectively. *Improved environmental performance of PetroEcuador:* (i) grant the Environmental Management Unit of the MEM the authority to design and implement plans and programs, (ii) implement a plan to modernize infrastructure and clean waste collection pools, and (iii) improve agreements with local communities (especially with indigenous peoples). *Improve governance, accountability, and transparency of public forestry institutions:* (i) strengthen the monitoring and evaluation systems by expanding scope and raising the participation of civil society, (ii) create a national consultative forestry council that includes stakeholders, (iii) generate and disclose public information about the sector, and (iv) develop a decentralization strategy to involve local governments and local stakeholders in decision-making processes. *Design output-oriented regulations, norms, and incentives to ensure sustainable use and conservation of forests and other ecosystems:* (i) promote standards and indicators of sustainable forest management, (ii) recognize and support third-party certification schemes, (iii) promote market-oriented strategies for payment of environmental services, and (iv) develop and implement integrated management plans for sustainable mangrove areas. *Improve management of the Galápagos Islands:* (i) establish and enforce strict limits on the number of tourists and their activities, (ii) manage migration, (iii) support capacity building for local residents, (iv) ensure the institutional capacity of agencies operating in the Galápagos, and (v) strengthen inspection and quarantine systems.

Annex

Table A.1. Selected Characteristics of Ecuador's Rural Zones

	Land Surface				*Land*			*Crops*[a]					
		Crops		*(%)*	*Gini*	*Productivity*			*US$*		*US$*		*US$*
Subregions	*km²*	*(%)*	*Agricul.*	*Irrigated*	*coeff.*	*Land*[b]	*Labor*[c]	*First*	*000*	*Second*	*000*	*Third*	*000*
Oriente	114,374.2	2.35	9.16	0.23	0.494	334.55	43.1	African palm	6584	Plantains	6249	Bananas	4310
Peasant Costa	24,419.9	32.93	71.47	15.64	0.719	264.95	153.2	Bananas	103010	Rice	92937	Hard maize	45016
Entrepreneurial Costa	24,031.4	28.13	45.48	54.05	0.779	565.74	267.4	Bananas	621405	Rice	70111	Sugarcane	41205
Northern Costa	17,950.7	11.21	31.45	4.60	0.608	190.98	129.4	African palm	30611	Bananas	8757	Cacao	5834
Transition areas	18,838.6	19.15	56.86	14.77	0.633	361.00	106.7	Bananas	69898	African palm	17327	Soft maize	9445
Galápagos Islands	8,010.0	0.34	2.11	2.99	0.733	205.16	58.9	Bananas	230	Plantains	39	Hard maize	9
Peasant Sierra	13,636.7	18.90	53.06	32.99	0.732	335.49	30.0	Soft maize	9250	Bananas	7206	Potatoes	6882
Entrepreneurial Sierra	19,212.9	13.23	32.68	47.87	0.826	690.88	48.9	Potatoes	16014	Soft maize	6359	Sugarcane	4732
Seigneurial Sierra	13,827.0	10.16	39.50	65.70	0.819	363.67	28.5	Soft maize	4954	Potatoes	2467	Bananas	1492
All Ecuador	254,301.4	11.66	29.24	28.77	0.801	377.13	100.0						

Sources: Own calculation from cantón-level data from population and agricultural censuses, SIISE, Infoplan *Tablas Dinámicas,* and work files of World Bank (2004).

Note: For definition of subregions, see section "Agrarian Structure and Production Characteristics."

a. *Crops* = first, second, and third in importance, by value, in the subregion.

b. *Land productivity* = gross value of output per hectare, in U.S. dollars.

c. *Labor productivity* = index based on gross value of output per labor-week.

Table A.2. Ecuador: Main Dynamic Rural Territories

	Agriculture/Agroindustry		*Rural Nonfarm*	
	Area	***Cluster Type***	***Area***	***Cluster Type***
Medium and large entrepreneurial development	Cantones Quito, Cayambe, Pedro Moncayo	Dairy basin and flower production	Marcelino Maridueñas and Milagro in Guayas	Industrial development around sugar complex
	Cotopaxi	Dairy basin, flower production, and broccoli	Galápagos Islands	Tourist complex
	Banana area in El Oro province	Banana production and export complex	Beach areas in Esmeralda province	Tourist complex
	Sugar area in Milagro, La Troncal and Marcelino Maridueñas	Sugar production and refining complex	Cantones Salinas and Santa Elena in Guayas	Tourist complex
	Quevedo, Mocache, Santafe, Cumandá	Palm oil and maize-mill complexes		
	Quinindé, Santo Domingo de los Colorados, La Concordia	Palm oil and beef complexes	Railway in Chimborazo province	Tourist complex
	North of Esmeraldas	New palm oil and cocoa areas		
Small entrepreneurial development	Cantón Salinas in Bolivar province	Cheese and other products, and small industry	Artisanal area in Otavalo, Cotacachi, Antonio Ante in Imbabura	Artisanal and Tourist complex
	High coffee areas in El Oro, Loja, and Zamora Chinchipe	Coffee complex	Artisanal areas in Cuenca and cantones Gulaceo, Chordeleg, Sigsig	Artisanal complex
	Aromatic cocoa areas in cantones Vinces, Pueblo, Viejo,and Baba in El Oro	Cocoa complex	production zones of straw hats in Azuay and Cañar	Straw hats and other crafts
	Potato production area in Carachi	Potato production	Production areas of rugs and leather products in Guano	Rugs and leather products
	Fruit and vegetable highlands areas of Tungurahua and Chimborazo	Highland fruit and vegetable production	Cantose Jipijapa and Montecristi	Natural fiber handicrafts
			Various locations in the Oriente	Community tourism

Notes

1. *Development with identity* was embedded in the concept of "ethnodevelopment," a term coined by Rodolfo Stavenhagen in 1986 to emphasize the need for cultural revitalization as part of development. It was implemented initially by NGOs and now internalized as part of governance practice.

2. No data are available on general economic performance at the cantón level. In view of the importance of agriculture in the rural economy and the connection that usually exists between the farm and rural nonfarm economies, we used as entry point the cantón-level agricultural productivity estimates calculated by World Bank staff for the preparation of the poverty assessment. These estimates of land and labor productivity by cantón were based on the agricultural census. The methodology is explained in World Bank (2004).

3. In a recent study using 1990–2001 data, Vos and León calculated a –0.8 percent change in total productivity growth for primary agriculture, forestry, and fisheries.

4. The DRC compares the opportunity cost of domestic resources (the numerator) with the value added generated by tradable inputs (in the denominator). For comparative advantage to exist, the DRC measure should lie between 0 and 1.0. The closer the measure is to 0, the greater the comparative advantage. If the DRC is greater than 1, then the cost of domestic resources is less than the net income (or savings) generated by the use of tradable inputs. The economy then does not have comparative advantage in the particular good, since the cost in terms of use of domestic resources exceeds the net returns earned from those resources. Thus, the DRC measures competitiveness by evaluating simultaneously both social efficiency, defined in terms of the opportunity costs of productive inputs, and net returns, defined by potential value.

5. Some large and well-established NGOs with a long tradition of development work enjoy a very good reputation and standing within Ecuador's development community. *The Central Ecuatoriana de Servicios Agrícolas* (CESA) and the *Fondo Ecuatoriano Populorum Progressio* (FEPP) are two of these NGOs; both were created under the umbrella of the Catholic Church with the intention of providing services to small farmers. CESA and FEPP, however, are special cases, for most NGOs are small, and many face considerable difficulties. They are often caught between the increasing reluctance of donors to support them on a sustainable basis (rather than just use them to implement specific and well-defined programs), the increasing competition from private service firms, and the desire of many membership organizations to become technically and organizationally self-sufficient.

6. The nationalities are Kichwa, Achuar, Shuar, Cofán, Chachi, Awa, Eperá, Tsáchila, Huao, Siona, Zápara, and Shiwiar. The peoples are characterizations among the Kichwa geographic settlements, with the largest denominated "Kichwua del oriente."

7. "Development with identity" refers to an integrated process of economic and cultural production to bring about social change with equity. It involves a merging of modern and traditional discourses and practices, in a process of cross-cultural flows, providing new meanings to traditions and creating improved ways of life.

8. Both PRODEPINE and PROLOCAL were supported by the World Bank.

Bibliography

Balarezo, Susana. 1998. "Desarrollo local: experiencias de la visión rural-urbana en las planificación local." Conferencia electrónica sobre gobiernos locales y desarrollo rural en los Andes: casos y experiencias. IICA, Quito, Ecuador.

Barril, A., and L. Martínez. 1995. *Desafíos del Desarrollo Rural frente a la modernización Económica.* Quito: IICA.

Bebbington, Anthony. 1997. "Social Capital and Rural Intensification and Islands of Sustainability in the Rural Andes." *Geographical Journal* 163 (2).

———. 2002. "El capital social y la intensificación de las estrategias de vida: organizaciones locales e islas de sostenibilidad en los Andes rurales." In *Capital social en los Andes,* ed. Anthony Bebbington and Víctor Hugo Torres, 11–38. Quito: Abya-Yala.

Berdegué, J. A. 2002. Evalauación del Componente de Transferencia Tecnológica del Programa de Modernización de los Servicios Agropecuarios: Informe Final.

———. 2004. "Estratégia Agropecuaria Ecuatoriana, 2005–2015." Documento de Trabajo. CORPEI, Guayaquil.

Bretón Solo de Zaldívar, Víctor. 2001. *Cooperación al desarrollo y demandas étnicas en los Andes ecuatorianos. Colección Atrio.* Quito: FLACSO-Universidad de Lleida-GIEDEM.

Cameron, John. 2001. *Local Democracy in Rural Latin America: Lessons from Ecuador.* Paper presented at the meeting of the LASA. Washington, DC, September 6–8.

Carroll, Thomas, ed. 2002. *Construyendo capacidades colectivas. Fortalecimiento organizativo de las federaciones campesinas-indígenas en la sierra ecuatoriana.* Quito: Rispergraf.

Chiriboga, Manuel, and L. Rodríguez. 1999. Análisis de las estrategias para reducir la pobreza rural. Consultoría para PROLOCAL, Quito.

De Ferranti et al. 2003. *Inequality in Latin America and the Caribbean: Breaking with History?* Advance Conference Edition. Washington, DC: World Bank.

Desai, M., S. Mehta, K. Smith. 2004. *Indoor Smoke from Solid Fuels. Assessing the Environmental Burden of Disease at National and Local Levels.* Environmental Burden of Disease Series, No. 4. Geneva: WHO.

Donoso-Clark, M. 2003. "Desarrollo rural." In *Ecuador: una agenda económica y social del Nuevo milenio,* ed. Frete-Cibils et al., 301–22. Bogotó: World Bank e Alfaômega.

Echeverría, Ricardo. 2004. *Análisis Económico-Financiero del Sector Forestal Ecuatoriano y del Sistema Nacional Tercerizado de Control Forestal.* Ministerio del Ambiente del Ecuador, Banco Interamericano de Desarrollo.

Espinel, R. 2003. *Analysis of the Functioning and Efficiency of Ecuador's Rural Markets and the Impact of the Expansion of Supermarkets.* Report prepared for Rural Development Strategy Report, World Bank, Washington, DC.

Flores, Rubén. 1998. *Diagnóstico de los Gremios de Productores Agropecuarios: Una propuesta de Trabajo para su fortalecimiento.* MAG – Programa Sectorial Agropecuario, Quito.

Gasselin, Pierre. 2001. "La Explosión de la Floricultura de exportación en la región de Quito: Una nueva dinámica agraria periurbana." In *Dinámicas Territoriales, Estudios de Geografía No. 10*, ed. P. Gondard, Juan B. León, 15–40. IRD-PUCE-CGE, Corporación Editora Nacional, Quito.

Gondard, Pierre, and Hubert Mazurek. 2001. "30 años de reforma agraria y colonización en Ecuador (1964–1994) – Dinámicas Espaciales". In: *Dinámicas Territoriales, Estudios de Geografía No. 10*, eds. Gondard, P. y Juán B. León, 15–40. IRD-PUCE-CGE, Corporación Editora Nacional, Quito.

Huttel, Charles, Claude Zebrowski, and Pierre Gondard. 1999. Paisajes Agrarios del Ecuador, Geografía Básica del Ecuador, Tomo V Geografía Agraria, Volumen 2. IRD-IPGH-IFEA-IGM-PUCE, Quito.

Jácome, Hugo, and Jorge Cordovez. 2004. "Microfinanzas en la economía ecuatoriana: una alternativa para el desarrollo." In *Microfinanzas en la economía ecuatoriana: una alternativa para el desarrollo*, ed. H. Jácome, 13–108. Quito: FLACSO-Fondo de Solidaridad.

Jokish, Brad. 1998. "Landscapes of Remittances: Migration and Agricultural Change in the Highlands of South-Central Ecuador." PhD thesis, Graduate School of Geography, Clark University, Worcester, MA.

———. 2001. "Desde Nueva York a Madrid: Tendencias en la migración ecuatoriana." Revista Ecuador Debate No. 54. Quito: CAAP.

Kyle, David. 2001. "La diáspora del Comercio Otavaleño: Capital Social y Empresa Transnacional." Revista Ecuador Debate No. 54. Quito: CAAP.

Lanjouw, Peter. 1998. "Ecuador's Rural Nonfarm Sector as a Route Out of Poverty." Policy Research Working Paper 1904, World Bank, Washington, DC.

Larrea, Carlos, Malva Espinoza, and Paola Sylva. 1987. "El Banano en Ecuador." FLACSO-CEN, Quito.

Larrea, Carlos, and Fernando Montenegro Torres. 2004. *Indigenous People, Poverty and Human Development in Latin America: 1994–2004.* Washington, DC: World Bank.

———. 2001. *Política y Estrategia Nacional de Biodiversidad del Ecuador 2001–2010.*

Ministerio del Ambiente del Ecuador, EcoCiencia, and Unión Mundial para la Naturaleza (UICN). 2001. La biodiversidad del Ecuador. Informe 2000. Quito: Ministerio del Ambiente.

Ministerio de Economía y Finanzas. 2004. Propuesta de Estrategia Nacional para la Reducción de la Pobreza. Quito: MEF.

North, Liisa. 1999. "Salinas: una experiencia de desarrollo micro-regional, en Cambiar se Puede, Las Experiencias del FEPP en Desarrollo Rural." Abya Yala-FEPP, Quito.

Otañez, Guillermo. 2002. "Ecuador: Breve análisis de los resultados de las principales variables del censo nacional agropecuario 2000." Ministerio de Agricultura Ganadería, Acuacultura y Pesca del Ecuador. http://www.sica.gov.ec.

Ponce, Juan. 2005. "Los Afro-Ecuatorianos." In *Mas Allá de los Promedios. Afrodescendientes en América Latina*, ed. Josefina Stubbs and Hiska Reyes. Washington, DC: World Bank/SIISE.

Prats, Susan. 2001. "El Consorcio Cachi: un ejemplo de coordinación institucional al nivel local." In *Los Páramos del Ecuador, Particularidades, problemas y perspectivas*, ed. Patricio Mena et al., 267–77. Quito: Abya-Yala Proyecto Páramos.

Proaño, Mauricio, and Susan Prats. 2003. "El Consorcio Carchi: un espacio para pensar,m analizar y actuar en cuenca hidrográfica." In *Foro de los Recursos Hídricos. Segundo Encuentro Nacional. Documentos de discusión*, 62–69. Quito: Foro de los Recursos Hídricos.

Salomon, Frank. 1986. *Native Lords of Quito in the Age of the Incas: The Political Economy of North-Andean Chiefdoms.* Cambridge; New York: Cambridge University Press.

Southgate, Douglas, Rodrigo Sierra, and Lawrence Brown. 1991. "The Causes of Tropical Deforestation in Ecuador: A Statistical Analysis." *World Development* 19 (9): 1145–51.

Suárez, Luis, and Carmen Josse. 2001. "Las prioridades de la conservación de la biodiversidad." In *La Diversidad Biológica del Ecuador, Informe 2000.* Ministerio del Ambiente, EcoCiencia, UICN.

Torres, María del Lourdes. 2001. "La diversidad genética en Ecuador." In *La Diversidad Biológica del Ecuador-Informe 2000.*

UNESCO (United Nations Educational, Scientific, and Cultural Organization) and IUCN. 2006. *Galápagos Islands World Heritage Site.* Report to the World Heritage Committee.

Villoria, N. 2001. *The Andean Price Band Policy: An Economic Analysis of Agricultural Protection, Producer and Consumer Welfare.* Unpublished master's thesis, Cornell University.

Vizcaíno, D. 2001. *Diagnóstico de la Agrotecnología en Ecuador.* Andean Competitiveness Project, Central American Institute of Business Administration (INCAE).

Vos, R., and M. León. 2003. *Dolarización, Dinámica de Exportaciones y Equidad: Como Compatibilizarlas en el Caso de Ecuador?* Paper prepared for United Nations Development Program Project on "Export-led Economic Strategies: Effects on Poverty, Inequality and Growth in Latin America and the Caribbean."

World Bank. 2003. *Case Study Ecuador: National Research Capacity Building by Introducing Competitive Research Funding.* Washington, DC: World Bank.

———. 2004. *Ecuador Poverty Assessment.* Washington, DC: World Bank.

———. 2007. "Note on Climate Change." Development Research Group, Knowledge in Development Note 13, Climate Change and Development, June 2007. World Bank, Washington, DC.

10

Enhancing Public Sector Transparency and Accountability

Edgardo Mosqueira

Executive Summary

Governance problems in Ecuador have not substantially changed in recent years, and may have indeed even deepened in some areas as a consequence of the political instability of the past four years. According to Latinobarómetro 2005, Ecuadoran citizens report more corruption within the public administration and are among the most pessimistic in Latin America regarding progress made on corruption. Other governance indicators developed by the World Bank Institute show deterioration in voice and accountability, regulatory quality, government effectiveness, and rule of law.

Modest reforms have taken place in key public sector areas. Public sector financial management has shown improvements, both accomplished and planned, to the Integrated Financial Management System (SIGEF). Some public sector transparency measures have begun but require considerably more work. Public procurement has benefited from the efforts led by the Civil Commission for the Control of Corruption (Comisión Civica de Control de la Corrupción—CCCC) through the implementation of Contratanet, a system designed to publish the main public procurement activities.

After the selection of a new Supreme Court, the judicial branch has recovered some legitimacy and credibility, but it still needs reforms to reach acceptable standards of transparency and improved service delivery. The judicial sector is vulnerable to corruption, not easily accessible, ineffective, and inefficient. These issues are associated with ineffective oversight models, inadequate administration of scarce resources, and low professional standards of quality of key operators (mainly judges and administrative and court staff).

This chapter was written by a team led by Edgardo Mosqueira and composed of Stefania Abakerle, Ana Bellver, Henry Forero, Jeff Rinne, and David Varela.

In spite of some recent progress, the administration of justice has not yet offered tangible results to the population.

The reforms of recent years in public management and the judicial sector may constitute a starting point for improving transparency and accountability in the public sector and could help the state recover the confidence of its citizens. The main incentives driving these reforms (improving management of public expenditures and civil society demands) should stay in place in the upcoming years, contributing to their implementation. The new administration's main objectives—of increasing public sector transparency and improving governance—seem aligned with the deepening of these reforms. The challenges are enormous, but progress in the areas addressed in this chapter would have a significant impact on transparency and accountability of public operations, and would contribute to improving Ecuadoran citizens' perceptions of the functioning of the state.

I. Three Key Governance Problems: Corruption, Lack of Transparency in Public Management, and Weak Delivery of Justice

There is a wide consensus among Ecuadorans that corruption, lack of transparency, and limited access to justice are some of the main problems on governance. The first section of this chapter describes the current situation on corruption in comparison with other countries in the region and the weaknesses of the governance situation in the country. The second section describes the lack of access of information on public management issues as well the limited progress in the implementation of the Freedom of Information Act. Finally, the third section describes the condition of justice delivery.

The Ongoing Challenge of Reducing Corruption

Ecuador has shown a slight improvement in the control of corruption, but the country still ranks among the most corrupt countries in the region and the world. The country scored 2.4 in Transparency International's 2006 corruption perceptions index (CPI), ranking 128 out of 163 countries (together with countries such as Cameroon, Niger, and Venezuela), a slight worsening from the 2.5 it scored in 2005. Although citizens' perceptions about progress against corruption improved slightly, from 18 percent in 2004 to 21 percent in 2005, this number remains very low compared with the rest of the region (figure 10.1). More citizens report corrupt acts (16 percent in 2005 compared with 13 percent in the previous year). The poll also found that Ecuadorans perceive that 82 percent of public officials are corrupt, the highest percentage in Latin America (figure 10.2).

The difficult problem of corruption in Ecuador is accentuated by the poor conditions presented in other governance indexes, such as voice and accountability, regulatory quality, government effectiveness, and rule of law. All these indexes deteriorated in the period 1998–2005 (figure 10.3). The reforms initiated in public financial

Figure 10.1. Respondents Who See Progress in Fighting Corruption, 2005
(percent)

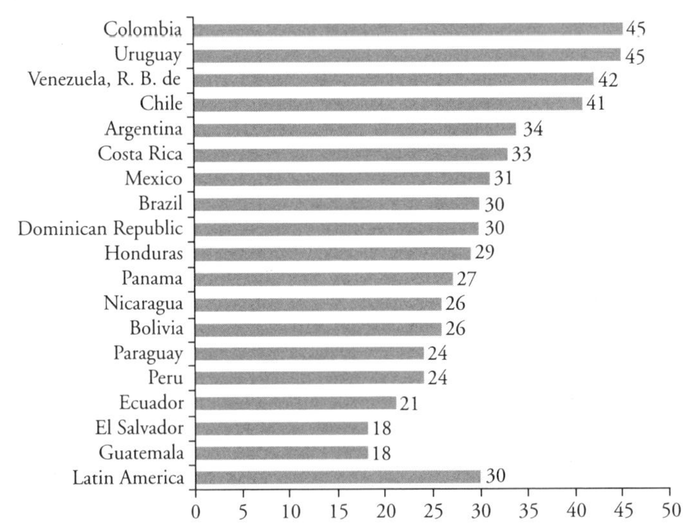

Source: Latinobarómetro (2005).

Figure 10.2. Respondents' Perception of Percentage of Corrupt Public Officials, 2005
(percent)

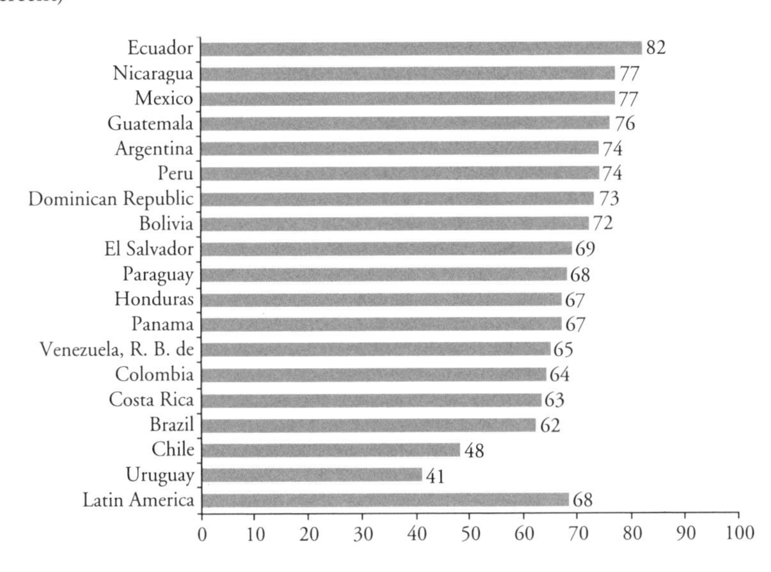

Source: Latinobarómetro (2005).

Figure 10.3. Governance Indicators, 2005 versus 1998

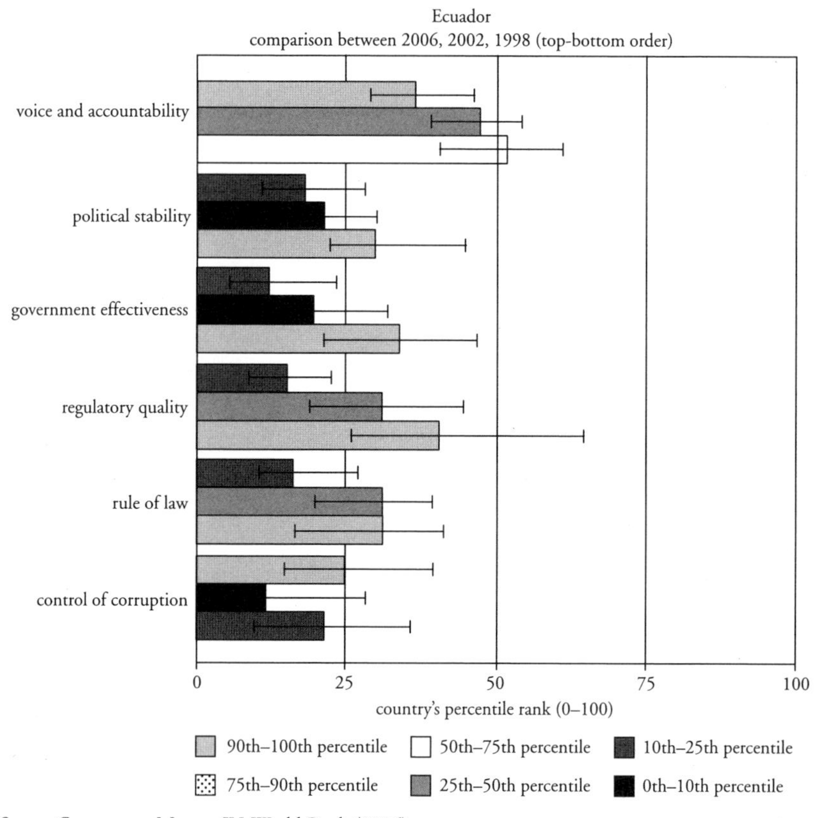

Source: Governance Matters IV. World Bank (2006).

management, civil service, and procurement have created conditions to increase transparency and accountability in key areas of public management and influence citizens' perceptions of corruption. Moving forward with judicial sector reform would send the right messages to the citizens.

Lack of Transparency's Limits to Public Expenditure Oversight and Accountability

Ecuador ranks below global and regional averages regarding economic and institutional transparency. Political transparency is about at the global average. Ecuador has made some progress in the publication of economic and financial indicators, following international best practices regarding data dissemination. However, information related to social expenditures, human development, and public service delivery is still not widely disseminated. This is particularly worrying given the need to monitor poverty reduction strategies, measure effectiveness and efficiency of social programs, and demand accountability for pro-poor spending.

In a study of budget transparency of 10 Latin American countries, Ecuador ranked last, after countries like Brazil, Nicaragua, and Peru.[1] Ecuador scored 31 out of 100 on the Open Budget Index 2006. The index evaluates the quantity of information provided to citizens in the seven key budget documents that all governments should make public during the course of the budget year. Ecuador's performance indicates that transparency of the central government's budget and financial activities is still poor.

Two years after the approval of the Law of Transparency and Access to Information, the progress in implementing it remains slow (box 10.1). Though most of the civil society organizations working on social accountability consider it crucial to have access to information from public sector entities, two-thirds of those surveyed by the local chapter of Transparency International (CLD) said they received the information they requested only occasionally, rarely, or never, and almost 80 percent considered that they got the information they needed to carry out their work only occasionally, rarely, or never. Only 15 percent of those surveyed consider that the information received from the state is sufficient.

Local governments were perceived by civil society survey respondents as better at providing citizens with information (table 10.1). At the central level, the Central Bank

Box 10.1. Progress in Implementing the Law of Transparency and Access to Information

Even though the Law on Transparency and Access to Public Information has been passed, the level of transparency and access to public information remain low in Ecuador. Through a series of monitoring exercises over the course of 10 months, *Coalición Acceso* found that public institutions and their private affiliates have not complied with two major provisions of the law: (i) responses to inquiries from civil society, and (ii) dissemination of public information explicitly mandated by article 7 of the law.

In the first phase of monitoring in May 2005, the Human Rights Clinic of the Catholic University of Ecuador (PUCE) made 22 information requests to public institutions, of which only three received a response. To assess the progress in disseminating public information, the local chapter of Transparency International (CLD) reviewed the Web sites of 100 randomly chosen public institutions. None of the Web sites reviewed displayed all of the information mandated by article 7. The majority of the sites did not contain information regarding budget management, procurement, collective contracts, or public salaries. Only half published detailed program implementation plans, which

(*Box continues on the following page.*)

Box 10.1. (continued)

would allow citizens to monitor performance. More than half did not provide forms for citizens to request information, nor instructions on how to make information requests. Half the Web sites did not supply contact information for the official responsible for distributing information to the public, office hours of operation, and internal procedures and regulations for information requests. A more recent monitoring exercise found that compliance had not improved. The Ministry of the Environment is the only institution that publishes the list of individuals and firms that have been contracted by the institution and all related costs.

The majority of municipalities also fail to publish all of the information mandated by article 7. Only the municipality of Guayaquil publishes the information considered most sensitive, such as salary schemes, detailed contract information, and information about loans and finance agreements. Of the 785 local assemblies in the country, only the local assembly in Cuenca de Jubones has a Web page. Only three local governments have Web sites (Otavalo, Cotacachi, and Guamote, which all benefited from participatory budgeting experiences). Otavalo's Web site contains, for example, the municipal government's accountability report to citizens, carried out at the end of 2005 to report on the projects, public works, and spending of the municipality. It also has a site called "Clear accounts," which provides information on all public works and contracts to date. Cotacachi's Web site provides information on some salaries in the municipality and the projected budget (for 2005, not 2006), including the portion subject to participatory budgeting. It also provides a link for citizens to send direct e-mails, addressing questions or complaints to the major or members of the municipal council. However, none of these Web sites publish even half of the information required by the law.

In early 2006, the Web pages of 36 public institutions were surveyed (courts and institutes for higher education) under the jurisdiction of the law. Although the Web pages of all of these institutions include information about procedures for requesting information, none publish information on five aspects mandated by the law, including full text of institutional contracts, firms and individuals hired by the institution, and finance agreements made by the institution.

Source: World Bank (2006).

Table 10.1. Public Institutions Perceived as Most and Least Transparent

	Percent
Least transparent public institution	
1. Ministry of Finance	17
2. Congress	7
3. Local governments	7
4. Presidency	6
5. Armed Forces	5
6. All	4
Most transparent public institution	
1. Local governments	15
2. None	14
3. Civil Commission for the Control of Corruption	11
4. Internal Revenue Service (SRI)	7

Source: CLD.

is perceived as one of the public institutions better at providing information, though still not nearly as good as local governments. The public entity that was perceived by far as least transparent was the Ministry of Economy and Finance (MEF). This perception is notable, because the systems of financial management, civil service, and procurement are important areas of opportunity for improving transparency, yet they are controlled or supervised by the MEF. Improvements in these areas could change citizens' perceptions about lack of transparency.

The factors most often cited by survey respondents as causing this slow progress were lack of awareness of public officials about their legal obligation to provide information, fear that the information would be used against them, an ingrained habit on the part of public officials to retain information, and the lack of operational mechanisms to disseminate information. Other factors cited were lack of incentives for public officials to provide information and the costs of gaining access to information. These responses resonated with the focus group discussions and interviews with civil society leaders, which coincided in their stating that Ecuador still lacks a public sector culture of transparency and access to information, that systems to generate information are still poor, and that incentives for public officials to provide information are not in place.

Deepening reforms in public sector financial management, civil service, and procurement will contribute to increased transparency and accountability in public resource management.

Unfinished Judicial Sector Reform

Reforming Ecuador's inefficient and corrupt judicial sector remains a high priority. The new Supreme Court is in a privileged position to lead this effort and rally the support of key stakeholders in Ecuador and the international cooperation. The court is currently preparing a long-term plan to ensure more efficient management, improve the professional quality of judges and administrative and court staff, and increase access to justice. The plan will build on previous efforts (Fretes-Cibils, Giugale, and López-Calix 2003). Below is a brief overview of the main challenges facing the sector.

Insufficient procedural transparency. Although the recent modernization of court management reduced case processing time, there is still considerable room for improving transparency. Under the new Code of Civil Procedure, a transition from the traditional written system to an oral argument–based system will take place. This change is critical not only for quality control, but also to achieve greater transparency in judicial proceedings: oral argument provides direct access to the evidence submitted, immediate discussion of its procedural significance, and understanding of the rationale for the court's ruling. The actions of judges and attorneys are fully open to public scrutiny. Since the judiciary is already empowered to make major policy decisions on the regulatory framework of court and case management, no major reforms are necessary to implement the modern management tools required for oral argument.

Ineffective accountability mechanisms. The justice system has the extremes of accountability mechanisms: some agencies are not subject to congressional oversight, whereas others are exposed to impeachment by a congressional majority. A modern system of internal controls reinforced by external oversight is lacking. Such a system should be applied to the investigation of corruption cases. Measures are also required to enhance transparency through public disclosure of information on the performance of judges and court staff, such as cases handled, rationale of decisions, compensation levels, attendance records, and itemized expenditures.

Transparent personnel selection and evaluation processes. Effective rules are missing that would ensure transparency and participation of civil society in filling judicial vacancies. In spite of some recent progress, no permanent systems are in place for selection, performance evaluation, and training of judicial staff to improve quality and provide objective criteria for appointment, promotion, and removal. Modern personnel management tools should be the backbone of a judicial career based on merit rather than seniority.

Weak public information and communications. The positive results of judicial reform programs that began in the 1990s have not been adequately disseminated and, consequently, negative public perceptions of the judiciary remain. Authorities need to design outreach campaigns that capture the attention of users and potential users of justice services, and request the active involvement of representative groups. A permanent dialogue space should be established for civil society organizations to maintain regular interaction with authorities. Citizen awareness and monitoring of judicial sector issues could also help improve public perception. No mechanism to preserve the independence of the judiciary is more effective than public support.

Barriers to social inclusion. The establishment of appropriate procedures to meet the due process needs of the poor without the high costs of regular court proceedings remains a top sector priority. Implementation of the small claims courts has been postponed; although the territorial jurisdiction of family courts has been defined, their effective operation is also delayed. Underutilized courts in Quito, Guayaquil, and Cuenca could be converted into family courts. Mediation offices attached to the courts could allow low-income parties to settle disputes without judge involvement; trained mediators could facilitate direct agreements among the parties. However, this alternative dispute resolution (ADR) mechanism is limited to a few cities. The constitutional mandate that empowers indigenous authorities to resolve the internal disputes of their communities according to customary law is not yet effective.

Unbalanced sector development. While the civil courts have improved performance, other key courts have lagged behind, for instance (i) the administrative courts (*contencioso administrativo*) that review decisions of the executive branch in areas such as public contracts and expenditures, and (ii) the tax courts (*tribunales fiscales*) that adjudicate disputes between the tax authority (SRI) or the customs service and taxpayers.[2] The complexity of certain civil cases with high economic and social relevance often overwhelms the capacity of civil courts (for example, insolvency and bankruptcy, antitrust, consumer protection, and environmental degradation). The traditional resources and capacity of a civil court are clearly inadequate to meet demand. Although the Judiciary Organic Law allows specialization of certain courts or judges for the rapid adjudication of more complex cases, this power has not been fully exercised.

II. Foundations for Further Reform

This section describes advances in introducing transparency in some areas of public affairs, as well as the opportunities created for those advances. Demand by citizens for greater transparency is rising, accompanied by gains in modernization and openness within Ecuador's financial and procurement systems and opportunities for improvement in the judicial system.

A Strong Demand for Transparency

Traditionally, public sector reforms have focused on the "supply" side of institutions and systems (that is, technical administrative and judicial reform programs). Though the reforms are important, experience shows that they could be much more effective when combined with actions that enable citizens to exert accountability over public institutions, budget decisions, and public services provision—the "demand" side of governance. By doing so, politicians tend to gain credibility, and citizens move beyond demands and protest toward engaging with politicians in a more informed, constructive, and systematic manner.

In the 2000s, Ecuadoran civil society has demanded greater transparency and accountability from the state. The role assumed by civil society organizations (CSOs) responds to a weakening formal governance system, an obsolete party system, low levels of public accountability, and a high degree of corruption and lack of transparency. This has prompted CSOs to gradually engage in a series of activities, including lobbying, budget formulation and management, procurement processes, social auditing of public service provision, and demands for accountability from the public institutions (table 10.2). Constitutional provisions recognizing the rights of citizens to participate have fostered this CSO activity.

Table 10.2. Key Areas and Activities of CSOs in Ecuador

Area	*Activities and supporting organization*
Public expenditure monitoring	• Jubileo 2000 (*Observatorio de Política Fiscal*)
Budget literacy	• Monthly bulletins and education brochures on macroeconomic issues and fiscal policies (*Observatorio de Political Fiscal, Grupo Faro, Jubileo* 2000)
Dialogue on the national budget	• Observatorio de Política Fiscal
Transparency and access to information	• Lobbying for Transparency Law (*Coalición Accesso*) • Monitoring Transparency Law implementation (Coalición Accesso, CLD) • Electoral information Web site (*Participación Ciudadana*)
Monitoring of public policies and services	• Monitoring of public policies (*Fundación Futuro Latinoamericano, Asamblea Ecuatoriana por los derechos de los Jóvenes*) • Monitoring of public works (*Red Cántaro* coordinated by Secretariat for National Administrative Development [SENDAS], *Cabildos Metropolitanos*) • Monitoring of the quality of public services (Citizen Report Cards by *Fundación Esquel*) • *Veedurías* (*Asociacion Cristiana de Jóvenes*, CAMAREM, CEDOCUT, *Coordinadora Política de Mujeres*, FODIMUF, CEDENMA, CARE)
Oversight	• Procurement oversight (CLD) • Observatories (*Comite Ecuménico de Proyectos*, Observatorio de Política Fiscal, SENDAS, CEDOCUT, Participación Ciudadana, *Observatorio Social del Ecuador-Habitus, Federación de Barrios de Paute*, SERPAJ, *Movimiento Mi Cometa*)
Judicial sector	• Justice Network (*Red de Justicia*) • Justice observatories (Fundación Esquel)
Civil society and laws	• Lobbying for the approval of laws (CLD, *Coalición de Control Social, Jubileo* 2000) • Monitoring of respect for the rights of indigenous peoples in elections (*Fundación QUELLKAJ*) • Monitoring of implementation of the consumer law (*Tribuna Ecuatoriana del Consumidor*)

Source: World Bank (2006).

The following are evidence of the role civil society is playing in improving the governance arena in Ecuador, demanding accountability from the state, monitoring national government actions, and influencing public policies:

- The enactment of the Law of Transparency and Access to Information in 2004, which guarantees free access to all public information for the first time in Ecuador's history, was passed after a two-year campaign led by a coalition of civil society organizations.[3] The law has been a key factor facilitating citizens' participation in decision-making and enabling citizens to monitor the use of public resources.
- The Civil Commission for the Control of Corruption (or the Anticorruption Commission—CCCC) was established to carry out an array of programs with the aim of preventing, identifying, and investigating corruption within the public sector. The organization is a public entity, with autonomy from the executive, a board designated by civil society, and programs that are carried out in partnership with civil society organizations. To pursue its mandate, the CCCC promotes anticorruption networks and supports the creation of public auditing committees at the local, regional, and national levels.
- In January 2006, a regulation for the creation and functioning of public auditing committees was approved by Congress, requiring periodic reporting to the CCCC.
- The Code of Penal Procedures for the Electoral Law was defined with the oversight of CLD and *Participación Cuidadana.*
- Elections and electoral spending, and information campaigns to the public on the work of parliamentary commissions, are monitored by CLD and *Participación Cuidadana.*
- Additionally, observatories are gathering information, generating public debate, and constituting bodies for public oversight. For example, the Observatory of Public Policies monitors public contracts and public works (OFIS, SENDAS), the Observatory of Foreign Debt monitors the level and impact of foreign debt, and the Observatory of Fiscal Policy and the Observatory of Cooperation monitor the inflows of foreign assistance.
- At the local level there are also experiences of participatory planning and budgeting, in which citizens take part in formulating local development plans and prioritizing their investment preferences through the budgeting process. An estimated 10 percent of municipalities in Ecuador have participatory budgeting processes.
- Indigenous people's organizations (IPOs) have also had a historical trajectory on advocating indigenous rights and public policies on accountability. Since 1998, legislative reforms enabled indigenous leaders to take part in the formal political arena. IPOs have developed a governance approach in a number of municipalities, and a provincial government is applying a participatory budgeting process consistent with traditional and cultural practices.

While still weak, the supply of transparency mechanisms by the state has made some promising progress that needs to be deepened. While overall the implementation of the Law of Transparency and Access to Information has been slow, there are encouraging examples of public entities at both the national and local levels that have made significant efforts to increase citizens' access to information. The agreements signed between the MEF and Grupo Faro with the Observatory of Fiscal Policy to provide budgetary information represent innovative and encouraging initiatives. The collaborative relationship between both institutions has proved fruitful, with the MEF consistently responding to the information requests presented by civil society.[4]

Continuing to strengthen transparency and accountability relations between government and civil society will require special attention in some areas:

- Increasing public access to information by (i) raising awareness about the transparency law among public officials, (ii) enhancing public sector capacity to generate and disseminate information, and (iii) developing user-friendly information systems and tools for the public.
- Strengthening the capacity of public sector institutions to establish relationships of accountability with civil society by establishing accountability of systems, tools, and processes toward citizens and service users' engagement and feedback.
- Increasing civil society's technical capacity to actively engage in decision making of public policies at the local level. Despite improvements, civil participation at the municipal level is amongst the lowest in the region.

Progress in Modernizing Public Sector Financial Management

In 1999, the use of the Integrated Financial Management System (*Sistema Integrado de Gestión Financiera*—SIGEF), which has both budgeting and accounting modules, was made official in the entities of the nonfinancial public sector. SIGEF is currently used in 168 institutions, managing 78 percent of the central government's budget. A total of 2,300 institutions feed monthly information to the central level in order to integrate it and enable the creation of comprehensive reports. At present, 99 percent of the central government budget's aggregated information is available through SIGEF. (Civil service reform is also a critical aspect of governance improvement in Ecuador. This issue is discussed in detail in the chapter 11, on labor markets.)

The development of SIGEF induced an important positive change in public financial management. Still, problems related to the processing and timely provision of information generated strong critiques against the system from within the public sector. An assessment of SIGEF in comparison with other similar systems in the region noted that despite the noticeable progress made in terms of standardization, coverage, and institutional culture in the use of SIGEF, some conceptual, technological, organizational, and legal problems remained.

Among the strengths identified were the following:

- Standardization of information that renders the central government's information comparable.

- Broad coverage.
- Strengthened capacities of both the managing entity and the institutions that use the system.
- Contribution to better internal control.

The following weaknesses were identified:

- No solution is provided to adequately integrate the approximately 2,300 financial entities in the central government or to facilitate the participation of the sectoral level in the system. This produces a decentralized model wherein the details of financial operations are available only among the financial agencies, rather than being integrated into a comprehensive system; and the comprehensive level only requires aggregated monthly information from the operational level, meaning that detailed operative information is lost and there is no synchronization between the MEF and the financial entities.
- The connection between planning processes and budget development is weak, which translates into an excessive number of budget modifications.
- Control over commitments and extrabudgetary movements are insufficient.
- The system lacks knowledge and control over the floating debt.
- From a technological point of view, the instruments on which the system was developed are now obsolete and do not take advantage of the communication and interaction of Internet facilities. The current technological environment renders the maintenance of the system costly and complex, limits scalability and performance, and leads to extremely high support costs in terms of human and financial resources.

As a result of these assessments, the MEF concluded that it was necessary to establish a new organizational model, to update the legal and regulatory framework, and to develop a new integrated system that will take advantage of the new technology. Modernizing and updating the system would generate undeniable benefits in terms of expanded coverage; the evolution to a transactional system that carries out internal budget control; improved information management and productivity; reduced development, operation, and maintenance costs; adaptability to new rules and procedures; and increased transparency and reliability in financial management data.

After evaluating the alternatives and examining the characteristics of the systems of Guatemala, Colombia, and Argentina, authorities opted for the Guatemalan model, which has one of the best designs and performance records in the region. At the beginning of 2006, an agreement was signed between the governments of Ecuador and Guatemala to provide technical assistance in the development of a new version of SIGEF.

The modernization process that has been launched broadly seeks to (i) attain 100 percent coverage of the financial information from 2,300 financial entities; (ii) provide an instrument that offers solutions and integrates dispersed sectors; (iii) perform the budget execution process in a Web environment; (iv) perform financial planning of the four-month budget execution of commitments and the monthly execution of accrual (commitment control and cash harmonization); (v) realize the basic operation registries under the accrual principle; (vi) enable the MEF to perform different payment concepts (cash programming, wire transfers) using the single account system; and (vii) develop an interoperability framework between the financial system and other public administration and financial management systems.

Progress in Modernizing the Procurement System

The current procurement system does not create a transparent, efficient, competitive, and predictable environment. The current rules include much too burdensome requirements and have spawned a proliferation of procedures, the results of which are neither economically efficient nor transparent. Among the main constraints of the procurement system are the following:

- The system is highly fragmented, as a large share of fiscal resources is subject to special procurement regimes; subnational governments follow their own rules; there are neither oversight nor follow-up policies and no standards have been developed for the preparation of bidding processes and procedures.
- Open and competitive buying procedures are only applicable to acquisitions over US$171,284 for 2006, leaving a significant percentage of purchases outside of these procedures.
- Some of the existing regulations hamper transparency (that is, the lack of clarity in contract-assigning rules, multiple exceptions, barriers to foreign bidders, contract negotiations, and exclusion mechanisms) and restrict efficiency (that is, excessive discretionality in buying modalities for less competitive bids, a large number of approval and control procedures, excess bureaucracy, and duplications). Also, numerous provisions were developed exclusively for a written process and are incompatible with electronic transactions.
- The selection of consulting services is regulated by another body of legislation, which needs improvements related to the use of open competitiveness instead of preselection, parallel negotiations, and so forth.
- As for executing bodies, the main problems are related to the low education and training levels of human resources, ineffective planning of acquisitions and internal controls, contract fractioning, delayed payments to contractors, cost and time indexation in labor contracts, and inefficient or nontransparent practices protected by weakness of the regulatory framework.
- The lack of a definition of objectives for a solid procurement system, unsustained leadership within the government to jump start reforms, and lack of a sustained and coordinated national dialogue are some of the main conditions that prevented the establishment of procurement policies. This lack of policies was also a consequence of not having a leading agency in charge of formulating policies and supervising the bidding process system, or able to function as the champion for the proposed regulatory reforms.

- The absence of a responsible body has induced public agencies to de facto take on some responsibilities that either do no lie within their competence or are inconsistent with their mandate. Some of these responsibilities have been formalized but do not necessarily correspond to or are incompatible with agencies' main roles. For instance, the CCCC is in charge of the management of the Contratanet system, and review of bidders' protests—which is a primarily administrative issue—is done by the comptroller general. When a clear definition of responsibilities for policy design and supervision is missing, not only are key implementation instruments not adopted, but spontaneous positive developments can be reverted. For instance, the bidding standards prepared by the comptroller general were briefly used, but they are not compulsory and are employed just as a reference.

Progress in Modernizing the Judicial Sector

A judicial reform project began in the late 1990s, implemented by ProJusticia (*Unidad de Coordinación para la Reforma de la Administración de Justicia*), a unit that reports directly to the chief justice and is in charge of coordinating initiatives for the reform and modernization of the judicial sector (World Bank 1994, 2002).[5] The focus of the reform effort was to (i) increase effectiveness and transparency in the judicial process, (ii) expand the use of ADR within the court system, iii) improve access to justice by the public in general and, in particular, women, and (iv) foster initiatives on court reform, legal research, and education.

The reform project financed specific investments that improved case management as well as court infrastructure in selected pilot courts (figures 10.4 and 10.5; tables 10.3 and 10.4). An ADR program allowed trial courts to refer selected cases to specialized mediation units; this component alleviated the workload of certain courts and provided effective dispute resolution services. A grant scheme was also established to promote increased participation of civil society stakeholders in judicial reform activities. A particularly successful subcomponent financed pilot projects for

Figure 10.4. Average Delay Reduction in Pilot Courts

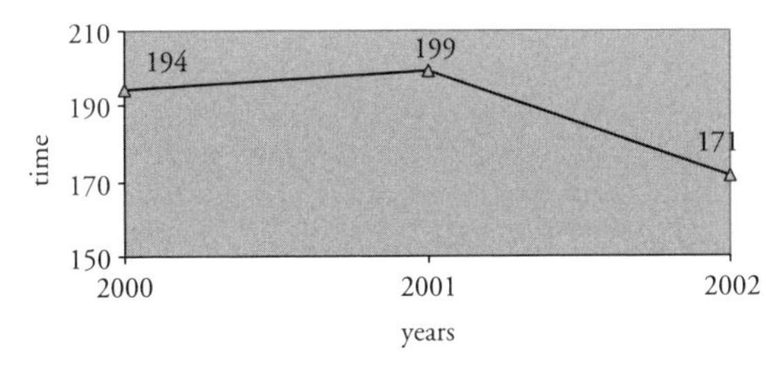

Source: World Bank (2002).

Figure 10.5. Number of Cases Adjudicated by Civil Court per Month

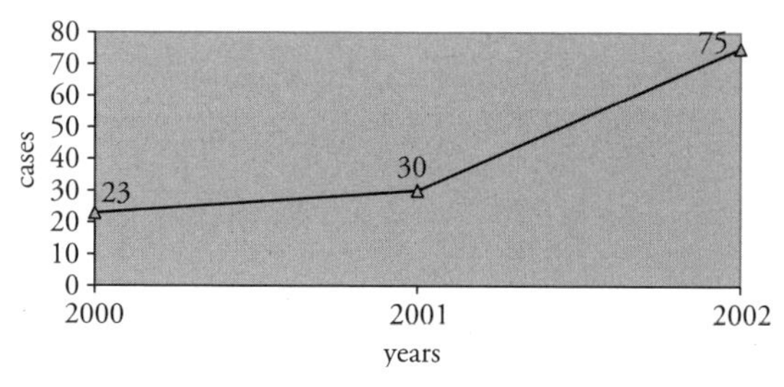

Source: World Bank (2002).

Table 10.3. Average Duration of a Civil Case in Quito (Days)

Court	*Baseline*	*Final project result*
First	1,185	266
Second	1,207	175
Third	1,732	332
Fourth	1,260	297
Fifth	1,096	204
Eleventh	1,717	422
Twelfth	840	236

Source: World Bank (2002).

Table 10.4. Clearance Rate in Pilot Courts (Incoming Cases Adjudicated) (percent)

City	*2000*	*2001*
Quito	8.56	27.38
Guayaquil	19.1	54.29
Cuenca	44	134.66

Source: World Bank (2002).

the provision of legal services for eligible poor women and their children aimed at enabling them to obtain and secure their legal entitlements, and take other actions to improve their socioeconomic position. An independent evaluation study confirmed the success of this component (Rodriguez 2000; also see Dakolias 2003).

The reform effort concentrated on formal justice in Ecuador's most populous cities (Quito, Guayaquil, and Cuenca) and recommended that the reforms be expanded to the rest of the country. The project demonstrated that the real locus for change may be outside the capital. The reforms undertaken in a small city like

Cuenca, and to a lesser extent, Guayaquil, were more sustainable than in the Quito courts. The support of the highest authorities of the judiciary and the judges of the superior courts was critical in all cities.[6]

The project provided the judiciary with concrete experience in implementing major judicial reforms. Donor assistance and financing should supplement the effort and resources available in the country to pursue further reforms in the medium and long terms. Otherwise, in the short term the limited capacity of sector institutions may erode public confidence. More recent donor-supported work included efforts to strengthen the solicitor general's managerial capacity, policy formulation, and legal skills, and a project to improve access to alternative means of dispute resolution and qualified legal representation for poor rural and urban communities, indigenous peoples, poor women, and children.

III. Policy Alternatives to Increase Transparency and Accountability in Public Administration

The policy options outlined below are all designed with a view to improving the transparency and accountability of Ecuador's public sector, reducing corruption, and—in the end—helping to reestablish a bond of trust between the citizenry and public institutions.

Financial Management

The ongoing modernization of SIGEF and the design of the new version of the system appear headed in the right direction (box 10.2). The technical diagnosis performed on the basis of international best practices has provided an adequate road map for the needed changes and improvements. This road map has received a degree of consensus from MEF technical staff on the importance of the new attributes of the system. The new system's conceptualization and design are almost complete and ready to be tested.

SIGEF's operation and maintenance responsibility lies exclusively in the hands of MEF officials, which will smooth the adoption process once the new version of the system is ready. The following are the main recommended policy options to enhance the process for SIGEF modernization, to improve the quality of the information the system provides, and to facilitate greater transparency and accountability in public financial management:

- Ensure political support from the MEF's highest-level officials to complete the SIGEF modernization plan, and confirm technical support currently being provided by the government of Guatemala.
- Establish an oversight mechanism to detect and quickly correct obstacles to successful implementation.

Box 10.2. Preconditions for the Development of a Financial Management Information System

1. *Authorities' commitment and ownership are clear.* They have a clear institutional designation, clear authority to implement, and active involvement with no undue delegation to suppliers.
2. *Preconditions are ready for reform.* Authorities are prepared to reengineer work practices, the environment encourages reform, sufficient skills and training are available, users are sold on the system, and the steering group is active and representative.
3. *Project design is sound.* Adequate time is being taken on the design phase, users are fully involved in the specification, design is not too ambitious in scope, and the timetable is realistic.
4. *Management of project is capable.* Managers have adequate management skills; they are motivated to reform; a full-time implementation team has been identified; and an in-house or outsourced maintenance capacity is identified, in place, and properly costed.
5. *Adequate resources are assured.* Sufficient funds are available to cover costs, which might exceed anticipated costs, to meet resource demands caused by operating two parallel systems, and to cover long-term operation and maintenance of the system.

Source: Diamond and Khemani (2005).

- Undertake the necessary legal, institutional, and procedural changes to support the new version of SIGEF and improve the current public financial management arrangements. This should help to simplify processes and procedures, increase transparency, and introduce more efficiency in the management of public finances.
- Create coordination mechanisms with the comptroller general, tax agency, and central bank, as they are key players of the system. Some preliminary steps have been made, but it will be useful to institutionalize these mechanisms.
- Bring budget classification in line with the GFSM2001.
- Continue strengthening MEF officials' awareness and capacity to provide the public with reliable, timely, and relevant information while fostering dialogue with citizens, in part through the new SIGEF.

Civil service reform, which is also an essential aspect of public sector financial management and governance in general, is discussed in detail in chapter 11, on labor markets.

Public Procurement

Efforts developed by the CCCC through the implementation of Contratanet, the comptroller general's office's design and approval of procurement standard documents, and the characteristics of the current regulatory framework all provide an opportunity for changes that may have important impacts in fiscal savings, increased transparency, and efficiency in the public procurement area. These short-term reforms can focus on high-priority actions that do not involve legislative reforms and can be executed in the short run by the executive. However, they could contribute to integral normative and institutional reforms in the medium term.

Short-term reforms could be introduced by focusing first on pilot agencies (for instance, in the health, education, and public works sectors, PetroEcuador, and some selected municipalities). In a second phase, once tangible results have been produced, they could be adopted as a national policy.

The following interventions would strengthen government acquisitions in the short term:

- *Institutional arrangements to facilitate synergies.* An interinstitutional agreement (the MEF, SRI, CCCC, and General Management Office) could define the roles and responsibilities of each entity in terms of public procurement. Considering the role of the MEF in financial management, the advances in the development of the new version of SIGEF, and its potential procurement module, it may be advisable to assign the MEF the leading role.
- *Transparency mechanisms.* Decree 122 for acquisitions over US$171,000 and Decree 1565 for acquisitions under US$171,000 established transparency mechanisms for these acquisitions. To enforce these rules, the MEF could approve financial management regulations that will condition the disbursement of resources on the compliance with the decrees. Another possible measure is to improve the Contratanet system to enable the use of information at the acquisition analysis stage.
- *Minor procurement processes.* The standard documents for procurement activities approved by the comptroller's office could be revised, improved, and adopted. Regulations can be approved to provide incentives for entities that adopt the developed standards, such as quick value-added tax return (the tax authority, SRI) and transparency seals (CCCC).
- *Provider registry.* Creating a unique provider registry and linking the electronic acquisition systems (Contratanet and the SIGEF procurement module) to the SRI and superintendencies will improve tax supervision.
- *Quick gains programs.* Following successful experiences implemented in other countries, the MEF could develop these programs to coordinate public acquisitions and improve quality of goods and fiscal savings. Such a program can have a strong impact in the short term, as the quick gains program implemented in Brazil's Ceará state has proved; that program resulted in over 15 percent savings

in public procurement costs (box 10.3). Although a thorough analysis of the government's expenditure profile is needed, preliminary data indicate that with a better procurement strategy, Ecuador could save US$50 million to US$100 million per year, depending on the items to be included, the participating buyers, and the level of coordination and support from key institutions.

In the medium and long term, it would be advisable to complete the institutional framework for public procurement. Looking at the experience of procurement

Box 10.3. Quick Gains: The Case of Ceará, Brazil

The first World Bank–sponsored "quick gains" experience was in the state of Ceará in northeastern Brazil, which resulted in savings of US$70 million per year. Investment costs with consultants for the initial work and six categories was only US$226,000. Two categories were subsequently done in-house using the same methods, and four additional categories were contracted for US$213,000. The price today would be roughly US$100,000 per category. The enormous success and total engagement by the Ceará government provided the impetus for efforts to replicate the program in Brazil and elsewhere. Activities, savings, and reforms are summarized below.

	Savings/year		
Group	*US$ million*	*% of 2004*	*Principal actions taken*
Fuel/gasoline	0.6		New, global contract for various agencies, with 9.6 percent price savings
Fuel/credit card	0.4		Control of consumption in small municipalities
Telephone	2.5		New, global contract for various agencies
Medicines	8.9		Bulk contracts, e-procurement, standardization of medicine/prices
Security services	6.1		Three global contracts based on space and other building characteristics
Electricity	1.1		Changed working hours to avoid peak price period 17:30–20:00
Air fares	0.4		
E-procurement	51.4		29 months of savings on common goods and services
Total	71.4	25	
Estimated for 10 additional categories	21.6	12	Food, office materials, and IT equipment, to be implemented in February 2007

reforms elsewhere in the region can provide valuable lessons (box 10.4). Recommended policy options include the following:

- Create a specialized oversight entity for public procurement.
- Complete the development of the Electronic Procurement System, ensuring that it will include transactions for minor acquisitions and electronic bidding. The benefits of such a system include increased transparency, decreased corruption, improved competitiveness, reduced transaction costs for providers

Box 10.4. International Best Practices for Improving Procurement Systems

Peru's CONSUCODE is an entity specialized in public procurement with technical, functional, administrative, and financial independence. It plays three main roles: (i) *normative*, by providing technical and legal assistance on issues related to regulatory compliance; (ii) *administrative*, by managing the providers' national record system; and (iii) *conflict resolution*, by solving conflicts derived from ensuring that regulations are complied with at the bidding stage. Peru has implemented a national system for conciliation and arbitration. It does not act as an arbitrator, but instead provides education and certification to independent professionals on local practices and regulations related to acquisitions, enabling professionals to arbitrate and resolve disputes arising in the execution phase of the contract. The agency has committed to implementing the public e-procurement system, SEACE.

Brazil's COMPRASNET offers services through the Internet to public servants and providers. The site contains information for the general public, including the legislation and a manual. Public functionaries have access to specific applications such as a discussion forum, prices of government contracts, and modules for processing bidding documents and amendments, among other services. This connection enables the public servants to download a catalog of goods and services and search for documents. It also includes updated news and a section to identify companies that have acquired the documents for presenting offers.

Mexico's COMPRANET enables buying agencies to announce their acquisition of goods and public works online. Bidding can be done electronically, online and in real time, with statistical data to monitor the performance of providers of goods and services. It also has a safe electronic exchange for the general public and individuals interested in specific information on processes, coded applications, and electronic signatures to protect privacy. The system is supported by a legal statute, and all transactions and electronic signatures are legally binding.

and government entities, and shortened procurement processes. Contratanet may be a good starting point for the development of an integral system.

- Develop interfaces between SIGEF and the procurement system. The procurement module to be used in the new SIGEF version will be the underpinning for this effort.
- Promulgate a new public procurement law that addresses, among other things, outstanding legal issues such as the compulsory use of the procurement system (Contratanet or the new one to be developed) and standard documents by all public sector entities, and amendments to ensure consistency between the law and possible free trade agreements (such as the threshold for the application of standard tender procedures and the lifting of preferences, preparation times, bases for granting tenders, and review procedures).

Judicial Reform

This section describes the improvements in service delivery and operations the judiciary could implement in the short and medium term.

Improved Transparency and Accountability of Judiciary Management

The judiciary has already adopted the modern court management model, which includes the separation of administrative and jurisdictional functions, and now seeks to incorporate an oral argument–based system that requires new management tools. The judiciary could implement a national court management system based on a model that seeks to ensure optimal court productivity while protecting due process guarantees. This would include a thorough review of internal policies and procedures to identify opportunities for possible reorganization, redefinition, and redistribution of functions and responsibilities, and overall process reengineering. A major input into the integrated management system will be the statistical information generated by judicial districts and specific court offices to ensure that this input is appropriately collected, analyzed, and disseminated.

The judiciary could also develop and implement standard information and communications technology (ICT) systems at the central level so that information from decentralized units can better inform sector decision making. Strategic planning with a focus on the needs of end users should inform the choice of services and technological platforms. This would require policies to consolidate some functions; varying levels of technological development will gradually meet the same standards within a limited resource envelope. The judiciary may also wish to conduct an assessment of its ICT resources and prepare an investment plan (including the possible implementation of the electronic signature for judicial processes).

Three additional areas may be proposed to strengthen the judiciary's transparency and accountability in case processing: (i) monitoring and evaluating judges' performance as managers of caseloads and courtrooms, (b) experimenting with different courtroom staffing patterns, and (c) analyzing medium- and long-term user demands, including possible revision of jurisdictions and incentives to use ADR mechanisms. Also, the judiciary may develop statistical databases on caseloads, individual and court performance, impact and outcome indicators, and user profiles.

Sector authorities should make available to the public basic information about how the judiciary functions. The Law of Transparency and Access to Information provides the right framework to strengthen the transparency of the judicial sector's structure. The authorities that are not yet prepared to meet the challenges of the law should gradually develop the mechanisms to provide the right level of public disclosure. Information disclosed may include judicial decisions, compensation packages, performance indicators of judges, administrative and court staff, attendance records, court dockets, and so forth.

Predictability and Reliability of Judicial Decisions

To increase the predictability and reliability of its decision making, the judiciary should focus on strengthening its capacity to handle highly complex cases relevant for economic and social development. A coordinated approach to handling these cases within strict cost-effectiveness and sustainability parameters should be developed. Personnel from the central offices of the judiciary, judges, and court staff should be involved in this exercise to analyze results and prepare proposals for further changes. It should target selected administrative, fiscal, labor, and civil courts that handle complex cases involving antitrust, insolvency and bankruptcy, consumer protection and environmental degradation. Specific consideration should be given to promoting the use of in-court and out-of-court ADR mechanisms. Public and private ADR systems would allow courts to focus on the handling of the most complicated cases, because relatively simple cases are more efficiently adjudicated using mediation, conciliation, and arbitration.

A diagnostic should be conducted to determine the criteria for the selection of specific court offices. Because of the different levels of readiness at the court level (in terms of experience with prior reforms, as well as human capital available) and the particular priorities of local judicial staff and users, specific actions may be structured as a "menu" of potential investments designed to improve quality standards in the handling of complex cases. Specific annual work programs could determine the amount and sequencing of such investments, which may include infrastructure (common services areas, hearing rooms) and computer equipment (hardware and software for the operation of networks and workstations).

Promotion of Social Inclusion

Authorities should seek to address obstacles preventing or limiting marginal groups' access to justice (such as high costs of attorneys or long delays in the functioning of family and tenancy jurisdictions). They may focus on the following areas: (i) strengthening legal aid; (ii) making innovative mechanisms operational for a more accessible and equitable judicial sector, such as small claims courts and justices of the peace in selected geographical areas with major transportation or communication barriers (these courts deal with issues of immediate interest for poor families, such as intrafamily violence, tenancy disputes, neighborhood conflicts, and consumer protection);

(iii) expanding mediation centers ascribed to superior courts as an expeditious ADR mechanism in civil and commercial matters; and (iv) strengthening other ADR mechanisms (conciliation and arbitration) in partnership with the private sector and civil society organizations.

These activities should take into account Ecuador's rich cultural diversity and the progress made in the area of indigenous justice systems. Specific actions to be considered for the benefit of indigenous peoples would include gender studies and strategies to handle intrafamily violence cases and strategies for the effective recognition of traditional ADR mechanisms of indigenous communities.

Transparent and Accountable Human Resources Management

The judiciary needs to (i) recruit and retain quality judicial human resources and provide them with appropriate professional development, and (ii) introduce modern concepts of human resources planning and management (including the use of incentives). These efforts would enhance the judiciary's capacity to implement a new approach to human resources that considers present and future system needs and career development and covers not only judges but also administrative staff.

Technical assistance may be required to reengineer internal practices and resolve bottlenecks in the selection process. These efforts also would facilitate interinstitutional coordination in the selection and evaluation process. The exercise would include the development of a coherent selection methodology, the review of job profiles, the adoption of consistent selection criteria, and the creation of appropriate examination mechanisms.

The new judicial training unit would focus on developing practical approaches to enhance service delivery by first defining how performance should be improved and measured, and then designing programs to achieve that end. Local realities and preferences of judges and court staff should be taken into account through participatory processes; relevant economic and social issues must be preferred to traditional legal topics. This process would include continuing legal education programs for court staff on the benefits of ADR for commercial disputes, especially among small businesses. The possibility of outsourcing training services should be considered; agreements with public and private universities and law schools might ensure a consistent professional development of judicial sector operators.

The absence of effective accountability mechanisms represents a major issue for the operation of an effective human resources management system. To that end, sector authorities may (i) strengthen their capacity to sanction serious incidents of corruption by ensuring that internal disciplinary bodies are equipped with effective investigative tools for the identification and sanction of responsible parties; (ii) establish interinstitutional coordination mechanisms to bring together groups in charge of curbing corruption in the justice sector; (iii) develop partnerships with civil society (including indigenous organizations) to encourage informed oversight of justice sector agencies; and (iv) promote an ethical value system among judicial personnel that requires the highest ethical standards.

Policy Matrix

Technical area	*Objective*	*Policy option*
Public financial management	Strengthen the ability of the government to manage public sector spending in ways that improve efficiency and transparency.	• Continue modernization of SIGEF and broaden its implementation to cover all financial management units. • Make the necessary legal, institutional, and procedural changes needed to support SIGEF. • Create coordination mechanisms between the comptroller general, the tax agency, and the central bank on budget control.
Public procurement	Reduce the cost of public sector procurement, and increase transparency to help limit opportunities for corruption.	*Short term* • Implement an overall strategy for public purchases and contracting, which could result in quick savings of US$50–100 million, with no necessary procedural or rule changes. • Enforce transparency requirements and condition disbursements on compliance. • Develop standards for minor procurement processes. • Create a provider registry. *Medium and long term* • Create a specialized entity to oversee public procurement. • Complete the development and implementation of the electronic procurement system, with an interface with SIGEF. • Pass a new public procurement law addressing issues such as compulsory use of Contratanet, standard bidding documents, and consistency with all trade agreements.

(*Table continues on the following page.*)

Technical area	***Objective***	***Policy option***
Justice	• Improve transparency and accountability of judiciary management. • Foster predictability and reliability of judicial decisions. • Enhance social inclusion. • Establish transparent and accountable human resources management.	• Implement national court management system. • Develop standard information and communication systems. • Monitor and evaluate caseload and courtroom management performance. • Experiment different courtroom staffing patterns. • Analyze medium and long-term user demands. • Strengthen capacity to handle highly complex cases of economic and social impact. • Select specific court offices ready for modernization. Remove access obstacles of marginal groups through legal aid, small claims courts, justices of the peace, mediation centers, and other ADSR mechanisms. • Reengineer human resources management. • Strengthen judicial training unit. • Establish accountability mechanisms (internal disciplinary bodies, interinstitutional coordination mechanisms, partnerships with civil society, and ethical value systems).

Annex

Table A.1. Ecuador Governance Indicators

Governance indicator	*Year*	*Percentile rank (0–100)*	*Estimate (–2.5 to +2.5)*	*Standard error*	*Number of surveys/ polls*	*Sources and underlying data*
Voice and accountability	2005	41.5	–0.16	0.12	11	List
	2004	43.0	–0.13	0.15	10	List
	2002	46.4	–0.11	0.18	8	List
	1998	55.1	+0.30	0.23	6	List
Political stability/no violence	2005	22.6	–0.83	0.22	8	List
	2004	18.9	–0.93	0.21	10	List
	2002	22.2	–0.84	0.21	9	List
	1998	23.1	–0.65	0.26	6	List
Government effectiveness	2005	13.9	–1.01	0.16	10	List
	2004	21.5	–0.83	0.16	11	List
	2002	15.3	–0.90	0.16	10	List
	1998	17.7	–0.84	0.28	6	List
Regulatory quality	2005	20.8	–0.83	0.17	9	List
	–2004	28.6	–0.58	0.18	9	List
	2002	29.1	–0.61	0.19	8	List
	1998	48.3	+0.12	0.40	5	List
Rule of law	2005	22.7	–0.84	0.14	14	List
	2004	30.8	–0.70	0.13	14	List
	2002	29.3	–0.69	0.14	12	List
	1998	30.3	–0.73	0.20	10	List
Control of corruption	2005	24.6	–0.81	0.15	11	List
	2004	26.0	–0.79	0.16	11	List
	2002	12.3	–1.04	0.16	10	List
	1998	20.6	–0.81	0.23	8	List

Source: Kaufmann, Kraay, and Mastruzzi (2006).

Table A.2. Comparison of Governance Indicators with Other Countries of the Region

	Control of corruption		*Voice and accountability*		*Political stability*		*Govt. effectiveness*		*Regulatory quality*		*Rule of law*	
	Rank 2005	***% change (1998–2005)***	***Rank 2005***	***% change (1998–2005)***	***Rank 2005***	***% change (1998–2005)***	***Rank 2005***	***% change (1998–2005)***	***Rank 2005***	***% change (1998–2005)***	***Rank 2005***	***% change (1998–2005)***
Argentina	41.9	–11	59.4	3.8	37.7	–17.5	47.8	–22.1	25.2	–52.6	36.2	–22.9
Bolivia	23.6	–16.1	44	–15.4	15.1	–26.9	23.9	–29.7	32.7	–46.1	27.1	–11.4
Brazil	48.3	–15.4	57	–6.3	40.6	13.2	55	0.5	55	2.3	43	–9.9
Chile	89.7	4.4	82.6	17.9	75.9	18.8	86.1	–1.5	90.6	0.5	87.4	2.3
Colombia	53.2	26.7	36.7	–3.9	4.2	–2.4	53.1	–3.8	54	–7.1	32.4	1.1
Costa Rica	66.5	–9.5	76.3	–10.7	70.3	–13.7	64.1	–8.6	68.8	–12	65.7	–10.3
Dom. Rep.	32.5	–2.3	51.7	3.9	47.6	11.8	41.1	17.7	45.5	–4.7	33.3	–17.2
Ecuador	24.6	4	41.5	–13.6	22.6	–0.5	13.9	–3.8	20.8	–27.5	22.7	–7.6
El Salvador	44.3	–5.7	52.7	2	40.1	–9.9	45.9	–12	57.4	–36.7	44	0.7
Grenada	71.9	12.6	71.5	–7.2	61.8	4.3*	62.7	17.2	62.9	13.6	59.4	–1.7
Guatemala	17.7	–6.8	35.7	0.9	21.7	2.4	29.7	–18.6	46.5	–30.8	14.5	–7.1
Guyana	37.9	–13.1	60.9	–13.5	32.5	–8.5	34.4	–16.3	39.6	–14.6	26.1	–31.1
Haiti	1.0	–11.7	10.1	–19.9	3.8	–5.6	5.3	–8.1	11.9	–2.9	1.9	–12
Honduras	31.5	12.4	42.5	–11.6	25	–13.2	31.6	–8.6	37.1	–28.4	27.5	2.0
Jamaica	39.9	–11.6	63.3	–4.3	34.9	–7.6	51.2	26.8	60.4	–6.1	37.2	–9
Mexico	43.8	3.1	54.1	15.9	36.3	10.8	57.4	–6.7	62.4	–9	39.6	2.1
Nicaragua	35	16.9	46.9	–0.4	39.6	8.9	24.9	–9.5	42.6	–16	32.9	14.1
Panama	49.8	0.8	61.8	0.4	43.9	–3.3	58.9	2.4	60.9	–30.2	51.2	–3.6
Paraguay	7.4	–0.4	41.1	1.5	28.3	2.4	23.4	13.8	22.8	–10.2	16.4	–5.7
Peru	40.9	–14	48.8	23.2	18.4	–6.6	33	–32.6	55.9	–22.4	28.5	–4.2
Uruguay	74.4	4.3	76.8	8.2	65.6	1.9	68.9	–6.2	61.4	–20.4	61.8	–3.1
Venezuela, R. B. de	16.7	–0.9	31.9	–22.7	11.8	–17.4	23	6.7	12.4	–33.9	9.2	–20.6

Table A.3. Regulatory Quality, Selected Countries, 2005

Country	*Percentile rank (0–100)*	*Standard error*	*Number of surveys/polls*	*Sources and underlying data*
Argentina	25.2	0.17	10	List
Bolivia	32.7	0.17	9	List
Brazil	55.0	0.17	10	List
Chile	90.6	0.17	10	List
Colombia	54.0	0.17	10	List
Costa Rica	68.8	0.17	9	List
Dominican Republic	45.5	0.17	9	List
Ecuador	20.8	0.17	9	List
El Salvador	57.4	0.18	8	List
Guatemala	46.5	0.18	8	List
Honduras	37.1	0.18	8	List
Mexico	62.4	0.17	10	List
Nicaragua	42.6	0.18	8	List
Panama	60.9	0.17	9	List
Paraguay	22.8	0.18	8	List
Peru	55.9	0.17	9	List
Uruguay	61.4	0.17	9	List
Venezuela, R. B. de	12.4	0.17	10	List

Source: Kaufmann, Kraay, and Mastruzzi (2006).

Table A.4. Rule of Law, Selected Countries, 2005

Country	*Percentile rank (0–100)*	*Standard error*	*Number of surveys/polls*	*Sources and underlying data*
Argentina	36.2	0.13	15	List
Bolivia	27.1	0.14	14	List
Brazil	43.0	0.13	15	List
Chile	87.4	0.13	15	List
Colombia	32.4	0.13	16	List
Costa Rica	65.7	0.14	13	List
Dominican Republic	33.3	0.14	13	List
Ecuador	22.7	0.14	14	List
El Salvador	44.0	0.15	11	List
Guatemala	14.5	0.14	12	List
Honduras	27.5	0.14	13	List
Mexico	39.6	0.13	15	List
Nicaragua	32.9	0.15	11	List
Panama	51.2	0.14	13	List
Paraguay	16.4	0.14	13	List
Peru	28.5	0.13	15	List
Uruguay	61.8	0.14	13	List
Venezuela, R. B. de	9.2	0.13	15	List

Source: Kaufmann, Kraay, and Mastruzzi (2006).

Notes

1. The International Budget Project coordinated a study of budget transparency in 10 Latin American countries (Argentina, Brazil, Chile, Colombia, Costa Rica, Ecuador, El Salvador, Mexico, and Nicaragua) using indicators such as accountability of the budget, citizen participation in budgeting, budget monitoring, changes to the budget, and information on public debt (CDES 2005).
2. Tax courts are located in Quito, Guayaquil, Cuenca, and Portoviejo.
3. *Coalición Acceso a la Informacion Publica* was created in 2002 by several civil society organizations (such as *Instituto Latinoamericano de Investigaciones Sociales, Fondo Justicia y Sociedad of the Esquel Foundation,* and *Proyecto Latinoamericano de Medios de Comunicacion* of the Friedrich Ebert Foundation, among others) to lobby for a law on transparency and access to public information in Ecuador.
4. The World Bank has supported several government transparency initiatives with grants, including "Strengthening Governance in Ecuador: Support to Transparency, Fiscal Literacy and Social Auditing" (2004, on information and budget transparency); "Grassroots Capacity Building for Social Auditing for Enhanced Service Delivery to the Poor" (2005, being implemented by the CCCC); and "Andean Social Accountability Initiative" (2006, to take stock and learn lessons from existing accountability mechanisms in the Andean region).
5. This project was supported by a World Bank loan, and in part was based on two Bank sector assessments: Ecuador Judicial Sector Assessment (World Bank 1994) Washington DC, August 1994; and Ecuador Legal and Judicial Sector Assessment, World Bank, Washington DC, December 2002.
6. ProJusticia has also established a unique reputation as a coordination unit for the justice sector that facilitates information sharing and decision making. After 10 years of existence it has a track record for the implementation of donor-financed projects that should benefit any future initiative in the sector.

Bibliography

Bellver, A., and D. Kaufmann. 2005. "Transparenting Transparency: Initial Empirics and Policy Applications." World Bank, Washington, DC.

Burki, Shahid Javed, and Guillermo Perry. 1998. *Beyond the Washington Consensus: Institutions Matter.* World Bank Latin American and Caribbean Region Viewpoints series. Washington, DC: World Bank.

Corporación de Estudios para el Desarrollo. 1999. "La Ruta de la Gobernabilidad: Informe Final del Proyecto CORDES-Gobernabilidad." CORDES, Quito, Ecuador.

Corporation for Latin American Development. *Viviendo la Democracia.* Electronic Bulletin (issues 20, 24, 26, 27, 29).

Dakolias, Maria. 2003. "Impact of Legal Aid—Ecuador." World Bank, Washington, DC.

Diamond, Jack, and Pokar Khemani. 2005. "Financial Management Information Systems in Developing Countries." IMF Working Paper 196. International Monetary Fund, Washington, DC.

Facultad Latinoamericana de Ciencias Sociales. 2004. "Political Institutions, Policymaking Processes, and Policy Outcomes in Ecuador." Unpublished draft. Inter-American Development Bank, Washington, DC.

Fretes-Cibils, Vicente, Marcelo M. Giugale, and José R. López-Calix. 2003. *Ecuador: An Economic and Social Agenda in the New Millennium.* Washington, DC: World Bank.

Kaufmann, D., A. Kraay, and M. Mastruzzi. 2006. Governance Matters V: Governance Indicators for 1996–2005. Washington, DC: World Bank.

OECD (Organisations for Economic Co-operation and Development). 2006. "Methodology for Assessment of National Procurement Systems-Based on Indicators from OECD-DAC/World BankProcurement Round Table. Version 4. OECD, Paris.

OSCIDI (Oficina de Servicio Civil y Desarrollo Institucional de la Presidencia de la República). 1999. *Estadisticas del Recurso Humano y Estructuras Sector Publico Ecuatoriano.* Quito: Ministerio de Relaciones Exteriores.

Rodríguez, Marcela. 2000. "Empowering Women—An Assessment of Legal Aid under Ecuador's Judicial Reform Project."

World Bank. 1994. "Ecuador Judicial Sector Assessment." World Bank, Washington, DC.

World Bank. 2002. "Ecuador Legal and Judicial Sector Assessment." World Bank, Washington, DC." http://www4.worldbank.org/legal/leglr/LJR—Ecuador.pdf.

World Bank. 2004. *Foundations for Institutional Reform in Ecuador.* Background documents prepared for the Institutional Reform Project. Washington, DC: World Bank.

World Bank. 2006. *Civil Society's Role in the Governance Agenda in Ecuador: Assessing Opportunities and Constraints.* Washington, DC: World Bank.

World Bank and IADB (Inter-American Development Bank). 2006. *Ecuador: Actualización de la Evaluación del Sistema de Adquisiciones del País (ESAP)/Reporte Final.* Washington, DC: World Bank and IADB.

11

Labor Market and Civil Service in Ecuador

Jeffrey Rinne and Carolina Sánchez-Páramo

Executive Summary

Ecuador's economy requires a flexible labor market, both to absorb internal and external shocks and to promote the economic growth needed to curb poverty. Thus, despite the recovery of employment and labor incomes from the crisis that was ended by the dollarization, constraints still compromise the flexibility of the labor market. This inefficiency arises from the rigid salary-setting system, which bears no relationship at all to sectoral productivity, and from the challenging provisions of laws that cover permanent workers. Both productivity and labor conditions in the formal sector are deteriorating as a result of the rise of informality and extensive outsourcing. Ecuador can counter this condition by simplifying the current labor market regulation, which would allow salary-setting consistent with sectoral productivity and promote a greater flexibility in the formal permanent employment regulations. These reforms would best be set in motion by the involved sectors (employers and employees) through a tripartite dialogue.

Adequate provision of public services is important and requires that reforms to the civil service be continued and strengthened. Initiatives are ongoing to improve management and optimize human resources and to unify and control payrolls. However, their implementation is still weak, making it important for reforms to strengthen the involved institutions (especially the National Technical Secretariat for Human Resources Development and Public Sector Compensation), broaden the coverage, increase the support merit-based policies, further develop systems and database for human resources management, and speed up the rationalization of resources.

I. Labor Market in Ecuador

Employment is fundamental to improving life quality and curbing poverty, but it depends on productivity.[1] Labor incomes represent 90 percent of poor (80 percent of nonpoor) households' total expenditure in the urban areas, thus job creation is the most important channel through which the poor can move out of poverty (World Bank 2004a). Job creation relies to a great extent on labor productivity, which in turn relies on human capital accumulation and enterprises' expansion opportunities—these issues have clearly been identified by the current administration's government plan (box 11.1). Employment growth also depends on regulations regarding the interaction between the demand and supply of labor, which will be discussed in the following three sections: the first describes the recent developments in the private labor market, the second will assess its main problems, and the last section concludes with policy options to overcome the identified problems.

Box 11.1. Government Plan 2007–11 and Its Relation to Labor Markets

The current government, in its *Plan de Gobierno* 2007–11, calls for important changes in the labor market, within a framework of economic reactivation, incentives for investment, productivity increases, strengthening of human capital, and technological innovation and adaptation, with a vision of equity and active government participation under the main objective of promoting decent and well-paid jobs.

The government intends to promote private investment in labor-intensive sectors such as tourism, housing, and rural development, supported by public investment in infrastructure, public services, and education. Modifications in the regulatory framework point toward controlling extensive outsourcing, establishing salary protection against inflation, and limiting public sector salaries. Business comanagement will be promoted in the private sector in order to control excessive profits, especially as a result of monopolies and oligopolies. Hiring of youth and other marginalized sectors will be promoted by remunerated internships, direct incentives for hiring, and employment agencies, in addition to risk-shared projects through a development bank. Equal labor conditions for women will be promoted, guaranteeing benefits and seeking their economic independence. As employment creators, small and medium enterprises (SMEs) will be the focus of several promotion initiatives.

Background

Employment and Unemployment

Postcrisis labor market improvements were determined by macroeconomic performance. The 1998–99 crisis and the dollarization in 2000 have had profound and lasting repercussions for the labor market. The unemployment rate rose from 6 percent in 1990 to 14.4 percent in 1999, owing to the high volatility of the economic activity during that period (table 11.1). A countercyclical increase also occurred in the overall occupation rate, from 58.4 percent in 1994 up to 63 percent in 1999, as the households sought to deal with the shortfall in incomes. Since dollarization, unemployment decreased gradually to a level slightly under 8 percent in 2005, reaching levels equal to the precrisis era, despite a higher growth rate than in the 1990s. Contrary to other economic indicators, the overall occupation rate remained steady after the crisis, which could explain to some extent the slow reduction in unemployment statistics.

Table 11.1. Economic Growth and Key Indicators for Labor Market
(percentage)

			Employment rate			*Unemployment rate*		
	GDP growth	*Overall occupation rate*	*Total*	*Employment*	*Under-employment*	*Total*	*Open*	*Hidden*
1990	2.7	55.7	93.9	44.2	49.7	6.1	4.7	1.4
1991	5.2	60.3	91.5	45.8	45.7	8.5	5.7	2.8
1992	1.5	62.0	91.1	43.3	47.8	8.9	6.2	2.7
1993	0.3	60.6	91.7	44.5	47.2	8.3	6.4	1.9
1994	4.7	58.4	92.9	47.8	45.1	7.1	5.4	1.7
1995	1.7	58.8	93.2	47.3	45.8	6.9	5.4	1.5
1996	2.4	58.7	89.6	46.3	43.3	10.4	8.3	2.1
1997	4.1	59.6	90.8	50.4	40.4	9.2	7.1	2.1
1998	2.1	61.7	88.5	46.2	42.3	11.5	8.7	2.8
1999	–6.3	63.0	85.6	28.8	56.8	14.4	10.1	4.3
2000	2.8	60.2	91.0	30.6	60.4	9.0	5.9	3.1
2001	5.3	66.5	89.1	33.4	55.7	10.9	5.9	5.0
2002	4.2	61.6	90.8	37.1	53.8	9.2	5.5	3.7
2003	3.6	62.2	88.5	33.7	54.8	11.5	7.7	3.8
2004	7.9	62.8	91.4	37.3	54.1	8.6	5.8	2.8
2005	4.7	62.4	92.1	36.2	55.9	7.9	5.3	2.6

Source: INEC.
Note: Overall occupation rate: Number of employed/economically active population (EAP). Underemployment: Employed people who involuntary work fewer than 40 hours per week + employed people who work 40 hours or more per week but receive wages below the legal minimum. Open unemployment: Unemployed people who sought a job during the five weeks of reference. Hidden unemployment: Unemployed people who are willing to work but who did not search for a job during the weeks of reference.

Developments in the labor market have had some effects on women and children. Women showed a propensity to increase their participation in the labor market, even though it remained significantly below male participation. From 1997 to 2005, female participation increased from 43 percent to 48 percent, while male participation remained about 71 percent during the same period. The crisis and continued migration of Ecuadorans, especially males, could have created incentives for increasing the proportion of female labor, particularly in the informal sector. For example, women face worse labor conditions than men regarding salaries and benefits, despite an average education level superior to that of men (Beckerman and Solimano 2002). Similarly, an increase in child labor was shown to be a likely way to help compensate for the shortfall in the real family income after the crisis. Even though Ecuador signed all the basic agreements with the International Labour Organization (ILO) regarding child labor, implementation remains limited. In 2003, the United Nations Children's Fund (UNICEF) calculated that over a million children below 17 years of age, mostly boys, were working in Ecuador.

Though the labor market situation in 2006 was better than in 1999, suggesting that the negative effects of the crisis and dollarization may have been only temporary, other changes emerged during the same period that call that optimistic view into question. First, a large number of working-age Ecuadorans emigrated from the country and in this way relieved the pressure on the labor market (figure 11.1). According to Larrea and Sánchez (2004), 10 percent of the economically active population (EAP) may have migrated (Ecuador received more than US$1.5 billion in remittances during 2003). A clear reflection of this is that unemployment is below the national urban average in cities like Cuenca, which have had high outmigration rates.

Figure 11.1. Emigration from Ecuador

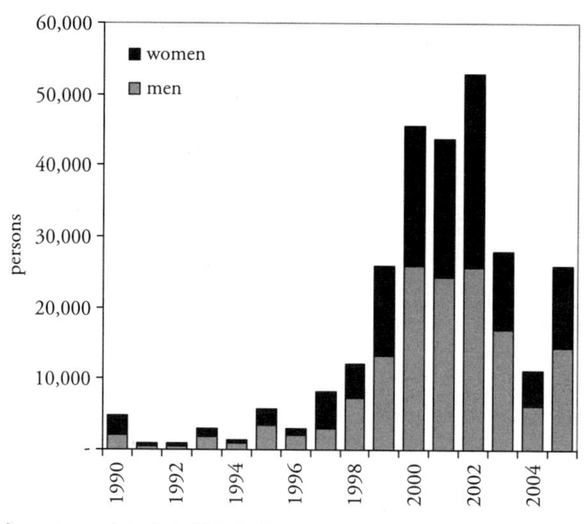

Source: SIISE Information and Analysis Unit 2007.

Despite the recovery of employment, other indicators hint at the precarious situation of the labor market. The urban underemployment rate rose noticeably in the wake of the crisis, reaching 60 percent in 2000. This number has since fallen slightly, to 56 percent in 2005, but is still well above precrisis levels. Despite some employment creation, labor rotation (hires plus separations, as a percentage of total employment) increased to over 50 percent in 2004, especially in medium enterprises, which reached rates above 70 percent (World Bank 2004b). This increase suggests that the employment recovery brought about more precarious and lower quality jobs. Furthermore, informal sector employment rose noticeably during the crisis and has remained high (table 11.2), ranking Ecuador as one of the Latin American countries with the highest rates of informality in its labor force (figure 11.2). An additional indication of precariousness is found in social security enrollment rates of the wage earners, which rose from 41 percent to 42 between 2000 and 2005, but still remains under the 51 percent observed in 1995.

Labor Income and Salaries

The crisis and dollarization have had profound repercussions on the compensation of the workforce (average real income fell 50 percent from 1995 to 1999), affecting every labor market sector equally (table 11.3). Following the crisis, real labor incomes recovered quickly, increasing almost 75 percent between 2000 and 2005, though unequally across sectors. However, during 2000–05, real salaries in the formal sector grew faster than in the informal sector, largely owing to salary increases in the public sector. The recovery of public sector employees' real salary was slow at the beginning, but during 2000–05 the growth of the real labor income of this sector sped up, reaching a level 150 percent higher than in 2000. The minimum salary followed the trend of average labor incomes, except in 2000–05, when its growth was slightly lower.

The impact has also been different among tradable and nontradable sectors. The real salary in the tradable sector registered a stronger recovery, particularly in mining, than the nontradable sector, probably owing to the strong competitiveness gained in 2000 during the continued currency devaluation prior to dollarization. However, this trend was reversed during the following years, owing mainly to the loss of real competitiveness of the Ecuadoran economy.

Table 11.2. Employment Distribution by Sector and Employment Situation (percentage of employed people)

	1995	*1999*	*2000*	*2005*
Modern sector	43.5	44.1	40.9	41.3
Informal sector	44.4	41.6	44.2	45.1
Agriculture	6.2	7.2	8.5	8.4
Domestic services	5.9	7.1	6.4	5.2
Public salaried (% total salaried)	23.0	18.1	17.2	16.6

Source: SIISE Information and Analysis Unit 2007.

Figure 11.2. Labor Force Informality in Latin America

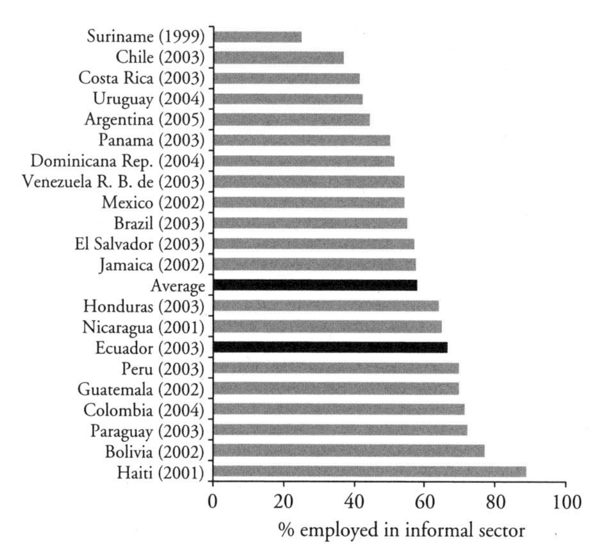

Source: World Bank (2004b).

Problems in the Labor Market

Economic recovery could have had a stronger impact on employment, particularly on formal employment, if companies had faced a better investment climate and less-restrictive labor regulations. According to the Global Competitiveness Report (GCR) of the World Economic Forum 2006–2007, the labor market's regulatory restrictions are an important binding issue for enterprises. Ecuador has restrictions for hiring and dismissing employees (106 out of 125), low flexibility in setting salaries (98), lack of relation between employees' salaries and productivity (96), and difficult relationship between employees and employers (97).

These regulatory restrictions encourage the labor market to adjust by employment quantity (or underemployment) rather than by prices. According to Doing Business 2007, the costs and difficulty to dismiss an employee are two times higher than the regional average, and firing cost is the highest in Latin America. Ecuador's employment rigidity index reached 51, compared with Latin America's average of 31.7, exceeding even sub-Saharan Africa's average (44.9), the highest regional average in the world (figure 11.3). Thus, employees by law receive 1.25 monthly salaries per year worked as severance pay, up to 25 years, in addition to other benefits. Finally, enterprises are forced by law to share yearly profits of 15 percent with employees. Within this framework, labor market shocks will be absorbed mainly by adjusting employment rather than prices, which increases unemployment, underemployment, and labor informality.

Table 11.3. Real Monthly Labor Income
(constant 2,000 US$)

	1995	*1999*	*2000*	*2005*
Minimum salary	144.6	70.0	97.7	141.8
Average labor income	214.5	102.2	146.1	254.2
Nontradable	220.1	105.7	122.2	177.0
Tradable	193.7	89.8	124.5	149.6
Farming	178.0	94.1	124.1	153.6
Mining	250.1	165.5	319.2	448.2
Manufacture	198.0	85.9	124.1	252.1
Electricity	341.0	170.3	297.6	386.8
Building industry	196.8	111.1	113.9	211.5
Commerce	213.9	101.1	158.8	219.7
Transportation	281.9	121.9	170.5	270.8
Financial services	329.3	177.7	211.9	382.6
Other services	200.0	92.1	132.6	298.6
Informal	176.2	73.2	113.3	181.5
Employer	356.5	150.5	318.6	378.5
Self-employed	169.0	68.0	114.9	171.4
Private salaried	110.2	48.1	70.7	144.2
Formal	273.1	139.6	199.1	366.0
Employer	849.3	399.9	618.2	829.5
Self-employed	300.1	146.3	272.2	347.9
Public sector salaried	265.6	140.3	184.1	461.4
Private sector salaried	230.4	115.3	174.7	295.2

Source: SIISE Information and Analysis Unit 2007.

Figure 11.3. Labor Regulation in Ecuador

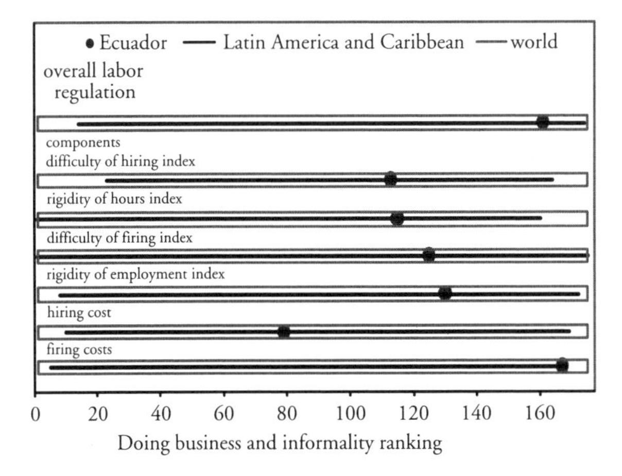

Source: World Bank (2006).

The restrictions described above explain, to a large extent, the tenuous formal job creation since 2000. Low job growth does not seem to be related to enterprises' lack of interest in hiring. In fact, according to the World Bank (2004a), a 2002 survey showed that permanent job creation intentions among companies reached 8 percent, while effective permanent job creation barely reached 0.1 percent in the same sample. According to enterprises, this gap is explained by termination costs, especially for small enterprises, and by nonsalary labor costs in large enterprises (figure 11.4).

The negative effects of regulations are partially lowered by weak compliance, owing to the large degree of informality present in the economy. Ecuador is ranked 54 out of 117 in degree of informality, behind Colombia and Panama, according to the GCR. Compliance with labor regulations is not enforced systematically by authorities, lowering the impact. Consistent with the situation described above, results coming from the *Investment Climate Assessment* of Ecuador (World Bank 2005a) showed that 87 percent of enterprises' employees are permanent.

Salary-setting mechanisms and restrictions on permanent contracts stand out as the most binding constraints that promote informality and outsourcing. First, salary negotiation is a complex process in Ecuador, both because it involves many agents who negotiate at different levels and times, and because, until recently, salaries represented only a part, and sometimes a very small part, of what workers receive, the rest consisting of supplements and allowances. Furthermore, these salary negotiations are led by the state and only marginally reflect productivity evolution. Second, formal employment has been under markedly restrictive rules. Over the past 10 years those rules have promoted extensive use of outsourcing using employment agencies

Figure 11.4. Constraints for Job Creation

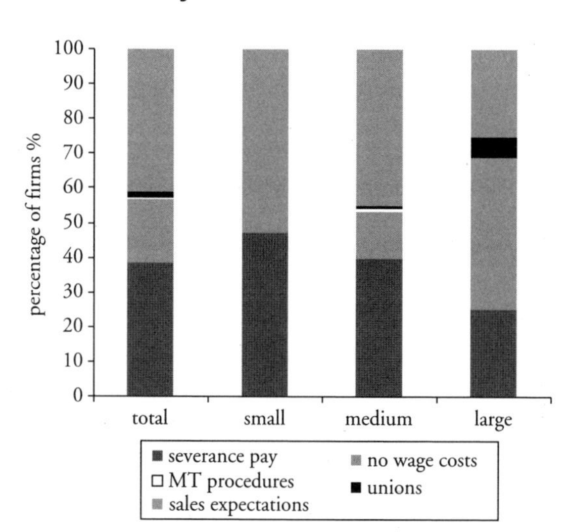

Source: World Bank (2005a).

through which temporary employees are hired to do permanent work, thus avoiding the payment of contractual obligations that a permanent employee entails.

Salary-Setting Mechanisms

Salaries are set at three levels:

- The National Wages Council (CONADES), which is a public entity, regulates the base salary and annual increases for each occupation in the different sectors of the economy, as well as the minimum salary for each sector not specifically identified by CONADES. When no agreement is reached between employers and workers' representatives within the CONADES framework, the Ministry of Labor establishes an annual increase in the base salary equal to expected inflation in the upcoming year.
- Minimum salaries specific to each occupation are established in each sector through fixed salary programs called "sectoral tables," which employers and workers' representatives renegotiate periodically. In the past, tables had to be updated once a year, but this is no longer the case. Except in the petroleum, electricity, and telecommunications industries, the tables appear to be binding, implying an automatic indexation of the entire salary distribution to increases in the minimum salary.
- Employers and workers' representatives can agree on additional salary increases (but not reductions) through collective agreements by sector or company.

This wage-setting mechanism transmits salary increases automatically through the entire salary distribution, equally across each company in every sector, and bears no relationship at all to productivity. The interaction between the tables and decisions made through CONADES and the agreements have the following effects:

- The tables, by setting relative salaries, have the ability to automatically transmit the increase in the minimum salary to the entire salary distribution. Although it may be reasonable to index the minimum salary according to inflation in order to preserve the buying power of those less favored by the distribution, it is not clear that this is the best method for all salary levels, without regard to productivity, between companies of a given sector and between different employees.
- The tables do not reflect differences in productivity between companies in a single sector and thus create considerable salary rigidity at a time when dollarization has diminished the competitiveness of Ecuadoran companies. In addition, renegotiation could create a tool for unfair competition between large and small companies in the same sector, given that the former are more productive than the latter and thus have more negotiating power in the renegotiation process.

The Economic Transformation Law (also known as TROLE I) in 2000 sought to simplify pay policy in the private sector ("salary unification," with the exception of the 13th and 14th salaries and a small number of other remunerations) and introduce more flexible and modern hiring methods, such as hourly and temporary contracts. The 2001 Social Security Law also provided that all workers, regardless of the nature of their contracts, must contribute to social security, thus equalizing to some extent the contractual obligations of so-called regular workers and those hired through temporary agencies. However, excessive rigidities remain, especially those related to salary indexation, consistency with productivity evolution, profit sharing, and termination costs.

TROLE I established the incorporation of several allowances in the minimum salary, in an attempt to expand the tax base for social security and other employment-related taxes that are traditionally paid exclusively on the basis of salaries. As a result, these measures will increase the cost of employment for employers; however, they have been implemented over five years, so that in each year during this period the base salary has incorporated 20 percent of all nonsalary components of the workers' pay.

Rigidities in Hiring Permanent and Formal Employees

Despite the efforts made at the beginning of the decade to allow some flexibility in labor regulations, informality has been rising as a share of total employment, from 42 percent in 1999 to 45 percent in 2000. A more recent but preliminary estimate suggests informality is around 60 percent of employment (World Bank 2007). In addition, temporary workers and outsourcing have been used increasingly to do permanent work, thus avoiding the payment of contractual obligations for permanent employees. According to the Survey on Employment, Unemployment, and Underemployment (INEC), employees hired through outsourcing have increased from 1 percent of salaried employees in 2003 to 1.8 percent in 2005, although this could be an underestimate (since 2003, INEC has included a question about outsourcing in its survey). Because temporary employment is exempt from some labor costs, it will likely continue, despite the introduction of hourly and temporary contracts in 2000. Some companies choose to use temporary workers because these workers often receive salaries that are below the legal minimum and also are denied special allowances or enrollment in social security (only 15 percent of these temporary workers have social security, versus 45 percent of private permanent employees).

The fear is that informality, temporary employment, and outsourcing have contributed to the deterioration of relations between employers and employees, as well as to a decrease in training and other types of company investments in human capital. *Ecuador's Investment Climate Assessment* (World Bank 2005a) points out that large turnover and the extensive use of outsourcing are related to low total factor productivity, owing to fewer incentives to invest in temporary workers' training and fewer incentives for employees to increase their productivity. A 20 percent increase in temporary workers will reduce capital and value added, per employee, by 26 percent. Similarly, a 20 percent increase in the turnover rate will induce a 14 percent decline in total factor productivity. By contrast, employee training is related to a 15 percent increase in labor productivity, controlling for other factors. Young workers, less-qualified employees, and small companies are the most affected by these conditions.

Recommendations for the Labor Market

Recommendations for Setting Salaries

The process used to set salaries must be simplified, be more sensitive to productivity, and avoid government leadership. The following recommendations could be considered:

- Suspend the indexing of annual salary increases to expected inflation in order to prevent greater deterioration of competitiveness and inflationary pressures.
- Make the recommendations of sectoral tables optional and not compulsory. The Ministry of Labor has already taken some steps toward transforming the tables into a specific minimum salary for each sector. The new minimum salary should only be a reference point and should not be compulsory.
- Increase the role of collective agreements for setting salaries. Collective agreements by sector and, particularly, by company should be the principal instrument for setting salaries that exceed base salary, so as to leave room for greater sensitivity to economic conditions.
- Gradually make rules on profit sharing optional (as an incentive to employee performance) rather than obligatory.

Recommendations Concerning the Rigidity in Hiring Formal and Permanent Workers

Current labor rules must be more flexible, the role of temporary employment agencies must be revised, and temporary employment must be controlled in order to improve the employment effective quality. The following recommendations could be considered:

- Reduce the costs to terminate formal permanent employees under new contracts, including the cost of pensions for employers. For economic policy reasons, it would be extremely difficult to take this step with existing contracts, unless a compensation mechanism could be found.
- Promote the use of temporary and hourly contracts when labor flexibility is needed. These contracts give the employer flexible arrangements and give workers formal employment and the benefits that go with it.
- Consider as a fair justification for employee termination poor economic performance of the company.

- Along with more flexible formal employment rules, control the use of temporary employment agencies and monitor the work and pay conditions of temporary employees in order to ensure that they reflect the provisions of the law, avoiding an increase in informality.
- Ensure the use of temporary contracts for temporary activities, controlling their renewal as well.

The government already has an institutional instrument to assess policy options, including those presented above, that requires strengthening. Several policy options regarding labor market issues were evaluated during a tripartite forum in 2004 hosted by the Ministry of Labor, reactivating the dialogue tables created in 1996, with participation of both employee and employer sectors. As a result of the meetings, the National Council of Workers was created and the impacts and challenges of the free trade agreement were assessed. These results were also taken into account by Congress for the elaboration of the labor reform project; however, the loss of continuity of this coordination instrument limited its impact (box 11.2).

In addition to strengthening labor market measures, the investment climate has to be improved to boost labor demand, as well as the education level and training of workers to strengthen the labor supply. Specific recommendations on these issues can

Box 11.2. Tripartite Table Dialogue

In 1996, under the leadership of the Ministry of Labor, the *Pacto Social* was created with the aim of establishing an institutional framework to define and assess policies related to productivity and employment (León 2004). A matter of concern was the impact of the dollarization and of the free trade agreements on the labor market. Since 1996, the Pacto Social has contributed to the social security reform, the creation of the National Council on Training and Professional Formation, and the Salary Unification Law (in 2000).

In 2003, under a dollarized economy and in the middle of negotiations with the United States for a free trade agreement, the government reactivated the dialogue in order to begin a forum on labor market reform. The forum also included the discussion of salary unification, the revision of salary-setting mechanisms, the hiring and firing process, social security reform, and human capital development. In addition, as part of the taxation framework reform, the elimination of the 15 percent of profit sharing rule in public enterprises was also included in the agenda (World Bank 2003).

Under the joint leadership of the Ministry of Labor and the Ministry of Economy and Finance, and the auspices of the World Bank, the Inter-American Development Bank, and the International Labour Organization, two forums took place during 2004. The first created the National Labor Council, with eight employers' representatives, eight workers' representatives, and one non-voting government representative. The second forum assessed in detail the impacts and challenges brought by the free trade agreement in negotiation with the U.S. government, especially those regarding the labor market. In addition, the forums promoted the approval of regulations for temporary employment agencies. However, the effect of both results still remains limited because of the lack of continuity of the meetings and the fact that the regulations mentioned above did not follow the coordinated mechanisms proposed by the dialogue.

Finally, by compiling the information, debates, and conclusions raised during the forums, the Labor Committee of the Congress started a labor reform project, which remains in discussion.

be found in the *Ecuador Poverty Assessment* (World Bank 2004a), the *Investment Climate Assessment* (World Bank 2005a), and other chapters of this document.

II. Civil Service

Background

Since 2000, the number of public sector employees has remained stable at around 17 percent of total salaried workers, after a gradual decrease from 23 percent in 1995. Public employees account for almost 12 percent of total employment, ranking Ecuador slightly below the average of the region (figure 11.5). The number of central government employees, without counting autonomous and decentralized agencies, is around 270,000, equivalent to 2.2 percent of the population. In addition, Ecuador currently has around 34,000 municipal and provincial employees. The data on state companies are not easy to obtain owing to a noncompliance with a Ministry of Labor requirement to provide data on employees.

Though the number of public employees increased only slightly between 1998 and 2005, government salary expenses fluctuated sharply the first years after dollarization, increasing from less than 5 percent of GDP in 2000 to 8 percent of GDP in 2002—equivalent to an increase in current expenditure from 25 percent of total expenditures in 2000 to 45 percent since 2002. Since then salary expenses have stabilized around this level. The 1998–99 fiscal crisis fueled inflation and a decline of over 70 percent in the real value of base salaries between 1997 and 1999. Though GDP fell more than 5 percent between 1998 and 2000, the central government's

Figure 11.5. Public Employment in Latin America

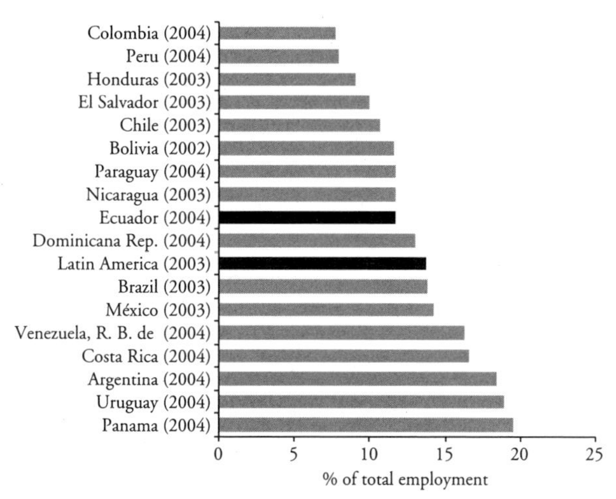

Source: ILO (2005).

personnel expenses shrunk as a portion of GDP, from 7.7 percent to 5.2 percent (BCE 2002). The 2000 dollarization stopped the deterioration of real salaries and triggered a reversion between 1999 and 2000, in which the real labor income of a public employee increased 31 percent (figure 11.6). Recovery continued during the following years: real labor income grew 150 percent between 2000 and 2005. As a portion of GDP, Ecuador's salary expenditure is in line with the standards of the region.

Different categories of public employees have different regulations (table 11.4). The legal code for civil service employees is the 2003 Civil Service and Administrative Career Organic Law and the Public Sector Salary Unification Law (box 11.3). The National Teaching Corps, regulated by the Teaching Career and Teaching Salary Scale Law, has approximately twice as many employees. Another 7 percent of public employees are regulated by the Labor Code, as are private sector employees. Physicians are in the category of "scheduled professionals" but have their own salary schedule, whereas the other eight professions also in this category receive a single salary and grading system. Finally, the police and armed forces have their own salary schedules, as do the judiciary, the legislature, and foreign service personnel. Contract employees are governed by the Law on Contracted Professional Services.

As a consequence of the promulgation of the new Civil Service Organic Law in September 2003 (box 11.3) and its amendment in January 2004, the National Technical Secretariat for Human Resources Development and Compensation in the Public Sector (SENRES) was created, unifying in a single institution the responsibility for management, recording, and control of public employees as well as the establishment of the unified salary scale. This law brought about the dissolution of the previous human resources and pay institutions, known as the National Council for Public Sector

Figure 11.6. Personnel Expenses in the Nonfinancial Public Sector
(% current expenditure and % GDP)

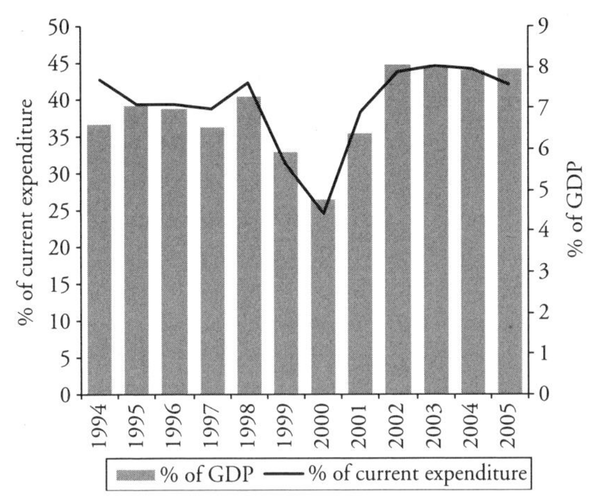

Source: BCE, MEF.

Table 11.4. Structure of Government Jobs under the Public Employees System, 2002

Employment system	*% Total*
Civil service and administrative career law	16.3
Labor code	7.3
Teachers	34.5
Armed forces	17.6
Police	8.0
Scheduled professionals (excl. physicians)	0.9
Physicians	2.1
Judiciary	1.5
Legislature	0.1
Foreign service	0.2
Contracted professional services	0.8
Others	10.7

Source: MEF.

Renumeration (CONAREM) and the Civil Service and Institutional Development Office (OSCIDI). Prior to the promulgation and implementation of the law, each government agency had to carry out an administrative restructuring in 2003 that included process definitions, organizational structure design, and the assignment of skilled human resources (which consequently served to identify redundant personnel). This law, as well as the centralized electronic system of compensation and benefits payments set in motion by the central bank, allowed the government to tighten payroll control.

Box 11.3. The New Civil Service Law

Civil service reform was started by the 2003 Civil Service and Administrative Career Organic Law and the Unification of Public Sector Salary Law of 2003 (amended 2004). The aim of these two laws was to base public employment on merit and to establish proportionality between public employees' remuneration and responsibility level. The new law reduced the number of salary categories (from 21 to 14), eliminated a substantial number of monetary payments that distorted the common salary scale, and froze public employee salaries that were above the levels established by the new scales. However, the law does not include teachers, soldiers, police, or subnational public servants, who represent 55 percent of the 360,000 current public employees. The law created a new institution called the National Technical Secretariat for Human Resources Development and Compensation in the Public Sector (SENRES), in charge of the supervision, registration, and oversight of public employees. SENRES also is responsible for establishing the Unified Monthly Salary Scale. The salary scale unification began in January 2005 and is to be completed within five years. In parallel, at the beginning of the law's implementation, the government checked the staff of each ministry and found redundant employees in several of them. The Central Bank of Ecuador has implemented a consolidated electronic database to register the payments and benefits of public employees. Finally, the SIPREM (Budgetary Remuneration System of the Public Sector) was created in the Ministry of Economy and Finance (MEF) to maintain up-to-date public employment and compensation data.

In January 2005, regulations for the new law were issued, establishing the remuneration system and setting the floors and ceilings for public sector salaries, based on designated compensation bands (*bandas remunerativas*). The floor of this band is determined by the monthly unified remuneration, and the ceiling is set by labor market conditions, establishing the possible range for each level of the salary scale. Modifications to the salary bands will be related to the growth of the economy.

Base pay in the past typically represented barely a fraction of a public employee's total compensation. Countless monetary allowances were added over the years. Consequently, it was not uncommon for an employee's salary to include between 20 and 30 different items. Unification of the vast majority of these allowances paid to central government employees (excluding teachers and police) is under way. This process will be carried out gradually and will end by 2010 in order to mitigate the incremental-costs effect, which could be around US$240 million according to the Ministry of

Labor's calculations. This increase arises because of (i) the difference between the basic salary of the new scale and the former basic salary plus allowances,[2] (ii) the new payroll classification, based on academic and work histories, of some employees according to the new 14-grade scale, and (iii) indemnities to be paid because of the termination of redundant employees. In addition to the basic salary, the 13th and 14th salaries, overseas allowances, cost-of-living allowances, overtime, and supplemental time compensation will remain.

These public administration reform measures are consistent with the general framework of the 2002 Fiscal Law, aimed not only at consolidating the spending and public debt management, fiscal prudence, and modernization of the financial control system, but also at developing a database for investment, human resources, and public sector purchases. The long-term objectives of this new framework are to strengthen and safeguard fiscal account sustainability. However, steps toward full implementation of the law are still unrealized.

Principal Problems

The recording, management, and control of the payroll, assigned to SENRES, have shown marked delays in their implementation. No government agency has a complete overview of the number of public employees in each department, their positions, and categories. There is no department for tracking employees who have been terminated in the public sector (and who have received indemnities) and for ensuring that they have not returned to government employment through some other avenue. In addition, since the disappearance of the National Personnel Directorate in 1998, no agency is working to ensure that the merits of the applicant are considered when vacancies are filled. Finally, the current coverage of the Civil Service Law (about 45 percent of public employees) is insufficient.

The implementation of adjustments suggested by the assessment of redundant personnel, plus other related measures, has been too limited. The possibility for savings through reducing personnel based on evaluations in each ministry is considerable, as are the opportunities to increase efficiency through the reassignment of personnel (box 11.4). However, in the 37 ministries, departments, and agencies that went through this restructuring process before the salary unification law was approved, staff cutbacks amounted to an average of only 3 percent. The cost of the indemnities is an important factor that limits the restructuring process.

Part of the logistics infrastructure necessary for the full implementation of the reform has not been completed. The government had to establish a human resources management information system within SENRES that is linked to the Integrated Financial Management System's (SIGEF's) database and that offers public disclosure through a Web page. However, the MEF set in motion SIPREM, although with a much more limited scope, which allows for the creation and management of payroll, covering at this stage the following sectors: police, education, and armed forces. SIPREM is expected to be linked with SIGEF in order to unify

Box 11.4. Human Resources Management Systems: Some Examples of Positive Fiscal Impact

In Argentina, the provinces of Misiones and Salta consolidated personnel information and pay processing in a single, electronic database, which led to a more transparent payroll and elimination of improper or unnecessary salary payments. These modernization efforts generated considerable savings. In Misiones, an analysis carried out in October 2000 identified approximately US$1 million in annual savings realized since the Integrated Personnel Administration System (SIAP) was implemented, covering approximately 18,000 staff members.

The sources of these savings included the following:

- Fifty eight employees with improper multiple employments (116 positions)
- Special payments that should have expired
- Payments for functions that were not performed
- Additional pay where the personal requirements for the payment were not met
- Duplicate payments for family members
- Payments for employees that exceeded those of their superior (prohibited by law)
- Employees eligible for retirement

As a result of these system improvements, provincial governments can readily produce detailed, disaggregated information on the wage bill for the budget process. Moreover, the impact of proposed personnel policies can be modeled before they are enacted.

In Indonesia, the implementation of the salary system found that there were 300,000 fewer civil servants than were registered in the salary system (out of 4.1 million). In Paraguay, a census of public employees developed in 2003 identified more than 4,000 civil servants in some sort of irregular situation (ghost employees, inappropriate salaries, and so forth). Bolivia is implementing a very important modernization effort through the creation of a salary control and payment database system. The system has allowed the registration of 318,000 central government public employees. About 90 percent of these employees receive their payment through the banking system using a biometric system, which will prevent irregularities in the payment of salaries.

payroll information, and with other databases (tax, social security, and civil registry) to detect inconsistencies. However, SIPREM's current design will not be useful in other spheres of human resources management (selection, performance assessment, and so forth), though the information contained in SIPREM could be used in the future by a more complete and dynamic system.

Policy Options

Ecuador's public administration reforms that began in 2003 have made important advances to reestablish reliable information and government control over public employment and the government wage bill. However, additional steps will be needed to complete this process, as well as to bring about improved quality and performance in Ecuador's public administration. The following recommendations could be considered:

- Strengthen the SENRES, the institutional development of SENRES is insufficient. Although it received the resources belonging to the former OSCIDI, those are not enough to ensure compliance with the large responsibilities assigned to this institution.
- Broaden the coverage of the Civil Service Law to labor categories not considered initially.
- Deepen the development of information systems and the database of public employees (including state companies that are the responsibility of SENRES) and link them with SIGEF.
- Assess the feasibility of sanctions against agencies that do not comply with information requests or set up systems related to human resources management.
- Identify sources of financing to cover the cost of indemnities due to the termination of redundant personnel who are already identified. In this case it could be useful to assign part of the income from the rise in oil prices.
- Carry out evaluations to identify potentially redundant employees and regularly monitor the human resources requirements of public agencies.
- Keep separate lists of those who have left civil service, including the causes, and link those lists with the unit in charge of authorizing appointments, so that employees who have received indemnities do not return to civil service.
- Enforce the legal provisions regarding merit-based recruitment, thus reducing clientelism.

Policy Matrix

Area	*Problem*	*Policy option*
Private labor market	Salary-setting mechanism that is complex and rigid	*Short term* • Reduce the role of sector tables, and make them optional. *Medium term* • Suspend the indexing of annual salary increases to expected inflation. • Increase the role of collective agreements for setting salaries. • Gradually make rules on profit sharing optional, as an incentive to employee productivity rather than compulsory.
	Rigidities for formal and permanent hiring	*Short term* • Promote the use of temporary and hourly contracts when labor flexibility is needed. • Ensure that temporary contracts are used only for temporary activities, and control their renewal. *Medium term* • Consider a company's poor economic performance as a fair justification for employee termination. • Control the use of temporary employment agencies and monitor the work and pay conditions of temporary employees. • Reduce the termination costs for formal permanent employees under new contracts.

Civil service	Institutional weakness of SENRES	*Short term* • Take measures to strengthen the authority of SENRES. *Medium term* • Deepen the development of information systems and database for human resources management.
	Insufficient coverage of new Civil Service Law	*Medium term* • Broaden the coverage of the Civil Service Law to other labor categories.
	Insufficient rationalization of public employment	*Short term* • Identify sources of financing to indemnify redundant personnel and set in motion the early retirement program for public employees. • Limit new hiring. *Medium term* • Eliminate vacancies and promote early retirement. • Carry out evaluations to identify potentially redundant employees and regularly monitor the human resources requirements of public agencies. • Enforce the legal provisions regarding merit-based recruitment, thus reducing clientelism.

Notes

1. All figures on activity, employment, and unemployment discussed in this section are based on the Survey on Employment, Unemployment, and Underemployment (INEC), except where noted otherwise. Independent experts and other users in Ecuador have expressed concern regarding the survey's sampling method and the comparability of its data over the time.

2. The law establishes, wisely, that it would be neither legal nor politically possible to reduce the current wage of an employee. Therefore, the new basic salary will be calculated by dividing by 12 all the payments received by an employee (excluding the 13th and 14th salaries, and a small amount of other allowances).

Bibliography

BCE (Central Bank of Ecuador). 2002. *Boletín Anuario No. 24*, 104. Quito: BCE.

Beckerman, R., and A. Solimano. 2002. *Crisis and Dollarization. Stability, Growth and Social Equity.* Washington, DC: World Bank.

Government of Ecuador. 2006. *Plan de Gobierno del Movimiento Pais 2007-2011. Un Primer Gran Pasó para la Transformación Radical del Ecuador* (proposed plan of government).

ILO (International Labour Organization). 2005. *Labour Overview 2005. Latin America and the Caribbean (First Semester Advance Report).* Lima: ILO.

Larrea, C., and J. Sánchez. 2004. *Proyecto de Apoyo en la Elaboración del Plan de Empleo para Ecuador: 2004–2006.* Final Report to subregional ILO office for the Andean Countries. Lima: ILO.

León, G. 2004. *Dialogo por el Desarrollo Productivo y Laboral Avances e Impactos.* In: *El Mercado Laboral del Ecuador (II): Evaluación del Dialogo Tripartito sobre la Modernización del Mercado Laboral.* Washington, DC: World Bank.

Rinne, J. 2003. Administración de recursos humanos del estado. Los avances y el camino por recorrer. World Bank presentation. Washington, DC: World Bank.

Unidad de Información y Análisis. 2007. *Informa de Desarrollo Social 2006. Evolución y Estructura del Mercado Laboral Ecuatoriano: Análisis 1990-2005.* Quito: Secretaría Técnica del Frente Social.

World Bank. 2004a. *Ecuador Poverty Assessment.* Poverty Reduction and Economic Management Sector Unit, Latin America and the Caribbean Region. Washington, DC: World Bank.

World Bank. 2004b. *El Mercado Laboral del Ecuador (I): Tendencias y Recomendaciones de Política.* Washington, DC: World Bank.

World Bank. 2004c. *Project Appraisal Document on a Proposed Loan in the Amount of US$20 Million to the Republic of Ecuador for an Institutional Reform Project.* Washington, DC: World Bank.

World Bank. 2005a. *Ecuador—Investment Climate Assessment.* Washington, DC: World Bank.

World Bank. 2005b. *Republic of Ecuador—Country Financial Accountability Assessment.* Washington, DC: World Bank.
World Bank. 2006. *Doing Business 2007. How to Reform.* Washington, DC: World Bank.
World Bank. 2007. "The Informal Sector: What It Is, How We Measure It, and Why We Care," Draft. Washington, DC: World Bank.
World Bank and IADB (Inter-American Development Bank). 2005. *Creation of Fiscal Space for Poverty Reduction in Ecuador. A Fiscal Management and Public Expenditure Review.* Washington, DC: World Bank.
World Economic Forum. 2006. *The Global Competitiveness Report 2006–2007. Creating an Improved Business Environment.* Geneva: WEF.

12

Decentralization

Jonas Frank

Executive Summary

Ecuador faces the challenge of how its intergovernmental system can lead to better services, more equity in resource distribution, and strengthened fiscal responsibility. The take-off period of decentralization between 1997 and 2003, which was based on aggressive transfers of revenue, appears to have concluded. Much of the fiscal cost of increasing grants from central to subnational governments has been absorbed in the national budget. Reforms now should focus on how the intergovernmental system, as problematic as it may be, can set the right incentives to deliver better services and more equitable subnational government spending. The current period of relative calm and inertia may, ironically, constitute a favorable setting to achieve this shift in policy. Rather than transferring new responsibilities on a large scale—which may not lead to the desired service improvements—an effort should be made to set the conditions so that the present set of responsibilities already under the control of subnational governments contribute to improving services. This requires (i) setting minimum levels of transparency as the underpinning for successful decentralization, (ii) shifting the focus from transfer of expenditures to expenditure coordination, and (iii) establishing equity-enhancing measures in order to reverse the antipoor bias in subnational government expenditures.

The author would like to thank Fernando Rojas, Edgardo Mosqueira, Omar Arias, and Juan Manuel Quesada for valuable comments to earlier draft versions, as well as, in Ecuador, Verónica Gallardo and Mario Piñeiros (of CONAM), and Maria Dolores Almeida and Amelie Torres (of GTZ) for supporting the elaboration of the document and valuable discussion.

I. Introduction

In 2003, the debates on a reform of the intergovernmental system and the fiscal as well as administrative framework centered on increasing transfers to subnational governments. The challenge for Ecuador was the extent to which these transfers could be increased—following the demands of subnational governments—and still be compatible with fiscal responsibility in the context of the recent dollarization of the economy. The country had just emerged from an intense debate on provincial autonomy, which suggested a deep regional conflict over political and fiscal powers, although the concept of autonomy was never really clarified. All 22 provincial councils and roughly two-thirds of municipalities signed agreements for the transfer of expenditure responsibilities in four sectors (roads, environment, tourism, and agricultural assistance), and the country was set to embark on a large-scale decentralization process.

Since then, many of the structural elements of the intergovernmental framework have remained unchanged. Ordinary transfers kept increasing—by the end of 2003 the full amount of the 15 Percent Law had been transferred—but have now stabilized; however, a wave of discretionary grants from the central government to individual provincial councils and municipalities has occurred. Only a handful of municipalities and provincial councils have effectively adopted and are managing new responsibilities in some sectors. They execute a higher share of total public expenditures, but this is not the result of a transfer of responsibilities; rather, it reflects the increase in intergovernmental grants. Subnational debt management is still not fully transparent, and sanctions have proved ineffective. Only 140 municipalities (out of 220) regularly report their expenditures. All in all, many of the problems of the country's intergovernmental framework have still not been fully addressed.

This inertia requires a new look at decentralization policy and strategy. The take-off period and aggressive revenue decentralization process from 1997 to 2003 appears to be over now, momentarily at least, and much of the fiscal cost of increasing transfers has been absorbed in the government budget. The focus today should be how this intergovernmental system, as problematic as it may be, can set the right incentives to deliver better services and more equitable subnational government spending. This period of relative calm and inertia may, ironically, constitute a favorable setting to achieve this shift in policy. Rather than transferring new functions on a large scale—which may not lead to the desired service improvements—an effort should be made to set the conditions so that the present set of responsibilities already under the control of subnational governments contribute to improving services.

As a country with 45 percent of the population living in poverty, Ecuador cannot afford to continue having low coverage in basic public services (World Bank 2004b). These basic public services are, above all, responsibilities for municipalities. Although public service coverage has improved since 1990, there are still significant deficiencies in sewerage, electric lighting, water, and solid waste removal (table 12.1). These deficiencies

Table 12.1. Basic Services Coverage
(percent)

	Sewerage		*Electric lighting*		*Water*		*Waste removal*	
	1990	*2001*	*1990*	*2001*	*1990*	*2001*	*1990*	*2001*
Costa	33	37	78	91	34	42	39	66
Sierra	48	62	80	93	44	56	49	64
Amazon	19	34	44	65	18	26	25	40
National average	**40**	**49**	**78**	**91**	**38**	**48**	**43**	**64**

Source: SIISE, INEC.

are particularly pronounced in certain regions of the country, particularly in the coastal (*Costa*) and Amazon lowlands.

Ecuador's subnational governments—220 municipalities and 22 provincial councils—play an increasingly important role in service delivery. In 2004 they executed about a quarter of public expenditures, worth 4.5 percent of GDP. The bulk of municipal spending is in basic urban services; provincial councils spend most of their resources on roads. The share of subnational spending has been growing over recent years: whereas in 2000 the share of subnational expenditures in total public expenditures was 10 percent, today subnational governments execute about 22 percent. As is explained further below, this increase is not the result of a process of transferring expenditure responsibilities; rather it reflects the trend of increasing intergovernmental grants. On the expenditure side, Ecuador has reached the average level of many other countries in Latin America.[1] Municipalities and provincial councils are less important in terms of collecting tax revenue: in 2004, subnational governments raised 1.2 percent of GDP in taxes, while the central government raised 17.1 percent of GDP. As in other countries, expenditures of subnational governments exceed their revenue-raising capabilities, leading to vertical fiscal imbalances (figure 12.1).

Given this context and the challenge of improving services within a tight fiscal space and within an intergovernmental framework that does not induce fiscal responsibility or expenditure coordination, this chapter focuses on four major areas:

- Own-source revenue generation
- Intergovernmental transfers
- Subnational debt and fiscal responsibility
- Subnational expenditures

The chapter first discusses the issues and problems of the intergovernmental framework, followed by a strategy for reform in the short and long term.

II. Issues

This section discusses the main issues of the present intergovernmental system in Ecuador. It focuses on the following areas: own-source revenue generation at

Figure 12.1. Vertical Fiscal Imbalances, 2004

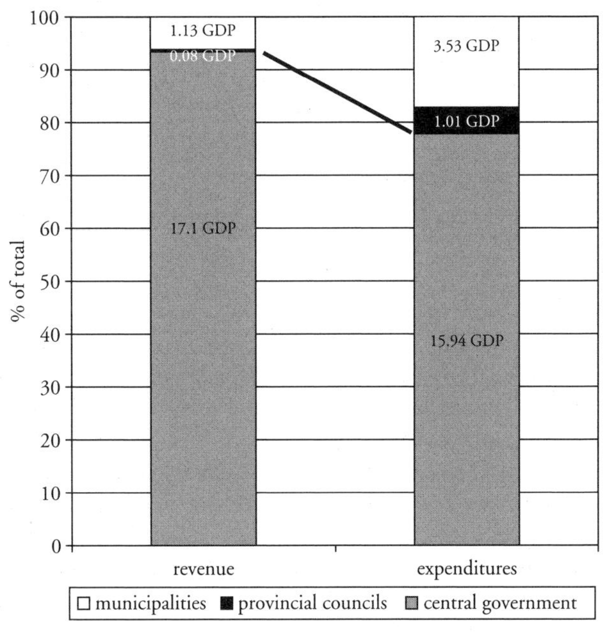

Source: Author's calculations based on data provided by CONAM (2006).

provincial and municipal levels, intergovernmental transfers, subnational debt and fiscal responsibility, and subnational expenditures.

Own-Source Revenue of Provincial Councils and Municipalities

The two main sources of revenue that originate in municipalities (own-source revenues) are the urban and rural property taxes and the improvement levies (*contribuciones de mejoras*). Municipalities also collect the patent tax, the tax on total assets, and a series of minor taxes (CONAM 2001b). Provincial councils raise only the tax for change in ownership of land. The share of municipal taxes in total taxes has increased from 2.6 percent in 2000 to 6.2 percent in 2004,[2] although significant differences in fiscal capacity across the different jurisdictions remain a large and unsolved structural problem for service delivery.

In recent years, there have been several improvements with regard to the subnational tax system, particularly for municipalities. They have been granted more autonomy to set tax rates for the property tax, within centrally established bands. As well, the 2006 reform of the municipal code eliminated some of the obstacles for tax administration and setting of user fees, which will most likely aid revenue-raising efforts, which are important for improving service delivery. On the other hand, some municipalities, such as Quito, have simplified payment of the property tax, which has created incentives for timely payment on behalf of taxpayers.

Despite these recent advances, three main problems of the subnational tax system remain. First, provincial councils lack access to more of their own revenue. As in many other unitary countries in the region—such as Bolivia, Chile, and Peru—most of the revenue of provincial councils originates from central transfers. They have very limited access to their own tax revenue. The main revenue is the real estate transfer tax (set at 1 percent of the value of the land) and improvement levies. In 2004, their transfer dependence was roughly 90 percent, and has remained largely constant over recent years (transfer dependence is defined as the percentage of transfers in total revenue). Yet given the high proportion of transfers in local budgets, mayors and particularly prefects do not feel the pain of the marginal tax dollar they spend. This, in turn, does not create incentives for efficient, cost-effective, and fiscally sustainable service delivery. In addition, it weakens accountability to voters and taxpayers, which are important conditions for effective service delivery.

Second, some types of subnational taxation are not based on fiscal correspondence, and they negatively affect national-level efforts to improve tax administration. In 2002 a law was adopted that allows taxpayers to donate up to 25 percent of the income tax to the country's municipalities. This tax revenue is problematic from several perspectives: it is provided without any link to expenditures and consequently undermines national-level efforts to improve collection of one of the few direct taxes it has for redistributive purposes. As well, there is no fiscal correspondence, since each taxpayer can freely decide to which municipality the resources will be allocated, even though he or she may not live in that jurisdiction and receive certain services and benefits in return. This separation violates the principle of fiscal federalism, that there should be a correspondence between taxes and the services citizens receive in a specific locality.

Third, the municipal tax code does not differentiate for municipalities with different financing needs. This is particularly evident with respect to large metropolitan areas that do not have sufficient own-source revenue in light of their expenditure responsibilities. In contrast to the many small and medium municipalities, the two large metropolitan cities and economic centers of Quito and Guayaquil deliver services that have positive externalities that spread beyond their jurisdiction. Also—and to illustrate this dilemma with an example—they have to cope with much of the traffic and environmental problems implied in the considerable increase in the country's stock of new automobiles, which grows at a rate of close to 90,000 new cars per year, and which affects the urban centers the most. This asymmetrical level of responsibilities is not matched with asymmetrical opportunities to access more own-source revenue. The tax code does not differentiate between the small rural municipality and the large urban municipalities. This requires new ways of financing metropolitan areas in order to strike a balance between providing more local financial autonomy while maintaining the central government's ability to redistribute revenues toward poorer areas.

Transfers

In recent years, decentralization in Ecuador was essentially transfer driven. The approval of the 15 Percent Law in 1997 set a milestone in this regard. Starting with a transfer of 3 percent of current revenue, transfers have gradually increased, eventually reaching the target of 15 percent of current revenue (in 2003). The full amount of resources was provided despite the central government's efforts to delay the increase in transfers and, sporadically, to tie the new resources to subnational governments' effectively assuming new expenditure powers. Transfers increased from 1.23 percent of GDP in 1996 to a peak of 2.53 percent in 2003, then stabilized at 1.92 percent of GDP in 2005 (figure 12.2). These developments created additional fiscal pressures at the central level, which came to full effect following dollarization in 2000. In this regard, the 15 Percent Law is a missed opportunity to put the intergovernmental framework on a more solid fiscal footing and to create better conditions for efficient service delivery.

Several problems remain with the transfer system. First, the central government carries all the risk of economic volatility. In January of each fiscal year, the Ministry of Economy and Finance (MEF) commits itself to a certain level of transfers, formalized

Figure 12.2. Intergovernmental Transfers, 1996–2005

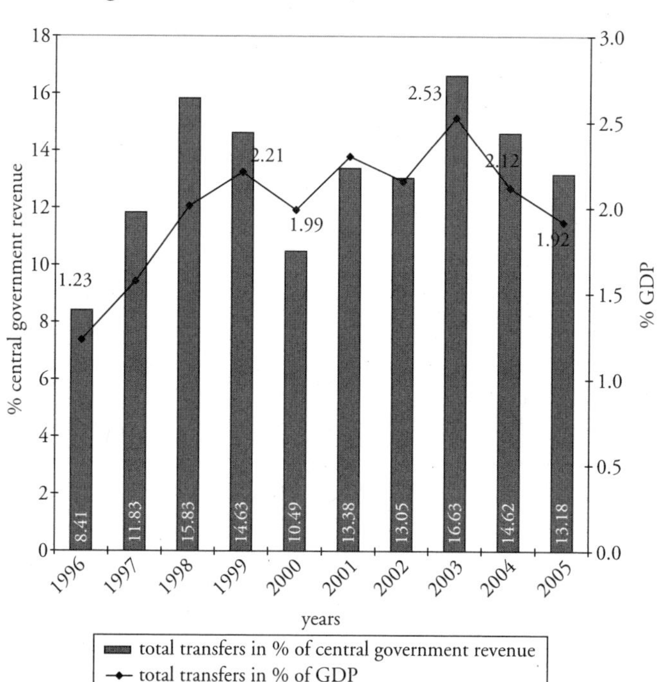

Source: Author's calculation based on information provided by MEF and CONAM.

in *acuerdos ministeriales* (ministerial accords), which list both the revenue source and amounts. These usually take into account the level of revenue available in January. Local governments then take the accords as a reference for their own budget formulation. However, this method can create inconveniences for budget execution, because the amount of revenue usually deviates substantially from initially planned levels of transfers.[3]

Second, the execution of transfers is erratic. Budget execution in the MEF typically involves a cycle of "savings" (when monthly available revenue exceeds the planned level of transfers) and "borrowing" (when monthly available revenue is lower than the planned level of transfers). These savings then become contingent liabilities of the central government that are claimed by mayors and prefects. The amount of transfer payments fluctuates strongly. In 2003, for instance, transfers remained relatively low until the middle of the year, when the MEF scaled up amounts to meet the overall target of resource amounts defined in January (figure 12.3). Similar oscillations—both in timeliness and amounts—can be observed in 2001 and 2002 (World Bank 2004b). Given the unforeseeable nature of resources, it is unrealistic to introduce multiyear subnational budgets as mandated by the Fiscal Responsibility Law (article 20), and even the mandatory quarterly budgetary projections are difficult to achieve (article 34). Finally, this does not allow subnational governments to plan and execute expenditures in a reasonable manner, which are fundamental for efficient service delivery.

Figure 12.3. Execution of Payments to Municipalities and Provincial Councils, under 15 Percent Law, 2003

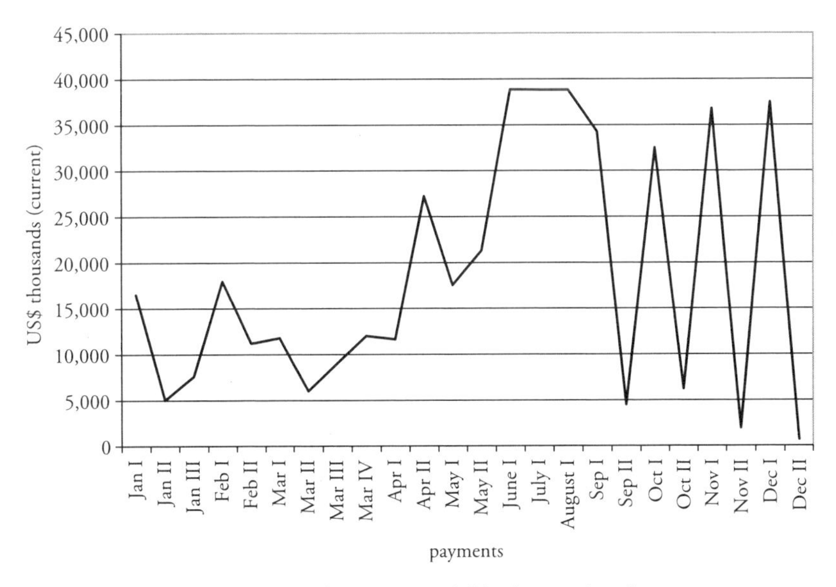

Source: Author's calculation based on information provided by the MEF (2004).

Third, considerable discretionary transfers occur. Although a precise estimate of the size of these transfers is difficult, they amount to roughly two-thirds of the amounts of the 15 Percent Law (CONAM 2006, 48). These transfers distort the compensatory goals established by the transfer system, weaken budget constraints, contribute to inequity, and undermine accountability, all of which negatively affect service delivery.

Fourth, the transfer system does not establish a coherent framework for compensation and service delivery. The system uses 17 different transfers, each establishing different criteria for resource distribution (see annex table A.3). Each transfer applies its own distribution principles and different spending conditions. Although subnational governments receive most funds from the 15 Percent Law and from the Sectional Development Fund (*Fondo de Desarrollo Seccional*—FODESEC), and previous studies claim that the distribution of these transfers disproportionately benefits municipalities with a high share of poor population (CONAM 2006, 62), the many discretionary transfers distort this incentive framework. On the other hand, the many different ordinary transfers have multiple rules limiting their use for current and investment spending. Yet monitoring and sanctions of resource use remain cumbersome and are not applied regularly.[4] It is a highly complex system that makes it impossible to create a framework conducive to efficient service delivery.

Subnational Debt and Fiscal Responsibility

The subnational debt stock has been growing over recent years. In 1997 the stock of debt was 0.63 percent of GDP, while in 2004 it was 1.4 percent of GDP. Similar to other countries—for instance Bolivia and Peru—most of the debt is concentrated in larger municipalities: roughly 60 percent of the debt stock is held by municipalities with a population larger than 100,000. In most smaller and medium municipalities, a significant share of debt is floating debt. This framework of subnational debt management and fiscal responsibility does not contribute to better service delivery from several perspectives.

First, a risk of service delivery stoppage is likely in the most populous jurisdictions due to inefficiency. This seems to be a problem in the water sector, particularly, as evidenced by the cases of Quito, Guayaquil, and Cuenca (CONAM 2006, 57). To preempt stoppage of service delivery, in these municipalities the central government has absorbed debt of municipal enterprises. It is clear that weak fiscal responsibility puts subnational government service delivery at risk, and the central government might have the ultimate responsibility.

Second, external debt is passed on to municipalities as unconditional transfers. For some of the larger municipalities—primarily Guayaquil and Quito—the central government contracts and services debt and makes these resources available for investment programs that are executed directly by municipalities. This type of debt is estimated at 1.7 percent of GDP, that is, more than the size of the debt stock held directly by all subnational governments. These debt arrangements do not induce fiscal responsibility for, or accountability of, the public services that are being financed.

Third, the precise size and types of subnational debt are unknown. Although there are recent efforts to improve reporting on municipal debt with automated systems managed by the MEF, municipalities underreport their level of debt. On the other hand, some types of debt, such as floating debt, are difficult to monitor.

Fourth, the current debt limits are too lax by international standards and do not address important sources for weak fiscal responsibility. While the limit for the debt stock (at 100 percent of current revenue) is largely in line with international benchmarks—in Colombia, for instance, it is set at 80 percent—the limit for debt service, set at 40 percent of current revenue, leaves too wide a margin for municipalities to contract debt. Also, the given indicators do not take into account the subnational government's disposable revenue that can be effectively used to service debt. At the same time, subnational governments are excluded from national rules established by the Fiscal Responsibility Law establishing limits for yearly budget growth (2.5 percent in real terms; article 3).

Fifth, sanctions for noncompliance are not applied or are ineffective. Several municipalities do violate the debt limits, but no sanctions or debt-restructuring programs have been applied, though they are compulsory for overindebted municipalities under the Fiscal Responsibility Law. In turn, the Law on Financial Administration and Control (*Ley Orgánica de Administración Financiera y Control*—LOAFYC) in article 129 stipulates that absorbed debt must be discounted on future transfers, but only a fraction of these resources were effectively reported and discounted (CONAM 2006, 57).

Subnational Expenditures

As a result of the growing level of intergovernmental transfers, provincial councils and municipalities today execute a higher share of public expenditures. In 2004, they executed roughly a quarter of all public expenditures. There are four major problems with regard to the expenditure responsibilities of subnational governments.

First, expenditure assignments among levels of government are blurred and diffuse. There is no clear delineation of responsibilities among municipalities, provincial councils, and the central government and its many implementing agencies.

- The dual political structure on each subnational level, whereby elected and delegated authority coexist, is a major obstacle for accountability.[5]
- A series of autonomous agencies exist in parallel with sector ministries and subnational governments. In 2004, regional development authorities executed roughly a third of the expenditures of provincial councils, but in some jurisdictions they exceeded the value of expenditures by provincial councils.[6] Regional development authorities execute many responsibilities that could be

decentralized, including rural roads, secondary roads, school buildings, hospitals, rural development programs, water and irrigation systems, and electrification programs, among others.
- Whereas municipalities are responsible for many urban services—streets, water and sewage, electricity, and markets—no clear delineation with regard to provincial councils has emerged.
- The jurisdiction of provincial councils is ambiguous with regard to urban and rural areas. Though they are constitutionally responsible for rural areas, involvement in urban areas is common.

Second, there is lack of investment coordination among levels of government. A higher share of investment is executed by subnational governments: in 1994 they executed 37 percent of public investment; in 2004 they executed 47 percent (CONAM 2006, 100). This raises the need for municipalities and provincial councils to better coordinate investment based on clear priorities. However, national investment is highly fragmented across social funds, regional development agencies, and sector ministries, which offer financing instruments to subnational governments in an uncoordinated fashion. This lack of coordination undermines the quality and efficiency of public services.

Third, mechanisms for transferring functions (*convenios*) are institutionally weak and do not induce clear delineation of responsibilities. The large-scale transfer of functions that was initiated in 2001, with all 22 provincial councils and 140 out of 220 municipalities signing a framework agreement for the transfer of responsibilities in roads, tourism, and agriculture, did not proceed to implementation. Only a few subnational governments effectively assumed new responsibilities, among them the municipalities of Cuenca and Manta (airports), and seven provincial councils were delegated (not transferred) the responsibility of road maintenance of the primary road network. In the meantime, the Guayaquil municipality devolved the responsibility for civil registry to the central government, after only two days of operation (the municipality had previously devolved education to the central government, in 1994).

Several problems exist with regard to how the transfer of functions proceeds:

- Coordinated approaches have been abandoned, and instead the transfers proceed in a one-to-one fashion that, if scaled up, does not lead to a better delineation of responsibilities.
- Municipalities and provincial councils do not fulfill minimum transparency requirements before adopting new expenditures.
- No service quality indicators are part of the agreements, undermining monitoring and public oversight as effective means for achieving efficiency in services.
- Arrangements for human resources are nonexistent. This is unlikely to lead to a better delineation of responsibilities across levels of government.

Figure 12.4. Subnational Government per Capita Expenditures and Consumption-Based Poverty, 2005

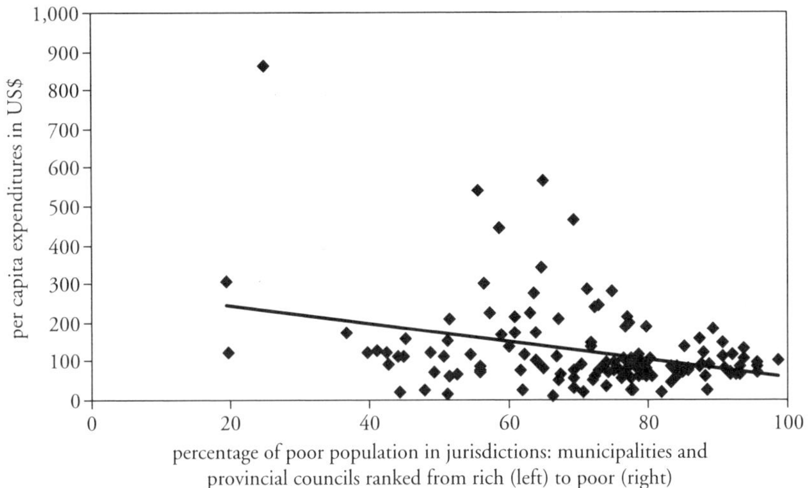

Source: Author's calculation based on SIM (2005) and SIISE (2001).

Fourth, subnational government expenditures (expenditures by both municipalities and provincial councils) are inequitable and do not contribute to poverty reduction. Municipalities with a high share of poor people living in their jurisdiction—as measured by consumption-based poverty[7]—tend to have lower per capita expenditures (figure 12.4). Not enough is known about the incidence of municipal expenditures on the population residing within the jurisdiction. In some cases, municipal expenditures might indeed be progressive. Yet it is clear that a country with such high levels of poverty as Ecuador cannot afford for a fifth of public spending, worth 4.5 percent of GDP, to be executed in an inequitable fashion.

III. Moving Forward: Strategy and Policy Options

Addressing the above-mentioned issues requires a strategy that fits within the institutional and incentive context of the country. There is a high level of informality and low level of transparency in the public sector (documented by a separate chapter on governance). Also, this strategy needs to be based on the track record and lessons learned from at least the past four years (since 2002). In addition, such a strategy needs to take into account the political economy of decentralization, where, ironically, the winners of partial decentralization provide the greatest obstacle to complete this process.[8]

Considering these different factors, the strategy for a reform of the intergovernmental system should be based on the following three elements:

1. Establish minimum levels of transparency in an incremental fashion. There is a high level of discretion in the distribution and management of resources. It would be important to continue with measures that would gradually create a constituency of actors benefiting from higher levels of transparency. The track record illustrates that the central government alone is not able to enforce sanctions for non-compliance solely in a top-down fashion. This implies that citizens and users of public services have an important role to play to create additional incentives for both central and subnational government officials. The same holds for private banks in the case of subnational debt.

2. Move the focus from transfer of expenditures to expenditure coordination. The large-scale effort to transfer expenditures to subnational governments that was set up following the year 2000 has stalled and, time and again, ended in deadlock. This process will most likely proceed on a one-to-one basis, following the initiative of individual provincial councils and municipalities. Efforts should now be put into coordinating the increasing size of subnational expenditures among the manifold executing agencies and levels of government, instead of putting too much energy into transferring new responsibilities.

3. Give priority to horizontal equity. Whenever there is a conflict between providing more fiscal autonomy to subnational governments and achieving horizontal equity, preference should be given to equity. The level of inequity in expenditures suggests that the intergovernmental fiscal system overall is not sufficiently equity-enhancing. It is paramount to address this issue over the coming years.

To present these three strategic directions, the following section lays out the specific policy options that could be adopted. These policy options should contribute to a reform of the intergovernmental system in order to improve services. If well managed and implemented, decentralization presents an opportunity to achieve this goal. Successfully strengthening the intergovernmental framework for these purposes could be very salutary. At the same time, it is clear that these policy options do not provide a comprehensive blueprint for this task.

Own-Source Revenue

Objective: The objective would be to give subnational governments more flexibility in their access to tax revenue, provided they meet minimum transparency conditions. Providing access to more revenue is particularly important for provincial councils as well as large cities. Efforts to protect national revenue collection are important, as well as efforts to keep the central government's ability to redistribute to poorer areas. While Latin American countries have generally had constraints to provide more subnational revenue authority, useful international experience is found in France (tax-base sharing) and Spain (*fuero* system), although these countries exhibit very different institutional contexts than Ecuador, particularly with regard to transparency and information sharing among levels of government as preconditions for revenue decentralization.

Short-term policy option:

- Eliminate the possibility to donate up to 25 percent of income tax to municipalities.

Long-term policy options:

- Allow large metropolitan areas (Quito, Guayaquil) greater flexibility for their resource needs, while maintaining the ability of central government to control horizontal inequity and achieve redistribution.
- Analyze the effects of giving financially responsible provincial councils (those with a good track record of collecting existing taxes as well as fiscal responsibility) access to more own-source revenue: surtaxes to national taxes, transfer of existing municipal taxes, or creation of new taxes.

Transfers

Objective: In the short term, priority should be given to providing the conditions for improved service delivery through better management of the existing transfers. In the long term, efforts should also include equity-enhancing measures. Useful international experience includes Canada (fiscal pact 1999) and different countries in Latin America that have tried to reform the transfer system at the margin (although with mixed success) include Bolivia (distribution of hydrocarbon revenue), Peru (compensation policy, royalty revenue management, sector transfers), Colombia (pooling of transfers and compensation policy), Argentina (complex distribution criteria), and Nicaragua (options to achieve fiscal neutrality in transfers).

Short-term policy options:

- Make the execution of payments of transfers more regular by improving cash-flow management at the MEF.
- Study distributional impact and incentives of the transfer system for service delivery, complemented by a study on budgetary allocation within subnational governments.

Long-term policy options:
Establish compensation policies:

- Align transfer criteria for the two most important laws: 15 Percent Law and FODESEC.

- Include social funds in a system of current transfers.
- If discretionary transfers cannot be stopped, at least publish these discretionary transfers. Strengthen public oversight mechanisms for monitoring the use of funds.

Share the risk of economic volatility among levels of government:

- Analyze the possibility of providing subnational governments with a stable and foreseeable flow of revenue without compromising fiscal sustainability and the ability of the central government to adjust during times of revenue shortfall. Consider adopting moving-average type of transfer stabilizer, which would give subnational governments more time to adjust their expenditures downward should a revenue shortfall occur, while providing the central government more budget flexibility.

Subnational debt

Objective: The policy options would need to create more transparency in subnational debt management. To achieve this, the central government needs support from the private sector as well as from other creditors, who would in turn need to exercise pressure on subnational governments to establish minimum transparency criteria. In addition, it would be important to design flexible solutions that are tailor-made to the type of debt. Also, sanctions need to be graduated to be credible and successful. Useful international experience includes Peru, Bolivia, and Colombia, which all faced similar challenges of subnational debt management. Peru's experience involved efforts to tailor policies to different types of debt and use of a different set of fiscal responsibility criteria; Bolivia's was municipal debt restructuring; and Colombia worked with a "traffic-light" debt system and tight, regular monitoring of subnational debt, mostly in a top-down and administrative fashion, as opposed to a market approach as followed by Brazil.

Short-term policy options:

- Announce that the national government will not assume the debts of local governments.
- Issue financial sector regulations stipulating that subnational debt is recognized only on balance sheets of private banks if minimum transparency criteria are met.
- Tighten existing debt regulations for debt stock and debt service.
- Regulate indebtedness with additional indicators that show real ability to pay debt (disposable revenue) and portfolio risk.
- Unify rules for subnational debt regulations (rules were adopted by the Ecuadoran Development Bank (BEDE) and the Fiscal Responsibility Law).
- Publish debt cancellations over the past five years.

Long-term policy options:

- Track and publish forms of indebtedness (contingencies, floating debt, late payments) in local governments and design specific policies for each type of debt.
- Undertake the Debt Reconversion Plan for overindebted municipalities and provincial councils.
- Make access to credit for Quito and Guayaquil contingent on evaluations of credit risk conducted by international firms.
- Establish and enforce graduated sanctions for noncompliance.

Expenditures

Objective: The policy would strengthen expenditure coordination among levels of government; it would transfer new responsibilities on a large scale only if preconditions of transparency, expenditure coordination, and basic institutional capacity were met. The policy would emphasize equity in expenditures, particularly in the key urban services (municipalities) as well as roads (provincial councils). Useful international experience includes Chile (most gradual approach in Latin America; expenditure coordination at the regional level), Colombia (most uniform transfer of responsibilities; sector approach for transfers), and Peru (established minimum service quality standards).

Short-term policy options:
1. Delineating functions of levels of government:

- Empower the *Comisión de Competencias* to be the final arbiter in resolving disputes over responsibilities.
- Align the jurisdictions of regional development authorities with the administrative division of the country to facilitate coordination with provincial councils and municipalities.
- Delineate the election of provincial councils with their area of responsibility: either urban or rural, or both.
- Coordinate external funding for regional development authorities and align with state reform priorities.
- Separate responsibilities among the deconcentrated public sector (*régimen dependiente*) and the autonomous subnational governments (*régimen autónomo*).
- Proceed with gradual transfers of responsibilities.

2. Strengthening the agreements for transfer of expenditures:

- Clarify arrangements for transfer of human resources, including labor rights and severance payments, and clarify provision for liabilities. Conduct in-depth discussions with unions with precise data on public employees affected by decentralization.

- Make access to the transfer of powers contingent on subnational governments meeting minimum standards of accounting, budgetary management, and regular submission of financial reports.

3. Achieving more equitable municipal expenditures (see also options to reform the transfer system):

- Study in-depth effects and incidence of present transfer system.
- Stop discretionary transfers and make public commitment.

Long-term policy options:
1. Coordinating public investment:

- Provided that transparency requirements are met, have the central government set up and offer a matching grant with different cofinancing shares to coordinate public investment. These shares could be differentiated by sectors and according to national priorities. The system would need to be financed out of existing resources.
- Align different social funds and other financing means with this new investment framework.

2. Strengthening the agreements for transfer of expenditures:

- Define and monitor basic (nonbureaucratic) indicators for quality of service delivery of transferred responsibilities; make indicators publicly available.
- Consider differentiating the transfer system by types of municipalities: large-scale metropolitan areas, medium municipalities, and smaller rural municipalities.
- Analyze the role of unequal fiscal capacity in subnational governments' revenue-raising ability, and analyze budget allocation decisions of municipalities, particularly with regard to the use of own-source revenue.

Policy Matrix

Area	*Problem*	*Policy option*
Own-source revenues	Own-source revenue base for subnational governments is weak, especially for provincial councils. Donations of income tax are disconnected from service provision and create horizontal inequities. The tax code does not differentiate for financing needs for municipalities.	*Short-term:* Eliminate the possibility to donate up to 25 percent of income tax to municipalities. *Long-term:* Establish greater flexibility for municipal taxation according to resource needs. Analyze giving financially responsible provincial councils access to more own-source revenue.
Transfers	Fiscal transfers are irregular, making it difficult for subnational governments to plan in the short and long term. Transfers are not sufficiently linked to incentives to promote improved service delivery. Many transfers do not work to promote greater equity in resource allocation in the country.	*Short-term:* Improve cash-flow management at the MEF for regular transfer execution. Study distributional impact and incentives of transfer system for service delivery; complement with a study on budgetary allocation within subnational governments. *Long-term:* Regarding compensation policies, align transfer criteria for main laws; include social funds in a system of current transfers; publish discretionary transfers and strengthen public oversight mechanisms for monitoring the use of funds. Consider adopting moving-average-type of transfer stabilizers.
Subnational debt	Central government has little effective control over subnational debt and weak fiscal responsibility.	*Short-term:* Announce that the national government will not assume the debts of local governments. Publish debt cancellations over the past five years.

(*Table continues on the following page.*)

Area	*Problem*	*Policy option*
		Issue financial sector regulations stipulating that subnational debt is recognized only on balance sheets of private banks if minimum transparency criteria are met. Tighten existing debt regulations and regulate indebtedness with additional indicators for debt service. Unify rules for subnational debt regulations. *Long-term:* Track and publish forms of indebtedness in local governments and design specific policies for each type of debt. Undertake the Debt Reconversion Plan for overindebted municipalities and provincial councils. Make access to credit for Quito and Guayaquil contingent on evaluations of credit risk, conducted by international firms. Establish and enforce graduated sanctions for noncompliance.
Expenditures	Expenditure responsibilities are not clearly delineated, and investment coordination is weak among municipalities, provincial councils, and the central government and its many implementing agencies.	*Short-term:* (i) Jurisdictions: Empower the *Comisión de Competencias* to be the final arbiter in resolving disputes over responsibilities. Align jurisdictions of regional development authorities with administrative division of the country. Delineate election of provincial councils with their area of responsibility: either urban or rural, or both. Coordinate external funding for regional development authorities and align with state reform priorities.

(ii) Transfer of expenditures:
Strengthen arrangements for transfer of human resources.
Make access to the transfer of powers contingent on subnational governments' meeting minimum transparency standards.

(iii) More equitable municipal expenditures:
Study in-depth effects and incidence of present transfer system.
Stop discretionary transfers and make public commitment.

Long-term:
(i) Coordination of public investment:
Set up mechanisms for investment coordination.
Align different social funds and other financing with new investment framework.

(ii) Transfer of expenditures:
Define and monitor basic indicators for quality of service delivery of transferred responsibilities.

(iii) More equitable municipal expenditures:
Differentiate the transfer system by type and size of municipalities.

Annex

Figure A.1. Subnational Government per Capita Expenditures and Poverty (based on unsatisfied needs), 2005

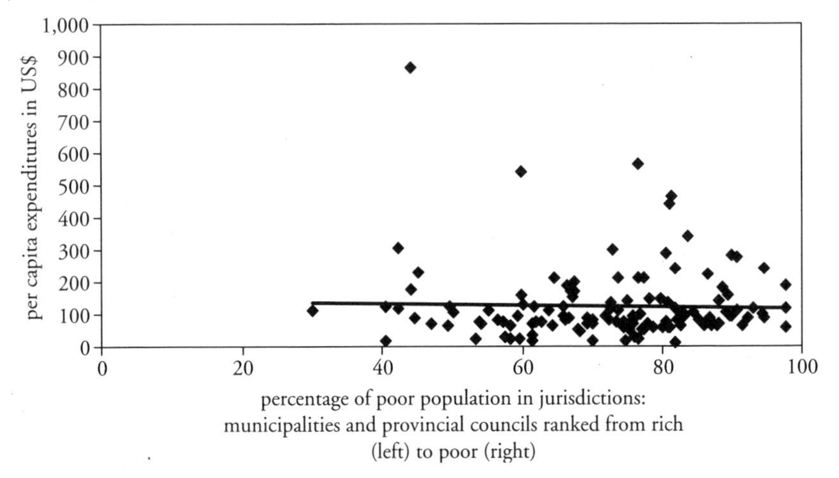

Source: World Bank calculation, based on SIM 2005 and SIISE 2001.

Table A.1. Special Laws Governing the Transfer of Resources and Revenue Sharing for the Benefit of Municipalities and Provincial Councils

Law	*No.*	*R.O.*	*Date*	*Amt./%*	*Source*	*Criteria*	*Use*
Cultural Heritage Recovery Fund	82	838	12/23/87	0.03	Local public performances		Restoration, conservation, and protection of historical, artistic, and cultural assets
				0.1	National Emergencies Fund (FONEN) budget		Investments
Bolivar Provincial Development Fund	46	281	9/22/89	7.5%	1% of credit operation transactions in domestic currency	20% provincial council 16% Guaranda 16% Chillanes 16% Chimbo 16% San Miguel 16% Echeandía	Environmental sanitation Sewers, urban development
Legislative decree on allocations to the provinces of Azuay, Cañar, and Morona Santiago	47	281	9/22/89	5%	Energy bills from INECEL to electric companies for generation at power stations in Pisayambo, Paute, and Agoyán	60% municipalities of Azuay, Cañar, and Morona Santiago 40% CREA (Centro de Reconversión del Azuay, Cañar y Morona Santiago)	100% for infrastructure 80% execution of projects 20% forestation
Environmental Sanitation, Roads, and Irrigation Fund of the Province of El Oro (FONDORO)	57	344	12/28/89	10%	Puerto Bolivar Port Authority revenues	20% provincial council	Irrigation, drainage, and roads
				5%	1% of operations in domestic currency	60% municipalities; 20% municipalities based on population	Sanitation and roads

(*Table continues on the following page.*)

Table A.1. Special Laws Governing the Transfer of Resources and Revenue Sharing for the Benefit of Municipalities and Provincial Councils *(continued)*

Law	*No.*	*R.O.*	*Date*	*Amt./%*	*Source*	*Criteria*	*Use*
Provincial Development Fund (FONDEPRO)	65	395	3/14/90	2%	Total current budget revenues	47.5% contribution to the capital of the Banco del Estado (BdE)	To back BdE credits
						47.5% provincial councils and INGALA (Instituto Galapagos): 25% based on population and 75% by equal shares	Development projects
						0.5% CONCOPE	CONCOPE
Sectional Development Fund (FODESEC)	72	441	5/21/90	2% distributed	Net current budget revenues	Municipal provincial capitals: 25% Quito, 25% Guayaquil; 50% of others level	
				98%		20% provincial councils: 60% population, 20% unsatisfied basic needs (UBN), 20% administrative efficiency and fiscal effectiveness	70% current expenses and investment; 30% rural area investment
						75% municipalities: of which: 60% municipalities (60% population, 30% UBN,	BdE: Investment fund

						10% administrative efficiency and fiscal effectiveness); 40% BdE	
						5% emergencies	Sectional agencies
				3 billion	Prior to distribution of petroleum revenues received by the state		
Rural Roads Program of the Province of Manabí	75	455	6/11/90	10 billion up to 2002 other budgetary allocations	General government budget	BdE credits counterpart	BdE credit trust
Irrigation Fund of the Province of Cotopaxi	93	501	8/16/90	1 billion since 1991	General government budget		Provincial irrigation plan
Fund for the Agricultural Sector of the Province of Chimborazo	115	612	1/28/91	12.5%	1% of credit operations in domestic currency	30% provincial council	Neighborhood roads, irrigation, forestation
						20% municipality of Riobamba	Area market and environmental sanitation
						50% evenly among the remaining cantons	Collection centers and environmental sanitation
Development Funds for the provinces of the Amazon Region	122	676	5/3/91	2.5%	Billing for petroleum services to PetroEcuador from national companies	50% provincial council 20% provincial capital 30% evenly among remaining provincial councils	Urban and rural infrastructure projects in Sucumbíos, Napo, Pastaza, Morona Santiago, Zamora Chinchipe, and Orellana
				4.5%	Billing for petroleum services to PetroEcuador from foreign companies		

(*Table continues on the following page.*)

Table A.1. Special Laws Governing the Transfer of Resources and Revenue Sharing for the Benefit of Municipalities and Provincial Councils *(continued)*

Law	*No.*	*R.O.*	*Date*	*Amt./%*	*Source*	*Criteria*	*Use*
	40	S. 248	8/7/89	5 U.S. cents	Per barrel of petroleum transported by pipeline	Evenly for Napo, Esmeraldas, and Sucumbíos	50% municipal infrastructure projects 50% provincial council infrastructure projects
	10	30	9/21/92	10 U.S. cents	Per barrel of petroleum produced in the Amazon region	BdE distributes 30% provincial councils 60% municipalities (55% by equal shares, 45% population) 10% regional fund	80% road and environmental sanitation projects 20% current expenses
Development Fund of the Province of Pichincha	145	899	3/23/92	15%	1% of credit operations in domestic currency	25% provincial council 25% Quito 50% by equal shares among remaining cantons	Studies, construction, improvement of neighborhood roads and infrastructure projects in urban and rural parishes
Development Fund of the Province of Carchi	146	899	3/23/92	15% 15%	Exchange differential in weekly transactions of the BCE 1% of credit operations in domestic currency	20% provincial council 27.5% Tulcán 16.5% Montúfar 11% Espejo 9% Bolívar 9% Mira 7% Dacha	Road and urban and rural infrastructure projects
15% Distribution of the central government budget	s/n	27	3/20/97	15%	Revenues from central government budget with the exception of revenues from internal and external credits	70% municipalities (50% UBN, 40% population, 10% by equal shares)	Economic, social, and cultural development plans

						30% provincial councils (50% UBN, 40% population, 10% area)	
Law replacing the law creating the Roads Fund of the Province of Loja (FONDVIAL)	92	335	6/9/98	100%	1% tax on the purchase and sale of used vehicles	70% municipalities 30% provincial council	Road projects Highway equipment
Creation of CORPECUADOR	10	S. 378	8/7/98	100%	Tolls, rehabilitated roads		Reconstruction of areas affected by the El Niño phenomenon Investment in proportion to damage caused by El Niño
				25%	Annual net income from Solidarity Fund; donations and subsidies		
				10%	State share in increased petroleum exports		
				0.7%	Banana exports		
					Loans on behalf of the state		
					Loans on behalf of CORPECUADOR		
					Budgetary allocations		

Notes

1. Ecuador by far exceeds the expenditure decentralization indicators of Central American countries where subnational governments execute only about 5 percent of total public expenditures on average. However, the country is not as decentralized as the federations of Brazil and Argentina, where subnational expenditures reach just above 40 percent, including responsibilities for health care and education.

2. This goes hand in hand with a lowering of transfer dependence, from 74 percent in 2000 to 67 percent in 2004. *Transfer dependence* is defined as the percentage of transfers in total revenue.

3. This is a general disadvantage of revenue-sharing arrangements, not attributable to the particular circumstances in Ecuador. However, even in the current system, adjustments are common; therefore, in practice, local budgeting becomes a year-long and continuous exercise, negatively affecting budget execution.

4. Each year roughly 150 out of 220 municipalities are accused by the Comptroller's Office of inappropriate budget management practices. Most of them are able to justify budget management ex post, but a small number of municipalities are subject to judicial processes. However, monitoring of classifications for current and capital investment is always difficult to establish. In addition, the LOAFYC rules that municipalities can, by request to the MEF, amend their budget classifications so that current spending is classified as investment expenditures, for instance, by listing human resources for investment.

5. Dual authorities exist on each subnational level: on the provincial level an appointed governor and elected prefect, on the cantonal level the appointed political lieutenant and elected mayor, and on the parish level the appointed political chief and elected president of the rural parish association. The constitutional reform of 1998 eliminated both the political lieutenant and the political chief, but they still exist in practice.

6. The more important regional development authorities include, among others, CREA (Centro de Reconversión Económica del Azuay), CEDEGE (Centro de Desarrollo de la Cuenca del Guayas), CRM (Centro de Reconversión del Manabí), and UDENOR (Unidad de Desarrollo del Norte). No data are available with regard to sectoral allocation of investments carried out by regional development authorities. Expenditures of provincial councils were US$140 million in 2003 and US$84 million in 2004 (CONAM and GTZ 2005, 9).

7. When measuring poverty based on the unsatisfied needs index (the 15 Percent Law takes this criterion partially into account in its distribution formula), this effect is less significant; however, the huge dispersion in per capita expenditures still remains. Refer to annex figure A.1.

8. Subnational governments have been empowered through higher transfers and exercise de facto veto powers over both the enactment and implementation of central government policies.

Bibliography

BCE (Banco Central de Ecuador). 2003. "Estadísticas de los Gobiernos Seccionales y Provinciales en el Ecuador: 1996–2001." Cuadernos de Trabajo 131. Quito: BCE.

BdE 2001. *Sistema de Información Municipal, 1990–2000.* Quito: BdE.

———. 2002. Metodología para la Calificación de Riesgo y Capacidad de Endeudamiento de Municipios y Consejos Provinciales del País. Gerencia de Riesgos, Quito, October 2002.

CONAM (Consejo Nacional de Modernización del Estado). 1998a. "Caracterización del Estado Ecuatoriano." Documento de Trabajo. Quito: CONAM.

———. 1998b. "Estructura del Régimen Dependiente: Las Gobernaciones." Documento de Trabajo. Quito: CONAM.

———. 2000. *Propuesta del Nuevo Modelo de Gestión para el Ecuador.* Quito: CONAM.

———. 2001a. Descentralización en el Ecuador (CD-ROM). Quito: CONAM.

———. 2001b. *Proyecto de Tributación Subnacional. Determinación de la Capacidad Potencial Tributaria Subnacional.* Quito: CONAM.

———. 2006. *Síntesis del Diagnóstico Descentralización en Ecuador al 2006. Propuesta de Políticas para la Descentralización Fiscal.* Quito: Consejo Nacional de Modernización del Estado.

CONAM and GTZ. 2005. *Análisis de las Finanzas de los Organismos de Desarrollo Regional.* Quito: CONAM.

Frank, Jonas. 2001. *Competencias: ¿Qué Descentralizar? Un Estudio de las Posibilidades de la Descentralización Administrativa en el Ecuador.* Quito: Proyecto Descentralización, GTZ-CONAM.

———. 2003. "Decentralization." In *Ecuador—An Economic and Social Agenda for the New Millennium,* ed. Marcelo Giugale, Vicente Fretes-Cibils, and José Roberto López-Cálix, 479–513. Washington, DC: World Bank.

———. 2003. "La Ruta Critica de la Descentralización en el Ecuador (1950–2002)". In *Línea de Referencia, Segunda Edición, El Proceso de Descentralización en Argentina, Bolivia, Brasil, Chile, Colombia, Ecuador, Perú y Venezuela.* Quito: GTZ/CONAM.

———. Forthcoming. *The Politics of Decentralization in Ecuador: Actors, Institutions, and Incentives. Baden-Baden*: NOMOS.

GTZ (Gesellschaft für Technische Zusammenarbest). 2002a. *Identificación de Unidades Ejecutoras Sectoriales en el Ecuador.* Quito: Cooperación Técnica Alemana, Proyecto de Asesoría en el Marco de la Modernización y Descentralización.

———. 2002b. *Investigación de la Situación de las Organizaciones de Desarrollo Regional, Preparación Programa de Fortalecimiento del Nivel Intermedio.* Quito: Cooperación Técnica Alemana.

———. 2002c. *Recursos de las Unidades ejecutoras de los Sectores: Vías, Ambiente, Turismo, Agricultura, Bienestar Social, Salud y Educación, en Ecuador. Proyecto de Asesoría en el Marco de la Modernización y Descentralización.* Quito: Cooperación Técnica Alemana.

INEC. 2002. *VI Censo de Población.* Quito: National Institute of Statistics and Censuses.

Larrea, Carlos. 1999. *Desarrollo Social y Gestión Municipal en el Ecuador: Jerarquización y Tipología.* Quito: ODEPLAN.

MEF. 2004. *Gastos e Ingresos de Gobiernos Seccionales. Base de datos.* Quito: Ministerio de Economía y Finanzas.

MEF (Ministry of Economy and Finance) and CONAM. 2002. *Indicadores de Endeudamiento Gobiernos Seccionales. Ministerio de Economía y Finanzas/Consejo*

Nacional de Modernización del Estado, Borrador de Discusión. Quito: Ministerio de Economía y Finanzas.

MEF and GTZ. 2000. *Estadísticas Fiscales del Ecuador: Nacionales, Provinciales y Cantonales, No. 1.* Quito: Ministerio de Economía y Finanzas.

Ministerio de Educación y Cultura. 2002. "Sistema Nacional de Estadísticas Educativas del Ecuador (SINEC), Año Escolar 2001." Dirección Nacional de Planeamiento de la Educación, Quito.

Ministerio de Salud Pública. 1997. "Cuentas Nacionales de Salud." Informe Final, Quito.

STFS (Secretaria Técnica del Frente Social). 2002. *Sistema Integrado de Indicadores Sociales del Ecuador (SIISE).* Quito: STFS.

Vargas, César. 2001. *Análisis y Homogenización de las Finanzas Públicas Nacionales. Asignación Territorializada de Ingresos y Gastos Nacionales.* Quito: CONAM.

Wiesner, Eduardo. 1999. *La descentralización, el ajuste y el desarrollo municipal en el Ecuador. Informe de consultoría.* Washington, DC: Banco Interamericano de Desarrollo.

World Bank. 2001. "Programa de Reforma de Descentralización en el Ecuador." Informe 22218-EC. World Bank, Washington, DC.

World Bank. 2002. "Convenios de Descentralización en el Ecuador: Revisión de los Convenios para la Transferencia de Competencias en Perspectiva de la Experiencia Internacional." Working Document. World Bank, Washington, DC.

World Bank. 2004a. *Creating Fiscal Space for Poverty Reduction in Ecuador. A Fiscal Management and Public Expenditure Review.* Washington, DC: World Bank, Inter-American Development Bank.

World Bank. 2004b. *Ecuador Poverty Assessment.* Washington, DC: World Bank.

World Bank. 2005. *Ecuador Fiscal Management and Public Expenditure Review: Creating Fiscal Space for Poverty Reduction in Ecuador.* Washington, DC: World Bank, Inter-American Development Bank.

13

Basic Infrastructure: Water Supply and Sanitation, Telecommunications, Transport, and Urban Planning

Franz Drees-Gross, Eloy Vidal, Emmanuel James, and Alexandra Ortiz

Executive Summary

The water supply and sanitation, telecommunications, and transport sectors face problems of poor coverage (especially in rural areas); inefficiency and poor service quality; high dependence on national government transfers to cover shortfalls in operational income; and deficient frameworks for policy setting, regulation, and service provision. In general, the national government could face these challenges by promoting better models for service provision and by consolidating institutional and legal arrangements. In addition, especially in the water supply and sanitation sector and transport sector, the government could use resource transfers to subnational governments (provinces and municipalities) to promote the adoption of better models for service provision and appropriate cost-recovery policies.

In addition to these general problems, the water supply and sanitation (WSS) sector is characterized by poor cost recovery through tariffs and a high dependence on transfers from the central government to cover operational and investment deficits. An integrated national system for managing water resources is also lacking. Since all water and sanitation services are provided by decentralized providers that depend on municipal governments, the central government has two main tools at its disposal to improve the quality and efficiency

This chapter was prepared by World Bank Staff members Franz Drees-Gross (coordinator, sector leader for Infrastructure, Rural and Social Development and Environment), Eloy Vidal (lead telecommunications engineer), and Emmanuel James (lead transport specialist). The section on urban development in this chapter was prepared by Alexandra Ortiz.

of services and to guarantee coverage to urban and rural populations not yet served. The central government can reform the use of transfers to encourage cost-effectiveness among service providers, and it can improve the institutional and legal framework.

The telecommunications sector faces specific challenges, including artificially low, unsustainable local rates for fixed telephone service; lack of competition in the cellular market, resulting in user costs that are among the highest in the region; and very limited Internet access. It is essential that the government consolidate the institutional and legal framework and look for greater participation from the private sector to attract private capital to Andinatel and Pacifictel so that they can make the large investments that the sector requires, and to break the duopoly in the cellular market.

The challenges in the transport sector arise from the relatively poor condition of all segments of the road network, the lack of transport services in rural areas, inadequate attention to environmental and social safeguards, uncoordinated and deficient sectoral and modal planning, and inadequate institutional capacity and resources at the sectional government (provincial and municipal governments, or SGs) level to upgrade and maintain provincial and rural roads. The latter is becoming a critical factor given the increasing transfer of responsibilities to the SGs that are associated with the decentralization process. Some of the key first steps to be taken by the central government should include contracting road maintenance services on the basis of performance and promoting private sector participation, including an expansion of the use of microenterprises to maintain roads. The central government must also pay increased attention to the environmental and social impacts of road projects and take steps to improve institutional capacities in this regard. The current plans to transform the Ministry of Public Works into a new Ministry of Transport that is charged with sector regulatory and planning functions marks a good step forward. Options and strategies for establishing a dedicated road maintenance fund that could be funded by a small surcharge on fuels should also be considered.

Rapid urbanization in Ecuador has led to an urgent need for infrastructure planning. The urban growth rate is one of the highest in the region, and the share of urban population is expected to grow from 64 percent in 2003 to 80 percent in 2025. At least four cities with current populations of over 700,000 will need to triple their built-up urban area by 2030. Also needed are a well-designed housing policy; urban upgrading with the cooperation of national, community, and donor resources; and planning for improved financial management and administration.

I. Introduction

The development of basic infrastructure is fundamental to the quality of life of Ecuador's citizens, the country's economic growth, and its competitiveness in the global economy. This chapter presents a summary of the situation facing Ecuador in 2007 in three key sectors that comprise a significant part of its public infrastructure: water supply and sanitation, telecommunications, and transport (highways and roads, railroads, ports, and airports). Other infrastructure sectors, including electricity and hydrocarbons, are treated in separate chapters, and the annex contains a discussion of urban planning. This section describes each sector's structures, main actors, and legal and regulatory frameworks. The subsequent section then summarizes the main challenges faced in each sector. The final section of this chapter looks at policy options. The main recommendations are also summarized in a short- and medium-term action plan.

Several of the challenges facing these sectors (especially coverage and quality of services) are closely linked both to urban population growth and to the country's urban-rural divide. On the one hand, between 1995 and 2000, Ecuador had an urban growth rate of 3.6 percent, compared with the 2.1 percent average for South America as a whole. On the other hand, despite strong population growth in urban areas, Ecuador continues to be one of the most rural countries in South America, with only 63 percent of its population living in urban areas, compared with the regional average of 80 percent. These two facts pose a double challenge: first, the need to mobilize significant investment for rural areas, where the coverage of services is generally lower than in urban areas, and second, the urgent need to restructure providers of urban services in all infrastructure sectors, so that they are able to efficiently meet the technical and financial challenges posed by urban areas undergoing rapid change.

II. Description of the Sectors

Key actors and sector structures for the water supply and sanitation, telecommunication, and transport sectors are summarized in this section, along with legal, regulatory, and institutional settings.

Water Supply and Sanitation

Over the past two decades, more than any other public service sector in Ecuador, water supply and sanitation service provision has undergone a profound decentralization from central control to municipal responsibility.

History

The structure of the water supply and sanitation sector in Ecuador from the 1950s to the 1980s was characterized by centralized planning, primarily by the Ecuadoran Institute for Water and Sanitation Works (IEOS). From the time of its creation in 1965 until its abolition in the mid-1990s, IEOS built, operated, and maintained potable water systems at the national level, financed by central government resources derived mostly from oil exports. When these resources diminished in the early 1990s, the central government decided to transfer the systems it had built to municipalities and communities. These communities were to operate and maintain their systems as part of a broader nationwide decentralization and modernization process. IEOS was replaced by the Subsecretariat of Potable Water and Basic Sanitation (later renamed the Subsecretariat of Water Supply, Sanitation, and Solid Waste, SAPSyRS) of the Ministry of Urban Development and Housing (MIDUVI), and its staff was sharply cut from about 2,500 public employees in the early 1990s to about 150 at present. Along with this reduction and with the support of two studies prepared by external consultants in 1999 and 2002, SAPSyRS began a transformation of its role from that of a direct project executor to that of a lead sector agency in charge of planning the development of the sector; establishing policies and regulations; providing technical assistance to municipalities, communities, and operators; and developing and maintaining a sector information system. This transformation has been slow and is still largely incomplete.

In addition to SAPSyRS, several other institutions have overlapping functions related to the sector (table 13.1).

Service Providers

As a result of decentralization in the 1990s, Ecuador today has a very large number of service providers, with public utilities in large and medium cities, and municipal water supply and sanitation departments as part of municipal governments in most small cities and towns (see table 13.2).[1] In these municipal water and sanitation departments, staff is typically shared with other municipal functions, and income and expenditures often become confused with the municipality's general accounting system. In rural areas, water and sanitation user associations (JASS) provide water supply (and occasionally sanitation) services in small communities, usually with very limited technical support from the municipal water supply and sanitation department in the cantonal capital. Between 2001 and 2006, under MIDUVI's Rural and Small Towns Water Supply and Sanitation Project (PRAGUAS I),[2] 28 municipalities

Table 13.1. Institutions Related to the Water Supply and Sanitation Sector

Institution	*Functions*
MIDUVI/SAPSyRS	Formulates sectoral policies, establishes regulations, and defines the development strategy for the sector at the national level.
Ministry of Public Health	Regulates the quality of potable water.
Ministry of the Environment	Is responsible for environmental protection, conservation, and water pollution control.
National Council on Water Resources (CNRH)	Is responsible for managing water resources, including granting water extraction rights, through eight regional development authorities.
Ecuadoran Development Bank (BdE)	Channels resources to municipalities.
Ministry of Economy and Finance	Channels resources to municipalities.

Source: Authors.

Table 13.2. Service Providers

Population	*Number of municipalities*	*Type of service provider*	*Population (million)*	*Pop. growth 1990s (%)*
More than 1 million	Guayaquil (1.7 million) Quito (1.6 million)	Concession (W + S) to the private sector (Interagua) Municipal water company (EMAAP)	3.35	2.3
100,000 to 300,000	12	Municipal water companies: 11; municipal department: 1 (Loja); of which: 1 PRAGUAS (Riobamba)	1.92	7.8
30,000 to 100,000	37	Municipal water companies: 11; of which: 6 PRAGUAS (Guaranda, Tulcán, Ventanas, Cayambe, Vinces, and Pujilí); plus 29 municipal departments	0.80	–2.2
Less than 30,000	169	Municipal water companies: 21; of which: 21 PRAGUAS (Pedernales, Gualaceo, Eloy Alfaro, Valencia, Morona, Saraguro, San Miguel, Pedro Moncayo, Colimes, Chimbo, Bolivar, Espejo, Pimampiro, Chunchi, Caluma, Echeandía, Sucúa, Pedro Vicente Maldonado,Cumandá, El Tambo, Las Naves); plus 1 municipal company with a private operator (Pedro Moncayo), 1 mixed-capital company (Caluma), 2 cooperatives (Echeandia, Las Naves) (all PRAGUAS); plus 144 municipal departments	1.30	3.5
Rural areas		Approx. 2,000 JASS	4.72	0.9
TOTAL	220		12.09	2.1

Source: World Bank.

adopted new management models, including one mixed-capital (municipal plus community-owned) company in Caluma, two cooperatives (Echeandía and Las Naves), and 25 municipal companies (7 have a majority of municipal representatives in their boards of directors and 18 have a majority of community representatives). A summary of service providers nationwide is provided in table 13.2.

Telecommunications

This section summarizes the key public and private actors in the fixed-line and mobile telephony markets, as well as the key features of Ecuador's legal and regulatory framework.

Structure of the Sector and Main Players

The telecommunications sector in Ecuador has had mixed results over the past few years. The country has been among the last to open up to competition in the region. Private companies operate the majority of the mobile telephony services, while state-owned enterprises operate the majority of the fixed-line telephony services. The main fixed-line operators are Andinatel S.A. and Pacifictel S.A., which operate in the mountain and the coastal areas, respectively. The exception is ETAPA Telecom, a wholly own subsidiary of ETAPA (Empresa Pública Municipal de Telecomunicaciones, Agua Potable, Alcantarillado y Saneamiento de Cuenca), a municipal company that provides services exclusively in the city of Cuenca. Three small, new, wireless local-loop private operators also have a small number of customers. The main players in the mobile-telephone market are CONECEL (PORTA), a subsidiary of the Mexican company America Movil S.A., and OTECEL (Movistar), a subsidiary of Spanish Telefonica. The market has grown an average of 50 percent in the past two years, with more than 8 million lines in service in 2006 (see figure 13.1). A third player, a state-owned company (TELECSA [Alegro PCS], owned by Andinatel S.A.), has not been able to compete effectively with the two main private operators. The largest cable television operator is TV CABLE, which provides cable television, Internet access, and, recently, telephone services in the cities of Quito and Guayaquil and many other smaller locations. However, 184 registered cable TV companies operate in Ecuador, most of them very small and serving several cities and towns.

Figure 13.1. Mobile and Fixed Telephony, 1999–2006

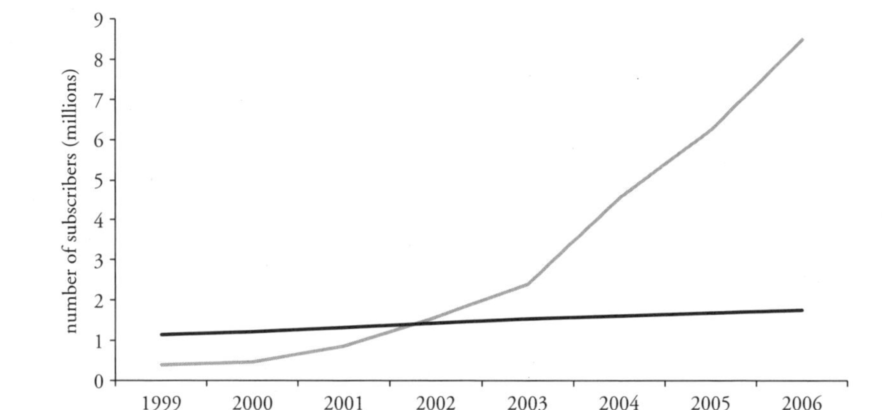

Source: ITU.

Legal and Regulatory Framework

In general, it has not been possible to consolidate the legal reform of the telecommunications sector. The lack of political support has meant that, despite several attempts at legal reform over the past seven years, no new law has been passed. According to the most recent ranking of the telecommunications sector by the Pyramid Research consultancy firm, the regulatory framework and the level of competition in Ecuador are among the poorest in the region (Ecuador ranks 16th and 13th in those two categories, respectively, of 18 countries studied).

The main challenges now are the existence of contradictory regulations, delays in the approval of the new telecommunications act, and, finally, the confusion and overlapping of responsibilities among the three regulatory authorities. Although it is argued that each of these has a different function, there is in fact a great deal of confusion regarding their functions and responsibilities: the National Telecommunications Council (CONATEL) is responsible for setting national policy in the sector and establishing interconnection regulations and the terms for concessions; the National Secretariat of Telecommunications (SENATEL) prepares the National Telecommunications Development Plan, signs concessions contracts with telecommunication companies, and is the executive arm of CONATEL. The Telecommunications Superintendency (SUPTEL) is by law the only independent body responsible for the control of telecommunications in the country, including the control of the radio-frequency spectrum. Finally, the National Council of Radio and Television (CONARTEL) issues concessions and regulates the radio and television companies. International experience shows that having a single regulatory authority, independent of any operator and with sufficient power to supervise private operators in the sector, is the best way to ensure transparency, boost private investment, and support sector development.

Regarding regulations, CONATEL has approved the adjustment of local fixed-line telephone rates. However, the executive branch of government has been reluctant to authorize rate increases for Andinatel and Pacifictel. CONATEL ordered an important reduction in the interconnection rates between fixed and mobile telephones in 2005, which had a profound impact on the growth of the mobile market. The concession contracts for the two largest mobile operators expire in 2008, and the extension of these contracts will be a major decision by the government.

Transport

The following sections provide an overview of the large number of actors involved in the planning, regulation, and provision of transport services in Ecuador.

Characteristics of the Sector

The transport sector represents 6.2 percent of GDP, a percentage that has remained relatively constant since 1995. About 7 percent of the national budget is typically assigned annually to the transport sector by the Ministry of Economy and Finance (MEF). Furthermore, almost 10 percent of transfer payments to SGs is also earmarked for the transport sector.

Institutional Framework

For road transport various governing bodies, with differing degrees and levels of interdependence, are responsible for the planning, construction, maintenance, and operation of the land transport system in Ecuador. By way of example, figure 13.9 provides an overview of the national ministries, councils, and commissions involved in the Participatory Planning Process for Rural Roads. Among the most important in terms of road transport is the Ministry of Public Works (MOP), which is responsible at the national level for building and maintaining the main or national segments of the road network. At the moment, certain stretches of the national network are operated under concessions to private companies working in different regions of the country. At the provincial level, the Consortium of Provincial Councils of Ecuador (CONCOPE) are responsible for construction and maintenance of the provincial or secondary segments of the road network. As for rural roads, the sectional governments, the Ministry of Social Welfare, the Social Investment Fund (FISE), the Corporation for the Reconstruction of Areas Affected by El Niño (CORPECUADOR), CONCOPE, and now the MOP, with its Decentralized Roads Management Unit (DGVD), are all involved in upgrading and maintaining rural roads in different provinces throughout the country.

The Civil Aviation Office (DAC) is responsible for the construction and maintenance of national airports. Although the construction of private runways is very common, only the DAC can authorize this. Construction projects for new airports in the cities of Quito and Guayaquil are under the management and responsibility of the respective airport corporations created by the municipal councils of these cities. The National Merchant Marine and Ports Council (DIGMER) is responsible for maritime transport, administrating and controlling the largest ports, such as Esmeraldas, Manta, Guayaquil, and Port Bolívar. DIGMER is also responsible for regulating river traffic on the navigable rivers of the Costa, Sierra, and Oriente regions of the country. The National Railway Company (ENFE) is responsible for the railway sector. This form of transport is not heavily used and is not really significant at the national level. Its tracks and trains are obsolete, service is poor, but it does have some potential for tourism purposes.

Regulation and Control of the Transport Services

Passenger and cargo transport by road, both nationally and internationally, is handled by the National Land Transit and Transport Council (CNTTT), which regulates passenger rates. The CNTTT is attached to the Ministry of the Interior and has 14 members. At the national level, a rate was established for popular (basic) transport. Freight transport rates are not explicitly regulated and depend on the competitiveness of the transport market in question. Air freight rates are established by the National Civil Aviation Council and by the Civil Aviation Authority. Rail transport rates are established by the Ecuadoran National Railway Company (ENFE), with different fares for national and foreign passengers. At the regional level, the 20 Provincial Land Transit and Transport Councils, the Guayas Transit Commission, and the Quito Metropolitan Transport Service and Administration Company are all involved. DIGMER determines policies and regulations for water transport. Finally, it should be noted that the institutional arrangements outlined in the sectoral chart are currently being reformed by the new government, and plans are well advanced for the transformation of the MOP into a Ministry of Transport and Public Works (MTOP). This is a welcome development.

III. Diagnosis of the Main Problems and Challenges

The key challenges faced by the water and sanitation, telecommunication, and transport sectors are summarized in the following sections.

Water Supply and Sanitation Sector

The water supply and sanitation sector in Ecuador is characterized by (i) low levels of coverage, especially in rural areas; (ii) low-quality services and inefficiency; (iii) low cost recovery through tariffs and high dependence on transfer payments from central and municipal governments to close deficits; (iv) an incomplete legal and regulatory framework, leading to overlapping functions and confusion within the national government and among different levels of government; and (v) the lack of an integrated national water resource management system.

Coverage

Despite significant improvements made over the past decades (total water supply and sanitation coverage rose from 48 and 43 percent in 1980 to 73 and 67 percent, respectively, in 2001), water supply and sanitation coverage in Ecuador remains relatively low compared with other South American countries. Though urban coverage rates are relatively good (water supply and sanitation both stand at approximately 85 percent),[3] rural coverage (53 percent for water and 37 percent for sanitation) lags behind the Latin American average.

Inequalities in the Provision of Services

Coverage of adequate water supply and sanitation services is characterized by a number of inequalities (Yepes, Gómez, and Carvajal 2002):

- *Regional inequalities.* As table 13.3 shows, the lowest levels of potable water and sanitation coverage are on the coast (Costa) and in the east of the country (Oriente).

Table 13.3. Coverage of Potable Water Supply and Sewerage Services, 2001
(percent)

		Region			
Service	*National*	*Sierra*	*Costa*	*Oriente*	*Islands*
Potable water	73				
Urban	85	94	78	80	95
Rural	53	70	33	32	39
Sanitation	67				
Urban	85	94	78	79	88
Rural	37	42	30	22	27

Source: Census.
Note: Coverage numbers below the national average are shown in bold.

- *Inequalities between urban and rural areas.* As percentages, rates of coverage with an adequate service are higher in urban areas than in rural areas (1.6 times higher for water supply and 2.3 times higher for sanitation).
- *Inequalities between income levels.* In urban (*urbano*), consolidated rural (*rural amanzanado*), and rural areas, low-income families are far less likely to have access to water and sanitation services (figure 13.2). In addition, poor families (with and without water connections) are far less likely to have the means or the awareness to treat the water available to them (figure 13.3).

Quality of Services

At the national level, most large and medium cities do not have continuous supplies of potable water. In 2003, the last year for which data are available, 90 percent of the population of Quito and Cuenca had 24 hours per day of water supply; but only 50 percent of the population in Guayaquil and Machala did. Other medium-size cities are between 70 percent and 80 percent, for an average of 72 percent (ANEMAPA 2003).

Efficiency of Service

Available figures on the efficiency of water supply and sanitation services provided in large and medium-size cities of Ecuador are very alarming, since the number of employees in almost all these companies—except Guayaquil (International Water Services [INTERAGUA]) and Cuenca (ETAPA)—is two to five times higher per 1,000 water connections than the best levels in Latin America (table 13.4).

The conclusion is that in addition to low tariffs, high personnel costs deprive companies of the resources they need to finance coverage expansion to reach the unserved poor. Because of limited data, it is difficult to reach a conclusion regarding the efficiency of service in small municipalities, where employees are often shared with other services and separate accounts are not kept. However, regional experience suggests that the absence of economies of scale in these small systems (needed to maintain technically skilled personnel and specialized equipment) goes hand-in-hand with inefficient service.

Figure 13.2. Access to Water Supply (Connection), by Income Level

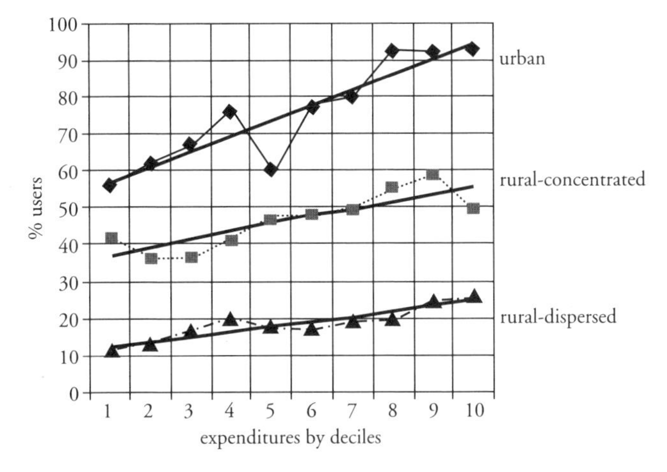

Source: PAHO (2001).
Note: 1 = lowest; 10 = highest.

Figure 13.3. Water Treatment by Income

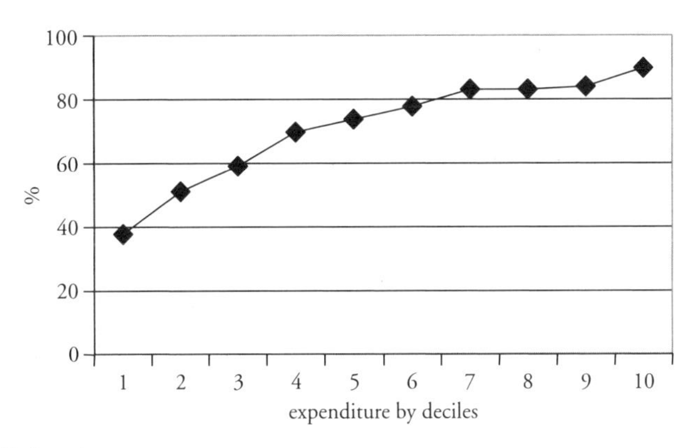

Source: PAHO (2001).
Note: 1 (poorest); 10 (richest).

Financing and Impact on the Poor of Tariffs and Transfer Payments

The WSS sector is characterized by low tariffs and high dependence on transfer payments from the central government and municipalities. Nationwide, cumulative income from tariffs covers only about half of the cost of operating a system adequately, with sufficient funds provided for routine maintenance. The deficit is closed in part by transfers to the WSS sector by the national government and by municipalities, and in part by undermaintenance.

Table 13.4. Operational Efficiency of Water Supply Companies in a Selection of Large- and Medium-Size Cities

Company	*Employees (N) per 1,000 water connections*
Cities with more than 1 million inhabitants	
Quito (EMAAP)	5.98
Guayaquil (INTERAGUA)	3.88
Cities with fewer than 1 million inhabitants	
Cuenca (ETAPA)	3.74
Ambato	7.91
Ibarra	6.84
Guaranda	4.95
Sta Rosa	10.35
Examples of high-performing water supply utilities in Latin America	
Santiago (Chile)	2.0
SANEPAR-Paraná (Brazil)	2.2
SABESP (Brazil)	3.0

Source: ANEMAPA 2003; Brazil (SNIS 2005).

Low tariffs are commonly justified by references to widespread poverty and by the fact that water is both a social and economic good that is vital for life itself. Unfortunately, the poorest are not the ones who benefit from the lowest rates and transfer payments to the sector. As figure 13.2 shows, almost 40 percent of the poorest residents in urban areas (the three lowest income deciles) do not have access to piped water supplies. The situation is even worse in rural areas with limited infrastructure, where more than 60 percent of the poorest population (the three lowest income deciles) do not have household connections. These people, who often get their water from untreated sources far from home (in rural areas) or from tanker trucks (in marginal urban areas) spend much more time and money getting water of unreliable quality than their connected neighbors. In Machala (table 13.5), for example, it is estimated that a poor family connected to the water supply system spends only 0.4 percent of its monthly income on its water bill, while an unconnected family spends approximately 9 percent (Yepes, Gómez, and Carvajal 2002).

The World Health Organization recommends that no more than a maximum of five percent of household income be spent on water supply. When the figures above are compared with this standard, it is clear that low tariffs deprive water and sanitation service providers of the resources they need to extend services to unserved areas, where users pay much more for water of unreliable quality. Operational deficits are only partly offset by national and municipal transfer payments that become little more than a subsidy for the relatively privileged population that already has access to services.

Table 13.5. Machala: Monthly Expenditure on Water Supply and Sanitation Services—Families with and without Home Connection, 2002

	User	
Expenditures	*With household connection*	*Supplied by tanker truck*
Monthly consumption, poor family (m^3)	15[a]	4 to 5[b]
Monthly expenditure per family (US$ per unit)	1.2[c]	29.0
Monthly expenditure—percentage of family income	0.4	9.0

Source: Yepes, Gómez, and Carvajal (2002).
a. World Bank estimates.
b. World Bank estimates based on approximately 30 liters/day/person consumption (2002).
c. The rate depends on the type of housing. The amount indicated is for the most inexpensive housing.

Regulatory and Legal Framework

A National Water and Sanitation Policy (Executive Decree 2766 of July 30, 2002) established guidelines and basic principles to increase water supply and sanitation coverage. It also aimed to improve the quality of services provided and make the use of water resources more efficient. However, the document did not take a clear position on key issues such as subsidies to the sector and objective criteria for the municipalities receiving them.

Management of Water Resources

Although, in general, Ecuador appears to have sufficient water resources to cover its needs, there is increasing competition for its use and greater conflict over its allocation. This leads to environmental degradation that particularly affects poor and indigenous communities. Government efforts made to date to protect water quality, promote efficient water use (especially in agriculture), increase the availability of water resources year-round, and control flooding have been insufficient. Ecuador needs a systematic, long-term program to modernize the management of its water resources and to guarantee sustainable management both at the local and national levels.

The main problems affecting the sustainable management of water resources are (i) the lack of updated information on quantity, quality, and seasonal availability of water and its use by different subsectors (human consumption, agriculture, and so forth), which impedes sectoral planning (stock of water resources was last taken in 1985); (ii) the lack of political consensus regarding water as a social and economic good; (iii) weakness of the institutions responsible for managing water resources and overlapping functions among the National Council on Hydraulic Resources (CNRH), the Ministry of Agriculture and Ministry of the Environment, provincial councils, regional development councils, and municipalities; (iv) degradation of water quality in several rivers (some already considered dead) due to chemical effluents and pesticides; (v) flooding (especially on the coast) and erosion (accelerated by deforestation); (vi) sedimentation of hydroelectric reservoirs; and (vii) increasing conflict among different users of water resources, which is especially harmful to poor and indigenous groups.

Telecommunications Sector

The key issues affecting the telecommunication sector are summarized below.

Fixed-Line Telephone Service

During the past three years, Ecuador's fixed-line coverage increased only slightly, from 12.2 lines per hundred inhabitants in 2003 to 13.1 lines in December 2006. Compared with other countries in the region, Ecuador is below the Latin American average of 18 lines per 100 inhabitants. However, considering its per capita income, Ecuador has an average level of penetration similar to other countries with the same level of development (figure 13.4). However, there are great differences in coverage within Ecuador: the province of Pichincha (where Quito, the capital, is located) has one telephone line for every four people, while provinces such as Orellana, Los Rios, and Sucumbíos have only one telephone line for every 20 inhabitants. Guayas province, where Guayaquil, Ecuador's largest city, is located, had only one phone per eight inhabitants in 2006. This is the result of the inefficiencies of Pacifictel S.A., where poor management has been endemic (figure 13.5).

Figure 13.4. Fixed-Line Density and GDP per Capita

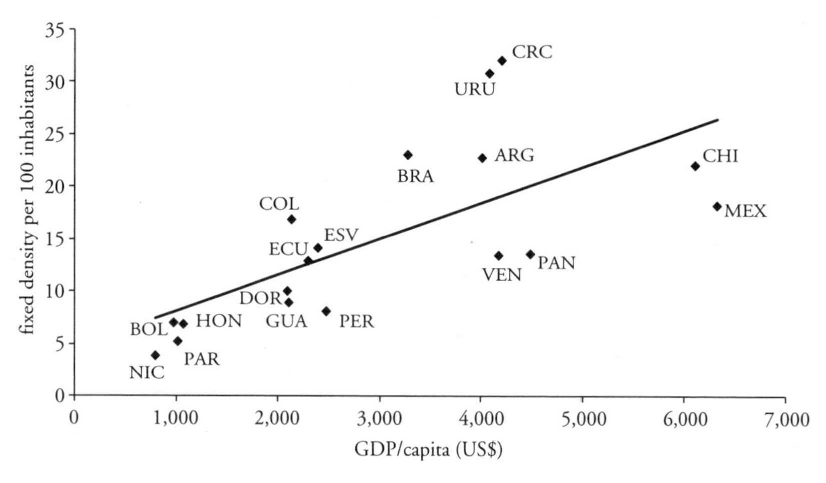

Source: ITU.

Figure 13.5. Fixed-Line Density Rate, by Province

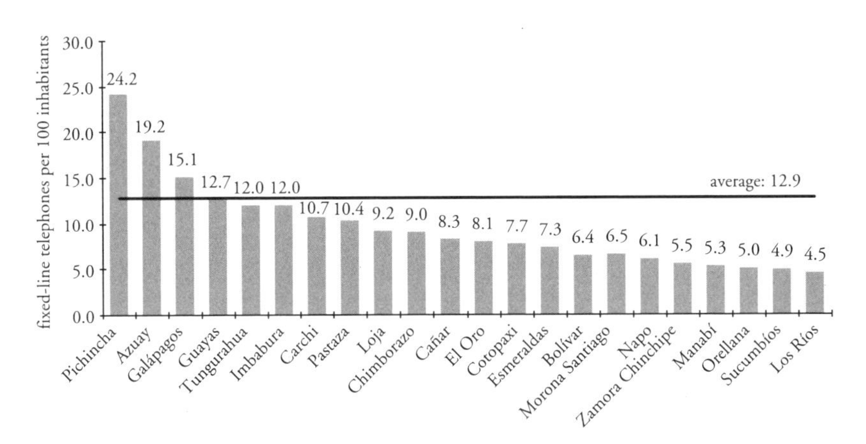

Source: Telecomunications Superintendency (SUPTEL).

Subsidies

Despite the market's having been opened to competition, serious distortions remain in the basic telecommunications services market. For several years, the operator responsible for basic phone service, EMETEL, and its successors, Andinatel and Pacifictel, maintained a cross-subsidy to offer very low local service rates at the cost of maintaining artificially high international long-distance rates far above the international average. This led to a large percentage of international calls being made using "by-pass," or the Internet, giving rise to a boom in cyber cafés, some of which are operating illegally. In 2000, CONATEL agreed to a rate adjustment plan to solve this problem and balance the market before the sector was opened to competition.

Nonetheless, this process was brought to a halt that same year, when the executive branch of the government ordered a rate freeze. As a result, the local Pacifictel rate for the residential sector in November 2002 was 60 percent lower than originally planned in the adjustment program that should have concluded in January 2003. The price of a local call is now one of the lowest in the region, and both Andinatel and Pacifictel offer below-cost local service. Because of the low number of telephones in Ecuador, this is a subsidy to the rich, who can afford a telephone in the first place. The present system of low rates is ineffective because it is based on the geographic location of the household rather than income level.

The long-distance market has been opened to competition and international rates have dropped, meaning that both companies face financial difficulties, as local rates have not been adjusted to real costs. Adjusting rates is necessary because both companies urgently need fresh capital to continue to make investments, build new networks, and provide access to the Internet. The necessary increase in local rates will undoubtedly affect a small portion of the population, especially the middle class. One possibility would be to use the system that has been very successful for mobile telephony services: prepaid cards. This way, each individual user has complete control over his or her spending.

The situation of Pacifictel is especially bad. The company has been mismanaged for the past eight years and provides poor service to its customers. No audit has been performed on Pacifictel. As a result of this poor performance, the residents of the coastal region, especially those who live in Guayaquil, either have poor service or do not have service at all. This imposes a serious impediment to economic development in the region. Several sectional governments have replaced managers, taken direct control of the company, and used other methods to try to fix this problem. None of these attempts has worked. The World Bank believes that the only option that has a chance of being effective in this context is radical restructuring by divestiture.

Long-Distance Telephone Service

CONATEL opted for the presubscription system instead of the teleselection system (dialing an access code for each call) for choosing a long-distance operator. International experience indicates that markets become more competitive when consumers can easily choose the operator that offers the best service and prices, which is made possible by dial-up selection. This advantage is the case in markets such as Chile's and in those recently opened to competition, for example, Bolivia. Another problem has arisen in countries that have opened up to competition but do not have an advanced and well-defined monitoring system; that problem involves illegal changes of operator, known as slamming. The new national long-distance regulations consider the possibility of implementing the dialing system after two years, if this becomes economically viable. However, this strategy may be insufficient, given that once competition has become established and consumers have decided which service to subscribe to, a dominant operator is highly unlikely to lose its market share. This is the case of Telmex in Mexico, which, after nine years of open competition, still controls about 70 percent of the long-distance market. The presubscription system for choosing an operator tends to stifle competition, since it means that each customer has to change operators, and consumers are generally not very proactive when it comes to taking this step.

Mobile Telephone Service

In contrast to the problems in fixed-line service, mobile-line penetration has increased exponentially over the past several years, to the point that Ecuador now has 8.5 million cellular lines, or 64 percent penetration, a level that compares very favorably with other Latin American countries (see figure 13.6). The remarkable growth of 51 percent annually over the past three years was mainly due to the reduction in prices as a result of reduced rates for interconnection between fixed and mobile lines,

Figure 13.6. Mobile Penetration

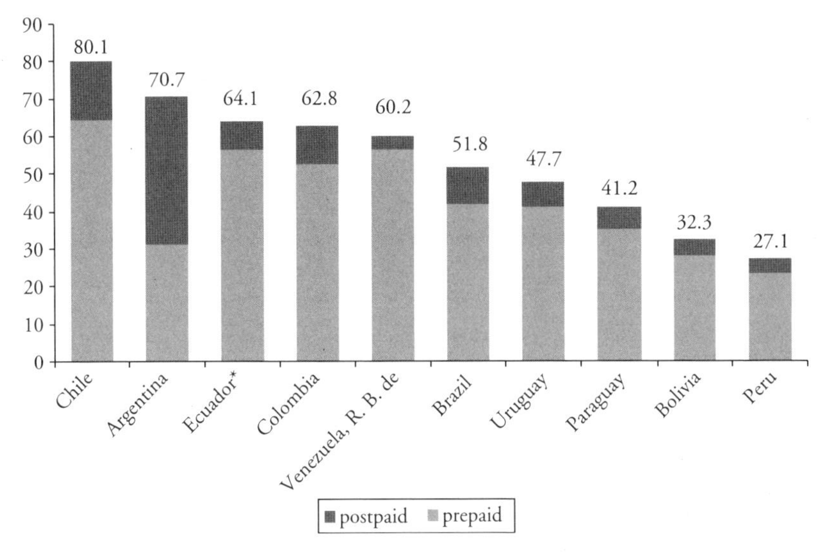

Source: Wireless Intelligence, ITU, SUPTEL.
*Ecuador: December 2006.

a change mandated by CONATEL in 2005. To a lesser degree, the increased coverage was also the result of the entry of a new third operator, Alegro PCS. Alegro PCS has captured only 4 percent of the market share in the past four years, and its future is questionable, considering the strength of its competitors.

Internet Access

Ecuador has only 170,000 Internet accounts, for about 1.2 percent of the population. SUPTEL estimates that about 750,000 users have access to the Internet (about 5.6 percent of the population). As figure 13.7 shows, this is low compared with other countries in Latin America: Ecuador ranks well behind Peru, Colombia, and the República Bolivariana de Venezuela, which have access rates of 16.5 percent, 10.4 percent, and 8.8 percent, respectively. The low level of Internet penetration in Ecuador is attributable to the low fixed-line penetration and the lack of competition for this service. In other countries, such as the United States, cable TV companies are actively competing with fixed-line service providers to provide Internet access. In Ecuador, the total number of cable TV subscribers is only 127,000, according to SUPTEL (although many small companies do not report the number of subscribers). TV CABLE, the largest cable company, is providing Internet access through cable modems and recently has started providing telephone service. This is a good development; however, the coverage of the cable network is still limited. Another factor that limits Internet access is the price per

Figure 13.7. Internet Users in the Region

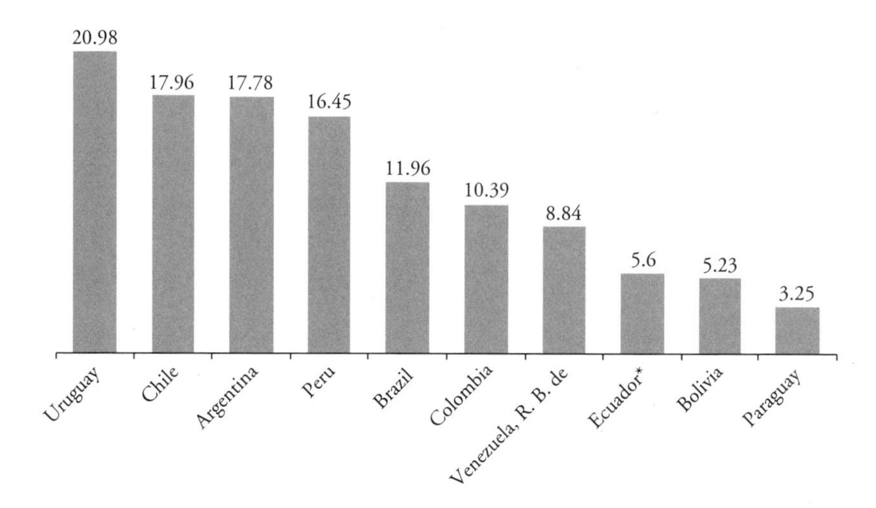

Source: Wireless Intelligence, ITU, SUPTEL.
*Ecuador: December 2006.

minute of the phone call to access the Internet service provider (ISP). Two-thirds of the subscribers use dial-up to reach the ISP in Ecuador. This means, for example, that a small business pays the phone company about US$28 a month for about 20 hours of use per month and pays the ISP US$22 per month. A flat rate could be a solution. To increase service, the government could promote new wireless access providers, by auctioning spectrum.

Rural Access

As explained earlier in this section, the majority of Ecuador's rural areas have either limited or no access to telephones. The Chilean success story suggests that to reduce inequality in access to telecommunications services, the most effective strategy for increasing low coverage in poor and rural areas would be to introduce competition and private investment to the sector and to create a development fund to which the companies themselves contribute. Although Ecuador has already created the Telecommunications Development Fund (*Fondo de Desarrollo de las Telecomunicaciones*—FODETEL), the contributions to the fund (1 percent of operators' gross annual income) are not included in the telecommunications act; therefore, FODETEL does not have resources for development of rural areas.

To address rural access, an ongoing World Bank project (*Proyecto de Mejora de los Sectores de Electricidad y Comunicaciones Rurales*—PROMEC) is installing telecenters in 1,100 small towns that do not have telephones in rural areas. The public-private partnership is a step in the right direction to reduce the gap of service to rural areas.

These telecenters are of two types: (i) a small telecenter, equipped with two telephones and two computers with Internet access, and (ii) a large telecenter, with four telephones and four computers. Four pilot projects will also be implemented to support small and medium enterprises and increase their production and export capacity. Modifying the law to include the contribution to FODETEL would ensure future development of rural telecommunications service. Another alternative is to use mobile networks, which companies have extended their coverage to outside of cities. Their networks are quite extensive; however, operators have focused on selected urban areas and still do not cover large parts of the country. One alternative to further expand service to rural areas is to negotiate with companies to extend their coverage by installing new cell sites in rural areas.

Transport Sector

The following sections outline the key issues facing the road, rail, air, and maritime transport sectors, with special consideration of urban transport issues in Quito and the particular challenges surrounding rural accessibility.

Characteristics of the Sector

The transport system in Ecuador has never been systematically planned, but rather has developed in response to specific needs, public demand, or government policy during any given period. The development of the different transport systems has never been coordinated adequately, and each one has acted independently of the others. Problems in the sector arise from the inadequacy of the policies and strategies applied, and from a weak regulatory, legal, and institutional framework. These weaknesses then translate into operational, financial, and management problems. Investments and maintenance are not adequately planned, efficiency is low, and budget allocations to the sector remain below real investment and maintenance needs. Although the government dominates the sector in terms of formulating policy, acting as the regulatory authority, and providing infrastructure and services, the poor coordination among institutions prevents government plans from achieving the desired benefits. Provinces and municipalities have very little technical, administrative, and financial capacity to take on the growing responsibilities imposed by the Special Law on Decentralization and Social Participation. At these administrative levels, political influences, limited institutional capacity, and shortages of resources all contribute to the current inadequate sector management.

Highway administration is generally a public sector function, with several institutions sharing responsibility, thus preventing proper planning and a clear division of powers. Urban and rural cargo and passenger transport service are overwhelmingly managed by individuals and small private companies without proper planning or operational efficiency. This structure results in inefficiencies, to the detriment of users.

The following sections summarize the situation and present certain problems and conditions related to transport subsectors.

Road Transport

ROAD NETWORKS

All forms of transport are present in Ecuador, but highway transport is the most important, carrying 85 percent of domestic cargo and passengers. Though extensive, the road system is poorly operated and maintained. According to an inventory carried out by the Ministry of Public Works (MOP), Ecuador has about 43,200 kilometers (km) of roads, of which 8,161 km are paved, 23,055 km are gravel, and 12,000 km are dirt. The national highway network is officially broken down by jurisdiction into (i) the National Highways Network (*Red Vial Estatal*), which includes roads managed by the MOP (8,682 km); (ii) the Provincial Highways Network (*Red Vial Provincial*), which includes the group of roads managed by each of the provincial councils; and (iii) the Cantonal Roadways Network (*Red Vial Cantonal*), which includes all the urban and interparish roads managed by the provincial and cantonal councils. Approximately 51 percent of all the roadways in the country are rural roads.

In terms of geographical coverage of roadways, there is a relatively extensive system of roads in the Costa region (except in Esmeraldas) and in the mountains (Sierra): 16,492 km and 22,052 km, respectively. Amazon or Oriente regions have only 4,470 km of roads, of which 89.3 percent are gravel or dirt roads. In the Galapagos Islands there are 184 km of roads, of which 92 percent are gravel. The eastern part of the country, characterized by a low level of development, sparse population, and numerous rivers, is sparsely covered by roads (table 13.6).

The length of the road network, its functional distribution, and the type of surface applied are comparable to other countries at similar levels of development. A total of 0.7 km paved and 3.6 km of total roads per thousand inhabitants is typical of low- and medium-income countries but well below regional averages of 5.4 km per thousand inhabitants. Several factors, including the institutional environment, unreliable budgets, and mountainous terrain contribute to the poor state of the highway network, resulting in long travel times and many accidents. Maintenance is poor throughout the network, especially the provincial and municipal rural network, only 30 percent of which is in good condition. In general, most of the primary network is paved, except in the eastern part of the country, where gravel and dirt roads predominate.

Difficult topography limits the technical quality of the network, and winding roads increase travel time. For example, the distance between Quito and Guayaquil is only 270 km as the crow flies, but the highway is 420 km long, and travel time for a heavy vehicle is over eight hours. The long distances and adverse terrain also make highways more vulnerable to rockslides, floods, landslides, land sinkage, and earthquakes, as well as to interruptions due to other causes (public demonstrations, strikes, blockades, and so forth). Given the topographic and geological conditions that characterize

Table 13.6. Characteristics of the Ecuadoran Road System, by Region

Concept	*Coast*	*Mountains*	*Eastern*	*Islands*	*Total*
Total intercity network (km)	16,492	22,052	4,469	184	43,197
Population (inhabitants)	5,989,543	5,463,934	546,602	18,555	12,018,634
Network service index km/1,000 inhabitants	2.75	4.03	8.18	9.92	3.59
Network segment (km)					
Primary	1,830	2,586	1,120	72	5,608
Secondary	1,461	1,847	534	34	3,876
Tertiary	4,705	5,091	1,294	16	11,105
Rural	8,354	12,239	1,499	61	22,153
Local	141	290	21	0	452
Road surface (km)					
Paved	4,040	3,628	478	14	8,160
Gravel	6,665	12,405	3,816	169	23,055
Dirt	5,787	6,019	175	0	11,981

Sources: MOP 1997; Ecuadoran Development Bank (BEDE) Rural Roads Team, July 2002.

the Andes, better policies need to be put in place in order to mitigate the threats to environmental degradation.

In summary, the length and coverage of the network is adequate, but road surfaces are in poor condition because of a lack of maintenance and institutional weakness. An extensive program of routine and periodic maintenance of the main MOP network is now necessary; at present, the MOP has plans for a routine maintenance program to be carried out by microenterprises. It is also absolutely essential to prepare and implement a comprehensive maintenance and repairs program for the secondary and rural systems, which are in such a bad state that many rural communities are cut off for weeks at a time during the rainy season.

VEHICLES AND TRAFFIC

The size of the vehicle fleet (about 625,000 vehicles, of which 90 percent are passenger cars, 8 percent are trucks, and 2 percent are buses) is commensurate with Ecuador's per capita GDP, but the distribution of vehicles is concentrated in two provinces (Pichincha and Guayas). Traffic volumes are not very high, with most stretches of trunk highway carrying annual average daily traffic (AADT) of 6,500 vehicles a day. Nonetheless, four stretches of highway carry an average of 10,000 vehicles a day. Most stretches with high volumes of traffic are located near big cities and are held in concession or are in the concession process. In practice, areas have periodic problems of traffic congestion owing to the state of the roads, special holidays, and the presence of slow trucks on mountain highways, but for the most part, limiting factors involve the structure and condition of the highways.

The volume of vehicle exhaust emissions generated by the transport sector and the atmospheric conditions of cities such as Quito lead to high levels of air pollution in densely populated areas. Air quality monitoring systems have been installed in some of these cities.

Rail Transport

Ecuador's rail network has a total length of 965 km, of which 31 percent is in service. The network is divided into three sectors: Southern Division (Durán–Quito, 446 km), Northern Division (Quito–San Lorenzo, 373 km), and Southern Branch (Sibambe–Cuenca, 145 km). The system is operated by the Ecuadoran National Railway Company (ENFE). This means of transport is used mainly by tourists. The most recent figures available show a more than 50 percent drop in passenger levels from the 197,855 passengers transported in 1996.

Airports and Air Transport

Ecuador has about 200 runways, aerodromes, and airports, five of which are international airports: Mariscal Sucre (Quito), Simón Bolívar (Guayaquil), plus the Manta, Tulcán, and Esmeraldas airports. There are also 23 important airports for domestic flights. In 2005, about 3.6 million passengers were transported—more than 2 million on international flights. Owing to the increase in passengers at the country's two main airports (Quito and Guayaquil), combined with increasing noise and urban pollution levels and the need to modernize and relocate the airports, new concessions have been awarded and are operational in both cities. In the case of the Quito airport, the existing terminal has been refurbished adequately by the concessionaire to meet travel needs in the medium term, while a new airport is being built outside the valley of Quito (partially to reduce the number of weather-related airport closures).

Ports and Maritime Traffic

It is estimated that 10 million tons of cargo were moved at the country's main ports in 2005. The largest port is at Guayaquil, which handles 75 percent of the country's foreign trade. The previous national government decided to grant concessions for the management of four state-owned commercial ports, through "landlord" contracts, by which the concessionaire assumes all responsibility and risk for the administration of existing infrastructure and for any investments that may be required, depending on the activities. At present, all national port authorities are free to provide cargo handling services through operators with short-term contracts.

Urban Transport Planning

Except in Quito, urban transport in most cities is organized, planned, and controlled by the National Land Transit and Transport Council (CNTTT). Specific urban transport plans for Ecuadoran cities are very scarce, and in most cases official information does not exist. The only city government that has an official plan is the Municipality of the Metropolitan District of Quito (MDMQ). This body has the authority to plan, regulate, and coordinate public and private transit and transport in its area of jurisdiction. In Quito, urban transport has many problems but has undergone relative improvements in recent years. For instance, the MDMQ has implemented projects such as the trolleybus system, which has partially rationalized public transport on its main route.

The MDMQ covers 4,228 km^2 and has about 1.5 million inhabitants, which equals about 10 inhabitants per vehicle. Public transit and transport demand is approximately 1.8 million trips a day, of which the trolleybus system handles 220,000 trips a day and Ecovía handles 30,000 trips a day. These two services are managed by the MDMQ through the Trolleybus System Operating Unit (UOST). The trolleybus system is currently operating near or at capacity and, hence, service quality is beginning to decline. Invasions of the dedicated road lanes are also becoming more frequent. It is necessary to plan now and in earnest to expand system capacity. There is a high concentration of public transport on the main routes, where the services overlap and generate congestion. Service is poor, routes are poorly organized, environmental impact due to gas emissions is high, and regulations and standards are not properly monitored. Private operators handle 82 percent of movements on public transport, representing 1.4 million urban trips. About 15 percent of these have been operating for more than 10 years, which means that the fleet is relatively new, though there is a great diversity of makes and models. Transport in Quito is divided into 132 routes and includes about 55 operators.

General Framework of the Rates System

The national rates system for transport is established by the CNTTT, except in the cities of Quito and Guayaquil, where this is handled, respectively, by the Municipality of Quito and by the Guayas Transport Commission. In general, urban passenger transport rates depend on the type of vehicle used. Prices vary between 10 and 36 U.S. cents. As for interprovincial transport rates, because there is a great variety of companies and cooperatives with routes throughout the country, there is fierce competition and prices are too low to permit operators to modernize their bus fleets.

Subsidies

In the roads sector, user charges include taxes on fuel, on vehicle imports, on tires, and on spare parts, plus charges for driving licenses and vehicle license plates. In Ecuador, the price of gasoline is at about market levels (US$1.50 per gallon) and is higher than the price of diesel fuel (US$0.90 a gallon). Therefore, although the total amount collected from users is greater than the cost of maintaining the network, there is clearly a cross-subsidy for heavy vehicles using diesel fuel, which also happen to be the vehicles that cause the most damage to the road network.

Highway Safety

The 1966 Land Traffic and Transport Law includes an adequate traffic code. However, a number of institutions share the responsibility for traffic safety, and the management of this sector is not properly coordinated. There is a high rate of traffic accidents, almost all trucks fail to obey laws on weight limits, theft of cargo en route is very common, and secondary and rural roads are practically abandoned in terms of sign posting and highway safety.

Rural Roads Project

Given Ecuador's significant share of rural residents and the importance of agriculture to its economy, it is worthwhile reviewing the issues and challenges facing the improvement of road transport in rural areas. This problem was analyzed in detail in the context of the Fiscal Stability Law (LOREYTF) and the preparation requirements for the World Bank's Rural Roads project (Ln7403-EC, approved in mid-2006). In Ecuador as in many other countries, road transport is the dominant mode of transportation. However, the existing road network certainly cannot provide the efficient, least-cost surface transport linkages needed to support economic growth and to meet the country's poverty-alleviation objectives. The level and quality of transport services are not commensurate with the country's needs, the road network provides limited access to many production centers and especially to rural areas, and investment in village roads and footpaths has largely been neglected. Moreover, maintenance and rehabilitation arrangements have been inadequate for most of the road network and, in particular, for secondary and rural roads. For rural residents, this has all resulted in a sense of isolation and reduced hopes for breaking out of poverty. Some of the overarching issues affecting rural roads from a national perspective are summarized in the following paragraphs.

INADEQUATE ACCESS

The lack of adequate access to rural economic or social centers has been highlighted in various World Bank consultations with stakeholders over the years as well as in workshops held at local levels during preparation for the Rural Roads project. Clearly, addressing road transport needs is a key requirement for supporting economic growth and meeting the needs of the rural poor. At a country level, the overall road service index is roughly 3.6 km per thousand inhabitants, which is well below the regional average of 5.4 km per thousand inhabitants, and for poor rural cantons the service index is further below the national average. In sum, the rural road network that is managed by the SGs receives too limited road-service coverage, and too little of that coverage (40 percent on average) is in maintainable condition, that is, good or fair. Furthermore, in the Sierra region, the topography is very difficult, which leads to the building of steeply graded, winding roads that are difficult for freight vehicles to traverse and makes travel times inordinately long; the adverse combination results in very high transport costs. This situation has been exacerbated by the lack of road rehabilitation and maintenance, and by the relatively high degree of vulnerability of road networks to natural disasters, such as mudslides, floods, earthquakes, and volcanic activity.

Economic and Social Isolation

Many rural communities can be reached only by tracks and trails (bridle paths, or *caminos de herradura*) that are often suitable only for nonmotorized transport because of their narrow, steep slopes, multiple river crossings, and often unstable soils. Poor rural accessibility has contributed to a general sense of isolation and reduced hopes for improvement in the livelihood of the people affected. Furthermore, during the rainy season many roads in rural areas are closed or remain impassable for weeks, which heightens the sense of isolation for the local population. This makes it very difficult and costly to provide services, public or private, to the affected rural residents on a reliable basis. In terms of self-improvement, considerable disincentives face isolated peoples, as they can neither take advantage of employment opportunities in the region nor reach markets to sell their goods. In reality, isolated peoples tend to engage in subsistence activities and need transport linkages in order to develop exchange economies with other communities. This is why improved access is usually one of their most frequently expressed priorities.

Lack of Comprehensive Road Maintenance Programs

Maintenance plays a key role in minimizing road deterioration, extending the useful life of roads, and reducing vehicle operating costs, but it is not being carried out adequately. Several factors cause this. Foremost among them are the lack of adequate budgetary allocations and untimely releases of funds as well as the institutional and other weaknesses in the SG that hamper the planning and implementation of maintenance. There is a pressing need to develop the institutional capacity of the provincial roads agencies (PRAs), which are typically part of the public works department at the provincial or municipal government level. This includes developing the PRAs' capacity to carry out condition inventories of the roads, design and implement annual and multiannual road rehabilitation and maintenance programs, seek least-cost solutions to technical and engineering problems associated with road and bridge maintenance, and promote the development of the local construction industry. Given the World Bank's experiences with similar projects elsewhere, it will require a long-term program of technical assistance to help accomplish all of these goals.

Incomplete Decentralization Process

The government of Ecuador had long ago diagnosed the difficult situation in the road sector and had taken steps to transfer the responsibility for managing the secondary and rural roads segments of the network to the provinces and municipalities. The objectives behind the decentralization attempt were to promote more efficient deployment of resources and to permit the SGs to address local problems more directly. A large measure of the underlying legal and regulatory framework supporting decentralization has been enacted during the past 10 years. Nevertheless, the process of decentralization has been only partially completed; there remains considerable tension among sectoral agencies about responsibilities and fiscal arrangements. Decentralization is a politically sensitive issue and progress is difficult, as Ecuador has multiple layers of government and has yet to establish well-functioning transfer principles that embody clear responsibilities and appropriate incentives for the road sector.

The decentralization law established that roughly 15 percent of the total national budget should be allocated to a general decentralization fund, of which municipalities and provinces would receive 70 percent and 30 percent, respectively. Allocation of funds is determined according to population and land area, among other criteria. On average, own-source generated revenues of local governments represent about 10 to 15 percent of their budgetary expenditures. Thus, most local governments, with the exception of Quito and Guayaquil, still depend heavily on revenue transfers from the central government. However, the actual percentage of central government funds that are finally made available to the SGs is often less than the theoretical level, owing to procedural complexities in transferring funds to the local governments. Hence, there is still some risk regarding whether financial resources that are commensurate with the SGs' increasing responsibilities (for the management of infrastructure) will be made available to them on a reliable basis.

THE NEED TO STRENGTHEN GOVERNANCE

The problems of poor governance and problematic levels of corruption are well known in Ecuador. The results of detailed surveys, carried out by the World Bank and other agencies, indicate that the issue of corruption is of considerable concern to Ecuadoran citizens in their daily lives, and more so if they need to win contracts awarded by the public sector, clear items through customs, or conduct transactions in which a public official has considerable discretion. Corruption has been shown in cross-country studies to be associated with worse rather than better levels of service, to affect the poor disproportionately in the allocation of public resources, and to increase public disaffection with the polity. Central to this issue also is the lack of transparency in public expenditures, which occurs largely because of the combination of (i) no truly centralized public payroll, (ii) a lack of controls on preallocated spending, and (iii) complex budgetary procedures.

In general, a reform plan is needed to focus on three areas: (i) strengthening existing regulations and institutions in the fight against corruption, which covers not only the public sector but also the private sector and civil society in general; (ii) educating the population regarding their rights to supervise public functions, which implies the development of mechanisms for monitoring public spending and guaranteeing public access to fiscal accounts; and (iii) improving administrative procedures to prevent corruption in its various forms, especially when linked to specific areas such as the administration of public procurement. In the short term, this could include modernizing budget management and making information accessible to citizens in electronic form; a good example of this could be the plans for the development of a Web site for the Rural Roads project and continued extensive use of informed public participation processes.

The Need to Integrate Environmental and Social Safeguards into the Project Planning and Implementation Cycle

An adequate framework and guidelines for environmental and social analyses currently exist at the national level (*Sistema Unico de Medio Ambiente* [Single Environmental Management System]—SUMA) and to a lesser extent at provincial and local levels. Usually these procedures tend to be applied somewhat late in the project cycle and typically are seen by many agencies as bottlenecks or obstacles to project development. Too often this also implies a less than desirable allocation of resources for environmental and social safeguards management and the inadequate application of environmental and social policies, plans, and procedures at the SG level. A strategic safeguards vision that could be deployed for rural roads would have the aim of (i) developing environmental and social policies that are appropriate to the sector; (ii) defining an adequate strategy that addresses the long-term environmental and social risks, and the indirect and cumulative impacts by ecoregion; (iii) developing mitigation measures to counteract the potential environmental and social effects; and (iv) defining environmental and social management procedures for the staff of SG road agencies.

Reorganization of Institutional Roles

Provincial governments have traditionally accepted responsibility for roads in rural areas of cantons; however, owing in no small measure to the unfinished decentralization agenda, weak and overlapping institutions with unclear mandates continue to characterize the rural transport sector. The MOP has tried to reduce the level of administrative duplication by defining and classifying three separate road networks corresponding to the national, provincial, and cantonal levels. As the main central government entity in the sector, the MOP is responsible for the administration of the road network, but several specialized agencies share the responsibility for the overall policy setting and regulatory functions of the sectors. The MOP is trying to gradually consolidate the planning functions within the sector to foster the integration and coordination of road sector activities among provincial capitals and economic centers. In addition to the overlapping responsibilities among the various levels of government, institutional capacity remains weak, especially in local government entities, including some where decentralization has already taken place. Key issues that have emerged in road network management at the SG level include (i) the dependence on national government transfers; (ii) inconsistent allocation by the SG of funds needed for road network improvements; (iii) inadequate provision for maintenance activities; (iv) lack of available technical data and statistical information that are necessary for decision making; (v) weak planning units; (vi) inadequate financial management and expenditure tracking systems; (vii) weaknesses in the procurement process, which have led to implementation delays and cost increases; and (viii) inadequate numbers of professional and technical staff.

During preparation of the Rural Roads project, the World Bank assisted the MEF in carrying out detailed institutional and financial assessments of each of the 22 provincial governments to ensure compliance with LOREYTF. The findings of the institutional capacity analyses showed that many road management issues affect the road transport sector in the majority of PRAs. The main findings of the assessments, which are instrumental to mapping the way forward, are presented below.

1. Inadequate planning, programming, and budgeting systems in road networks. The analysis indicates that provincial governments do not have integrated and adequate planning, budgeting, and execution capacity for roads management. Moreover, in most cases, at the provincial level, the operational planning is not based on technical criteria but rather responds to the ad hoc requests of municipalities and communities, as well as to decisions adopted by individual provincial governments. This shortcoming is being countered by requirements under the Rural Roads project for the preparation of adequately prioritized rural road improvement plans. However, most provinces have not yet started using the Participative Provincial Roads Plan procedures and recommendations for their own-financed projects. Figure 13.8 details the planning process.

2. Reliance on "force account" execution of works. The predominant road project management model in most provincial governments is via force account. This model is used to identify the dimensions of work programs and to organize, execute, and deploy financial resources in accordance with the capacity of a province's own equipment and personnel. To a large extent, the current weak planning environment is also derived from the use of the force account as the predominant system of project execution, because this system does not really depend on the use of rational planning criteria. It is also suboptimal for life-cycle management of roads because the organization of resources (equipment and personnel) is oriented to road construction projects and gives little or no priority to addressing subsequent preventive maintenance, thereby leaving roads to deteriorate again. On the financial side, the negative impact of the force account model arises from the fact that the provincial decision to carry out projects is traditionally accompanied by spending to acquire new equipment and also by the need to hire additional personnel, because it is felt that this is the way to augment a PRA's implementation capacity. This, in the long term, tends to escalate recurrent budgets and to deploy them in a way that is unsuitable for the various stages of the road project cycle and even less so for other provincial program needs.

3. Incipient development of management capacity for private sector participation. The assessments showed that experiences with private sector participation in project design and implementation are very limited at the provincial level. To enhance efficiency and promote capacity development at local levels, private sector participation should be promoted through a progressive expansion strategy

Figure 13.8. Participative Planning Process for Rural Roads

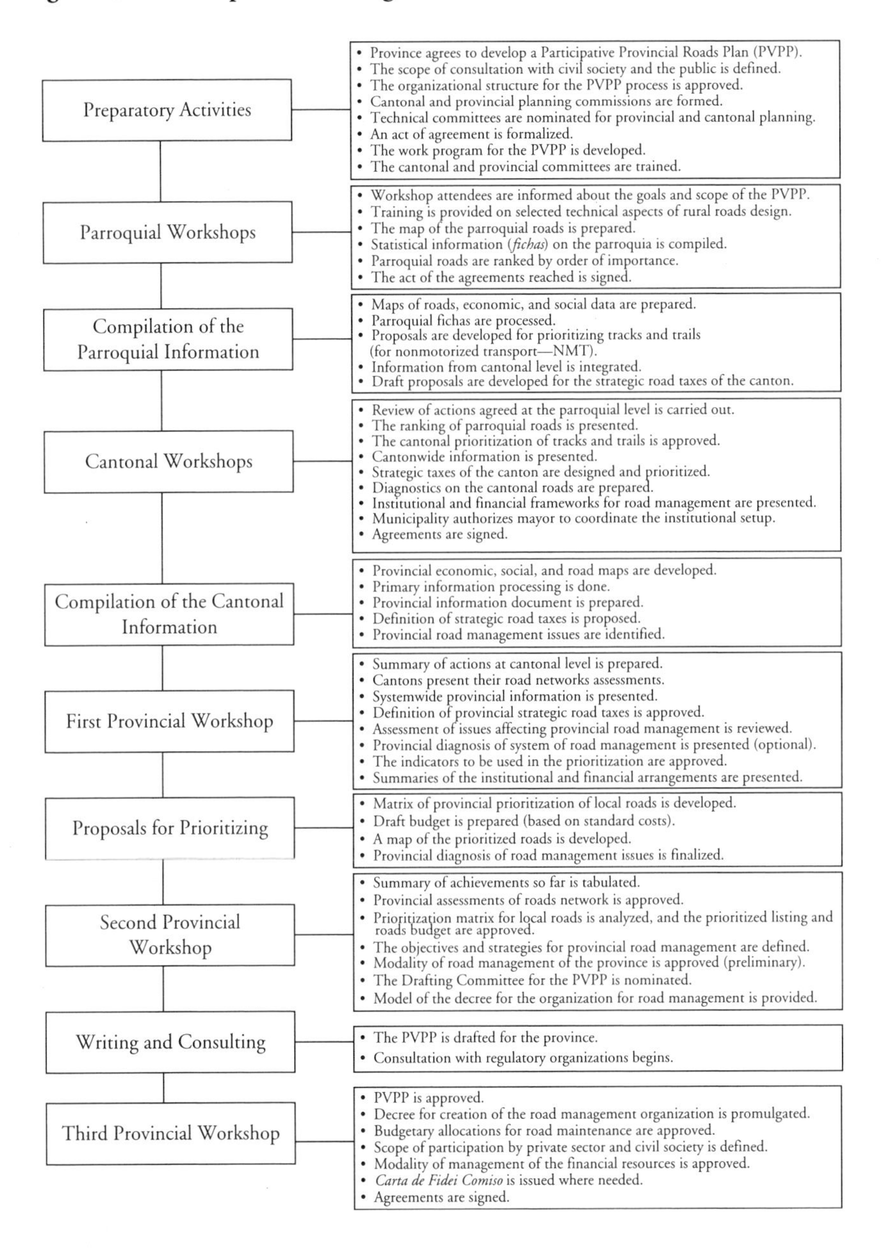

that would consider it as the primary modus operandi for road rehabilitation and maintenance projects instead of the current reliance on the force account. This would require developing the PRA's capacity to procure services efficiently and to manage contractors.

4. Stocks of PRA construction equipment. Under the force account modality, it is assumed by PRAs that a greater supply of road equipment will imply an increased capacity for road project execution. Nevertheless, in most cases, equipment stocks have been acquired by provincial governments without adequate planning and without considering the organizational demands of project management or their internal operational capacity. As a result, each new acquisition of road equipment has too often been accompanied by the creation of new staff positions. Subsequently, the equipment falls into disrepair, and it was noted during the assessments that in most cases the PRA's capacity to carry out road rehabilitation and maintenance is too often limited by low levels of availability of their equipment fleets.

5. PRA staffing. The analysis has highlighted the need to rationalize and improve the pool of personnel dedicated to road networks with regard to the real needs of the organization in charge (the PRA or Road Infrastructure Directorate). It also noted that the total number of road network personnel, including professional and technical staff, administrative assistants, and laborers, represents between 30 percent and 50 percent of all personnel employed by provincial governments. The number of professionals employed was typically only 6 percent of total personnel. This situation is aggravated by the lack of trained professionals with experience in maintaining the road system efficiently. The existence of strong labor unions, acquired labor rights through old labor agreements, a great amount of equipment on the verge of becoming obsolete or inoperative, and the absence of an adequate institutional structure to optimize the use of resources are leading to an undesirable combination, that of a major economic burden on the provincial governments' current expenditures and limited capacity for managing road network investments.

6. Problems of institutional organization. In most cases, the PRAs do not have a clear distribution of responsibilities, functional structure, and adequate decision-making procedures to efficiently serve the different demands of the road network under the responsibility of the provincial governments. Also, high-performance road network authorities normally focus on road intervention based on project cycles (activities that are differentiated at various stages of the useful life of roads, considering the typology, situation, and level of service). The assessments showed that for rural roads, in most cases the PRAs limit their functions almost exclusively to tending emergencies and providing periodic maintenance to the road network sections for which they are responsible. Moreover, the study found that road construction and rehabilitation activities are not carried out in accordance with road deterioration patterns, and when they do occur, they are carried out partially (in annual installments or by tranches). In most provincial governments, no mechanisms or systems are applied to evaluate the performance and effectiveness of PRA activities.

7. Lack of coordination between provincial governments and municipalities. The assessments noted that, in most cases, there is incipient coordination between municipalities, parishes (*parroquias*), and other agencies involved in managing rural road networks. This means that although agreements and collaborative mechanisms exist between provincial governments and municipalities, in effect they are limited to emergency works. The short- and long-term goals of the government organizations involved are not defined, and the participation of or support from users' organizations and beneficiaries are practically disregarded.

IV. Sectoral Policy Recommendations

Recommendations with respect to water supply and sanitation, telecommunications, and transport vary depending on the maturity of existing institutional and legal arrangements and the degree to which the central government controls each sector. In the telecommunications sector, on the one hand, the legal and regulatory framework is still incomplete, as is a clear designation of regulatory responsibilities (several bodies have overlapping responsibilities). Improved coverage and quality of services also depend on greater private sector participation, for which a legal and regulatory framework must first be put in place. Since the central government controls Andinatel and Pacifictel and also controls the issuing of licenses, improvements in the telecommunications sector depend mostly on the central government. In the water and sanitation and transport sectors, on the other hand, most services are provided by decentralized entities under provincial or municipal governments (municipal water companies, PRAs, and so forth). Here, too, the central government must finish an incomplete institutional, regulatory, and legal framework and foment better provision of services, using fiscal transfers as an incentive. In both sectors, improvements in the quality and coverage of services depend on greater private sector participation in the design, construction, and operation of the services (water and sanitation, and transport) or the delegation of service provision to independent public, private, mixed-capital, or cooperative operators (water and sanitation).

Water Supply and Sanitation Sector

The water and sanitation sector's principal challenges—(i) coverage, service quality, and efficiency; (ii) cost recovery; (iii) high dependence on transfer payments from central and municipal governments to close operational deficits; (iv) an incomplete legal and regulatory framework; and (v) the lack of an integrated national water resource management system—need to be met with an integrated package of measures at the national, municipal, and community levels.

National-Level Recommendations

At the national level, key recommendations comprise (i) consistent financial policies that provide incentives to subnational actors as well as arrangements to improve the quality of public expenditure; (ii) completion of the restructuring of the SAPSyRS; and (iii) overhaul of the legal framework for the WSS sector.

FINANCIAL POLICIES AND QUALITY OF EXPENDITURE

The national government spends upward of US$100 million annually[4] on the water supply and sanitation sector, but the use of resources is not monitored systematically, nor do the municipalities and water companies that receive resources use them strategically to leverage performance improvements in favor of the poor. A multitude of national and subnational actors—the Solidarity Fund, the BdE, the FISE, regional development corporations, various government ministries (including the MEF, MIDUVI, and the Ministry of Social Welfare), and agencies (Council for the Development of the Indigenous Nations and Peoples of Ecuador, provincial and municipal governments, and others) provide financing for urban and rural water supply investments under different eligibility criteria and financing rules. To overcome this situation, the government boldly decided, at the MEF's behest, to improve Ecuador's incentive framework for investments in the WSS sector by adopting Executive Decree No. 2562, published February 21, 2005. Under the decree, about US$75 million a year in national government transfers to municipalities, which were already earmarked for WSS investments under a special consumption tax on telephone calls (*Impuesto sobre Consumos Especiales*—ICE), were linked to operator performance, the service model, and poverty indicators. In the past, the ICE transfers for the water sector had generally returned funds to those municipalities that had generated the phone calls. In effect, this meant that Quito and Guayaquil (which between them account for only about a third of the national population) received nearly three-fourths of all transfers.

To complete this nascent reform of financial policies, the government might consider the following:

- Require financial and technical audits of WSS utilities receiving ICE transfers to determine (i) how funds assigned in previous years were used (only water supply investments, not operating expenditures, are eligible); (ii) whether current funding requests are backed by a pipeline of projects with feasible least-cost designs; and (iii) whether the utility data used to calculate the ICE assignment are accurate. While such audits are mandated under the executive decree, they have never been carried out in practice.

- Extend uniform financing rules to other central government programs in all ministries and agencies under a uniform "sector financial policy."
- Audit the use of government funds (not just ICE funds) by WSS utilities to improve the quality of government expenditures. In practice, many utilities currently use government transfers to cover operational deficits rather than to extend coverage to the unserved poor.

It is estimated that in order to raise water coverage to 85 percent (90 percent urban and 75 percent rural) and sanitation coverage to 83 percent (87 percent urban and 75 percent rural) by 2011, total investments of approximately US$650 million would be needed. In addition, another US$120 million would be needed to improve service quality (continuity of service and quality of water). Reaching those goals would mean doubling current national government spending of US$100 million a year in the s7ector or, alternatively, using existing government transfers as incentives to increase revenue generation by municipalities and utilities themselves.

COMPLETE RESTRUCTURING OF SAPSYRS

Restructuring of SAPSyRS proceeded at a slow pace over the course of the past five years, in part because of high turnover in ministerial and subsecretary ranks at MIDUVI. Though a new organizational structure for SAPSyRS has been adopted, SAPSyRS has yet to assume the normative and sector planning functions of a true lead sector agency and continues to act as a direct implementing agency. Few of SAPSyRS's working groups (for sector planning, benchmarking, norms, and so forth) actually produce the products for which they were designed. The government might consider the following steps:

- Jump-start the preparation of each of SAPSyRS working group's main products, giving priority to (i) collecting data for the existing (but unused) sector information system, SISASAR, and publishing benchmarking data on utility performance; (ii) producing five-year plans for sector development (investments, priority areas, and so forth); and (iii) updating sector norms (for example, appropriate discharge standards for sewage; preparation of environmental guidelines for water supply, sanitation, and solid waste); and (iv) monitoring potable water quality in rural and cantonal systems through its provincial water and sanitation teams (*equipos provinciales de agua y saneamiento*—EPAS).
- Secure accreditation (by the Ministry of Environment) of MIDUVI's in-house environmental unit to facilitate environmental review of low- and medium-impact WSS investments.
- Promote strategic reassignments within the government to improve the skill mix of SAPSyRS staff (there are currently no economists, financial experts, lawyers, or technical staff with a background in business administration).

LEGAL FRAMEWORK

Although SAPSyRS prepared a draft water supply and sanitation sector law over the past several years with support from external consultants financed by the World Bank and the Inter-American Development Bank, the draft law was never presented to Congress. The law would clarify the roles and responsibilities of sector actors at various levels, thereby eliminating costly overlaps and inconsistencies. The incoming government may wish to review this draft law, make the adjustments it deems necessary, and present it to Congress for approval.

Municipal-Level Reforms

The financial policies discussed above could provide incentives for municipalities across Ecuador to adopt better management models for WSS service provision, particularly in those (mostly small and medium) municipalities that continue to provide WSS services directly through the municipal government. MIDUVI should offer municipalities technical assistance to choose a model (municipal, mixed-capital, or private company; cooperative; and so forth) appropriate for their needs from a menu of alternatives and promote regional operators serving a number of municipalities with greater economies of scale (for example, through the World Bank-financed PRAGUAS program). Finally, municipal councils need to approve tariff increases (gradually if necessary) required to allow WSS utilities to cover at least their operation and maintenance costs as well as the cost of replacing essential equipment such as pumps and valves.

Community-Level Reforms

Several thousand water users associations (*Juntas de Agua Potable y Saneamiento*, JAPS) operate in Ecuador, many with poor sustainability characteristics. The large number of juntas precludes direct technical assistance (TA) for service improvements by SAPSyRS. Instead, SAPSyRS should (i) inventory juntas already developed for Ecuador and classify them (using the scale of A, best, to D, least sustainable); (ii) promote the creation of regional associations of JAPS and strengthen these associations to provide technical, financial, administrative, and legal assistance to their member juntas; and (iii) strengthen municipal sanitation teams (*equipos municipales de saneamiento*—EMS) to provide technical assistance to juntas under their jurisdiction.

Water Resources Management

The sustainability of the quality and quantity of the water supply of urban and rural communities depends on integrated management of the resource at the level of water basins, where all users (including rural municipalities and communities) can openly discuss the use, management, and prioritization of the resource. The management of water resources at the level of water basins is fundamental, especially in places where one municipality's sewage (or agricultural effluents) has a significant impact on raw water quality in other municipalities downstream. Two short- and medium-term measures are recommended below.

MONITORING OF WATER BASINS
In water basins where conflicts over use or significant risks of flooding already exist, it is important that the National Council on Water Resources, supported by development corporations, provincial councils, and municipalities, monitor both the supply and the demand for surface and underground water and evaluate its quality to prepare more systematic management in the medium term.

LEGAL FRAMEWORK
Although Ecuador already has its National Strategy for the Management of Water Resources, it is important that the government review the country's legal framework in this regard, in order to establish a more efficient and fairer system for managing water basins and allocating water resources.

Telecommunications Sector

The following sections outline key areas of action essential to the modernization of Ecuador's telecoms sector.

Regulatory and Policy-Making Agencies

To provide greater coherence to the institutional and regulatory framework, the organizational structure that regulates and sets policy in the sector must be reformed. There is great confusion regarding the functions of SUPTEL, CONATEL, and CONARTEL. For example, SUPTEL controls and monitors the use of the radio-electric spectrum, CONATEL approves the frequencies planned and uses of the spectrum, and CONARTEL regulates the radio and television subsector. The difficulty in defining the lines of authority and responsibilities makes investors hesitant and uncertain. The consolidation of CONATEL, SUPTEL, and CONARTEL in two agencies with sufficient authority and functional capacity—one for regulatory functions and the other to set policy in the sector—will provide the simplicity and clarity necessary for a dynamic, competitive sector. While the international trend is toward the convergence of telecommunications services, the Ecuadoran telecommunications sector is still extremely fragmented, beginning with the organization of its regulatory agencies.

Legal Framework

A new legal framework must be found to replace the existing one, which is based on regulations characterized by duplications, inconsistencies, and lack of clarity. For example, article 15 of the general regulations prohibits private networks being connected to public ones, while article 36 allows it. Furthermore, this same article indicates that operators of public networks must lease their infrastructure to third parties but limits this leasing to a maximum of two years; however, article 7 of the interconnection regulations requires that the network and other elements be broken up with no time limits.

A National Digital Agenda

Government ministries and agencies have different levels and capacities to use information and communications technologies (ICTs). Though a few of them have computer systems and use the Internet effectively to deliver their services, many do not have computers and do not provide services online. It would be advisable for the new government to consolidate the different ICT initiatives under one single ministry or policy unit, which would be charged to prepare and supervise the implementation of a national digital agenda. This entity would provide training and supervise the different ministries to carry out a program of modernization by using ICTs. Many services can be offered online, for example, thereby saving citizens the inconvenience of waiting in lines to receive services. Elimination of unnecessary (or redundant) processes and waste would reduce costs and increase the effectiveness of the government. This program was implemented very successfully in Chile, reducing the costs and improving service to citizens.

State-Owned Companies

It is clear that state-owned companies have not expanded to meet demand, and several attempts to fix them have been ineffective. Although there was an attempt to attract private capital to Andinatel and Pacifictel, the strategy has not been sufficiently clear, nor have the necessary incentives been offered. The situation of Pacifictel is especially difficult and requires an urgent decision at the highest level to change the company for good. A package must now be put together that is attractive enough to convince international operators and investors. For example, combining Andinatel, Pacifictel, and Telecsa (Alegro PCS) would be attractive for private investors, who would be attracted by the growth opportunities of the cellular company and who would want to turn around Pacifictel, a daunting task, but possibly facilitated by the cash flow of Andinatel. A strong, third cellular operator would be good for the cellular subsector, as increased competition would reduce cost for consumers.

Access to the Internet

Ecuador has one of the lowest penetration rates of Internet service. It is well known that countries that have better access to the Internet have better opportunities to compete in a globalized economy. Better opportunities mean better jobs, more exports, and lower costs to citizens. To improve access to the Internet, the World Bank proposes two measures. The first is to introduce a flat rate tariff for Internet access. This tariff will stimulate more users to access their ISP using the dial-up method. The second is the implementation of a National Digital Agenda, as described above, that would stimulate the use of the Internet. More users would like to use the new online services that government ministries and agencies would make available. They would get connected to the Internet to reduce time and the cost of trips to offices and waiting in lines. Thus, this measure has a double benefit: it would reinforce the development of the Internet at the same time that it would reduce the government's costs.

Rural Access

Ecuador's poorest inhabitants do not have access to telecommunication services. An ongoing World Bank project (PROMEC) has demonstrated that with limited funds it is possible to give access to 1,100 towns through the FODETEL. However, FODETEL does not have funds. To reduce the rural gap, two measures are proposed: (i) modify the law to create a fee to fund FODETEL (a 1 percent levy on gross revenues of all telecommunications operators would be enough), so that FODETEL can implement more projects similar to PROMEC; and (ii) negotiate with the cellular companies to extend their networks to rural areas. Part of the financing for this expansion could come from FODETEL, and the other part from the companies' own cash flows.

Transport Sector

Institutionally, the agencies responsible for planning, regulation, and control of transport are spread out among different ministries at different administrative levels, generally without proper coordination. Medium- and long-term sectoral and modal planning are deficient; in this regard, there is a clear lack of leadership. Adequate planning is also absent at the provincial and municipal levels. An exception is the metropolitan district of Quito, which has a properly functioning planning unit. Deficient planning was partially compensated for by the National Modernization Council (CONAM), but this was not sustainable in the medium or long term. The greatest need is to complete institutional restructuring in the sector. This could include turning the MOP into a ministry of transport in charge of planning, regulating, and controlling the different forms of transport—functions now in the hands of different ministries, councils, and commissions. In this scheme, independent agencies would be responsible for the administration of each form of transport, with greater private sector participation in the creation of infrastructure. A concessions superintendency could even be established to administer all projects of this kind in the sector and to improve the sector's institutional framework. A recent decision by the new government to restructure the MOP and other sector institutions could go a long way toward fulfilling this agenda.

Decentralization

As was mentioned earlier, Ecuador is engaged in a long and difficult process of decentralization, with significant implications for the transport sector. At present, there is a theoretical consensus on the definition of the types of network (primary, secondary, and tertiary) but administrative responsibilities are not clear. This issue also involves strengthening regional councils; financing provincial highways; maintaining and improving local roads, concessions, and tolls; and enhancing environmental and social management. The case of local roads merits special comment, since national agencies have participated in their financing and construction, and now, theoretically, their maintenance will be turned over to municipalities. However, provinces and municipalities have little technical, administrative, or financial capacity to take on the new responsibilities imposed by the Special Law on Decentralization and Social

Participation. At these levels of government, political pressures, insufficient training, and a critical lack of resources conspire to prevent change in the situation.

Linked to decentralization is the system for transferring 15 percent of the total government budget to the sectional governments (the 15 Percent Law). A fundamental problem is that this system of transfer payments is nearly automatic, and few incentives are in place to promote efficient use of the transferred funds by SGs. The other problem is that SGs claim that the system is not adequate for managing the infrastructure network that has been transferred to them as part of decentralization and, furthermore, that at the end of each year the central government typically transfers only 10 percent of the budget. While steps are being taken to rectify this situation, it would be best if transfers above the mandated level were earmarked to (i) projects focused on special issues such as targeted poverty alleviation, and (ii) SGs that demonstrate adequate ability to manage resources and to plan and implement projects. This approach provides double benefits: the efficient use of resources and an incentive for weak SGs to improve their performance.

The transport sector will not be successfully modernized without greater private sector participation in several areas: in concessions (not only highways, but also concessions of maritime infrastructure, urban transport, and railways), the design and implementation of infrastructure works, and the provision of transport services. Clear rules and appropriate sector management policies are essential to increase private sector participation.

Rural Roads

Without question, one of the main problems faced by rural and indigenous communities is the poor state of local roads (both for motorized and nonmotorized vehicles), as well as poor coverage by transport services. The combination of these factors in rural areas makes economic activities more costly and weakens government programs aimed at poverty alleviation. Considering the goals of the decentralization process, the need for social participation by the rural population, and the needs of the transport sector, reforms should emphasize satisfying the transportation needs of rural communities. For rural transport services, Ecuador could test small truck cooperatives created with mixed capital (municipal, community-raised, and funds supplied by individual companies), as well as other more traditional forms of mixed-capital ventures.

Main Network

The MOP has decided to substantially improve its highway maintenance system by contracting maintenance services on the basis of performance, standards, and quality of service, rather than by simple administrative decision. In this framework, a routine maintenance pilot project has already been implemented with 14 microenterprises in the province of Loja. Results have been positive, and the plan is to use this approach for the routine maintenance of the entire main network.

Sectoral Action Plan

Problem	Policy measures: Short term	Policy measures: Medium term	Progress indicators	Objectives/goals
Water supply and sanitation				
Lack of consistent financial policies that would provide incentives for improved performance by WSS sector utilities	• Audit past use of and proposed future use of ICE transfers by WSS utilities as well as key performance data to provide a sound basis for ICE allocations in the future. • Publish a list of all resources (ICE, FISE, and others) effectively transferred by the central government to municipalities and WSS service providers.	• Develop a uniform financial policy for all national resource transfers to the WSS sector. • Audit the use of national government transfers and vet proposed investments to improve the quality of public expenditures.	WSS service providers that receive ICE resources are audited by independent auditors. National government resource transfers to municipalities and WSS service providers are published regularly on the web. A uniform financial policy for the WSS sector is published and applied. Use of national government transfers by municipalities and WSS service providers is audited.	Have service providers with modern, efficient structures operating with tariffs that cover at least O&M and major equipment replacement so as to free up funds for extending coverage and improving the quality of service provision.

(Table continues on the following page.)

Problem	Policy measures: Short term	Policy measures: Medium term	Progress indicators	Objectives/goals
SAPSyRS has yet to assume its role as lead sector agency	• Jump start SAPSyRS working groups by (i) collecting data for the existing sector information system (SISASAR) and publishing benchmarking data on utility performance; (ii) producing five-year plans for sector development (investments, priority areas, and so forth); and (iii) accrediting an environmental unit for MIDUVI.	Deepen SAPSyRS' function as sector leader by (i) updating sector norms and (ii) monitoring potable water quality in rural and cantonal systems through SAPSyRS' provincial water supply and sanitation teams (*equipos provinciales de agua y saneamiento*, EPAS)	SISASAR contains data on a least 50 major WSS service providers and benchmarking data are published. SAPSyRS produces five-year sector development plans. Key sector norms are updated. Water quality in 500 rural and 50 cantonal potable water systems is monitored on a regular basis by the end of 2008.	Strengthen SAPSyRS so it is able to produce the information products that improve sector planning and promote improved performance by all sector actors (municipalities, service providers, and so forth).
Incomplete regulatory and legal framework	Prepare and pass a new water supply and sanitation law		• Draft law is reviewed and finalized. • Law is passed.	Establish a clear legal and regulatory framework that encourages modernization of services and eliminates wasteful overlaps in roles and responsibilities.
Inefficient organization of service provision at the municipal level	• Hire a specialized international or regional water operator or consulting firm (*empresa consultora de apoyo a la delegación—ECAD*) to advise municipalities on alternative WSS management models.	• Provide interested municipalities with technical assistance on service delegation as well as financial assistance to jump start new models.	At least 30 additional municipalities adopt improved management models and receive financial assistance to jump start their operations.	Implement efficient management models and appropriate cost-recovery tariffs that allow depoliticized and solvent operators to improve and extend WSS services.

Failure of many water user associations to operate rural WSS services sustainably	• Define areas for creation of JAPS on a pilot basis and determine their portfolio of services. • Begin classifying JAPS on a scale of A to D.	• Create and strengthen several associations of JAPS with a critical mass of member JAPS to ensure their viability.	• Areas for pilot associations of JAPS are defined. • Several associations of JAPS are created and strengthened. • Juntas are classified. • Associations provide member JAPS with services they are willing to pay for.	Strengthen JAPS to provide high-quality and sustainable WSS services to rural populations.
Poor management of water resources	Unify and modernize the legal and institutional framework for water resources management.	Improve and modernize the administration and management of available water resources (and related water infrastructure) in priority water basins.	New legal and institutional framework is implemented and under way at the national level and in at least one priority water basin.	Put in place an integrated water resources management system that includes a legal and institutional framework that is coherent at the national level and has sufficiently decentralized administration and management.
Telecommunications				
Poor performance of Pacifictel and ineffectiveness of Telecsa (Alegro PCS)	Combine Andinatel, Pacifictel, and Telecsa into one single company, and invite strategic investors to participate in the purchase of shares of the new company to turn around the companies, bring profitability, and improve services.	Monitor the performance of the new operator.	1. Number of lines in service (Alegro PCS). 2. Quality of service indicators (Pacifictel). 3. Number of Internet connections (all).	1. Promote competition in the market. 2. Promote investment and development of the sector.

(*Table continues on the following page.*)

Problem	Policy measures: Short term	Policy measures: Medium term	Progress indicators	Objectives/goals
Overlapping responsibilities and confusion regarding the role of SUPTEL, CONATEL, and CONARTEL	Create a structural plan for the new organization of regulatory institutions in the sector.	Implement institutional reorganization according to the plan.	1. Reduction in number of regulatory agencies. 2. Consolidation of authority and functions in a single regulatory authority.	Establish a single regulatory authority that is separate from the agency that sets policy in the telecommunications sector.
Contradictions between regulations and confusing legal framework	Prepare a new draft of a general law on telecommunications to eliminate legal inconsistencies in the existing regulatory framework.	Carry out negotiations and make agreements necessary for the draft law to be passed by Congress.	Approval of a new law on telecommunications that is inclusive, clear, and effective.	Establish a transparent regulatory framework that encourages private investment.
Local telephone rates not fixed according to real costs	Continue adjusting rates; complete this before opening bidding for private participation in the companies.		Rates are established according to costs.	Eliminate distortions in the market that discourage private investment.
Low coverage in rural and marginal areas	Negotiate with cellular companies the extension of cellular services in rural areas.	Introduce a bill to Congress to modify the telecom law to create the contribution to FODETEL to promote investment in rural areas.	Rural population is covered by mobile networks.	Increase penetration of telecommunications services in rural and marginal areas.
Little use of ICT for development in Ecuador	Appoint a single ministry or policy unit to design and supervise the implementation of the national digital agenda. Introduce a flat rate for Internet access.	Implement the national digital agenda in all ministries and agencies of the government.	A higher percentage of schools, health centers, national government ministries, municipalities, and other public entities are using ICT effectively, providing online services, and rationalizing work flows.	Improve citizen access to government services to 24 hours a day, seven days a week. Reduce government cost and waste. Promote the use of the Internet to improve productivity and create jobs and exports.

Transport				
Ineffective highway maintenance and rehabilitation practices	Establish microenterprises to maintain the main network.	Prepare and implement a project for maintaining and improving the main network.	At least 50 companies are formed, trained, and working throughout the main network.	Improve the state of the network. Increase the network's useful economic life. Increase highway safety. Provide more employment for skilled and unskilled people.
Outdated sector institutions and management	Carry out a strategic institutional assessment.	Rationalize and clarify the role of various agencies in the highway sector.	The strategic plan for the sector has been completed.	Improve service. Reduce costs to users. Guarantee more efficient use of resources.
High levels of rural poverty not addressed	Prepare a rural roads project with the MOP and sectional governments.	Implement the Rural Roads project (World Bank project).	Road network improvement plans (PVPP) at the provincial level are being prepared. Support for rural roads is sustained through budget.	Eliminate bottlenecks impeding economic growth. Provide isolated areas with social services. Provide employment. Support agricultural production.

Annex

Urban Development in Ecuador
I. Description

Urbanization

Ecuadoran cities are still growing rapidly because of rural-urban migration. The urban population of 8.4 million (in 2003) represented 64 percent of the country's total population, almost 10 percentage points above 1990 figures (United Nations 2004). Although this urbanization level is still moderate compared with some of its highly urbanized neighbors such as Argentina, Colombia, and Venezuela, Ecuador's urban growth rate is one of the highest in the region. Between 2000 and 2005, Ecuador's urban population growth rate was 2.3 percent, the fourth highest in South America, after Paraguay (3.5 percent), Bolivia (2.7 percent), and French Guyana (2.7 percent), and higher than the growth rate for Latin America as a whole, 1.9 percent. Moreover, urban population growth constituted 92.3 percent of Ecuador's total population growth between 1995 and 2005 and continues to account for almost all population growth in the country.

The distribution of the urban population in Ecuador is not evenly spread among the country's diverse regions. In 2001, of a total urban population of 7.0 million in cities with 10,000 or more people, 48.5 percent resided in Guayaquil (population 2.0 million) and Quito (1.4 million). Secondary cities with an average population of 162,000 housed an additional 30.2 percent (2.1 million) of Ecuador's urban population. Finally, tertiary cities with an average population of 35,000 housed about 15.6 percent of this population (1.0 million). The growth of the urban population also responds to size differentials. Despite the attention drawn by primary cities, they have in fact grown at a slower rate—2.4 percent per annum between 1990 and 2001—than secondary or intermediate cities. The average annual growth rate in small and intermediate cities was of the order of 3.1 percent per annum.[5]

Future Urban Growth

According to a recent World Bank study, the population in cities of developing countries is expected to double in the next 30 years: from some 2 billion in 2000 to almost 4 billion in 2030 and built-up areas are expected to double and triple (Shlomo, Sheppard, and Civco 2005). According to United Nations projections, Ecuador will be 80 percent urbanized by 2025. Preliminary estimates of spatial projections of future urban growth, carried out in five intermediate Ecuadorian cities, show that by 2030, four of these cities will require a threefold increase in their present urban areas to accommodate their projected population and increases in built-up areas.

II. Main Issues

The severe economic and financial crisis in Ecuador in the late 1990s had a devastating effect on already high poverty levels and income distribution. The number of people living in extreme poverty (income insufficient to cover a basic basket of goods) increased from 12 percent to 21 percent during the crisis. The incidence of poverty (per capita) nearly doubled from 34 percent to 56 percent of the population between 1995 and 1999. This means that the number of poor Ecuadorans grew by over 2 million during the crisis. The crisis severely affected the poor and the indigenous population, particularly those living in the rural Sierra region, where the poverty rate increased by 7 percent just between 1998 and 1999, and those living in the Costa region, which suffered at least US$2 billion in damage and a doubling of urban unemployment rates in cities like Guayaquil (World Bank 2004a).

Migration

As a response to the crisis, millions have immigrated internationally and millions moved within the country into marginal urban areas. First, international emigration of about 200,000 people—about 7 percent of the labor force—since 1997 (World Bank 2004a) has transformed the country into an "exporter of people and importer of remittances" (Jokisch 2001). Until the mid-1990s, the United States was the preferred destination for Ecuadoran immigrants. Provinces located in the southern area of the Ecuadoran Sierra, such as Azuay, Cañar, and Loja, have traditionally produced large immigration waves headed to the United States. Since 1997 however, the migratory process has reached unprecedented levels. Much research has been produced about the exodus initiated from Ecuador during the last years of that decade due to the economic and institutional crisis (Mora 2006).

Popular belief holds that urban overloading will not happen in Ecuadoran cities because of the substantial waves of Ecuadorans that are migrating from rural and semirural areas directly to the United States or Europe (Mora 2006). Table A.1's data regarding the proportional migration from each province challenge this belief. The data indicate that the proportion of Ecuadorans who migrate internationally per province varies between 0.5 percent in the Amazonian province of Morona Santiago to 8.5 percent in the highland province of Cañar.

Second, although internal migratory movements have been common in Ecuador for decades, they have risen substantially in the years since the crisis. In 2000, poverty levels rose to 77 percent of the rural population and to over 90 percent among indigenous rural communities. The degree of deterioration in these indicators reveals the depth of the crisis and the greater vulnerability of the rural poor in dealing with income losses. Poverty levels in Ecuador's urban areas rose due to both the impoverishment of its existing population and the urban-to-urban and rural-to-urban migratory flows. Medium-size cities were hit most severely.

Table A.1. Measures of Migration as a Proportion of Total Population, by Province

Region/province	*Total migrants*	*Total population*	*Percentage of population*
El Oro	22,568	525,763	4.3
Esmeraldas	5,207	385,223	1.4
Guayas	89,344	3,309,034	2.7
Los Ríos	8,018	650,178	1.2
Manabí	16,174	1,186,025	1.4
Total Costa	**141,311**	**6,056,223**	**2.3**
Azuay	34,053	599,546	5.7
Bolívar	1,942	169,370	1.1
Cañar	17,625	206,981	8.5
Carchi	1,323	152,939	0.9
Cotopaxi	5,745	349,540	1.6
Chimborazo	11,720	403,632	2.9
Imbabura	9,919	344,044	2.9
Loja	24,201	404,835	6.0
Pichincha	99,279	2,388,817	4.2
Tungurahua	14,588	441,034	3.3
Total Sierra	**220,395**	**5,460,738**	**4.0**
Morona Santiago	5,770	115,412	0.5
Napo	832	79,139	1.1
Pastaza	1,458	61,779	2.4
Zamora Chinchipe	4,271	76,601	5.6
Sucumbíos	1,812	128,995	1.4
Orellana	718	86,493	0.8
Total Amazonia	**14,861**	**548,419**	**2.7**
Undefined Areas	562	72,588	0.8
Country Total	**377,908**	**12,156,608**	**3.1**

Source: Project team's calculations, based on population data from the 2001 Population Census and migration data from Mora (2005) citing Camacho (2005).

A particular feature of the internal migratory movements is that, although nearly half of the urban population is concentrated in two cities, which continue to grow at an elevated average rate of 2.3 percent, secondary or intermediate cities (100,000–300,000 people) are growing even faster, at an average rate of 8 percent (National Census 2001). This phenomenon finds its origins in both rural-to-urban and interurban migration.

Population growth in urban areas is, in turn, the result of natural growth of the urban population, rural-urban migration, and the reclassification of rural parishes as urban as a result of the creation of new cantons. In addition to natural urban growth and migration flows driven by Ecuadorans searching for work, the country also receives international waves of migration in its northern cities, such as displaced rural inhabitants of Colombia. According to the 2001 Population Census, 30 percent of the population lives in a place different from the one they were born in.

- Most migratory movements (over 60 percent) are urban-to-urban, rather than rural-to-urban, although there are some differences across regions (such as rural-to-urban flows are more common in the Sierra and the Oriente than in the Costa). This should not be surprising given that a majority of the population resides in urban areas.
- Quito and Guayaquil alone are the destination of 29 percent of all internal migrants (13 percent and 16 percent, respectively).
- More than two-thirds of the population lives in the province, canton, and parish they were born in (80 percent, 70 percent, and 67 percent, respectively). These figures suggest that about one-third of all internal migration occurs within provinces, while two-thirds occurs across provinces (World Bank 2004b).

Ecuador Poverty Assessment

The World Bank's *Ecuador Poverty Assessment*, completed in 2004, concludes that poverty has become an urban phenomenon in Ecuador. Increases in urban poverty in the period between 1990 and 2001 were largest (over 80 percent) in the urban areas of the Costa and Sierra regions, while poverty remained constant in the rural Costa and increased by 15 percent in the rural Sierra. As a result, the number of poor people living in urban areas increased from 1.1 million to 3.5 million, surpassing the number of rural poor in the country. The urbanization of poverty is the result of the 1998–99 crisis and the migratory movements discussed in the preceding section. The report also shows that city-level poverty numbers can hide important welfare differences across neighborhoods, and that this effect tends to be higher in larger cities.

Urban labor markets were deeply affected by the 1998–99 crisis and the 2000 dollarization. Employment levels and real labor income dropped dramatically as a consequence of the crisis and did not recover until 2002. Urban poverty levels have followed the same trends. According to the surveys, poor urban households were headed mostly by a jobless or informally employed individual (table A.2). The informality rate and the unemployment rate are significantly higher among women, and hourly wages earned by women are significantly lower than those earned by men.

Characteristics of Intermediate Cities in Ecuador

Table A.3 summarizes characteristics related to access to infrastructure in 12 intermediate cities. Clearly, coverage rates vary a great deal in the 12 cities. In general electricity coverage is very good with the exception of Azogues. On the other hand, the service with the lowest coverage is piped sanitation, as a few striking cases demonstrate; for example, the coverage for Daule, Milagro, Azogues, Manta, Ambato, and Duran range from about 22 percent to 56 percent. The coverage rate for water exhibits great variation, with rates ranging from 50 percent to over 90 percent. Solid waste collection services never reach 100 percent of the population. Extreme cases of low coverage are Azogues (40.51 percent) and Machala and Milagro (68 percent), while Riobamba and Sangolquí enjoy rates above 90 percent.

Table A.2. Characteristics of Poor and Nonpoor Urban Households in Ecuador, 1997–2002
(percentage, except where noted otherwise)

	Poor			Nonpoor		
	1997	*1999*	*2002*	*1997*	*1999*	*2002*
Household characteristics						
Household size (no. of persons)	4.5	4.8	4.1	4.5	4.2	4.1
Dependency ratio	33.5	30.6	36.3	20.0	19.0	19.7
Labor force participation (LFP) rate	38.6	52.3	42.7	63.9	69.2	66.7
Female LFP rate	29.1	39.2	34.1	47.9	56.1	52.8
Employment rate	81.2	79.4	80.8	94.8	93.0	95.4
Unemployment rate	18.7	20.5	19.2	5.1	6.9	4.5
Informality rate	70.0	75.5	71.2	50.8	50.2	53.7
Underemployment rate	14.8	18.7	19.8	7.4	11.6	11.7
Household head characteristics						
LFP rate	62.1	77	64.9	92.1	93.5	92.1
Employment rate	90.1	86.2	85.5	98.3	97.6	98.4
Unemployment rate	9.8	13.7	14.4	1.7	2.3	1.5
Public sector employed	3.3	4	5.4	17	16.3	13.4
Private sector employed	32.2	42.3	37.7	35.1	38.7	37.9
Employer	4.7	8.9	5.3	13.2	15.6	14
Self-employed	52.4	41.4	43.4	32.4	27.6	30.8
Informal	73.9	67.5	72.7	45.5	41.8	49.1
Underemployed	16	17.4	24.5	5.2	8.2	10
Multiple jobs	2.4	2.4	1.6	4.6	4.9	3.2
Hours worked weekly	41.7	42.8	38.3	46.7	46.8	44.8
No schooling	7.7	7.1	8.1	3.4	3.3	3.3
Primary	54.8	51.7	48.6	37.2	34.1	35.5
Secondary	29.2	31.2	31.2	35.2	34.8	35.7
Tertiary	8.2	9.7	12	23.9	27.6	25.4
Years of schooling	7.0	7.4	7.3	9.6	10.0	9.5

Urbanization Trends in Intermediate Cities

A study on urbanization trends in five intermediate cities (Durán, Milagro, Riobamba, Sangolquí, and Santo Domingo) was carried out in December 2005 (Shlomo 2006). The study noted four aspects of the pattern of urban growth in Ecuador that merit attention: the urban-rural balance, the distribution of the urban population, urban growth rates, and the distribution of urban growth.

Urban-rural balance. In 2003 only 64 percent of the Ecuadoran population lived in cities, compared with 76.8 percent for Latin America and the Caribbean and 81.1 percent for South America. In South America, only Guyana and Paraguay were less urbanized than Ecuador.

Table A.3. Access to Basic Services in 12 Intermediate Cities in Ecuador

City	*Density: habitations per hectare*	*No. of households*	*Households with water connections (%)*	*Households with piped sanitation connections (%)*	*Households with door-to-door solid waste collection service (%)*	*Households with electricity (%)*
Ambato	50.1	40,693	67.0	56.2	79.9	96.0
Azogues	19.4	6,648	61.4	36.8	40.5	68.5
Daule	25.0	7,201	89.0	22.4	78.5	93.9
Durán	43.5	34,507	67.0	56.3	80.0	96.4
Machala	66.6	39,130	87.3	71.3	68.0	94.0
Manta	44.3	40,880	79.0	54.0	86.0	95.6
Milagro	40.0	28,209	75.0	24.0	68.0	94.0
Portoviejo	36.0	38,143	83.6	60.9	78.5	94.0
Puyo	21.5	6,115	85.4	75.4	87.0	96.0
Riobamba	42.0	31,482	97.4	96.3	93.0	98.3
Sangolquí	24.9	14,314	97.5	94.9	95.7	97.8
Santo Domingo	44.0	36,606	57.8	73.7	86.2	95.8

Source: CONSUL Centro (2006).

Distribution of the urban population. The distribution of the urban population in Ecuador is highly skewed. In 2001, of a total urban population of 7.0 million in cities with 10,000 or more people, 48.5 percent resided in the two large cities (Group 1) of Guayaquil (1.9 million) and Quito (1.4 million). In group 2, 13 secondary cities with populations between 100,000 and 300,000 and an average population of 162,000 housed an additional 30.2 percent of this population (2.1 million). In group 3, 31 tertiary cities with populations between 20,000 and 100,000 and an average population of 35,000 housed an additional 15.6 percent of this population (1.0 million). Cities with populations between 10,000 and 20,000 people housed 390,000 people, or 5.5 percent of the total, and had an average size of 13,000.

Urban growth rates. Ecuadoran cities are still growing rapidly because of rural-urban migration. The urban growth rate in Ecuador between 2000 and 2005 was 2.3 percent, the fourth highest in South America after Paraguay (3.5 percent), Bolivia (2.7 percent), and French Guyana (2.7 percent), and higher than the growth rate for Latin America as a whole (1.9 percent). Urban population growth constituted 92.3 percent of Ecuador's total population growth between 1995 and 2005 and continues to account for almost all population growth in the country.

Distribution of urban growth. The rapid growth of the urban population is not evenly distributed. Large cities grew at a slower rate than smaller cities—2.4 percent per year—between 1990 and 2001. The average annual growth rate in secondary and tertiary cities was of the order of 3.1 percent annually. One city grew very rapidly—at a rate more than 7 percent per year—Durán. At that rate of growth, the city can be expected to double its population in a single decade.

Table A.4 provides population, built-up area, and density figures for five intermediate cities.

Table A.5 contains estimates of urban areas, built-up areas, and densities for the five cities in 2030. These projections were based on the assumption that (i) urban population growth in Ecuador will decline between 2000 and 2030 at the rates estimated by the United Nations (2004); (ii) the urban population in these five cities will grow at the same rate it grew between the two latest census periods—0.15 percent annually; (iii) built-up area densities will decline at the rate of 2 percent per year; (iv) the urban limits will encompass one-third more area than the built-up area, to account for open space and vacant lands. These projections are being perfected using a more sophisticated model for the population projections, and basing built-up area projections on the classification and measurement of satellite images of the cities in two time periods corresponding to the census periods. In the meantime, only preliminary conclusions can be drawn. By 2030, Eloy Alfaro Durán, Santo Domingo, Milagro, and Sangolqui will require a *threefold* increase in their present urban areas to accommodate its projected population and built-up area increases. Riobamba will require a doubling of its urban area.

Table A.4. Population, Built-Up Areas, and Densities in Five Intermediate Cities in Ecuador, 2006

City	*Population 1990*	*Population 2001*	*Percent annual growth*	*Population 2006*	*Urban area (km²)*	*Built-up area (km²)*	*Density (persons/km²)*
Sangolquí	30,760	53,816	4.40	70,104	32	19	3,664
Milagro	93,111	111,319	1.80	123,684	30	21	5,816
Riobamba	97,632	125,553	2.60	141,403	29	17	8,177
Durán	80,954	167,589	7.10	242,821	59	29	8,273
Santo Domingo	98,911	207,375	5.20	255,871	73	44	5,863

Sources: Population data for 1990 and 2001 are from the census. The 2006 population estimates were obtained by linear extrapolation of census data. Urban area and built-up area estimates are from interviews in municipalities.

Note: Density is measured as a ratio of the population and the built-up area, not the urban area (the administrative area within the city limits).

Table A.5. Population, Density, Built-Up Area, and Urban Area Projections for 2030 for the Five Intermediate Cities in Ecuador

	Projections for 2030				*Growth ratios 2006–30*			
City	*Population*	*Density (persons/km²)*	*Built-up area (km²)*	*Urban area (km²)*	*Population (millions)*	*Density*	*Built-up area*	*Urban area*
Sangolquí	188,949	2,211	64	85	2.70	0.6	3.3	2.7
Milagro	178,184	3,510	72	96	1.44	0.6	3.4	3.1
Riobamba	222,061	4,935	40	53	1.57	0.6	2.3	1.8
Durán	842,547	4,993	127	170	3.47	0.6	4.3	2.9
Santo Domingo	902,505	3,538	161	214	3.53	0.6	3.7	2.9

Source: Author's calculations.

III. Recommendations

Given the rapid growth of Ecuador's urban areas (both in terms of population and urban built-up areas), national government policy should focus on the following:

1. **Planning**. Start planning for urban growth over the next 25 years through simple schemes such as land acquisition for the urban grid, large-scale land titling, and creative, low-cost, progressive urbanization that takes advantage of partnerships among municipalities, interested communities, and private developers.

2. **Urban upgrading**. Leverage national government (or donor) resources as well as local government and community contributions to finance participatory,

demand-responsive urban upgrading programs that provide the physical infrastructure necessary for overcoming urban poverty.

3. Policy making. Strengthen MIDUVI's role as a policy maker, especially through the design of a new and comprehensive housing policy.

4. Financial management and administration. Promote good financial and administrative management, particularly in intermediate municipalities, using loans to municipalities as an incentive to reward solid municipal administration.

Notes

1. In addition to public WSS utilities, there is one private sector WSS concession in Guayaquil.
2. The World Bank supported the PRAGUAS I project with a US$32 million loan. On July 25, 2006, the Bank's board approved a second loan (for US$48 million) in support of the program's second phase (PRAGUAS II).
3. Potable water service is available either within or outside of the house (but within the lot). Sanitation service is either via sanitary sewerage system (without treatment) or on-site disposal systems (septic tanks).
4. Overall national sector financing includes approximately US$75 million per year in grants to water companies from the ICE, as well from the Solidarity Fund (*Fondo de Solidaridad*), regional development corporations, and other sources in addition to loans made by the Banco del Estado (BdE).
5. Large, or primary, cities are defined as those having more than one million inhabitants (2), secondary cities have between 100,000 and 300,000 inhabitants (12) and tertiary cities have between 30,000 and 100,000 inhabitants (57).

Bibliography

MOP (Ministry of Public Works). 1997. "Planning and Decentralization of the National Roadways Administration." Prepared by Isra and Majón. Quito: MOP.

PAHO (Pan American Health Organization). 2001. "Desigualdades en el acceso, uso y gasto con el agua potable en América Latina y el Caribe." Ecuador, Technical Report Series No. 5, PAHO, Washington, DC.

Shlomo, Angel, Stephen C. Sheppard, and Daniel L. Civco, Robert Buckley, Anna Chabaeva, Lucy Gitlin, Alison Kraley, Jason Parent, and Micah Perlin. 2005. "The Dynamics of Global Urban Expansion." Transport and Urban Development Department, World Bank, Washington, DC.

Shlomo, Angel. 2006. "Preparing for Urban Expansion in Intermediate Cities in Ecuador." Draft paper prepared for the World Bank.

United Nations. 2004. World Urbanization Prospects: The 2005 Revision Population Database. http://esa.un.org/unup/.

World Bank. 2004a. "Ecuador Development Policy Review. Growth, Inclusion and Governance: The Road Ahead." Ecuador Country Management Unit, World Bank, Washington, DC.

World Bank. 2004b. *Ecuador Poverty Assessment.* Washington, DC: World Bank.

Yepes, G., B. Gómez, and E. Carvajal. 2002. "Plan Nacional de Desarrollo del Sector de Agua Potable y Saneamiento Básico." National Plan pp. 11–14, unpublished report prepared for the government of Ecuador.

ECO-AUDIT

Environmental Benefits Statement

The World Bank is committed to preserving endangered forests and natural resources. The Office of the Publisher has chosen to print ***Revisiting Ecuador's Economic and Social Agenda in an Evolving Landscape*** on recycled paper with 30 percent post-consumer waste, in accordance with the recommended standards for paper usage set by the Green Press Initiative, a nonprofit program supporting publishers in using fiber that is not sourced from endangered forests. For more information, visit www.greenpressinitiative.org.

Saved:

- 10 trees
- 7 million BTUs of total energy
- 911 lbs. of CO_2 equivalent of greenhouse gases
- 3,780 gallons of waste water
- 485 pounds of solid waste